"Daniel McCoy has assembled a tremendous team of contributors who are passionate experts in their respective fields. *The Popular Handbook of World Religions* is a true "Swiss Army knife" for every reader interested in understanding various religious systems. This highly unique and multifaceted volume not only presents the facts about the world's most prolific religions, but it also offers the reader compelling and practical ways to move the religious discussion forward—*in love*! For this reason, *The Popular Handbook of World Religions'* clear and concise content is a must-read for anyone seeking to make a real and measurable difference in an often misunderstood and contentious discipline. Every serious student, missionary, pastor, and evangelist must read this volume!"

Joseph M. Holden, PhD
President, Veritas International University
Author, *The Harvest Handbook™ of Apologetics*

"I've been wishing for a long time that a book like this would be published! This is a truly accessible guide to world religions with just the right amount of detail and written in a compelling way. I have no doubt it will be my go-to recommendation on the subject for years to come."

Natasha Crain, speaker and author of three books, including *Talking with Your Kids about Jesus*

"*The Popular Handbook of World Religions* is an excellent resource with a wealth of insight on an array of critical topics for anyone ministering cross-culturally. Rather than settle for dry, encyclopedic entries, the contributors use an engaging narrative style that provides valuable context without sacrificing nuance. The chapters offer balanced perspectives with concision and clarity, which makes the book useful for practitioners and scholars alike."

Jackson Wu
Theologian in Residence, Mission ONE

"The twenty-first century church must return and recommit to Jesus's command to make disciples who make disciples. This excellent handbook encourages and equips disciple-making among people of the world's religions. Not only are the authors intent on describing the religions accurately and graciously, but they are also effective in helping us carry out our core mission: to make disciples of all nations."

Bobby Harrington
Point Leader of Renew.org and Discipleship.org

"One of the biggest apologetics challenges today is explaining how Christianity can be the one true religion in light of the various claims made by the world's religions. *The Popular Handbook of World Religions* not only provides a wealth of information about the distinctive religions of the world, but it also serves as a tool chest for Christians who desire to be informed and to interact with people who embrace these religions. This work is a valuable resource for Christian education, evangelism, and apologetics."

Kenneth Samples
Senior Scholar, Reasons to Believe

The POPULAR HANDBOOK OF WORLD RELIGIONS

DANIEL J MCCOY
GENERAL EDITOR

I dedicate this book to my five precious children:

Beth, Sarah, Hannah, John, and Elijah

I love you, and I pray that God would use you
to help make disciples of all nations.

Acknowledgments

I am so grateful to so many people for making this project possible. Thanks to Win Corduan for motivating my interest and guiding my study in world religions. Thanks to Lindsey Medenwaldt for not only contributing the chapter on Jehovah's Witnesses but also doing an excellent job looking over all the chapters and making the project far better as a result. Her help was invaluable. Thanks to my editors at Harvest House for entrusting me with this project. I am thankful for getting to work with more than 20 capable scholars who agreed to contribute chapters.

I will always gladly make use of any opportunity to thank my wife, the lovely Susanna McCoy. I don't deserve such a wonderful wife, and I sure am grateful for her. I'm also grateful for our five children. They fill our home with joy, each in his or her unique way.

Jesus has given us a very clear purpose: to make disciples. I'm thankful to my parents, David and Nancy, for discipling me throughout my childhood. I'm thankful to be working with the Renew Network (renew.org), an organization whose purpose is to fuel disciple-making. I'm also thankful to be able to offer this book toward that same end, that we as His disciples might become dedicated and effective disciple-makers.

Contents

Introduction

Daniel McCoy

If you're like me, you've got bookshelves crammed with well-intentioned purchases. In fact, multiple shelves aren't enough; book stacks spring up around the house like firework stands in summer. There are the theology books on *what* Christians believe and apologetics books on *why* Christians believe. There's that stack of Christian books on marriage you have been meaning to read. With parenting growing more complicated, you really ought to get to those books on how to be a Christian parent. There's the devotional you started twice but never finished—last January and the January before that. And of course, as your preacher keeps reminding you, there are lots of great plans for reading through the Bible itself.

When there's already not enough time to read all the books you'd like to about your own religion, why should you take the time to study a book on *other* religions? Sure, there are theology students who read such books as part of a three-credit-hour class. But why should everyday Christians bother to learn the basics about other religions? Here are three reasons you should consider.

Clarify the Facts

It's too easy to misunderstand other religions. On the one hand, some writers will make religions seem more similar than they really are. Such authors fudge the facts in order to bring about peace between the religions. On the other hand, some writers will make other religions seem worse than they really are. They exaggerate the embarrassing features of the religion, since a "straw man" is easier to knock down than the real thing.

Christians should seek truth. This means learning and growing. This means being able to recognize phoniness on either side and steering between it. It means hunting for answers, not settling for stereotypes. It means being able to enter discussions on other religions and offer light, not merely adding to the heat.

So what is the difference between Hinduism and Buddhism? Do Christians and Muslims and Jews worship the same God? What was Siddhartha Gautama's fundamental insight? Are Hindus pantheist (all is god), or polytheist (there are many gods)? Is Islam a peaceful religion? What has changed in

Judaism since the writing of the New Testament? What did Confucius teach? Is a Sikh basically a Muslim, or a Hindu, or something else? Do African traditionalists worship their ancestors as gods? What religion does the yin-yang symbol come from?

Clarifying such facts is part of seeking truth and understanding the world.

Love Your Neighbor

Followers of Jesus already know that we can't compartmentalize the command to love. Jesus taught us in the parable of the good Samaritan (Luke 10:25-37) that it's not enough to love the next-door neighbor; we are to *be* a neighbor, showing love to whomever is in need. The way of Jesus is to be a neighbor to Buddhists and Hindus, Jews and Muslims. Just as the victim's Jewishness didn't stop the Samaritan from showing love, another person's religious identity should never stop us from loving.

This opportunity to be a neighbor to people of other religions is no longer theoretical. This is because "neighbor" is no longer merely metaphorical. You have people of other religions as your coworkers, your clients, your classmates, your neighbors.

Part of learning to love is getting to know. And part of getting to know is learning the religion. So invite your "neighbor" over. Ask questions. Offer help. Share a meal. Appreciate the culture. Learn the holidays. Understand the taboos to avoid offense. Do your homework.

It was after dinner at the McCoy household. YouTube was on autoplay, and it had started playing a song by a choir in an old, darkly lit church. I didn't pay attention to the video until my five-year-old daughter who was watching the video from across the room said, "Ooh—creepy people."

I said, "Creepy people? What do you mean?"

So she got closer to the screen, and suddenly she said, "Oh, not creepy people. Just people."

That's the invitation to you and to me: Move in. Get closer. Get to know people of other religions. Learn to love them as precious people for whom Jesus left heaven to die. Part of this is learning their religion.

Preach the Gospel

It's one thing to teach your kid about Jesus or to remind your uncle that he ought to get back in church. It seems like quite another to evangelize someone of a different religion. Your family has a religion; his or her family follows another religion. Why feel compelled to preach the gospel to someone of a different religion, especially when the person already seems culturally established, basically content, and adequately virtuous?

This was the dilemma the Catholic priest Thomas Merton wrestled with concerning his friendship with the Buddhist D.T. Suzuki. He could try to convert Suzuki to accepting the truths of Christianity, but he was afraid this would "simply confuse and (in a cultural sense) degrade him." Besides, Merton mused, "Who says that Suzuki is not already a saint?" Merton concluded that he would concentrate on "the most important thing": cultivating the friendship.[1]

Is it safe to assume that a person's saintliness equals the person's salvation? Are we to see friendship with us as a more important end result than the person's friendship with God? The only way these can be safe bets is if we fundamentally change the message of the New Testament. Either we feel compelled to convert the person, or we have to convert Christianity.[2]

It's entrancing to consider the heavenly vision of "a great multitude that no one could number, from every nation, from all tribes and peoples and languages, standing before the throne and before the Lamb" (Revelation 7:9). In the meantime, there is work to do. There is every reason to connect that future vision with our current orders: "Go therefore and make disciples of all nations" (Matthew 28:19).

When the Apostle Paul preached the gospel to the Jews, he taught the Law and Prophets. When he preached to pantheists, he quoted their poets. When he preached to pagans, he spoke of rains from heaven and fruitful seasons.

Part of preaching the gospel to people of other religions is to learn their religions.

This Book

There are many books on world religions that do a good job clarifying the facts. There are fewer books that both clarify the facts and teach practical ways to love your neighbor of a different religion. There are still fewer books that clarify facts, teach how to love your neighbor, and give you insights on how to preach the gospel to people of other religions. This book seeks to do all three. In fact, each chapter on a particular religion typically follows a basic threefold structure. The first section of a chapter typically focuses on the religion's history and beliefs; this information helps you clarify the facts. The next section describes the religion's lifestyle and culture, thus equipping you to better love your neighbor. The final section of the chapter, comparing and contrasting the religion with Christianity, provides a frame of reference for evangelism.

The book was written with you, the reader, in mind. We intentionally wrote chapters to be clear and readable, yet still unwavering in their aim to teach truth. We hope you find this book helpful.

Part 1

RELIGION AND CHRISTIANITY

What in the World God Is Up To (and How You Can Join In)

Miriam Adeney

Amina is Egyptian. Raised in a religious family, she was veiled when she was six, and began to say regular prayers. Every morning, she and her mother would wake to roll out their prayer rugs. Rubbing sleep from her eyes, Amina would ask, "Why are we doing this?"

"It's just our duty to God, dear," her mother would answer.

"I wish God was like Daddy," Amina would say. "When I talk to Daddy, he answers me. When I talk to God, why doesn't he ever answer?"

When Amina was 12, a woman gave her a little book. It was a religious scripture, Amina noted. At that age, she didn't want to read it, but she knew it should be treated with respect. She put it on a closet shelf, then forgot about it.

Years passed. Amina was awarded a scholarship to a national university. She was determined to use her education to benefit the Egyptian people. As a result, she often found herself joining protest marches in the streets. One afternoon, she came upon a music concert in a park. After a few songs, she realized it was a Christian concert. Then the lead singer spoke to "Father," and she wondered, *Is he speaking to God? Do Christians know God as a Father?*

Going home after the concert, she remembered the Scripture she had received years before. By now she knew that it was part of the Christian Scripture, the Gospel of John. *Do I still have that little book?* she wondered. Rummaging around, she found it and sat down to read.

The words of Jesus touched her powerfully. How wise, how compassionate, and how beautiful were His thoughts. And the idea that the eternal Word would become flesh! Then she came to chapter 8 and read about a woman who had been caught in adultery. The woman's accusers brought her to Jesus. They wanted to stone her. That was the law.

Jesus said, "Let him who is without sin among you be the first to throw a stone at her." At that, all the accusers slipped away. Jesus told the woman, "Neither do I condemn you; go, and from now on sin no more" (John 8:7,10).

That penetrated Amina's heart. What wisdom, what holiness, what compassion, what justice she saw. This was what she wanted for her society, for Egypt. Jesus was the Lord who was worthy of being followed. Amina went out and found a pastor, and he discipled her. Today, Amina and her husband work to spread justice and compassion through their society, following Jesus actively.

Amina was a Muslim. She followed the religion of Islam, but her life changed radically when she met God in Jesus. Amina represents the millions of people of diverse faiths whose worlds turned upside down when they encountered God through Jesus.

How shall we understand this global movement? How should we view the various faiths around the world? These topics are complex, and there are multiple dimensions to consider, which will be probed in the chapters that follow. In this introductory chapter, we will explore three areas: (1) Christian worldview, (2) God's people, and (3) practical actions.

Christian Worldview: The Cosmic Center

In the Beginning

"In the beginning, God created the heavens and the earth" (Genesis 1:1). The Bible opens with these words. Before humans existed and before the earth had a shape, there was God. Who is this God? What kind of superpower is He? Around the world, many people believe in some kind of deity. Various religions speak about an ultimate power. What kind of being is the God of Genesis, the one who was present from the beginning?

Is God a great force? Or is He like the Tao of Chinese religion, an ordering principle that gives structure to everything in the universe—rational structure, social structure, and moral structure? Or is God like Brahman of Hinduism, a great soul, a great consciousness that underlies all consciousness in the cosmos? Or is God a lawgiver like Allah of Islam, who creates us, and sends us prophets, and teaches us principles?

The biblical story tells about a shockingly different kind of God. A Creator who chooses to live as a human being, experiencing our pain to the point of death, then erupting back to life and offering us power for new beginnings. This is the God who comes close to us in Jesus.

Yet Jesus is so much more than just our Savior and friend. Jesus is the center of the universe. Where I live in the state of Washington, we have snowy mountains. One of our great mountaineers was once asked, "Why do people climb mountains?" He answered, "Because when you stand on the top of a mountain, all the lines come together. The top of a mountain is the only place where you will find convergence."

This is a picture of Jesus. He is the place where all the lines in the universe come together. He is our cosmic mountain. Ephesians 1:10 says the mystery of the ages is that God will bring all things in the cosmos together in Christ. Colossians 1:16 says it is in Christ that all things hold together. Revelation 4:11 says that Jesus created all things, and for His pleasure, they continue to hang together.

What kind of God existed in the beginning? A God who combines power and love. This is the God who was present before history began. This is also the God whom Amina encountered in the twenty-first century.

In God's Image

When God made humans, He said "it was very good" (Genesis 1:31). Behind the miracle of a baby, there is God. Behind the love that causes some people to give their lives for others, whether in a great event or in quiet daily faithfulness, there is God. Behind all our lives, there is an awesome personality who brought us into being.

Nature's intricate designs and complex meshing are breathtaking. Yet we humans are more valuable than all the rest because we are made in the image of God (Genesis 1:27). We are not just animals, machines, consumers, or producers. We are personalities, generated by a great personality. That is why humans are not disposable. Many scholars have noted this. For example, American political scientist Francis Fukuyama said, "Writers from Hegel to Tocqueville to Nietzsche have traced modern ideas of equality to the biblical idea of man-made in the image of God."[1] Equal rights are not an invention of the United Nations. They do not flow automatically from logical thinking. Human rights stem from the biblical understanding of humans.

Two years ago, I published a book on migrant working women in Dubai and other places in the Arabian Gulf. Filipino maids are some of these women. By the world's standards, they are not important. They may spend their days scrubbing toilets. They may be yelled at and even hit. They may be confined for weeks at a time with no days off.

But the maids who are real Christians know that their main master is the King of kings and Lord of lords and that they are princesses in His palace, even while they scrub toilets. So they hold their heads high. They walk with dignity. They laugh. And they witness to and disciple fellow migrants, and sometimes even their local employers. Are they victims of a global economic system? Are they unimportant? From the world's standpoint, yes. But a Christian worldview tells them they are created in God's image, liberated by Jesus's death, empowered by the Holy Spirit, and commissioned for active service in God's world.

Every person in every culture and religion is made in the image of God, endowed with creativity, and called to develop it.

> When God made the earth, he could have finished it. But he didn't. He left it as a raw material—to tease us, to tantalize us, to set us thinking, and experimenting, and risking, and adventuring. And therein we find our supreme interest in living. He gave us the challenge of raw materials, not the satisfaction of perfect, finished things.
>
> He left the music unsung, and the dramas unplayed.
>
> He left the poetry undreamed, in order that men and women might not become bored, but engaged in stimulating, exciting, creative activities that keep them thinking, working, experimenting, and experiencing all the joys and satisfactions of achievement.[2]

Sin and Brokenness

Although there is beauty in humans, there is also evil in this world. And in our communities. And in us. God gave humans the freedom to choose, and to our shame, we often have chosen selfishness. This has resulted in tragedy across the globe. Racism and ethnic hatred stain our societies. Women and children are abused. Families fall apart. The earth's resources are destroyed. Corruption gives birth to poverty and famine.

Our popular stories and movies show how this works. Every story has a villain. Many stories tell about betrayal. In *Star Wars*, for example, the greatest Jedi, Anakin Skywalker, turned to the dark side and became Darth Vader. In *The Lord of the Rings*, Saruman, who was once a friend to the free peoples, went wrong in order to gain power.

Shakespeare's *The Tragedy of Julius Caesar* shows how that emperor was sold out and stabbed by a friend.[3]

Although we human beings have great value, paradoxically we have turned ourselves into enemies. Feeling deprived by our environments, we deprive others by the environments we create. Like abused children, we abuse others. Optimistic humanists may insist that we have within ourselves the power to develop a good society, but Christianity paints a strikingly different picture. We are not the owners of the universe but creatures within it. Further, we are creatures who sin—who often willfully choose what is false.

The Cosmic Center

Confucius taught good ethics. So did the Buddha. So did the Prophet Muhammed. But by and large, they did not get involved with hurting people. They did not voluntarily hang around with sinners. Instead, they expected people to follow their ethics and pull themselves up.

How different God in Jesus is. One poet put it in these words:

> The other gods were strong,
> but You were weak.
> They rode, but You stumbled
> to your throne.
> To our wounds only a wounded
> god can speak
> And not a god has wounds
> but You alone.[4]

In Jesus, the Creator who spoke the universe into being came close to us humans. He became vulnerable. He experienced our pain to the point of death. There are raped women of central Africa who have felt a connection with Jesus because He, too, was stretched out and tortured. His body was damaged and bloody. There are African Americans who have seen a parallel between the cross and the lynching tree. Human pain is profound—but at the bottom of the abyss, we find God because He has chosen to be with us in that pit. God does not leave us in our brokenness. Among all the world's religious leaders, He is the wounded God. He comes near. He shares our vulnerability and our agony, not only by living with us, but also by dying with us.

But death cannot hold God. Jesus absorbed death into Himself and exploded right out because God is stronger than death. God ultimately overpowers evil. Jesus broke through and generated the power for new beginnings. Resurrection power, Holy Spirit power, is showered on people who ask for it. They experience renewal.

In John 3, Jesus speaks of the new birth to explain how this happens. If people turn wholeheartedly from their self-centeredness to follow Jesus, if they ask Him to forgive and purify and fill them, He will. Regeneration will happen and will shape a new humanity (2 Corinthians 5:17; 1 Peter 1:23; James 1:18; Ephesians 2:15; 4:24). Without renewal, we remain far from God. But with renewal, even when there is no change in a person's personality, we will have a new orientation, motivation, and energizing power. We will experience life in the Spirit day by day (Galatians 5).

Our new birth is part of a broader restoration, a cosmic renewal, an ultimate universal reversal of decay (Matthew 19:28; Acts 3:19; Isaiah 65:17; 66:22; 2 Peter 3:10-13; Revelation 21:1). Resurrection reverses the rules. It snowballs change with far-reaching effects. A new heart, a new covenant, and a valley of dry bones coming to life are other word pictures that biblical writers painted in order to describe this change.

But restoration does not come cheap. It

cost Jesus His life. Jesus died not just to stand alongside us in our vulnerability. He died to restore us, to give us new life, peace with God, forgiveness, and deliverance. In the simplest words, He died for our sins. Consider these biblical passages:[5]

> He was pierced for our transgressions,
> he was crushed for our iniquities;
> the punishment that brought us
> peace was on him, and by his wounds
> we are healed.
> We all, like sheep, have gone astray,
> each of us has turned to our own way;
> and the LORD has laid on him the
> iniquity of us all
> (Isaiah 53:5-6 NIV).

> Look, the Lamb of God, who takes away the sin of the world! (John 1:29 NIV).

> The Son of Man [came]...to give his life as a ransom for many (Mark 10:45 NIV).

> Christ was sacrificed once to take away the sins of many (Hebrews 9:28 NIV).

> He himself bore our sins in his body on the tree (1 Peter 2:24).

> For Christ also suffered once for sins, the righteous for the unrighteous, to bring you to God (1 Peter 3:18 NIV).

> God made him who had no sin to be sin for us, so that in him we might become the righteousness of God (2 Corinthians 5:21 NIV).

> Christ redeemed us from the curse of the law by becoming a curse for us (Galatians 3:13 NIV).

People who risk their lives for others are not unknown to us. Mothers may shield their children with their own bodies. Think of doctors and nurses in epidemics, or how firefighters and soldiers may lose their lives while serving. But Jesus's death was something more. He died to pay for our sins and to wipe them out. He was the ultimate sacrifice.

"The missionary among Moslems (to whom the cross of Christ is a stumbling-block and the atonement foolishness) is driven daily to deeper meditation on this mystery of redemption," reflected Samuel Zwemer, pioneer missionary to Muslims. "One comes to realize that literally all the wealth and glory of the gospel centres here. The cross is the pivot...Although the offense of the cross remains, its magnetic power is irresistible."[6]

We stand in awe at this cosmic struggle, this divine atonement, every time we take the cup and bread of the holy communion supper.

Shockingly, Jesus is our friend. But as C.S. Lewis says in the Narnia books, He is not a "tame lion." He is not just a dialogue partner to consult whenever we need advice. He rules a cosmic kingdom, and one day will throw a party that will blast all other celebrations out of sight.

Charlene was friends with an Iranian immigrant family. One day, Merva, the 20-year-old daughter, asked, "Charlene, what do you think of the Prophet Muhammed?"

"Honestly, I'm no expert on the Prophet Muhammed," Charlene answered. "The only one I can talk about with any authority is the Lord Jesus Christ."

A year later, that family came to Jesus as Lord. Later Merva told Charlene, "If you had said anything else at that point, it might have been the end of our friendship."

Apparently, God used Charlene's ignorance for good. Her story reminds us to keep the main thing the main thing: Jesus. He is more important than all our arguments to defend Him. When we interact with people of other religions, we must remember that we are not just God-fearing people. We are not just nice ethical people. In fact, sometimes we are not very nice at all. We make stupid mistakes. We get mad. We certainly are not perfect. But we are being renewed. We are walking with the Holy Spirit—because we are Jesus's people. Again and again, we will get snared into tangential discussions. We will find ourselves running down cul-de-sacs. Then we must retrace our steps to the straight path: the Lord Jesus Christ, who shows us an incomparable, vulnerable, cosmic God.

The Magnificent Metastory: The People of God

In the 2019 Pulitzer prize–winning book *The Overstory*,[7] "overstory" connotes the crown level of trees in a forest. The term is also used as a metaphor for the overarching human story. It implies culmination and integration. We humans hunger for that kind of completeness and connectedness.

A grand unifying story is rare in our time. According to a postmodern perspective, we once aspired to a coherent worldview. But now in the postmodern world, we think in bits and pieces, in compartments. Yes, we progress technologically. We aim for excellence in our professional fields. And in the personal arena, we have people whom we love. But these realities seem to operate in separate spheres. There seems to be no overarching truth, no unifying metastory.

Yet we thirst for one. Like people in every era, we long for a big story that will help us understand relationships, justice, beauty, spirituality, and hope. This is where the Bible resonates powerfully. Flowing over thousands of years, the biblical story shows God communicating with people, progressively revealing more and more of the purpose of life. As well, God speaks through nature, conscience, and special revelation. In nature,

> The heavens declare the glory of God;
> the skies proclaim the work of his hands.
> Day after day they pour forth speech;
> night after night they reveal knowledge.
> They have no speech, they use no words;
> no sound is heard from them.
> Yet their voice goes out into all the earth,
> their words to the ends of the world
> (Psalm 19:1-4 NIV).

Abraham. Throughout time, God has spoken to certain people, not only for their benefit, but also so that they might transmit His truth and blessing to others. Abraham, for example, lived about 4,000 years ago in what is now Iraq. God called him to pack up his family and travel west. Eventually, he passed through the land of Palestine and dipped down to Egypt. God intended Abraham to be a channel of God's good news to everyone: "I will bless those who bless you…and all peoples on earth will be blessed through you" (Genesis 12:3 NIV).

Trusting in God was a key virtue that Abraham learned. The New Testament book of Romans says,

> If, in fact, Abraham was justified by works, he had something to boast about—but not before God. What does the Scripture say? "Abraham believed God, and it was credited to him as righteousness"…It was not through law that Abraham and his offspring received the promise that he

> would be heir of the world, but through the righteousness that comes by faith... Against all hope, Abraham in hope believed and so became the father of many nations (Romans 4:2-18 NIV).

The book of Hebrews says, "By faith Abraham, when called to go to a place he would later receive as his inheritance, obeyed and went, even though he did not know where he was going...For he was looking forward to the city with foundations, whose architect and builder is God" (Hebrews 11:8-10 NIV). In the magnificent metastory that stretches through time, God gave special revelations to certain people like Abraham. God invested in these people with the expectation that they would share what they had learned until it spread to "many nations," even to "all the peoples on the earth."

Moses. Moses was a descendent of Abraham born several hundred years later. History had taken some turns so that Moses was born in Egypt. In that foreign land, his family and his people were struggling to survive as slaves. But Moses received some unexpected benefits, and eventually, God empowered him to lead his people out of bondage and into freedom.

Moses is remembered for giving people the law, writing it down, and teaching it. While this may sound like a dry and restrictive focus, the law was intended to surround a vigorous, dynamic, full-bodied, joyous lifestyle. Consider these words of Moses:

> All the commandments which I command thee this day shall ye observe to do, that ye may live, and multiply, and go in and possess the land...
>
> For the LORD thy God bringeth thee into a good land, a land of brooks of water, of fountains and depths that spring out of valleys and hills;
>
> A land of wheat, and barley, and vines, and fig trees, and pomegranates; a land of oil olive, and honey;
>
> A land wherein thou shalt eat bread without scarceness, thou shalt not lack any thing in it; a land whose stones are iron, and out of whose hills thou mayest dig brass.
>
> When thou hast eaten and art full, then thou shalt bless the LORD thy God for the good land which he hath given thee (Deuteronomy 8:1,7-10 KJV).

Like Abraham, Moses had a universal, or at least transcultural, vision. Although his people had suffered greatly under an alien power, he did not allow that to turn him sour or xenophobic. Instead, he employed it to cultivate empathy with other peoples. Under Jewish law, he transmitted these words from God: "When a foreigner resides among you in your land, do not mistreat them. The foreigner residing among you must be treated as your native-born. Love him as yourself, for you were foreigners in Egypt. I am the LORD your God" (Leviticus 19:33-34 NIV). This care for foreigners included some economic protections as well as welcoming them to the regular public readings of the Scripture, the record of God's revelations to His people. Through those sacred words, people of other religions and cultures, too, could come to know what God was like. If they were so moved, they could choose to join His people—the ones who had been called to be a channel of God's good news to all peoples. There were procedures for joining the people, and some foreigners followed these and became "proselytes." Two of the four women who are named in Jesus's genealogy in Matthew—Rahab and Ruth—were foreigners who were welcomed into the people of faith.

David. Years passed. Around 3,000 years ago, David the humble shepherd boy was raised from obscurity to become the greatest king that Israel would ever have. He consolidated the scattered and sometimes quarrelsome inhabitants and formed them into a nation of significance. He conquered the Canaanites who held Jerusalem and took it for his capital city. This became Israel's golden age.

David regularly and wholeheartedly worshiped God. True, he sinned grievously. But he repented quickly and amended his ways. David became the measuring rod for all who followed. For example, when the young king Josiah wanted to turn the nation from corruption and licentiousness to wholesome living, he determined to follow the example of David, his precursor on the throne. It was expected that the Messiah would come from the line of David.

What was David's attitude toward God's larger world? How was God working in the world through David? In his early years, when he was hiding from the vitriolic king Saul, David took refuge with other people groups, such as the Philistines. He may have learned ironworking there and brought that valuable skill back to Israel. Later as king, however, he would find it necessary to enter into a fierce battle with the Philistines to ward off two massive attacks.

It would have been natural to focus on his kingdom and minimize attention to other peoples except when necessary for trade or security. But that is not what we see in David's writings. Many of his psalms speak about the nations worshiping God. This seems to have been a strong emphasis in his worldview. Consider these words:

> The LORD reigns, let the earth be glad;
> let the distant shores rejoice...
> The mountains melt like wax before
> the LORD, before the Lord of all
> the earth.
> The heavens proclaim his righteousness, and all peoples see his glory
> (Psalm 97:1,5-6 NIV).

> Sing to the LORD a new song;
> sing to the LORD, all the earth.
> Sing to the LORD, praise his name;
> proclaim his salvation day after
> day.
> Declare his glory among the nations,
> his marvelous deeds among all
> peoples...
> Ascribe to the LORD, O families of
> nations, ascribe to the LORD
> glory and strength.
> Ascribe to the LORD the glory due
> his name; bring an offering and
> come into his courts.
> Worship the Lord in the splendor of
> his holiness; tremble before him,
> all the earth.
> Say among the nations, "The LORD
> reigns..."
> He will judge the world in righteousness and the peoples in his
> faithfulness
> (Psalm 96:1-3,7-10,13 NIV).

Although David gloried in his nation, it was evident that his people were not God's owners. God was not their private possession. God is bigger than any one nation. He is intimately connected to all peoples on earth. Further, David made it clear that the Jews were not the only people who knew God. Indeed, it was possible for people from every nation to worship God aright. David urged them to do so: "Make a joyful noise unto the LORD, all ye lands" (Psalm 100:1 KJV). Jerusalem and the people of Israel were called to shine as a model because they had the most detailed and close experience with God. But all nations were welcome. It is possible that when foreign peoples marched into Jerusalem to pay tribute, some also may have visited the temple to worship God. Psalm 87 may refer to this:

> Glorious things are said of you,
> city of God:
> "I will record Rahab and Babylon
> among those who acknowledge me—
> Philistia too, and Tyre, along with
> Cush—and will say, 'This one
> was born in Zion'..."
> The LORD will write in the register
> of the peoples,
> "This one was born in Zion"
> (Psalm 87:3-9 NIV).

Isaiah. Sadly, the kingdom deteriorated after David. Corrupt kings would be interspersed between godly rulers. During this period, the Bible's great prophetic books were written. Among these is the book of Isaiah. Expanding David's broad view, Isaiah wrote at length with great hope for all nations as well as judgment for their sins. At one point, for example, Isaiah foresaw a highway of peace stretching from Egypt to Israel to Assyria (now Iraq). All three of these nations would be "a blessing on the earth" and "the LORD Almighty will bless them, saying, 'Blessed be Egypt, my people, Assyria my handiwork, and Israel my inheritance'" (Isaiah 19:24-25 NIV). At another point, Isaiah described the splendor of an epic parade of nations in which even the two oldest sons of Ishmael—Kedar and Nebaioth—bring offerings that are acceptable on God's altar (Isaiah 60:7 NIV).

The crux of this universal hope appears in Isaiah chapters 42–56, which feature the "Servant Songs."

Who is the servant? Three levels of meaning may be enfolded in this term. The "servant" may alternately refer to the coming Messiah, to a leader living in the author's time, and/or to the people of Israel. One meaning need not cancel the others.

It is clear that God's people are expected and commissioned to be a medium of God's revelation, "a light for the Gentiles, to open eyes that are blind" (Isaiah 42:6-7 NIV). Theologian Arthur Glasser comments, "Isaiah's Servant Songs...present Israel as a people with a vocation. Israel is charged by God with the sacred task of mediating the divine message to women and men and of leading the whole world into the Kingdom."[8]

The result will be striking:

> "And foreigners who bind themselves
> to the LORD to minister to him,
> to love the name of the LORD, and to
> be his servants,
> all who keep the Sabbath without
> desecrating it
> and who hold fast to my covenant—
> these I will bring to my holy
> mountain
> and give them joy in my house of
> prayer.
> Their burnt offerings and sacrifice will
> be accepted on my altar;
> for my house will be called a house of
> prayer for all nations."
> The Sovereign LORD declares—
> he who gathers the exiles of Israel:
> "I will gather still others to them
> besides those already gathered"
> (Isaiah 56:6-8 NIV).

Isaiah's final chapter peals out the strongest clarion call to take God's good news to the rest of the world, to people of all cultures and all religions:

> I...[will] gather the people of all nations and languages, and they will come and see my glory.
>
> I will set a sign among them, and I will send some of those who survive to the nations—to Tarshish, to the Libyans and the Lydians (famous as archers), to Tubal and Greece, and to the distant islands that have not heard of my fame or seen my glory. They will proclaim my glory among the nations. And they will bring all your people, from all the nations, to my holy mountain in Jerusalem as an offering to the LORD... They will bring them, as the Israelites bring their grain offerings, to the temple of the LORD in ceremonially clean vessels. And I will select some of them also to be priests (Isaiah 66:18-21 NIV).

Daniel. Many other prophets echoed international themes. However, the Old Testament narrates the sad story of the Israelites ultimately failing their commission. Rather than exemplify God's love, grace, and wholesome righteousness to the peoples beyond their borders, they focused selfishly on their interests. Some became legalistic. Others actively exploited and oppressed the vulnerable. Others wallowed in their lusts, consumed with satisfying their desires. There were exceptions, and God noted them, but they could not stem the general trend of ungodliness.

So God allowed the great empires of Babylon and Persia to take the people captive, destroy the temple, obliterate the borders of the land, and scatter the population across many nations.

At this low point, out of the depths of exile and slavery, many biblical books were written, including Jeremiah, Ezekiel, Daniel, Esther, Nehemiah, and others.

Around 600 BC, Daniel was taken to Babylon as a young man. He rose in the ranks of civil service and functioned as a high official under several emperors. Through it all, he worshiped God wholeheartedly. Sometimes that meant suffering, as when he was thrown into the lions' den. His authentic and trustworthy character impressed the rulers, however. In particular, King Nebuchadnezzar seems to have grown in his understanding of God through interaction with Daniel. We see this from the king's proclamation in Daniel 4. Surrounded by people of another religion, Daniel had myriad opportunities to witness to the true God. Perhaps he had that experience in mind, as well as his astronomical studies, when he wrote in the last chapter of his book, "Those who are wise will shine like the brightness of the heavens, and those who lead many to righteousness like the stars for ever and ever" (Daniel 12:3 NIV).

The Hinge of History. All these dreams—and all these failures! Good rules and good intentions had been tried, but human zeal proved not to be enough. Was there any way to turn the tide? Clearly, it was time for something more. Then Jesus came—not to impose peace and prosperity, but to offer choices. For transformation of the heart. For experience of the renewing power and presence of God. For opportunities to love and serve as channels of God's grace.

Peter. Jesus's followers spread the good news cross-culturally. At first, that was not intentional. Peter, for example, was sent by God to a Roman named Cornelius. God told Peter to eat the food that he was served, including dishes prohibited to Jews, like pork. He was horrified, but he did it. "I now realize how true it is that God does not show favoritism but accepts from every nation the one who fears him," he said (Acts 10:34-35 NIV). Later he explained to fellow Christians,

"God, who knows the heart, showed that he accepted them by giving the Holy Spirit to them, just as he did to us. He did not discriminate between us and them...It is through the grace of our Lord Jesus that we are saved, just as they are" (Acts 15:8-11 NIV).

Earlier, at the feast of Pentecost in Jerusalem, Jesus's followers experienced the Holy Spirit with unusual manifestations. Those around them wondered what was happening. Peter spoke up, and after his public talk, 3,000 people committed themselves to Jesus. These included many travelers who had come to celebrate Pentecost, including some from as far away as Iran in one direction and North Africa in the other. Eventually, Peter would describe Christian cultural diversity in these words: "You are a chosen people, a royal priesthood, a holy nation, God's special possession...Once you were not a people, but now you are the people of God" (1 Peter 2:9-10 NIV).

Paul. Other believers took the good news to people of other nations, such as Philip, who explained it to an Ethiopian official (Acts 8). Still, global evangelism was not a planned activity until it became clear to those in Antioch (Acts 13:2-3 NIV). Only then did Jesus's followers envision what Jesus meant when He said,

> You will be my witnesses in Jerusalem, and in all Judea and Samaria, and to the ends of the earth (Acts 1:8 NIV).
>
> Therefore go and make disciples of all nations (Matthew 28:19 NIV).

Paul was a key part of the Antioch-based outreach. Originally, Paul was a zealous,

1A. Saint Paul preaches to the Areopagites in Athens. An engraving of Raphael's painting *St. Paul Preaching in Athens*. Metropolitan Museum of Art (https://creativecommons.org/publicdomain/zero/1.0/).

theologically educated Jew who persecuted Christians. Then God zapped him with a vision. Overnight, everything changed. Paul became passionate about Jesus—and about taking the good news to people of other nations and faiths. In the opening of the book of Romans, Paul acknowledged his "obligation" to share the gospel with both Jews and Greeks, two broad cultural divisions (Romans 1:14-16). At the end of the book, he announced his plans to witness in Spain, the outer edge of the known world: "It has always been my ambition to preach the gospel where Christ was not known" (Romans 15:20 NIV). Christian elders formally recognized Paul's call to witness to people of other faiths and cultures (Galatians 2:2,7-9).

John. John the Apostle wrote the book of Revelation while imprisoned on the island of Patmos. Here John gave a preview of the magnificent metastory's final chapter. In chapters 5, 7, 20, and 21, John described Jesus reigning over the whole cosmos, surrounded by strobes of dazzling light, jewels, unimaginable heavenly creatures, and a river of life and a tree with leaves to heal the nations. As part of the revelation, John saw the truly multicultural people of Jesus,

> A great multitude that no one could count, from every nation, tribe, people, and language, standing before the throne and before of the Lamb...And they cried out in a loud voice: "Salvation belongs to our God, who sits on the throne, and to the Lamb" (Revelation 7:9-10 NIV).

Theologian Justo Gonzalez has paraphrased this vision in these words:

> We know and we believe that on that great waking-up morning when the stars begin to fall, when we gather at the river where angel feet have trod, we shall all, from all nations and tribes and peoples and languages, we shall sing without ceasing, "Holy, Holy, Holy! All the saints adore thee, casting down our golden crowns before the glassy sea, cherubim and seraphim, Japanese and Swahili, American and European, Cherokee and Ukrainian, falling down before thee, who wert, and art, and evermore shall be." Amen.[9]

Jesus's People Today. What is God doing in this world today? He continues to unroll a magnificent metastory, stretching from the beginning of time through the present and into the future. Now Jesus's people are present in every nation, among Buddhists, Hindus, Muslims, and historic Christians. They are so widespread that even if the United States and Europe were to fall off the map tomorrow, the church of Jesus Christ would go gloriously on.

In China, there are nearly 100 million Christians. These people have believed during the faith-suppressing Communist period, as ordinary grassroots Christians have shared their faith with neighbors and colleagues.

Six hundred Arabic-speaking churches as well as 250 Iranian churches are spread across Europe. Most of their members were Muslims just a few years ago. In their homelands, too, Muslims like Amina are coming to Jesus. Twenty thousand former Muslims in one ethnic group in the Horn of Africa now worship Jesus as Lord. More than a million Iranians are Christians, many of them inside Iran despite strong persecution. All in all, it is estimated that more Muslims have come to Jesus in the past few decades than in all former centuries.

Hindus are joining the family as well. Across North India—the least evangelized part of the country—there are now many thousands of house churches. They are fostering not merely converts, but authentic disciples/followers of Jesus. These Hindu-background believers grow in their understanding of the faith through teaching appropriate for a nonliterate culture, such as stories, dramas, and songs that transmit a biblical curriculum. Many of these Jesus followers also participate in microloan programs to increase their minuscule incomes. Coaching and accountability are hallmarks of these programs.

Witnessing remains essential in the twenty-first century. It is in Christ—and uniquely in Christ—that God has most fully revealed Himself. It is by relationship with God through Christ that people poor and rich find their deepest hunger met, find the surest prescription for wholeness, find their place of belonging. Although there are Christians in every nation, there are still many people who have never heard a clear word about Jesus as Lord. God is their creator. Their savior. Their lawgiver. Their peacemaker and reconciler. The one who, on their behalf, conquers the powers of darkness, both macrocosmic and microcosmic. This good news must be shared.

Witnessing can provoke persecution, unfortunately. In some countries, it has been understood that Muslims are born into Muslim families and Christians are born into Christian families. If Christians now begin to testify that Jesus is the way to God for *everybody* (John 14:6), the balance is upset. Those simple words become inflammatory.

And because we know that Christians are far from perfect, we may wonder: Do we really have the right to witness to non-Christians? When we read history, we cringe at some records of Christian-Muslim encounters or Christian-Jewish encounters. On the other hand, we must not forget that history also shows some very beautiful Christian contributions. Throughout time and all over the world, Jesus's model and the Spirit's empowering have propelled Christians to serve blind people, drug addicts, trafficked women, homeless children, lepers, prisoners, and many other needy populations. When Christians truly follow Christ, caring action flows out into the community. Witnessing is not peripheral. However, it must be done humbly. We are not experts or authorities but storytellers, channels of the grace that is greater than we are.

Imperfect as we are, we must witness. Like the early church, we "cannot help speaking about what we have seen and heard" (Acts 4:20 NIV), in particular, that "there is no other name under heaven...by which we must be saved" (v. 12). While many religions and ideologies contain wisdom and ethics, the God/man Jesus is unique. His Lordship is distinctive. He is the true center of the cosmos and our lives.

How You Can Join In

We serve an activist God. He is not static. He is not quiet. He moves, He loves, and He fights. Most gloriously He moved when the Word became flesh, took on the form of a human being, humbled Himself to the point of death, and then blasted right back to life. This God does not sit still. He moves because He cares.

The normal Christian life moves too. God calls us to action. In relation to the religions of the world, here are some simple steps that we can take:

- Relate to people of other faiths both locally and globally. Appreciate their giftedness. Feel for their brokenness and their need to be delivered from any system that derails them from worshiping Jesus as Lord.

- Serve needs when that is appropriate (hunger, English tutoring, legal consultancy, etc.), but remember that these needs are temporary, secondary to their eternal need for Jesus. Also, keep in mind that we are not primarily the givers while they are the receivers. It is a two-way street, a mutual exchange. All of us can learn from and bless each other mutually. Certainly, in relation to the grace of God, we are all receivers.
- Offer to pray for anyone's needs, and do it immediately, simply, and joyfully.
- Offer to share briefly the story of your spiritual journey.
- Offer to tell some stories of Jesus, and be ready with 10–30 stories for repeat sessions.
- Know each story well, so you can maintain eye contact. Show emotion in your face and body as you tell the story. (Online, you can look up "Discovery Bible Studies" for story suggestions.)
- Know the basic beliefs and practices of your friend's religion. Know where it conflicts with the gospel. Also know some bridges for explaining the gospel to these people. Be ready to discuss beliefs, but recognize that most people are not very interested in abstract doctrines. They are much more moved by prayer, stories, moral lives, and loving friendship.
- Pray for some ethnic group every day. Get a news app on your phone (CNN, BBC, NYT, etc.) so that in just a few seconds, you can learn what is happening in the world. Encourage your fellow church members to do the same.
- Ask the businessmen and businesswomen in your church what countries they sell to and buy from, and then pray publicly in church for those countries. Many will be nations with Confucianist, Buddhist, Hindu, or Muslim majorities.
- Ask your high school and college students what world issues they are studying (hunger and poverty, global trade, human trafficking, global art, climate change, ethnic and religious violence, media restrictions, epidemics and global health, sports, etc.) and then pray publicly about those issues. When you pray, mention the Hindu, Muslim, or Buddhist majority nations where these issues are important.
- Organize an adult church class that traces the biblical basis of missions—Abraham, Moses, David, Paul, John—to remind us of the great story surrounding our outreach to people of all faiths.

God is telling a magnificent metastory. Like Amina, we are actors in that story, with roles and parts to play and lines and movements to bring to life. Through these, we can inform, challenge, comfort, and bless those around us, near and far. The rest of this book will show us how.

Miriam Adeney (PhD, Washington State University) is an anthropologist and missiologist and professor at Seattle Pacific University who teaches on six continents. Among her many publications are *Kingdom Without Borders: The Untold Story of Global Christianity* and *Daughters of Islam: Building Bridges with Muslim Women*. Miriam has received a Lifetime Achievement Award from Media Associates International and has served as president of the American Society of Missiology.

Tough Questions About Religion

Winfried Corduan

The Uniqueness of Studying Religions

The topic of religion is drastically different from other areas of learning. For many disciplines, a simple description of the subject along with some explanations will suffice without calling for any further direct personal engagement. For example, let us say that I'm a biologist studying birds (an ornithologist). The project would be—for most people, at least—almost entirely intellectual. Knowledge of, say, the circulatory system of birds could conceivably be of personal advantage to someone, but even then, it's unlikely that there is a lot of deep subjective involvement. Of course, we may have a sense of fascination when we look at the beauty and complexity of God's creatures, but that's not directly derived from our present research; it's just one instance among many. Most likely, the topic will speak only to our minds, not our hearts and souls. We are not birds. I don't believe that I should strive to become more like a bird, and I'm pretty sure that a bird would not want to be me.

However, the study of religion is quite different. Religion, wherever we find it, addresses human beings. Religions differ in their beliefs: They do not all share a common goal (e.g., heaven, paradise, nirvana), and they certainly do not advocate the same method to attain it. It may surprise you to learn that not all religions promote the worship of gods or spirits. However, one thing that all religions do share is that they are about you and me: human beings trying to find help along the way through a puzzling universe.

When a religion tells us about a deity, it probably wants us to worship that god or goddess. Religious truth claims are often dismissed by critics as fantasies merely intended to stroke our emotions; however, that is not the nature of the claims themselves. They are not intended to convey greeting-card-style bromides, but they are meant to inform us about certain realities that are assumed to be just as real as mountains, happiness, and text messages. They may be false, but we do them an injustice if we do not treat them as the kinds of statements that are capable of being true or false. And if they are false, we gain nothing by insisting that they convey some pseudotruth that lies beyond their obvious meaning.

In short, the study of world religions can never be purely detached, as though one is reading through a telephone book or *The Handbook of Chemistry and Physics*.[1] If done with sincerity, it will always present us with alternative ways of thinking. It will raise two questions: (a) whether we truly believe what we claim to believe and (b) whether we should rethink our beliefs. Even if we are absolutely sure that our answers are (a) yes and (b) no, we must first consider these questions. What we designate as a "religion" may not be about *other* beings, such as gods or spirits, but it will always be about human beings, and it will demand our response to its claims. Even atheists who reject all religions as false still had to have come to a personal decision regarding the content of one or more religions.

Also, let us keep in mind that religious statements do not come to us as individual propositions. The many facets of a religion, including its claims about gods, worship, prayer, and morality, are all part of a package. Their adherents want you to believe them, and they want you to follow the practices. Religions do not just tell you what there is (ontology); they also tell you what you should do (deontology). For example, if I read the Qur'an, it tells me what I should accept as a fact: There is one—and only one—God. But it doesn't leave things there. Together with this existence claim, it also conveys the exhortation that I should worship that one God and him alone. Religious implications demand decisions.

What Is Religion?

Before trying to attempt a large-scale definition of "religion," it will be helpful to introduce two words that will help us define it: *cultus* and *transcendent*.

1. All religions have a "cultus." By "cultus," I mean all the rituals, moral exhortations, worship practices, and material things (e.g., buildings, altars, literature) in which a religion is embedded. Frequently, they are purely cultural and not based on the teachings of the religion.
2. I will use the term "transcendent" for any item of belief that goes beyond our everyday experience of the world. Transcendence includes gods and spirits but will also include other metaphysical concepts, such as an afterlife. Frequently it includes what we might term the "supernatural," but this word has become rather wiggly these days.

In order for something to be a religion, does it really need to include transcendence? After all, earlier I said that a religion need not center on gods or spirits. In saying that, I had already set aside a very common definition. Religion, we may read here or there, is a human being's attempt to placate one or more gods or spirits. So have I painted myself into a corner?

No, I have not. A definition of religion that focuses on "otherworldly" beings, though perhaps relevant in many cases, is not universally applicable. Some religions, such as certain forms of Buddhism or Jainism, recognize the existence of various gods but deny the existence of a divine Creator. Furthermore, they consider someone's devotion to the gods to be an obstacle to enlightenment, which is the intended outcome of their teachings.

Of course, we could just make it easy on ourselves and simply declare that, consequently, Buddhism and Jainism are not religions. But that very idea runs counter to our basic intuitions. If they are not religions, what else could they possibly be? For that matter, on a popular level, they certainly function as many other religions do: Laypeople worship deified versions of the original teachers as well as other gods. It is the monks and an educated majority who break the mold; nonetheless, despite their lack of interest in gods, their beliefs and practices are still religious, as I shall demonstrate below.

If one doesn't look too closely at the details of religions, one could say that they are merely codes for living, rules to benefit us in our moral and personal growth, usually accompanied by some unique motivation. But this definition is too broad. There are many people, both individuals and groups, who have a rigid moral code without being considered religious. Boy Scouts are expected to live by certain rules, yet "scouting" does not constitute a religion. Many people do not think of themselves as religious and, indeed, would be horrified at the thought, but they still attempt to live according to some strict ethical rules.

To get closer to a definition of "religion" that will not collapse immediately, let's take a look at the context in which such a code of behavior may be embedded. First, consider a college sports team, whose members have dedicated themselves to winning a trophy in the upcoming season. To do so, they must be physically and mentally fit. In order to achieve their goal, they must live according to some clear rules governing their diet, physical exercise, mental discipline, and so on. Still, as all-encompassing as it may be, this regimen per se is not religious in nature.

Contrast that description with the stereotypical life of monks in various religions. They, too, seek a goal, and they, too, must live all day every day according to some clear rules governing their diet, physical exercise, mental discipline, and so on. But they do so in order to attain a spiritual goal, not just an athletic victory. Both groups have a goal, but one is the purely human victory in an athletic contest, while the other is spiritual in nature. The religious goal is rooted in something transcendent.

It's no surprise, then, that even those religions that do not stress gods or spirits still recognize a transcendent context for their practices in that they teach about purported realities that we don't usually encounter in our daily lives. For example, in many forms of Buddhism, an important idea is the recognition of impermanence, sometimes even nonexistence, of everything we think exists, including ourselves. In Jainism, followers must learn to live so as to rid their souls of stipulated material particles they acquire by their actions, particularly when they harm another living being. In both cases, the hoped-for end will be the state of nirvana, the reality of which cannot be adequately understood by us mere humans, let alone described with our finite vocabulary.[2]

In short, dispensing with gods and spirits does not imply the absence of some form of transcendence. Thus I believe that a helpful working definition of religion is, as I have advocated elsewhere, "a system of beliefs and practices that by means of its cultus directs a person toward transcendence and, thus, provides meaning and coherence to a person's life."[3]

Where Did Religion Come From?

In order not to get swept away into an opaque world that can only be traversed by speculation, let us limit our understanding of human beings to *homo sapiens*, our species. My initial question for this section is whether, to the best of our knowledge, there has ever been a time before humans engaged in religious activities. The answer is a rather clear "no." The discovery of ancient ceremonial objects by paleo archaeology and the conclusions of ethnology leave little doubt that, as the Latin-inspired saying goes, "Homo sapiens have always been *homo religiosus*." We need to clarify both of these sources of knowledge.

Paleo archaeology looks for artifacts of human beings all the way back to the Old Stone Age (the Paleolithic Period). Artifacts are objects made and used by human beings; thus, since nothing other than stone would have survived over the ages, it is practically impossible for us to find any earlier ones. As the physical aspects of cultures become more sophisticated, the diversity in the materials and functions of artifacts increases dramatically. Archaeologists can look for evidence of religion among human beings in two directions.

For one, they may find "ritual" or "ceremonial" objects. These artifacts are usually identified either by their resemblance to similar things carrying a religious function in later times or by stipulating that no conceivable use for them in everyday life seems plausible.

Another direction is to find artifacts accompanying human remains in burial sites. An ax head, a spear point, a coin, a spindle, or some other object can tell us a lot about the beliefs of its presumed owner.

Ethnology is the study of ethnic groups around the world. Different people obviously have distinct cultures, and we can discover many levels of material development, from the digitized and industrialized nations to those who still live on a cultural level not so distant from what we know of Stone Age humans. The latter ones are usually referred to as "tribal" or "traditional," and they are of greatest interest here. A basic assumption is that the materially lesser-developed people groups are most likely to manifest a culture akin to that of the earliest human beings.

Since the eighteenth century, many prominent writers have asserted that religion began with a cultus that they considered to be childish, primitive, and savage. For example, many have thought that the first religion of human beings consisted of the veneration of various spirits, including those that live throughout nature as well as those of departed human beings. Such a religion would be saturated with magic and ritual.[4] One can find many traditional cultures that fit this description. The question arises, however, whether these people truly exist at the "lowest" level of material development. Are there perhaps people who are less developed in their general culture and, consequently, should be thought of as older yet?

It is indeed possible to establish the relative ages of different traditional cultures.[5] A culture in which the warriors used metal-tipped arrows most likely displays a later development than one using stone arrowheads, which, in turn, is probably younger than one in which only sharpened sticks were used. Clearly, not all factors are as easy to delineate as the above example, but we can discover which cultures are older than others by taking into account all their utensils, dress, economic activities, lore, weaponry, and similar factors. Some examples of cultures that are clearly on the lowest level of material development include certain pygmies in Africa, a few tribal groups around the Philippines, and a small number of Australian aborigines.

The German anthropologist Wilhelm Schmidt (1868–1954) has demonstrated that people who struggle through the lowest levels of material cultures have a religion that is directly opposed to the earlier preconceptions.[6] They are not spirit-crazy, magic-obsessed, amoral savages, as the common stereotype would have it. Their religion is a monotheism in that they worship only one God, and they don't occupy themselves much with ghosts or ancestor spirits. Their moral code stresses monogamy and the value of human life and property. In short, Schmidt's observations and conclusions were utterly at odds with what other scholars had blindly presumed the earliest religion should be.

It is no secret that much scholarship of the nineteenth and twentieth centuries (and its continuing vector into the twenty-first) has been firmly grounded on a presumptive rejection of religious beliefs. Schmidt's conclusions about this primordial monotheism are, of course, consistent with the Bible, and he was a Christian. Since he based his conclusions on empirical data, he created a dilemma for a large segment of the academic world. If you start with the assumption that there is no God, it's hard to go along with the thesis that worship of the one true God is a part of our most basic human nature. So if other academics stayed on factual ground, they could not avoid Schmidt's conclusions; if they did not work with the facts as Schmidt had gathered them, they would look like bad scientists. Thus they simply avoided Schmidt's work and wrote him off as a religious crank, out to justify his religious beliefs. Nonetheless, the empirical facts and their logical inferences are firmly on the side that human religion began with the worship of the one true God. Though many of the cultures that constituted the evidence have now disappeared, the records are still as available as they were then, and they still add up to an original monotheism.[7]

Do All Religions Share a Common Core?

It would be a lot easier to answer this question if there were an objective definition of the "core" of a religion accepted by a majority of religious people and not prejudicial to anyone. The rather broad definition of "religion" above is certainly inadequate for such purposes. My definition is intentionally vague in order to place the concept of religion somewhere on the map of human knowledge, and the nature of "the core" would need to be filled in more concretely before we could learn anything more substantial. Transcendence per se is not a thing. If someone were to claim to have encountered transcendence, there must have been a transcendent reality to be encountered.

We must also note that a common core is not necessarily shared truth. After all, the common core could be nothing more than a fundamental illusion.

Shared Truth? Most people are rational and understand that mutually exclusive beliefs cannot be true. Thus their reaction to learning about other religions would probably be logical, rejecting one or more of them as false and recognizing shared truth only where they obviously agree. People who believe that their religion is the only true one must logically accept that all other religions are false insofar as they are inconsistent with it. However, sometimes rationality seems to be put on hold in the context of religious truth.

Some people believe that truth is distributed in unequal portions across the various religions, in which case their religion usually becomes the one with the most truth, and the others are somehow contorted to fit into their favorite religion. This approach is frequently called "inclusivism," but perhaps a more fitting title is religious "colonialism" or "imperialism."

Yet another not-so-rational group of people ties itself to the logically impossible notion that all religions are equally true. They sometimes call themselves "pluralists" and thrive on the notion that they are the epitome of tolerance. The truth, however, is that such "tolerance" mocks the claims of individual religions and contorts reason.

Still, others may reject all religions as false and embrace atheism. However, since they cannot reject what they don't know about, somewhere along the line they must have first confronted the claims of various religions or religion in general in order to make a meaningful personal decision about the matter.

A Shared Core? The fact is that adherents of different religions would undoubtedly give drastically different answers to the question, "What is the core of your religion?" Here are some sample answers. I'm not claiming that they are "official" representative declarations, just some statements a person might make. The "core" of a religion could be the following for each:

- Christian: "redemption from sin through Jesus's death and resurrection"
- Muslim: "submission to God (Allah) by keeping the rules of the Qur'an"
- Hindu: "release from the cycle of reincarnations by devotion to my god"
- Another Hindu: "realization of the identity of my Self with the Ultimate, Brahman"
- Jain: "to avoid doing harm to any living being and always telling the truth"
- Observant Jew: "to live according to God's law, the Torah"

These sample statements made by adherents of various religions differ drastically from each other. Adding further religions would only add to the problem of finding commonality in what each of these people might say. They cannot be reconciled by rational means without drastically altering their intended meanings. If these assertions are allowed to stand, then religions definitely do not share the same core.

However, this simple logic is frequently considered to be shallow and uneducated by various scholars and certain religious groups. Some writers on religion regard their beliefs and practices as the only true and proper ones, and then they proclaim that, even though followers of other religions may not know it, they are actually worshiping the writer's God. One such example is the doctrine of the "anonymous Christian" coined by the twentieth-century theologian Karl Rahner, who held that anyone sincerely committed to full humanity was worshiping God, whether he knew it or not.[8]

A similar idea is often propagated under the misquoted slogan from the Hindu Rig Veda, "Truth is one, the wise call it by different names." Thus we would all be "anonymous Hindus."[9] In each case, the practical outcome is that Christianity or Hinduism, respectively, arrogate themselves the standing as the most authentic religion, while others are merely their lesser imitations. Once again, we are encountering versions of religious colonizing. One obvious alternative is the one that I hold: The message of Christianity is based on God's revelation in the Bible, and sadly, people of other religions do not have a kind of backdoor into it.[10]

Feel free to substitute the names of other religions into the following example. An easy response by, say, a Buddhist to a religiously colonizing Hindu would be that the Hindu in question is simply mistaken, since the two religions hold to some mutually exclusive beliefs and practices. It would be one thing to assert that Hinduism is the only true religion, a statement that can at least be debated sensibly, but quite another to ignore the obvious distinctions and redefine Buddhism as Hinduism in disguise. The latter would have to contort Buddhist beliefs and vocabulary to such an extent that it could not even be discussed rationally, though there seems to be no limit to irrational proclamations.

Some scholars of the twentieth century have made this commonsense response just a little harder, not by substituting the vocabulary of one religion for all the others, but by inventing a term that is not found in any of the specific religions but supposedly expresses the core of all religions. I'm going to use a famous example that clearly indicates the illogic behind these attempts—namely, the thought of John Hick.[11] He stipulated that (1) the aim of all religions is to get people to treat each other better, (2) no single religion has an advantage over the others in that respect, and (3) all (mature)[12] religions boil down to motivating their adherents to make contact with what Hick called "the Real," which would improve their spiritual state as well as their disposition toward humanity.

So in the case of Hick's system, our earlier examples of core beliefs for Christians, Muslims, Hindus, Jains, and Jews are only apparently correct, given the limited understanding by people of their own religion, but they are false from the more exalted vista of Hick's thesis. According to Hick, all of them are stuck on the naïve level of thinking that the language about their gods and their practices is meant to be taken literally. They treat the assertions of their religion as facts, although they are mere images meant to transport us to the deeper actuality of the Real. Had they adopted Hick's supposedly more insightful perspective, their only true response should have been, "The core of my religion is to relate myself to the Real."

What makes Hick's proposal of the Real so convenient for those seeking to reduce all religions to an amorphous abstraction is that the Real cannot be directly known or described with words and concepts. One cannot actually explain it. It is something deep, holy, and mysterious, an expression of the numinous (sacredness), which cannot be captured by human thought. Thus, although Hick might declare that in my religious cultus I am really establishing a relationship with the Real, rather than with God through Jesus, both he and I would be hard-pressed to provide any more information on this synthesized Real, except to speak of it in negative terms, for example, it is *not* limited.

There have been quite a few other attempts to distill an "essence" of all religions, but they all founder on the simple reality that the supposed core they are advocating is either (1) an idea taken from one religion and then imposed on "colonized" religions by distorting them or (2) an invented notion that, if actually applied, entails that the adherents of all religions are actually in the dark about what they believe and practice. Hick's scheme is sometimes presented as an implementation of tolerance among the religions of the world because he treats them all equally; however, a little bit of reflection reveals that he treats them all equally badly.

But wait! Having said all this, isn't it still true that all religions teach us to love and respect each other, to get along in peace and not make war, to aid the helpless, and to encourage those who have many resources to share with those who have little or none?

No, it is not true, at least not when you take a close enough look at what different religions might mean by these terms. For many of them, the perfect ending of history includes the victory of one people or class of people over inferior human beings. Not all religions teach what you and I might call "love and compassion for all." For example, we do not see this type of benevolence toward "infidels" among many Muslims.

I once received a note from a young man informing me that he did not know much about Jesus and Krishna (a Hindu god) except that they both taught love and peace. I had to answer him that he was right about Jesus, but not about Krishna. There are no passages in Hindu scriptures where Krishna taught self-sacrificial love in the same sense as Jesus did. As to advocating peace, the most important work concerning Krishna is the Bhagavad Gita. Its initial theme is Krishna's rebuke of the warrior Arjuna for not wanting to take up arms against his enemies, who also happened to be his cousins.[13] Love and peace for all? A rare find among the religions of the world.

Speaking of South Asian gods, the internet is filled with site after site claiming identity between Christ and Krishna, Buddha, or other spiritual leaders. Some of the reasons given may overwhelm someone who does not have accurate knowledge of the facts involved, particularly if the arguments involve forced and improbable derivations from Sanskrit or other ancient languages.

2A. Krishna and his brother Balarama fight King Kamsa's warriors. Public domain.

There are a number of questions one can ask in order to discover whether the "identity" is fraudulent. For our purposes, the most important issue is the alleged identity of Christ with various figures.

- *Is the comparison accurate with regard to Christ and His life and work in the Bible?* The Bible is the only reliable source of information on Christ. If it is being distorted for the sake of claiming identity, you know the comparison is worthless. Identity with Christ is not the same thing as identity with an invented revision of Christ.

- *Is the comparison accurate with regard to the figure to whom Christ is being compared?* That question is obviously far more difficult for a Western Christian to answer. Let's say someone claims that Buddha and Christ are the same person and that they taught the same message. Clearly, we cannot tell a Buddhist what he or she should believe as a Buddhist, let alone declare to Buddhists what true Buddhism is or should be. However, we can study Buddhism sufficiently to be able to tell whether the description of the Buddha in question conforms to the common understanding of him in traditional Buddhist societies and their contemporary continuations. Identity with the Buddha as recorded in traditional scriptures is not the same thing as identity with an invented revision of Buddha.

- *Are the supposed resemblances significant or trivial for the religious figures?* I once heard in a radio discussion someone declare that Islam and Christianity were extremely similar because they both shared an affinity for the color green. It is true that in Islam, green is an important color, which is sometimes used to represent the religion, though it has nothing to do with Islam's actual message. The example of green in Christianity was even more trivial. The speaker pointed to the color of branches in Christmas decorations, something that surely is on the farthest edge of what Christianity is all about.

- In short, please keep in mind the principle that *all things are the same if you ignore the differences.* A triangle and a square are the same if you ignore that one has three, possibly unequal, sides, while the other has four equal sides and that, consequently, they must be studied with different geometric formulas. Or, to use another illustration, a boat and a car are the same kind of vehicle as long as you ignore the facts. One is made for water, the other for dry land; one has four wheels, the other a keel; one runs with a motor that turns a crank shaft, the other (possibly) runs with a motor and a propeller; one is steered with a wheel attached to the front axle, the other with a rudder. Subtract all that's different between the two and, voilà, you're looking at identical things.
- So we can say that yes, Jesus and Krishna and Buddha and even, say, Erasmus of Rotterdam and Wyatt Earp are one and the same—if we ignore every aspect in which they differ from each other in favor of creating an artificial figure that does not do justice to any of them.[14]

2B. A worshiper kneels before the Buddha at a temple in India. Photo by Evan Loveley (https://creativecommons.org/licenses/by/2.0).

If you study the contents of various religions, as presented in this book and similar ones, you will realize that, beyond empty truisms, you can find a substantial "common core" among them only if you put it there first.

Do We Need Religion Now That We Have Science?

The relationship between religion and science has historically been stormy. Religious authorities have often condemned the methods and conclusions of science, while certain scientists frequently ridicule religion and dismiss it as unnecessary, even harmful, mythology.

Given the historical turbulence, it is advisable to express one's beliefs on the subject without leaping into dogmatism. Sweeping statements such as "Science tells us *what* and *how*, while religion tells us *why*," simply do not stand up unless we endow these words with preconceived meanings. Of course, science tells us *why* it is colder at the north pole than at the equator, and religions frequently tell us *how* the human race came into being, just to pick out two simple examples.

As a matter of fact, the question does not have much meaning unless we observe some important distinctions, including the following:

- *The differences among religions.* They do not all relate to science in identical ways.
- *The differences between religions and religious people.* What even apparently devout adherents of various religions believe may be drastically different from what the "official" version of the religion teaches.
- *The differences among sciences and among their subdisciplines.* Different areas of inquiry may lend themselves to various degrees of accommodation with religions.
- *The differences between scientists and their sciences.* Scientists are human beings who will have their own personal beliefs, which are not necessarily dictated in any way by the science they practice. Some scientists believe, in light of their observations, there must be a God who created the universe, while others insist that the discoveries of science make belief in a Creator superfluous.

Some scientists think of their science as the culmination of religion and turn themselves into virtual oracles for the ultimate truth to all questions. For example, theoretical physicist Michio Kaku believes that he has found the key to the meaning of the universe in a relatively "simple" equation out of string theory.[15] Conversely, some religious people assert that their beliefs or their scriptures contain all the science that one needs, and to go any further in the quest for knowledge is downright sinful. Such arrogant attitudes on both sides not only are unhelpful but can become dangerous. Scientists may be quick to point out that the church persecuted Galileo, but they seem to forget the persecution of Christians in the name of science during, for example, the French Revolution or the Lenin and Stalin eras of the Soviet Union.

We mentioned earlier in this chapter that religion includes a transcendent dimension, something that lies beyond our everyday experiences, often called "supernatural." If we accept this phenomenon, we may hold a key that helps us understand the distinction between science and religion. Nevertheless, one-sidedness is a frequent occurrence.

Let's look at a crass example. Frequently, religion becomes its own worst enemy by trying to play up to the agnosticism promoted by a number of scientists. A case in point is the German New Testament scholar Rudolph Bultmann, who wrote in the 1950s, "It is impossible to use electric light and the wireless and to avail ourselves of modern medical and surgical discoveries, and at the same time to believe in the New Testament world of spirits and miracles."[16]

It is difficult for me to make a logical connection, let alone find any force, in Bultmann's statement. Consider a healing miracle recorded in the New Testament. A paralyzed person is brought to Jesus, who says to him, "Take up your bed and walk." The person does exactly that. Now, this event is predicated on the belief that there is a God who is omnipotent and who gave Jesus the power to perform something that cannot be done without such divine power. In what sense is it reasonable to state that modern medicine has erected a barrier to believing this event occurred? It is, indeed, not possible for today's medical practitioners to duplicate that kind of healing, but that's the point of it. That's why it's called a miracle; it's not an everyday kind of thing.

Further, we rightly observe that in biblical times, people made light at night by means of oil lamps and torches, while today we rely on electricity derived from various kinds of power plants, thereby allowing lightbulbs to glow. In each case, there is a source found in nature, such as oil or tar in one case, coal, nuclear fission, or hydraulic power in the other. To the Christian believer, all of them are created by God and used by humans. The latter methods are technically more sophisticated, but they give us no reason to believe that now we can get along without God and the things He has created, including us.

As to the reason the existence of radios should be a hindrance to belief in a religion, I must say that I cannot even come close to understanding why that should be the case. Nor does the argument become any stronger if we fast-forward from Bultmann to now and consider the advances in physics and technology that would have been unknown in Bultmann's time. Religion has clearly not been obviated by contemporary digital technology.

Now, there should be no question when a religious person asserts the existence of a god or maybe the efficacy of a particular ritual, he or she is intending to state a truth that is meant to be just as objectively factual as a scientist's report on a certain phenomenon. But religious people are not just meddling in the workshop of the scientist. They add something that science, due to its limits in methodology, cannot provide. Science may lead a person to the threshold of religion. It can show, for example, that the universe has features for which the best explanation is that it must have been created by an intelligent all-powerful being. But science cannot go further and reveal to us how we must relate to this Creator. Scientific methodology may be used in history or philology to confirm factual statements of the various religious scriptures, but it cannot provide the spiritual information that the scriptures seek to communicate. In short, science is a gift from God insofar as it enables us to explore the world He has created; religion is an essential element for letting us get a deeper look at the Creator.

At the heart of what I'm saying is that there is only one kind of truth—namely, whatever corresponds to what is real. There is no such thing as "truth-with-a-little-t" for factual matters and "Truth-with-a-big-T" for religious knowledge. Some beliefs are accessed and tested by science—for example, water is a compound of hydrogen and oxygen. Others are considered to be true only on the basis of religious authority, an example being that God is a Trinity or that there is a Buddha named Amitabha. Still others can be held on the basis of faith but can also be examined by means of scientific, scholarly methods. In the latter category, we might put the historicity of the battles described in the Hindu epics or the existence of Jesus of Nazareth. Saying that religious claims are immune from truth-testing is a lame excuse for holding on to something unbelievable. When believers state what they consider to be true about their religion, they mean their statements to be just as factually true as descriptions of the furniture in their houses.

How Does "Religion" Connect with the Idea of "Worldviews"?

To put it simply, a religion must entail a certain worldview, but a worldview is not necessarily a religion.[17]

What is a "worldview"? The term refers to the fact that the collection of our various beliefs gives us a specific way of looking at the world around us, and since people differ in their beliefs, they look at the world differently as well. The term is usually used with reference to groups of people who share central tenets in their belief systems, like a "communist" or an "environmentalist" view.

Obviously, when we come right down to it, every person sees the world in a unique way. To stick with the illustrations above, every communist or environmentalist will hold any number of personal beliefs that are based on their own experiences and thus cannot be shared by others. So when we use the term "worldview," we usually overlook the personally distinctive beliefs and focus on the larger, more central ones that organize a person's thinking and link them up with other people who share their main ideas. So most communists will also hold a materialist worldview, though not necessarily so.

We can find a fascinating account of how a religious worldview arose and perpetuated itself in the life of the Buddha Gautama. When he was still known as Prince Siddhartha, he took a chariot ride, during which he was overcome by the reality of old age, disease, and death. Subsequently, during a large social gathering crowded with handsome men and gorgeous women, his mind would not allow him to see their youthful beauty. Instead, all he could see was how they would look in just a few years or decades. He could not get away from picturing them as putrid, decaying blobs of flesh sagging off crumbling skeletons. This morose mode of perception paved the way for the foundational Buddhist belief in the impermanence of everything. Monks in the more traditional branches of Buddhism to this day are taught to meditate by bringing similar visions to their minds.

On the other hand, a biblically based Christian worldview should take a very different approach. If I may resurrect the idea of the "core" of a religion here, at the heart of Christianity, there are the notions of God as Creator and Redeemer. We are weak, finite, mortal beings, to be sure, but we are the creatures of an all-loving, all-powerful God. Our bodies are a gift from God, and we are to cherish them even if they come with defects due to the imperfections of a fallen world. Speaking of fallenness, we are born as sinners and spiritual corpses due to our sin, but God sent His Son to die on our behalf and reconcile us to Him. When old age sets in and our physical disintegration is near, we are also close to the full realization of eternal life with Him.

Unsurprisingly, given what we said earlier, religious worldviews come with certain demands in how we act and respond to various realities. Anyone who might claim to be a Baha'i and is not concerned for peace in the world is not living according to his worldview. A Hindu worldview prohibits the slaughtering of cows. Similarly, a nonreligious worldview, such as the illustration of communism above, entails working toward the revolution of the proletariat, as prescribed in the works of Marx, Lenin, and Mao Zedong, among others. However, some worldviews, such as purely materialistic atheism, without any authoritative sources—neither human nor divine—are hard put to provide any injunctions with moral force.

How Should Christians Relate to People of Other Religions?

Let me begin this answer by reflecting on who and what I am under two headings. These are fundamental points to keep in mind at all times and in all situations, but they are worth spelling out, particularly in this context.

First, I'm a human being who was born into sin, alienated from God, with my will misdirected by my self-centered desires. For a reason that I will never know, God in His love allowed me to grow up in a home in which the Bible was accepted as the Word of God, and consequently, I had the opportunity to become a child of God by receiving Jesus Christ as my Lord and Savior early in life. Growing up in a Christian family does not mean that I would automatically become a Christian. Being a father myself, I know that Christian parents do not take the salvation of their children for granted; they pray for it daily. Looking back on my life, I am aware more than anyone else of the times when I was not living up to my identity as God's child, and I can only credit the fact that I did not fall away to God's astonishing patience. As the Apostle Paul said, "By God's grace I am what I am, and His grace toward me was not ineffective" (1 Corinthians 15:10 HCSB). As I apply this statement to myself, I include not only my salvation but the cultural, material, and professional successes I have been blessed with over my life.

I trust that if you are a Christian, you realize that you are in the same position. None of us deserve what we are and have, and it is only because of God's astonishing love for us that we are born-again creatures rather than spiritual corpses. The negative aspects of our situation before coming to Christ apply to all human beings—no matter how charitable, kind, or religious they may be—unless they have found new life in Christ, as described in the Bible.

Second, I am also privileged to live in a society whose founding philosophy includes the intrinsic liberty and worth of every human being, regardless of one's spiritual state. Clearly, the extent to which this point of view has been implemented in my country needed to increase over its history, is subject to criticism today, and comes with no guarantee for survival in the future. Few, if any, countries do not at least lay claim to a similar view. The nearly universal claim to these values demonstrates their significance for a full human life, no matter how poorly they may be put into practice in reality.

And of course, this description applies to those who do not share our culture, religion, or values. No matter how distorted other people's views may be, and even if you see their religion as a threat to your rights, that perception does not deprive them of theirs. The fact that all humans share certain fundamental rights does not eliminate the need for the government to punish those who violate the rights of others, but it is not up to us as individuals to disrespect other people who are humans created in God's image.

At first reading, you may consider this quick lesson in theology and civics to be unnecessary, irrelevant, and maybe even a bit patronizing. Of course, you know that you should treat others, including those of different faiths, respectfully and lovingly.

Nevertheless, at this point, I'm going to ask a "tough question" back of you. Do you really practice these virtues? What is your feeling deep inside toward the thousands of Muslims who have immigrated into your country (assuming that you live in a "Western" country)? For a century or more, missionaries have gone to Muslim nations and spent many decades with little or no fruit. Now Muslims are coming here en masse. Are you now wanting to send them back to locations where we cannot interact with them? Do you really think that you can put an end to Islamic terrorism around the world by being contemptuous of the Islamic people who may be attending a mosque in your neighborhood? I doubt it. Should you perhaps take advantage of the opportunity to show some Muslim individuals that biblical Christianity is not the Christianity of the Crusades or of Western exploitation? God willing, you should.

A short while ago, I was invited to dinner by a Christian couple living in a village in Germany. The wife told me of an immigrant woman from Thailand who had just established a hair and nail salon in that location and had placed an image of the Buddha in her display window. My friend continued to relate that the villagers, most of whom would have been nominal Christians at best, were resolved to rid themselves of her presence, which they considered disruptive to their local culture. They had informed my friend that they were just going to "ugly her out." She was aghast (as was I) and told them that doing so was 180 degrees in the opposite direction of how Christians should relate to folks like this Thai woman. They should show her love and help her in whatever concrete ways might arise, even taking their business to her so that, by the power and love of God, she might become a Christian. It has happened before.

Of course, for people whose "Christianity" is merely a cultural artifice in which baptisms, weddings, and occasional church attendance are just things respectable people do, a negative attitude is possibly the only response that makes sense. However, for a New Testament Christian who is aware of the points I made above, respectfully embracing the person (so to speak) in order for her to see her need of salvation is ultimately the only biblical option.

Obviously, evangelism is not always the immediate motive for establishing a relationship with people of other religions. It may just be a matter of getting along with each other in the workplace, merely trying to learn from them about their religion for the sake of attaining greater goals in the future, or maybe even just building bridges to a new community in your neighborhood. Needless to say, whatever your immediate objective might be in this case, letting others see Christ and His redemption in your life should be true regardless of where you go and to whom you may be talking. In that light, let me make some further suggestions.

First, in many non-Western cultures, it is hard to conceive of friendship without mutual hospitality. I realize that it is not possible for many people to become involved with others on that level regardless of the context, and any rational person of good faith would understand that. Still, if you are in a position to do so, it is a good idea to accept invitations and to open your door and dining room to acquaintances of other religions.

Second, most people cherish their religion and take a certain amount of pride in it, even if to our eyes they don't seem to be very committed to it. I have found that, if you are able to show interest in what they believe without displaying an aggressive or superior attitude, most people of other faiths are not just willing to talk about what they believe but actually delighted to do so. Still, keep in mind (1) they may not know very much about the history and theory of their religion, which you may have read about in a book such as this one, and (2) if there is a negative stereotype about their religion, they may not even be aware of it. As such, it would be unfair to hold them, as individual adherents, responsible for it.

Third, if you have demonstrated a genuine interest in a person's religion, courtesy, if nothing else, may lead them to ask you about what you believe. Feel free to be open and share with them kindly, without compromise, what you accept. However, don't make people feel like you have placed a target on their backs as subjects for conversion; nobody likes to be thought of as a potential trophy. If they ask questions, answer them to the best of your ability, but avoid heated discussions if possible. Few people come to Christ on the basis of someone speaking disdainfully of their religion. Allow the Holy Spirit to do His work over the course of time. Only He can change people.

Fourth, most houses of worship (temples, shrines, churches, synagogues, mosques, etc.) welcome visitors, though under various conditions. If you are in doubt, and there are no signs, go ahead and ask someone. Even for one religion, places of worship may have different rules. Some may allow visitors only during times when there is no service going on, some may allow you unrestricted access, some may allow you to be there with or without restrictions on taking pictures and videos, and some may simply not allow any visitors at all. And there may be some places that not only welcome you but invite you to take part in their practices. Usually, if you explain that you are a Christian and that you cannot participate, they will respect your convictions. If they do not, you do not want to be there.

What Is "Contextualization"?[18]

Let us consider the option mentioned above, that your objective in meeting people from other religions is very specifically to convey the gospel to them. As we just said, it is not up to you to do the work of the Holy Spirit to change a person's mind and heart, but it is up to you to convey the gospel in such a way that your friends can understand and respond to it, should God lead them to do so. A good point to keep in mind is that even people of roughly your Christian background are often clueless as to the content of the gospel. How much less can people from other religions come to grips with ideas that may be entirely alien to them! Consequently, we must be sure to present the Bible's teachings in ways that make sense to them, a task that includes (1) separating those of our interpretations that are purely rooted in our culture from pure biblical teachings and (2) if possible, use concepts from the other culture to help it make sense. This process is called "contextualization."

Contextualization means to express the message of the Bible in terms that make it relevant to the people of a different culture. Now, when I say "culture," I do not mean a different religion. Contextualization is not religious colonialism as we discussed it above. It is not a fusion of Christianity and another religion. The Christian gospel itself must not be compromised, and so we must be sure to differentiate between the gospel and the language and cultural references with which we express the gospel. It is not easy to do so, though again, we may rely on the Holy Spirit to do things that are impossible for us as finite humans.

Many people around the globe think of Christianity as a religion of the West, by which they mean the European-originated industrialized culture that has swept the world. In fact, some people from Eastern cultures have adopted a Western-style church-going habit simply for the sake of being seen as in touch with the modern world.

The first step in contextualization is to recognize that, as we practice Christianity, many things that are a part of our Christian cultus have simply come with Western culture and are not direct mandates from the Bible. That's okay as long as we recognize this fact; after all, Christianity did spend its formative years, so to speak, in the Near East, North Africa, and Europe. We worship in houses that usually have a steeple, we sit on wooden benches, and the preacher stands in front of the worshipers behind the pulpit or lectern. Most Western churches observe an order of worship even if they do not subscribe to an actual liturgy. We meet on Sunday mornings, dress up in nice clothes, and the service usually takes not much more than an hour. More often than not, offering plates are passed through the congregation. Our music, whether traditional (accompanied by organ, piano, or harmonium) or contemporary (with electric instruments and drum sets), is definitely Western in style. We hold private devotions in our homes where we have access not only to a Bible but to a multitude of English versions of the Bible along with devotional literature to help us understand and apply biblical teaching. The list could go on, but I trust that you see the point that much of what we do in Western Christendom may not be contrary to the Bible, but it is not based on biblical requirements either.

Many of these practices potentially build an unnecessary barrier between the gospel and the people whom we are trying to reach because they are alien—and possibly even alienating—to them. Clearly, one cannot easily separate the biblical message from the culture in which we have heard it, and obviously, it is not possible at all to do so if we are not familiar with the content of the Bible. So a thorough knowledge of God's Word is essential.

Having highlighted the biblical message from its embodiment in our own culture to the best of our ability, the next part is to express it to our non-Christian neighbors in terms that they will hopefully understand. Now, I'm assuming that people in non-Western cultures are just as capable of reading and interpreting the Bible as we are, but first, they need to hear the gospel in their terms and learn what the Bible is all about.

The development of synergism, which we have called religious colonialism above, is an ever-present danger. For example, a number of years ago, a friend and I were talking to a Buddhist professor who was giving up a lot of her time to take us to various Buddhist temples and arrange for interviews with scholars on Buddhism. When we asked her why she was doing so, she responded, "I love the Lord too," and went on to tell us that she believed that Jesus was a great Bodhisattva, a Buddha in the making, who extends His benevolence and loving-kindness to all living beings and shows them the way to nirvana out of karma and reincarnation.

Not more than an hour later, we were talking to a Christian couple who had converted from Buddhism and asked them what Christ meant to them. They explained to us that, in their view, Jesus was a great Bodhisattva who was more successful than previous ones in showing living beings the way to nirvana out of karma and reincarnation. Except for the idea of Christ's superiority among all the other Bodhisattvas, they were echoing the same idea that our Buddhist friend had just voiced. There is no question that their former Buddhism was still providing the paradigm into which they had forced their recently acquired version of Christianity.

On the other hand, our Western forms of music, architecture, worship order, and so forth are certainly not a part of the gospel message, and we may wind up not reaching people if we put those matters into the foreground. Obviously, how we specifically contextualize the biblical message without falling into a synergistic trap depends on the particular culture we are addressing. Still, if we start to draw false equivalences that compromise the uniqueness of Christ as the Son of God incarnate or His atonement for our sins on the cross, we may wind up creating serious misunderstandings.

Is Reading Textbooks Enough to Learn All That Is Necessary to Understand a Religion?

We contributors to this anthology thank you for reading and studying this material. However, the next time you have a conversation with an adherent of a religion covered here, you may wind up hearing things that are quite different from what is in print before you or in other books. For example, you may read a treatment of Buddhism that emphasizes the way toward enlightenment as taught by the Buddha. Subsequently, you may encounter a Buddhist who tells you that his religion is all about chanting a mantra while facing a piece of inscribed rice paper, displayed in a beautifully carved cabinet. Did the author get it wrong? Worse yet, did the Buddhist to whom you talked get his religion wrong? Well, I can't vouch for the accuracy of some hypothetical author, though I would assume the author is correct, and I certainly cannot tell a Buddhist that his faith, no matter how peculiar, isn't really Buddhism. There are many schools, subschools, and derivative schools of Buddhism. In the example just now, the Buddhist would be a member of one of the sects of Nichiren Buddhism that does indeed vary a great deal from the Buddhism practiced by, say, the monks in Thailand, and a description thereof may simply not have fit into whatever you may have read.

There may be even greater surprises in store for you. Sticking with Buddhism as an example, you may encounter people who call themselves Buddhist but are mostly concerned with protecting themselves from evil spirits while worshiping various gods. Whatever the textbooks may say about their religion, in their own world, their "Buddhist" practice may have more in common with spirit-centered religions (animism) rather than Buddhism.

The same thing is true for people in other religions, including some that call themselves Christians. Common people frequently do not know the scriptures, let alone the basic beliefs of their religion. They just want supernatural help of some kind to make it through life. So, for example, many think Christianity teaches us to be nice people who are rewarded for one or more good deeds by getting angel wings after they die. For many Muslims, the focus of their faith is to protect themselves against the "evil eye." We use the term "folk religion" for this phenomenon, according to which people are not concerned with, or possibly not even aware of, what the books say they "should" believe and practice.

Thus the answer to the question above is "no." Reading is an important start, but to get the full picture, experience and personal interaction are also necessary. Wherever you go, adherents of a religion do not see it as their duty to exemplify what has been written about them in books, but they are trying to live a long and prosperous life with the spiritual aid of the main figures of their religion, though often without paying attention to their actual teachings.

A short while ago, when I had misplaced my cell phone, a kind elderly lady told me she would pray to St. Stephen for me to find it. When I found the phone, she thanked St. Stephen on behalf of me. As a Christian who accepts the Bible alone as God's revelation, I do not believe in St. Stephen as the patron saint for finding lost articles, but I was thankful to the lady for wholeheartedly bringing her folk Christianity to bear on my frustration. Look for folk religion wherever you go; you may find a talking point with adherents of a religion easier if you start there rather than by trying to bring up the abstract philosophies of some of their writings.

Although there are many more questions surrounding the study of world religions, I hope the answers to the questions in this chapter will be of help as you seek to study religions and cultivate relationships.

Winfried Corduan (PhD, Rice University) is a world-traveling expert in a great many subjects, most notably philosophy and world religions. From 1977 to 2008, he served as a professor of philosophy and religion at Taylor University. He is the author of over ten books, including *Neighboring Faiths: A Christian Introduction to World Religions* and *In the Beginning God: A Fresh Look at the Case for Original Monotheism.*

3

How to Contextualize the Gospel

I'Ching Thomas

Having grown up in a small town in Malaysia during the preinternet era, the only windows to the world were the world news section in our local newspaper as well as the nightly world news segment on our cathode-ray tube television. And of course the constant diet of Hollywood television series like *Dallas* and *Little House on the Prairie*. All my friends were Malaysians, albeit mostly from two other ethnic groups—Indians and Malays. The only friend from another country I had (we used to call them "pen pals") was a girl my age from Sweden, and we were "connected" via the American television program *The Big Blue Marble*.

Some of you reading this may have no idea of the world I'm describing here because today we live in a world that's characterized as a global village or a globalized world. Many of us live in communities where our neighbors are from either a different ethnic group or another nationality. Hardly anyone has pen pals anymore because we now have Facebook and Instagram to connect.

So has the globally connected world we live in led us to a greater understanding of our cultural, religious, and social differences? Global immigration and accessibility to travel have brought foreign peoples and cultures to our doorstep—and many of these do not know Christ. As followers of Jesus who want to witness Jesus Christ as the Savior of the world as a universal truth to those who do not know Him, a key question to ask is whether we are prepared to have such cross-cultural discussions about the gospel in a meaningful and impactful way with our friends.

I met "Andrew," who is from China, when I was speaking on the relevance of the Christian faith for the Cultural Chinese at a church in Perth, Australia. While he looked like he had only just graduated from college, he was actually on a yearlong professor exchange program to teach math at one of the largest universities in Perth. Upon introducing himself, he confessed that he was not a believer and was struggling with his fear that if he became a Christian, he would have to give up being Chinese. Many Chinese people grapple with this question of identity even though they are interested in the Christian faith because it is perceived as a Western religion. He was therefore relieved when I affirmed in my teaching that one can be a Christian and Chinese without any contradiction. He ended our conversation by saying that he was now interested in becoming a Christian—that is, of course, barring no opposition from his mother!

Is Christianity a Western Religion?

My encounter with Andrew is packed with many cultural nuances, but one that may stand out and surprise you is the perception that Christianity is a Western religion. I have to admit that I, too, was astonished by the fact that Andrew, who has been attending the church in Perth for months and was a highly educated man living in the connected global world, still held on to this age-old misconception about the Christian faith.

We do not have the luxury of space to trace what precipitated this misperception, but according to missiologist Paul G. Hiebert, there are three historical eras[1] in the West's reaction to cultural pluralism that have profoundly influenced the way Westerners relate to those of a foreign culture and the way they have done missions: (1) the colonial era, (2) the anticolonial era, and (3) the present global era.[2] The first two eras each resulted in consequences we will have to work through in the global era.

Evangelism and missions during the colonial era were motivated by deep convictions about the truth of the gospel and the desire to share this good news with all people. Unfortunately, however, the means of achieving this were often colonial in nature.[3] Many Western Christians were unaware that their theology was culturally conditioned and simply assumed that it was universally valid and applicable.[4] Believing that they were messengers to universal truth, well-meaning missionaries unknowingly approached their tasks with a sense of arrogance and power. Since they were going to convert them to the righteous way of life, very few saw the need to understand other cultures, which they believed to be steeped in paganism.

As such, native converts were encouraged to reject their cultural traditions and values as incompatible with Christian practice and values. They were supposed to embrace the way of doing Christianity as modeled by the Western missionaries. African theologian Felix Muchimba laments how the African church, to this day, struggles with this dilemma:

> I am surprised that many churches in Africa demand that a preacher on Sunday morning wears a tie and suit before

3A. Native schoolchildren in uniforms at Yukon's Holy Cross Mission. Photo by J.C. Cantwell. Public domain.

> he can be allowed to preach from the pulpit. Perhaps this is tolerable during the cold season. But can you imagine preaching in a building with poor ventilation in temperatures of 104 degrees Fahrenheit (40 degrees Celsius) in a thick woolen suit and tie, graciously donated as second-hand clothing by Christians in another country? Surely, a thick woolen suit and tie is not a national or "rational" dress for an African country.[5]

The consequence of this was the presentation of the Christian faith as one that is characteristically Western, and should one become a Christian, one would have to reject one's culture and ethnic identity. In other words, becoming a Christian required accepting not only the faith but also Western cultural ways.

However, conversion into Christianity does not require that one reject his culture or ethnic identity. Instead, the biblical faith works to transform new believers as they live out their cultural identity as followers of Jesus. In other words, it is the redemption of their previous cultural identity rather than a rejection. Obviously, there will be values, beliefs, and practices that a new believer needs to shed in light of his newfound faith, but embracing the Western culture or cultural identity is not a requirement to becoming a Christian!

Furthermore, since the nineteenth century in other parts of the world, like China, Christianity has been associated with Western imperialism. For example, the Chinese associate Catholics and Protestants with the Western imperialists because they came to China together. Many Western missionaries of that generation rode on the coattails of the European opium traders to bring the gospel to the Chinese.[6] A scholar aptly described this historical baggage when he compared the arrival of Buddhism and Christianity in China: "Buddha rode into China on a white elephant, while Jesus rode in on a cannonball."[7] The anti-Christian feeling was understandable in view of the circumstances under which the modern Christian missionary movement in China began: The door that was forced open by Western powers to expand trade was the same door through which missionaries entered China. This tainted the gospel in the eyes of Cultural Chinese for the next century.

Lest you think that this is a problem of the past, a European missionary in the Mekong area recently told me his frustration of working with a native church there: "They just don't understand what worship means!" Curious, I probed further only to discover he was frustrated with the local Christians' inability to adapt to a Sunday worship service patterned after his home church in Europe. As far as he was concerned, if the local Christians didn't appreciate traditional hymns or sing them soberly, they were not worshiping the right way. I'm sure the frustration was mutual!

The reaction to this colonial era—anticolonialism—was sadly not promising either. In trying to counter and remedy the perspective that identified the Christian faith with Western culture and identity, many missionaries sought to find ways to build bridges with non-Christian worldviews. They started to seek aspects of common faith, such as forms of worship and beliefs in a transcendent God, in order to moderate the foreignness of the Christian faith.[8] Unfortunately, this desire to contextualize the Christian faith often led to an uncritical approach where the good in other religions and cultures was affirmed, but the evil in them was unchallenged and even embraced.[9]

There is no doubt that all peoples exist in historical and conditioned environments and that the gospel can be lived and expressed in any and every culture. For example, as we learn in the book of Acts, not every church needed to be culturally Jewish (Acts 10:9-29). However, it must be recognized that all cultures have aspects of fallenness, and hence context needs to be approached with a good deal of caution. If the gospel is to truly take root within a culture, it needs to also challenge and purify that context and not just assimilate.[10]

3B. El Greco painting depicting Jesus's followers being given the supernatural ability to speak in other languages on the Day of Pentecost. Painting by El Greco, 1597. Public domain.

In the era of anticolonialism, encounters with other religious worldviews were no longer confrontational but dialogical. While dialogue is a respectful way to understand another's worldview and beliefs, the anticolonial notion of dialogue came to denote not just understanding of other religions but the synthesis and embrace of such differences. As such, for example, we are told we should not be so arrogant and offensive to proclaim that salvation is only through the work of Christ. Rather, we should recognize that within others' cultures and contexts, they also possess truth, and we must honor that. Accordingly, we fall into a kind of religious relativism where the truth of a belief system is relative to culture and context. I still vividly remember when a group of young missionaries we were training accused us of being patronizing and arrogant for claiming that Jesus is the Savior of humanity. Apparently, as Christians, we have no right to claim that we are the only ones who have found the "way."

Obviously, such a strategy of contextualization is problematic on many fronts. Most significantly, in denying the uniqueness of Christ and His work of salvation, one is denying the very foundation of biblical faith. Consequently, even though this anticolonialist reaction helped challenge Western cultural arrogance by questioning the relationship between the gospel and the Western culture, anticolonialism also breeds what Hiebert calls theological relativism.[11] Instead of differentiating the gospel from Western culture, we end up challenging the idea of theological absolutes and seeing all forms of claims to universal truth as arrogant and imperialistic—especially when proclaimed by the West.

Hiebert added, "Anticolonialism does not move us from our initial prejudices to mutual respect. It leaves us as separate islands of subjective being. Furthermore, it lives in reaction, not proaction."[12] In trying to counter colonialism, we may have overcompensated for our past errors and compromised our task to evangelism and discipleship as commissioned by Christ.

Jesus Is the Answer, but What Is the Question?

A friend who has been trying to share the gospel with her Buddhist neighbor relates an interesting encounter:

> I've known "Susan" for almost two years—since she and her family moved next to us. We've gotten to know each other quite well socially and she seemed very curious about the Christian faith. After having shared some of my Christian beliefs with her, I thought it was time to ask if she would want to consider Jesus for herself. I explained that if she accepted Jesus as her Lord and Savior, her sins would be forgiven and that she would not die but have eternal life. However, "Susan" was shocked by the prospect of an eternal life. She asked, "Why would anyone want to live eternally? Life is full of suffering and we're trying to be released from the cycle of life, and you're offering us eternal life—why would one want an eternal life of suffering?!"

Good question!

In addition to the obstacle of misperceiving the Christian faith as a Western religion, many have found the gospel that's been presented to them existentially irrelevant as well. Whenever we share the gospel with someone from a different culture or religion, we need to realize that various cultural factors are involved in the interaction. First, the gospel in its original form was set in the biblical New Testament Jewish and Greco-Roman cultures. Next, our understanding of the gospel message has been shaped by our culture, and now we are trying to share it in a way that makes sense in our friend's culture—the third culture in the equation. In short, any evangelistic conversation would involve the interplay of at least three cultures: the biblical culture, your home culture, and your friend's culture.[13] Hence for the gospel message to be existentially relevant, it has to be communicated in ways that are culturally faithful (to the original biblical context) and relevant and meaningful to the listener's culture.

In addition, even when we use the same language to communicate, we may forget that some terms in our Christian culture mean something else in another worldview. As the above story shows us, the phrase "eternal life" had a completely different meaning for Susan than for her friend. When we use familiar terms like "salvation," "sin," and even "God," we must never assume they convey our intended meaning. Often they do not, and we must carefully define and explain these key terms and concepts.

I met "Evan" when I spoke at the college Bible study meeting he leads. He comes from a tribe in the eastern part of Malaysia where the majority of the community are professed Christians. As one who takes his faith seriously, Evan said that he cannot understand why the faith of his community is still so shallow even though the gospel has reached them for decades. In addition to their involvement in church, many also practice shamanistic rituals. In fact, syncretism is common and accepted in the Christian community. He bemoans the fact that the gospel has been so powerless in rooting out the community's previous pagan beliefs: "The faith of our community is an acre wide but only an inch deep. It takes so little to shatter their faith."

One possible explanation to the biblical faith's lack of impact on the worldview of this community could be due to the gospel they received from the foreign missionaries. These Western missionaries most likely preached a gospel that emphasized humanity's guilt and the forgiveness of sins. Such good news about a God who loves them was appealing; hence they all converted to follow this God. However, this aspect of the gospel (humanity's guilt and the forgiveness of sins) does not necessarily impact the existential problem that the community faces. The facet of the gospel that is more meaningful to them is about a God who can protect and deliver them from the threats of evil spirits. Because He is the King of kings and Lord of lords, He can defeat all other spirits this community was appeasing previously. The aspect of the gospel that would be most significant to a community of this cultural perspective is the power of Christ to deliver them from fear if they submit to His lordship and enter into His kingdom.[14] Therefore, if the first missionaries who reached out to this community had contextualized the presentation of the gospel according to this people group's cultural perspective, perhaps the gospel could have been more effective in stamping out their paganistic beliefs.

Often syncretism happens when the professed faith or belief system is perceived as inadequate in helping the believer make sense of his or her existential reality. Hence the gaps are filled either by their previous beliefs or by new ones from another belief system. Syncretism and compromises are real risks in any cross-cultural evangelistic endeavor, and we must constantly be on guard against it. However, it is indeed a great tragedy when we fail to identify the existential questions of the ones we are trying to reach and help see the relevance of Christ in their culture and reality.[15]

Recently, a Christian Chinese economics professor at a large university had an urgent question for me: She wanted to know if the "spirits," which are released among us on the seventh month, could harm us if we are Christians![16] One could imagine this kind of question from a young believer, but this came from someone who has been attending church for many years. Another risk of noncontextualization is that wrong beliefs of one's worldview are not exposed and confronted. Deep-seated cultural values, such as belief in the spirit world, ancestor veneration, communal expectations, suffering, and witnessing, as minority communities may not be adequately examined and dealt with. Consequently, the gospel's power to transform one's worldview is limited.[17]

It is important for us to recognize that whenever an interreligious encounter takes place, it always occurs in contexts influenced by culture, religious belief systems, history, associations with the past, and as present realities. All these factors influence the dynamics of the interaction. Sometimes, they help clarify the message, and other times, they are an obstacle. Whenever we present the truth of the gospel to someone from another culture, we are essentially declaring that all they have believed and known about life and reality is flawed. What's more, we are suggesting they alter their worldview by abandoning their previous values and erroneous beliefs to conform to this newly presented truth. We must empathize with them because this is a significant and complex decision that will affect their social and cultural identities and their lives even long after they become Christians.

Jackson Wu rightfully asks, "Are we biblically faithful if our gospel message is not culturally meaningful?"[18] I would go even further to ask, "Jesus is the answer—but do we know the question(s)?"

Both the colonial and anticolonial approaches fall short in helping us relate more meaningfully and intimately cross-culturally. However, the task of the Great Commission is still at hand while the world continues in rapid globalization. No doubt, contextualization is necessary and crucial, but the risk of falling into syncretism and theological or religious relativism may discourage us from considering it. However, there is no need for us to throw the baby out with the bathwater. Instead, we need to revisit what good contextualization looks like and correct our misconceptions.

Contextualization: A Posture of Our Heart

Often, when we think of contextualization, the first image that comes to mind is a Western man dressed in a traditional costume that is not of his own culture—for example, Hudson Taylor in his Chinese Qing dynasty pigtail, trying a dish of local delicacy like chicken feet. Contextualization in some settings certainly requires that we adapt to local outward cultural forms such as dress, food, language, and manners. However, more essential in our current global era is finding concepts and images that are relevant and meaningful to the respective culture.[19]

There is no need to attempt another definition for contextualization, since many lengthy books have been written on the subject.[20] The following by David Hesselgrave and Edward Rommen is probably a standard definition:

> Christian contextualization can be thought of as the attempt to communicate the message of the person, works, Word, and will of God in a way that is faithful to God's revelation, especially as it is put forth in the teachings of Holy Scripture, and that is meaningful to respondents in their respective cultural and existential contexts. Contextualization is both verbal and non-verbal and has to do with theologizing, Bible translation, interpretation, and application, incarnational lifestyle, evangelism, Christian instruction, church planting and growth, church organization, worship style—indeed with all those activities involved in carrying out the Great Commission.[21]

In practical terms, contextualization includes trying to locate themes of the gospel

3C. Though British, Amy Carmichael, missionary to India, wore traditional Indian clothes. Photo by Heroes of Faith. Public domain.

in our unbelieving friend's culture as well as, in some instances, adapting to the foreign culture as much as possible to gain us a hearing. This means it may involve outward cultural adaptation, but even more important for us, it means to think through the most culturally appropriate concepts and images we can use to communicate the message. Both complex and nuanced, contextualization seeks to present the gospel as the practical solution to culture-specific existential questions and problems. Hence if our unbelieving friend rejects the gospel, it should at least not be for reasons of irrelevance.[22]

Contextualization is also obviously biblical. Immediately we can think of Paul the Apostle. He writes about his approach to ministry to the church in Corinth:

> For though I am free from all, I have made myself a servant to all, that I might win more of them. To the Jews I became as a Jew, in order to win Jews. To those under the law I became as one under the law (though not being myself under the law) that I might win those under the law. To those outside the law I became as one outside the law (not being outside the law of God but under the law of Christ) that I might win those outside the law. To the weak I became weak, that I might win the weak. I have become all things to all people, that by all means I might save some. I do it all for the sake of the gospel, that I may share with them in its blessings (1 Corinthians 9:19-23).

Paul summed up the spirit of contextualization here: "I have become all things to all people, that by all means I might save some" (1 Corinthians 9:22). He is willing to adjust his message according to whom he is trying to reach for the sake of the gospel and the lost. Authentic contextualization is, therefore, not merely a technique or a process of doing something; rather, it is about the willingness to step out of our comfort zone to identify with those we are trying to reach. It is profoundly and fundamentally about the posture of our heart—first, toward God and the gospel, which would, in turn, affect our posture toward those who do not yet know Jesus. In the case of Paul, he was willing to forgo his freedom and privilege of power to identify with the weak.

In fact, the Christian gospel itself is about contextualization. The incarnation of the divine Son of God was a project in contextualization:

> Though he was in the form of God, did not count equality with God a thing to be grasped, but emptied himself, by taking the form of a servant, being born in the likeness of men. And being found in human form, he humbled himself by becoming obedient to the point of death, even death on a cross (Philippians 2:6-8).

Though Christ is radically different from humanity in that He is divine and has all the power that comes with it, He was willing to put all that aside to enter into our world and our culture and become one of us. His love for the Father and for the lost compelled Him to sacrificially be confined by the limitations of time and space. How humbling it must have been for the Son of God to be bound by the constraints of being human. Nonetheless, He was able to successfully reveal the Father to humanity and fulfill His mission on earth (John 14:9). What is even more astounding is how He now bears those marks of humanity for eternity (Revelation 5:6-12).

Some Considerations as We Seek to Contextualize the Gospel Message

A few years ago, we had the opportunity to train a group of local university students in Christian apologetics in a city around the Mekong region. As none of us spoke the local language, we had to use an interpreter. As soon as we began, we ran into a problem we had not anticipated: Our interpreter informed us he was having difficulty finding the right words in the local language that convey the idea of "loving God with our mind." Looking back, this should not have been unexpected in view of the local dominant religion, which dismisses the value of thinking and of the mind. However, we were not prepared for this complication because we entered into our cross-cultural engagement with many assumptions about the way to engage in theological discussions.

Historically, much of the early theological development of the church was couched in Western vocabulary and philosophical tradition. As a result, it was the general assumption that this is the way to examine these ideas. That is, until we come across a worldview, culture, and language radically different from our own. However, realizing the limitations of cultural forms of expressions should not lead us to think the biblical truths we seek to communicate are inappropriate or irrelevant in an Asian (or any other non-Western) context.[23] Part of the challenge of evangelism is finding understandable and relatable terms, images, analogies, or parables that convey the truth about Christ. So what are the considerations we should pay attention to as we seek creative and appropriate ways to contextualize the presentation of the gospel message? Here are two crucial questions to answer.

Question #1: What Is the Gospel?

The first step in evangelism is, of course, to have a firm grasp of what exactly the message is. The term "gospel" has its roots in the idea of it being a "good story" or "good news." As followers of Christ, we are commissioned to go and make disciples of Jesus (Matthew 28:19). This includes the task of preaching the good news. However, what exactly is our message? Why is it good, and why should it matter to someone who already has his or her own belief system or religion? Why should anyone listen to our message and even consider it to be true?

As discussed above, any cross-cultural or interreligious conversations involve the influence of at least three cultures. Hence we must first discern the gospel message in its biblical setting. Second, as much as possible, we must ensure that nothing in our culture supersedes or diminishes the gospel message. Finally, we must relate the message in a way that not only is clear to our listener but also will lead him or her back to the biblical message itself.[24]

It is tempting when we share the gospel to merely condense it into an elevator pitch that affirms the basics of our faith. For example, "*God loves us and has a wonderful plan for us. But we have sinned and are therefore separated from Him. Jesus Christ on the cross is the answer to our sinful state, and if we will accept Him as our personal Savior, we will have eternal life.*" While this transactional narrative summarizes the message of the gospel and affirms the basics of our faith, it does not give a thorough presentation of what the gospel is about. In fact, such a simplified presentation can wrongly convey the message that the gospel is primarily about our own fulfillment and satisfaction: "God loves *you* and has a wonderful plan for *you*." A truncated message like this seems to place *us* in the center of the gospel and not *Jesus*.[25]

Some of us may have learned that we should share our personal testimony of how God has transformed us and given us purpose in life. However, it will not be long before you meet a Buddhist or a Muslim with a similar testimony or experience that affirms his or her beliefs.

Any witnessing that is limited to sharing our personal testimony without the validation of the truthfulness of the gospel is inadequate because the truth of the gospel is both personal and universal. It is universally and objectively true for all people, regardless of their context.

The Apostle Paul was aware of the universal relevance of the gospel when he presented it to the Athenians in Acts 17. Paul was in Athens among a pluralistic community with worldviews that were diverse and distant from the Judeo-Christian tradition. The diverse cultural and religious environment in Athens at that time was not very different from any major cosmopolitan city in the world today. As Paul was compelled to present the claims of Christ to those around him, he prefaced his presentation by courteously esteeming the Athenians' reverence for God. Then he took his listeners back to the beginning—to the drama of creation—and identified the Creator of all as one who is transcendent and personal, holding command over the history of His creation. Next, Paul described God's mercy in relation to the human condition, setting the stage for the climax of his message: redemption through the death and resurrection of Jesus and the need for all people to repent.[26] By presenting the grand narrative of humanity, Paul demonstrated the relevance and truth of the Christian worldview for his audience. We should aspire to do the same in our witnessing, sharing the gospel as a grand story of God and His relationship with humanity. This way, no one people group or culture can claim that it is irrelevant to them.

Question #2: What Is Relevant?

A main task of contextualization is surveying to find the roadblocks keeping people from accepting Christ as their Lord. To engage the unbelieving world effectively, we need to understand the beliefs that they subscribe to and the ideas that compete for their minds and hearts. Good contextualization seeks to be scriptural as well as meaningful to a given culture. Therefore, we must be able to understand where our non-Christian friends are coming from and their basic assumptions about the world so that we think about how we can present the gospel in a way that resonates with their existential longings and questions. This requires studying Scripture alongside the reading of contemporary cultures and religious histories and philosophies of societies.[27] This is no small feat that calls for humility and commitment to persevere in the hard work of rigorous reflection.

While it is essential we familiarize ourselves with the beliefs of the various religious systems (this is, after all, a handbook on world religions), we must also be careful to not typecast adherents of the various religions according to simplistic categories. As you engage socially with individuals from other religions or cultures, you will find that they do not fit neatly into textbook descriptions (even those you find in this text). This is because their worldview is shaped not just by their religious beliefs but also by their culture, family upbringing, nationality, and so on. It is not enough for us to merely quote various scripture verses or compare our beliefs to the beliefs of other religions and assert that we are correct. We need to drill down further. We need to consider their cultural context too. For example, the worldview of a Buddhist who grew up in Hong Kong would be very different from a Buddhist who grew up in California. For one, the Buddhist from Hong Kong is likely ethnically Chinese, and his Chinese cultural upbringing would have shaped his values and beliefs rather differently from our Californian friend. As we seek to share the gospel appropriately, we need to pay attention to the religious, cultural, national, and even generational differences.

Missiologists have discovered that there are typically three responses to sin in human cultures: guilt, shame, and fear.[28] These three types of cultural perspectives define a group's cultural inclinations, which affect their values, ethics, identity, and understanding of salvation. For example, recall the Chinese economics professor I referred to earlier. Though truly forgiven of her sins, she also needed to know and experience God's salvation from her fear of spirits of the dead.

According to Jayson Georges, a missionary who has served many years in a cross-cultural context, the three cultural perspectives are as follows:

1. *Guilt-innocence cultures:* individualistic societies (mostly Western) where people who break the laws are guilty and seek justice or forgiveness to rectify a wrong
2. *Shame-honor cultures:* collectivistic cultures (common in the East) where people feel shame when they fail group expectations and seek to restore their honor before the community
3. *Fear-power cultures:* animistic contexts (typically tribal or African) where people afraid of evil and harm pursue power over the spirit world through magical rituals[29]

Identifying the cultural orientation of a given individual or people group will help us contextualize the emphasis of our gospel presentation accordingly. While God desires that people in all cultures experience His complete salvation, we tend to focus on only one aspect of salvation (i.e., forgiveness of sins), thus neglecting other facets of the gospel, such as delivery from fear and shame.[30] Contextualizing the gospel according to a given people's cultural orientation will also help mitigate the risk of syncretism because the salvation that Christ offers addresses their existential predicament relevantly and thoroughly.

In Acts 17, you will notice that the Apostle Paul did not explicitly quote the Hebrew scripture in his presentation on Mars Hill. Instead, he quoted from the writings of pagan Greek poets—something that his audience was familiar with. By doing so, he sets an example for us: Sometimes we need not quote verses from the Bible to bring across the gospel message. There will be instances when our audience will be more receptive to our message when familiar contextual expressions like cultural folk stories or anecdotes are used as illustrations.[31] God has revealed truth about Himself through general revelation to all peoples and nations throughout history. However, this knowledge can be suppressed or concealed by many factors because of sin. For instance, traditional cultural practices or values may impede our access to truth, but our culture could also provide the context in which we may encounter the one true God.

So in our effort to contextualize the gospel, we need to learn about the cultural world our friends inhabit in the hope of finding common ground. If there are areas of agreement between a worldview/religion and the Christian faith, then possibilities of bridge-building can be explored. For example, a conversation with a Buddhist could see us agreeing with their diagnosis of the problem of suffering—our attachment to the things of the world (1 John 2:15)—but the solution to the problem proposed by Christianity and Buddhism are radically different. The common concerns we have with the Buddhist could serve as a point of connection with them as we enter into deeper conversations about the truth and falsity of the beliefs we have about reality.

Alternatively, we may discover biblical themes or values embedded in a given culture. For example, there is a common existential recognition found across civilizations and cultures that something has gone awry with humanity. Consequently, we were not able to fulfill our destiny. Thus there is a need to find a way to resolve this existential crisis of humanity. This describes the account of humanity's fall as depicted in Genesis 3. However, Confucius, the sage and philosopher whose teachings have most influenced the worldview of Cultural Chinese around the world, believed the same about humanity's existential dilemma. In fact, there is a strong parallel in many of the aspects of Confucius's ideal of human flourishing and the biblical vision of Shalom in addressing the inadequacy of the human condition. However, what has fallen short in Confucius's solution was his optimism in the very nature of humanity that needs restoration.[32] Nonetheless, this parallel could draw us into a meaningful conversation about Christ with our Cultural Chinese friends.

Another example of a bridge is Jesus's role as the one mediator between man and God (1 Timothy 2:5-6). Chinese culture greatly honors relationships. This means confrontation is never done directly but through an emissary or mediator who mitigates the risk of loss of face. In doing business, engaging a reputable person as a guarantor rather than signing a contract is a cultural practice familiar to the Cultural Chinese. Since Cultural Chinese are well acquainted with the need for and the role of a mediator or middle person in any major undertaking, the idea that Jesus is the mediator and reconciler of relationships is one that is culturally familiar and could lead to a greater understanding of the gospel message.[33]

Contextualization: A Journey

As we begin to pursue ways to contextualize the presentation of the gospel, it is critical that we recognize the universals of the biblical faith so that the localized expression does not fall into syncretism. Since the biblical faith is a creedal faith, it is not too difficult to identify the universals of Christianity: the Trinitarian nature of God; Creator as distinct from creation; Jesus as the incarnate Son of God, crucified and risen; and salvation by faith in Christ as the only way to the Father.[34] We must find creative and relevant ways to express these truths in the cultures we seek to reach, but all contextualized expressions of Christian truth have to be faithful to the core beliefs of the universal church.[35]

In addition, as the world continues to change, the context in which we preach the gospel changes, requiring us to adapt the presentation of the gospel accordingly. This means that we can never claim to have arrived at a definitive pattern of contextualization. Hence our efforts in contextualization make for an ongoing journey.[36] If we are to be faithful to the task that Christ assigned us in proclaiming the good news and making disciples, then we must also be diligent in continually learning about the cultural roadblocks that are standing in the way for the nations to embrace the Christian faith as their own and seek to articulate the gospel in terms that they find relevant and significant.

I'Ching Thomas (MA, Biola University) is a Malaysian Chinese whose present sojourn is in Singapore. She's an aspiring Sinologist who serves as Operation Mobilization's International Director of Leadership Development. Before that, she was Director of Training for RZIM in the Asia Pacific. She moonlights as an apologist and a writer in all things related. Her first book *Jesus: The Path to Human Flourishing: The Gospel for the Cultural Chinese* was published in 2018.

Objections to Cross-Cultural Evangelism

Daniel McCoy

During my senior year of college, I went on a rather difficult mission trip for spring break. Oh, another country or even hemisphere, perhaps? A Saharan desert or Siberian wasteland? No, it was none of those places. It was Hawaii, okay? But difficult it was nonetheless. In fact, I got seriously close to dying. After passing the surfboard on to someone else, I tried swimming back to shore but got caught in an undertow and had to be rescued by the lifeguard.

But since I didn't die, I was able to walk away from the near fatality with two lessons: Number one, I am a Kansan landlubber, and I have no business doing surfboard ministry. After all, when you're underwater, the word *surfing* sounds a lot like the word *suffering*. Number two, having to get saved isn't a cool thing. For those who grew up in the church, "getting saved" is standard lingo. The concept, though, is still humbling.

What could be less cool than saying, "I need to get saved"? I can think of one statement, and that's telling someone else, "*You* need to get saved."

Why is evangelism seriously uncool? Let's play word association. I say "Evangelism," and you think "Door-to-door evangelism." I say "Door-to-door evangelism," and you think "Don't let them in the door." I say "Don't let them in the door," and you think "Flies." I say "Flies," and you think "Pesky." Not very cool.

So does *cross-cultural* evangelism fare better in the game? Perhaps if it's pesky at home, it's okay across the sea. Unfortunately, no. I say "Missions," and you think "Western enculturation." I say "Western enculturation," and you think "Colonialization." I say "Colonialization," and you think "Hernán Cortés." I say "Hernán Cortés," and you think "Pirates of the Caribbean." I say "Pirates of the Caribbean," and you think "Should have ended a long time ago." In short, telling others "You need to get saved"—whether during personal evangelism or overseas missions—is often seen as something pesky that should have ended a long time ago.

In this chapter, we will be looking at three reasons given for why cross-cultural evangelism is a problem that should have ended a long time ago. To give the chapter context, we'll apply these problems to Christianity's relationship with Buddhism. Should the followers of Jesus try to convert the followers of Gautama? In the end, we will see why—whatever the pushback—followers of Christ don't have the option of making cross-cultural evangelism optional.

Context: Proposed Marriage Between Christianity and Buddhism

The religious "romance" between Christianity and Buddhism began the way countless relationships do: in a harmless noticing of the other. Process theologian John Cobb tells us that prior to World War I, the typical popular Western response to this foreign "god" named Buddha was that it was all idolatry, pure and simple.[1] The postwar West had time to appreciate the exotic. In place of easily dismissed superstition, Western scholars began to take notice of a religion with sophisticated philosophy and cultivated spiritual technique.

Many less reflective Westerners have leaped from an uncritical demonization to a sort of "puppy love" fascination with Buddhism. Self-help meditative techniques spice up secular dullness. Products with the "Zen" catchphrase sell. Living room Buddha statues exhibit one's cultivation.

Not surprisingly, such impressionability does not impress real Buddhists. After describing such popular repackaging as "Zen Light" or "McBuddha," one scholar informs us that his Japanese Buddhist friends of the Kyoto school grow weary of the tourists seeking "the Instant Buddhist." One abbot told him, "I give them a meditation cushion and tell them to come back again after they have meditated at home for six months."[2] Despite the reluctance of some Easterners to export their religion uncritically, it seems that an

4A. D.T. Suzuki's writings and interfaith dialogues popularized Buddhism in the West. Photo by Shigeru Tamura (1909–1987). Public domain.

uncritical West imports anything Eastern with open arms. Western culture is accommodating: "Sermon and catechism give way before mantra and meditation; guru and avatar displace pastor and savior; resurrection and judgment founder before reincarnation and karma."[3]

In the meantime, however, a serious relationship has been developing. A celebrated intersecting of East and West had already occurred in 1893 at the World's Parliament of Religions in Chicago. There, Zen Buddhist Soyen Shaku met Paul Carus, head of the Open Court Publishing Company and editor of *The Monist*. Carus saw in Buddhism a modern alternative to "unscientific" Christianity. Shaku went on to mentor Daisetsu Teitaro Suzuki, the illustrious popularizer—or, to many, the controversial oversimplifier—of Zen to the West.

With the help of his new publishing partner Carus, Suzuki blessed the West with more than 100 books and articles and became a sought-after lecturer. The matchmaker died in 1966.[4] In the same decade, the Second Vatican Council was repositioning the Roman Catholic stance toward other religions. Many saw an implicit blessing on a Buddhist-Christian courtship in Vatican II's more inclusive posture.[5]

With many Christians feeling freer to look around at other religions, and with Buddhism in the neighborhood, both sides decided to officially meet. In 1980, Honolulu hosted the first international conference on Buddhist-Christian encounters.[6] In 1984, Zen Buddhist Masao Abe and Christian process theologian John Cobb initiated a series of annual "theological encounters," in which both sides presented and discussed papers centering on a shared theme.[7]

Many observers recognized a match made in heaven (or nirvana?). Historian Arnold Toynbee saw in the meeting of the two an event perhaps as historic as the invention of nuclear fission. Hoping a Buddhist-Christian alliance could unite and guide humanity, Toynbee speculated, "A thousand years from now, historians looking back upon our century, may remember it less for its conflicts between democracy and communism than for the momentous encounter between Christianity and Buddhism."[8] After all, according to religion scholar Ninian Smart, Buddhism and Christianity are "those two great shapers of East and West."[9] What could possibly go wrong?

Objection #1: Cross-Cultural Evangelism Is Imperialistic

Like a disapproving parent, something threatens to ruin the courtship: evangelism! As long as Christians believe they're right and Buddhists are wrong, the marriage that interfaith scholars want to see between the two religions won't work. Why? First, because cross-cultural evangelism is said to be imperialistic.

Let us take all the purported injury done by Christians toward Buddhists and bundle it together with the word suggested by these interfaith scholars: *imperialism*. In this context, the word is used to describe any form of aggressive Christian expansion—from the steamroller of proselytizing plus power politics to its residual fumes of a religiously superior attitude. We will look at five embodiments of Christian imperialism that keep interfaith dialogue staffed with its villain. It is historic imperialism that brings agitation to the discussion and sympathy to the cause. And for the sake of the relationship, it is imperialism in all its forms that must be disowned.

But first, a tragic love story: He was a brilliant tutor; she an admiring student. Peter Abelard and Heloise are most famous for the passionate love letters they left behind. Looking back, he probably shouldn't have moved into her uncle's house to give Heloise one-on-one tutoring. She ended up pregnant, followed by a secret marriage, followed by the uncle's henchmen breaking into Abelard's room and castrating him. From there, Peter and Heloise paid for their scandal by going separate directions: he to pay for his sins as a monk in a monastery, and she as a nun at a convent. They continued to write letters, but of a more philosophical than romantic nature.

It was clear that Peter Abelard had a wealth of romantic passion to give. And romance can be channeled in nonscandalous ways. But because he had violated society's trust, the new monk was now prevented from romance altogether.

In the past, Christianity sometimes crossed the line from evangelistic to imperialistic. Thus as we shall see, the whistle will be blown at any attempts at evangelizing whatsoever, even when it's intentionally done without any trace of coercion or Western dominance. It is better to retreat into the monastery where no damage can be done.

There are five forms of imperialism of which the church is said to be guilty. First, there have been incidents of *statist subjugation*. Born in the historic headquarters of the Inquisition, the Spanish philosopher Santayana's view of the matter can be summarized as follows:

> Christianity persecuted, tortured, and burned. Like a hound it tracked the very scent of heresy. It kindled wars, and nursed furious hatreds and ambitions. It sanctified, quite like Mohammedanism, extermination and tyranny. All this would have been impossible if, like Buddhism, it had looked only to peace and the liberation of souls...Buddhism had tried to quiet a sick world with anesthetics; Christianity sought to purge it with fire.[10]

Perusing any church history book will reveal an embarrassing catalog of brutalities carried out through church-state coalition and in the name of God.

Second, and more recently citable than actual episodes of Christian-led persecution, is the matter of *colonial collaboration*. Buddhism is often a national as well as religious identity. Hence it is often difficult to distinguish a person's religion from the person's culture. There is a similar difficulty in separating the mission of the Christian missionary from the Westerner's historic colonizing. Thus it is natural to accuse Christian missionaries of "taking advantage of the power of Western colonialism" in their proselytizing.[11] Indeed, the approach of the missionary and colonizer is easily conflated: "A triumphal conversion approach toward Buddhists is too much akin to the early British colonial approach of cultural superiority."[12]

The third embodiment of imperialism, and one that flows naturally from the discussion of colonial collaboration, is Christianity's *expansive evangelization*. Again, note how seamlessly the two are affixed, according to Buddhist John Makransky:

4B. A fleet of ships for the British East India Company, which brought trade and conquest while opening up nations for Christian missions. Photo by Royal Museums Greenwich. Public domain.

> The traditional Buddhist allergy to the notion of learning important religious things from religious others, including Christians, has been exacerbated in the modern period by the Asian experience of Western colonialism, which many experienced, in part, as an aggressive assault by Christian missionaries on indigenous Asian beliefs in support of the Western domination of their societies.[13]

Now, to be fair, Buddhist beliefs once supplanted indigenous Asian beliefs. Thus those supplanted Asian cultures must also have felt they were experiencing the "aggressive assault" of Buddhist missionaries on "indigenous Asian beliefs." Nonetheless, in asking why there seem to be so many more Christians interested in Buddhism than Buddhists in Christianity, Buddhist Rita Gross suggests that Buddhists historically pressured by proselytizing feel naturally more defensive than the progressive Christian who feels "free to admire the Buddha without facing any resulting pressure from Buddhists to convert."[14]

Fourth, Christianity is said to be imperialistic because of its *extensive enculturation.* For many, Christianity's cultural dominance in the West has become a troublesome truism. We are told—perhaps overstatedly depending on one's definition of *Christian*—that "the academy remains dominated by Christians, Christian concepts, and hermeneutical frameworks derived from Christianity." Asian Buddhists have to "adopt the language of their Christian oppressors in their efforts to compete and to help their religion survive in the face of overt cultural imperialism."[15]

Finally, Christianity is said to be imperialistic because of its *adamant affirmations.* In other words, Christians truly believe that what they preach is from God. Paul Knitter explains, "The game of dialogue is not possible when one religion enters the game claiming that God has dealt them all the aces."[16] To Knitter, dialogue is the deuce that trumps any ace the Christian thinks God has dealt him. Therefore, to keep saying, "Thus says the Lord" is counterproductive and immoral. "What impedes a moral imperative," Knitter writes, "can be considered, I believe, immoral."[17]

True, Christians in recent times have been behaving far better. No witches have been burned or inquisitions have been called in the name of Christ for centuries. However, though such scandalous incidents are less available for tallying, the potential, we are told, is always there. This is because Christians may have changed their customs since then but not their fundamental convictions.

Buddhist-Christian Knitter contends that "holding that there is only one true religion promotes violence" because even though such religions might not necessarily be the direct cause of violence, "they can condone it, encourage it, and strengthen it."[18] His reason is simple: "If you are a president or a king seeking to advance your cause, or if you are a political or popular leader seeking to defend your cause, it sure helps to have at your disposal a religion that holds itself up as God's privileged faith." Just take the signs reading "*Gott mit uns!*" posted by German soldiers in the trenches during World War I. Those who "are struggling for God's truth and doing God's will, not only will be braver, they also can be more brutal—ready to give their lives."[19]

As we can see, the five accusations of imperialism often get sloshed together. Even the missionary who tries wiping the message free of the last traces of Western veneer still gets labeled as imperialistic. Why? Because the missionary believes that Christianity is truly true.

By way of consolation, however, Christians who think one has to believe in Jesus to be saved aren't the only religious people branded as imperialists. Catholic theologian Karl Rahner taught that non-Christians open to God's grace were actually "anonymous Christians," even though they didn't know it. Yet even Rahner's gracious attempts to get non-Christians saved was "demeaning and imperialist," we are told.[20] We are told that even the most renowned pluralist in recent times, John Hick, imposed his own "vision of reality, the vision of one's religious commitment" and thus "still disguise[s] an unintentional religious imperialism."[21]

In the end, the slightest hint of any superiority of any position will simply not be tolerated—all in the name of tolerance and for the sake of love.

Objection #2: Cross-Cultural Evangelism Is Exclusivistic[22]

The police whistle blows. "Everybody is to leave immediately! This café is closed until further notice! Clear the room at once!"

The owner of the café demands to know why: "How can you close me up?"

The police chief responds, "I'm shocked—shocked—to find that gambling is going on in here!"

It's a straightforward explanation. That is, until the roulette croupier walks up to the police chief with a wad of bills: "Your winnings, sir."

"Thank you," the police chief responds. Then, remembering himself, he continues, "Everybody out at once!"

Keep zooming out to get more context. The scene comes from the movie *Casablanca*,[23] which tells the story of a Nazi concentration camp escapee whom the officials are trying to recapture. It just so happens that the escapee has been seen in the very restaurant that the police are closing down. Add in the fact that the restaurant-bar has always been a favorite spot to gamble. It's simply where people go to gamble.

With each new fact we learn, it becomes clear that the original explanation (closed down because of gambling) was inadequate.

The same goes for the second accusation against cross-cultural evangelism. Why is cross-cultural evangelism a problem? The explanation given is that Christianity is *exclusivistic*.

As in, when a Christian invites a Buddhist to place faith in Christ, the interchange assumes that the Christian is correct and the Buddhist is wrong. The implication is that Buddhists are lost and Christians are saved. Christian salvation excludes nonbelievers (hence, the label *exclusivistic*). After all, how is a marriage supposed to work out with one partner ending every conversation before it starts by saying, "I'm right; you're wrong"?

Zoom out. There are four general views about who gets saved and who doesn't:

1. *Exclusivism:* All can be saved (but some will be lost).
2. *Inclusivism*[24] *and/or Universalism:* All will be saved (but through my religion).
3. *Pluralism:*[25] All paths will save.
4. *Relativism:* All questions of religious truth are dismissed as unanswerable.

Going clockwise (starting with exclusivism), the views get gradually less concerned with truth. Both exclusivism and inclusivism still associate with a particular revelation from God (e.g., the Bible). The further one

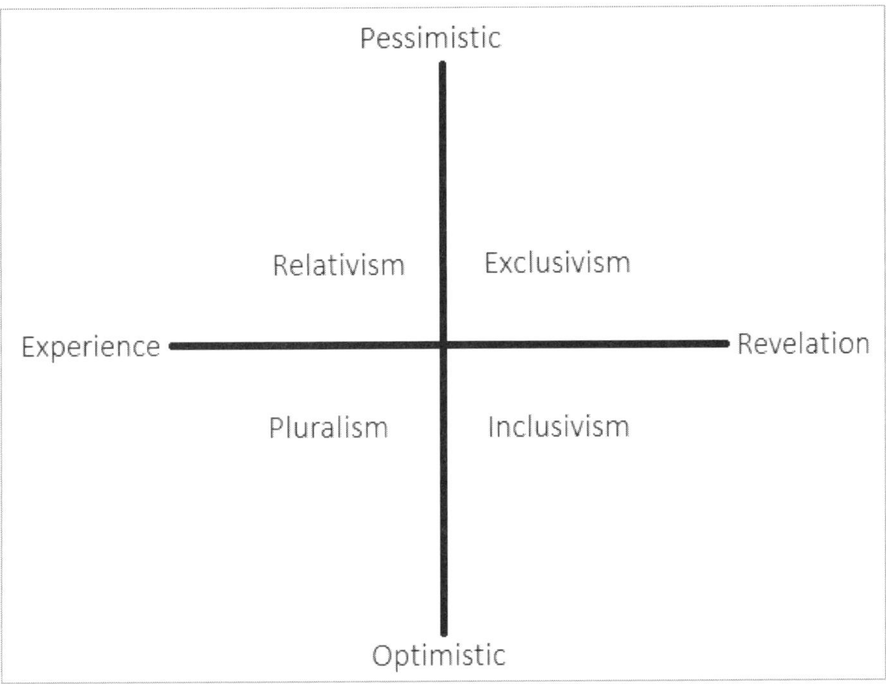

4C. Table. Exclusivism, inclusivism, pluralism, relativism.

drifts from exclusivism down to inclusivism, the more optimistic the person becomes about the salvation of non-Christians. Moving leftward to religious pluralism, revelation is traded for experience as the source of truth. In pluralism, the spiritual experiences of all religious people are seen to be valid paths to the Ultimate. Moving up toward relativism, the person experiences more pessimism regarding salvation. This is not because the person worries that another person won't be saved (as in exclusivism), but rather because the person begins to doubt that there is salvation at all (or, if there is, that we could possibly know about it).

So which one of these four is exclusivistic? The obvious answer to the question would seem to be "exclusivism." But we've asked the wrong question. The real question is, "Which of these four *isn't* exclusivistic?"

First, *exclusivism.* This shouldn't take long. After all, "exclusive" is in the name. Is it exclusivistic? Absolutely. Exclusivists believe they're right, and other people are wrong.

Why exactly is it a problem to believe you're right and others are wrong? Gross explains, "Their claim to exclusive truth lands them in the ethical position of causing harm to others by denigrating the religions of others and using all possible methods to get them to change religious allegiance."[26] She goes on to categorize these methods: "All possible methods have included physical force and often include psychological coercion..."

Of course, embarrassing uses of physical force chronicled in church history books are commonly apologized for and repented of; Christians can accommodate Gross's grievances in that category. But what exactly does Gross see as "psychological coercion"? She explains, they "often include the psychological coercion of threatening others about eternal consequences for not converting to the perspective of the religious exclusivist."[27]

In other words, physical force is put into the same category as psychological coercion, which, when defined, translates to "You won't be saved otherwise," and hence simply restates the exclusivist position. In other words, exclusivism should not be tolerated by the pluralist because it can cause physical force, but even when it does not, then exclusivism harms others because it is exclusive.

Second, *inclusivism*. Surely, a position with such a welcoming name couldn't possibly be exclusivistic, could it? But according to many interfaith matchmakers, inclusivism is still too exclusivistic. In fact, inclusivism might even be perceived as more insulting to the religious compared to exclusivism! This is because whereas the exclusivist is content to take the religious other's claims at face value (albeit as false), the inclusivist often presumes to know better what the religious other *really* believes (e.g., "You might think you are a Buddhist, but you are really an 'anonymous Christian'"). According to interfaith theologian Amos Yong, "The inclusivist vision finally subordinates the insights of the alien faith to that of the home tradition."[28] Both exclusivism and inclusivism present too particular a salvation for the matchmakers' tastes.

Third, *religious pluralism*. Finally, we arrive at a belief that contains no unacceptable exclusivity. Right? Pluralist John Hick was the quintessential pluralist. Hick began with Immanuel Kant's belief that we can't truly know ultimate reality (e.g., God) in itself. If so, Hick continues, then any time we talk about God, we're really just talking about our experiences with God, and not about what God is really like. And even if religious experiences differ from religion to religion, we can't really be wrong about our experiences. Thus, according to Hick, no religion is more right than another. They are all equally valid paths to "the Real" (Hick's name for God).[29]

But even Hick's pluralism is seen as too exclusivistic! Why? It's because he forces each religion into the mold of being paths up to the same summit (the Real). To be fair, he doesn't make any positive claims about "the Real." The summit remains obscured in metaphysical mist. But the fact remains that "Hick thus demythologizes each religion...on the basis of his meta-theory of 'The Real,' which becomes the privileged account of ultimate reality."[30] Similarly, even specifically Buddhist-Christian pluralists anchor their pluralism to particular views of ultimate reality (e.g., Cobb's process theology,[31] Paul Ingram's process theology,[32] and Knitter's "Buddhist Ontology"[33]). Even pluralists can't escape having too particular a view of ultimate reality.

Thus we move on to the fourth option: *relativism*. After all, the three traditional categories of how religions relate to truth—exclusivism, inclusivism, and pluralism—err on the side of exclusivity. Buddhist-Christian interfaith scholars tend to castigate the first two options and only identify with the third in a highly nuanced way. Those with process theology or Buddhist views of ultimate reality might be able to be "pluralists" when it comes to Buddhism and Christianity. But then what prevents them from being exclusivists with regard to all the other religions? Simply adding one to make two religions that get along is not religious pluralism.

Could it be that in relativism we have at last found a view that is nonexclusive? But relativism is the view that dismisses all religious claims to truth whatsoever. Hence anybody who has taken her religious beliefs to be truly true has been wrong. Relativism excludes Christians and Buddhists alike.

Well, what about the Buddha himself?

Can he escape the charge of exclusivity? Although the Buddha spoke skillfully, reinterpreting Indic terms and speaking Buddhist truth in the language of other worldviews, he clearly critiqued opposing views. If there is an edge Buddhism has over Christianity in being less exclusivist in its doctrines, it is that the Buddha recognized the ability of other paths to potentially help its adherents along in the virtues (e.g., nonattachment) conducive to the Buddhist path. Yet even where there are said to be alien elements conducive to the path, we must not rule out that such words of commendation could be merely *upayana* (skillful means) meant to move as many as possible, by whatever means possible, onto the *true* path.

The Buddha's successors, the scholars and branch founders throughout the centuries, have carried themselves with the same conviction of correctness. Makransky concludes after a comparison with Catholic writings, "Most Buddhist thinkers, just as the authors of the Vatican documents, have *not* accepted a theological pluralism. They viewed the teaching of their tradition as uniquely efficacious in its salvific function."[34]

To dramatize this point, let us consider Chinese Shin patriarch Shandao's (613–681) parable of the white path.[35] Attacked by thugs and beasts, a traveler flees west until he stops short at what he sees just below him. If he keeps going, he will surely fall into one of two rivers, which are separated by an incredibly narrow four- to five-inch path. One river swells with violent waters; the other leaps up and down with flames. Both are immeasurably deep and long. If he goes back or stays, there is certain death. His only option is to continue west along this narrow path, with flames licking at his feet and waves sloshing over the path.

As the traveler takes his first steps, a voice from the east says, "O traveler, just resolve to follow the path forward! You will certainly not encounter the grief of death. But if you stay where you are, you will surely die."

4D. A depiction of Amida's Pure Land. He is in the center surrounded by bodhisattvas. Photo by Rubin Museum of Art. Public domain.

Just then, a voice from the west echoes, "O traveler, with mind that is single, with right-mindedness, come at once! I will protect you. Have no fear of plunging to grief in the water or fire."

With new resolve, the traveler "advances directly forward with mind that is single, forthwith reaches the western side, and is free forever of all afflictions."

According to the parable, the attackers are one's own treacherous attachments to the ego. The fire and water are the poisons of greed and anger. The encourager from the east is none other than Sakyamuni, the historic Buddha, and the speaker from the west is Amida Buddha from his western paradise. The narrow path going west is the pure mind, set on rebirth in Amida's Pure Land.

The point, of course, is that if both Christianity and Buddhism claim in various ways to be the "narrow gate" (e.g., Matthew 7:13), it seems difficult, if not impossible, to please both religious founder and interfaith matchmaker. Indeed, even cycling through the progressively more open views provided by interfaith dialogue—inclusivism, pluralism, and relativism—it is next to impossible to land anywhere that is not labeled too exclusivistic in some sense. Even if you somehow disavow all connections to particular saviors, salvations, and ultimate realities, you find yourself in a secularistic wasteland, according to which every religious adherent is patronized as an "anonymous simpleton." The question becomes not, "What is exclusivistic so that we might banish its last traces from our midst?" but rather, "What is not exclusivistic so that we might actually have something to build upon?"

"I'm shocked—shocked—to find that gambling is going on in here!" I doubt it. Everybody gambles here, including you.

In the same way, everyone is exclusivistic in their own way. This is because all people who believe something—from Christianity to Buddhism, from exclusivism to relativism, and all in between—believe they're right. Otherwise, they wouldn't believe it.

In the end, those who accuse Bible-believing Christians of exclusivity are not so much attacking exclusivity as they are averse to the possibility of certain types of reality.

Objection #3: Cross-Cultural Evangelism Is Pessimistic

So why shouldn't Christians do cross-cultural evangelism? First, because we are told it's imperialistic. Yet it is possible to evangelize people without coercing them or forcing the evangelist's home culture on them. And if evangelism is still "imperialistic" when it's just a matter of persuading people to believe a particular way, then what seriously held view isn't "imperialistic"? As we've seen, even theologians as accommodating as Rahner and Hick can't escape the charge of imperialism, even when they crafted theologies as all-embracing as they could muster.

Why else? The second reason Christians shouldn't do cross-cultural evangelism, we are told, is that evangelism is exclusivistic. True, but what view isn't? As we've seen, even pluralists and relativists believe in particular versions of ultimate reality that exclude others. It doesn't matter that Jesus got crucified for claiming to be the Son of God or that the Buddha vowed to either find true enlightenment or die trying. Their convictions are patronized as being only "true," not even rising to the seriousness of being a truth claim worth testing.

So in being labeled "imperialistic" and "exclusivistic," the cross-cultural evangelist finds herself not unique at all. By those definitions, all strongly held views imperialize and exclude. So if those aren't strong enough reasons to stop evangelizing, is there one? It seems there must be a good reason, with evangelism having fallen out of fashion with so many people, even Christians.[36]

How about the one we're all thinking: God is love. If God is so all-loving, then why should we feel compelled to evangelize people as if their eternities depended on it? Where is the divine love in such pessimistic possibilities? God so loves the world, so shouldn't that good news give us optimism about everybody's eternity? John 3:16, remember?

Yes, about John 3:16. Christianity's apple pie verse. It's familiar and comforting. It feels good.

Zoom out. The verse is set in a conversation between Jesus and an Israelite judge named Nicodemus. The fact is, John 3:16 is so comforting that it seems almost out of place in John 3. For in John 3, Nicodemus meets serious Jesus. Very serious. The conversation will get tense. They won't agree. They won't connect. In fact, there's a whole lot of negativity in the chapter, such that "God so loved" clashes with the serious tone of the conversation.

It's surprising the conversation didn't go better. We finally find a Pharisee who seems genuinely impressed with Jesus. And Nicodemus is not only a Pharisee (quite a righteous guy), but he's also a member of the Sanhedrin (quite an important guy). And he's interested in Jesus—just the kind of guy to stamp the Jesus movement with some major legitimacy. Yet by comparison, Jesus responds coldly:

> This man came to Jesus by night and said to him, "Rabbi, we know that you are a teacher come from God, for no one can do these signs that you do unless God is with him."
>
> Jesus answered him, "Truly, truly, I say to you, unless one is born again he cannot see the kingdom of God" (John 3:2-3).

All at once, Jesus's words offend Nicodemus's sense of goodness and confuses his sense of logic: "How can a man be born when he is old? Can he enter a second time into his mother's womb and be born?" (John 3:4). Huh? It's not like I can get back in my mom, can I? If Nicodemus is trying to lighten the mood, it's not working.

Jesus remains serious. He tries explaining. Nicodemus still doesn't understand. So Jesus gives another really serious, almost rude reply: "Are you the teacher of Israel and yet you do not understand these things?" (John 3:10). I mean—you're the doctor-professor-reverend of Israel, and you don't get this?! And whereas Nicodemus had said, "We know that you are a teacher come from God," Jesus turns the tables on Nicodemus: "Truly, truly, I say to you, we speak of what we know, and bear witness to what we have seen, but you do not receive our testimony" (John 3:11).

The conversation is getting really serious.

Meanwhile, we're wondering when we can get past this serious, tense talk and get on to the good stuff: "God so loved." If we could simply skip ahead to the "God so loved the world" part, we wouldn't have to get bogged down in the pessimistic pronouncements about "unless one is born again." Can't we skip ahead to the good news? If we know that "God so loved," then we shouldn't have to talk about uncomfortable ideas like, for example, "Nicodemus, I know you think you're a good person. But even you have to be born again before God will let you into His kingdom."

Where I'm from in the American Midwest, basically everybody knows about God's love. Even people who have never read a Bible assume there's a God and that He loves them. Thus they often assume that it doesn't really matter what they believe or how they live: "Why would a loving God care what I believe or how I live anyway?"

Now, from the Bible, is it true that God loves everybody? Absolutely! John 3:16. Romans 5:8. Ephesians 2:4. First John 4:9. And is this good news? Oh yeah! Very good news! But get this: Some good news is really serious. Some good news compels you to get really serious, sit up, and pay focused attention.

Let's say you're trying to get through Chicago, but your smartphone is out of battery power. You can't use the GPS, and you find yourself downtown, unable to find your way through. You drive and drive but just get more and more lost. Finally, you decide to pull into a gas station. You walk up to the counter and tell the guy, "I'm lost. Is there any way you can help me?"

And the guy says, "Sure."

"You—will help me?" you ask.

"Yeah, of course."

And you start laughing with relief. "Oh, that is such good news! I'm going to be okay! Oh, thank you so much for the good news!" And before he can say another word, you skip out of the store, jump in your car, and with a smile on your face, drive away because you have heard good news.

Now, what's wrong with that response? It's definitely good news—someone is going to help you. But this good news you have heard doesn't mean it's time to turn your brain off. Rather, it means it's time to get serious. To pay close attention. That's the kind of good news it is.

You go to the doctor. He confirms you have a life-threatening condition. It could be a matter of months before you die. So you ask the question that, for you, means the difference between life and death: "Doctor, is there a cure?"

And he says, very slowly, "Yeesss..."

But before he can say another word, you jump up and say, "Oh, that is such good news! I was so scared! Thank you, thank you, doctor!"

Now the doctor is trying to say, "But you're going to have to—" But you're already out in the hallway, on your way to the vehicle, shouting, "Yes! Yes! There's a cure!" You didn't stay long enough to hear what the cure was. What you're going to have to do now to be cured. The diet changes, the procedures, the exercises. You see, it's definitely good news. But this isn't the time to turn your brain off; it's time to get serious.

You're in college. You have a crush on a particular young woman. You have a friend who is friends with one of her friends. One day, your friend tells you that he heard from her friend that she might like you."

Good news.

She's in the cafeteria. So you go up to her in the cafeteria and say in front of all her friends, "Hey, you like me!" And you laugh. Your voice gets louder: "Hey, everybody! I just want to announce that this here's my girlfriend!" You post on Facebook, "Good news, everybody: I've got me a girlfriend!"

Now was that good news? Yes, but you're ruining your chances. The window of you winning her heart is getting smaller and smaller. It's definitely good news, but this isn't the time to turn your brain off. It's the time to get serious.

"God loves you."

Good news? Absolutely. "God loves me!" you say. "That means no worries, right? Now I can believe whatever I want. I can live however I feel. God loves me, I'm in, and everything's great!"

Now, hang on. God does love you—more than you can imagine. And it is good news. But this isn't the time to turn your brain off. It's time to get serious.

Don't you think you ought to stick around and listen to the directions? Don't you think you ought to stay put and listen to what the cure is? You hear that God loves you, wants to be in a relationship with you. Don't you think you ought to figure out what getting into a relationship with God looks like? How it's done so that you don't ruin the relationship?

Why is Jesus so no-nonsense with Nicodemus? Why is this such a serious kind of good news? There are two reasons.

First, *your situation is dangerous*. You're being offered rescue, and "rescue" is a serious word. Rescue from what?

In the Old Testament, people were dying

from snakebites. Thus God told Moses to make a bronze serpent and hoist it up on a wooden beam. That way, when people got bit and were dying, they could travel to where the wooden beam was set up, and they could look up at the serpent and be healed. The serpent was "lifted up."

Someone in the New Testament would be similarly "lifted up" on a wooden beam:

> As Moses lifted up the serpent in the wilderness, so must the Son of Man be lifted up, that whoever believes in him may have eternal life (John 3:14-15).

Those are the verses immediately before John 3:16. Here are the verses after John 3:16:

> For God did not send his Son into the world to condemn the world, but in order that the world might be saved through him. Whoever believes in him is not condemned, but whoever does not believe is condemned already, because he has not believed in the name of the only Son of God (John 3:17-18).

Judgment is already on us. We've already rebelled against God's rule. We've already been bitten by the snake. Our situation is dangerous.

There's a second reason Jesus is so serious about this good news. Not only is your situation dangerous, but *your receptivity is limited.* Limited by what? "And this is the judgment: the light has come into the world, and people loved the darkness rather than the light because their works were evil" (John 3:19). Jesus came to earth; the Light of the World dawned. And people responded by squinting and shielding their eyes and getting unnaturally irritated. Why? Because people like the darkness. And why would anyone prefer darkness?

> For everyone who does wicked things hates the light and does not come to the light, lest his works should be exposed (John 3:20).

People want to protect their habits from Jesus. For when Jesus gets in charge of a life, who knows how things are going to change? Because sins become addictive, people protect them from Jesus as if His attempts to rescue them were actually attempts to rob them. In this way, people's sins affect their receptivity to Jesus. The everyday decisions people make affect how they respond to Jesus. If people keep shielding their sins from Jesus, they'll find that the window of their willingness to come to Jesus gets smaller and smaller.

Having zoomed out to the context, let's focus back in. John 3:16 says, "For God so loved the world, that he gave his only Son, that whoever believes in him should not perish but have eternal life." God loves us, so we can stop worrying about eternity, right? No, this is the kind of good news that means it's time to get serious. Our situation is dangerous. Our receptivity is limited.

We know God is love not because nature is always benevolent or because that's the universal teaching of the world's religions. Rather, we know that God is love because of the cross. And we know the cross is love—and not just an unfortunate tragedy—only against the backdrop of holy judgment against our sins.

Therefore, may it never be that we would yawn, "God loves me? Well of course He would. Why wouldn't He?" May it never be that we shrug at the love of God or treat the cross as a triviality. May it never be that we would twist our reason for hope into an excuse for complacency. With the world's situation dangerous and its receptivity limited, it's time to get serious about cross-cultural evangelism.

Or do you presume on the riches of his kindness and forbearance and patience, not knowing that God's kindness is meant to lead you to repentance? (Romans 2:4).

Daniel McCoy (PhD, North-West University) is the editorial director for Renew.org. He also teaches classes on philosophy, world religions, and ethics for Ozark Christian College. He is author of *Mirage: Five Things People Want from God That Don't Exist* and coauthor with Christian apologist Norman Geisler of *The Atheist's Fatal Flaw: Exposing Conflicting Beliefs.*

Part 2

MISSIONARY RELIGIONS

Christianity

Karin Stetina

There are more than two billion Christians in the world—approximately a third of the earth's population—making Christianity the most widely practiced religion on the planet.[1] While it began with only 12 disciples, Christianity has grown to be the most influential religion in human history. But what is Christianity? What are the key beliefs, authoritative writings, history, and the major movements that define Christianity and make it so significant?

In a nutshell, Christianity revolves around the life, death, resurrection, ascension, and promised return of Jesus Christ. Christians believe that God the Father sent His Son Jesus, the promised Messiah, to save the world. The Apostle John declares that the purpose of his Gospel and the Christian faith is belief in Jesus Christ. He writes, "Now Jesus did many other signs in the presence of the disciples, which are not written in this book; but these are written so that you may believe that Jesus is the Christ, the Son of God, and that by believing you may have life in his name" (John 20:30-31). This disciple of Jesus uses the verb "believe" nearly 100 times in his account of Jesus. The belief that Jesus is "the Christ" (i.e., Messiah) and "the Son of God" is what sets apart Christianity from all other religions. Jesus is the Messiah who came to earth to reconcile humans to God the Father. Faith in Jesus stands at the center of the Christian faith.

While many other religions seek to know the divine through human means, Christianity recognizes that God can only be known when God reveals Himself. God condescended to us and made Himself and His ways known most fully in Jesus Christ.[2] In other words, Christianity is not primarily about human knowledge or human self-improvement but about God, the eternal Creator of the universe, coming to us to reconcile us to Himself so that He may be truly known and worshiped.

The Bible, the Holy Scriptures of the Christian faith, speaks about Jesus Christ as the long-awaited Messiah, sent by God the Father. In the record of His birth in the Gospel of Matthew, the author writes,

> "She will bear a son; and you shall call his name Jesus, for he will save his people from their sins." All this took place to fulfill what the Lord had spoken by the prophet: "Behold, the virgin shall conceive and bear a son, and they shall call his name Immanuel"

(which means, God with us) (Matthew 1:21-23).

Many religions recognize the significance of Jesus Christ and His teachings. Christianity, however, does not depict Jesus merely as a prophet or an enlightened man who teaches us the truth about God or how to live our lives. Instead, Christianity acknowledges that He is Immanuel, "God with us."[3] It is only through belief in Jesus that one is reconciled to God.[4]

While other religions seek to please the divine through human effort, Christianity acknowledges that we can do nothing to earn salvation from God.[5] It is only by God's grace—His unmerited favor—that we can be saved from the consequences of sin. Humans, by nature, are fallen, sinful people, who desperately need saving.[6] Christ came to do just that.[7] When we confess our sins, ask for God's forgiveness, and put our trust in Christ, who died to pay the penalty for our sins, God promises to forgive us and to make us righteous.[8] Christianity, therefore, centers on the historical person Jesus Christ as God's Son and our Messiah.

What Are the Authoritative Writings of Christianity?

What Is the Bible?

To understand Christianity, one must recognize the significance of the Bible for Christian teaching and practice. The word *Bible, biblia* in Greek, literally means "books." It is a collection of writings that Christians hold as authoritative for faith and life. The Bible includes the essential teachings of the prophets and disciples of God as well as an outline of Jesus's life and teachings. The Bible has two parts: the Old Testament and the New Testament.

What Is the Old Testament?

Adherents of both Christianity and Judaism consider the writings of the Old Testament (or Hebrew Scriptures) as authoritative. It consists of 39 books, starting with Genesis and ending with Malachi. It is primarily written in Hebrew, with some Aramaic, and covers the narrative of God and His people, the Israelites. The Old Testament includes several genres: the Law, Historical Books, the Prophets, and Wisdom Literature.

The Books of the Law. Genesis, Exodus, Leviticus, Numbers, and Deuteronomy are also referred to as the books of Moses, the Pentateuch, or the Torah. These first five books of the Old Testament cover the creation of the world and the beginning history of the Israelites, including the giving of the Law by God to Moses.

The Historical Books. Joshua, Judges, Ruth, 1 and 2 Samuel, 1 and 2 Kings, 1 and 2 Chronicles, Ezra, Nehemiah, and Esther are considered the Historical Books. They cover various aspects of the history of the Israelites, from their entrance into the Promised Land to their return from exile in Babylon. These books, which are arranged roughly in chronological order, include the establishment of kings in Israel as well as the division of Israel into the kingdom of Israel in the north and Judah in the south.

The Prophets. The 17 prophetic writings, which are arranged chronologically, are generally divided into the Major Prophets and the Minor Prophets based on their length. Under the inspiration of the Holy Spirit, these prophets (messengers of God) delivered God's message of judgment, repentance, forgiveness, and hope. The Major Prophets include the books of Isaiah, Jeremiah, Lamentations, Ezekiel, and Daniel. The 12 Minor Prophets include Hosea, Joel, Amos, Obadiah, Jonah, Micah, Nahum, Habakkuk, Zephaniah,

Haggai, Zechariah, and Malachi. These 12 works are separate books in the Christian Bible but are consolidated into one book known as the *Nevi'im* in the Hebrew (Jewish) Scriptures. From these writings, numerous prophecies of the coming Messiah are quoted in the New Testament as referring to Jesus.

Poetic Writings. Job, Psalms, Proverbs, Ecclesiastes, and Song of Solomon are the Poetic or Wisdom Literature of the Israelites. They explore various issues, including wisdom, love, suffering, death, worship, and the nature of God. These works include sayings, petitions, prayers, songs, and poems. The Psalms are often used as prayers and songs in Christian worship services.

What Is the New Testament?

Christians also embrace the New Testament as God's Word. The New Testament is composed of 27 books attributed to eight authors (Matthew, Mark, Luke, John, Paul, James, Peter, and Jude). These books were written in Koine Greek in the second half of the first century. The New Testament makes up the second part of the Christian canon and is a continuation of the Old Testament narrative of God's story. It begins with the birth of Jesus in the Gospels and ends with a vision of the future in the book of Revelation. The New Testament includes four Gospels, the Acts of the Apostles, the Epistles (i.e., letters), and the apocalyptic book of Revelation.

The Gospels. The books of Matthew, Mark, Luke, and John are the four narrative accounts of the life and teachings of Jesus Christ. The word *gospel* means "good news," in reference to Jesus as the promised Messiah. The Gospels are historical, narrative, and theological biographies of Jesus Christ. The first three are considered "synoptic" Gospels (*syn* = "same"; *optic* = "see") because much of the content overlaps among these Gospels, whereas the last Gospel, John, is more distinct in style and emphasis. The Gospel of Matthew focuses on Jesus as the fulfillment of Jewish prophecy. Mark puts more emphasis on Jesus as the suffering, sacrificial Son of God. Luke proclaims that Jesus is the Savior of all people. The Gospel of John focuses on Jesus as the Word, the eternal Son of God, and the revelation of God the Father.

The Acts of the Apostles. The Gospels are followed by the book of Acts. This book continues Luke's Gospel narrative, telling of Christ's ascension to heaven, the spread of the gospel, and the beginnings of the early church.

The Epistles. The Epistles (Romans; 1 and 2 Corinthians; Galatians; Ephesians; Philippians; Colossians; 1 and 2 Thessalonians; 1 and 2 Timothy; Titus; Philemon; Hebrews; James; 1 and 2 Peter; 1, 2, and 3 John; Jude) are the 21 letters of the New Testament written to early churches and individuals. The Epistles are sometimes separated into the Pauline Epistles, written by the Apostle Paul, and the General (or "Catholic") Epistles, attributed to James, Peter, John, and Jude.

Prophecy. The last book of the Bible, Revelation, is written to seven churches in Asia Minor (modern-day Turkey), telling of the Apostle John's revelation from Jesus Christ to churches which were struggling in the face of persecution. The Greek word from which the name "Revelation" comes is *apokalupsis* (apocalypse), meaning the unveiling of something previously hidden. This prophetic book encourages the church to stand firm while it waits for Christ's triumphal return and final restoration of the world.

What Is the Apocrypha?

The Apocrypha (or Deuterocanonical works) is considered an authoritative part of the biblical canon by the Roman Catholic and Orthodox traditions, but not by most

Protestants. The word *Apocrypha* comes from the Greek word meaning "hidden," "secret," or "covered." These 14 "intertestamental" works, written between the Old and New Testaments, approximately between 450 BC and AD 50, include such works as 1 and 2 Esdras, Tobit, Judith, the Wisdom of Solomon, Ecclesiasticus, and Baruch. These works include essays, psalms, and historical narratives. Since Jesus and His apostles never refer to these works, many Christians have not placed much weight in their authority.

What Are Creeds, Confessions, and Catechisms?

Creeds, confessions, and catechisms are formal written summaries of the Christian faith and practices. The word *creed* comes from the Latin word, *credo*, meaning "I believe." The Apostles' Creed (written in the first four centuries), the Nicene Creed (325/381), the Athanasian Creed (probably written in the fourth or fifth century), and the Definition of Chalcedon (451) are creeds widely accepted by most Christians, whether Catholic, Orthodox, or Protestant.

Confessions are longer statements of faith that are often used in worship services or the education of believers. Some of these include the Augsburg Confession (Lutheran, 1530), *Professio fidei Tridentina* (Roman Catholic, 1564), the Belgic Confession (Reformed Tradition, 1561), Thirty-Nine Articles (Anglican, 1571), and the Mennonite Confession of Faith (American Mennonite, 1963).

A catechism is a more comprehensive instructional tool used to train children or new converts in the faith. Catechisms are often written in question/answer format. For instance, the Westminster Shorter Catechism, written in 1647 by the Westminster Assembly in London, continues to serve as a teaching tool for Presbyterians and other Christians. The Roman Catholic and Eastern Orthodox churches emphasize their official doctrinal teachings, often called Tradition, seeing them as another source of authority alongside the Bible. Although many Protestants consider catechisms to be helpful summaries of God's Word, most uphold the Bible as the sole authority.

What Is the Overarching Story of the Bible?

While Christianity officially began as a distinct faith with the establishment of the church in the first century, the Bible traces its roots to the beginning of creation. The Bible tells God's story of creation, fall, redemption, and restoration. Before discussing the major beliefs of Christianity, it is important to briefly summarize this overarching story of the Bible.

God's Creation of the World

The Bible begins in Genesis 1 and 2 with God creating the world and specially making humankind in God's image. God places Adam and Eve, the first humans, in the Garden of Eden to care for creation. God pronounces creation as good.

The Fall of Humanity

Genesis 3 describes how sin and its consequences entered into the world. The term "the fall" refers to the first man and woman's rejection of God's rule by disobeying God. Their rebellion results in human alienation from God, each other, and the world as well as physical and spiritual death.

Redemption

The biblical story continues, describing how God, who is just and loving, redeems humanity. Jesus Christ, the eternal Creator of the universe, takes on human flesh, lives a perfect life, suffers, dies on the cross and pays the penalty for our sin, resurrects from the dead, and ascends into heaven. Christ's redemptive work enables humanity to be reconciled to God.

Restoration

The biblical narrative doesn't end with redemption. God promises to renew all things. Christ, the ruler of the universe, promises to return to judge the living and the dead and to establish His kingdom on earth and in heaven.

What Are the Basic Beliefs of Christianity?

What Do Christians Mean by "God"?

Christians believe in the existence and knowability of God—that God has revealed Himself to us but can never be fully understood due to our finite nature. While God is beyond us, He can be known through His self-revelation. Some of the things that God reveals about Himself include His eternality (Revelation 4:8), independence (Acts 17:24-25), unchanging character (Psalm 102:25-27), knowledge of all (Psalm 147:5), power over all (Jeremiah 32:17), presence everywhere (Psalm 139:7-12), holiness (1 Samuel 2:2), justice (Romans 3:26), glory (Hebrews 1:3), and loving nature (1 John 4:9).

Christians are monotheistic as well as trinitarian in their beliefs about God. *Monotheism*—from the Greek words *monos* (only) and *theos* (god)—is the belief that there is only one supreme God. God alone is the Creator and Ruler of the world. There are three major monotheistic religions: Christianity, Judaism, and Islam. Christianity is distinct from Judaism and Islam, however, in its *Trinitarianism*. Trinitarianism is the belief that there is one God who eternally exists as three distinct persons—the Father, the Son, and the Holy Spirit. Each of these persons shares the same essence, being fully,

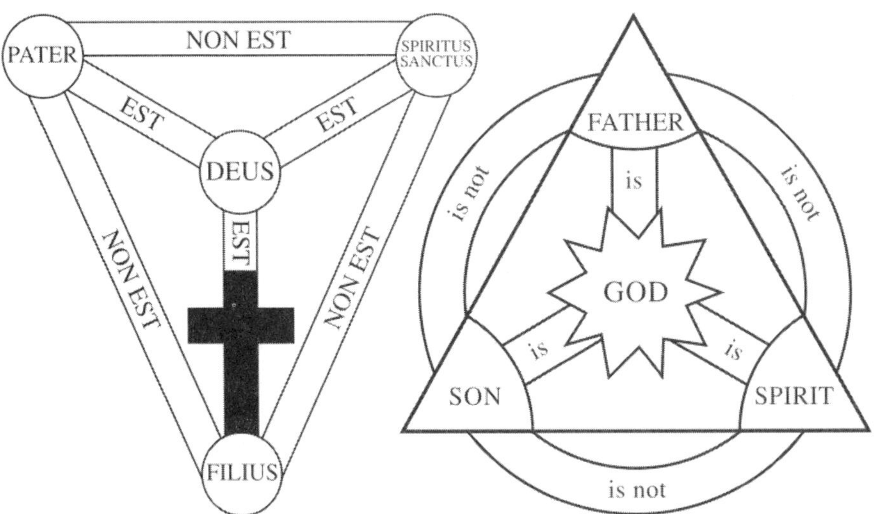

5A. This ancient diagram helps illustrate the great paradox of the Trinity. Graphic by AnonMoos. Public domain.

eternally, and equally God, yet each person is distinct.

While the word *Trinity* never appears in the Bible, the Bible identifies God as one and yet three: Father (1 Corinthians 8:6), Son (Titus 2:13), and Holy Spirit (Acts 5:3-4).[9] Each member of the Trinity is fully and eternally God. Colossians 2:9 proclaims the full divinity of Christ saying, "In him all the fullness of Deity dwells in bodily form" (NASB). As theologian Wayne Grudem helpfully notes, we should not see God as three pieces of "pie," but each "equal to the whole being of God."[10] Each member is a distinct person. "Person" is used in reference to an independent, personal being, not in the sense of a human being. In other words, the Son and the Holy Spirit are not mere forces, divisions, or actions of God the Father, but they are distinct individuals that relate to one another and to creation separately. The members of the Trinity act together as one God. This is evidenced in John 14:9, when Jesus replies to Philip, "Have I been with you so long, and you still do not know me, Philip? Whoever has seen me has seen the Father. How can you say, 'Show us the Father'?" Therefore, Christians affirm that there is one God who exists as three Persons, each fully God and worthy of worship. The ancient diagram on page 83 helps illustrate the great paradox of the Trinity.

5B. The Pantocrator, a sixth-century icon from Saint Catherine's Monastery, Mount Sinai. Public domain.

Who Is Jesus Christ?

An essential tenet of Christianity is that Jesus is the only "Son of God," as well as the "Savior" of the world.[11] Christians believe that Jesus Christ is both fully God (John 10:30) and fully man (Philippians 2:7) in one person (Colossians 2:9), and will be so forever (Hebrews 13:8). Christian theologian J.I. Packer proclaims, "Here are two mysteries for the price of one—the plurality of persons within the unity of God, and the union of the Godhead and manhood in the person of Jesus...Nothing in fiction is so fantastic as is this truth of the Incarnation."[12]

The Eastern Orthodox image of the Pantocrator is an attempt at illustrating this divine mystery. "Pantocrator" means the "creator of all." The left side of the painting depicts Christ's human nature and the right side His divine nature, both coexisting in one man. Jesus was born of the Virgin Mary, who conceived by the power of the Holy Spirit without a human father, as was foreshadowed in the Old Testament (Matthew 1:18-25). Jesus had a real human mind, soul, and body, thus being able to represent us and exemplify true humanity (Hebrews 2:14-17). While living on earth, He had real human weaknesses and limitations, and He was tempted, yet did not sin. The Bible tells us Jesus grew both physically and intellectually.[13] He felt genuine human emotions such as love, sadness, exhaustion, joy, and righteous anger. When He was tempted by Satan in the desert, He did not sin, but He relied on the power of the Holy Spirit and the Word of God. Jesus lived a perfect life of obedience to God, the Father, and paid for our sins through His death.[14] Christians affirm that Jesus was more than a perfect man—He was also fully God. The word *incarnation* is the theological term used to refer to God the divine Son taking on human nature.[15] Jesus, as God alone is able to do, created the world, sustains the world, and forgives sins.[16] Christians acknowledge the divine miracle of the incarnation: God became man, lived a perfect life, died on the cross, and was resurrected from the dead so that humans may be reconciled to God. Christians also look forward to when Jesus will return to earth. This is known as the second coming.

What Is Faith?

The Bible describes faith as "the assurance of things hoped for, the conviction of things not seen" (Hebrews 11:1). Biblical faith is not blind hope, an opinion, or belief in empirical facts; instead, biblical faith is placing one's trust in the person Jesus Christ, as revealed in Scripture. Christians understand faith as the means of receiving salvation. Romans 5:1 proclaims, "Therefore, since we have been justified by faith, we have peace with God through our Lord Jesus Christ." Faith guides Christians in living their lives. Reformer John Calvin writes of faith that it is "a firm and certain knowledge of God's benevolence toward us, founded upon the truth of the freely given promise in Christ, both revealed to our minds and sealed upon our hearts by the Holy Spirit."[17] Faith is like being given a sixth sense, where one can apprehend what they could not previously—that is, the beauty, glory, and love of God.

What Is Salvation?

Christians believe that salvation comes by faith in Jesus Christ. Christians acknowledge that all have sinned and disobeyed God and are therefore justly condemned by God (Romans 3:23). Salvation is deliverance from sin, condemnation, and eternal death. It is found in Christ alone. Ephesians 2:5 tells us, "Even when we were dead in our trespasses, [God] made us alive together with Christ—by grace you have been saved." In other words, God, who is holy, just, and loving, saved us from His just wrath by sending His Son. Jesus's life, death, resurrection, and ascension secured salvation for whoever believes in Him.[18] Jesus, who lived a perfect life when we were unable to, died in our place so that we don't have to pay the penalty for our sins. His resurrection from the dead broke the power of sin and death over us. Jesus ascended to heaven and now sits at the right hand of the Father, making intercession for those who put their trust in Him.[19] Salvation is a gift from God and not earned. As 1 John 1:9 proclaims, "If we confess our sins, he who is faithful and just will forgive us our sins and cleanse from all unrighteousness." Our salvation not only frees us from the consequences of sin but also enables us to live holy lives, glorifying, and serving God.[20] Protestant reformer Martin Luther reportedly said, "We are saved by faith alone, but faith is never alone."[21] A change of heart that results in holy living always accompanies true faith. Faith is not a mere intellectual assent to the idea that Christ is

God, for even the demons recognize that (James 2:19). True faith is becoming a disciple of Christ. It is crucial, however, to realize that our holy lives do not earn salvation; instead, they become a testimony of God's saving grace. Salvation is being born again as a child of God and living according to the new nature put within you.[22]

What Happens When We Die?

Christians believe that we continue to exist even after death. The Bible speaks of a literal heaven and hell.[23] All humans will spend eternity in one of these two places.[24] Heaven is the dwelling place of God. It is where Christ reigns today and where Christians go when they die.[25] Heaven is a perfect paradise where believers will eternally worship, serve, and enjoy God. Jesus is the only way to heaven. Christ said, "I am the resurrection and the life. Whoever believes in me, though he die, yet shall he live" (John 11:25-26). Those who do not put their trust in Jesus will be condemned to hell, where they will be eternally separated from God due to their sin. This eternal penalty, however, can be avoided by confessing that Jesus is Lord and placing faith in Him as the risen Savior (Romans 10:9).

What Is the History of Christianity?

What Was the Beginning of the Church?

According to the book of Acts, the story of the church begins with the resurrection and ascension of Christ, the Day of Pentecost (the day the Holy Spirit came upon the church in Acts 2), and the spreading of the gospel to both Jews and Gentiles (non-Jews). The early church faced persecution and martyrdom due to the conflict between Christianity and society until the rule of Constantine (AD 306–337). In the first century, the apostles helped spread the gospel and build the foundation of the church, fulfilling Christ's words in Acts 1:8: "But you will receive power when the Holy Spirit has come upon you, and you will be my witnesses in Jerusalem and in all Judea and Samaria, and to the end of the earth." For example, Philip the evangelist went to Samaria; Peter to Asia Minor (Turkey) and Babylon (Iraq); Paul to Antioch, Asia Minor, and Rome; and Thomas to Persia (Iran) and India.

Prior to Jesus's apostles, the good news of the Messiah was primarily for the Jews, God's chosen people. Indeed, in the beginning, Christianity was often considered a sect of Judaism. They differed primarily in their belief about Jesus being the Messiah and God's covenant extending to the Gentiles. The apostles witnessed not only to Jewish people but to Gentiles as well. Questions, however, began to arise regarding the status of Gentiles and whether they needed to follow the laws of Israel. The first recorded church council (Acts 15) recognized Gentile believers as full members. The Gentiles were required, however, to abstain from offensive pagan practices. Thus early Christianity had the critical task of both defining and distinguishing itself from Judaism as well as paganism.

How Did Christianity Expand?

Christianity began to spread quickly throughout the world as the apostles went out and shared their faith. In addition to Jerusalem, other cities emerged as significant centers of Christianity, most notably Rome, Alexandria (Egypt), Carthage (Western North Africa), Antioch (Turkey), and Constantinople (Turkey). Each of these areas helped shape the theology and practices of Christianity, particularly regarding how to interpret Scripture and articulate doctrine about Christ. During the first few centuries, there was an increase in persecution, with Christians falsely accused of ungodly practices such as cannibalism and incest. They were crucified, burned, stoned, boiled, starved, and skinned for their faith. Martyrdom, however, only seemed to further the gospel. As Tertullian famously proclaimed in AD 197, "The blood of martyrs is the seed of the church." The martyrdom of Christians such as Polycarp, the bishop of Smyrna, as well as that of other Christians, served as a catalyst for the growth of Christianity.

The writings of the Apostolic Fathers (Clement of Rome, Ignatius of Antioch, Polycarp of Smyrna, Didache, Shepherd of Hermas, Barnabas) give us insights into the life and thought of the early church. This time period was filled with inner divisions among Christians, persecution, and conflict with Jews and pagans. The general character of their writings is far below the depth and the force of the New Testament. Yet these works reveal an enthusiasm for a simple faith, love, and loyalty to Jesus Christ. There is a conscious preservation of the New Testament teachings, a simple understanding of the biblical truths, and a very practical, ethical focus. In these works, we see the development of *sacramentalism* (the belief that God gives grace through visible church practices such as the Lord's Supper) and *asceticism* (strict practices that are thought to lead to holiness). During this time, some began to suggest that the bishop of Rome (the Apostle Peter's successor) has primacy over the other bishops.

The Greek apologists such as Aristides, Justin Martyr, and Tatian, who were concerned with defending the faith from false accusations and relating Christianity to Greek culture, were important figures in the early church. They sought to explain Christian beliefs and practices and to counter paganism. Some of their key ideas included the importance of monotheism: that all truth is God's truth, that the orderliness of the world reveals the glory of God, and that reason—while useful—has its limits. As is the case with many Christians today, the Apologists viewed Christianity as more than personal faith; they saw it as a comprehensive worldview.

How Did the Church Go from Persecuted to Favored?

What impact did the Roman emperor Constantine have on Christianity? Before Constantine's reign (AD 306–337), Christianity was tolerated, at best. The church experienced a particularly extensive persecution beginning in 303 under Roman emperor Galerius. Christian buildings were leveled, and bishops were imprisoned and released only if they made sacrifices to the pagan gods. Constantine the Great, however, reversed course by attempting to unite the Roman Empire under the Christian faith. Under his leadership, the church went from persecuted to tolerated and finally to favored. In February 312, Constantine helped establish the "Edict of Milan," which officially granted legal toleration to Christians.

During his reign, Constantine adopted measures that would set Christianity above other religions, allowing the church to become the dominant force in the Roman Empire. During this time of relative peace, Christians began to pursue monasticism (an isolated life of self-discipline in a religious community) as a substitute of sorts for now-obsolete martyrdom, seeing monastic life as an alternate form of self-denial and discipleship. Favoring Christianity allowed for the building of churches and the opportunity for church leaders to produce theological

5C. Church leaders gathered at the Council of Nicaea. http://www.saint.gr/518/saint.aspx. Public domain.

treatises and spiritual works without the threat of losing their lives. This period also blurred the line between being a citizen of the world and a citizen of heaven.

What Were the Church Councils?

To iron out doctrine, the church called together gatherings of church leaders. These became known as church councils. Although many only influenced this or that group of Christians, some councils influenced the trajectory of all the major branches of the church. The four most formative early councils were held in Nicaea, Constantinople, Ephesus, and Chalcedon.

Council of Nicaea. The church faced a major doctrinal dispute during Constantine's reign. Arius (ca. 250–336), a Christian priest in Alexandria, clashed with Alexander, the bishop of Alexandria, over the eternality and divinity of Jesus Christ. Seeing the danger of a divided kingdom, Constantine convened the Council of Nicaea in 325 to resolve the conflict. Contrary to Arius, the vast majority of councilmembers affirmed that Jesus is the "Son of God, begotten from the Father, only-begotten, that is, from the substance of the Father, God from God, light from light, true God from true God, begotten not made, of one substance with the Father...for our salvation."[26] The resulting Nicene Creed not only helped affirm the essential doctrinal beliefs about Christ and the Trinity but also helped cement the relationship of the church to the Roman Empire. Some of the fundamental teachings of the Nicene Creed that are still held today by Christians are as follows:

1. Christ is true God from true God.
2. Christ is consubstantial (of the same essence) with the Father.
3. Christ was begotten, not made or created.
4. Christ became a human for us and for our salvation.

Council of Constantinople. In 381 at the Council of Constantinople, the church clarified the role of the Holy Spirit in the Nicene Creed in response to a group called the *Pneumatomachi* (the killers of the Spirit) who denied the divinity of the Holy Spirit, thus challenging the doctrine of the Trinity. The council added into the Nicene Creed, "And in the Holy Spirit, the Lord and Giver of life, who proceeds from the Father, who together with the Father and the Son is worshipped and glorified."

Council of Ephesus. Would you be willing to lose your freedom and possibly your life over one word or one letter in one word? Particularly if the word wasn't even a word found in the Bible? This was the very situation that some Christians found themselves in during the third and fourth centuries. After the Council of Nicaea, which focused on the church's Trinitarian doctrine, debate continued among Christians about how to speak about Christ, particularly about Christ's essence or nature. Should Christ be considered the same substance (*homoousios)* or of a similar substance (*homoiousios)* with God the Father? What does it mean for Christ to be fully human? What is the relationship between the two natures? In the West, beliefs about Christ had been fairly well established since the time of Tertullian (AD 155–220). Even prior to Nicaea, the West had taught that Christ had two complete natures (human and divine) in one person. The West was not very specific, however, about the union of those two natures.

In the East, two different Christologies (doctrines of Christ) had emerged. The teaching in Antioch emphasized the distinctiveness of the two natures of Christ and placed an emphasis on Christ's human nature saving us. Opponents argued that this Christology risked Christ being seen as two distinct persons. In Alexandria, however, priority was given to the unity of the two natures at the risk of neglecting the full humanity of Christ. In 431, the third ecumenical council (in Ephesus, a city in Asia Minor) set out to help resolve the tension regarding the nature of Christ. In particular, the council responded to Nestorius's view that Mary was the *Christotokos* (the mother of Christ), but not the *Theotokos* (the mother of God). Nestorius (ca. 386–451), the patriarch of Constantinople, was opposed to the idea that God Himself suffered and died on the cross. Byzantine Emperor Theodosius II called the council to resolve the controversy. In response to Nestorius, the Council of Ephesus (431) affirmed the virgin Mary as *Theotokos* (the Mother of God incarnate) and the *hypostatic* (real) union of Christ's two complete natures in one person.

Council of Chalcedon. Like a pendulum swinging between extremes, an opposite error arose in relation to Nestorianism. Whereas Nestorius had been too drastic in demarcating the two natures of Jesus, a church leader in Constantinople named Eutyches taught that Christ had only one nature. In Chalcedon, another city in Asia Minor, the fourth ecumenical council (451) attempted to further clarify the church's views of Christ, especially in response to the Eutychian doctrine, which became known as *Monophysitism.*

Regarding the doctrine of Christ, the Council of Chalcedon affirmed the following:

1. The Virgin Mary as *Theotokos* (bearer of God) in terms of Christ's manhood
2. Christ as fully human, with a rational soul and body, yet without sin
3. Christ as fully God, coequal and coeternal with the Father and the Holy Spirit
4. The real union of Christ's two complete natures in one person, without confusion or separation

From Chalcedon on, Eastern Christianity had two orthodoxies (i.e., correct standards). The Eastern Orthodox Church accepted the Council of Chalcedon while the Oriental Orthodox, which is often described as *Monophysite* (emphasizing one nature), did not. Monophysites still exist today in Syrian Jacobites, Coptic, and Ethiopian churches. The Council of Chalcedon remains a stumbling block to full reconciliation between the Eastern and Oriental Orthodox traditions.

How Did Monasticism and Scholasticism Mark the Medieval Church?

The medieval period (roughly AD 500 to 1350) was marked by Monasticism and

Scholasticism. Historian Mark Noll writes, "The rise of monasticism was, after Christ's commission to his disciples, the most important—and in many ways the most beneficial—institutional event in the history of Christianity."[27] The monastic movement was one expression of Christ's directive to be in the world but not of it (John 17:14-19). *Monasticism* comes from the Greek word *monas* meaning "alone." It allows for an inward, individual spirituality, often practiced in community. As Christianity grew in favor and martyrdom became less common, monastic communities enabled Christian men and women to show their radical devotion to God by separating from the world and following *The Rule* of discipline. *The Rule*, a book written by Saint Benedict (AD 516), helped promote obedience, stability, and continual conversion. Living a life according to *The Rule* involved the submission of every aspect of one's life to a practiced awareness of God's presence. Life in the monastery was guided by three things: *cruce, libro, et arto*—the cross, the book, and the plow—or put more simply, faith, knowledge, and work.

Monasteries and convents (the female counterpart) helped Christians live a devoted life to God by practicing the spiritual disciplines of silence, chastity, prayer, fasting, confession, good works, and obedience. These communities, which still exist today, produced bishops (Anselm of Canterbury), preachers (Bernard of Clairvaux), scholars (Augustine), missionaries (Saint Patrick), Bible translators (Jerome), mystics (Julian of Norwich), and philosophers (William of Ockham). As Philip Mitchell points out, monasticism is also arguably responsible for the survival of education in the Western world, the perpetuation of manuscripts, the development of important medicines, Western capitalism, cultural advances, social stability, the spread of Christianity, and the reform movements of the sixteenth century.[28] Monasticism also encouraged a theology of salvation by faith and works, ascetic privation of the body, and physical or spiritual withdrawal from the world.[29] For better or worse, some of these practices still mark some Christian groups, such as Roman Catholic monks and the Amish.

Scholasticism, a largely speculative or theoretical system, emerged during the later medieval period (twelfth through sixteenth centuries). It has been suggested that Scholastics would often discuss abstract matters, such as how many angels can dance on the head of a pin. Whether this is true or not, these scholars devoted their attention, as their Latin name *scholasticus* suggests, to learning and disputing ideas in great detail. These scholars wanted to attain logically defensible truths and sought to reconcile reason and doctrine. They understood reason to be in the service of faith rather than a challenge to it. They also advocated for the use of sources outside of the church, such as the writings of Aristotle, as well as Arabian and Jewish theologians. Thomas Aquinas and his *Summa Theologica* helped shape the Western church's thought and practice. His theology reveals a synthesis of classical philosophy and Christian theology, a trend that still exists today in both the Protestant and Catholic traditions. Aquinas's classic arguments for the existence of God are still influential in theological and philosophical education. In contrast, the Eastern Orthodox tradition has a stronger appreciation for mystical contemplation and the mysteries of Christianity.

Both Monasticism and Scholasticism have had a systematizing effect on Christianity and have impacted the way Christians have understood their relationship with the outside world.

What Are the Pillars of the Medieval Church?

There are three main pillars that define the Western church during the late medieval period: growing papal supremacy, salvation in the Roman Catholic Church alone, and salvation by grace and works. During this time period, the pope (the bishop of Rome) was increasingly seen as having primacy over other bishops and rulers. Innocent III's statement in 1198 is indicative of this perspective:

> Just as the founder of the universe established two great lights in the firmament of heaven, the greater light to rule the day, and the lesser light to rule the night, so too He set two great dignities in the firmament of the universal church...the greater one to rule the day, that is, souls, and the lesser to rule the night, that is, bodies. These dignities are the papal authority and the royal power. Now just as the moon derives its light from the sun and is indeed lower than it in quantity and quality, in position and in power, so too the royal power derives the splendor of its dignity from the pontifical authority.[30]

Innocent's claim of spiritual and political authority was echoed by Pope Boniface VIII (1294–1303) and Pope Leo X (1513–1521). The popes used excommunication (excluding from communion with the church) and ecclesiastical censure (spiritual punishment) to control the church and political alliances. In *Pastor Aeternus* (1516), Leo X declares that the "pope alone has the power, right, and full authority...it is necessary for the salvation of souls that all Christian believers be subject to the pope at Rome...the Holy Scriptures and the Holy Fathers testify."[31] While the pope's supremacy and infallibility (his inability to err when officially speaking from the "throne of Peter") was not officially declared until Vatican I (1870), it was implied much earlier.

A second pillar in the medieval church was the doctrine of salvation. With a shorter life expectancy due to plagues, wars, and famines, the salvation of the soul was a preoccupation in medieval Europe. The Roman Catholic teaching emphasized that salvation was accessible only in the Roman Catholic Church, upholding Cyprian's statement (ca. 250) "You cannot have God for your Father if you do not have the Church for your mother." The church understood salvation as mediated through the church's hierarchy and the sacraments. Priests were given special authority to act as spiritual mediators between God and humans in the absolution of sins and the administration of grace through the sacraments. Anyone outside of the church had no hope of salvation.

Connected with seeing the church as mother, the medieval church taught that salvation was a transaction between God and humans, a synergy of both grace and works. In *Cur Deus Homo?* (*Why God Became Man*), Anselm (1033–1109) helped establish the church's understanding of salvation, specifically the satisfaction view of the atonement. In this work, Anselm explained how humanity has defrauded God of His honor and how it is necessary that God's justice be satisfied. He writes, "Everyone who is obliged to repay to God the honor of which he has stolen. This [repayment of stolen honor] constitutes the satisfaction which every sinner is obliged to make to God."[32] Christ's self-sacrifice on the cross provides satisfaction for the infinite debt that humans owe but cannot pay. The medieval perspective depicts the receiving of this gracious work of God as a lifelong, cooperative activity within the church. As nominalist theologian Gabriel

Biel (1420–95) proclaims, "If we do not add our merits to those of Christ, the merits of Christ will not only be insufficient, but nonexistent."[33] In the Catholic tradition, salvation is tied to the sacraments and practices such as Catholic baptism to remove original sin, communion with the church, confession of personal sin, good works, pilgrimages, indulgences, and Christian burial. If you die in a state of sin, you are sent to purgatory (a state between heaven and hell), where you will be purged of your sins by fire. Your loved ones, however, can assist you by having a mass (church service that includes the Lord's Supper) said for you or by buying indulgences to prompt the mercy of God. According to the Catholic Catechism, an indulgence is "remission before God of the temporal punishment due to sins whose guilt has already been forgiven, which the faithful Christian who is duly disposed gains under certain prescribed conditions through the action of the church which, as the minister of redemption, dispenses and applies with authority the treasury of the satisfaction of Christ and all of the saints."[34] Today, the Catholic Church still teaches that it has a vital role in dispensing Christ's grace to the individual.

What Was the Great Schism of 1054?

Who commissions and sends out the Holy Spirit? Was it God the Father alone (John 15:26 says, "The Spirit…who proceeds from the Father") or also God the Son (in John 16:7, Jesus says, "I will send him to you")? When the Nicene Creed was translated into Latin at the Council of Toledo in Spain in 589, the phrase "and the Son" (*filioque*) was added so that the Holy Spirit "proceeds from the Father *and the Son*," an insertion that became known as the *filioque* clause. In 1014, Pope Benedict VIII officially inserted the clause into the Roman mass. The Eastern church's mass, however, did not include it, seeing it as subordinating the Spirit to the Son and diminishing the Spirit's equality. The *filioque* clause has been considered one of the primary reasons for the split between the Eastern (Orthodox) and Western (Roman Catholic) churches in 1054, known as the "Great Schism of 1054." Still today, the *filioque* clause remains a dividing point between the Eastern and the Western liturgies.

This division occurred not merely because of theological differences but also due to political and geographical matters. Even prior to the official break, there was tension, particularly over the hierarchy and practices of the church, with each side failing at times to acknowledge the authority of the other. For example, Pope Leo III's naming of Charlemagne, the king of the Franks, as the Holy Roman Emperor in AD 800 was seen as an attack on the Byzantines' claim to be the true successors of Rome and resulted in weakening the authority of the Byzantine Empire based in Constantinople. In response, the Byzantines (now the Eastern Orthodox Church) looked to the patriarch of Constantinople, rather than to the pope, as the key authority of the church. There were also notable differences in each community's expression of faith and practices. The addition of the *filioque* clause into the Nicene Creed is just one example. Language remained a significant dividing point between the two, with the West using Latin and the East using Greek in their preaching, doctrinal statements, and worship.

The final break between the East and the West came on Saturday, July 16, 1054, when Cardinal Humbert, representative of Pope Leo IX, entered the Hagia Sophia, the patriarchal cathedral of the Eastern church, and excommunicated Michael Cerularius, patriarch of Constantinople. Differences had arisen over the use of Greek customs when the Eastern bishops had been replaced with Western ones after the Normans had conquered the Byzantine area of southern Italy. In the 1040s, the Western bishops had begun to challenge Greek practices such as clerical marriage, the use of leavened bread for the Eucharist, and the Greek days of fasting. These disagreements culminated in Cerularius's excommunication. A week later, the Eastern Patriarch returned the favor by condemning the Western cardinal. While this was not the first time for the East and the West to excommunicate one another, this event had a more decisive and permanent impact.

Recently, dialogue between the two churches has improved, with the Second Vatican Council (1962–65) acknowledging the validity of the Eastern church's sacraments, and the Joint International Commission for Theological Dialogue (1979) making strides toward reconciling some differences. Many of the doctrinal, linguistic, political, and geographical breaches between the Roman Catholic and Orthodox churches, however, continue today.

What Led to the Dividing of Western Christianity into Roman Catholicism and Protestantism?

Protestantism, the second-largest branch of Christianity after Roman Catholicism, developed as a separate movement in the sixteenth century. Five hundred years ago, on October 31, 1517, Martin Luther, a relatively unknown Augustinian monk, challenged the Roman Catholic practice of indulgences when he posted his *95 Theses* on the door of Castle Church in Wittenberg, Germany. While there were calls for reform long before Luther, the events that ensued after his initial protest led to a decisive break of Western Christianity into two parts: Roman Catholicism and Protestantism. The splintering of the Western church had significant religious, political, intellectual, and cultural implications, including diminishing the authority of the Roman Catholic Church and reconfiguring the church-state relationship away from Christendom.

The Protestant Reformation centered on the Reformers' call to purify the church according to teachings found in Scripture. Figures such as Luther, John Calvin, Ulrich Zwingli, and Henry VIII challenged the pope's supreme authority and the Catholic Church's role in defining the Christian faith and practices. Initially, Luther hoped to reform the Catholic Church from within, appealing to the pope to rid it of unbiblical theology and practices. In *Freedom of the Christian* (1520), Luther attempted to persuade Pope Leo X that the theology of the Reformation was consistent with the Bible. He urged the pope to recognize that Christ alone saves and to convince him to reform any practices that challenge the Gospel writing: "One thing, and one alone, is necessary for life, justification, and Christian liberty; and that is the most holy word of God, the gospel of Christ."[35] In 1521, however, the Catholic Church denied the validity of the Reformers' teachings and excommunicated Luther at the Diet of Worms when he refused to recant his writings. This act began a seemingly irreparable breach between Protestants and Roman Catholics.

Some of the key ideas of the Reformers (often referred to as the *solas*) are as follows:

1. *Sola Scriptura.* Scripture alone is authoritative for faith and practice.
2. *Sola Gratia.* Grace alone saves. Humans cannot accomplish their own salvation.

3. *Sola Fide.* Humans are justified by faith alone, placing their trust in Christ's work, not by any works of their own.
4. *Solus Christus.* Salvation is accomplished and mediated by Christ alone, not by the church.
5. *Soli Deo Gloria.* God alone should be glorified. Our whole life should be centered on bringing God glory.

The Reformation became the basis for the establishment of Protestantism, one of the three major branches of Christianity. Today, there are many types of Protestant churches, including but not limited to Lutheran, Presbyterian, Anglican, and Baptist.

What Was the Counter-Reformation and the Council of Trent?

In 1545, the Catholic Church formed the Council of Trent to respond to issues raised by the Protestant Reformation. Pope Paul III established the council with the hopes of restoring church unity and reform. Initially, the council was to be for all Christians, but Protestants never attended any of the sessions. Bishops and theologians convened over an 18-year period to help define Roman Catholic doctrine and practices. The documents and proclamations produced by the Council of Trent are referred to as "Tridentine" works.

The Council of Trent had two main directions of reform: the reform of customs and laws of the church (such as affirming clerical celibacy) and the defining of dogma (teachings) of the church over and against Protestants (such as justification by faith and works). At the start, it was thought that Protestants and Roman Catholics may be able to reunite; however, the anathemas (formal denouncements) issued in later sessions against Protestants cemented the break between the two.

By the end of the sixteenth century, many of the abuses that initiated the early calls for reform were rectified, including the improper sale of indulgences and simony (the buying and selling of church offices). There, however, remained doctrinal and practical differences that made reconciliation between Protestants and Catholics impossible, particularly regarding their views on justification and the authority of Scripture.

What About the Further Fracturing of Christianity?

In 2001, the *World Christian Encyclopedia* reported that there are more than 33,000 Christian denominations in the world.[36] While it is likely that this number is greatly inflated, especially considering that some of the denominations included do not qualify as Christian denominations (such as Latter-day Saints and Jehovah's Witnesses), it is clear that the Reformation was just the beginning of the fracturing of Christianity. In particular, the Protestant doctrine of *sola scriptura* contributed to its fragmentation. This doctrine maintains that the Bible, not the church, is the ultimate and infallible source of truth and is self-interpretative. In his commentary on the Psalms, Luther wrote, "Scripture is its own expositor."[37] This principle implied that the church was no longer necessary to understand the Bible. The essential truths of the Bible are clear enough that "even the humble miller's maid, nay, a child of nine if it has faith" can interpret it.[38] Therefore, the Reformation advocated that the Bible be available for all to read. *Sola scriptura* and the connected principle of the priesthood of all believers (that God is equally accessible to all believers) opened the door for the common person to question the church's judgments.

Shortly after the Reformation, many Protestants attempted to establish confessions and catechisms to unite believers. *The Canons of Dort*, which emerged from an international gathering of Reformed believers in Dordrecht, Netherlands, in 1618–19, is one example. This Synod (assembly of clergy) set out to resolve a theological controversy initiated by the rise of Arminianism. Jacob Arminius, a theology professor in Leiden, questioned the Reformed teaching regarding God's unconditional election in salvation. His followers presented their views in the *Remonstrance* of 1610. In this document, the Arminians advocated for the belief that God's election is based on the foreseen faith of the individual, not on God's will alone. Without the church as the final authority, there was no way to fully settle the dispute. While Arminians were condemned at the Synod of Dort, the issue was not fully resolved, nor was unity established between Reformed believers and Arminians. Instead, doctrinal differences like this served to further divide believers.

What Are Some of the Distinguishing Marks of the Major Branches of Christianity?

What Is Roman Catholicism?

Roman Catholicism is the largest Christian church, with an estimated 1.2 billion members worldwide.[39] Catholics share many of the same beliefs as other Christians, holding firmly to the teachings expressed in the Apostles', Nicene, and Chalcedonian creeds. Catholics uphold the Trinity, the divinity of Christ, the sinfulness of humanity, and the necessity of Christ for salvation. However, Catholicism differs from Eastern Orthodox and Protestants in its structure and some of its teachings and practices.

Many historians date the beginning of Roman Catholicism as an institution to the fifth or sixth century, with the formal development of the papacy and the hierarchical structure. Catholics, however, consider the beginning to be with the founding of the church by Jesus Christ and His giving of authority to the Apostle Peter. The Roman Catholic Church claims that Apostolic succession (the uninterrupted transmission of spiritual authority passed down from the apostles) is found in the Catholic Church alone. At the top of the Catholic hierarchy is the pope, followed by cardinals, archbishops, bishops, priests, deacons, and the laity. The pope, also known as the supreme pontiff or the bishop of Rome, is seen as the "vicar" (representative) of Christ on earth. The pope's supremacy is based on being the successor of Peter, upon whom Christ built the church and conferred the "keys of the kingdom of heaven" in Matthew 16:19. When the pope speaks *ex cathedra* ("from the chair," i.e., from the throne of Saint Peter), his statements are said to be infallible (unable to err in matters of faith or practice). In the Catholic tradition, clergy are to be celibate men with the exception of Eastern Rite Catholics and married Anglican priests who convert.

Catholics, unlike Protestants, accept both the Bible and tradition as authoritative. For Catholics, the Bible is comprised not only of the Old and New Testaments but also the Apocrypha (also known as the Deuterocanonical writings). Bishops who are in communion with the pope have the divine task of interpreting and teaching the Bible and tradition to the church. The Catechism of the Catholic Church maintains that this role "has been entrusted to the living, teaching office of the Church alone."[40] Laypeople are not encouraged to interpret the Bible but are to "receive with docility the teachings and directives that their pastors give them in different forms."[41]

Catholic doctrine is based on both Scripture and tradition. Some of the essential tenets of the Catholic Church are as follows:

- *Devotion to the Blessed Virgin and the saints.* Catholics are committed to showing devotion to the Virgin Mary, the mother of Christ, whom they teach was born without sin (immaculate conception), was taken up into heaven (the Assumption of Mary), and intercedes for believers in heaven (the Intercession of the Blessed Virgin Mary). Devotion can be shown by honoring Mary and invoking her help in prayer. Those who adore Mary with a sincere heart receive Christ's healing grace and forgiveness and grow in holiness. In addition, Catholics practice adoration of the saints (holy persons formally recognized by the church) through special prayers, rituals, pilgrimages, and the use of icons (sacred images). Catholics do not consider adoration the same as worship, which is reserved for God alone.

- *The seven sacraments.* Catholics understand the sacraments as visible signs of Christ's invisible presence and a means for receiving His grace. The Catholic Church celebrates seven sacraments: baptism, confirmation, communion (Eucharist), reconciliation, last rites (extreme unction), marriage, holy orders, and baptism. In baptism, original sin is washed away, and the Holy Spirit gives new life in Christ. Confirmation and communion are sacraments of initiation. Confirmation seals a life of faith in Christ. The Eucharist nourishes the life of faith. Reconciliation and last rites are sacraments of healing. Reconciliation, also known as confession or penance, enables the sinner to receive

5D. St. Peter's Basilica in Rome. Photo by Eugene Pivovarov, September 4, 2009 (https://creativecommons.org/licenses/by/3.0)

Christ's healing grace through confession and the pardoning of sin by the priest. Last rites or anointing of the sick is the sacrament that unites a sick person with Jesus and brings about forgiveness through the anointing with oil and the laying on of hands by a priest. Marriage is the uniting of a man and a woman as Christ is united to His church. Holy orders is the ordaining of bishops, priests, or deacons to be spiritual leaders. Bishops are to pass on the teachings of the apostles, priests are to be the spiritual leaders of their communities, and deacons are to serve the church.

- *Transubstantiation.* The Catholic Church teaches the "Real Presence" of Christ in the celebration of the Eucharist. Christ is literally present in the bread and the wine. When an ordained priest blesses the elements, the bread is transformed into the body of Christ and the wine into the blood of Christ, though they appear unchanged. The celebration of the Eucharist unites one with Christ. Worship of the Eucharist is an expression of faith in the real presence of Christ, takes away sin, and unites one with Christ. The Council of Trent summarized the doctrine of transubstantiation:

  > Because Christ our Redeemer said that it was truly his body that he was offering under the species of bread, it has always been the conviction of the church of God, and this holy council now declares again, that by the consecration of the bread and wine there takes place a change of the whole substance of the bread into the substance of the body of Christ our Lord and of the whole substance of the wine into the substance of his blood. This change the holy Catholic Church has fittingly and properly called transubstantiation.[42]

- *The dignity of the human person.* The Catholic Church proclaims that all human life is sacred. The dignity of the human person is the foundation for the church's moral vision. Pope John Paul II wrote in the doctrinal statement *Centesimus annus*, "Human persons are willed by God; they are imprinted with God's image. Their dignity does not come from the work they do, but from the persons they are."[43] Based on human dignity, the Catholic Church condemns, among other things, artificial contraception, abortion, euthanasia, slavery, prostitution, human trafficking, and disgraceful working conditions.[44]

- *The nature of salvation.* The Catholic Church teaches that salvation is a lifelong process of good works accompanied by faith in the sacrifice of Jesus. The Catholic Catechism proclaims,

  > Justification establishes cooperation between God's grace and man's freedom. On man's part it is expressed by the assent of faith to the Word of God, which invites him to conversion, and in the cooperation of charity with the prompting of the Holy Spirit who precedes and preserves his assent.[45]

What Is Eastern Orthodoxy?

While Eastern Orthodoxy is the third largest branch of Christianity with 200–300 million members worldwide, most Westerners know little about it. In the West, most Eastern Orthodox churches have Eastern European roots and are composed of immigrants from Greece, Russia, Ukraine, Armenia, Romania, or Serbia. Eastern Orthodoxy shares most of the same beliefs and traditions as Roman Catholicism, recognizing seven ecumenical councils: Nicaea (325), Constantinople I (381), Ephesus (431), Chalcedon (451), Constantinople II (553), Constantinople III (680–81), and Nicaea II (787). Like the Catholic Church, the Eastern Orthodox Church recognizes itself as the "one, holy, catholic (universal), and apostolic Church" described in the Nicene Creed. It maintains that it alone has an unbroken chain of apostolic succession, meaning that it can trace its teaching directly from the apostles of Christ. The word *orthodox* comes from the Greek words *orthos* (correct) and *doxa* (belief). Orthodox churches developed in the Eastern part of the Roman Empire, whose capital was Byzantium (the city that became Constantinople and later Istanbul), and is therefore sometimes referred to as Byzantine Christianity. It is composed of 15 self-governing churches that are united in faith and practices. Most of the churches have a geographical title—including the Church of Greece, the Church of Russia, the Church of Serbia, and the Orthodox Church in America. Not all Orthodox churches, however, are considered Eastern Orthodox. For example, the Oriental Orthodox Church and the Coptic Orthodox Church are theologically distinct from Eastern Orthodoxy. Furthermore, not all Eastern-tradition churches are Orthodox. For instance, there are Eastern Catholic Churches.

The Orthodox Church shares with Catholicism the beliefs in the authority of

5E. Moscow's Cathedral of Christ the Saviour is the tallest Eastern Orthodox Church in the world. Photo by Isik5 (https://creativecommons.org/licenses/by-sa/3.0).

both Scripture and tradition, the real presence of Christ in the Eucharist (transubstantiation), salvation by faith and works, the affirmation of church hierarchy, and the veneration of the Virgin Mary and the saints. At the same time, it differs from Protestantism and Catholicism in several ways. Some of the distinctions of Eastern Orthodoxy are as follows:

- *Church hierarchy.* While Orthodox Christians hold to apostolic succession, they do not accept the authority of the pope as Christ's vicar on earth or as having supremacy over other bishops. Instead, they regard him as simply the bishop of Rome. Also, Orthodox priests may marry prior to taking their holy orders, but bishops must remain celibate. The Orthodox Church has the role of interpreting and preserving God's revelation found in both Scripture and tradition.

- *The Holy Spirit.* The Holy Spirit, the third person of the Trinity, has a central place in Eastern Orthodox thought. Orthodox theologian Athanasios N. Papathanasiou writes,

  > The church ceaselessly seeks the action of the Spirit, which is also what makes the body of believers into the Church. This is especially clear in the anaphora prayer at the liturgy, where the celebrant prays for the Spirit to be sent down not only upon the eucharistic gifts but upon the community as well.[46]

  Bishop Kallistos Ware observes, "Orthodox theology never treats the earthly aspect of the Church in isolation, but thinks always of the Church in Christ and the Holy Spirit. All Orthodox thinking about the Church starts with the special relationship which exists between the Church and God."[47] In keeping with its emphasis on the Holy Spirit, the Eastern Orthodox Church insists that the Holy Spirit proceeds from the Father alone, not from both the Father and Son. To the Orthodox mind, the *filioque* clause (from the Son) subordinates the Spirit to the Son and diminishes the Spirit's equality.

- *Communion of saints.* Orthodox Christians hold that believers can have communion with the saints (or the great cloud of witnesses) in this present life. Although there is one true Mediator—Christ—and saints are not substitutes for Christ, saints can intercede with God on our behalf, as Ware explains:

  > In God and in His Church there is no division between the living and the departed, but all are one in the love of the Father. Whether we are alive or whether we are dead, as members of the Church we still belong to the same family, and still have a duty to bear one another's burdens. Therefore just as Orthodox Christians here on earth pray for one another and ask for one another's prayers, so they pray for the faithful departed and ask the faithful departed to pray for them. Death cannot sever the bond of mutual love which links the members of the Church together.[48]

- *Ancestral sin.* The Orthodox Church holds that everyone bears the consequences of Adam and Eve's original sin, including death, but not their guilt. In the Orthodox tradition, the preferred term for original sin is "ancestral sin" to describe our "inclination towards sin, a heritage from the sin of our progenitors," and this is removed in baptism.[49] In contrast, Roman Catholicism teaches that everyone receives from Adam and Eve a fallen nature and its consequences as well as their guilt. The Catholic sacrament of baptism regenerates (spiritual transformation), freeing one from both fallen nature and guilt.
- *Deification.* The Orthodox Church understands salvation as "deification." Christ's incarnation allows humans to be united with God (deification). This union with God enables humans to participate in God's divine energies, though not His essence. The process of deification, or *theosis*, is a communal one involving prayer, asceticism, charity, and receiving the holy sacraments of the Orthodox Church. The Orthodox tradition proclaims, as Athanasius did in the fourth century, "God became human that we might be made god."[50] Deification is both a gift from God and something to be humbly sought.
- *Veneration of Mary and the saints and the use of icons.* Like Catholics, Orthodox Christians are dedicated to venerating the Virgin Mary, the mother of Jesus, and they believe in her bodily assumption (she was taken to heaven at the end of her earthly life). She is sometimes even referred to as the "co-Redemptrix" for her vital role in agreeing to give life to the Redeemer. Orthodox Christians differ from Catholics, however, in that they deny the Immaculate Conception due to their views on original sin. The church uses icons of Christ, Mary, the saints, and angels to teach about God and to aid the faithful in prayer. They do not consider the use of icons idolatrous since they venerate the person depicted rather than worshiping the physical image.
- *Theological approach.* The Eastern Orthodox Church also differs in its theological approach. It has been influenced by more Eastern philosophy and mysticism than the Western church has been. This approach encourages focus on the spiritual over literal interpretation of Scripture as well as an emphasis on mystery and personal experience, which transcend logic. In contrast, the Western tradition tends to rely more on reason and a literal approach. Orthodox Christianity views God as incomprehensible; therefore, there is less emphasis on the development of systematic theologies (organized, topical studies of Scripture).

What Is Protestantism?

Protestantism, the second-largest branch of Christianity, arose in the sixteenth century during the Reformation. The term initially described German princes and cities that declared religious independence and exercised territorial sovereignty from the Roman Catholic Church in response to the Diet of Speyer (1529). In the beginning, Protestantism primarily applied to Lutherans and Reformed churches. However, the term eventually began to be used for all who held to the teachings of the Reformation and were not in communion with the Roman Catholic or Eastern Orthodox churches. Protestants affirm many of the same core teachings that Catholics and Orthodox believers do, including the teachings from the Nicene and Chalcedonian creeds regarding the Trinity and Christ. Protestants largely reject the teaching of an unbroken apostolic succession down through particular church hierarchies. They also hold to a different authoritative canon than Roman Catholics and Eastern Orthodox believers, including only the Old and New Testaments in their Bible, not the Apocrypha. The five solas—*sola scriptura* (Scripture alone), *sola gratia* (grace alone), *sola fide* (faith alone), *solus Christus* (Christ alone), and *soli Deo gloria* (for the glory of God alone)—are some of the core foundational teachings of Protestantism. The Protestant movement includes several denominations as well as independent churches, including Lutherans, Presbyterians, Methodists, Episcopalians, and Baptists. Some of the essential ideas of Protestants are as follows:

- *Scripture.* Scripture alone is the infallible and authoritative source of truth. While tradition can be a valuable source, it does not hold the same authority as Scripture.
- *Salvation.* Salvation is an unmerited gift of God. Salvation is offered by grace through faith in Christ alone, not by works. This stands in contrast with both the Catholic and Orthodox traditions, which emphasize receiving salvation through a lifelong process of faith, works, and sacraments.
- *The priesthood.* Rather than seeing the priesthood as a church office of mediators between God and people, Protestants hold to the priesthood of all believers. They do not think priests are necessary for mediating God's grace, nor do they believe that the Lord's Supper is an actual sacrifice of Christ's body and blood (transubstantiation), which needs to be consecrated by a priest.
- *Sacraments.* Most Protestants adhere to only two sacraments: baptism and the Lord's Supper. There are several perspectives regarding the role that the sacraments have in the life of the church. Some see them as reminders of God's grace (e.g., Baptist), whereas others view them as vehicles of grace (e.g., Anglican).

What Is Evangelicalism?

The Greek word for "good news" (gospel) is *euangelion*; this is where we get our word *evangelism* (telling the good news about Jesus), and subsequently the term "Evangelicals." Evangelicals are considered a branch of Protestantism. "Evaungelicalles" was a term used by Sir Thomas More in 1531 to refer to advocates of the Reformation. As late as the eighteenth century, the term meant simply "of the gospel" in a nonpartisan sense. For example, in 1723, Isaac Watts wrote about an "Evangelical Turn of Thought." The term "Evangelical" with an uppercase letter began to be used in the 1730s to refer to the Evangelical movement of church renewal according to biblical beliefs. Historian David Bebbington points to four marks that define the Evangelical movement:

1. *Conversionism* (the belief that lives need to be changed, or "born-again")
2. *Activism* (the expression of the gospel in missionary and social effort)

3. *Biblicism* (the Bible as the ultimate authority)
4. *Crucicentrism* (stress on the redemptive sacrifice of Christ on the cross)[51]

In the late nineteenth century, an emphasis was placed on biblicism as the first and leading principle of the Evangelical movement. In the twentieth century, however, conversion began to be given the highest priority by the movement.

"Fundamentalism" is a fairly precise term used to designate a particular type of militant evangelical. The movement began in the late nineteenth and early twentieth centuries as a reaction to modernism and theological liberalism. Fundamentalists advocated for upholding the fundamental doctrines of the Christian faith found in Scripture. The Fundamentalists emphasized biblical inerrancy (the Bible is without error or fault in the original manuscripts). Over time, Christian Fundamentalism has become associated with more strict separatists or with right-wing politics. It should not, however, be considered synonymous with Evangelicalism.

Evangelicalism is a much broader term than Fundamentalism and can be used to describe a more diverse body of Protestant believers, including the following: Holiness churches, Pentecostals, Traditionalists, Methodists, Presbyterians, black churches, Fundamentalists, Pietist groups, Reformed traditions, Baptists, some Episcopalians, Anabaptists, Lutherans, and nondenominational believers. Historian George Marsden suggests that in the 1950s and 1960s, Evangelicals could be identified as "anyone who likes Billy Graham."[52] Now, however, there is no recognizable leader. Evangelicals often differ in worship styles, lifestyles, politics, and ethics.

Christianity is the world's most popular religion today. Like many movements, as it has grown, it has struggled to stay united, splintering into different branches. Yet most Christians still agree on one thing: the life-changing significance of the life, death, resurrection, and ascension of Jesus Christ. Jesus is to be believed in and confessed as Lord by all.

Karin Stetina (PhD, Marquette University) taught theology and church history for nearly 20 years at Wheaton College, and she now serves as associate professor of theology at Biola University. Among her publications are *Jonathan Edwards' Early Understanding of Religious Experience* and *The Fatherhood of God in John Calvin's Thought*. She has also served as consultant and editor for *Luther Digest*.

Islam

Mark Durie

In the world today, followers of Islam make up a quarter of the world's population. Represented in every nation, this vast religion—second only to Christianity in number of followers—traces its origins back to the teachings and influence of one man, Muhammad, who was born in Mecca in Arabia, around the year AD 570. Almost everything we know about Muhammad comes from sources written by Muslims after his death.

History and Beliefs

Muhammad was born into a prominent Meccan clan, the Quraysh, but he lost his father before he was born; his mother, Amina, when he was six; and his paternal grandfather, Abdul-Muttalib, when he was eight. After this, his uncle Abu Talib took him under his wing. As an orphan, Muhammad's status in his clan was not high, and tradition reports that he was mocked as a child by his wealthier and more powerful relatives. Later, Muhammad became a merchant, and his fortunes improved when he married Khadijah, a widow who was 15 years older than he.

When he was around 40, Muhammad reported an encounter with an angel, Jibril (Gabriel), who gave him verses of poetry to recite. This was the beginning of his religious awakening. For the next 23 years, more poetry to recite was "sent down" to Muhammad via this angel, and after Muhammad's death, the verses were compiled together to form what came to be known as *al-Qur'an*, "the recitation," the core scripture of Islam.

At first, Muhammad was troubled by his spiritual encounters. However, three years after receiving the first revelation, Muhammad had come to believe he was commanded to recite these verses to others and to call them to accept the message that had been given to him through these revelations. This message developed over time, but its basic elements were as follows.

God. There is only one God, Allah, who has created human beings and placed them on this earth to serve him exclusively. The eternal destiny of all people is determined by the path they take in this life. Those who are obedient to Allah, believing and trusting in him, paying attention to the reminders provided by his guiding signs, and obeying his commands, are on the "straight path," and they will do well.

Humans. By nature human beings are

not evil, but weak and ignorant, so they can easily go astray, wandering or being led off the straight path. Satan tries to lead people off this path. To keep humanity on track, Allah sends messengers to call attention to the guiding signs. Muhammad is one of these messengers. Anyone who follows this guidance, repenting and returning to Allah's path, will receive mercy and be successful. Those who reject this guidance will be punished in both this life and the next.

Duty. People who accept this message should devote themselves to daily prayers, give alms to help people in need, including the poor and orphans, and worship Allah as the one and only God.

Afterlife. There will come a day when all who have died will be resurrected. Then it will be too late to repent. On that day, those who have accepted Muhammad's guidance will enter Paradise, which is a garden full of delights and pleasure. However, others who reject the truth brought by Muhammad and past messengers will be counted as "losers." They will be punished by Allah, in the fires of Hell.

In the early part of Muhammad's career as the "Messenger of Allah," the Qur'an draws attention to what it calls the "nearer punishment," a destructive act in which Allah punishes those who reject the guidance brought by his messengers. The Qur'an emphasizes that, again and again in the past, whole communities were destroyed by traumatic events such as flood, fire, thunderbolt, wind, or stones falling like hail from the sky. Surah 7:4 states, "How many a city did we destroy! Our punishment caught them unawares, by night, or while they were snoozing in the middle of the day."

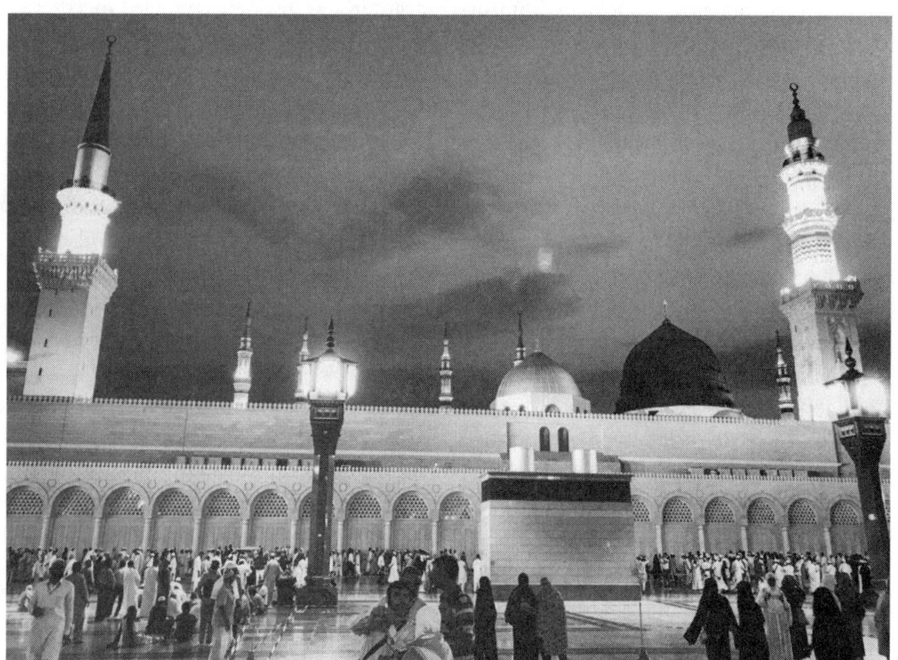

6A. The Al Nabawi Mosque in Medina is famous for being spearheaded by Muhammad himself and for the site of his tomb. Photo by Hadibeh, 2016 (https://creativecommons.org/licenses/by-sa/4.0).

Mecca and Medina

Muhammad presented this dire warning to the Arabs of Mecca. A few believed and joined his new religious group, but it was a small community at first, comprised mainly of poor people and slaves. They were initially known as *mu'min* (believers), and later as *Muslims* (surrendered ones). However, most Meccans were skeptical, and the townspeople mocked Muhammad, his message, and his followers. The fledgling Muslim community had to deal with an economic boycott by the rejecters, and at times, they experienced overt persecution. Some believers were driven from their homes.

Islamic tradition reports that some early Muslims fled from this persecution across the Red Sea, where they enjoyed the protection of the Christian Ethiopian king. Some of these refugees stayed in Ethiopia, becoming Christians, but others returned to join Muhammad when he migrated from Mecca to the oasis city of Yathrib, later known as Medina, in June 622. Islamic tradition records that the people of Medina accepted Muhammad's message, even before he left Mecca, and they agreed together to become his allies, submitting to his leadership. Islamic tradition celebrates the migration to Medina as the start of the Islamic calendar because it was at Medina that a properly constituted Islamic community—in effect a fledgling Islamic state—was established on a firm footing.

Not everyone in Medina was pleased with Muhammad's offer to them to follow the "straight path." Medina's Jewish tribes were resistant to the new preaching, and Muslim traditions report that some Jews had long, difficult dialogues with Muhammad. This stubbornness annoyed him considerably, and after some time he began to drive the Jews out of Medina, until he destroyed the last tribe, the Qurayza, by executing the men and enslaving the women and children. After unifying Medina under his leadership in this way, Muhammad launched a series of military campaigns to extend his power and the Islamic community's reach. He returned in triumph to Mecca, and over time, more and more tribes joined his cause, and the rule of Islam was secured over the whole of Arabia.

According to Islamic tradition, the early chapters (surahs) of the Qur'an were "sent down" to Muhammad in Mecca, and the later ones came when he was in Medina. So there is a "Meccan Qur'an" and a "Medinan Qur'an." Within the Qur'an itself, the surahs are not laid out in chronological order, so the reader needs some kind of a guide in order to tell which surahs are Meccan and which are Medinan. (Some translations provide this information at the heading of each chapter.)

There are striking differences between the Meccan and Medinan chapters. The Qur'an's famous calls to fight unbelievers are in the later Medinan chapters, not the earlier Meccan ones. In Mecca, the warning messages are about an expected "Act of God" coming in judgment upon rejecters in this life, followed by a grim future in the fires of Hell. However, in the Medinan chapters, the emphasis on the punishment of God shifts to the sword of believers, who are called to "fight until there is no more persecution" (Surah 2:193; 8:39) and "fight and kill the polytheists wherever you find them" (Surah 9:5).

There are also stylistic changes in the Medinan Qur'an: Verses become longer as time passes, and the language becomes less poetic. However, more important than mere style is a profound shift in the way the Muslim community and its relationship to Muhammad is portrayed. In Mecca, believers are described as pious people who help the poor and devote themselves to practices such as prayer and fasting: There are very few regulations beyond these basics. At the same time, Muhammad is described as "only" a messenger, whose sole function is to deliver the message given to him by the angel Jibril.

In Medina, all this changes. Muhammad becomes a leader of a highly regulated community, acting as its king, judge, and general. The Medinan verses include several detailed instructions directing many aspects of life, including marriage, sexual activity, raising children, inheritance, clothing, financial transactions such as borrowing and lending, punishment of serious crimes like theft and murder, the conduct of war, slavery, prostitution, legal contracts and processes, the correct way to enter a house, caring for livestock, greeting others, paying contributions for the religion, hunting, permitted foods, and the correct way to relate to Muhammad.

Hadiths and Sharia

In the Medinan verses, Muhammad is portrayed as both a leader and a role model for other Muslims to follow. He is described as a "good example" (Surah 33:21), who is to be obeyed as one would obey God himself: "O believers, obey Allah and obey the Messenger" (Surah 4:59). Building on this teaching about Muhammad, early Muslims collected many traditional reports concerning the details of Muhammad's life and teaching as well as the life of his companions, and they used this material to compile guidance for believers to follow. Even the smallest details of what Muhammad did and said were combed through in order to help shape the life path of believers. Muhammad's whole way of life is called the *Sunnah*, and it was passed on in the form of collections of individual reports, called *hadiths*.

The hadiths are as important as the Qur'an for determining the religious practices of Muslims, and this means the scriptures of Islam consist of not only the Qur'an but also the Sunnah, as recorded in the hadiths. Sunni Muslims recognize six canonical collections of hadiths: *Sahih Al-Bukhari*, *Sahih Muslim*, *Sunan Abu Dawud*, *Sunan al-Tirmidhi*, *Sunan al-Nasa'i*, and *Sunan Ibn Majah*. These, together with the Qur'an, form the primary holy books or scriptures of Islam. The hadith collections are a much larger body of text than the Qur'an.

It is recorded in a hadith that one day, when he was asked about faith, Muhammad said that faith consists of five key elements. The first is belief in *tawhid*, or the absolute "oneness" of Allah, who created all things. A second key belief is in angels, spiritual beings who serve Allah. The angel Jibril, in particular, plays an important role in transmitting the verses of the Qur'an to Muhammad. Angels also record the deeds of humans, whether evil or good, and they are involved as Allah's servants at the final judgment. A third key belief is in "books." These are revealed texts sent to humanity from Allah. The Qur'an is the final such book, superseding and completing the messages contained in all previous books. A fourth key belief is in messengers, men sent by Allah to impart his guidance to human beings. The Qur'an reports that many biblical figures were in fact prophets of Islam, including Adam, Noah, Abraham, Lot, Moses, David, Solomon, and Jesus. There are also messengers mentioned by name in the Qur'an who are not found in the Bible. Muhammad himself is considered by Muslims to be the last of the messengers, or the "seal" of the prophets. A fifth key belief is in a future *resurrection* and *judgment*. Islam teaches a physical resurrection, followed by a universal judgment of all people. After being raised bodily, the heavenly record of everyone's deeds will be opened, and each person will be judged according to what he or she has done in this life, whether good or bad. People will then be sent to the Garden or the Fire. An additional final key belief is in destiny, that it is Allah's sovereign will to determine all things.

After Muhammad, early Muslim scholars pored over the Qur'an and the hadiths and extrapolated rules and principles for Muslims to live by. Some questions they could answer directly from the Qur'an or the hadiths, but for other issues, they had to apply reason and analogy. The collected wisdom produced by these efforts is a system of guidance for humanity to follow. In Islam, the word for this guidance is *sharia*, which literally means a "path to follow." The study of this guidance is the queen of the religious sciences in Islam, and this is why the religious faculty in Islamic universities will often be called the faculty or school of Sharia.

Guidance and Submission

In Islam, the fundamental problem of humankind is ignorance combined with weakness: Ignorant of the right way to go, people are easily led off the right path. The solution to this state of ignorance is guidance. The metaphor of the straight path plays a central role in Islam. The promise of Islam to those who are rightly guided, keeping on the straight path, is that they will be successful in both this life and the next. So Islam offers success through being rightly guided. The whole religion is itself understood as a system of guidance not just for individuals but for whole societies and states.

In Islam, right action is more important than right belief: Islam prioritizes orthopraxy over orthodoxy. There is great emphasis in Islamic tradition on practical guidance on what to do in every conceivable situation. Possible actions are divided into five categories: those that are obligatory for all Muslims to follow (*fard* or *wajib*), those that are recommended (*mustahabb* or *mandub*), those that are neutral (*mubah*), those that are dispreferred or disliked (*makruh*), and actions that are forbidden (*haram*). The category of *halal* (permissible) is sometimes contrasted with *haram* (forbidden).

In Islam, the fundamental metaphor for the relationship between God and humanity is the master-slave relationship. The word *Muslim* literally means "submitter" or "one who surrenders," and the word *Islam* means "surrender" or "submission." This terminology is derived from warfare. The Arabic root *slm* means "to be safe." The concept of *islam* (surrender) is that in warfare, someone becomes safe through surrender. In other words, in the culture of warfare at the time of Muhammad, a person would become the slave of the person who had conquered him, and in becoming a slave, one's life would be saved. So a Muslim, as "one who surrenders," is someone who has become safe through surrender to God, becoming his slave. Or, as Muhammad himself used to put it, *aslim taslam*: "surrender (i.e., become a Muslim) and you will be safe."

In many ways, the central characteristics of Islam were set by the character and role of Muhammad at the very start of the religion. Muhammad combined in himself the roles of high priest (supreme religious leader), chief justice, general of the army, and head of state. Spiritual, legal, military, and political power were united in one person. This set a model that has deeply influenced the course of the religion. For example, in Saudi Arabia today, which is strongly influenced by sharia principles, the chief judge of the nation is also the supreme religious leader. Islamic tradition knows no distinction between religion and politics, and a core duty of any head of state in an Islamic society is to use available power to promote and impose Islamic faith and observance.

Islam was originally established by warfare and conquest, and with some exceptions, it spread astonishingly rapidly by this means. Immediately after the death of Muhammad, many Arabs desired to revert to their pagan beliefs, and a bloody Ridda (Apostasy) War was required to reimpose Islam across Arabia. Muhammad's successors, the Caliphs, led Muslim armies south, north, east, and west to extend the borders of Islam. Just 100 years after Muhammad's death, Muslim armies were crossing from North Africa into Spain.

Shia and Sunni

After Muhammad died, there were disputes over who should succeed him, and a split of allegiances developed. The *Shia* party believed that Muhammad's cousin and son-in-law Ali had been designated by Muhammad as his rightful successor, while the *Sunni* party believed that Muhammad did not choose anyone. Thus they believed that the community's appointment of Abu Bakr, the father-in-law of Muhammad, as the first Caliph, was legitimate. In essence, this was a family feud between Muhammad's daughter Fatimah (married to Ali) and his young wife Aisha (the daughter of Abu Bakr).

Over time, the Shia-Sunni split developed theological features, and while Shia and Sunni Islam have a great deal in common, they do not accept all the same hadiths. The Shia consider that Ali and his descendants, the 12 imams, were sinless and rightly guided, so they serve as models for guidance as much as Muhammad. In contrast, the Sunnis stress the importance of following the example of Muhammad and his companions. The word Shia means "followers" (of Ali), and the word Sunni means "people of the Sunnah" (way of life) of Muhammad and his companions. Because these two traditions look to different sources for guidance, their interpretations of sharia are not the same. A well-known example is that the Shia maintain an institution of temporary marriage (i.e., an intentional short-term marriage), based on a tradition of Muhammad, but the Sunnis reject this based on a ruling by the Caliph Umar, whose authority the Shia do not accept.

Today around 85 percent of Muslims are Sunnis, and 15 percent are Shia. The Shia are themselves divided into many sects, but the majority (around 95 percent) are "Twelvers" (named after the 12 imams). Other Shia sects are the Ismailis and the Zaydis (also known as "Fivers"), and there are other smaller groups. Ismailis are themselves split into multiple groups. A group distinct from Sunni and Shia is the Khawarij, who exist today only in a sect known as the Ibadis, who form a majority in Oman.

Today, Shias form a majority in Iran, Bahrain, Iraq, Lebanon, and Azerbaijan, and a significant minority in Pakistan, Syria, Yemen, Saudi Arabia, and Kuwait. The relationship between Shias and Sunnis has been marked by warfare throughout history, and today the distinction has become associated with conflict once again, with proxy conflicts raging in Yemen, Iraq, and Syria that are driven by the struggle for regional power between Shia Iran and Sunni Saudi Arabia.

Sunni Muslims are not religiously uniform. Traditionally they are divided into four main schools of Islamic jurisprudence, known as Hanafi, Maliki, Shafi'i, and Hanbali. These schools emerged just over 1,000 years ago. Some schools came to dominate in particular regions. For example, Southeast Asia, East Africa, Kurdistan and parts of India are Shafi'i; Hanafis predominate in Russia, Iraq, Turkey, South and Central Asia, most of Egypt and the Levant; Malikis are dominant in North and West Africa and are also found in some Gulf states, parts of Arabia and Upper Egypt; and the Hanbali school is mainly found in North and Central Arabia. While many differences between the schools are quite minor, some are significant. For example, it is only in Shafi'i jurisprudence that female circumcision is obligatory; in other schools, it is only permissible or recommended. This explains, for example, why the practice is widespread among Muslims in Southeast Asia.

Sufism

Both the Qur'an and Islamic theology stress the otherness of Allah—that he is utterly separate from, distinct from, and unlike human beings. Nevertheless, Islam does have a long tradition of facilitating mystical encounters with Allah. Islam's tradition of mysticism goes under the general heading of Sufism. Sufis are Muslims who belong to an order (*tariqah*) that defers to a leader known as a *wali*. These orders meet for mystical practices. These can include *dhikr*, repetitive praises and prayers, recited together. Some orders practice ritualized dhikr, which involve dancing (e.g., the whirling dervishes), singing or chanting, beating of drums, burning of incense, trance states, and the use of prayer beads. For Sufis, these practices are a way to achieve annihilation of the self, seeking the divine presence in order to achieve union with Allah. Sufi teachings share some features in common with New Age spirituality, and in the West, participation in Sufi groups is one pathway into Islam for non-Muslims.

Finally, it is important to note that Islam is a missionary faith. Its followers are instructed by the Qur'an to "call" others to Islam, and many Muslims are proactive in seeking ways to present the message of Islam to others.

Lifestyle and Culture

For Muslims, the core practice of the faith is a total way of life based on the Qur'an and the Sunnah of Muhammad. The sharia in an Islamicized society is integrated into the culture. There are many specific provisions required of Muslims, including limitations on foods they can eat and rules for going about their daily lives, such as how to enter a room, how to maintain bodily cleanliness, how to greet an acquaintance, which hand to use for eating food (the right), and on which side to sleep (also the right).

Especially important are Islam's five core religious practices, known as the "five pillars of Islam." These are the profession of faith, the *shahada*, which is an affirmation in Arabic that "there is no god but Allah and Muhammad is his Messenger"; daily ritual prayers (the *salat*) that Muslims are expected to perform five times a day (for Shia it is three times); giving alms (*zakat*), which is directed to specific purposes, including helping the poor; fasting during the month of Ramadan, which consists of refraining from food and drink from sunrise to sunset; and, for those who have the means, a pilgrimage to Mecca (the *hajj*). The highlight of the pilgrimage is to walk around the Ka'ba, a building believed by Muslims to have been built by Abraham as a house of worship.

Societal Structures

Many details of family life are regulated by the sharia. The Sunnah of Muhammad provides much guidance for matters such as marriage, sexual intimacy, respect for parents, and the nurturing of children. When a child is born, the words of the call to prayer (the *azhan*) are recited in the newborn's ear. Important milestones for children are circumcision for boys and, in some schools of sharia, for girls also. An Islamic marriage is

6B. Pilgrims walk around the Ka'ba during the Hajj. Photo by Adli Wahid, 2018 (https://creativecommons.org/licenses/by-sa/4.0).

constructed as a civil contract rather than a religious ceremony. It requires two witnesses and the payment of a gift (*mahr*) to the bride by the groom. The bride is represented in the process by her guardian, so the contract is conducted between the groom and the guardian. The guardian will normally be the bride's father, or else another close male relative, such as her grandfather or brother. Islam permits a man to have up to four wives. Divorce is not difficult for a man to enact; he does so by telling her three times that he is divorcing her, saying, "*Talaq*" (I divorce you). Divorce is more difficult for women to initiate because it can require a ruling from an Islamic court. Islam stipulates that a son's inheritance is double that of a daughter's. Like birth, death is marked by religious rituals: A body is washed by relatives of the same sex, wrapped in a white shroud, and buried lying on its right side, facing Mecca.

Not all nations recognize the authority of the sharia in family-related legal processes such as marriage, divorce, and inheritance. On the one hand, some Islamic nations intervene in the application of sharia principles, for example, by banning the triple-talaq divorce (e.g., in Pakistan, Morocco, and, since 2017, India)[1] or by moderating sharia principles when assigning custody of children (e.g., Egypt). On the other hand, in nations that do not incorporate the Islamic sharia into their legal systems, Muslim communities often establish sharia tribunals outside the official legal system, to enable them to settle family issues in accordance with the religion. The status of these tribunals is controversial and often contested.

One of the most visible markers of Muslim identity is the head covering worn by women. The sharia requires women to cover themselves in the presence of males, except for close relatives. Although there are different opinions as to the degree of covering required, the general consensus is that women should cover everything except the face, hands, and feet (and men should cover from the navel to the knees). The veil that covers the hair and neck but not the face is known as a hijab. Some Muslim scholars also require women's faces to be covered, either with a face veil (*niqab*), leaving the eyes showing through a slit, or with a single garment that covers the body, head, and face completely (*burqa*), with mesh to see through. Some Islamic nations, such as Iran and Saudi Arabia, require women to wear a head covering in public. On the other hand, other Muslim countries have, in modern times, banned the wearing of the hijab, regarding it as a sign of Islamic conservatism. For example, Turkey banned headscarves at universities and government offices until 2010.[2] Some non-Islamic nations have also banned or limited the wearing of the burqa and even the hijab. For example, France prohibits the wearing of religious symbols in schools, including female head coverings.

The Islamic system of guardianship, which requires men to be guardians of women (Surah 4:34), has become increasingly controversial, with many Muslim women seeking more autonomy. The sharia requires that every woman have a guardian—her husband if she has one, or else her father, grandfather, or another close male relative. In some contexts, this guardianship can include control over whether a woman can marry, or even whether she can go outside the family home.

It is the duty of every Muslim to seek guidance in matters of religious practice. Islam highly values knowledge and learning, and it is considered meritorious to learn to recite the Qur'an in Arabic. Learning to recite at least portions of the Qur'anic text is considered to be a fundamental aspect of a child's formation. However, most Muslims will acquire their knowledge of Islam, not from the primary texts such as the Qur'an and hadiths, but from others in their community. Indeed, a good deal of Islamic practice becomes embedded in culture to the point where Muslims may consider all their cultural practices to be Islamic.

Fasts and Festivals

Islam follows a 12-month lunar calendar. The Islamic calendar is used to determine the dates for the fasting month (Ramadan), the timing of pilgrimage to Mecca, and various festivals throughout the year. Since each lunar month is 29.53 days, an Islamic year is 354 or 355 days, about ten days less than a solar year.

Ramadan, the fasting month, is the ninth in the Islamic year. During Ramadan, Muslims fast from sunrise to sunset. This means abstaining from food, drink, smoking, and sexual relations during daylight hours. Exemptions are provided by the sharia for the sick, travelers, pregnant, breastfeeding and menstruating women, and the elderly. It is customary to begin each day with a meal, just before dawn, and to break the daily fast after sunset with a feast known as the *iftar*. Muslim cultures typically have specific cultural practices and preferred foods that are eaten during the season of Ramadan.

Muslims also engage more in spiritual practices during this month, such as communal prayers. In Muslim societies, business tends to run at a slower pace during Ramadan. It is also considered to be a special blessing for someone to die during Ramadan. Some particular days in Ramadan have special significance. For example, the "Night of Power" occurs sometime during the last ten days of the fasting month. It is believed that the first verses of the Qur'an were "sent down" on this night, and special blessings await those who set this night aside for worship and contemplation. The festival of Eid al-Fitr celebrates the end of Ramadan, making the return to a normal pattern of eating and drinking.

Another important Muslim festival is Eid al-Adha, the tenth day of the last month of the lunar year, when the pilgrimage is taking place. Many Muslims show acts of kindness and generosity to others at this time. Another festival celebrated by many Muslims is Mawlid, the birth of Muhammad, which falls on the twelfth day of the third month in the Islamic calendar. The manner and degree to which Muslims celebrate these and other festivals vary in different parts of the world.

Because the Islamic calendar is ten days shorter than the solar calendar, the date of Ramadan gradually moves, starting ten days earlier each year. This can cause problems for Muslims living in higher latitudes. When Ramadan falls during winter and days are shorter, Ramadan is easier to observe because fasting is for only a few hours each day. Because the weather is cool in winter, going thirsty is not so onerous. However, where summer hours are very long, such as in Alaska, Iceland, or Norway, fasting could become very difficult, as a Muslim might have only a few hours in which to eat and drink each day, or no night hours at all. Fasting from drinking can also be difficult at the height of summer, when days are both long and very hot, as in the southern regions of Australia. One solution put forward by Islamic scholars is to follow the fasting hours of Mecca in regions that experience unique fasting challenges because of sunlight hours.[3] The difficulty of summer fasting presented a challenge for Muslim athletes during the London Summer Olympics in 2012, when there were only four to five hours of nighttime in which to break one's fast; however, some religious authorities addressed this by providing a religious ruling to allow Muslim athletes to eat and drink during the day.[4]

6C. Ramadan celebration at a mosque in Indonesia. Photo by Rhmtdns, 2019 (https://creativecommons.org/licenses/by-sa/4.0).

Fatwas and Muftis

There is, in principle, no limit on the kinds of questions Muslims might seek guidance on in order to be rightly guided. While the answers to many questions are well known and not controversial—for example, all schools of Islam agree that eating pork is forbidden—modern conditions and advances in technology are always creating new issues and situations that could require guidance. Muslims can also encounter complex situations for which they may need more expert guidance than is readily available at the local mosque. In such circumstances, Muslims can turn to a religious scholar for advice. A *fatwa* or ruling can then be provided to answer the question. For example, there is a hadith in which Muhammad prohibited men from wearing silk or jewelry made of gold. In response, one Muslim asked a Saudi scholar, Muhammad Saalih Al-Munajjid, whether it is permissible for a Muslim man to wear a gold watch on the basis that it is not jewelry, but a tool. The scholar's reply was that it is *haram* (forbidden) for a man to wear a gold watch, or even to repair a man's gold watch.[5] Another inquirer wanted to know on which hand it was permitted to wear a watch. Since Muhammad did not wear a watch, his example cannot provide any direct guidance; however, the Leicester-based scholar Muhammad ibn Adam replied that since Muhammad used to wear signet rings on either hand, and a watch is a tool, like a signet ring, a watch can be worn on either hand, but the right is probably preferable because Muhammad preferred to use his right hand for good things, and a watch is a very good thing because it helps Muslims keep track of prayer times.[6]

In Islam, a *mufti* is an Islamic scholar who is qualified to offer a fatwa on a legal question. Some Islamic countries have a state-appointed official, the grand mufti, who administers a state-funded office devoted to answering people's requests for guidance. In traditional Islamic societies, Muslims could turn to anyone more knowledgeable than they themselves to seek guidance—such as the person who led prayers in their local mosque—but the availability of the internet has given rise to many fatwa websites offering Islamic guidance on a vast range of topics. In Egypt, the current grand mufti, Sheikh Shawki Ibrahim Abdel-Karim Allam, oversees a large fatwa team that runs a website and a call center, answering requests for fatwas over the phone, by email, or by ordinary letter.

The application of analogy and reason to new situations allows Islam to be a flexible faith in changing circumstances, as fatwas can help believers find solutions to questions of guidance that could have never come up in the past.

Folk Islam

"Folk Islam" is a term used to refer to expressions of Islam that incorporate local beliefs and practices. These can include the use of sacred objects, amulets, or talismans, often incorporating Qur'anic verses; the veneration of Muslim saints or spirits (*jinn*); the practice of witchcraft (*sihr*); the incorporation of animistic beliefs and rituals (such as fertility rituals); belief in the "evil eye"; and adherence to a wide variety of rituals, often in combination with Sufi practices.

Let us consider a folk Islam practice from Southeast Asia. In Aceh, Indonesia, the *rapa'i* drum, used in ritual dances, gets its name from Sheikh Ahmad bin Rifa'i, the founder of the Rifa'iyyah Sufi order. Originating in southern Iraq, this order spread through India to Southeast Asia, where it played an important role in spreading Islam. Groups of men would gather in local communal meeting places (*meunasah*) on religious festivals or other special occasions such as funerals to perform religious songs (*dikr*, *ratib*) together in praise of Allah, Muhammad, and other prophets. Some groups perform dances in which drummers and dancers seek physical invulnerability and union with God while repeating the names of Allah and Islamic prophets, stabbing themselves with knives, or threading rattan through their flesh.

Islam teaches that in addition to human beings and angels, Allah has also created *jinn*. These are spirits, some of whom are Muslims, and some are not. The Qur'an reports that a group of *jinn*, on hearing the Qur'an recited by Muhammad, converted to Islam on the spot (Surah 72:1-2). There is a resulting openness to the spirit world in most Islamic communities, and although Muslim scholars frown on it, many Muslims will consult people who offer guidance received from spirits and who can enact spells on their behalf. Muslims practice exorcism (casting out *jinn*) by means of reciting the names of Allah, reciting verses from the Qur'an, especially the last three surahs, and other religious formulae.

Prayer

Muslims are required to perform personal ritual prayers called *salat* five times a day (three for most Shia). These are performed before sunrise, after noon, in mid-afternoon, at dusk, and then later in the night, preferably before midnight. These are performed facing Mecca. The prayers are preceded by the ritual washing of hands, feet, and face (including nostrils, mouth, and ears). While making prescribed gestures, including raising hands and prostrating, the person praying recites phrases in Arabic, uttering praises to Allah, invoking his name, including verses from the Qur'an, such as the whole of the first chapter, *al-Fatihah*:

> Praise to Allah, Lord of the worlds. The Merciful. The Compassionate. Master of the Day of Judgment. You we worship, and you we seek for help. Guide us to the straight path: the path of those whom you have blessed, not (the path) of those on whom (your) anger falls, nor of those who go astray.

This short chapter of the Qur'an is a prayer for guidance, which is the very essence of Islam. The precise form of the daily prayers varies across the five daily times while maintaining a common basic structure.

6D. A Muslim prostrates himself and prays toward Mecca. Photo by Jonathan David Chandler, 2011. Public domain.

On Fridays, congregational ritual prayers are held in mosques, just after noon. Mosques vary in design around the world, depending on local conditions, but they are often open buildings, with a large flat level area. On one side of the mosque, there will be a niche on the wall, a *mihrab*, marking the direction of Mecca, which sets the direction in which people pray. Anyone who enters a mosque is expected to remove his shoes first. Mosques can be quite ornate, but the decorations never depict human figures, unlike the decorations in many Christian churches.

The Friday prayers are considered obligatory for men, but not for the elderly, women, or children (Surah 62:9-10). Normally most of those who attend Friday worship are men. The Friday service is preceded by the call to prayer by the *muezzin*, and after a short interval, a sermon (*khutbah*) is delivered to the gathered congregation. The preacher normally commences with verses from the Qur'an (in Arabic) and praises of Allah and Muhammad. In addition to exhorting the congregation to the practice of Islam, the preacher is expected to recite from the Qur'an and to offer commentary on contemporary events that impact Muslims. Once the sermon is finished, the communal prayers begin, led by an imam.

Food and Hygiene

Muslims are constrained by food laws as a part of the sharia. In principle, all foods are permitted (halal) for Muslims unless they have been explicitly prohibited. Animals that are absolutely forbidden include pigs, cats, and most small vermin such as ants, rats, and mice. Also forbidden are most predators. Horses and camels can be eaten, but not donkeys. Carrion (unslaughtered dead meat) is also prohibited. Islam does not prohibit the eating of shellfish (unlike Judaism). When land animals are permitted to be eaten, it is necessary that they be ritually slaughtered, which is done by cutting the animal's throat with a sharp knife, with the animal facing toward Mecca. At the same time, the slaughterer recites *bismillah* (in the name of Allah) and blesses Muhammad. There has been controversy in Western countries about whether halal slaughtering methods are humane.

In the second half of the twentieth century, the practice of halal certification has become widespread particularly in Western nations. A Muslim organization provides a seal or symbol attached to a product's packaging to show that its means of production complies with sharia halal principles. The halal certification industry is expanding rapidly at the present time, with sales of halal-certified products valued in the billions.

Cleanliness and purity are important in Islam. Not only are the daily prayers preceded by ritual washing, but the left hand is designated for use when going to the toilet and other dirty tasks, and the right hand is for handling food. This division of labor between the right and left hand is deeply embedded in most Islamic cultures, but it is also mandated by the religion, since Muhammad said in a hadith, "Eat from the right hand" and "No one among you should eat with his left hand or drink with it, for the devil eats with his left hand and drinks with it."

Relationship with Outsiders

The Qur'an instructs Muslims not to make friends or allies with nonbelievers (e.g., Surah 5:51), but Muslims disagree on how to interpret these verses. Some, of a more radical orientation, will take these instructions literally, and deliberately limit their circle of friends to fellow Muslims. There is a tradition of Muhammad that states, "No-one has (genuine) faith until he loves for his brother what he loves for himself," and a well-regarded commentary by Ibn Hajar al-Asqalani explains that it is fellow Muslims who should be loved.[7]

However, many Muslims take exception to such interpretations and insist their religion calls them to do good to all others. They point out that the Qur'an also speaks of making friends with people you might be at enmity with and treating them kindly as long as they are not fighting against you (Surah 60:8-9). In practice, the attitude of Muslims toward non-Muslims varies greatly depending on the circumstances. For example, in Pakistan, Christians and Hindus are looked down upon and discriminated against; non-Muslims are often forced to take on the dirtiest and most dangerous jobs, such as cleaning blocked sewers. However, in some parts of Africa, families can be made up of both Christians and Muslims, and people following these two faiths can sometimes live and cooperate well within extended family structures.

Revival Movements

It is impossible to understand Islam and the place of Muslims in the world today without grasping the context of the global Islamic revival. As a faith, Islam promises to its followers success in this life and the next. For centuries, this success included the conquest of other nations and their subjugation under Islamic rule. A great deal of the historical growth of Islam happened through armed conquest, and these victories were regarded by Muslims as proof of God's favor toward Islam and the superiority of its message. The Qur'an itself teaches that Muslims are the "best people" (Surah 3:110) and repeatedly asserts that Islam's destiny is to triumph over other religions (Surah 4:28; 9:33; 61:9).

It was, therefore, a theological shock to Islam when, from around 1700 on, the technological superiority of the Europeans enabled "Christian" armies to prevail over Muslim states, conquering and containing Islamic power at every turn. Muslim leaders did much soul-searching as the enormity of Islamic decline became apparent to them. In some cases, their response was to embrace secularization and Westernization, as Ataturk did after WWI, turning Turkey into a secular state.

A contrary response has been a global, grassroots revival of Islam. The big idea of all the Islamic revival movements of the past two centuries is that Muslims have been losing on the world stage because of their lack of adherence to the sharia, and if only Muslims would return to their origins and reimplement Islam properly, they will once again rise and become dominant. One of the manifestations of this utopian vision of a resurgent Islamic order has been the birth of many jihadi movements, such as Al-Qaeda and ISIS, who seek to restore the glory days of Islam through warfare. Another fruit is the re-Islamization of societies in the wake of decolonization. For example, Pakistan began as a secular state, but as the decades have passed, the nation has become more and more Islamicized, including the reintroduction of sharia courts. Another fruit was the creation of the Organisation for Islamic Cooperation as a kind of Islamic United Nations, formed in 1969 to strengthen the position of Islam and Muslims in the world.

Alongside such significant political developments has been a trend toward greater sharia compliance in many Muslim societies. The veiling of women, a practice that declined greatly during the first part of the twentieth century, has returned all over the Muslim world. In Iran and Afghanistan, where in the 1960s women quite commonly wore short skirts with bare legs and unveiled hair, today the burqa, niqab, or hijab has become the new norm. Whether the global Islamic revival will usher in a new golden age for the dominance of Islam remains to be seen. However, there is some evidence that many Muslims have been deeply disappointed by the failed fruit of the revivalist movement, such as the Iranian Islamic Revolution and the attempt of ISIS to revive a caliphate in Iraq and Syria.

Islam in the West

The final observation to make about Muslim lifestyles and cultures is that, in the past 50 or so years, there has been an unprecedented movement of Muslim peoples out of Islamic societies into Western nations. The global Muslim diaspora numbers in the many millions and has seen the establishment of influential Muslim minorities in European nations and also across North America. Muslim migrant communities have worked hard to establish themselves in their new homes, building mosques, Islamic centers, and training institutions. While many Muslims have become secularized and are barely distinguishable in their lifestyles from their non-Muslim neighbors, the global Islamic revival has also taken root in the West, and many Muslims who are the children and grandchildren of immigrants are more committed to Islam than their parents were when they migrated.

For all the complexity of thought and doctrinal systems Islam offers, Islam gives many devout Muslims a sense of place and identity in the universe and in time, making clear to them what God expects of them. "Eva," a Swedish convert to Islam, finds that her faith helps her stay focused on what is important in life. She is very conscious that she is only in the world for a short time, and she wants to make it count. Her faith also offers her a way of accepting what happens around her, good or bad. With Islam, she does not have to go deeper to ask "why" about everything. Her faith helps her stay calm and live in peace. She is troubled, however, by the many signs of discontentment and alienation she sees around her in the world. She wishes people would take better care of the world in which we all live. For her, religion itself cannot fix things, but it does offer instruction and guidance to help keep her on a good, straight path. She finds that this helps her live as a good person with humility, respecting others. It also pushes her to stand up for others who cannot fight for themselves.

Eva believes that at death, her body will be left behind, as her soul leaves. The life she has lived will have been a test. She hopes that, based on the way she has lived and practiced her faith, she will pass the test and be prepared for what comes next. Eva is aware of Christian teachings, but for her, Jesus was just a great human being and a prophet, one of many sent to guide humanity and call them to the right way of practicing faith.

Like all people on this earth, Muslims are very diverse. There is no "one size fits all," and it is unhelpful to stereotype Muslims. In the end, the only way to really get to know other people is to come alongside them and listen to them. Eva also wishes that people would take the time to look beyond what is highlighted to them about Islam in the media and that they could be curious and open-minded, to be unafraid to look for answers, and to think outside the box. She wishes they would ask themselves, "What have I got to lose if I knew more?"

Islam and Christianity

Islam's relationship to Christianity is complex. The teaching of the Qur'an, and of orthodox Islamic doctrine, is that Islam is the original religion, the faith of Adam, and also of biblical figures such as Abraham, Moses, and Jesus, whom it considers to have been prophets of Islam. By this understanding, Jesus's followers were Muslims, and if Solomon ever built a temple, it must have been a mosque. The Qur'an teaches that the message taught by Jesus was Islam, so although Christians have "gone astray" (as *al-Fatihah* puts it), their faith was originally Islam, and for Christians, it should only be a small step to "revert" to their original faith by embracing Islam. According to this view, Muhammad was sent by Allah to clear up any misunderstandings that had developed over the centuries, and to call Christians and Jews back to their original religion, which was Islam.

In making this case, the Qur'an declares that the God of the Bible and Allah of the Qur'an are one and the same, and Muslims should announce to the "People of the Book" (Jews and Christians) that they believe in the revelation the other two faiths had received: "Do not dispute with the People of the Book... but say 'We believe in the revelation which has come down to us, and in that which has come down to you. Our God and your God are one'" (Surah 29:46).

There is an important subtlety in this declaration of respect—namely, that the Qur'an is asserting that the *Islamic* revelations to Jesus and Moses, as prophets of Islam, are accepted by Muslims. This is not an assertion that Muslims accept the Bible as the Word of God, but that an original revealed book, once sent down to Jesus (and another to Moses) are what Muslims believe in. In many places, the Qur'an asserts that these original scriptures have become corrupted, and are no longer reliable, so the scriptures in the hands of Christians and Jews today cannot be relied upon.

What the Qur'an is saying is that Islam is the true Judaism and the true Christianity, so a really genuine, open-hearted Christian or Jew would embrace Islam, recognizing in it the fulfillment of their faith.

The affinity Islam claims with Christianity and Judaism is manifested in a tradition of tolerance of Christians and Jews under Islamic rule. Unlike pagans, who had to choose between Islam and death, conquered Christians and Jews, as "People of the Book," were permitted by the sharia to keep their religion, provided they submit to Islamic rule and pay a (quite heavy) annual tribute to Muslim conquerors. This accounts for the enduring presence of Christian churches under Islamic rule after conquest. Nevertheless, under the system of Islamic "tolerance," Christians suffered many disabilities. There have been repeated pogroms and violent acts against Christians, and everywhere under Islam, the church underwent a slow history of decline as a result. In some regions, such as Northwest Africa and Afghanistan, it died out altogether.

View of God

The Qur'an includes many references to biblical figures and stories. Islam clothes its message in biblical garments. However, many core theological features of the Qur'an are in conflict with the message of the Bible despite superficial similarities. For example, Allah is portrayed in the Qur'an with characteristics that are distinct from those of Yahweh in the Bible. Some of the features of God in the Bible that are lacking or very underdeveloped in the Qur'an include the following: holiness, a capacity to make Himself present with His people, faithfulness, and unconditional love (even for enemies). These attributes play a key role in God's capacity (in the Bible) for intimate, personal relationship with human beings. Allah of the Qur'an is much more impersonal: Nothing is like him, human beings are not made in his image, and it is considered an unforgivable sin to associate anything with him as being similar to Allah in any respect. What Allah in the Qur'an and the God of the Bible have in common is that they are both considered the creator of all things, powerful, omniscient, and compassionate.

Islam's emphasis on Allah's supreme mastery and submission to Allah as the fundamental human duty promotes a kind of slave mentality: The faithful Muslim sees himself or herself as the slave of Allah. By contrast, the biblical understanding of a relational, covenantal God points to a family relationship between humankind and God, so believers in Christ are not just servants or slaves but "children" of God and brothers and sisters of Jesus, the Son of God.

View of Humans

Another important contrast is that Islam sees human beings not as sinners in need of salvation but as weak and easily led astray. The fundamental human problem according to Islam is not sin but ignorance and weakness. The solution to this problem is not salvation but guidance. In a sense, for Islam, sin is not a problem at all, since Allah can forgive whatever and whomever he chooses.

These contrasting understandings of the human problem are reflected in differing visions of heaven. In Islam, the "Garden" is a place of what seems to be all-too-earthly pleasures, a kind of five-star oasis with abundant sexual partners and rivers flowing with wine—things that were actually forbidden to Muslims on earth. On the other hand, the heavenly vision in the book of Revelation is of dwelling in the abundant, undiminished presence of God.

From an Islamic perspective, the solution to injustice is justice, which is the punishment of the wicked and imposition of God's way by force of law. In contrast, the solution to injustice in the Bible is freedom. Consider, for example, the story of Moses and the Egyptians. In the Bible, Moses leads the Israelites out of bondage into freedom, but in the Qur'an, after the Egyptians are killed in floodwaters, Moses leads the people of Israel to take over the Egyptians' gardens, farms, and buildings. This reversal of injustice thus results not in freedom but in material success as the righteous followers of Moses take over the homes and farms of the unjust (Surah 44:25-28; 6:136-37).

Muslims Coming to Christ

For Christians witnessing to Muslims, there is something of a dilemma presented by the idea that the Qur'an affirms Jesus as a Muslim prophet, and the assertion that "we worship the same God." This is, in a sense, a bridge between the two faiths. Yet it is a thoroughly Islamic bridge, not a Christian one, being grounded in Islamic doctrines that reject Christ as the Son of God and insist that He was only a human messenger, like Muhammad. Yes, Muslims venerate Jesus, but only as a human being. Some Christians seek to find in this bridge common ground from which to present the gospel. However, it can also be seen as a tactic to replace Christian truth rather than a bridge of truly shared understandings. Islam affirms Jesus and Christianity only to repurpose Jesus as an Islamic prophet, and it declares the Christian faith to have originally been Islam. The Qur'an respects Jesus as a miracle worker but derides belief in Him as the Son of God or Lord. In most readings of the text, the Qur'an also denies the death of Jesus on the cross (Surah 4:157).

For the human problem of sin, the solution the Bible offers is forgiveness, leading to salvation, which is a restored relationship with God. This is a relational solution to the problem of broken relationship. Because Islam sees the human condition very differently from the Bible, this schema—of sin being resolved through forgiveness, resulting in salvation—makes little sense when viewed from the perspective of Islamic fundamentals. Furthermore, the Qur'an explicitly rejects key biblical claims about Christ, including His divine sonship, and it contains within itself multiple arguments against core Christian beliefs. Even the simplest Muslim will be aware of Islamic objections to the claims of the gospel, and many will be able to present these objections quite forcefully to a Christian who tries to share the gospel with them. For this reason, Christians who desire to reach out to Muslims can benefit greatly from receiving some training first.

In the past, Christians took the view that leading Muslims to faith in Christ was very difficult, and many missionaries labored long and hard among Muslims to glean only little fruit. The reasons for the lack of response are complex. One reason has been Islam's inherent opposition to Jesus as the Son of God and Savior. Another is Islam's view that people are not sinful but ignorant and weak. Another factor is Islam's apostasy law, which prescribes death to people who leave Islam. Under sharia conditions, it is not a crime for a Muslim to kill someone else who has rejected Islam, and a decision to follow Christ can result not only in severe rejection from family and friends but in putting a convert's life at risk. Another reason is Islam's own self-confident claim to be the superior, original, and final faith, in contrast to Judaism and Christianity, which are considered to be flawed corruptions. A traditional reading of *Al-Fatihah*, mentioned above, which is a prayer for guidance, is that those who incur Allah's wrath are the Jews, and those who have gone astray are Christians. This is an interpretation that, according to a hadith, Muhammad himself favored. One could say that, in reciting the daily prayers, every Muslim asks several times a day not to become a Christian or a Jew; resistance to Christianity (and Judaism) is, through daily ritual, hardwired into Islam.

Despite these obstacles, more Muslims are turning to Christ now than at any time before in history.[8] Why is this so? One reason is the failure of the global Islamic revival to deliver improved conditions for Muslims. In Iran today, there is widespread disillusionment with Islam, especially among younger people. The Iranian Islamic Revolution in 1979 promised a better life for Muslims, but it delivered repression, corruption, and pain. Hundreds of thousands of Iranians have turned to Christ, and often they reject Islam before finding Jesus. Likewise, many Arab Muslims, observing the mayhem and destruction caused by ISIS in Iraq and Syria, have responded with, "If that is the real Islam, then I do not want to be a Muslim." Among the Muslim refugees who have fled Iraq and Syria, many are embracing Christ. Every recent attempt at Islamic revivalism has resulted in suffering and disillusionment, including the Muslim Brotherhood gaining power in Egypt in 2012 and the rise of the Taliban in Afghanistan. The motto of the Muslim Brotherhood was that "Islam is the Solution"—to everything—but when the Brotherhood assumed power and things began to get worse for ordinary Egyptians, some concluded that Islam was actually the problem, promising utopia but delivering dystopia.

Another reason for Muslims to turn to Jesus is that the old system of control and dissemination of knowledge in Islam is breaking down. Although Muhammad in popular Islamic piety is the perfect example for humankind and the best person to have ever lived, some of what Muslims have found in the hadith and the early biographies of Muhammad have caused them to doubt Muhammad altogether. Today Muslims can explore questions about Islam for themselves. For example, they can read the hadiths of Muhammad translated into their own native language on the internet. This great unveiling of primary Islamic sources is causing some Muslims to reject Islam because the primary sources—which often do not present Muhammad in a flattering light—are reaching ordinary Muslims in unfiltered form.

Research has been undertaken to find out why Muslims turn to Christ. One reason is disillusionment with Islam, not only in terms of contents of the Qur'an and the hadiths, but also because of disappointment with the fruit of Islamic revivalism. These are "push factors." There are also "pull factors." One is the love, openness, and kindness Muslims can experience among Christians. One ex-Muslim reported to me that he chose to become a Christian because a Christian man he knew was gracious and helpful in answering his questions. His Christian friend gave good, thoughtful answers to every question he asked. He found through this process that his humanity was affirmed because he was being respected as an inquiring human being. In Islam, his experience had been just the opposite: To ask questions would bring an angry rebuke from Muslim teachers.

Another pull factor is that today the Bible is more available to Muslims than ever before, and many Muslims are turning to Christ through encountering the Gospels. They find in Jesus someone who is compellingly attractive. One Muslim man chose to follow Christ after reading Matthew 5:27-28: "You have heard that it was said, 'You shall not commit adultery.' But I say to you that everyone who looks at a woman with lustful intent has already committed adultery with her in his heart." This call of Jesus for men to live alongside women with a pure heart was very different from what he had experienced in the Islamic environment where he grew up. This was so radically different from everything he had ever heard before, and so powerfully liberating, that he gave his life to Jesus on the spot.

Another pull factor reported by many Muslims who have turned to Christ is a miraculous encounter with Jesus: a vision or dream, an answered prayer, or a dramatic deliverance from evil. The Holy Spirit has been declaring "it is time" over the nations of Islam, and is reaching out to millions, even including many who have never before heard the gospel. This makes it a very exciting time to be engaging Muslim people with the message of Jesus Christ.

Christians can be inhibited by fear and lack of knowledge from reaching out to their Muslim neighbors. This is a great pity and a loss for both the Muslim and the Christian. This is a great time to be sharing Jesus with Muslim people. A good starting place can be Muslims' openness to Jesus, if only as a prophet of Islam. This can give an opportunity to read the Gospels together with your Muslim friend and to pray with them and share with them your personal relationship with Christ. There are few things sweeter than being able to introduce your Best Friend to your Muslim friend.

Mark Durie (PhD, Australian National University) is a pastor and academic in Melbourne, Australia, who writes on a wide range of topics, including the origin and history of Islam, faith and culture, and freedom of religion. Mark is a Shillman-Ginsburg Writing Fellow at the Middle East Forum and an Adjunct Research Fellow of the Arthur Jeffery Centre for the Study of Islam. His books, including *The Third Choice: Islam, Dhimmitude and Freedom*, have been translated into over a dozen languages.

7

Buddhism

Winfried Corduan and Daniel McCoy

If university religious studies degrees are any indicator, Buddhism attracts fascination in the West. Likewise, if pop culture catchwords such as *mindfulness* and *Zen* are any indicator, Buddhism has made inroads into Western culture, attempting to replicate its success in the Eastern world since the religion's inception. Who was the Buddha, and what was his story? Do all Buddhists believe basically the same things? How are the ways of Jesus and the Buddha similar, and how are they different?

History and Beliefs

Siddhartha Gautama was born in privilege. We are told that the future Buddha had been a god in a Buddhist heaven. Right before he was born on earth in the sixth century BC, he was able to pinpoint the perfect time to be born (when the life span was around 100), the perfect (sub)continent to be born on (in India where Buddhas are born), the perfect family to be born into (the warrior caste), and the perfect parents to be born to ("King Suddhodana shall be my father…The mother of a Buddha…has fulfilled the perfections…and has kept the five precepts unbroken from the day of her birth. Now this queen Maha-Maya is such a one; and she shall be my mother.").[1]

Thus Queen Maha-Maya dreamed that after circling her three times, a "superb white elephant" entered her womb. When she told the king about her dream, he summoned 64 priests and told them what had occurred. They prophesied that the queen would have a son who would choose between two possible paths: If he continued on the same path as his father, he would become a "universal monarch," but, if he renounced such a life, he would become a Buddha.[2]

When Gautama was conceived, we are told that "the ten thousand worlds suddenly quaked," and all manner of wonders broke out. The blind, deaf, hunchbacked, and lame were cured. People became kind, the weather became lovely, and diseases became benign. Even the fires in the hells were blown out. When it came time for the birth, the future Buddha emerged spotlessly clean. The infant looked around, surveyed the landscape in all ten directions, and upon seeing no equal, exclaimed, "This is the best direction." He walked seven steps and shouted, "The chief am I in all the world."[3] The point conveyed in these tales is not to be missed: Gautama was privileged in every way, even prior to his conception, and he was clearly no ordinary child.

Now, the king naturally desired his son to continue the lineage and so fulfill the prophecy's alternative of glorious kingship. The king reasoned, "We must not have Gotama declining to rule. We must not have him going forth from the house into the homeless state. We must not let what the Brahman soothsayers spoke of come true."[4] So the king kept his son close to the palace and indulged him with all imaginable pleasures, all with the hope that Gautama would continue enjoying himself and not stop long enough to consider any futility in his current path. This explains why, when finally allowing his son to take a chariot ride through the city, the king commanded the area cleared of any sights that would propel his son into monkish pursuits. Yet it was at this time that the gods intervened, making sure that the chariot rode by an old person, a sick person, and a dead person. The pampered prince had to ask his charioteer basic questions about the sights he saw: What is old age? What is sickness? What is death?

7A. A statue of the Buddha in Kamakura, Japan. Photo by Dirk Beyer, 2005 (http://creativecommons.org/licenses/by-sa/3.0/).

The images of sickness, old age, and death stuck in his mind: "Am I too subject to old age...to fall ill...to death?" And as it would turn out, the worst possible image the king could have imagined would lodge itself most stubbornly in Gautama's thinking: "And he saw, as he was driving to the park, a shaven-headed man, a recluse, wearing the yellow robe."[5] And where thoughts of sickness, old age, and death could have filled him with despair, Gautama saw *hope* in the tranquility of the monk. After all, it was only those who were intoxicated with health, wealth, and youthfulness who would be horrified by such inevitable experiences as sickness, old age, and death. According to his own account long after he had renounced the householder path, Gautama would reflect, "Monks, I lived in refinement, utmost refinement, total refinement...I had three palaces." Yet when he came to realize that he, too, was subject to old age, sickness, and death, all the intoxications of youth, health, and life "entirely dropped away."[6] He realized that, since there was nothing but futility in all the sensuous pleasures that had surrounded him, there was no reason to panic at the inevitability of losing them.

He famously left his wife and son the night his son was born, but not before naming him Rahula, meaning "fetter."[7] From that moment on, Gautama had renounced the "householder life." Gautama went on to study with skilled monks, but he soon surpassed their meditative abilities. He went on to his own methods of severe asceticism, eventually growing so emaciated that he said, "The skin of my belly became so stuck to my spine that when I thought of touching my belly, I grabbed hold of my spine as well."[8] As he became aware that such an approach was getting him nowhere, he reasoned that perhaps the path to enlightenment lay *between* the extremes of asceticism and sensuality. It was no use testing this new approach when he was famished, so, to the disgust of fellow renunciates, he ate some food. Then he sat under a fig tree, resolving to find enlightenment or die trying. His meditations under the famous "Bodhi" tree yielded progress, such that Gautama would later reflect,

> There are two extremes that are not to be indulged in by one who has gone forth. Which two? That which is devoted to sensual pleasure...and that which is devoted to self-affliction. Avoiding both of these extremes, the middle way realized by the Tathagata... leads to calm, to direct knowledge, to self-awakening, to Unbinding.[9]

7B. King Ashoka constructed the Mahabodhi Temple at the site where the Buddha attained enlightenment. Photo by Cacahuate, 2006 (https://creativecommons.org/licenses/by-sa/2.5).

Under the Bodhi tree, Gautama accomplished such feats as entering the four *jhanas* (meditations), manifesting supranormal powers, and remembering his past lives.[10] The meditative struggle all culminated in his enlightenment. Thus Gautama became the Buddha, or "the enlightened one."[11]

Once enlightened, Gautama sat in the shade of the Bodhi tree for seven days, dwelling on how "this" leads to "that."[12] He emerged having discovered the 12-step chain of how suffering can be traced back to ignorance. Since all life is suffering, the 12 causes in the chain essentially explain how all life arises in the first place. Buddhists call the process "dependent co-arising" because all the conditions depend on each other, arising from each other, with no official beginning point. In short, it all exists because it all exists.[13] Thus any need for a Creator God is replaced by causal interdependence.

After becoming the Buddha, Gautama was persuaded by the god Brahma to teach what he had discovered to the world. In Gautama's first sermon, he unveiled the Four Noble Truths, the first three of which summarized Gautama's view that (1) all life is suffering, (2) suffering is caused by craving, and therefore (3) one is able to overcome suffering by eliminating craving.[14]

In his fourth truth, Gautama showed his audience the way to eliminate craving, and he called it the "Noble Eightfold Path": "And what is the middle way realized by the Tathagata that—producing vision, producing knowledge—leads to calm, to direct knowledge, to self-awakening, to Unbinding? Precisely this Noble Eightfold Path."[15] Depicted by an eight-spoked wheel, the path consists of eight attitudes, skills, and behaviors to cultivate in order to achieve nirvana: right view, right intention, right speech, right action, right livelihood, right effort, right meditation, and right concentration. Gautama's language of "middle way" calls to mind his discovery that neither austerity nor sensuality was conducive to enlightenment. With this sermon, Gautama began attracting a following called the *sangha*, or community of monks (*bhikkhus*). Later, he allowed an order of nuns (*bhikkhunis*) as well. Many of these monks and nuns would go on to achieve enlightenment themselves under Gautama's teaching, and these would be called *arhats*.

Although Gautama ministered to countless people, one story will serve as a snapshot of his message and method. Kisa Gotami was a poor woman whose in-laws treated her as beneath them until she bore a son. One tragic day, however, her young son was outside playing when he suddenly died. Kisa's grief drove her mad. Though the child was clearly dead, she picked up the corpse and went door to door asking for medicine to treat him. "What good is medicine?" they would explain, but she did not understand.[16]

Taking pity on her, someone finally told her about the Buddha residing nearby, encouraging her to ask the Buddha for medicine. So she hurried to find the Buddha, and here is what he told her: "Go, having entered the city, into whatever house has never before experienced any death, and take from them a mustard seed." With renewed hope, she again went house to house asking for the special seed. Yet her optimism diminished with each visit as each person informed her the house had been visited by death multiple times. Death was everywhere! Suddenly, she discovered the Buddha's "medicine": the acceptance that death is just what happens. She exclaimed, "This indeed is what is true—impermanence." Still carrying the corpse, she went that very moment to the graveyard, left the corpse there, and returned to the Buddha. He explained what she had already discovered:

> A person with a mind that clings,
> Deranged, to sons or possessions,
> Is swept away by death that comes
> Like a mighty flood to sleeping town.[17]

In other words, the problem was not the death of a son, but the clinging to that son that had made grief inevitable. That day, Kisa joined the community of nuns, and it would not be long before she attained arhathood.[18]

Gautama's reputation as an "incomparable teacher" of enlightenment continued to spread[19] until he had spoken to "many hundreds" of assemblies.[20] He was able to convert kings[21] and outcasts alike.[22] He continued his itinerant ministry of teaching into old age. The day came when Ananda, one of Gautama's foremost disciples, noticed and commented to Gautama that "the Blessed One's complexion is no longer so clear and bright; his limbs are flabby and wrinkled; his back, bent forward."[23] Gautama ministered until his eightieth year, when he finally told Ananda, "Now I am frail, Ananda, old, aged, far gone in years. This is my eightieth year, and my life is spent. Even as an old cart, Ananda, is held together with much difficulty, so the body of the Tathagata is kept going only with supports."[24]

After predicting his imminent entrance into *nirvana*, Gautama ate a meal that gave him dysentery and sharp pains. Yet we are told he "endured them mindfully, clearly comprehending and unperturbed."[25] He had Ananda prepare a couch for him between two trees where he lay down. Tree blossoms and flowers from the sky rained down upon him while voices sang from the heavens. All the deities gathered to watch. When Ananda began to weep, Gautama corrected him, "Enough, Ananda! Do not grieve, do not lament! For have I not taught from the very beginning that with all that is dear and beloved there must be change, separation, and severance?"[26] Gautama ended a brief final lesson with the famous last words, "Strive with earnestness!" Then, after cycling through the appropriate meditations, he entered nirvana. We are told there were earthquakes below and thunders above and weeping deities declaring the event's significance. Gautama's body was cremated, and the bones were dispersed among various groups who had played a role in his life. Each promised to construct a *stupa* (monument) over their particular relic.[27]

So what became of Gautama? What exactly is *nirvana*? This is what Gautama said about it:

> There is, monks, a domain where there is no earth, no water, no fire, no wind, no sphere of infinite space, no sphere of nothingness, no sphere of infinite consciousness, no sphere of neither awareness nor non-awareness; there is not this world, there is not another world, there is no sun or moon. I do not call this coming or going, nor standing nor dying, nor being reborn; it is without support, without occurrence, without object. Just this is the end of suffering.[28]

"Nirvana" literally means an "extinguishing," a "blowing out," a picture made all the more obscure by all the *nos*, *nots*, *nons*, and *nors* in the above description.

Why would nirvana be an attractive destination? Well, consider what Gautama believed about the universe: All life is suffering. This doesn't mean that Gautama thought there was no pleasure to be had. Rather, it's that Gautama understood that even the greatest pleasures come to an end. All our attempts to grasp ultimate satisfaction end in futility. Even the noblest joys, such as a husband's devotedness to a wife, ends with one of them dying and the other grieving. All life, taught Gautama, is emptiness, or *sunyata*.

To illustrate, one of the icons of Buddhism is the *bhavacakra*, the "wheel of existence." In the center of the wheel are three animals: a pig, a bird, and a snake. The pig chomps on the bird's tail feathers, the bird's beak grasps the snake's tail, and the snake bites the pig's hindquarters. These animals in the inner circle symbolize the "three poisons" at the root of all our suffering. The pig symbolizes the poison of ignorance. The bird symbolizes the poison of greed. The snake symbolizes the poison of hatred. According to Buddhism, ignorance, greed, and hatred poison all life and keep us drunkenly staggering around the nauseating merry-go-round of the cycle of rebirths (a cycle Buddhism calls *samsara*). Further out from the center are pictures of Buddhist heavens and hells. Even further out

7C. The Bhavacakra, or the "wheel of existence." Public domain.

are step-by-step portrayals of the depressing cycle of birth-death-rebirth. And does the "wheel of existence" portray all the various seasons of Buddhist reality as being cradled in the hands of a loving God? Hardly. The entire wheel is pictured as held in the jaws of a ferocious demon. Nirvana is seen as a blessed escape.

It's not just what humans experience out in the world that makes the release of nirvana desirable. People are also drawn to nirvana by what they discover in themselves. Take Gautama's doctrine of *anatman*. To understand the concept of *anatman*, first consider the Hindu teaching, "*Atman* is *Brahman*."[29] *Atman* means a person's "true self." *Brahman* is the impersonal, pantheistic God of Hinduism. To say that "*Atman* is *Brahman*" is to say that my true self is identical with the divine reality. Now back to Buddhism. Whereas *atman* means a person's "true self," *anatman* literally means "not-self." According to Buddhism, although humans often see themselves as selves to be cherished and preserved, we are in reality not-selves. Think of a chariot. Is there such a thing as an actual chariot? Yes, there are the wheels, the axle, and the reins that comprise a chariot. But take away all those parts, and do you still have an enduring chariot that remains? No. According to the Buddha, humans, like a chariot, are merely a collection of parts. So what exactly is it that nirvana extinguishes? Something that never existed as an enduring entity in the first place. There is no point in getting attached to something that is merely an impermanent collection of parts.

In 400 BC, shortly after Gautama entered nirvana, a group of his followers called together the "First Council" in order to systematize the Buddha's teachings. The result was an enormous threefold collection of writings called the *Tripitaka* ("the three baskets"), also known as the Pali Canon. The first "Pitaka" is the *Vinaya Pitaka*, a handbook of rules for monks and nuns. The second is

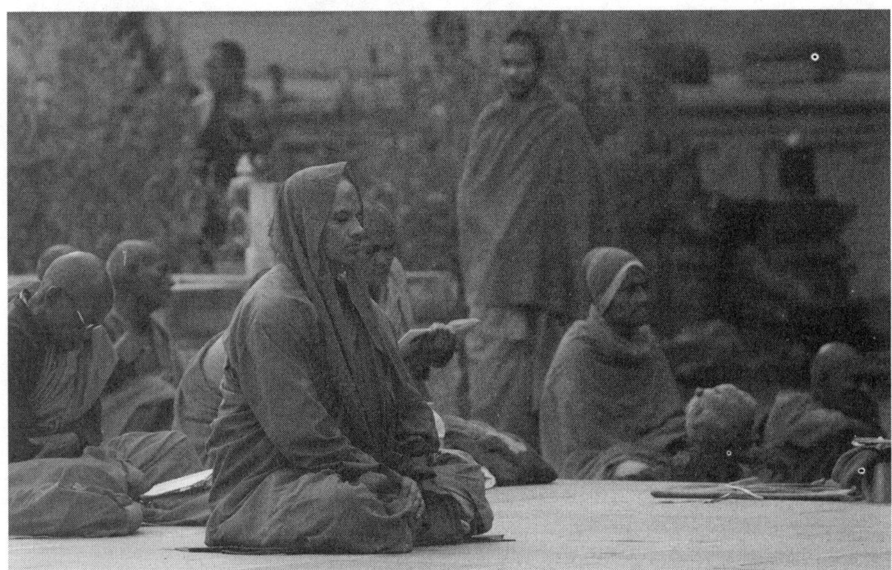

7D. Buddhist monks meditate in Bihar, India. Photo by Jakub Michankow, 2009 (https://creativecommons.org/licenses/by/2.0).

the *Sutta Pitaka*, which records the Buddha's many discourses (*sutras* or *suttas*). The third is the *Abhidhamma Pitaka*, a collection of Buddhist doctrines and philosophy.

A century later, the "Second Council" was called. There were Buddhists who thought that Buddhism ought to be less focused on monastic rules and more open to the laity. A couple hundred years later, this dissenting group would eventually split off and form their own more inclusive branch of Buddhism. One term to emerge out of this schism was *Hinayana* (little vehicle) to describe the original branch. The branch devoted to opening nirvana to the masses designated themselves with the term *Mahayana* (great vehicle).

Hinayana Buddhists follow the Buddha's teachings by becoming monks and nuns so they can devote themselves to this path completely and eventually achieve nirvana. The Hinayana branch that survives to this day is called "Theravada" Buddhism. Following Gautama's virtuous example, Theravada monks are expected to obey a list of ethical dos and don'ts. The "Ten Precepts," for example, include prohibitions on telling lies, harming living beings, drinking alcohol, attending amusements, sleeping on high and wide beds, or touching gold or silver. The Asian countries most associated with Theravada Buddhism are Sri Lanka, Cambodia, Laos, Myanmar, and Thailand. Because these countries are in southern Asia, Theravada Buddhism is sometimes called "Southern Buddhism."

As the "great vehicle," Mahayana Buddhism raises the goal higher than merely following the Buddha's teachings and thus attaining nirvana for oneself. For Mahayanists, the highest ethic to aspire to is to follow the Buddha's example by becoming actual Buddhas, starting out as *bodhisattvas* (Buddhas-in-the-making). As Buddhas, they can then devote themselves to helping others achieve nirvana. In fact, a bodhisattva vows not to enter nirvana himself until he has done whatever it takes to bring all other sentient beings into nirvana first (a vow called "Great Compassion").[30] The Asian countries/regions most associated with Mahayana Buddhism are China, Korea, Japan, Vietnam, Nepal, Mongolia, and Tibet. Because these areas lie north of the traditional Theravada countries, Mahayana Buddhism is sometimes called "Northern Buddhism."

Lifestyle and Culture

Wherever Buddhism has found a home, it has adapted itself to the local way of life. This observation is true for the more traditionally oriented Theravada branch, where one can notice significant outward differences between Buddhism as it is practiced in, say, Sri Lanka, in contrast to Thailand, even though the central beliefs of both are still quite similar. In the much larger world of Mahayana, there are schools that differ so much from each other that it becomes difficult at first glance to recognize them as belonging to the same religion.[31]

For this reason, if you are speaking or writing about Buddhism, let alone talking *to* a Buddhist, be as careful as you can not to make hasty generalizations. What complicates matters is that the members of different schools usually refer to their beliefs and practice simply as "Buddhism," not doing you the favor of specifying how your textbook would classify them. On the next page is a table with some quick information on the biggest schools of Mahayana Buddhism. Since we need to abbreviate some of the headings, let us specify that by "name" we mean the most common name used in the Western world, which may not be the most accurate

MAHAYANA BRANCHES		
Name	**Origin**	**Distinctives**
Tendai	Zhiyi (AD 538–597)	Gives priority to the Lotus Sutra over the Pali canon. All is emptiness (*sunyata*). Every sentient being can become a Buddha. Bodhisattvas are benevolent beings who delay their entry into nirvana in order to give aid to other people.
Zen, Chan	Bodhidharma (fifth or sixth century AD)	Enlightenment is achieved in an intuitive awakening of the mind. It can come gradually or suddenly, depending on the subdivisions.
Pure Land	Honen, Shinran (thirteenth century AD)	The Buddha Amitabha (Amida) has created a paradise to which he admits by his grace any person who calls on him. Meditation is replaced by visualization techniques.
Nichiren Shoshu	Nichiren (thirteenth century AD)	Buddhahood can be attained by regularly chanting the invocation of the Lotus Sutra, called the *Daimoku*, facing the *Gohonzen*, a piece of rice paper on which Nichiren wrote it.
Tibetan Buddhism	Around the eighth century AD	A combination of devotion to numerous Buddhas and bodhisattvas, along with other deities who may have been worshiped in pre-Buddhist Tibet. Elaborate rituals and emphasis on magic.
Humanistic Buddhism	Twentieth century	True Buddhism expresses itself in an overarching concern for the welfare of society and marginalized people. Traditional acts of worship are carried out in the context of a humanistic philosophy. Emphasis on world missions.

one. "Distinctives" refers to the beliefs and practices that mark the school and does not necessarily indicate that the adherents practice nothing else. For example, most schools of Buddhism encourage some form of meditation, and it need not be mentioned except where it is fundamentally different from the apparent norm.

So what is it like to live as a Buddhist? Not only in Buddhism but in virtually all religions, most people live what we might call "a normal routine life." We should not lose sight of that fact lest we start to imagine differences among human beings where there aren't any. Buddhists usually wake up in the morning, go to work, come home in the evening, go to bed at night, and eat their meals at the normal times for their culture. For Buddhist monks and nuns, the picture is different, of course, but laypeople, like most of us, are primarily concerned with the usual human goals of adequate food and shelter, good health, procreation, and maintaining harmonious relationships with other people.

Now, as soon as you read this list, you realize that the religion, Buddhism in this case, provides the glasses through which one sees each of these items, and devout Buddhists will take great care to apply their beliefs to these aspects of daily life.

Theravada Lifestyle

Let us take a look at the situation in Theravada (Southern) Buddhism in Sri Lanka and

Southeast Asia. We see a wide gulf between the religion of the monks (bhikkhus) and the laity. Full-time monks have separated themselves from the rest of the society and have committed themselves to the quest for enlightenment. They spend a great amount of time in meditation and in giving laypeople the opportunity to earn merit by serving them. For example, someone may build up a lot of merit by providing the monks with food, material for robes, or other supplies needed by members of the order. A layperson can also achieve a great amount of merit by providing offerings of flowers, scented oil, or money in a temple. A popular method is to apply patches of gold leaf to a smaller statue of the Buddha. Monks serve other people by teaching and preaching, not by clothing and feeding them.

Merit can only increase one's chances at a better life next time around and so has only an indirect bearing on the attainment of nirvana. The direct pursuit of nirvana is limited to the bhikkhus. In the Theravada branch, once a bhikkhu has attained enlightenment, his departure into nirvana and the end of all suffering are secured, but he does not yet become a Buddha. He is only an arhat, a holy man—the most likely way of becoming a Buddha.

Almost paradoxically, another good way for a young man to receive merit is by spending a year or so as a temporary monk in a monastery. He doesn't find enlightenment thereby but adds more merit to his spiritual trove. In Thailand, someone in that position traditionally will transfer that merit to his mother, who, as a woman, does not have the opportunity to gain it herself.

So a Theravada Buddhist layperson is allowed to carry out certain monk-like activities that will add to his merit. He has an overarching duty to support the monks. Monks are center stage, and they are the ones who are headed toward enlightenment. He can cheer for them, but he cannot attain for himself the results that he promotes for them. The implication is clear, but it may strike someone from a Christian background as backward. Obviously, there are bhikkhus who care for other people and participate in humanitarian events. However, if we may put it this way, doing so is not a part of their "job description." A bhikkhu's primary concern is supposed to be his liberation from the cycle of reincarnations, and it is the duty of other people to provide him with whatever aid is possible. Being helped by a monk does nothing for either person; helping a monk provides the helper with merit and hopefully aids the monk in his quest toward enlightenment.

Now then, we must ask an obvious question. Accumulating merit toward an event that may perhaps still be hundreds of lives in the future may be a good thing, but what about spiritual help in the present? What do you do when your crops fail, a child is ill, or your business is going bankrupt? To whom do you turn? If you need spiritual help, who will provide it?

It is at this point that the difference between the bhikkhu's Buddhism and that of the layperson comes to the fore again. Thai Buddhism provides a particularly striking and colorful example, though the same phenomenon is found in every Theravada country as well as in Mahayana settings. Common people recognize the Buddha as a great teacher, venerate him as though he were a god, worship whatever pre-Buddhist gods or goddesses may be available, and carry out activities to fend away evil spirits.

If you walk along the streets of Bangkok, you will find in front of many residences a little shrine on a pole, which contains representations of animals or people, sometimes from the Buddhist tradition, sometimes of departed relatives. These devices are called "spirit houses" in English, and they are intended to ward off evil as well as secure good from the supply of blessings that the Buddha left at the time of his death. One passes several of these on the way to Brahmanat Corner, a prominent street-side location for Buddhist worship. However, the central item of worship is not a statue of the Buddha, but a representation of the god Brahma, the creator according to Hindu scriptures. In the same location, you can find some Buddhist symbols along with various devices intended to deal with both destructive and helpful spirits. People come by and place little offerings such as flowers before the Brahma statue. For a certain amount of money, six women in Thai costumes, accompanied by a three-person instrumental ensemble, will perform a short traditional dance and tune, while the client kneels in a prayerful position next to them.

So here we have an example of a "folk religion" (see section "Is Reading Textbooks Enough to Learn All that Is Necessary to Understand a Religion?" in chapter 2) in which the actual principles of the religion are covered over by prayers and rituals associated with the gods of early Hindu scriptures and a general preoccupation with spirits.

Needless to say, the Buddha does fit into this synthesis. People come to his temples in order to secure his blessings. Even though according to the popular belief, the Buddha departed from this universe in order to vanish into nirvana, he left a storehouse of blessings, and people who worship him may receive benefits from him. Further, Buddhist scriptures function as moral exhortations on living so as to improve one's karma. Still, even where Thai Buddhist temples are focused on the Buddha, they frequently contain statues of Brahma as well as of the earth goddess.

We can say, then, that in Theravada Buddhism, to live as a layperson may not really be to live according to the ideas that we associate with the religion but to work your way through an array of spiritual beings and rituals that will hopefully make the journey through life easier and maybe lead eventually to the possibility of practicing true

7E. Sri Lankan monks walk through town with umbrella and alms bowl. Photo by AntanO, 2014 (https://creativecommons.org/licenses/by-sa/3.0).

Buddhism in a life far into the future. This description is clearly a generalization, though it is a true one. Just as we as non-Buddhists can study and write about the beliefs and practices of a Theravada monk, so can a Buddhist layperson. However, neither one of us can anticipate nirvana after passing from this life, albeit for different reasons.

Mahayana Lifestyle

As we move on to discuss Mahayana Buddhism, we cannot let go of two insights we have brought up: (1) Most people are more likely to make use of their religion in order to lead a rewarding life than to devote themselves to the religion itself for its own sake. (2) Given the variety of what constitutes Buddhism in the various Mahayana circles, the lives of the adherents may also look very different from each other.

One of the main differences between Theravada and Mahayana Buddhism is the Mahayana belief that all human beings—yes, eventually even all sentient forms of life—can and will attain Buddhahood. We see here, of course, a big distinction from Theravada, where enlightenment can only be attained by bhikkhus, and even then, they can only become arhats rather than full-blown Buddhas. Consequently, in some Mahayana schools, the distinction between monks or priests and laypeople may not be emphasized as much as in Theravada, but in others, it persists just as strongly, though in slightly different forms.

An obvious Mahayana case of there being a significant difference between monks and laypeople is found in Tibetan Buddhism. Tibetan Buddhism is far more complex than, say, Theravada. It has incorporated many elements that may have been derived from Hindu influence, a polytheistic pre-Buddhist religion in the region, and even from its surprising mirror-reversed religion called Bön. Ancient gods and goddesses have turned into Buddhas and bodhisattvas, and Buddhas and bodhisattvas have taken on spouses with or without their former Buddhist titles. Not only the laity, who clearly occupy a lower position, but also the religious orders work on achieving merit by using roughly the same techniques. For example, most people know about the "prayer wheels" of Tibetan Buddhism that allegedly supply continuous chanting of the Tibetan mantra "*um mani padme hum*," which one finds in monasteries and in the hands of laypersons. The fundamental difference is that the lamas (Tibetan monks) will have integrated such practices in their Buddhist framework, while for laypeople, the point of it all is, once again, to ward off evil spirits and to conjure up good ones. A Tibetan person will live all day with the symbolism and requirements necessary to survive in a world of hostile spirits. In Tibetan Buddhism, there is a greater intensity of this concern than in Theravada, with ever-present reminders in the forms of prayer wheels, prayer flags, sacred stones, obligations for daily meditative walks, and so forth.

How does one live as a Zen Buddhist? The question alone could be considered one of those celebrated enigmas, called *kōans*, which are popular in some of the subschools of Zen. Possibly acceptable answers to this particular question might be "One lives as a Zen Buddhist," or, perhaps even better, "One lives." Zen is said at times to provide people with a "third eye" to help them get a fresh comprehension of reality, but the "fresh" vision is actually the same reality we have looked at before, only perceiving it directly as it is rather than analyzing it theoretically with scientific, philosophical, or religious categories. Now, there is a strong religious tradition of Zen that, when taken to its logical extreme, teaches that the religious traditions themselves must nonetheless be surpassed for the sake of enlightenment. However, the religious dimension persists, and most people who are affiliated with Zen in some way (other than those Westerners for whom Zen seems to have become almost a hobby) also practice some other form of Buddhism. For example, in Taiwan, a number of large temples have sprung up recently that lay claim to both a Zen (Chan) and a Pure Land heritage.

For the layperson, Zen provides wisdom to live by even as he or she also venerates many bodhisattvas. As a matter of fact, Zen takes very seriously the idea that any person can become a Buddha and applies the title "bodhisattva" not only to the large figures of mythology but also to anyone who is seeking truth and enlightenment. If you practice Zen, chances are that you will attend regular meditation sessions, perhaps once a week, and that you will work on going through life with equanimity. Yet from a practical standpoint, there could be very little outwardly visible difference between you and your neighbors who hold other religions or no religion at all.

The schools based on the teachings of Nichiren began their existence with a strict division between priesthood and laity. Still, the lay membership has been at the heart of the religion because each person must chant the *Daimoku* (*namu myo horengekyo*), preferably two or more hours a day, and attend regular group meetings each week. Nichiren Buddhism has created a formal scheme, according to which a person can, through regular and rigorous chanting, pass through ten hierarchical stages, beginning with "hell" and "anger" at the bottom and ending with "Buddha" at the top. So rather than giving a promise of what might happen many lives into the future, Nichiren makes the potential for Buddhahood a real possibility in one's present existence. The more you chant, the more you will advance. Furthermore, chanting the *Daimoku* while facing the *Gohonzen* (a piece of paper on which Nichiren wrote the Lotus Sutra) may have this-worldly benefits as well. Chanting changes the vibrations of the world around us. Therefore, it may change your material circumstances, including financial and medical ones. So not only are laypersons eligible for full Buddhahood, but once they have been initiated and have found an officially approved place to chant, they can pretty much proceed without monks or priests, as exemplified in the worldwide lay organization Soka Gakkai. Still, their lives are heavily beset with religious duties.

Pure Land Buddhism is another very popular school of Buddhism, geared toward laypeople. If you are a member of this school, your devotion will be directed primarily to another Buddha than the historical Gautama of the sixth century BC. His name is Amitabha (Japanese Amida), the "Buddha of Light." According to the mythology, he is a Buddha who is located in heaven as the lord of the Western quadrant of the universe. There he has built a paradise, called a Pure Land, to which he welcomes all people. Regardless of how sinful someone may be, by acknowledging Amida, they will be reborn in this land, which is beautiful and hospitable.

If you are a Pure Land Buddhist, you will celebrate Amida's mercy and grace. Chances are that you will also give special veneration to the bodhisattva associated with him. His original name was Avalokitesvara, but under Chinese influence, he became known as Guanyin, the Goddess of Mercy, and she has been recognized as the goddess Kannon in Japan. You will probably attend weekly worship services, which are nowadays modeled to a great extent after Protestant church services. You will express your gratitude to Amida by frequently repeating a mantra dedicated to him: *Namu Amida Butsu* (I worship the Buddha Amida). This phrase is referred to as the *Nembutsu*, and to highlight one form of Pure Land belief, some writers have claimed that repeating the *Nembutsu* once, simply out of gratitude to Amida, will allow you entry into his paradise after you have died.[32]

Buddhism and Christianity

Different Worlds, Different Problems, Different Solutions

When a Buddhist and a Christian talk, they may sound very much alike. Often, they may use some of the same words (e.g. *salvation*), but even when they don't, it may seem as though the subject matter is the same. As I (Win) remarked in the chapter on tough questions (chapter 2), any two things are the same as long as you choose to ignore the differences. So, yes, it is possible to paint with a brush broad enough to make them sound quite similar. Both Buddhism and Christianity worship a person who came to earth when people were suffering in order to show a way of salvation. He gathered a large following of disciples, taught many wise ideas, and ascended to heaven. His death left a strong and lasting impression on his followers, who recorded his teachings in scriptures and carried on his mission.[33]

Of course, if you start to look at the details, the similarities vanish rather quickly. In fact, beyond this obvious outline, the actual teachings find little in common. You can see a sharp contrast by looking at two "firsts": Genesis 1:1, the first verse of the Bible, and the first of the Buddha's Four Noble Truths:

Genesis 1:1	Noble Truth 1
"In the beginning, God created the heavens and the earth."	"To live is to suffer."

Genesis 1:1 gives us a very quick preview of what is to come. It will have to do with God, a God so powerful and wise that He can create a universe and did so. As we know, the story goes on with the human fall into sin and God's plan of salvation that centered on His Son, Jesus Christ, dying on the cross for our salvation. When we place our faith in Him, He will forgive our sins, adopt us as His children, and let us spend eternity with Him in heaven.

Buddha's first Noble Truth foreshadows that his teaching will address something very different than our relationship with a god—namely, the fact that human beings suffer. The Buddha will provide us with directions on how to eliminate our suffering, most notably by recognizing the impermanence of everything that we think exists and stop trying to attach ourselves to anything. At that point, we are on the road toward liberating ourselves from the bondage of karma and rebirth into new lives.

Whereas biblical religion emphasizes that God alone is our firm anchor and the rock of our salvation, in authentic Buddhism (rather than the god-populated versions of folk Buddhism), gods are also a part of the impermanent world, and to rely on them will not result in liberation. On the whole, Buddhism does not deny the reality of gods, but they could not ultimately deliver anyone into salvation—even if they knew the way, which they do not. So without getting into a lot of technical details, it should be obvious that Buddhism views the world differently from Christianity, focuses on a different matter as the main problem besetting humanity (suffering rather than sin), and appropriately proposes a solution geared to the problem (detachment from that which causes us to suffer). The Buddhist solution is thus very different from the Christian solution to its understanding of the main problem—namely, salvation from sin by faith in the person and work of Jesus Christ. The idea that Buddhism and Christianity are really the same religion in different words is not only too outlandish to be believable but also robs each religion of its integrity.

Busting Myths

Buddhism and Christianity are both "missionary religions." Both include the goal of spreading their message around the globe to all people. Even though in many circles today—sometimes even including Buddhists—words such as *conversion* or *proselytizing* may provoke immediate outrage and condemnation, Buddhism is a religion that constantly seeks the conversion of people. At times, Buddhists clarify that they intend to spread not Buddhism but the dharma (the "Way"). However, this is wordplay, equivalent to missionaries saying that they preach only the gospel and not the Christian faith. Neither distinction will satisfy an outsider who is opposed to the idea of evangelism in general.

Buddhism comes with an extra item to the religious marketplace. This is the doctrine of *upayana*, a term that is variously translated as "cleverness," "skill," "skillful means," and so forth. Now, one could think of it in a purely positive way as the need to be creative and resourceful in bringing the message to the people. However, in the Lotus Sutra, where it is treated at length, upayana includes the idea that there is nothing wrong with conveying a falsehood if it brings people closer to actual truth.[34] In the modern world, upayana manifests itself by the perpetuation of various stereotypes about Buddhism that have no grounding in facts. The following are some of these popular, yet mythical, stereotypes.

Buddhism is a truly (or the most, the only, etc.) peaceful religion. In the early 1980s, the BBC produced a documentary series, rebroadcast in the United States by Public Television, entitled *The Long Search*, a collection of one-hour presentations on the world's main religions. In the segment on Buddhism,[35] after a monk had talked about the mission to the world initiated by the Buddha, Ronald Eyre, the host, reads from his script, "and a mission, what is more, without bloodshed." One might suspect this comment to be a barb possibly aimed at Christianity, which spread at times by riding on the coattails of imperialistic conquests.

However, the situation is no different for Buddhism. Just like other religions, there have been times when the mission was helped along significantly by people wielding swords and clubs. In fact, during at least two periods in two different locations, in Tibet and in Japan, monasteries of different orders would recruit and ordain men simply for their prowess in battle against each other.[36] Persecutions of Christians by Buddhists is not unknown. In 1905, it was the Dalai Lama's own order, the Gelupka, that slaughtered all Christians in a particular area where they feared they were losing influence.[37]

Now, our intent is not to smear Buddhism but merely to point out that Buddhism has no more legitimate claim to be a religion of peace than others. In a conversation with Buddhists, we're happy to give them the chance to avail themselves of the usual explanations—for example, "Those were not true Buddhists." That's fine, but to assert unequivocally that the Buddhist mission has occurred without bloodshed is upayana at its crassest.

In contrast to Christianity, Buddhism has no strict rules, and—best of all—no such thing as hell. Looking at the comments on my (Win's) video, "Basic Buddhist Teachings,"[38] there are numerous people who think of Buddhism as a kind of recreational activity, compatible with their favorite vice or a desirable alternative to Christianity with all its rules and supposedly judgmental attitude. Again, this is simply not true. Whether you are a layperson or a monk, there are rules to follow. From Thailand to Tibet, on the lowest level of the Buddhist cosmos, there is a hell, a place of punishment for beings who have violated the rules that determine karma. One can, of course, omit that part, but then one can hardly claim to follow Buddhism as it has been taught for about 2,500 years.

Buddhism is particularly suited for science. Some people say that Buddhism is true science, a highly debatable point. But even more so, the myth is making the rounds that Buddhism provides a particularly good conceptual framework for contemporary physics, chemistry, and other "Western" natural sciences. This idea makes no sense, as the sciences grew out of the context of an orderly creation based on an intelligent Creator. If the idea is that the Buddhist doctrine of impermanence is particularly helpful for understanding quantum mechanics or Einsteinian relativity, that idea is based on a misunderstanding of both areas. Whereas the Buddhist worldview ultimately denies the reality of the experienced world, both developments in physics assume the reality of the cosmos and our accessibility to it by empirical evidence. And if we may take recourse to a somewhat subjective standard, surprisingly few Buddhists have won the Nobel Prize in any science.

Buddhism is a religion of love. Even many Buddhists who know their religion protest against this generalization. It is true that the bodhisattvas have postponed their entry into enlightenment in order to help out other beings; however, they are only to be thought of as compassionate and benevolent, not loving. "Love" supposedly carries the connotation of attachment, the root of human suffering. The Bible tells us that God loves the world; to the Buddhist for whom the world is impermanent, insubstantial, sometimes even nonexistent, love, as exemplified by God, only worsens the human condition.

God's Love as Shown in Christ

And that last point brings us to the point of contact as we seek to share the gospel with Buddhists. Please let us clarify what should be an obvious point. Buddhists do not need to find Christ as Savior because they are Buddhists; they need Him because, like all fallen human beings, they are separated from God by sin, and only Jesus can reconcile them with their Creator. To put it another way, dismantling Buddhism may be necessary in the course of a debate-like interaction. It may also be required to show people the difference between Christianity and Buddhism (e.g., so that they do not think of Jesus as yet another bodhisattva). However, no one is saved by becoming a non-Buddhist. Strip the Buddhist ideas and trappings away from someone, and you get a former Buddhist, not a Christian.

As we mentioned above, Buddhist laypeople are often not really involved with the actual content of their claimed religion. They find whatever spiritual encouragement they seek in either folk versions of Buddhism or the veneration of spirits and deities whose connection to Buddhism, if any, is tenuous at best. Furthermore, the gods and spirits are to be enticed to act for the sake of one's welfare while, at the same time, they are to be feared and guarded against lest they inflict evil.

As a generalization based on many decades of interaction, we feel free to state that many Buddhist monks and leaders appear to live in spiritual doldrums. They know what the people want them to attain, but they also know that they have not yet done so. Despite (or, maybe because of) their supposedly exalted state, they often interact harshly with the laity. Called upon to perform rituals, such as funeral ceremonies, one finds them reading the proper sutras in the monotone of ennui, ringing bells or clicking drums with expressions that say they have done this 1,000 times, and the next 1,000 won't be any more interesting—and they are probably correct.

The gospel comes to both of these groups, regardless of school or location, and proclaims that it is possible to have eternal life now. Lives are not just an exercise in eliminating whatever is considered superfluous and finding one's true self in a virtually catatonic isolation from the world. God has created the world, and when the world broke away from Him, He made the provision that we can return to Him as His children. Our lives are meaningful because we have a genuine relationship with God in Christ. This relationship is built on God's love for us, which in turn enables us to love Him and, consequently, love other people as well. We are naturally preoccupied with looking out for our own benefit; self-love comes naturally to us. But God's love turns our self-love into love for Him and enables us to love our neighbor with the same priority as our own desires. This love is found by becoming new creatures in Christ.

Because of the diversities found within Buddhism, in both culture and belief, we cannot prescribe a universally applicable list of things to do to help Buddhists see God's love. However, we are sure of this: Despite Buddhism's quasi-official rejection of the term "love," when Buddhists see Christians act out of visibly self-sacrificial love, they will take notice. After all, the gospel is not our creation, but God's, and its very nature makes it applicable to all human beings.

Winfried Corduan (PhD, Rice University) is a world-traveling expert in a great many subjects, most notably philosophy and world religions. From 1977 to 2008, he served as a professor of philosophy and religion at Taylor University. He is the author of over ten books, including *Neighboring Faiths: A Christian Introduction to World Religions* and *In the Beginning God: A Fresh Look at the Case for Original Monotheism.*

Daniel McCoy (PhD, North-West University) is the editorial director for Renew.org. He also teaches classes on philosophy, world religions, and ethics for Ozark Christian College. He is author of *Mirage: Five Things People Want from God That Don't Exist* and coauthor with Christian apologist Norman Geisler of *The Atheist's Fatal Flaw: Exposing Conflicting Beliefs.*

Part 3

MAJOR RELIGIONS

Judaism

C. Wayne Mayhall

The history of Judaism shows many centuries of cruelty toward Jewish people. To the church's shame, people who have claimed to be followers of Christ have been among those perpetrating hostility against Jewish people. This side of an often shameful history, how is a Christian to relate to a Jewish person? Obviously, with genuine kindness and love. But what about the issue of evangelism—an issue as sensitive as a fresh wound? One approach would be to avoid evangelism toward Jews.[1] But is this the approach Jesus modeled and the biblical writers took? Was avoidance an option for Paul—himself a Jew whose "heart's desire and prayer to God for [his countrymen] is that they may be saved" (Romans 10:1)?

In this brief introduction to the history, beliefs, and practices of Judaism, this chapter offers Christians many points to begin a conversation over coffee with Jewish friends and acquaintances. And in what may be viewed as equally controversial today as it was thousands of years ago when Christ and Paul confronted Jewish unbelievers, this chapter closes by embracing the Christian conviction and Christlike love that compel us to present the gospel. As we shall see, there are many points of connection between Judaism and Christianity, but as followers of Christ, our every breath is for a reality where every person hears a clear presentation of the gospel. Jesus is first and foremost their Messiah, and Jews need to hear the message. And they cannot hear the greatest message of love, forgiveness, and hope without messengers who know the message. With that in mind, let's discuss Judaic history.

Judaism in the Biblical Period (Early Second Millennium BC–AD 70)

The Time of the Patriarchs

All three of the major monotheistic world religions—Judaism, Christianity, and Islam—acknowledge the patriarch Abraham and his wife Sarah as among the most important figures of their faith. Abraham and Sarah belonged to one of many small tribal peoples indigenous to West Asia. They were set apart at some point from the polytheistic practices of other tribes when Abraham was called by the one God (Yahweh). In a series of encounters, Abraham was asked to enter into a covenantal relationship in the building of a new nation, to leave his present home in Mesopotamia, and to travel to the land of Canaan. Circumcision became the outward sign of obedience to the covenant (Genesis 17:8-12). This covenant was pledged to the patriarch and his descendants, which would secure for them "all the land of Canaan, for an everlasting possession" (Genesis 17:8).

The Exodus from Slavery and a Covenant with Moses

Abraham and Sarah had two sons, Isaac and Ishmael, the former from God's supernatural intervention and the latter born to Abraham's servant Hagar. Isaac's wife Rebekah gave birth to twin sons, Jacob and Esau. God gave to Jacob the name "Israel." Israel had 12 sons, from which the "12 tribes of Israel" emerged. Jacob's favored younger son, Joseph, despised by his brothers, was sold into Egyptian slavery, where, through a series of divine interventions, he became a prominent figure in the court of the pharaoh. When a famine enveloped all of Canaan and Egypt, Joseph's brothers went to Egypt in search of food. When they learned that the Egyptian official they were dealing with was the brother whom they had betrayed, they expected their brother's wrath but were instead met with forgiveness and reconciliation. Joseph was able to arrange a new life for his family in Egypt.

Generations passed in Egypt until the Egyptians began to feel threatened by the growing numbers of Hebrew people. The pharaoh in power at the time began to enslave the Hebrews. Eventually, God called Moses to lead his people out of slavery. The two most prominent messages contained in the exodus of the Hebrew people out of slavery in Egypt are that of *human freedom* ("You were a slave in the land of Egypt," Deuteronomy 15:15) and *divine deliverance* ("See the salvation of the LORD, which he will work for you today," Exodus 14:13). After a series of miracles in the form of plagues crippled the Egyptian nation, the pharaoh agreed to let the Hebrew slaves follow their leader out of Egypt. But in another moment of hardening his heart toward the Hebrew people, the pharaoh pursued them through the desert. In one of the most spectacular examples of divine intervention, God parted the Red Sea, allowing the Hebrews to safely pass through but collapsing the waters back upon their Egyptian pursuers when they followed. After rescuing the Hebrews, God gave them His laws at Mount Sinai, summarized in the Ten Commandments. Since He gave the instructions through Moses, Moses is considered not only the Hebrews' leader but also their lawgiver.

Canaan Is Conquered (ca. 1220–1020 BC)

Stories from the two biblical books of Joshua and Judges reveal Yahweh's desire to establish His people in the Promised Land of Canaan. Joshua tells a story of the Hebrews' defeat at the Battle of Ai as a result of Achan deliberately disobeying Yahweh by stealing and hiding loot taken from the enemy at Jericho. For his sin, both Achan and his family were stoned to death. In the book of Judges, Israel's cycle of disobedience, punishment, and deliverance continues. The Hebrews sinned by serving the false gods of the Canaanites and were punished when Yahweh handed them over to their enemies. Each time, they were eventually delivered from their captivity when God raised up "judges" or "deliverers," such as Gideon and Deborah. Unfortunately, as the book of Judges records repeatedly, whenever the people were again without the guardianship of a judge, the cycle would repeat itself.

The Reign of Kings (ca. 1020–587 BC)

After many years of migratory tribal existence, the conquest and occupation of

Canaan marked the Israelites' transition from a pastoral subsistence on animal husbandry and the absence of a priestly hierarchy to guide them, to the establishment of agricultural settlements where both a priesthood and a monarchy could be initiated.

The first Israelite king was King Saul, whose modest reign (1020–1000 BC) ended in his defeat by the Philistines. After his death and the deaths of three of his four sons in battle, a former shepherd boy, David, was chosen by his own tribe to reign as king of the southern kingdom of Judah (r. 1000–961 BC), eventually becoming king of both north and south. It was David who chose the centrally located Jerusalem as the kingdom's capital city. Arguably its most celebrated king, David, according to the prophet Nathan, had come into a kingdom whose "throne shall be established forever" (2 Samuel 7:16). King David's son Solomon, known to all for his gift of wisdom, was next in line to rule the kingdom, and he did so between 961 and 922 BC. During Solomon's reign, Israel experienced its greatest period of prosperity and growth. Further, it was under Solomon that the Israelites were able to construct a temple for offering sacrifices to Yahweh and for housing the Ark of the Covenant, a gold-covered wood chest specially signifying God's presence. The Ark was previously kept in the tent-like "tabernacle."

However, fractures were forming. Solomon's son Rehoboam was an arrogant leader against whom the northern tribes rebelled. Thus the kingdom divided into North and South, with the North often being called "Israel" and the South often called "Judah," after the tribe from which its kings came (David, Solomon, Rehoboam, etc.). From the outset, the northern kings of Israel veered into the worship of other gods, heedless of the warnings of God's prophets. This kingdom was conquered by the Assyrians in 722 BC.

Meanwhile, the Judean kingdom in the south had seasons of idol worship mixed with seasons of revival and reform. For example, King Manasseh (r. 687–642 BC) led his kingdom wholeheartedly into the worship of foreign gods. However, Manasseh's grandson King Josiah (r. 640–609 BC) refused to bow the knee. When during his reign a temple scroll was discovered containing the Mosaic covenant, King Josiah was so overwhelmed by its contents that he had it read to the people and began to implement immediate reforms. The result was a rejection of polytheism and idolatry and a return to sacrifices being performed exclusively in the Jerusalem temple.

Yet in the end, despite the repeated protests of God's prophets, idolatry won out. And that is why, according to the scriptural record, Judah lost its kingdom. In 598 BC, Chaldean King Nebuchadnezzar II (r. 605–562 BC) accepted the surrender of Jerusalem by King Jehoiachin and began a campaign of deporting the conquered Jews to Babylon. Less than a decade later, in 589, the Chaldeans again invaded and besieged Jerusalem. In 587, the city and temple were plundered and destroyed by fire.

The Time of the Prophets

A common theme of the prophets of God to the Hebrews was that devotion to Him would lead to peace and safety, but rebellion against Him would receive punishment. Amos warned those "who oppress the poor, who crush the needy" (Amos 4:1). Hosea explained that there would be no peace because "there is no faithfulness or steadfast love, and no knowledge of God in the land" (Hosea 4:1). God inspired Hosea to write, "For I desire steadfast love and not sacrifice, the knowledge of God rather than burnt offerings" (Hosea 6:6). The message was relentless and clear to His wayward people: "Seek good, and not evil, that you may live" (Amos 5:14) and "Let justice roll down like waters, and righteousness like an ever-flowing stream" (Amos 5:24). In the prophetic message was hope, too, and a promise that a remnant of Israel would survive and be reconciled to God and be reestablished in the land. Jeremiah proclaimed the "everlasting love" (Jeremiah 31:3) of God and a "new covenant with the house of Israel and the house of Judah" (Jeremiah 31:31) in which God's law would be written in their hearts.

The prophet Isaiah (742–701 BC) spoke of a Messiah—"anointed one"—who would deliver the Israelites from their enemies. A new king descended from the seed of Jesse would sit upon the throne of David and would usher in a new age "to establish [his kingdom] and to uphold it with justice and with righteousness from this time forth and forevermore" (Isaiah 9:7). According to Isaiah, when the Messiah comes, those in conflict "shall beat their swords into plowshares, and their spears into pruning hooks; nation shall not lift up sword against nation, neither shall they learn war anymore" (Isaiah 2:4).

From Exile to Roman Rule (598 BC–AD 136)

After the Chaldean conquest and the mass deportation to Babylon, Jerusalem was laid low. Psalm 137:1-4 captures the broken hearts of God's chosen, now in exile:

> By the waters of Babylon, there we sat down and wept, when we remembered Zion. On the willows there we hung up our lyres. For there our captors required of us songs, and our tormentors, mirth, saying, "Sing us one of the songs of Zion!" How shall we sing the LORD's song in a foreign land?

Babylon itself was conquered in 539 BC by the Persians, who had built a large empire in the East. The Jewish people were now no longer under the reign of the Chaldeans. The Persians allowed the Jewish people to return and rebuild their homeland, including what is today referred to as the Second Temple. Even after their return, however, it would not be long before they were again subjugated, this time under the brutal regime of the Seleucids from Syria. Yet under the leadership of a family of Jews known as the Maccabees, they would liberate themselves in what is today known as the Maccabean revolt, a victory in 165 BC commemorated in the festival of Chanukah (Hanukkah). This revolt led to the establishment of a Jewish state ruled by Maccabean descendants, known as the Hasmonean dynasty. Eventually, infighting led two Maccabee brothers who were vying for the throne to approach Rome for help. As a result, the Hasmonean kingdom became a vassal of Rome in 63 BC.

At the time of Roman emperor Augustus (27 BC–AD 14), the world population of Jews numbered around five million, one million of whom lived in the original Promised Land.[2] In an often violent relationship between Roman and Jew, Jewish factions such as the Sadducees and Pharisees competed for their countrymen's allegiance, each believing its side held the key to well-being in the land. The Pharisees were a movement dedicated to returning their nation to holiness as codified in rabbinic teachings. The Sadducees were composed of priests, merchants, and landowners who accepted only the first five books of the Old Testament (Pentateuch) as sacred scripture. The Sadducees rejected the belief in the resurrection of the body, the world to come, and the Messiah, and stressed that temple sacrifice and interpretation of *Torah* (the law of Moses) were

8A. Prayers at the Wailing Wall in Jerusalem, Israel. Photo by Paul Arps, 2013 (https://creativecommons.org/licenses/by/2.0).

priestly functions. It would not be until the destruction of the Second Temple that the Sadducees would lose their influence, and the Pharisees would take the helm of Judaism.

In AD 70, the Romans answered a Jewish rebellion by besieging Jerusalem, burning its temple to the ground and enslaving or killing many of its inhabitants. The ancient mountaintop fortress of Masada in southeastern Israel was the Jews' last stand against the Romans. There, atop the isolated mesa near the west coast of the Dead Sea, they chose to take their own lives rather than be taken by the Roman invasion. The dead included 960 men, women, and children, with only 2 women and 5 children surviving.[3] According to historian Josephus, the final exhortation of Eleazar, the leader of the Masada community, was as follows: "Since we, long ago…resolved never to be servants to the Romans, nor to any other than to God Himself…the time is now come that obliges us to make that resolution true in practice…Let us make haste to die bravely."[4]

A final Jewish rebellion against Rome was crushed in AD 136 (the Bar Kokhba Revolt). Rome had purposed to build a temple to the Roman god Jupiter where the Second Temple once stood. Jewish leaders revolted, and Rome responded even more forcibly than it had in AD 70.

The Period of Rabbinic Judaism (AD 70–1789)

Following the Bar Kokhba Revolt, the Jewish population, particularly in the south (Judea), was decimated, and Jewish religion was forbidden from being practiced. Now without a temple or homeland, Jewish people largely made their settlements outside of the Promised Land in surrounding makeshift settlements, guided by the stable influence of the rabbinic leaders. Rabbinic teachings thoroughly applied Mosaic law to all areas of life, including prayer, agriculture, festivals, Sabbath, marriage, divorce, property, sacrifice, and dietary rules.

Although Jesus and His 12 apostles were Jewish, they faced much persecution from Jewish religious leaders. For example, Stephen and James were martyred, and both Peter and Paul imprisoned, by Jewish religious leaders. In the AD 80s, a rabbinic edict closed synagogues to Christians and warned Jews to disassociate with them.

Rather than turning the other cheek (Matthew 5:39), some Christians in the next few centuries would turn to anti-Semitism. For example, in his *Eight Orations against the Jews*, the patriarch of Constantinople John Chrysostom (ca. 347–407) vilified Jews as thieves and animals who lived "by the rule of debauchery and inordinate gluttony. Only one thing they understand: to gorge themselves and to get drunk."[5] In his *Dialogue with Trypho* (a Jewish man), Justin Martyr seemed almost to gloat over the destruction of Jerusalem: "That you may be separated from other nations, and from us; and that you alone may suffer that which you now justly suffer; and that your land may be desolate, and your cities burned with fire...these things have happened to you in fairness and justice, for you have slain the Just One."[6] Other Christian leaders were more gracious to Jewish people, such as Augustine (354–430), who, according to one Jewish source, "quite unlike the violently anti-Jewish diatribes of his contemporary, John Chrystostom" demonstrated a gentler, missionary attitude "to the Jewish people as being destined ultimately to join in the fullness of the Divine promise as realized in the church."[7] Sadly, church-state alliances sometimes made for very little religious tolerance of Jews.

By the time of Charlemagne (742–814), emperor of much of Europe, many Jews lived in regions of northern France and western Germany. Jews referred to these areas as "Ashkenaz." The term "Ashkenazim" became a term for Jews associated with France, Germany, and Eastern Europe. Rashi, whose full name was Solomon ben Isaac (ca. 1040–1105), is probably the best-known Ashkenazi Jew of medieval Europe. Rashi was a rabbi whose commentaries proved influential for the study of the Hebrew Bible and Talmud. It was out of Ashkenazic Judaism that *Hasidism* emerged. Hasidism, a form of Jewish mysticism, originated in Poland. The first Hasidic master was Israel ben Eleazer (1700–1760), also known as the Baal Shem Tov (master of the divine name). According to his disciples, the Baal Shem Tov taught the core Hasidic beliefs: God is mystically present in all things; there is joy in all aspects of life; one must follow a "righteous man"; and one must study the Torah.[8]

Whereas Ashkenazic Jews are associated with France, Germany, and Eastern Europe, "Sephardic" refers to Jews traditionally from the Iberian Peninsula (Spain and Portugal). Perhaps the most influential Sephardic Jew of medieval Europe was Maimonides (Moses ben Maimon, also known as Rambam), who combined Torah scholarship with Aristotelian philosophy.

It was initially because of persecution in Muslim lands that many Jews settled on the Iberian Peninsula. However, with their recapturing of the rest of Spain from the Muslims, Ferdinand and Isabella felt it was time to unify Spain under Christianity. In 1492, the same year Columbus arrived in the New World, Ferdinand and Isabella expelled all Jews who refused to convert to Christianity. Many Jews found themselves back in Muslim lands, specifically under the rule of the Ottoman Turks. Once again living in exile, many Jews began rekindling messianic hopes. Sabbatai Zevi, a Jew born in Turkey, was for a time believed to be the Jewish messiah, but when imprisoned in Constantinople, he shocked his followers by converting to Islam.

Modern Judaism

Modern Judaism was born out of the emergence of modern Western nation-states as well as during the modern economic, intellectual, and political revolutions of the eighteenth, nineteenth, and early twentieth centuries. Five main periods best define this modern Jewish formation: Enlightenment, Emancipation, Reform Judaism, Holocaust, and Israel.

Enlightenment. The eighteenth-century period known as the Enlightenment marked a significant shift in worldview. This shift was characterized by faith in human reason and optimism about scientific advancements. Likewise, the miraculous was often dismissed as something only gullible, superstitious people would accept.

Emancipation. The world population of Jews was around half a million in Central Europe and over one million in Eastern Europe around the beginning of the eighteenth century.[9] These Ashkenazic Jews were accustomed to living in separate villages (known as *shtetls* in Eastern Europe), having their tranquility periodically shattered by *pogroms*, officially sanctioned violence against Jews. But in Europe, signs of peace and integration were beginning to appear. For example, Hapsburg emperor Joseph II (1741–90) was one of the first to attempt to integrate Jews and non-Jews by abolishing the Jewish badge of identity and striking restrictions on places of residence. On August 26, 1789, at the outset of the French Revolution, the French National Assembly adopted the *The Declaration of the Rights of Man and of Citizens.*[10] Article 1 read, "Men are born and remain free and equal in rights."[11] In September 1791, this was clarified to include Jewish men as full citizens.

Reform Judaism. In eighteenth-century Germany, a more "enlightened" form of the faith emerged, coinciding with the general removal of legal barriers to Jewish participation in public life. Reformed Judaism no longer bound themselves to traditional rabbinic Judaism. Only those religious directives compatible with modern life and "in accord with the postulates of reason" were to be practiced. Reformed Jews had no interest in a coming messiah. Moreover, they saw assimilation as preferable to a separate Jewish state, arguing that Judaism was a religion based on conviction rather than an ethnic-national way of life.

Holocaust. The German Third Reich's massacre of six million Jews between 1938 and Germany's 1945 surrender in World War II is today remembered as the *Holocaust* (a Greek word meaning burnt sacrificial offering) or *Shoah* (Hebrew for "extermination"). The Holocaust was the horrifying consequence of Nazi intolerance of Jews. What Nazis referred to as the "final solution" came within reach of annihilating the European Jewish population. Out of a prewar European Jewish population of 9.2 million, only 3.1 million survived. "One must not allow sentimentality to prevail...[in the] life and death struggle between the Aryan race and the Jewish bacillus," Minister of Propaganda Joseph Goebbels wrote in his journal.[12]

Concentration camps were first planned and then constructed throughout Germany as soon as Hitler and his governing Nazi Party acquired command of Germany in 1933. Built on the model of a barrack-style compound, the camps were surrounded by electric, barbed-wire enclosures and protected by guard towers. The barracks contained row after row of beds jammed with detainees packed from floor to ceiling. Over 100 labor camps and a handful of mass extermination camps were discovered when Allied armies smashed through German lines on all fronts in Germany, Austria, Poland, and other European countries. The prototype for the many camps was located in Dachau, in the vicinity of Munich; 80 percent of its estimated 40,000 victims were Jews. In Poland, carbon monoxide poisoning took the lives of over 400,000 Jews at Belzec, and nearly 800,000 were gassed at Treblinka. Roughly one million Jews and Gentiles were massacred, typically by hydrogen cyanide, at Auschwitz.

Israel. As a result of Zionist efforts and European and American disgust over the Holocaust, the nation-state of Israel was founded on May 14, 1948, as a homeland for Jews. Within days, Israel was attacked by the armies of Egypt, Jordan, Lebanon, Syria, and Iraq. Israel was victorious, and by spring of 1949, they had retained their allotted land and accumulated large areas that had originally been partitioned for Arabs. The Jews in Israel numbered around 630,000 when the War of Independence began, but by 1951, the "ingathering of the exiles"[13] from Displaced Persons camps and Arab countries grew the Jewish population to 1.2 million. Palestinians and Arab nations declined to recognize the right of Israel to exist and pledged "to throw the Jews into the sea."[14] In 1964, Palestinian refugees established the Palestine Liberation Organization (PLO). Israel's borders expanded again in June 1967, during what is now referred to as the Six-Day War. Israel took East Jerusalem and the West Bank from Jordan, the Golan Heights from Syria, and the Gaza Strip and Sinai Peninsula from Egypt.

Judaic Beliefs

Of the world's 17.5 million Jews today, the majority still subscribe to the basic concept of one God who is the sovereign creator of the world. Although Judaism focuses far more on practice than belief—and Jewish belief can vary widely—the following beliefs remain the basics of biblical Judaism.

God. The Shema (Hebrew for "hear") is a daily prayer recited by Jews: "Hear, O Israel: The Lord our God, the Lord is one. You shall love the Lord your God with all your heart and with all your soul and with all your might" (Deuteronomy 6:4-5). Moses Maimonides's "Thirteen Principles" aver that there is only one God, that "God is one," and that only God is worthy of worship.[15]

God's transcendence (existence outside of space and time) in classical Judaic theology speaks of His nature as eternal, incomparable, immutable (without change), incorporeal (immaterial), omniscient (all-knowing), and omnipotent (all-powerful). Biblical scholars often understand God's name for Himself in Exodus 3:14—"I am"—to indicate that God is Being Itself, transcending the finite creation, and incapable of being fully known by humans.

God is not only transcendent but also immanent. That is, He is active in time and space. His presence, often called His "Shekinah" glory, fills heaven and earth. It is taught that God was present in the temple, in the study of the Torah, in prayer, and in benevolent and just acts.

Word of God. Torah literally means "instruction." It is used to denote God's law as revealed through Moses in the first five books of the Hebrew Bible. Another word to describe Genesis, Exodus, Leviticus, Numbers, and Deuteronomy is *Pentateuch.* The word *Torah* is also used in a more general sense to refer to the entire Hebrew Bible, also known as the Tanakh. Tanakh is an acronym that comes from the three main divisions of the Hebrew Bible: *T* for "Torah" (or the *Pentateuch*), *N* for "Nevi'im" (the prophetic books), and *K* for "Kethuvim" (the writings).

Also authoritative is the *Talmud,* a massive collection of Jewish law and literature. Jews are able to read and understand the Tanakh through reading the Talmud. The Talmud contains both the *Mishnah* and the *Gemara.* The Mishnah contains rabbinic teachings on the Hebrew Bible, and the Gemara is a rabbinic commentary on the Mishnah.

Israel. In Jewish thought, Israel is both a land (Eretz Israel) and a people (Beth Israel). Both were featured in God's covenant with Abraham: "And I will establish my covenant between me and you and your offspring after you throughout their generations for an everlasting covenant" (Genesis 17:7) and "give to you and to your offspring after you the land of your sojournings, all the land of Canaan" (Genesis 17:8). As long as Israel remains faithful, it is called God's treasured possession (Exodus 19:5), a light of nations (Isaiah 42:6-7).

The World and the Afterlife. Judaism is far more oriented toward living faithfully in this world than focusing on the world to come. After all, according to Judaism, this world is good, not something to escape from. Creation was called "very good" (Genesis 1:31). Sexuality and marriage are gifts from God. Although fasting is a feature of Judaism, it is rare to see prolonged fasting or the denigration of marriage and sexuality. Permitted pleasures such as food and wine or dance and music are seen as so good that, according to a Talmudic passage, "a man will have to give account in the judgment day of every good thing which he might have enjoyed and did not."[16]

Life after death was a shadowy concept in the Hebrew Bible, although it took on more weight and clarity in rabbinical writings. This world began to be seen as preparation for the next: "This World is like a vestibule to the World to Come. Prepare yourself in the vestibule, so that you may be admitted into the banquet hall."[17] The righteous would be rewarded with Paradise, and the wicked judged in *Gehinnom* (hell). Jewish tradition did not limit salvation to Jews; for example, according to the Talmud, "The righteous of all nations have a place in the world to come."[18]

Suffering. All humans experience suffering. As one rabbi put it, "There is no man in the world to whom suffering does not come."[19] The problem is reconciling God's goodness with undeserved suffering. Shouldn't evil be punished and goodness be rewarded? After all, "The LORD does not let the righteous go hungry, but he thwarts the craving of the wicked" (Proverbs 10:3). Human freedom means that suffering happens, but what about undeserved suffering? A history of the Jews demonstrates that sometimes the people most faithful to God's law are the most persecuted. In response to this dilemma, the book of Job teaches that, from our human vantage point, we are incapable of understanding why undeserved suffering happens. If our suffering is not always caused by our sin, then what purpose could suffering serve in light of the goodness of God? The prophet Isaiah taught that suffering can be redemptive. He pictured Israel as God's suffering servant, a light of nations "that my salvation may reach to the end of the earth" (Isaiah 49:6).

Judaic Practices

As mentioned earlier, religious practice is more crucial to Judaism than correct doctrine. Even Jews who no longer follow biblical beliefs can still practice Judaism as part of their heritage. The following are observations about Judaic practice.

Halakah and Mitzvot. Jewish *halakah* is another term for Jewish law. The word means "to go" or "to walk," denoting the way in which we should go. The term can be used generically as referring to the entire Jewish legal system. It can also be used more particularly to refer to a specific law. Because the original Torah did not legislate on all possible scenarios that can arise, the Jewish community needed teachers of the law to clarify how halakah would be applied to their own time period. For example, in order to clarify what was meant by resting on the seventh day (the Sabbath), a Mishnah lists 39 classes of work that would be forbidden on the Sabbath, including planting, plowing, reaping, weaving, unraveling, carrying, burning, and slaughtering. Halakah includes the laws of Moses written in the Hebrew Bible as well as all the subsequent rabbinic clarifications and elaborations. The clarification and application of laws, such as Sabbath laws, continues to this day in order to accommodate modern scenarios.

The word *Mitzvah* means "commandment." A mitzvah may be either obeyed, resulting in a good deed, or broken, resulting in a sin. There are said to be 613 *mitzvot* in the law of Moses, 248 of which are positive commands ("You shall"), and 365 of which are negative ("You shall not"). There are also mitzvot in the Talmud, each of which originates from a passage in the law of Moses.

Worship and Festivals. Prayer plays a central part of everyday life and synagogue worship. Adult males are expected to pray at least three times a day—in the morning, afternoon, and evening. Prayers in the morning and evening include the previously mentioned Shema ("Hear, O Israel..."). But the term "Shema" is also used to refer to the daily prayers in their entirety, which include Deuteronomy 6:4-9; 11:13-21; and Numbers 15:37-41.

In the synagogue, there is a special prayer book used called the *Siddur*. In order for there to be congregational prayer or a business meeting held in a synagogue, there must be a minimum of ten Jewish men to comprise a quorum (*minyan*), although Reform

8B. In this synagogue in England, the Torah ark is opened, showing the scrolls inside. Photo by Rodhullandemu, 2017 (https://creativecommons.org/licenses/by-sa/4.0).

Judaism expands this to include a total of ten Jewish adults, whether male or female.

Sabbath (*Shabbat*) takes place weekly from sundown on Friday to sundown on Saturday. It is a day of rest to be remembered and enjoyed. The Sabbath rest is considered a foretaste of the eternal rest coming. As theologian Abraham Heschel (1907–72) put it, "The essence of the world to come is Sabbath eternal, and the seventh day in time is an example of eternity."[20] The Sabbath was such an important remembrance that rabbis once declared that the Messiah would finally come if only all Jews would observe it.

The Jewish calendar includes several holy days. The Jewish "New Year" is Rosh Hashanah, celebrated around September or October. Rosh Hashanah is a day of rest and prayer, with a shared meal in the evening in which families eat fruit dipped in honey in the hope that the year ahead will be a sweet one. The day ends with the blowing of a ram's horn (*shofar*). Rosh Hashanah commences a ten-day period of penitence, which concludes with Yom Kippur, known also as the "Day of Atonement." Yom Kippur is a time to seek God's forgiveness and reconciliation with other people.

Beginning five days after Yom Kippur, Sukkot is an eight-day festival that holds two purposes. First, it is when the Jews construct temporary shelters for living in so that they can remember the Hebrews' wilderness wanderings under Moses. This is why Sukkot is also called the "Festival of Booths." Second, Sukkot is a time of thanksgiving for the harvest. Another eight-day festival is Chanukah (Hanukkah), celebrated in November or December to remember the Maccabee victory over the Seleucids in 165 BC, in which they won their independence and reconquered the temple. Purim remembers the story of Esther, the Jewish queen in Persia who saved her people from extermination.

8C. Interior of the Spanish Synagogue in Prague, Czech Republic. Photo by Txllxt TxllxT, 2003 (https://creativecommons.org/licenses/by-sa/4.0).

Pesach (Passover) is another eight-day festival that celebrates God's deliverance of the Jews from slavery in Egypt. Seven weeks after Pesach, Jews celebrate Shavuot (Pentecost) as a way of remembering God's giving of the law at Mount Sinai.

Life Cycle Rites. On the eighth day after birth, male children are circumcised by a *mohel* (circumciser). When he reaches age 13, the young man becomes a "son of the commandments" (*bar mitzvah*). As part of the ceremony in the synagogue, the "son of the commandment" gives a benediction and reads from the Torah. He is now held responsible for his own actions and can be considered toward the ten adults needed for a quorum (*minyan*). Some forms of Judaism allow for a young woman to become a "daughter of the commandments" (*bat mitzvah*) in a similar ritual. When a Jewish man and woman marry, they stand under a canopy signifying that they will live under the same roof. Blessings are recited over a cup of wine, which the couple drinks. At the end of the ceremony, the groom crushes a glass under his foot, as a reminder of the destruction of the Jerusalem

8D. A temporary shelter in Tel Aviv for celebrating Sukkot. Photo by matan lantsiano, Pikiwiki Israel, 2015 (https://creativecommons.org/licenses/by/2.5).

temple. In this way, sorrowful remembrance is mingled with joyful celebration.

Sharing the Mission, Message, and Methodology of Christ with Jewish People

While it is great to talk to our Jewish friends with a working knowledge about their religion, worldview, and acceptance of Jewish history, beliefs, and practices, it is imperative to talk about Jesus Christ—His mission, His message, and His methodology. I would like to mention some of the key points we should always remember in our witnessing efforts.

Jesus Christ is our supreme example as we seek to share the gospel. We cannot accomplish much without following His example in what we say and do. Remember, Jesus came, as He said, for one purpose: "To seek and to save the lost" (Luke 19:10). He taught people so they could develop a right relationship with God. He healed people so they could understand divine forgiveness and the love of God. He performed miracles so people could experience the joy of knowing that God cares.

But in each situation, Jesus wanted the people to understand His supreme mission: to glorify God by drawing people to Himself. Yes, He provided for the people's immediate needs, but He also pointed out people's ultimate needs. Yes, He delivered people from the enemy, but He also directed them to the Father. Evangelism often begins with the immediate, but we must never forget the eternal.

We should be willing to understand what our Jewish friend wants us to understand about their religion, but we must not let them disarm us to the extent that we forget the urgency of our mission. Loving? Yes. Compromising? No.

Jesus went to people to meet their needs. Jesus, as we have mentioned, not only shared the good news with the people, but He also met their immediate needs. We should do no less. Evangelism should not be treated as a "sales call." The desire to witness must proceed from our deep burden for the lost. Burden for the lost generates love and compassion for those who are without the Savior. Spiritual needs are reflected in man's physical, social, financial, and other needs. As we help people with their immediate needs, we can point people to God, who can meet their ultimate needs. People are lonely these days. They want someone to talk to, someone who would listen to and share their burdens. Our interest in people can be transformed into their interest in the Lord.

Jesus exhibited an attitude of tremendous care for everyone He encountered. Statesmen to soldiers, mothers to members of His group, friends to foes—all came to see Him, to ask Him questions, and to observe His life. Of course, not everyone accepted Him. He was rejected; He was despised; He was abused. But He did not give up the cause, and He did not abandon the needy and the poor. Just like Christ, we may be rejected, despised, or even abused. But let us continue to care for people so they would see the care of the Lord Jesus Christ in the whole effort. Our care must always point to Christ.

Jesus demonstrated a life of prayer. Jesus prayed for the people for whom He was sent, as we can see from several moving prayers in the Gospels. Let us pray for the contacts we are going to make and let us not hesitate to pray in the presence of people, especially when we are witnessing to them. Jewish people need to see and observe our dependence upon the Lord for the work we do, and they need to experience the power of prayer through us.

Jesus never complained about His hardships. Jesus made the greatest sacrifice for our sake. He gave up the perfection of heaven to live in the wicked world; He gave up the fellowship of the Lord and the saints to be rejected of man; He gave up the glory of heaven to live and suffer as a man.

When we face the slightest difficulty in our work, not only do we typically get frustrated, but we also feel we have the right to complain. We seem to display the notion that since we are engaged in mission work, we deserve the right contacts, the right breaks, and the right compensations. Evangelism must be undertaken irrespective of the cost involved. If you are called of the Lord to become His messenger to a Jewish friend, consider the privilege; don't obsess about the sacrifice.

Jewish people seem to value sacrifice, especially in religious leadership. When they observe Christians witnessing out of genuine love for people, they are intrigued, and they begin to ask questions.

Jesus avoided common sociopolitical controversies. Jesus remained true to His calling, which was to bring people to God, the Father. His questioners tried to draw Him into controversial political situations, but Jesus refused to take sides (Matthew 22:21).

We are being asked to take the gospel of our Lord Jesus Christ to the Jewish people, not to get embroiled in controversial topics. It does not mean that we forget our responsibilities as citizens of this land, but that we remember our privilege as citizens of another, more permanent land. And we need to continue to direct the attention of Jewish people to that land without being distracted by the problems of this temporal world.

Jesus was guided by God, the Father. Jesus did not make a single move without express direction from God, the Father. "The Son can do nothing of his own accord" (John 5:19) sums up His approach to His work. We should do no less. Jesus clearly told His disciples, "As my Father hath sent me, even so send I you" (John 20:21 KJV). He came in total dependence upon the Father; we should go in total obedience to Jesus Christ, our Lord.

He has sent the Holy Spirit for this purpose. He is here to guide us in all things, including evangelistic efforts. We must listen to His instructions, receive His direction, and follow His leadership. He will bring us to the people to whom we need to go. He will give us the words we will need to share. He will prepare the people to be ready for our message before we meet them. Let us simply follow in His steps.

POINT OF CONTENTION, POINT OF CONNECTION	
Point of Contention	Point of Connection
Worship of Jesus as God?	Let us not forget that Jews were the first to worship Jesus as God. If Jesus's first followers were all devout Jews familiar with the Hebrew Scriptures, it would be reasonable to assume that they must have understood various Old Testament passages in a way that would have allowed them to accept Messiah as God with us (Isaiah 7:14). Jesus Himself, of course, was fully Jewish, a fact which biblical scholarship once neglected but is returning to. Likewise, the idea of a coming Savior who was both human and divine is not without precedent in Old Testament prophecy, as we see in Micah 5:2 and Isaiah 9:6.
Jesus and the Torah?	The message laid out for us in Hebrews could not be any clearer: "And every priest stands daily at his service, offering repeatedly the same sacrifices, which can never take away sins" (Hebrews 10:11). Jesus, however, "offered for all time a single sacrifice for sins" (10:12). We need not picture Jesus as having discarded the Torah's system of Temple sacrifices as if He were dismissive of His Hebrew heritage. Rather, He fulfilled the sacrificial system in Himself. There are similar parallels in the Torah that find fulfillment in Jesus's life, such as the sacrifice of the beloved son (i.e., the story of Abraham and Isaac) and the Passover lamb (John 1:29; Matthew 26:19,26-29).
Validity of the New Testament?	In many New Testament passages, first century Judaism is severely criticized (e.g., John 8:44; Thessalonians 2:14-16). In response, Jews have raised various objections to it, alleging, for instance, that the New Testament misquotes/misinterprets the Old Testament, contains historical inaccuracies, and portrays a mythical Jesus. Christianity invites seekers to share the perspective of the first-century Bereans, who were commended for searching out for themselves the Old Testament scriptures in order to know truth and the validity of teachings they heard (Acts 17:11). Jesus Himself told His Jewish followers, "If you abide in my word, you are truly my disciples, and you will know the truth, and the truth will set you free" (John 8:31-32). Clearly, the New Testament advances the teaching that God's people can know Him through scripture, which is trustworthy.

POINT OF CONTENTION, POINT OF CONNECTION	
Point of Contention	**Point of Connection**
But does the Old Testament teach that God's followers can understand His holy words themselves?	The resounding answer in the Tanakh is yes. Psalm 119:18 reads: "Open my eyes that I may see wonderful things in your law." Psalm 119 also tells us, "I have stored up your word in my heart, that I might not sin against you" (v. 11). Nothing here mentions the need for any rabbi or Talmud. Nowhere, in fact, does the Tanakh even mention the existence of any oral Torah. The Hebrew scriptures, like the New Testament, indicate that it is primarily God's Spirit who enlightens us to the scriptural truth, as David prayed, "Get wisdom; get insight; do not forget, and do not turn away from the words of my mouth" (Proverbs 4:5). Similarly, Deuteronomy 29:29 declares, "The secret things belong to the Lord our God, but the things that are revealed belong to us and to our children forever, that we may do all the words of this law." Again, nothing is said here about an "oral Torah" or sages/rabbis.
On the Trinity?	The Christian doctrine of the Trinity forcefully upholds the Old Testament teaching that there is only one true and living God. It should come as no surprise, therefore, that the first Jewish Christians were quite open to accepting the fuller revelation about God's nature that was thrust upon them by Jesus's appearance—i.e., that God exists as three "persons" who are the one God. The Tanakh leaves more than enough room for such a plurality in God's nature. For example, in the shema itself we find a fascinating implication in the Hebrew word *echad*, which is used to describe God as being "one" God. The term does not necessarily demand singular unity. It can very easily be used to describe compound unity, as in Genesis 2:24, where it describes a man and woman become one flesh in marriage. Another instance of *echad* being used to depict composite unity occurs in Exodus 30:13 where God commands that various pieces of tabernacle be brought together and united as one.
Consider just a handful of the prophecies pointing to Jesus as Messiah.	He would be descended from the line of David (Isaiah 9:6-7; Luke 1:31-32). He would be born in Bethlehem (Micah 5:2; Luke 2:4-7). He would be linked to a prophet: "Prepare the way of the Lord" (Isaiah 40:3-4; Luke 3:1-5). He would be preceded by a "messenger" (Malachi 3:1; Luke 7:24-27). He would be a prophet like Moses (Deuteronomy 18:15; Acts 3:19-20,22). He would have a ministry based in Galilee (Isaiah 9:1-2; Matthew 4:12-16). He would comfort the brokenhearted (Isaiah 61:1-3; Luke 4:17-21). He would raise the dead (Ezekiel 37:13; John 11:38-44). He would be sacrificed for humanity's sins (Isaiah 53:3-12).

POINT OF CONTENTION, POINT OF CONNECTION	
Point of Contention	Point of Connection
Jesus as Messiah?	Despite a widespread rejection of Jesus, many Jews listening to Jesus were able to see in Him the God of Israel, the incarnate Messiah prophesied to come. They ultimately understood that the salvation long promised was not a deliverance from earthly oppressors (Rome) or the establishment of any earthly kingdom (based in Jerusalem). Instead, the Messiah's mission was to rescue God's people from the oppression of their own sin, and then establish God's kingdom of righteousness through their yielded hearts. As Jesus's followers listened to Him teach, this truth about the kingdom grew more evident. Then, after His resurrection, it all became crystal clear. Jesus often alluded to the unearthly nature of God's kingdom and His rule over it. For instance, in reply to the Pharisees who asked when God's kingdom would come, He said, "The kingdom of God is not coming in ways that can be observed, nor will they say, 'Look, here it is!' or 'There!' for behold, the kingdom of God is in the midst of you" (Luke 17:20-21). And when standing before Pilate, He explained, "My kingdom is not of this world. If my kingdom were of this world, my servants would have been fighting, that I might not be delivered over to the Jews. But my kingdom is not from the world" (John 18:36). It cannot be denied, of course, that throughout first-century Israel the prevailing expectation among Jews was that Messiah would indeed "free" them and establish an era of peace via God's earthly kingdom. But many other expectations were also held, which in their fulfillment by *Y'shua*, indicated that He was truly the Messiah and that the freedom they were to enjoy and the kingdom they were to see was not the earthly kind that they had been expecting. *Y'shua* the Messiah had come to do far more. He had come to set the people spiritually free and deliver them from being slaves to sin (John 8:31-36; Romans 6:17-18).

When it comes to sharing our faith with those in the Jewish community, our duty is to demonstrate the reality of Jesus Christ through the testimony of our love, our life, and our lips. For as the Apostle Paul explains, the gospel of Jesus Christ "is the power of God for salvation to everyone who believes, to the Jew first and also to the Greek. For in it the righteousness of God is revealed from faith for faith, as it is written, 'The righteous shall live by faith'" (Romans 1:16-17).

C. Wayne Mayhall (MACT, Bethel University) has taught philosophy, religious studies, and ethics at numerous colleges, including Liberty University, North Carolina A & T State University, and Newberry College. He is a contributing editor to the *Christian Research Journal* and the author or coauthor of six books, including *Patterns of Religion, Religious Autobiographies*, and *On Martin Buber*, and is EdD (ABD) at Liberty University in curriculum and instruction.

9

Zoroastrianism

Michael Caba

One day, while working out at a local fitness center with a good friend, our discussion turned to a recent trip I had taken to a Zoroastrian fire temple. I had gone to the temple as a means of furthering my understanding of one of the various faiths I was planning to teach about in an upcoming world religions course. As I related my experience, we talked about the nice people I met and the good food I had consumed due to my Zoroastrian hosts' warm hospitality. Our talk lingered on until another gym member—having overheard our conversation—approached us and began to relate his encounters with Zoroastrian people, particularly regarding their emphasis on honesty and, specifically, how they would *never* tell a lie. In a manner typical of casual banter, the exchange was short and surface-level, but it was nevertheless clear the Zoroastrians this person had encountered had left an indelible mark on him due to their high moral standards. In addition, it turns out that not only had I and my newly found acquaintance been impressed with the Zoroastrians we had encountered, others throughout history have also noted the Zoroastrians' distinguished character. One such person was Benjamin Franklin, who wrote, "There is lately published in Paris… the Writings of Zoroaster…I have cast my Eye over the Religious Part; it seems to contain a nice Morality, mix'd with abundance of Prayer, Ceremonies and Observations."[1]

Who are the Zoroastrians, where do they come from, what do they believe, and (though not often asked directly) what is the meaning of the interesting name of their religion? As it turns out, the religion now known as Zoroastrianism is a long-enduring faith—which has, at times, withstood harsh persecution—having taken firm root initially in ancient Persia (modern-day Iran) in the first millennium BC. The founder of the religion was a teacher named Zarathustra,[2] in the earliest texts, and the customary English designation of "Zoroaster" is based on a Greek rendering of his name. Thus the common term for the religion comes from a Greek form of the name of the founder. Moreover, as is the case with most major belief systems, the current faith reflects the teachings ascribed to its founder, for it was Zoroaster himself who taught his followers the precept that has been called the "fundamental tenet of the faith"[3]—namely, the triad of good thoughts, good words, and good deeds. Thus we can see the strong emphasis on what is "good" both at the inception of Zoroastrianism through the teachings of its founder and in the lives of its modern practitioners.

History and Beliefs

Though the faith of modern Zoroastrians is deeply rooted in the teachings of Zoroaster, it is not fully clear when and where he actually lived, and scholars continue to wrestle with these enigmas even to this day. Concerning the time frame of his life, various ancient sources give significantly different dates. For instance, there are dates that are simply not believable such as a tradition ascribed to Aristotle that would place Zoroaster's life at about the year 6000 BC. Still, despite the ambiguities involved, modern scholars have generally settled on two possible eras for his life, specifically (1) the later part of the second millennium BC, say, 1500 to 1000 BC (the time of Moses and the Judges in the Bible), or (2) approximately 700 to 500 BC, the era of prophets such as Jeremiah, Isaiah, Daniel, and others portrayed in the biblical text. Either way, perhaps the most accurate general statement that can be made is that the religion is *about* 3,000 years old, as suggested by the UNESCO declaration that marked the years 2002–3 as the three-thousandth anniversary of Zoroastrian religion and culture, which was celebrated by a number of Zoroastrian communities around the world.[4]

Regarding Zoroaster's homeland, his forefathers originally shared a common culture with the ancestors of the people who are known today as Hindus; but the two groups diverged, with Zoroaster's predecessors migrating toward what became Iran, and the other group moving into what became India. Scholars are therefore able to place his native soil in the general area of central Asia—that is, modern-day eastern Iran and areas immediately to the north and east of it, though the exact location of Zoroaster's homeland is still unknown.

In any case, Zoroaster's teachings eventually became a major influence during

9A. Zoroastrian Fire Temple, Southern California. Note the wording above the entrance. Photo by Joshua Caba. Used with permission.

the mighty Persian Empire, which began around 550 BC and continued until the empire was conquered by Alexander the Great in 330 BC. Following this conquest, Zoroastrianism continued to flourish for more than 1,000 years through subsequent Iranian kingdoms in the region until the Muslim invasion in the middle of the seventh century AD. Eventually, for various reasons—particularly Muslim dominance and the desire for economic and community survival—a number of Zoroastrians migrated to the Gujarat area of western India, and here the migrating wing of the faith became known as the "Parsis" (i.e., people from Persia). Thus there are two primary geographic areas from which the modern Zoroastrian faith emerged, ancient Persia (modern Iran) and India.

Today, the Zoroastrian faith is one of the lesser world religions numerically, with one source indicating a worldwide population of just 111,691 in 2012.[5] As such, it is possible that most people around the globe have never met a Zoroastrian. Yet if you have ever been in a sports arena and heard the distinctive sound that starts with a simple stomp-stomp-clap followed by the crowd singing "We will, we will, rock you," you have heard a rendition of a song by the rock group Queen, whose lead vocalist, Freddie Mercury, grew up in the Parsi Zoroastrian tradition in Zanzibar, East Africa. (His given name was Farrokh Bulsara.) On the other hand, if rock is not your preferred musical genre, you can always turn to the classical music conducted by the famous maestro Zubin Mehta, a former music director of the New York Philharmonic Orchestra, who was also born into a Parsi Zoroastrian family. In effect, Zoroastrianism, though a small faith that is rooted in antiquity, has now spread around the modern world. Moreover, some claim that it has had a large impact on other faiths, including Judaism, Christianity, and Islam—a topic to be examined in more detail later in this chapter.

In general, Zoroastrianism is a long-standing faith with a strong ethical message, but what are the other essential components of the faith? What, for example, do Zoroastrians believe about God or gods, about humanity, or about life after death? Obviously, it is difficult to speak of Zoroastrianism as an entirely monolithic worldview with all persons agreeing on all issues. Nonetheless, we can explore some of the main contours of various Zoroastrian beliefs, around which there seems to be much agreement.

In a round-about manner, I encountered one such belief during a lunch I had with a Zoroastrian priest. We were a group of five who had decided to dine together at a local restaurant, including me, the priest, a young PhD in mathematics, a software engineer, and a young man studying for the Zoroastrian priesthood. As our conversation progressed, we naturally turned to the subject of religion, the existence of God, and so forth. Our interaction was quite friendly, and it turned out that four of the five in the group were believers in a single supreme God. The lone holdout was the young mathematician; he was not necessarily an atheist, just a curious seeker with questions and comments. As the conversation continued, what eventually struck me was the fact that the two Zoroastrians and the two Christians (myself and the software engineer) held comparable views on the issue of the existence and nature of God, using similar language and reasoning to present our opinions. As it turns out, Christianity and Zoroastrianism do, in fact, share a common conviction in what is technically known as "monotheism," the belief in one God, with the name of the Zoroastrian divinity being "Ahura Mazda," the Wise Lord.[6]

Ahura Mazda and the Amesha Spentas

Further, it seems that monotheism is one of the main theological developments that is traced to Zoroaster, who stood against the common viewpoint of his day—that is, the belief in multiple divine beings. Thus Zoroaster is thought of by some of his adherents as a revolutionary, one who transformed the course of his culture—so much so that his changes touched the participants in a lunch table discussion thousands of years later on the other side of the globe. The teachings ascribed to Zoroaster are also thought to have influenced kings of ancient Iran, such as Darius I, who ruled the Persian Empire (522–486 BC) and had the following inscribed above his tomb carved into a sheer cliff face near the ancient capital of Persepolis: "A great god is Ahuramazda, who created this earth, who created yonder sky, who created man, who created happiness for man, who made Darius king..."[7]

However, although Zoroastrianism is commonly described as a monotheistic faith, it has a number of aspects that distinguish it from the other monotheistic religions. For instance, in the Zoroastrian universe, Ahura Mazda is associated with six "Amesha Spentas," sometimes translated as "Holy Immortals."[8] One Zoroastrian author explains these as "six abstract concepts, essences or aspects of Ahura Mazda, the divinity, through which he is known. Though abstract ideals, they are personalized in the style of the religious poetry of the day."[9] Each of these six Amesha Spentas has an individual quality and is associated with a part of creation.

While these six[10] are often thought of as "essences" or "aspects" of Ahura Mazda himself, some speak of the Amesha Spentas as if they were entities with their own separate existence, having been individually created by Ahura Mazda, but nevertheless separate in a manner that has been compared to that of an archangel in the Christian tradition. Accordingly, as is common to many religious groups, there exists some internal dissonance regarding the precise nature of the divine realm—that is, the relationship between Ahura Mazda and the Amesha Spentas; specifically, are the Amesha Spentas simply aspects of Ahura Mazda or separate beings brought forth by him?[11]

Of additional interest is the fact that within Zoroastrian monotheism, there has historically been room for the dispersal of worship in directions other than expressly toward Ahura Mazda, which is an openness not commonly encountered in other monotheistic traditions—or at least not in their familiar "orthodox" expressions. For example,

AMESHA SPENTAS		
Name	**Idea**	**Associated creation**
Asha Vahishta	The highest truth	Fire
Vohu Manah	The good mind	Animal kingdom
Spenta Armaiti	Holy devotion, rightmindedness	Earth
Kshathra Vairya	Divine strength/power	Sky/metals
Haurvatat	Complete well-being	Water
Ameretat	Immortal bliss	Plant kingdom

one of the most ancient Zoroastrian texts says, "And now we worship this earth which bears us..." with the "earth" referenced being connected to Spenta Armaiti, one of the Amesha Spentas noted above.[12] In addition to the Amesha Spentas, there is another group of beings known as "Yazatas," who are designated as "beings worthy of worship."[13] Given this potential for the distribution of worship to various entities other than Ahura Mazda, one modern scholar has made the following interesting point concerning the nature of Zoroastrian monotheism:

> It seems to be the case, however, that the Zoroastrian model has been historically capable of encompassing many different dimensions that would ordinarily seem to be incompatible with the concept of monotheism. Nowadays, a more rigid understanding of monotheism has been adopted by many Zoroastrians, perhaps due to the impact of the other monotheistic religions of the Near East. Such standardization of theological terminology tends to leave no room for a broader definition.[14]

Along these same lines of openness, the Persian king Darius I, who declared that Ahura Mazda had created the earth, also authored an inscription in which he prayed that Ahura Mazda and "all the gods" would give him aid.[15] Thus Zoroastrian monotheism has exhibited its own unique nature over time—namely, the potential for a wider scope of worship than is typically the case in other monotheistic traditions. This feature was observed by the ancient Greek historian Herodotus, who said that the ancient Persians, in addition to worshiping the sky, also made offerings to "the sun and moon, to the earth, to fire, to water, and to the winds."[16]

Dualism

But the story of the Zoroastrian view of the heavenly realm does not stop there; in fact, one of the aspects of the faith that has become fairly well known—and is sometimes misunderstood—is its dualistic nature. Stepping back for a moment, when taken in its full-blown sense, the idea of dualism often means that there are two *equally* powerful and eternal forces that stand behind and operate within the universe and that our cosmos are essentially a meeting point between them, oftentimes as a battlefield. However, even though there are various schools of thought within the faith, normative Zoroastrianism—especially in its modern expression—rejects this idea of a thoroughgoing dualism and insists that Ahura Mazda is ultimately supreme. Still, there are dualistic aspects to the faith in the (1) *ethical* realm and in the (2) *cosmic* realm, though, again, in both instances, these dualisms should not be understood in the sense of an endless, equally balanced struggle.

In the *ethical* realm, Zoroastrian moral philosophy presents a clear conflict between good and evil; indeed, this ethical dualism and the mandate that humans participate in the promotion of the good is at the very heart of the Zoroastrian faith, and this is true regardless of the divergences of opinion on other matters. Beginning with Ahura Mazda as the supreme God, Zoroastrian ethical dualism envisions Spenta Mainyu, the good spirit, doing battle against Angra Mainyu, the evil spirit. Often, Spenta Mainyu is depicted as the inner force of Ahura Mazda himself, and at other times "as more of a separate power belonging to Ahura Mazda and also to humanity."[17] In any case, "The destructive evil spirit (*Angra Mainyu*) which opposes the beneficial spirit (*Spenta Mainyu*) is in constant conflict to capture the soul and mind of men, creating an ethical dualism."[18]

Concerning *cosmic* dualism, Zoroastrians use a dualistic approach in an attempt to answer the question of the source of evil as well as the reason for pain and suffering in the world. In Zoroastrian cosmic dualism, the origin of evil comes first through the incursion of Angra Mainyu into the created world; and this leads to not only the ethical conflict of good and evil but also the destructive forces in the material world, such as earthquakes, tornados, and so on. One author writes, "In the cosmic realm, Spenta Mainyu makes the good creation prosper, while Angra Mainyu, by its evil nature destroys the good creation of Ahura Mazda. This is cosmic dualism."[19] In effect, Zoroastrianism is dualistic in the ethical realm when it comes to good versus evil, and it is dualistic in the cosmic realm when explaining the existence of evil and disastrous occurrences in the natural world, but neither of these should be understood as a full-fledged dualism between equally powerful opposing forces.

Asha

But again, there is more to the story than just straight-up fights between good and evil; and with this next step into Zoroastrian doctrine, we discover "the axis around which the ethics of Zarathustra and the entire structure of his philosophical system revolves."[20] This fundamental axis is the idea of "Asha," which is often translated as "righteousness" in English texts, but includes much more than is contained in this single English word. As such, an explanatory quotation is in order.

> The Cosmic Law of Asha. In his Gathas, Asha is the divine law of God governing the universe. Zarathustra states that just as there are physical laws that govern the material universe—the movement of stars, gravity, evolution, etc.—there are corresponding laws governing relationships in the human arena. Both these laws exist, whether we obey them or not. Good and evil...are in reality, adherence to or deviation from the Law of Asha. In the physical world, examples of evil are earthquakes or volcanic eruptions. In the spiritual world, good and evil are not primordial entities, but the product of the human mind.[21]

As can be seen, Asha is the very created order of Ahura Mazda himself, both morally and materially, though corruption has crept into our world and now the dualisms are in play.

In addition, it is essential to understand that Asha is not simply an abstract ethical concept at the center of Zoroastrian beliefs: Its continued maintenance in a morally divided cosmos is the very goal of Zoroastrian practice in everyday life, and this preservation and perpetuation is important not only for the individual but for all of human society—and the entirety of creation as well. Starting with the idea that humans exist in a morally divided cosmos, people are expected to listen clearly, to think for themselves, and to ultimately choose good. In individual life, judgment after death occurs "at the Crossing-place of the Account-Keeper" at which "the thoughts, words and behavior of each 'breath soul' are tallied" with the result being that "the good receive a good reward, but the bad come to a bad end."[22] Further,

> There is no concept of redemption or intercession; and in the original teaching, there is no place for a plea of mercy. No person is regarded as intrinsically perverse. We are creatures of intrinsic free will. We make of ourselves what we choose and arrive at the appropriate ultimate consequences thereof. Such is

> the doctrine of the faith of Zarathustra—an essentially ethical religion.[23]

Thus individuals have a pathway laid out before them to reach the highest reward on a personal level.

Further, according to Zoroastrian texts, every human is also called to participate in the restoration of the full cosmos; indeed, "Ahura Mazda is a progressive God, who has created a dynamic universe in which everything is in progression toward perfection."[24] How, it might be asked, do humans participate in this progression to wholeness and incorruptibility of the entire creation? In answering this question, we have come full circle to the central tenet of the faith—that is, to good thoughts, good words, and good deeds. In essence, at the core of the faith, there is the idea that if humans, using their unconstrained free will, choose to follow the correct path, it will lead not only to "individual growth and increase, but also to the reinvigoration and healing of the natural world."[25] In other words, humanity can "help Ahura Mazda on the road of evolution" as it pertains to the perfection of both individual humans and all of the created reality.[26]

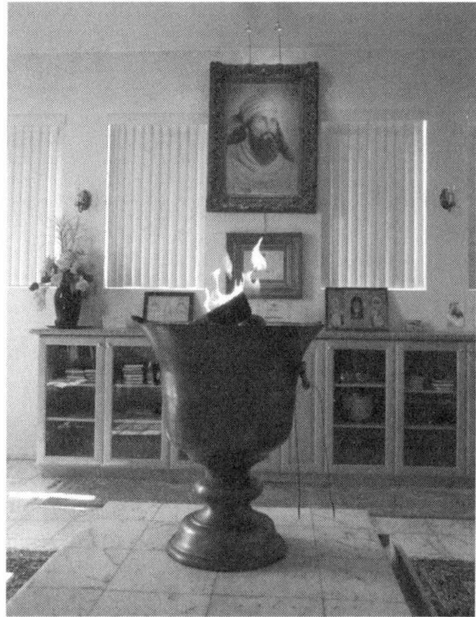

9B. Zoroastrian fire. Photo by Michael J. Caba. Used with permission.

The Religion in Practice

Yet despite these lofty ideas, Zoroastrianism is more than an ethical system designed to mend the world, a fact that was poignantly brought home to me during a visit to a Zoroastrian fire temple. My Zoroastrian guide and I were sitting in the inner sanctuary of the temple, staring at the fire, when I noticed a woman across the room also peering into the flame. The room itself was roughly the size of a standard living room, quite clean, with a picture of Zoroaster on the wall and a cabinet holding various types of religious reading material below the picture. But it was the woman, not the fire or the inanimate objects, I have thought about most since leaving that temple. Not wanting to breach any manner of proper etiquette, I didn't stare at her at length, but a glance or two told enough of the story to suggest that there was an earnest clamor in her soul. She sat bent over just a bit, closed into herself in posture, with a face that was drawn but aware. We were of no interest to her, for she appeared to be in prayer about some personal matter that was unrelated to us. Whatever the cause—perhaps the death of a loved one, anxiety about a family member, or some physical affliction—she was engrossed by the fire and her inner thoughts in a manner akin to many others around the world who cry out for help from on high. Indeed, though Zoroastrianism can lay claim to a weighty theological and philosophical heritage, it is also a religion of everyday people—people who hurt, pray, and have rituals and all manner of other customs and accoutrements with which they adorn their daily lives, and this fact was singularly portrayed by this one quiet, solitary woman in prayer.

Fire Temples

Why do Zoroastrians pray in front of a fire, and more broadly, why does fire take such a central place in the Zoroastrian tradition that their places of worship each contain a central flame within its confines? This mingling of fire and worship reaches back into antiquity. For example, as previously noted, Zarathustra's Iranian forefathers at one time formed a single culture with Indic people who paid homage to a fire god known as Agni, and reverence for fire still forms an important part of modern Hindu worship. Further, Herodotus also makes mention of a deeply rooted Persian reverence for fire, stating, "The Persians hold fire to be a god, and never by any chance burn their dead."[27] Nonetheless, even with this reverential attitude toward fire in the historical record, and despite the fact that Zoroastrian places of worship are now referred to as fire temples, it is abundantly clear that the faithful do not actually worship the fire. Indeed, Zoroastrian texts state this in unmistakable terms, and descriptive names such as "fire-worshippers" that are sometimes applied to the group are both mistaken and derogatory.[28] In point of fact, instead of being the direct object of worship, fire is simply seen as a symbol of Ahura Mazda, and "it is through the medium of a consecrated fire that a Zarathushti is able to develop an experiential link with the divinity."[29]

In the Zoroastrian classification, there are three levels of fire temples, each distinguished by the degree of consecration of the fire. The highest grade of fire (and fire temple) is known as an "Atash Bahram" (Victory Fire), in which the fire, consisting of flame from 16 different sources, has been taken through the requisite months-long process of elaborate and prayerful rituals. This grade of temple exists only in the city of Yazd, Iran, as well as in India. Next in line are the "Atash Adaran" (Fire of Fires) temples, which are established from fewer fires and fewer ritual ceremonies than the Atash Bahram, and these, too, are only located in Iran and the Indian subcontinent. Finally, an "Atash Dadgah" (which

9C. A well-kept Zoroastrian Fire Temple near San Jose, California. Photo by Michael J. Caba. Used with permission.

translates as "lawful place") fire is not necessarily consecrated, and the flame may not necessarily burn at all times. These last fires, which are at a similar grade to the fires kept burning in private homes, are located in the ancestral areas of the faithful and elsewhere in the Zoroastrian diaspora, including the United States and the United Kingdom.

Priests

Tending to the fires and performing rituals in the temples are Zoroastrian priests, who trace their spiritual lineage back to the time of Zoroaster himself. In addition to this spiritual heritage, the office of priest has also traditionally been one of physical heredity that has seen a father passing the title to his son. The priests, also known as "mobeds," have at times (e.g., during the Sasanian period) held positions of prominence in society. Yet in the modern era, "many Zoroastrians are painfully aware that the role of priests as perpetuators of the religion through counseling and teaching the laity, performing ritual and mentoring and training other priests is challenged through the lack of numbers."[30] Still, despite their diminished numbers, the central role played by the priests in ritual performance remains crucial—with ceremonies separated into two categories: (1) inner rituals performed within the confines of the fire temple and (2) outer rituals performed in such community spaces as the home or meeting halls. Of additional interest is the fact that a recent survey of priests about the ideal qualities to properly perform the duties of their office revealed that "sincerity, honesty and dedication" were believed to be important, which again points to the religion's emphasis on ethical comportment.[31]

Avesta

One of the tasks historically undertaken by the Zoroastrian priests has been the transmission and dissemination of the sacred texts of the faith that are collectively known as the Avesta. These scriptures contain many genres and were transmitted orally from the era of Zoroaster onward, or in written script beginning in the Sasanian era (AD 224–651). Some of the language contained in the oldest sections of the Avesta indicate a late second-millennium BC composition, a fact that tends to support the earlier of the aforementioned two dates for the life of Zoroaster.[32] For many modern Zoroastrians, the most important texts of the Avesta are the *Gathas*, which are five songs attributed to Zarathustra. In fact, of all the Avestan texts, only the *Gathas* are ascribed to Zarathustra directly. The word *Gatha* means "song," and the five songs are further subdivided into 17 sections.[33] They are "short verse texts, cast largely in the form of utterances addressed by [Zoroaster] to Ahura Mazda; and they convey, through inspired poetry, visions of God and his purposes, and prophesies of things to come, here and hereafter."[34] Because of their origin in deep antiquity and the difficulties in understanding the language in which they were originally composed, the *Gathas* are challenging to translate. Yet for many Zoroastrians, they form the foundation of faith. The following quote is a brief excerpt:

> I who have attuned my soul
> to Good Thoughts
> know that actions
> in the name of Ahura Mazda
> have their rewards.
> So, as long as I have the will
> and the strength, I shall teach others
> to strive for Righteousness
> (Song 1, verse 4).[35]

The Question of Influence

Based on the brief overview given above, it can be seen that the Zoroastrian faith has a rich theological heritage as well as committed followers striving toward ethical conduct. Yet given the rather small number of Zoroastrians, a reasonable question arises: Why would this belief system be given a full chapter in a book on world religions? Indeed, there are many denominations and subsects within larger faith traditions that significantly outnumber Zoroastrians, let alone the larger traditions themselves; so, from a purely practical perspective, why spend much time with this group?

To answer this question, we return to my good friend in the exercise facility at the beginning of this chapter. Prior to our previous related discussion, he had, in fact, already encountered Zoroastrianism, though not directly; instead, he heard about the faith in a college classroom setting. According to his retelling of the event, the professor attempted to explain that the Zoroastrian religion had been the original source for Christian beliefs my friend held dear. In the professor's viewpoint, the Judeo-Christian tradition is not necessarily based on a unique revelatory experience from God, but instead it has simply borrowed a number of its key doctrines from Zoroastrianism. This contention bothered my friend because it seemed to contradict his belief that the Judeo-Christian scriptures constitute a direct revelation from God that has not been mediated by anyone except the biblical authors themselves.

In fact, the belief that the Judeo-Christian tradition (and eventually Islam) borrowed much from Zoroastrianism is a noticeably thoroughgoing opinion in some circles, particularly those in academia. For example, one leading scholar has said, "Zoroastrianism is the oldest of the revealed credal religions, and it has probably had more influence on mankind, directly and indirectly, than any one single faith…Some of its leading doctrines were adopted by Judaism, Christianity and Islam."[36] Further, one text claims that

> there are five original ideas that arose from Zarathustra's teachings, that were absorbed into Judaism and then into Christianity and Islam: (1) the concept of a universal God, (2) the concept of existence of the soul after death, (3) the judgment of the soul after death, (4) the idea of a savior who will bring about the destruction of all evil, and (5) the idea of the final renovation of creation. These are fundamental contributions of the Zarathushti faith to the western world's religious ideas.[37]

Thus much of the heart and soul of Christianity, Judaism, and Islam is said to stem from Zoroastrianism.

On the other hand, the precise origin of many of these beliefs, and their subsequent migration from culture to culture, is a matter of considerable conjecture, disagreement, and debate among scholars. For example, the belief in "Aten" as the supreme God by the Egyptian pharaoh Akhenaten was once claimed by Sigmund Freud to be the true precursor to biblical monotheism. Freud wrote, "The kernel of our thesis, the dependence of Jewish monotheism on the monotheistic episode in Egyptian history, has been guessed and hinted at by several workers."[38] This is not to say that Freud's view is credible, but in view of such beliefs as this, one wonders why it is concluded with such *certainty* that the Judeo-Christian worldview obtained its monotheistic viewpoint from Zoroastrianism if others have found it entirely plausible to find an altogether different source for the very same belief.

Further, these borrowing theories often rely on dating schemes for the biblical writings (e.g., late dates) that appear to flourish within the very same schools of thought that advocate for the borrowing theories but are strongly challenged by others. As such, it goes without saying that a good bit of speculation is in play with these types of endeavors, and none of the large-scale cultural appropriation models are anything more than conjecture. Certainly, none are proven.

Nonetheless, it is likely that some modest exchange of ideas did occur between the ancient Persians and Jews. First of all, these two peoples had direct contact with one another, as is portrayed in such biblical texts as Ezra, Nehemiah, and Esther. Further, the "strongest evidence" for the belief in Persian influence on Judaism comes from a single Persian word for the name of a demon in the book of Tobit, which, though Jewish, is not part of the Hebrew Bible.[39] Additional inferences have been made along various lines. Nevertheless, despite some minor interplay, no direct evidence exists in the material at hand of a fully cut-and-paste project between faiths. As a result, one eminent historian has indicated that "not a few scholars have concluded that the earlier claims for the decisive influence of Persian beliefs on Judaism have been overvalued."[40]

Still, those of the Christian persuasion may need to adjust some aspects of their view of other religions in light of a close consideration of some New Testament texts. In this regard, we note that the writers of the New Testament did utilize other religions and philosophies in making their theological points. For example, in his speech to the Areopagus in Athens concerning the true nature of God as recorded in Acts 17:28, the Apostle Paul quotes from two non-Christian sources when he says, "'For in him we live and move and have our being.' As some of your own poets have said, 'We are his offspring'" (NIV). The first of these quotes is from a Cretan philosopher Epimenides, and the second is from the Cilician philosopher Aratus.[41] One can also consider the story of the Magi coming from the East to honor Christ at His birth (Matthew 2:1-12) as a testament by a biblical author to the fact that those outside his own tradition were more up to speed with the things of God than His own people. It is true that some have suggested that the Magi were Zoroastrian in heritage,[42] though this is unclear. However, if they were Zoroastrian, then it is also clear that they recognized the distinction and authenticity of the Jewish tradition in and of itself.

In essence, the New Testament recognizes the possibility that people outside the Judeo-Christian tradition may have some understanding of the truth, however abridged it may be. As a result, it would be fully in line with the scriptural pattern if some Zoroastrian thoughts were used by New Testament authors as support for their respective presentations; though interestingly enough, none are quoted in the text, and those who are claimed to have arrived via the channel of Judaism are conjectural and without empirical support. These facts suggest minimal, if any, Zoroastrian influence on Christianity; though it would not invalidate Christian beliefs if it had occurred. In reality, the New Testament was composed in a rich intellectual milieu, and the New Testament recognizes the fact that those outside the Judeo-Christian faith can know aspects of the truth, none of which undermined the security the authors felt in their own tradition. To them, the historical revelation of God in Christ was their central library of knowledge, to which others may add a few lines without altering the sovereignty of the core.

Thus it would seem that two misjudgments need to be avoided, specifically (1) the unsubstantiated claim of the wholesale derivation of significant aspects of the Jewish, Christian, and Islamic faiths from an alternative source other than what their respective followers have traditionally claimed, and (2) the belief that the biblical authors adhered to the idea that those outside their faith were fully devoid of any true understanding of the divine. If the two opposing positions are corrected, we are left with a small but evidentially authenticated space that contends that ordinary contact and interaction occurred between these various religious streams, but that nothing like a full-scale joining of these distinct waters transpired.

In summary, we can turn to a Zoroastrian scholar for a bit of wisdom and advice on the purported cross-pollination between these various theologies. Ali Makki says:

> Either in passing conversations or in various media we often hear of the attractive idea of influences of Zoroastrianism on other religions...But do we really know the extent and nature of these direct and indirect influences and how the original thoughts may have been transformed or altered in other religions after or even before they were borrowed?[43]

After a clear-cut presentation of the inherent weaknesses in the assertions of influence, Makki goes on to note that we are dealing with a "cloud of uncertainty" and that "in most instances it is truly difficult to take the notion of Zoroastrian influences on other belief systems at face value."[44] In light of this type of intellectual integrity and humility—traits we can find in those who claim to be seekers of the good in many traditions—nothing more needs to be added.

Conclusion

In conclusion, the Zoroastrians should, without question, be respected for their many good works. But there is one essential truth that Christians can add to the faith of their Zoroastrian friends—namely, the grace of God available through faith in Christ. For all its goodness, this is one missing element in Zoroastrianism, and this difference at the core of these two faiths shows convincingly that these two trees are truly of a different stock. With respect, Zoroastrians (and the rest of us, as well) should know that all their good works are not enough to make them righteous before God. In fact, Ephesians 2:8-9 is an appropriate conclusion to this chapter: "For it is by grace you have been saved, through faith—and this is not from yourselves, it is the gift of God—not by works, so that no one can boast" (NIV).

Michael Caba (Doctor of Arts, Harrison Middleton University) was one of the founders of Kilns College, where he served as an adjunct professor and Dean of Faculty. He has traveled widely, researching world religions, and has completed volunteer archaeology work in Israel. He has taught a number of classes over the years on modern philosophy, the Bible, and religious cultures for various organizations. He was previously a technical editor at *Artifax* magazine, the quarterly publication of the Near East Archaeological Society.

10

African Traditional

Anne Carlson Kennedy

One evening in Mali, when I was very small, I padded barefoot down the soft, dusty path in the growing twilight to the towering mango tree that stood halfway between my house and the mud-walled cluster of huts that made up the tiny Supyire village we were gradually getting to know.[1] I walked to the tree and then turned around and ran back, because I wasn't supposed to be out after sunset, especially in bare feet, lest I step on a scorpion, or worse. The next morning, a friend on his way to his field inquired if I had been out in the dark. "Someone thought he saw a djinn," explained our friend.

Djinn are very short, about the height of a small child, pale white, their feet pointing backward. They go about in the dusk, and you wouldn't want to accidentally meet one on the road. They are not necessarily malign, but they are tricksters. You might get caught up in one of their clever traps, in some kind of game that would bring you to ruin or some costly misery. You might be able to outsmart a djinn, but probably not. The Supyire folk tale of Piifungo, told by Ali Sanogo and Kutunucwo, illustrates the peril of ignoring the taboo to keep away from the places where they like to live.

Piifungo and the Helpful Jinns[2]

Long ago there was a certain place in the bush which people said no one should clear and make into a field. There was a man whose name was Piifungo. Piifungo refused to listen, and he went and got axes from the blacksmiths in order to clear that place. When he had got those axes, he went with his wife and children to clear that place in the bush. But that place belonged to some jinns. It was they who had said that no one should ever farm there. When Piifungo struck the first blow of the ax against a tree "cho!," the old man of the jinns said to the jinns, "Go out and chop the trees so Piifungo can rest." The jinns came out and chopped all the trees of that place for Piifungo.

Sometime later, when the wood had dried, Piifungo came to burn the trees. Then the old man of the jinns said again, "Go out and burn the trees so Piifungo can rest." They came out and set fire to all the trees, and all the trees were burned.

Later on, the rains came. Piifungo came with a big hoe. When he struck the first stroke of the hoe 'cha!' to turn the first mound, the old man of the jinns said, "Go out and prepare the field so Piifungo can rest." The jinns came out with big hoes and made mounds in the whole field.

When the mounds were made, Piifungo took the seed gourd and went to begin sowing. He dug the first seed hole and put in the seed, and the old man of the jinns said, "Go out and sow the seed so Piifungo can rest." The jinns went out and sowed the whole field.

Later, the weeds began to grow in the field. Piifungo came with a small hoe to begin weeding the field. When he started weeding, the old man of the jinns said, "Go out and weed the field so Piifungo can rest." They came out and weeded the whole field.

Later on, the beans that Piifungo had planted began to spread out. Soon the bean vines were too thick, in Piifungo's opinion. He went to thin those bean vines, so that they would spread out well and bear lots of beans. When he pulled up the first vine, the old man of the jinns said, "Go out and pull up the bean vines so Piifungo can rest." They came out and pulled up all the bean vines in the field and came and piled them up next to Piifungo.

Later on, Piifungo said there were too many seedlings in the seed holes. He would pull some of them up so that the others could get big. The old man of the jinns said, "Go out and pull up the crop so Piifungo can rest." The jinns came out and pulled up the field's entire crop and piled it up. It wasn't yet ripe, but they pulled it all up. Piifungo's wife came, and the children, and they all sat down next to the pulled up grain plants and the dried bean vines, and they cried. The old man of the jinns said, "Go out and cry so Piifungo can rest." So the jinns came out to help Piifungo. They all sat there crying.

Then, Piifungo saw a mosquito on one of his little children. He went and hit the mosquito. Then the jinn said, "Go out and give the beating so Piifungo can rest." The jinns came out and hit the child for Piifungo, and they killed it.

Piifungo sat down and cried again. Then another mosquito came and sat on the other little child and he hit that mosquito too. The jinn said again, "Go out and give the beating so Piifungo can rest." The jinns fell on that other little child and hit it for Piifungo and killed it.

Piifungo and his wife sat down and cried. Then another mosquito came and sat on Piifungo's wife herself, and she hit it. When she hit the mosquito, the jinns said, "Go out and give the beating so Piifungo can rest." The jinns came and hit the woman and killed her for Piifungo.

If you see people have stopped putting their fields in places where there are lots of trees, one of the reasons is this. Some stubborn people used to refuse to listen and they would clear a place belonging to the jinns and make it into a field. But what happened to Piifungo made the people afraid of places belonging to jinns.

History and Beliefs

A Definition

Human beings are, by nature, religious—searching for the sublime in the anxieties of life, trying to make sense of the ephemeral nature of time, grasping the riches of this mortal sphere before they disappear forever, coping, as theologian Langdon Gilkey says, with "the feeling of dependence and contingency, of being subject to uncontrollable forces...the experience of temporality and mortality, of an approaching 'deadline to one's powers and life.'"[3] Humanity reaches to the heavens and then, failing to ascend, looks down and into the grave, stretching back into the past and forward into the future for meaning.

The traditional religions of Africa are no different: They are attempts to understand the creation and existence of the cosmos, to face death, to explain trouble, and to combat evil. Even now, as Islam and Christianity have gone into every corner of the continent, shaping the destinies and outlook of almost every African society, there remain the deeply traced streambeds of an ancient African religious philosophy. African Traditional Religion (hereafter ATR) is the term used to refer to the broad scope of pre-Christian and pre-Islamic religious and philosophical worldviews indigenous to and spanning the whole continent of Africa south of the Sahara Desert.

It is difficult to miss the presumptuous nature of this attempt to sweep up into one heap the whole religious expression of a continent so wide, so diverse, possessed of so many different languages and systems of thought. Providentially, out of decades of ethnological research certain common themes emerge.[4] As we look at African cosmologies, time, humanity's relationship to God, the realm of the spirits and ancestors, the question of magic, the place of diviners, and the hope of Christianity for Africa, the first step is to discover that "in Africa, religion does not represent a philosophy of life that searches for ultimate meaning, as it does for many Western Christians today. Rather, it represents a view of life that acknowledges the existence of an invisible world, believed to be inhabited by spiritual forces that are deemed to have effective powers over one's life."[5]

What Is God Like?

As John Mbiti notes, "God is not a stranger to African peoples, and in traditional life there are no atheists."[6] But what kind of God is he?[7] Is he benevolent? Remote? Concerned with the affairs of humanity? Does he do anything?

While for the traditional African there are many ways of looking at God, I will focus on two. The first view arises from Mbiti and Bolaji Idowu's herculean labor to describe ATR on its own terms, which arose out of a desire to lift ATR out of a colonial, and often racist, mire of misconceptions. This view nonetheless takes the Western dichotomy between immanence and transcendence and imposes it over the African view of God. Desiring to militate against negative stereotypes of paganism, animism, and ancestor worship, Mbiti and Idowu defined God as essentially transcendent, as a Westerner would understand that term, who becomes immanent through the work and mediation of the spirits.[8] Mbiti writes:

> For most of their life, African peoples place God in the transcendental plane, making it seem as if He is remote from their daily affairs...But they know that He is immanent, being manifested in natural objects and phenomena, and they turn to Him in acts of worship, at any place and time. The distinction

> between these related attributes could be stated that, in theory God is transcendental but in practice He is immanent.[9]

This view corresponds superficially with the fact that many groups appear to conflate the concept of God with the sky, using the same word for both. God used to live very close to the earth, but then retreated and can no longer be directly encountered.[10] This is not to say God *is* the sky, but rather that he is fundamentally associated with the place where he lives.[11] Remote and yet often referred to in blessings—"May God/Sky make it go well"—God is transcendent and sovereign. Certainly, while it would not be exactly wrong to think of God in these categories, they do not get to the heart of the African worldview.

The second view is one of *holism*. People, animals, spirits, ancestors, and even God, all exist in one unbroken holistic hierarchy.[12] They are connected to each other, and this connection is constantly reinforced by the hierarchical order in which they are placed. There is no insurmountable separation, then, between God and any portion of the created order. When some ancestral spirit is appealed to for help or succor, that being can be counted on because of his connection to all the other spirits and ultimately to God. Yusufu Turaki writes:

> The question of a direct or indirect approach to the worship of God does not even arise. Rather, the assumption is that if God is active behind the various gods and divinities, He is automatically also approached when they are approached. Both the Supreme Being and the lesser beings are part of the same cosmic community.[13]

Look again at those same blessings, and you will see a whole spiritual community. May God make it go well. May God bring the rain. May God give health. May God give the money. God is invoked in an ultimate sense, with the trust that other spirits and forces are part of that invocation. A Westerner looking at the diffused, dispersed way that the African orders his material and spiritual world would imagine that there were many different, unrelated powers or actions, but this is not so.[14]

> Africans do not live in a confused world of non-integrated parts. Life is mysterious, but it is part of a whole. And that whole is governed by a law of harmony, the goal of which is to maintain a state of agreement or peacefulness. The traditional African seeks to live in harmony and to balance his life in a harmonious and peaceful existence with his entire world and especially with the spirit world.[15]

It is a spirit world that is connected to, rather than alienated from, God. It is essential to see this connection because, while the Westerner separates the physical/material from the spiritual, the secular from the religious, the family from the state, and the community from the individual in his negotiations with the world, for the traditional African, none of these separations exist. Kwame Bediako contends, quoting Harold Turner, "Man lives 'in a sacramental universe where there is no sharp dichotomy between the physical and the spiritual.' The physical acts as a vehicle for spiritual power whilst the physical realm is held to be patterned on the model of the spiritual world beyond."[16]

A helpful way of thinking about the difference between the way a traditional African might think of the universe and the way a Westerner would is to flip over, as Arnold Meiring did, the proverb "as above so below," rendering it, "as below so above." The weight of what God is doing is down here in this realm.[17] This is a reversed, though still hierarchical, order. Distinct beings within an ordered cosmos are so connected that each determines the behavior and destinies of the others. God may feel far away, but the very fact of human community makes him present.[18]

The tension or balance between holism and hierarchy will become crucial when we come to consider the human community and how it is ordered. God is not disconnected from that order. Indeed, he is supreme over it.

What Does God Do?

God created the world, and many traditional societies employ vividly physical metaphors for that creation—clay pots, the ground, or the weather, for example. Mbiti's comprehensive research across Africa is invaluable here. Investigating the Akan people, he discovered they use a word for God that means "Excavator, Hewer, Carver, Creator, Originator, Inventor, Architect."[19] Likewise, looking at the language and customs of the Banyarwanda, he discovered, "Women of child-bearing age are careful to leave water ready, before they go to bed, so that God may use it to create children for them. It is known as 'God's water'; and He is known as 'the Giver of children.'"[20] "Ila have three names for God by means of which they describe His creative work. They speak of Him as Creator, Moulder and Constructor."[21] This divine characteristic of creator pervades Africa and lends each culture a particular flavor.[22]

Outflowing from God's creative work is his provident care for and ordering of that creation. Mbiti writes, "The Ashanti believe that God 'created things in an ordered fashion,' and made an orderly and harmonious world where everyone could perform his own duties."[23] Likewise, "the Ovimbundu name for God means 'He who supplies the needs of His creatures.'"[24]

Africans, moreover, acknowledge their dependence on a God who creates and organizes. They value his gifts of children, fertile land, and the weather they need to grow food, particularly the rain: "Rain is, however, the most widely acknowledged token of God's providence. To African peoples, rain is always a blessing, and its supply is one of the most important activities of God."[25]

The chief creation of God, however, is humanity. ATR is deeply anthropocentric. Man is the center of the universe of which he is a part. His place within the cosmos is not directed toward the heavens as much as it is rooted in the ground where his ancestors are buried. He cannot go outside of this realm, but neither does he want to. God has given everything needful for his well-being—rain, earth, birth, death, ancestors, rituals, and the rhythm of life that connects him not just to his own self but to a long, far-reaching family of ever-loving spirits and ancestors.

Humanity and the Fall

Nevertheless, despite the unbroken circle that binds all of creation together, pragmatically, it is acknowledged that God is not close by:[26]

> But while everywhere there seems to be an underlying conviction that such a God *is*, it is accompanied, and usually overwhelmed, by the pragmatic knowledge that such a God has gone away. The African myth does not tell of men driven from Paradise, but of

> God disappearing from the world. It is man, not God, whose voice calls through the desolate garden, Where art thou?[27]

The severed relationship between God and the people of the earth is told in many ways. One society blames man for asking too often for help.[28] For another, it was the smoke from men's fire that drove God away.[29] "The Banyarwanda," writes Mbiti, "tell that when a woman decided to hide death, contrary to God's law not to do so, He decided to let men keep death, and so death has ever since remained with men."[30] The Supyire say that the first woman became irritated with God, who lived quite close to her hut. She "took her hot stir-stick and climbed up on the roof of her house and touched it against the sky/God, who was burned and offended and hence retreated." Now he never comes down here.[31]

However it came about, mankind was separated from God, and that division continues to be felt and must be superseded through various practical methods (as we shall see below). It is therefore incorrect to say, as some do, that the traditional African has no sense of sin. On the contrary, the idea of sin is expressed so plainly that many Westerners simply miss it. John Taylor articulates three kinds of sin experienced by the African. The first is the anxious preservation of a harmonious life here and now. The work to maintain peaceful order, and the many means by which repairs are made, speaks to a powerful sense of ruin.[32] The second is the prevalence of shame-and-honor cultures among African societies (see below).[33] The third is that the self, for many Africans, is frequently "externalized":

> Because of the different "myth" of human nature in which each lives, the European represses the things in himself that he is afraid of, the African projects them. The European is on guard against the self he has battened down in his own mind; the African is on guard against the self he has externalized into the world around.[34]

In illustration of the difference between internal and external causes, here is a description of the main road near the village where I grew up:

> There have recently been three accidents involving trucks at a particular place on the highway ten kilometers from where we live. To our Western eyes, this spot on the road seems potentially dangerous, because there is a curve, and a rise, and a steep embankment on one side of the road. Nevertheless, hundreds of vehicles get past it without mishap. We are inclined to attribute the recent accidents to such factors as incompetence on the part of drivers (driving too fast, falling asleep at the wheel, doing drugs) or their assistants (loading the back so that the load shifts, failure to repair the truck correctly). The rumor going the rounds among our neighbors, however, is that a particularly malignant *jinà* has taken up residence there and will continue to cause these accidents.[35]

Disharmony and disorder exist, certainly, as powerful forces in the ordinary lives of men and women, but their cause is not very often located inside of the self. Moral or ethical behavior can appear to be location specific and not universal. As we saw in the folk tale of poor Piifungo, he did not observe the taboo against cultivating where the djinn live.

The narration indicates no particular concern for the state of his interior sinful inclinations, or what one might call his heart. Why he did not adhere to the taboo is not of prevailing interest. The outcome—losing everything—points to the story's status as a cautionary tale.

To repair the breach, if that were possible, the offender, Piifungo in this case, would have to first discover what went wrong. He would need a diviner or a medium to find out what happened. It would not be immediately clear to him what he had done or what had been done by another. He would not look inward and measure his heart against some objective standard, but he would examine his spiritual neighborhood. It would be wrong, however, to imagine that what he discovered there was arbitrary or even, to an outsider, untrue. The mythological and symbolic expressions of sin and evil, though external and at times many, point to the internal quality of a person's nature, almost never in an individual sense, but always in how they related to others: "The essence of sin in the primal view is that it is anti-social."[36] Piifungo has lost that which is most precious—not his own sense of himself, but his family and his field.

A diviner, in trying to discern what has gone wrong through locating and remedying some evil for an individual or group, will rely on the metaphors of overshadowing, heaviness or weight, heat, and dirt. Many rituals, sacrifices, remedies against cursing, confessions of witchcraft, and other kinds of mediation all relate directly to these four ways of understanding sin. Cooling the stomach, taking some medicine to cool the mind, undertaking a ritual sacrifice or bath to cleanse away dirt, escaping from an evil "shadow" or overshadowing, finding ways to "lighten" the heart, or fleeing from some heaviness, are all part of escaping from the power of sin and evil.[37]

We cannot go much further without venturing into the spiritual realm that occupies what Paul Hiebert calls the "excluded middle."[38]

Spirits and Ancestors

The modern Westerner conceives of the self as an atom in the cosmic void that comprises space and reality. Brought about by chance and gone in the blink of an eye, increasingly humanity's very existence throws the earth itself into peril. In Western thought, the moral person will not materially extend the trace of the self upon the environment and ought to think twice before bearing and raising children. The African, in contrast, sees a world full of spiritual beings. The individual is caught in a web of relationships, not only material and temporal, but immaterial, eternal, stretching backward and forward in time.

These mystical and spiritual powers are knowable. They affect every course and action of each person's life. God gives life, but it is the spirits and ancestors who determine where each one will go. In this way of thinking, your life force is given and sustained by those buried under your feet, and they dominate the natural world. These spiritual entities have the power to give you a name, protect you from evil, govern what you will eat and drink, and order your relationships. This might seem like the sort of guidance and direction that you would be expected to want, but that is not always the case: "This belief is not a source of comfort but of fear, for it makes it difficult to distinguish between good and evil, thus fatalism dominates life."[39]

Spirits come in many different kinds, most often peculiar to the places they live. There are the small localized djinn,[40] guardian spirits,[41] the spirits of the witches,[42] and spirits born to die.[43] Robin Horton describes the categories of spirits of the Kalabari. The water spirits "are said to be 'like men, and also pythons.' They are the 'owners' of the creeks and swamps, the guardians of the fish harvest, the forces of nature."[44] Each kind of spirit in every place may be malign or benevolent.[45] An ordinary person wouldn't know. Some kind of expert divination would be required to discover if you had run afoul of a spirit or djinn. Essentially, Gerrie ter Haar concludes, "The moral nature of spirits traditionally [depends] largely on the quality of the relationship between the human and spirit world. For a prosperous and stable life, many Africans believe, humans need to maintain a good relation with the spirit world."[46]

In addition to location-bound spirits, the ancestors loom over everyday African life. Mbiti employs the term "the living-dead," disfavoring, for reasons of animist and colonialist connotations, the term "ancestors." I think, however, the term "ancestor" is currently more in favor, as language has shifted to accommodate new phenomena. Especially with the rise of apocalyptic zombie tropes, the term "living-dead" now has connotations Mbiti could not have foreseen. I think we might once again hear the term "ancestor" with fresh attention. Nevertheless, Mbiti's description is timeless:

> Because they are still "people," the living-dead are therefore the best group of intermediaries between men and God: they know the needs of men, they have "recently" been here with men, and at the same time they have full access to the channels of communicating with God directly or, according to some societies, indirectly through their forefathers. Therefore, men approach them more often for minor needs of life than they approach God. Even if the living-dead may not do miracles or extraordinary things to remedy the need, men experience a sense of psychological relief when they pour out their hearts' troubles before their seniors who have a foot in both worlds.[47]

To discover the nature of the ancestor, let us follow a man from his birth to his entrance into the land of the dead. Because he is an integrated person, bound holistically and hierarchically to God and to his community and to himself, he does not know himself apart from being known by others. Where a Westerner would say, "I think, therefore I am," an African "learns to say, I am because I participate. To him the individual is always an abstraction; Man is a family."[48]

Lifestyle and Culture

A Man on His Journey to the Dead

The custom, among the Supyire people of Mali, is that when you determine to go on a journey, you must first ask permission. "Give me the road" (*kuni kan*), you will say to all the people in your family and those to whom you owe some obligation. If you do not have some outstanding business or trouble, your family and friends will say, "There is the road." Then someone will go with you at least halfway to where you are going, before turning back and going home.[49]

Going from one place to another is, after all, a dangerous business. Poisonous snakes lurk. Stones obstruct the path. Unseen spirits, hoping not to be disturbed, inhabit streams and trees. It is not good to go alone. The journey to the land of the dead is no different: A man needs the whole community to bring him along. A child is not "incorporated into this human organism merely by birth...he is made a member by a series of mystically creative acts, each like a doorway leading into the next of a succession of rooms."[50] The first doorway is to be given a name.

Naming

At birth, a child is welcomed into a family and clan. The head of the family, "mediating between the living and the dead," might divine the name from the ancestors, who have given the soul of the child back to the land of the living.[51]

> The names of the ancestors are tried out in order, beginning with the recently deceased, until the baby indicates in some recognized manner that the choice is right. The shade of that particular ancestor is certainly regarded as taking on the guardianship of that child, and in many places, both in East and West Africa, the evidence points to a belief that, in an undefined way, the ancestor has been "restored" in the child.[52]

The naming practices of a group not only reflect the underlying theological myths that shape the communal mind but also set the child within his place in the family. P.T.W. Baxter's fascinating study of the Boran people in East Africa illustrates the central value of peace in every rite and ceremony, especially in the naming of a child:

> A *Jiila* [great festival] for an heir is held in the main when milk is abundant, and he can walk steadily...On the afternoon of the second day, the officiants, parents, and grandparents form a procession. All the males wearing check turbans and carrying their horsewhips and *danis* rods, file into the cattle enclosure. There the child's head is shaved with the exception of a small patch on the crown, *gutu*. The *gutu* is a symbol of virility which is not cut until that child himself, as an elderly man, "completes his head"...that is when he absolutely renounces virility for peace...Coffee beans are sacrificed, and the father names the child saying: Chosen name—thrive healthily.[53]

Rites of Passage

In childhood, this new member of the visible community will gradually be admitted to the ways of the communal family. His early life will unfold in a balance between dependence and responsibility. He will be instructed in the myths and genealogies of his clan. When he approaches puberty, he is, as he was at birth, once more in a precarious position. The rites and ceremonies he undergoes during this period are meant to settle him in his position as part of an unbroken family. In this transition, he risks becoming part of a "rising generation...tempted to anticipate its power by throwing off all parental control."[54] The community, then, must reassert his position, making him ready for his responsibilities to them and to his ancestors.[55] These rites and ceremonies will most likely include circumcision. He might undergo some kind of isolated trial in the wilderness. He will gradually be given secret knowledge. He may or may not be encouraged to experiment sexually with girls his age, depending on the mores of the group.[56]

In some places, there will be another initiation rite for men as old as 40 into the full secret knowledge of the clan. Thus he is welcomed into any number of secret societies—fetish groups, societies of hunters or blacksmiths, or other powerful groups that confer upon their devotees the practical aid of blood sacrifice, knowledge, and wealth.[57]

A Living Elder

Age, in Africa, is always a blessing. The older a man becomes, the more the community's respect for him grows. As our African traditionalist nears old age, he begins to be revered as a village elder. He will sit under the big tree in his courtyard, and young children will attend and wait on him. He will be consulted about matters of spiritual significance. His vast store of knowledge about family custom, taboos, rights, agriculture, the spirits and ancestors, and the life of his own clan make him an invaluable receptacle of knowledge and power.[58]

As he ages, he will become the head, or even chief, of his clan. As such, he may become the mediator between the living and the dead. It may be his job to perform important sacrifices. He may be the representative of the ancestors. In his connection to the ancestors, he may be "the fountain-head of the people's vitality." He may even be the mediator between man and the cosmos.[59] He may be believed to control the rain or other natural phenomena.[60] Finally, he may be called upon to perform some priestly function as head or elder of his clan.[61]

The Funeral

Nevertheless, his life is tenuous. As he nears his death, he must die peacefully and at home. He cannot die violently or in catastrophic circumstances:

> Another common requirement for a person to become an ancestor is that he or she must have died a "good death," not one caused by incurable sickness (such as leprosy, small pox, or AIDS), an accident, or violence. Most importantly, the deceased must transition at an old age, signifying wisdom and experience. In some societies, burials and formation of new ancestors are a

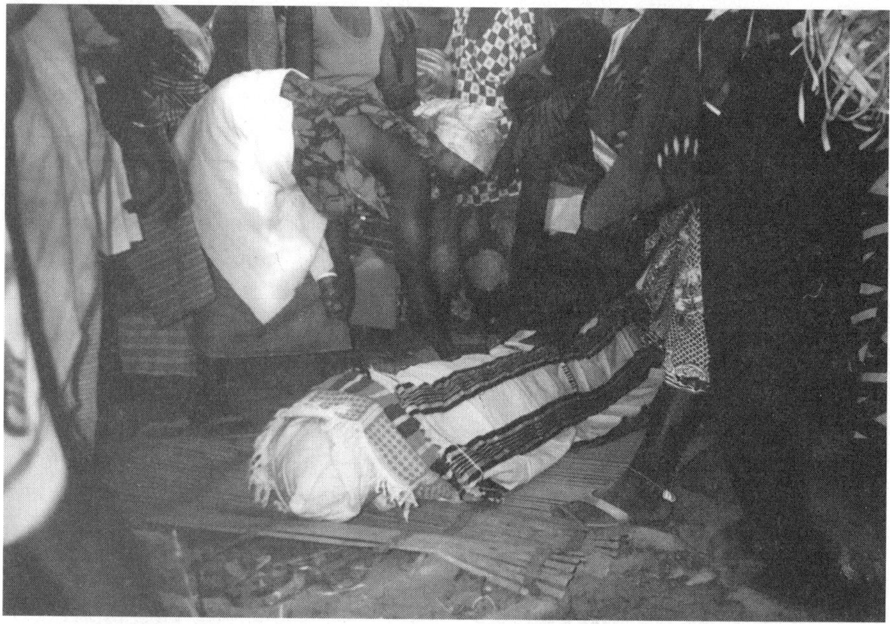

10A. A woman performing a funeral ritual over her mother. Photo by Anne Kennedy. Used with permission

> time of great instability. Great anxiety, confusion, and unpredictability infiltrate the Bambara of Mali. They consider death a liminal period when the fortunes of the deceased and his or her descendants are unpredictable.[62]

His family has to perform the complicated ritual of burying him precisely according to the preferences of the ancestors. If anything goes wrong in the burial process—or in the intervening months—that person will not successfully join the village of the ancestors: "Because the dead are still spiritually very much alive, the family of the living makes every effort during funeral rites to make sure that their new ancestor is pleased."[63]

I must pause here and make a personal note that in my experience in Mali, the invisible spiritual world comes very close to the visible, material world at a funeral. In the heat and dust, in the midst of the chaos of surging crowds of people, a complicated series of rites and ceremonies unfold one on the heel of another. Where the Christian might speak of sacraments or of copies of the heavenly temple, and where the Buddhist might speak of nirvana, many African Traditionalists would point to the funeral. The spirits and ancestors come very close, almost touching fingertips with the world of the living at the time of death.

Moreover, the land of the living finds its order and symmetry in the entrance of the soul into the village of the dead. Every individual's place within the village of the living is reasserted. Kinship relationships come sharply into focus. The relationship of each person not only to the dead but to every other living person is rearticulated.[64] The dead is honored and given to the world of the ancestors, taking his first steps along the path that will lead him into that rich and abundant time, which Mbiti calls *Zamani*.

Time

Although the question of how different cultures think about time is controversial, and the theories posited even as late as the 1960s are beginning to be irrelevant, the African concept of time continues to hold a unique flavor that many Westerners who encounter it for the first time are inclined to judge, unfortunately, in moral terms. Every scholar and ethnologist working south of the Sahara must grapple with Mbiti's theory of time in Africa. He employs two Swahili terms, *Sasa* and *Zamani*, to describe an ethos he believes extends widely over the continent. Sasa has to do with the present, day-to-day lived experience. It stretches no more than six months to two years into the future, encompassing those events that are sure to occur. Sasa is experienced cyclically—the harvest, the rains, the birth of a child, an upcoming festival. Zamani, on the other hand, is what we might think of as "macro" time. Zamani gathers up the present, adding it to the already enacted heritage of time. Sasa "disappears" into Zamani.[65]

Mbiti posits that Africans traditionally did not conceive of a long future. The present is the basis of African time stretching back into a long, rich past that provides the meaning and basis for the contemporary African community. Time, he writes, "is a two-dimensional phenomenon, with a long past, a present and virtually no future."[66]

> The question of time is of little or no academic concern to African peoples in their traditional life. For them, time is simply a composition of events which have occurred, those which are taking place now and those which are

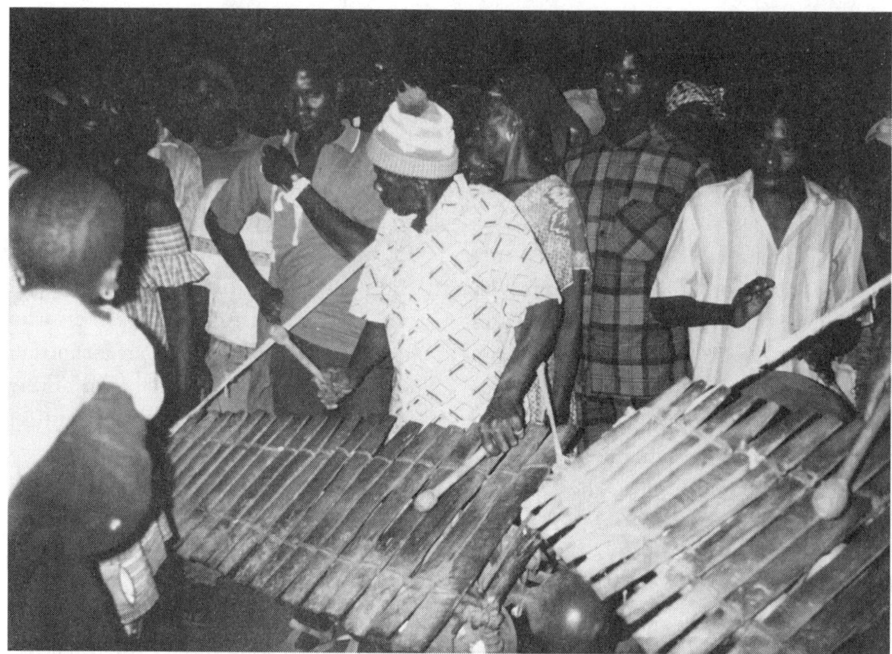

10B. Funeral dancing. Photo by Anne Kennedy. Used with permission.

> immediately to occur. What has not taken place or what has no likelihood of an immediate occurrence falls in the category of "No-time." What is certain to occur, or what falls within the rhythm of natural phenomena, is in the category of inevitable or potential time.[67]

Many have taken exception to Mbiti's view, arguing that of course Africans conceive of a future.[68] Answering these critics, Newell Booth writes, "[Mbiti] is not suggesting that the African view is of the same kind as the Western, simply reversed, but that Africans do not share the Western notion of abstract time which can be measured apart from events."[69] Time, in other words, is not an esoteric concept that drives behavior. A clock announcing an hour does not bring about a meeting. The meeting comes into being when all the people have assembled. Time becomes real when individuals and the community act to bring it into being: "The Tiv, who are acquainted with the use of clocks, use the word *awha*, meaning 'mark' or 'tally.' Thus, when they count 'hours' they are really counting the marks on the watch rather than artificial units of time."[70] Time, then, is not a commodity to be bought and sold, but a thing to be made: "Man is not a slave of time; instead, he 'makes' as much time as he wants."[71]

Mbiti claims that traditional Africans, having a truncated view of time, do not long for a future hope but rather are always looking backward into the past to the accumulated power and wisdom of the ancestors. Does this mean, then, that the African has no hope? It might be better, writes Booth, to think of the difference between Sasa and Zamani as the reality that there have been "events in the past, making it real, in contrast to the future, which is only an abstract idea."[72] It is not that the future does not exist; rather, it exists insofar as it is guaranteed by the past: "Crops that have been planted will be harvested, a child who has been conceived will be born; at least, one can reasonably expect these things to happen. But these events are already in some sense 'present;' in fact, anything that can be spoken of definitely in the 'future' is already part of the present."[73]

Power—Blood and Magic

This present life, overall, is of primary concern to the African traditionalist.[74] One question that often hangs in the air in the face of uncertainty is "Does it work?" The Westerner makes things work by manipulating a temporal material world. If something doesn't work, an expert is summoned to fix it. Restoration very often involves technology, and when that fails, we use self-help. The Westerner would not imagine that fixing the problem was a religious activity. For the African, however,

> the choice of terminology is not a neutral matter, as history shows, and in many cases African religious beliefs continue to be seen in terms that have a derogatory connotation and emphasize the difference between "us" and "them." Hence, while "we" are religious, "they" are superstitious, and while our beliefs may be "mystical" in nature, theirs belong to the "occult" just to mention some of the conceptual categories and terms that have been indelibly marked by the historical processes of Africa's evangelization and colonization.[75]

The African, as we have seen, looks to a rich spiritual past and a living spiritual present to find solutions to the problems of now. These temporal problems are often redressed with spiritual power.[76] So while some of the terminology used in this section on power—terms like "witchcraft," "sorcery," and "spiritual possession"—might seem questionable, we ought not to look down on them as inferior to the way a Westerner orders the material world. You or I are perhaps unlikely to go see a diviner, but we are statistically very likely to spend a lot of money on one-day shipping from the largest purveyor of material goods in the world.[77]

One of the easiest ways to get power is to appeal to the strength and resources of others, whether they be spirits, ancestors, family, or neighbors. The ancestors, though no longer alive, have more power than they know what to do with. If you pour out your libation on the ground or give them the meat they crave and listen to them, they will tell you what to do or give you some remedy to make you well or your enemy sick.[78]

If the ancestors are unhelpful, the African traditionalist will turn to the help of the spirits. One spiritual remedy among the Supyire of Mali, if you are suffering from madness, is to become a clown. This is not the scary clown of the circus or carnival, but rather a desirable person blessed with the tools of music, cross-dressing, and humor, who travels to festivals to entertain the crowds. This remedy has worked on more than one occasion. Some say that the spirits like to choose someone to be a clown because they love music and will drive that person mad until he or she goes to the diviner and there discovers the remedy—clowning.[79]

Hunting, blood sacrifice, and the collection of power-laden objects is another way to accumulate power. Hunters are particularly feared because the accumulated bones and frequent libations of the blood of hunted animals are a reservoir of power sought out by those suffering sickness, broken relationships, or material want.[80]

In the same way, devotees of a fetish are able to gain power through the life-force of the animals sacrificed to the spirit behind the mask.[81] Though this may feel spiritually dark, one man said of his fetish, "He is my shepherd."[82]

Small charms and sacred objects are powerful. If you want a particular spirit to guard your child, you might write a small Qur'anic verse on a paper, and then wrap it up and tie it around the waist of your baby.[83]

Words also have power, and the wise person is very careful about what he says and how. One ought never to look up at the sky and say, just as the millet is ready to be harvested and when rain would be a catastrophe, "Oh, I hope it doesn't rain!" Those words would tempt the spirit, who did have power over the rain, to make it rain. For this same reason, it is not good to say out loud that you fear something, such as disease or death. Those words could awake the attention of a supernatural being who may misunderstand or who wishes to bring you to harm.[84]

One great source of fear and anxiety is of witches and sorcery: "To Africans of every category, witchcraft is an urgent reality... African concepts about witchcraft consist in the belief that the spirits of living human beings can be sent out of the body on errands of doing havoc to other persons in body, mind, or estate."[85] Finding remedies against witchcraft is a central preoccupation, and often accusations—whether true or false—wreak havoc in every kind of community.[86]

In sum, all these methods and devices are useful ways to gain power over the unknown, to mitigate against very real evil.

Viewed normatively, the term "magic" has a neutral connotation. It means

10C. A fetish house. Photo by Anne Kennedy. Used with permission.

> ritual acts involving the manipulation of material substance (often inadequately translated as "medicines") and the use of verbal spells or addresses—all directed towards the influencing of forces—conceived of as impersonal and subject to direct human control if correctly handled—that are believed to govern the course of events. Magic may be used for either (a) productive, protective, and curative purposes, when it is sometimes referred to as "white magic," or (b) destructive purposes, when it is sometimes referred to as "black magic."[87]

As we saw earlier, the moral question is localized. Good and evil find their expression within the circumstances of everyday life. The use of magic may be good or bad, depending on who is wielding it and why.

Shame

One day when I was a child living in my Supyire village, I did the worst thing I could possibly have done. My sin was in two parts. First, while playing in the stream with my friend, I took her plastic sandal, as a joke, and threw it into the light-flecked water. The shoe floated gently away while I laughed, and my friend cried out in dismay. Stricken with remorse, I tried to go after it, to no avail. It was gone forever. My mother, as you can imagine, was mortified. The next day, we hurried to the village market and purchased the exact same sandals and took them, with great ceremony, to my friend's mother, explained about the unkindness and the loss, and said we were sorry. My friend's mother sat silent, her face a shadow. "Why are you making war on me?" she finally asked.

Most African societies could be classified as shame-honor cultures. The worst thing you can do is dishonor someone. Meiring works comprehensively through Van der Walt's treatment of guilt and shame and its implications for the work of reconciliation: "In a communal culture—such as in Africa—Van der Walt argues that a transgression is never directly addressed because it may undermine a person's honour. The insult may be even worse than the transgression itself."[88] Direct confrontation should be avoided at all costs even when a person has every possible good intention. Indirectness is the key ingredient. This reality presents problems for the work of forgiveness and restoration, since "repentance and admission of guilt shames the guilty person even more"[89] and, thus, to offer forgiveness "implies that the guilty party is bad."[90]

In my case, by buying and restoring the same sandal, I was saying to my friend that I did not think our friendship was very good, nor very strong. I had better keep very short accounts with her because I did not think she would be able to forgive me. I had shamed her, not by losing her shoe, but by making our friendship superficial and unforgiving.

A Woman on Her Journey to the Dead

Like her baby brother, a new baby girl in a traditional African society will likely be named according to the desires of the ancestors. Her name might also be useful in warding off the attention of malign spirits who wish to reclaim her for the village of the dead, though she is more likely to survive infancy than her brother.[91] Like her brother, she will not learn to walk until well into toddlerhood, being always tied to her mother's or another female relative's back. Once she can walk, her first jobs will be to fetch and carry. She, like her brother, will not be allowed to cry publicly and will obey immediately and without question.

As she nears her teen years, she, too, will go through some kind of initiation rite, probably involving female circumcision/mutilation overseen and carried out to the secret spiritual knowledge of her female relatives.[92] She may also spend some time in the wilderness, enduring trials or feats of physical and emotional strength designed to teach or to display a readiness for marriage and motherhood. She will be initiated into the secret knowledge of her female elders.[93] She will conform herself to the customs and rites of giving birth, cooking, medicinal cures, and the spiritual protection of her children when she has them.

Marriage and Mothering

When I was a child, we had to drive a young girl—ritually painted in beautiful henna designs and draped in cowrie-shell jewelry—to the village of her new husband. She wept loudly during the journey and then had to be almost forcibly removed from the car. She continued to weep as the final gifts were exchanged and the marriage ceremonies were accomplished. The groom was nowhere to be seen—for him to be present would have been very bad luck. The young woman cried and carried on loudly the whole time until I myself was overwrought. However, when we returned to visit a few weeks later, she was complacently calm and happy. The exaggerated weeping had been necessary to honor the ancestors of her own village, family, and parents, and to grieve over leaving her own clan. Taylor explains,

> The transfer for a girl and all her unborn children from one kinship group to become a wife in another represented a very serious loss of the life-force of her family which must be compensated by some exchange...The transaction was a public, ceremonial event, for the greater the number of kinsmen who contributed to the gift, or who shared in receiving it, the greater was the security of the marriage.[94]

The gifts a woman takes into her marriage are the foundation of her future. She may be given most of the cloth and clothing she needs for her whole life. Money may be exchanged in these modern times, though certainly cattle is still an integral part of many marriage negotiations. The marriage rite may include the ritual placing of her cooking stones. She will have her own house—one she will never be asked to share with a co-wife, who may nevertheless share her husband and compound. In ancient times, the bridegroom, or some members of his clan, may have farmed a certain number of years for her family before the marriage. In many places, the marriage will not be considered accomplished until the arrival of a child: "The primal view, regarding the child as the consummation of marriage, considered it more natural that sterility should annul it. It was hard on the childless wife; but she at least had a secure place in life and after death, in her own kinship group."[95]

Still, childlessness "assumes a tragic significance beyond our Western comprehension."[96] A woman's children are central to her position and her power. She has a right to them. They are part of the provident gifts of God. In some mystical way, they are the presence of the ancestors themselves. They will certainly honor and care for her in her old age.

Part of her role is to teach her own children the taboos, knowledge, and lore that binds the community together. She must raise children who attend to the spiritual underpinning of their common life. Indeed,

> the human solidarities of Africa do not depend upon the changes and chances

> of affection. The family is a delicately poised and interlacing organism in which each knows to whom he owes particular duties, from whom he can expect particular rights, and for whom he bears particular responsibilities. And this whole pattern of interdependence is symbolized and ratified by the way in which food is provided from one household and shared amongst others.[97]

Three Cooking Stones and Friendship

Most Western women would balk at the sheer physicality of village life. The African woman, but especially the village woman, works hard. Awake in the early dawn, she will feed her family some simple meal of millet porridge, milk, and tea, perhaps, and set children to the tasks of sweeping the compound, fetching, and carrying. She will share the task of pounding grain with mortar and pestle for the evening meal. She may have to work in the fields. In many places, the job of gathering firewood is hers, as is hauling clean water, however great a distance, from a stream or well to her compound.[98] She will often be seen with a child tied on her back, nursing in the midst of all her other work.

When she does sit down, it is apart from the men, perhaps in the shade of her hut in the heat of the day. If you visit her, she will stop what she is doing and give you a chair, a drink, and something to eat. Her hospitality, unhurried and generous, is a mark of her strength. You might feel embarrassed, sitting, having nothing to say, unable to breach the barriers of uncommon language, but she will graciously receive your presence as a gift. Indeed, the hurried, harried, and distracted work of the Westerner, which carries some morally good quality with it the busier it is, has no place in the traditional African context. To visit is itself a gift, and to stop and greet, and to sit and receive a visitor is the mark of true goodness.[99]

Her destiny seems ever more precarious, threatened by illness, the dangerous work of bearing children, and the ever-present anxiety of the spirits and ancestors. But she, like her husband, brothers, and father, has recourse to that same powerful realm. She might be well versed in the spiritual world of magic, able to prescribe some remedy for anyone with a problem or ailment. She cannot be initiated into the sacred cults of the fetishes, but as we have seen, she may be feared (if they are dark) or sought out (if they are benevolent) for her powers of witchcraft.

ATR and Christianity

Joining a Divided World Back Together

The preeminent heritage of the enlightenment for the Western mind was to successfully sunder the invisible spiritual world from the visible material one. In their sometimes frantic pursuit of scientific knowledge (and the inevitable backlash), Western people have become accustomed to intellectually organize the world into ever more secular categories and mores. While this has produced a highly technological society, full of material ease and convenience, it leaves Westerners with a fragmented sense of the world and self and an inability to know what they are about and what they are for. Science and its outflowing technology quenches the thirst for answers to the pressing questions of meaning and existence.

> Westernized man, having surrendered to the scientist the task of explaining the phenomena of his life, is prepared to take a great deal for granted. Assuming a mechanistic causation in every

> event he can afford to let a multitude of incidents pass as accidental with no sense of insecurity or wonder.[100]

But for the great portions of the human family, unmarked by the enlightenment—though much of its baggage has come to mar and trouble the continent of Africa—the sharp demarcation between the shadowy realm of the spirit world and the bright, sunlit world of observable materialism does not exist. He is a man "who assumes a personal causation in every event." Life is "an unceasing, Who-goes-there?" as he "alternates between triumph and anxiety."[101]

It would be, and in fact has been, a mistake for Westerners to approach, even with the best of intentions, traditional African settings with a God they have made in their own image. The person who enjoys an unbroken mystical connection to the invisible, spiritual realm, to spirits and ancestors, and most importantly to a living, breathing, knowable, familial community is not waiting to be told about a personalized, individualistic Jesus. Taylor explains, "The primal vision is of a world of presences, of face-to-face meeting not only with the living but just as vividly with the dead and with the whole totality of nature. It is a universe of I and Thou."[102] Mbiti says, "Unless Christianity and Islam fully occupy the whole person as much, if not more than, traditional religions do, most converts to these faiths will continue to revert to their old beliefs and practices for perhaps six days a week, and certainly in times of emergency and crisis."[103] The great failure of so many mission endeavors has been to offer Christ

> as the answer to the questions a white man would ask, the solution to the needs that a Western man would feel, the Saviour of the world of the European world-view, the object of the adoration and prayer of historic Christendom. But if Christ were to appear as the answer to the questions that Africans are asking, what would he look like?[104]

A Caution

I see at least three essential connecting points for Christianity in Africa, along with one great danger and a possible gift. The danger is for a Western Christian to continue to adopt a sentimental and paternalistic view of the continent. It is easy to look down on what we don't understand, or worse, to imagine that it is more romantic than it is.[105] As the West de-Christianizes, embracing pagan and pre-Christian categories, the traditional religious views and practices of Africa are enticing for those searching for ultimate meaning, including, occasionally, the Christian. The central connection of humanity to the earth, in which generations of ancestors are buried and who live on in a spiritual communion stretching into a rich mystical past, is a stark contrast to the isolated, community-starved Westerner, whose family consists of the individual, one or two parents, and a marriage partner, if dating or hookup apps did their work. The increasing rejection of the scientific, enlightenment-oriented worldview that explained everything except who you were supposed to be has failed to support the psycho-social identities of North Americans. This fragmented Western individualism is deeply rooted, even within the church. It is too easy to carry on exporting it in the name of the gospel.

Three Points of Connection

Christ came to save sinners—sinners who live in every place and who speak every language. The Jesus who came to die for

Africans long ago planted the seeds of His gospel, a gospel that comes into rich expression when the Bible is translated into every language. If that gospel is to be heard, it must speak about the world of (1) the spirits and ancestors, (2) power, and (3) the future.

Jesus is the one mediator and advocate between God and man. He is our brother and friend, the one who went on a long and difficult journey, away from His own home, to be a stranger among those who should have known Him. He went down into the place of the dead, to a place of shame and weight, to bring back to life, into the land of the living, those from whom we expected to be separated forever. The gospel itself—the life, death, resurrection, and ascension of Jesus—through its sheer human impossibility, is a gospel no one should be afraid of or ashamed to preach. Jesus is our Ancestor. He came back when we had pushed Him away. He spoke clearly and plainly, not in visions, not in strange rites, but with His own mouth to call us to Himself.

Moreover, Jesus came in power. All the spiritual forces of this world bowed to Him when He came here. They had to obey Him. They had to tell Him their names when He spoke. They had to leave when He cast them out. He was also Lord over the weather. By many signs, He calmed the storm, healed the sick, and—something that no spirit or ancestor can accomplish—raised the dead. His greatest power, though, was displayed in His strange and overturning work of the cross. When He had the power to rescue Himself, He chose instead to rescue us. Weakness, then, is in opposition to power. To throw yourself onto the power of Jesus means embracing the difficulty of defeat. This is a message no Westerner wants to hear anymore, nor any African. How could the power of the cross mean defeat in this life? To die, as Jesus did—young, alone, violently, and away from His village—is a peculiar kind of shame. And yet, it is the sign of His greatest power.

Finally, Jesus's view of time is not so very far from the traditional view of Africa. The Christian does hope in the future. While, to the outsider, it appears to be an unknown future that may still be 1,000 years away, it is not the partially imagined future of unrealized potential, the kind of hoped-for future of dreams and vacations on the beach, of a better car and a life of material ease. The future hope of the gospel is both Sasa and Zamani, the guaranteed future because the down payment has already been made. The seed has fallen into the ground and died; it will necessarily rise, yielding a full harvest. The woman is great with child, and the child will not fail to be born. The return of Jesus to gather His people is part of the time that has already come into being; it has already been enacted. It will come to the promised conclusion.

Can Africa Save the World?

The Western communion with the triune God is slowly fading away, slipping from consciousness. Bediako theorizes that, having not grappled with the primal imagination, with the rich spiritual world so essentially a part of the cosmos, but having instead suppressed it, the West is throwing off what it never really embraced—the gospel. There is, then, a turning back to the primal mind:

> For the signs of what appears to be a post-modernist rejection of the enlightenment in the West, which can be seen partly in the resurgence of the phenomena of the occult as well as in the various "quests" for spiritual experience and wholeness—even without explicit reference to God—all bear the marks of elements of a primal worldview.[106]

If Christian Africans, as they connect with the rest of the world, will show the way to "the viability of a Christian consciousness which retains its sense of the spiritual world of primal religions, as well as the theological encounter between the primal world-view and the Christian faith that is evident in African Christianity," there may yet be hope for the West.[107] There is certainly hope for Africa.

Anne Carlson Kennedy (MDiv, Virginia Theological Seminary) grew up in Mali, West Africa, and came to the United States in 1995 for college, where she earned degrees from Cornell University and Virginia Theological Seminary. She oversees liturgy, music, and catechesis at the Anglican Church of the Good Shepherd. She blogs at Patheos and is the author of *Nailed It: 365 Sarcastic Devotions for Angry or Worn-Out People.*

11

Hinduism

Amit Bhatia

In this essay, I am going to describe Hinduism, including a brief sketch of its history and beliefs, lifestyle and culture, and Hinduism's engagement with Christianity. Because Hinduism is very broad, encompassing all kinds of diverse ways of practicing this religion, I will primarily describe Hinduism as I lived and practiced it as a high-caste Hindu. Thus, while my description will be a very narrow slice within all that Hinduism encompasses, the understanding of the various religious and cultural terms that I explain will help you get a grasp of the basic and fundamental beliefs and teachings of this vast religion. In order to describe Hinduism's engagement with Christianity, I will not only narrate my own interaction with Christians as well as my conversion to the Christian faith but also offer some suggestions for effective evangelism among Hindus.

History and Beliefs

Where Did Hinduism Come From?

I was born and raised in a devout high-caste Hindu family, learning about my religion through many different avenues. At home, my mother taught me about the various Hindu gods and goddesses through stories in children's books. At school, I learned about Hinduism in history class and read the epic tales in English and Hindi literature classes. I also learned about some things through the dramatization of the stories of some of the Hindu gods. I quickly realized that while these stories are innumerable and the beliefs within Hinduism quite diverse, some core teachings are constant and form the foundational lens through which the varied beliefs of this religion need to be viewed in order to wrap our minds around the vastness and complexity of Hinduism.

The story of Hinduism begins with the migration of the Aryans into the Indus Valley on the northwest corner of the Indian subcontinent. There was already an indigenous group of people, the Dravidians, living there. Scholars have proposed various theories about the interaction between the Aryans and the Dravidians. For example, one theory is that the Aryans were warlike and pushed the agrarian Dravidians to the south of India (this is what I was taught in history class). Another theory is that the Aryans had a highly developed cattle-herding culture and moved into and took over the areas abandoned by the Dravidians because the rivers along which their towns were located were drying up.[1] I was also taught that the Aryans were fairer or lighter skinned than the indigenous Dravidians. The migrant Aryans brought their religion and culture with them, which displaced and/or got mingled with the Dravidians' religion and, over time, developed into what we know today as Hinduism. This migration and displacement occurred no later than 1500 BC.[2] As I learned and reflected on my history as a high-caste Hindu, having roots in the Aryan migration, I was always filled with a sense of pride at the presumed superiority of my religion.

Obtaining Release

Although there is incredible complexity in Hinduism, Hindus often hold the basic belief that every human is divine, yet in present life, humans exist in a state of separation from *Brahman*, the ultimate divine reality that is the source of all knowledge and everything that exists.[3] As long as people are ignorant that they are god, they will continue to exist in this world. After death, the body is burned and the ashes are sprinkled in one of the many rivers Hindus regard as holy. The *atman*, or soul, of the person will be reborn in this world in a different form. This cycle of death and rebirth, called *samsara*, continues endlessly until the person realizes the truth of his divine nature. The goal for every person is to obtain *moksha*, or release, from samsara.

As long as people exist in samsara, it is important they pay attention to their karma, or deeds, because as long as their soul has bad karma associated with it, their atman (soul) will continue to exist in samsara (the cycle of birth and death). People can work off their bad karma by paying the consequences for their bad deeds in their present life or subsequent lives. Once all the bad karma has been worked off, a person can obtain moksha (release). The goal of moksha is also spurred on by doing good karma.

Once a person obtains moksha, he becomes part of Brahman (ultimate divine reality). Because all bad karma must be worked off, when a person faces hardship in his life, such as the loss of a job or a serious accident, sometimes people say the reason the person is facing it is because he must have done bad karma in this or a previous lifetime. That is, he is simply reaping the effects of his bad karma, which he will reap in this life or another future life. For this reason, one way people respond (or at least I found myself responding this way) is by leaving the person to suffer through his misery because helping him out of his hardship would only serve to delay him from reaping the negative consequences of his bad karma. The dilemma, though, was that by helping someone who was suffering, the helper could obtain good karma, which would aid the helper in being able to obtain moksha sooner. These concepts are introduced in the Upanishads, one of Hinduism's sacred texts written around 1000 BC.

One of the things I came to realize was that a person could never know what life-form he would be born into in the next life. While the person's life went on, all relationships that he had in the present life would end. As I reflected on this, I was deeply impacted, being filled with a sense of fear at the lack of knowledge of the future as well as a feeling of loss because I would no longer be with my family. My family and I would all exist forever, but who we would be or where we would go was indeterminable. This experience filled me with a sense of uncertainty and emptiness, an element in my spiritual journey that Christ used many years later to reveal Christian truth to me when I encountered Him through the Bible.

11A. Krishna teaches Arjuna. Photo by Arnab Dutta (https://creativecommons.org/licenses/by-sa/3.0).

Three Paths

There are many different "ways" or "paths," called *marga* in Sanskrit, of obtaining moksha, and a person may either follow one of the three major paths or design his own path that draws elements from each. The purpose of these paths is to neutralize the effects of karma and accumulate positive karma by removing focus from an individual's "yearnings and concerns" and coming to realize the true nature of reality.[4]

Over the years I saw my parents practice *bhakti-marga*, the path of devotion to a particular god or goddess. This path comes from the teachings of Krishna to Arjuna that are recorded in the Bhagavad Gita, "The Song of God," which was written around AD 100. In this Hindu holy text, Krishna enjoins his followers to meditate on him by devoting all actions to him, worshiping him, focusing their minds on him.[5] The dialogue between Arjuna and Krishna takes place on the *Kurukshetra* battlefield, where two sets of cousins, the Pandavas and the Kauravas, have gone to war over the rightful heir to the throne. Arjuna, upon observing his relatives on the front of the other battle line, refuses to do his *dharma* (lawful duty) as a warrior because he fears the consequences of killing his kinsmen. Krishna explains that one does not have to give up action to achieve moksha, but the *fruit* of action. One needs to cultivate desireless action, or acting without attachment to the fruit or benefit of the action. Krishna encourages Arjuna to perform his duty as a soldier on the battlefield in his devotion, or *bhakti*, to Krishna.

The practice of bhakti-marga looks

different in the life of each family or person. In our family, during the festival of Diwali (described in detail below), the Hindu festival of lights, we stood before our little wooden temple in our home and worshiped Rama, the seventh avatar of the Hindu god Vishnu, as well as Laxmi, the goddess of wealth and prosperity. This was the only time during the year when we worshiped these idols. I saw high school friends express their devotion to Hanuman, the monkey god, by visiting his temple regularly as well as taking an annual trip to the temple of Shri Siddhi Vinayak that was dedicated to the god Ganesh, the elephant-headed god, in order to obtain his blessing to pass their final exams.

For the most part, my parents practiced yoga and meditation, focusing inward on their own souls as ways of coming to realize the truth that they were gods. This path is called *jnana-marga* (*jnana* in Sanskrit means "knowledge"). About jnana-marga, the Bhagavad Gita asserts:

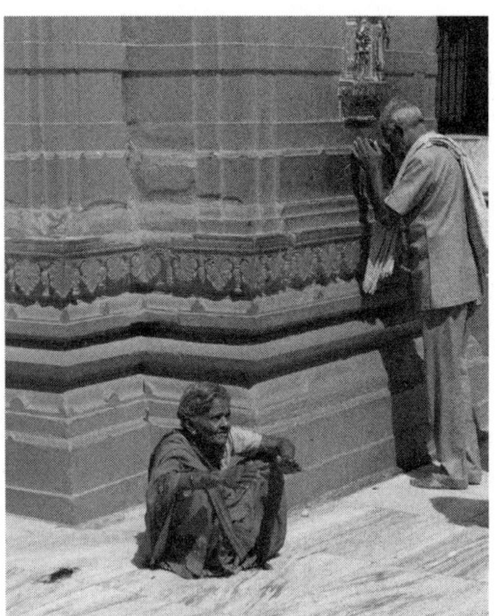

11B. A worshiper prays before a statue in a temple dedicated to the goddess Durga. Photo by Baldersdod (https://creativecommons.org/licenses/by-sa/4.0).

> No purifier equals knowledge,
> and in time
> the man of perfect discipline
> discovers this in his own spirit.
> Faithful, intent, his senses
> subdued, he gains knowledge;
> gaining knowledge,
> he soon finds perfect peace.[6]

Jnana-marga entails the focused study of the sacred texts as well as the intense reflection on the philosophical teachings of Hinduism. The goal of this path of wisdom is to come to realize the true nature of atman (the soul).

In my home, I saw this unfold in several ways. First, my mother engaged in the physical exercises that we call *yoga*, which in the West, for the most part, seems to have become separated from its spiritual connection and significance. She eventually enrolled in school and got trained to be a yoga teacher. My father, on the other hand, practiced meditation. He became part of a group of five or six friends who would meet in each other's living rooms to meditate, closing their eyes and focusing at an imaginary point in their minds to empty out all their thoughts. Through such techniques, they attempted to become aware of the true divine nature of their souls.

At one point, my father's hunger and search for truth took him to Sri Aurobindo's meditation center in Pondicherry in South India, where he spent time meditating and reading Hindu philosophical texts. He took me and my brother along, and I watched people from all over the world, dressed in saffron-colored clothes, seated around the *samadhi* (funerary monument) of Sri Aurobindo, meditating. Walking into this meditation center, I was filled with a sense of peace, another experience that became significant when I encountered the teachings of Christ. This was the first time I became keenly aware that there is an unseen but "felt" spiritual world that is deeply interconnected with the physical world that we see around us every day. However, I did not become aware until about nine years later that this was the point in my life when I began asking questions about spiritual matters. When I encountered Christ's teaching for the first time through my interactions with Christian students as a freshman in college, I began to articulate all the questions that I had been silently asking in my heart.

Karma-marga is a path that is theoretically practiced by those who are absorbed in activities of working and taking care of their families. This path emphasizes engaging in rituals and ethical deeds that are in keeping with dharma, which entails living in accordance with the social order. When one is young, it is their duty to live as a student and focus on education; when a person gets married, traditionally it is the husband's duty to work and provide for the family and the wife's duty to stay home and engage in raising the family and offering prayers to the god(s) on behalf of her family. These roles have become more fluid in contemporary times, since quite often women are out now in the workforce as well.

Performing a person's duty takes on many different forms and is lived out in different ways. Most recently, I saw this expressed by my cousin during the funeral rites for my father. According to Hindu custom after cremating his body, the ashes needed to be sprinkled in the River Ganges, one of Hinduism's holy rivers. While driving back from Haridwar, one of Hinduism's holy towns, when my American wife thanked my cousin for driving us all to perform this ritual, he simply responded by stating, "There is no need to thank me. I am just doing my duty."

11C. The Sanskrit word *Om* is both a recited syllable common in worship as well as a common symbol for Hinduism. The Unicode Consortium. Public domain.

This is a common response among Hindus as many actions are performed out of respect in order to uphold the social and cultural order.

The Caste System

Hinduism is also known for the caste system, a fact I became acutely aware of as an 11-year-old. One afternoon I was sitting at the back of the school bus waiting to be dropped off after school. Another student was sitting across from me, staring. When I asked him why he was staring at me, he responded by asking, "What class are you?" I quickly responded, "I am in class 6." He said, "No, not what class, but what caste are you?" So I told him that I was a *Kshatriya*, one of Hinduism's two high castes. I had learned in school of Hinduism's four castes: *Brahmins*, the priestly caste; *Kshatriya*, the caste of kings and warriors; *Vaishyas*, the merchants; and *Shudras*, the servants.

The caste system was initially connected with a person's profession but became embedded in society, and it is still very much prevalent even though outlawed. Its pervasive nature becomes most evident when people hoping to get married seek marriage partners from their own caste. Outside of the caste system is the group of people referred to as the *Harijans* (now called Dalits) or the "untouchables." Prior to that afternoon on the school bus, I had never reflected on the significance of the caste system in India—I did not need to because, as someone born and raised as a high-caste Hindu, I had never felt the system's negative effects.

Depending on where one lives, the negative effects can be keenly felt by people of the lower castes and the *Dalits*. In small villages where the caste of a person will presumably be common knowledge among the villagers, the social separation occurs in many settings. For example, low-caste people cannot go into a Hindu temple to present offerings. Rather, they must leave their offerings outside of the temple entrance to be picked up by the priest later and offered to particular gods and/or goddesses. At a bus stop, the low-caste travelers may be expected to sit a few feet away from the other travelers. If a low-caste person is sweeping the streets, she may physically face away and cover her head by her sari in order to physically separate herself from the high-caste Hindu walking by in order not to contaminate the other person. In large cities, on the other hand, because it is not possible to discern the caste of a person from their phenotype, the separation observed in villages is largely absent. This is why I never paid attention to the castes of the people I rode the train or the bus with. It never occurred to me to inquire of the caste of the servants who worked in my home.

Lifestyle and Culture

The lifestyle and culture of Hindus as practiced daily become most evident and are most easily understood in two ways: first, through the major religious festivals celebrated yearly; and second, through relationships with people they interact with regularly.

For Hindus, religion is bound up very closely with cultural practices. It is common for a Hindu to claim that Hinduism is more than a religion; it is a way of life. In explaining Hindu traditions, I will be selective, describing only the most popular of the festivals.

Diwali and the Epic of Rama

Diwali, connected with the Hindu new year, is a five-day Festival of Lights celebrated in autumn after the rice harvest. Adherents decorate their homes with *diyas* (oil lamps), dress nicely, light fireworks, and give each other sweets and gifts. Diwali commemorates the homecoming of Rama after a 14-year banishment from his kingdom. I grew up hearing the story, reading about it, being taught it by my mother, and seeing variations of it in movies and on television. Even today, when I watch movies with story lines based on variations of Rama's story, it strikes quite an emotional chord in me.

Rama's homecoming is narrated in the *Ramayana* (The Journey of Rama), written some time between 200 BC and AD 200. This holy book is one of the most important sources of Hindu notions of social and filial duty (dharma). It is a seven-volume tale of "political intrigue, romance, and philosophical speculation" written by the poet Valmiki.[7] *Ramayana* is the story of the ten-headed demon King Ravana, who performed fierce austerities and was granted a wish by the god Brahma. His wish was that he be protected from members of his own demon race, titans, snake people, gods, and so on. Having procured this kind of protection, Ravana and his demons controlled the earth, eventually enslaving even the gods of heaven. However, in his arrogance, Ravana forgot to ask for protection from humans and animals.

In the meantime, King Dasharatha of Ayodhya and his three wives, wanting an heir to Dasharatha's throne, performed sacrifices before the gods, urging them to grant their wish. The king and his three queens were blessed with four sons: Rama (son of Kausalya), Bharata (son of Kaikeyi), and Lakshmana and Shatrughna (sons of Sumitra). Rama, the eldest, married a princess named Sita. Because of his virtue and righteousness, Rama was respected and loved by all, and when King Dasharatha decided to step down from the throne, he announced that Rama would replace him as king. Then Kaikeyi, the king's favorite wife, called in the two wishes that the king had once granted her: First, she asked that Rama be banished from the kingdom into the forest for 14 years and, second, that her own son, Bharata, be made king instead. Even though the king was distraught, because of his integrity, he kept his word to Kaikeyi and did as she asked. Stricken with grief, the king died.

Rama, the dutiful son, obeyed his father without any protest and went into exile. Out of loyalty and a sense of duty, his wife Sita and brother Lakshmana accompanied him. While they were in the jungle, Surpanakha, the demon-king Ravana's sister, tried to seduce Rama and failed. Rejected by Rama, she tried to attack Sita, but Lakshama stepped in and cut off her nose and ears. In Indian culture, the proverb "getting your nose cut off" is a figurative way of saying that a person has been publicly humiliated. After this gross humiliation, Surpanakha ran to Ravana, and in order to avenge herself, incited his lust by describing Sita's beauty. Ravana then took the form of an old *sanyasi* (a person who has withdrawn from society in order to obtain moksha). Ravana tricked and kidnapped her, carrying her off to his demon stronghold in Lanka.

Rama and Lakshmana, both in great despair, embarked on a nationwide search to find Sita, but to no avail. Eventually, they met Hanuman, the monkey-headed deity from a sophisticated race of magical monkeys and trusted messenger of Sugriva, the recently deposed king of the forest-dwelling Vanaras. After Rama helped reinstate Sugriva to the throne, Hanuman and his platoons of monkeys, along with the support of the bear king Jambavan, went north, south, east, and west to search for Sita. Hanuman led the contingent south to the sea and leaped across the ocean, landing in Lanka, where Sita was held prisoner in Ravana's fortress.[8] Hanuman promised Sita that Rama would come get her soon.

Learning from Hanuman that Sita was held captive by Ravana, Rama and his army marched to Lanka to rescue her. A fierce battle was waged, during which Rama's arrow pierced Ravana's heart, and he died. Even though Rama and Sita were reunited, because she had spent a year in another man's house, she had to prove her chastity publicly through a trial by fire. With the fire-god Agni as her witness, she passed through the flames and was found to be virtuous. The exile now concluded, Rama, Sita, and Lakshmana returned to Ayodhya. Bharata returned the kingdom to Rama, the rightful heir, and Rama was crowned king.

The happiness, however, was short lived. Rumors spread in Ayodhya about Sita's chastity, and Rama was forced to abandon Sita in the forest. Unknown to Rama, Sita was, in fact, pregnant and gave birth in the forest to their two sons. The boys were raised by the hermit Valmiki in the forest. Valmiki, who had seen all this come to pass while meditating, composed the *Ramayana*, having Rama's two sons memorize it and sing it before their father. Soon afterward, Rama died, yearning for Sita.[9]

For Hindus, this is no ordinary tale. The *Ramayana* is a story about loss and separation, and Rama is a tragic hero who feels the despair of losing the love of his life whom he had fought so hard to rescue. The *Ramayana* wrestles with the question of *dharma* in the public, political, private, and family realms.[10] It was through this story that I learned about exemplary role models: The faithful and virtuous Sita is the ideal wife, dutiful and obedient Rama is the perfect king and ideal man, loyal Lakshmana is the best of brothers, and Hanuman is the selfless devotee. Virtue, faithfulness, duty, obedience, loyalty, and selfless devotion are all modeled in the *Ramayana*. Indian movies will sometimes feature a story line based on various aspects of the *Ramayana*. Seeing depictions of the banishment and separation from the father and the subsequent reunion of all family members evokes deep emotions for many, including myself.

Holi Festival

Another popular festival is Holi, Hinduism's most colorful festival. It is celebrated in February or March, right after the wheat harvest. Holi is based on the story of the demon King Hiranyakashyap, who demanded worship from all his subjects. However, when his son Prahlada became a devotee of Vishnu, Hiranyakashyap made many attempts to kill him, but to no avail. Hiranyakashyap then asked his sister Holika to wrap herself with her special scarf that was immune to fire and to sit in a fire with Prahlada so that he would be burned to death, while she would be protected by the special scarf. She took Prahlada in her arms, but when she attempted to sit in the fire, the scarf flew off her and covered Prahlada instead. Holika died but Prahlada survived. From that day on, Prahlada's survival and Holika's destruction is celebrated by lighting a bonfire on the eve of Holi. The next day, people throw colored water and colored powder on each other. Holi signifies the victory of good over evil.

I grew up celebrating Holi from a very young age, engaging other kids in water-balloon and water-pistol fights. A big part of the celebration is visiting friends and enjoying snacks together. Holi is celebrated even in American suburbs with a significant Indian immigrant population, with non-Indians also participating.[11] Even though it is a Hindu festival, I remember celebrating Holi with Sikh, Jain, and Muslim friends. While Holi is a celebration that has a religious beginning, for me (and perhaps for most Indians), it was primarily a cultural celebration without any religious associations. This is true even when Holi is celebrated at Hindu temples in the United States.[12]

Home Rituals

In addition to these religious festivals, Hindus often celebrate some major festivals as well as family rituals in their homes. For example, the festival of Ganesh Chaturthi, the worship of one of the most popular Hindu deities by the name of Ganesha (the elephant-headed god), is performed with great pomp. I observed a high school friend's family celebrate the worship of Ganesha every year. The ten-day ceremony began with bringing an idol of Ganesha into the home, where his family offered fruits, incense, and *laddoos*, a sweet Indian dessert, to honor Ganesha. On one of the days, they invited guests over for a religious meal in honor of Ganesha, and we sat on the floor, eating home-cooked vegetarian food on a banana-leaf plate. On the final day, after more worship of Ganesha, the idol was taken to the Arabian Sea (the most convenient body of water for us) and immersed into the water. Ganesha's devotees perform the same rituals each year, praying for the removal of any obstacles in life, which Ganesha is particularly believed to be able to do.

Hindus may also perform other ceremonies in their homes when they are seeking some kind of blessing from the divine. These ceremonies are called *puja*, meaning "prayer, service, and worship," and may be performed or offered at home, in the local *Mandir* (temple), at pilgrimage sites, or by sacred trees/rivers. Typically, puja involves making an offering to the deity, such as fruit, incense, flowers, or *prasad* (Indian pastries). Prasad has special significance because, once it is offered to the deity, it is believed to now be infused with the deity's blessing. One component of puja is called *arti*, a ceremony that involves offering worship with light. This includes lighting a five-flamed lamp that symbolizes the five elements, earth, water, fire, air, and ether—as well as the totality of the universe—and waving the lamp in a clockwise motion. This ritual is believed to remove evil influences and return the worshiper to an auspicious state. Puja may be performed by one individual, whether layperson or a priest, or led by one person with several other people joining in. Puja is often accompanied by the chanting of a *mantra*, a ritual formula used to produce a spiritual effect. A mantra is usually chanted in Sanskrit, and its recitation is believed to aid in the efficacy of an offering, to help focus the mind, induce a trance, and alter one's state of consciousness. A popular mantra on the lips of many a devout Hindu is the "Om Namah Shivaya" (obeisance to Shiva) chant, the recitation of which brings the devotee closer to Shiva.

Other ceremonies need to be led by a trained priest. In my family, on one particular occasion, the fire sacrifice was performed so that my father, who had been jobless for a protracted period of time, could find gainful employment. We invited a Hindu priest to lead us in this ritual every Saturday morning for several weeks. I distinctly remember sitting on the floor in our living room around a makeshift fire, tossing flowers into the fire and repeating after the priest as he chanted verses in Sanskrit from the Vedas. Hindus generally don't read the Vedas, as they are all written in Sanskrit. However, Hindu priests memorize these texts in order to perform the rituals. Hindus believe the Vedas were revealed and written down sometime between 1200 and 900 BC. The four Vedas—Rig Veda, Yajur Veda, Sama Veda, and Atharva Veda—were not originated by humans, but rather "heard" and written down by ancient sages. Verses from the first three Vedas are recited during

11D. The Arti ceremony in Hindu *puja*. Photo by Chris Shervey (https://commons.wikimedia.org/wiki/File:Ceremony_aarti HinduPujaIndiab.jpg).

yajana (sacrifice), and the fourth has spells and incantations to protect against demons, disasters, diseases, and so on.[13] After the priest finished reciting the Vedas and performing the fire sacrifices, he advised my mother to perform individual worship of the sun. I saw her do this regularly, bowing down and pouring out water and flowers from a bowl to the sun as it rose above the horizon.

Personal Interactions

Hindu culture revolves around showing respect for people around them. Showing respect is not unique to Hindus, but the way in which respect is shown is unique. Growing up, whenever I visited my relatives during the summer holidays, I always greeted them for the first time by bowing down and touching the feet of my aunties and uncles. This is a way of acknowledging age, seniority, and wisdom. They always responded to this show of respect by touching my head and saying to me, "*Jeete raho*," which is a wish for long life. This is called giving an *aashirwad*, or blessing. I never addressed my older relatives by just their first name. It was always *Masi-ji* (*Masi* is the term for mother's sister) or *Mama-ji* (*Mama* is the term for mother's brother), where *ji* is a gender-neutral honorific appended on to the title to show respect for someone older than oneself. This practice of not using the first name to address someone who is older than you is also practiced in relationships with people who are not family members. That is, older people are never addressed by their first name as it would show disregard for their age and bring them down to the addresser's age.

When Hindus greet each other, it is by joining the palms of the hands together, bowing down slightly and saying, "Namaste." I was in a church once and ran into a retired missionary who had served in India for 45 years. When she addressed me in perfect Hindi, I greeted her with the traditional Namaste. She responded to me by saying that I should not do that because the origin of that greeting is religious, and it is a way of one Hindu saying to the other, "I bow down to the god in you," an understanding that derives from the Hindu belief that we are all god. That was the first time I had heard this (it was quite amusing to me to learn something new about my Hindu background from a foreigner). This is because the religious significance of Namaste has largely been lost and now often just means, "Hello." Hindus will also follow this pattern of greeting when they visit a temple and seek to honor the idol of a god or a goddess. They will stand before the idol, join their hands at the palms, shut their eyes, and bow down slightly at the waist to show respect to the god before whom they have come to perform worship.

Hinduism and Christianity

My Conversion to Christ

My conversion to Christianity came five years after I encountered the person of Christ. My roommate and a friend first shared the gospel with me in my dormitory in fall 1987, just a couple of months after I arrived in the United States. I was talking with them about life in India and they wanted to know, among other things, what I believed as a Hindu. In just a few minutes, I explained to them what I felt were the basics of Hinduism—that there are many paths within Hinduism to finding God and all religions are basically true and just different paths leading to God. I explained to them the inviolable laws of karma, reincarnation (transmigration of all souls), and moksha ("release" from the cycle of reincarnation). They, in turn, explained the gospel of Jesus Christ, starting from John 3:16. In a matter of four or five minutes, in very simple terms, they explained who Jesus is, what heaven and hell are, the significance of the crucifixion, and the basics of sin and forgiveness.

My conversation with my two American friends was the first time I had heard that Jesus claimed that He is God, that He is the only God, and that all other gods of Hinduism are false gods. My first reaction was against the person of Jesus, and it was laced with anger. As a Hindu, I was convinced that every individual should faithfully practice the religion he was born into, and I was enraged at Jesus for making such an exclusive claim. The clear implication of Jesus's claim was that Hinduism is a false religion and that my parents and my Hindu culture are wrong and inferior.

While the claims of Jesus in the Bible were the cause of great offense to me, the conversations about spirituality with my roommate and other Christians I met on campus continued. Over time, I came to realize that I was on a spiritual quest, which had begun for me as a fifth-grade student in India. During these conversations, I began to articulate questions that I had been asking inwardly about truth, religion, and the meaning of life. I also wrestled with these questions when I would visit church (e.g., for Thanksgiving). As I reflected, I realized that I had been asking these questions since my first spiritual experience of peace at Shri Aurobindo's Ashram in Pondicherry, India. One significant element of my spiritual pursuit was to find peace. My life was in turmoil because of all the pressures of school, which I had to shoulder by myself as I was living alone in the United States, away from my family. My questions all seemed to center on the person of Jesus. In my conversations and reflections, it was always Jesus I encountered, and it was always Jesus I rejected.

I had an experience as a seventh-grade student in India that Jesus in His sovereignty used to orchestrate my life in the United States. One morning in history class, we were studying the Old Testament story of Abraham and Isaac. My history teacher was an Indian Jewish woman, and her nephew was a fellow student. Growing up in India, I was familiar with Hindus, Muslims, Sikhs, and Christians, but I had never heard of Jewish people. I remember being confused at not knowing what God Jews worshiped, and I remember asking my fellow student whether his God was Krishna or Allah or someone else. I became intrigued by Jewish people and was fascinated with narratives about Jews living in Europe around WWII. My captivation persisted, and when I came to the United States, wanting to meet some Jews, I asked my roommate if he knew any Jewish people. He told me of a Jew who lived in his hometown who had become a Christian in a meditation center in Pondicherry, India, practicing the kind of philosophical and mystical Hinduism that I grew up with. My friendship with this Jewish-Christian over the next four years included conversations about his conversion from Hindu meditation to faith in Jesus. The trust we developed through these conversations, as well and his prayers for me, were greatly influential in my conversion to Christianity.

I continued to believe that the Hindu worldview was the one that made the most sense and best explained life and the plethora of religions. However, I was also drawn to the person of Jesus. During my junior year in college I, along with four other Christian friends, formed a Bible study, meeting once a week to simply read through the Gospels and talk about what we read. I was the only Hindu in this group, and I interpreted everything I read from a Hindu perspective, while the other four were Christians and read the story of Jesus through the eyes of a Christian. Coincidently, the Bible study was led by an Indian, a Hindu convert to Christianity who had come to faith in India. The plan for the Bible study was for everyone to come together at my friend's apartment, eat dinner, and then read the Bible and talk about it. We made a covenant to set aside the two-hour meeting for spiritual fellowship and discussion, and we did not bring schoolwork to our meetings. In all the pressures that college life brought to me, this Sunday evening gathering was the only time of peace I had. Without realizing it, over time, I slowly began to associate the sense of peace that I felt with the person of Jesus. In this way, I was drawn to Him. However, I was also repulsed by the idea of converting to Christianity. I did not think very highly of the Hindu convert who had become a Christian. It felt to me as if he had done a bad thing in converting. There is so much social stigma attached to a Hindu converting to Christianity because it communicates that Hinduism is a deficient religion. Indian culture looks down on and stigmatizes the convert as well as his family. Thinking about converting always left a bad taste in my mouth. At the same time, I loved going to the Bible study and was drawn to Jesus, thoughts of whom always brought a sense of peace to my heart.

After college, I went on to graduate school on the US East Coast. By this time, my spiritual thirst and search had deepened. One vivid memory of my college years was the Bible study that I attended during my junior year. I continued to reject conversion to Christianity, but I was drawn to the person of Jesus and I wanted more. So as I started graduate school, I began looking for a campus Bible study that I could join. That week, there was an ad in the college newspaper published by the Protestant Campus Ministry inviting people to attend a three-part Bible study titled, "Where Is God When It Hurts?" I qualified because I was hurting and could not make any sense out of the seeming purposelessness of life, and I was completely devoid of peace, both of which resulted in serious depression.

So I called the campus minister and asked if I could attend. At my request, the three-part Bible study became a yearlong Bible study. During that year, I sought God in the pages of the Bible. Using the words of the psalmist, I cried out to a God I did not know and certainly did not believe in. There were times when my Jewish-Christian friend in Illinois prayed for me over the phone as I poured out my frustration and despair to him. But I still was not willing to commit my life to Christ. I wanted to know why I should choose Jesus over Krishna. After all, they both made similar claims about themselves, and I could not "see" either of them. I remember reading an autobiography of a 19-year-old American missionary, Bruce Olsen, titled *Bruchko*, as well as the story of Tal Brooke, an American who had begun practicing Hinduism and then came to faith in Christ in India.[14] I had reached the point where I wanted some proof that Jesus really was who He said He was. What that proof was going to look like I did not know, but if Jesus really cared for me and had a plan for my life, then I wanted Him to show Himself to me.

During the summer after my first year in graduate school, life completely unraveled for me. Due to an unforeseen turn of events, I lost my research scholarship for the second year of graduate school, and I no longer had the financial resources to finish my master's degree. I decided that I would look for a job, but after several weeks of writing letters and sending résumés to over 75 companies, I had no luck. The end of the summer was fast approaching, and in a matter of a few days, I would be completely out of money and have no place to live. I was very depressed and again turned to my Jewish-Christian friend in Illinois for prayer, pouring out my discouragement to him. He prayed and encouraged me.

One afternoon, I was sitting alone in my apartment desperately trying to figure out what I was going to do. Out of sheer hopelessness, I decided I was going to ask Jesus for help. I got up off the couch, walked into my bedroom, shut the door, got down on my knees, and prayed, "Jesus, I have no one else to turn to. Everything I have tried has come to nothing. If you really are God, please help me."

A few days later, I got a call from one of the companies I had sent a résumé to. I had worked for them over the summers as an undergraduate student, and they said they would offer me a job, but that meant returning to Illinois. I had enough money left for a train ticket back to Chicago and to ship boxes of my belongings back to me. I called up my Jewish-Christian friend and explained this turn of events, asking if I could stay with him for a few days. On the phone, he did not seem surprised at what had happened, suggesting that Jesus had answered his prayer. On the overnight train journey, one thought kept going through my mind: "Jesus is going to take care of me."

I got back to Chicago and stayed with my Jewish-Christian friend for a few days. That's when I started attending his church regularly. Eventually, I was able to move in with my college roommate's family for a few months until I got back on my feet. Jesus had answered my prayer and provided everything that I needed. This was the proof I had been looking for, and I knew that Jesus was real. I no longer cared what other Hindus would think about my conversion to Christ—this wall that had been a huge hindrance in my becoming a follower of Jesus came crashing down. On Sunday, October 4, 1992, I prayed the "sinner's prayer" and bowed my knee to Jesus, acknowledging that He is my Lord.

Over the course of five years, from September 1987 to October 1992, I had moved from anger at Jesus to a complete surrender to Him. Christ used the curiosity I'd had since seventh grade about Jewish people in order to lead me to Him through my Jewish-Christian friend. Years later, Jesus would use my interest in Jewish people to lead me into full-time ministry work in a Messianic Jewish congregation. He had been orchestrating my life for years, something I realized only after I came to faith in Jesus.

Talking with Hindus about Christ

Drawing from my personal experience and academic study, I will present some insights and proven approaches to sharing the gospel with Hindus. I also draw from the experiences of several Christians involved in evangelizing Hindus, some who hail from a Hindu background and others who have lived among Hindus in Northern India. There are some common components that are significant in evangelism for all people, like praying for wisdom, developing friendships, and loving people with the love of Christ and meeting their needs in the context of those relationships. However, there are some particular issues that are unique to evangelizing Hindus.

My friends introduced me to Jesus through what is sometimes called the "simple gospel approach." The evangelist, working from the assumption that the gospel is the same no matter whom you are speaking with, shares the message of Christ with the Hindu as he would with any other ethnic group in any part of the world. Missiologist H.L. Richard asserts that this simple gospel approach is, in fact, a Western way of presenting the gospel, as opposed to preaching a message that is relevant and that "reverberates in the local context."[15] For example, when entrepreneur and philanthropist Ram Gidoomal read about Jesus's death on the cross, what was meaningful to him was not so much Jesus's sacrifice for sin, but that he believed that Jesus died for his karma. He came to faith in Jesus "on those terms."[16] There is often a need for biblical concepts to be translated so that they are understandable to Hindus, keeping in mind their religious worldview as well as their cultural values. For example, some Hindus would appreciate the translation of some biblical terms using Sanskrit, the language of the Hindu scriptures. Culturally, for some Hindus, it is more acceptable to walk into a church service and be able to take off their shoes outside the sanctuary and to be seated on the floor rather than on pews.

While my spiritual quest was to find peace, and Gidoomal came to faith because he believed that Jesus died for his karma, I was intrigued to read the testimonies of two other Hindu converts who both arrived at Jesus from still different paths. Author Mitali Perkins's quest seemed to center on the notion of evil and how could a "God—if God existed—leave humanity alone to endure so much [pain and suffering]?" Her question led her to encounter Jesus in the pages of the Bible, and she made the decision to "follow Jesus."[17]

Screenwriter Manoj Raithatha, on the other hand, was facing a deep crisis in life, including extreme financial pressures and a "critically ill" two-year-old son "fighting for his life." An American couple, whom Raithatha and his wife had befriended, and their families' churches in the United States, prayed for his son. When his son became well quite unexpectedly, the only explanation that Raithatha could give was that God had done a miracle. Experiencing firsthand the power of prayer, a few weeks later he gave his life to Christ.[18]

Gidoomal, Perkins, Raithatha, and I came to Christ in different ways. All four of us have unique spiritual journeys, characterized by different spiritual needs, yet Jesus stepped into our worlds, and we encountered Him based on our spiritual needs.

Recently, I came across a research project in which one of the goals was to investigate "specific guidance [that] might be given to those evangelizing in terms of their own attitudes and what they say and do."[19] In light of this goal, one of the challenges that researcher Brian Nelson faced while interviewing Hindus who had come to faith in Jesus was that the interviewees "did not wish to cast the evangelist in a negative light."[20] The interviewees seemed to indirectly communicate the sentiment that the negative from the evangelists did not matter because "through this person I found Jesus." However, I want to suggest that it is important that we pay attention to the negative so that we don't make the mistakes others have made, otherwise becoming a hindrance rather than a help in the outreach process.

I had several interesting experiences with Christians during my freshman year in college, both negative and positive. The first time I stepped into a church on a Sunday morning, I was standing and singing hymns during the church service. I had never seen a hymnal before, and I was struggling to follow the song lines in the hymn paragraphs. It was uncomfortable to be in the strange setting of a church and even more embarrassing trying to sing a hymn when I couldn't follow the lines. I glanced sideways for help from the person who had invited me to church. Seeing my utter confusion, instead of explaining how lines flow, he stood there laughing at me. My confusion quickly turned to humiliation.

On another occasion, someone claimed that marriages are valid only if they are done in the presence of the Christian God. Because my parents were married in a Hindu ceremony, he asserted that their marriage was not a legal marriage. For this reason, he asserted, I was born out of wedlock, and that thus I was a "bastard." He looked quite amused explaining this to me, and his mother was sitting next to him chuckling. I also received ridicule from Christians who mocked Buddha, palm-reading, and so on. Needless to say, these incidents did not make the church or Christians attractive to me.

On the other hand, Raghav Krishna, another Hindu who became a follower of Jesus living as a university student in the United States, shares how he was impressed with the lives of the American Christians he befriended while attending university. Their lives were characterized by a pursuit of Jesus: "They were interested in God and wanted to talk about Him." Moreover, "not only were they interested in spiritual matters, but the lives they led were truly spiritual in spite of their being college students."[21] He continues,

> I saw one major difference in them from what I had seen in my own people growing up—Christ Himself and the reality of His presence in their lives... I saw that the difference between the lives they were supposed to live and the actual life they lived was very small.[22]

I, too, saw this in my Jewish-Christian friend's life, and it drew me to the person of Jesus. He lived and ministered in a church that was a Christian commune. His simple lifestyle was characterized by the sole purpose of seeking Jesus, which conjured up images of spiritual pursuit in the setting of an ashram in India and filled me with a sense of peace, softening my heart toward Jesus.

From the many conversion stories of Hindus, it is evident that there is no single reason as to why Hindus are drawn to put their faith in Christ. In the stories I've mentioned, we all encountered Jesus in unique ways. Perhaps it would be more accurate to suggest that Jesus reached out to each one of us in our particular life circumstances, engaging our spiritual needs, and revealing Himself to us in a manner that would resonate with us as individuals. Every Hindu will approach matters related to spirituality in different ways: Some will have an innate sense of their sinfulness and will seek the forgiveness that Jesus offers, others will have a severe medical need and then experience the healing power of Jesus, and still others will simply want to know why they should choose Jesus over Krishna. There is not just one way in which Jesus connects with Hindus. Engaging Hindus means that we must look to understand where they are in their lives and spiritual journeys, learn about their unique needs as articulated by them, and then present Jesus as the living God who is able to meet them where they are. For this to happen, the burden is on Christians to create a safe place where Hindus can engage with Jesus from the perspective of their unique questions and needs.

At the same time, it is important we

articulate the gospel clearly to Hindus in order to help them understand the exclusive claims of Jesus so they do not think of Jesus as just another god among the pantheon of Hindu deities. In all likelihood, Jesus's exclusivity will be offensive to Hindus, but it must be communicated. Developing relationships with Hindus becomes all the more important because only then can we help them work through their reaction to Jesus's claims. It is also significant to communicate to Hindus that Jesus is the *Sanatan* (eternal) Son—and not someone who was created by the Eternal Father. Using this Hindu terminology can help them realize that Jesus has always existed.

Hindus who come to faith in Christ will likely face opposition from their immediate family members. I told my family right away that I had come to believe that Jesus is the only God and that I had become a Christian. My parents were living in India, and I was in Chicago. So the only conflict I faced initially was over the phone or in letters. Indians are very family and community oriented, so converts usually experience distress from a sense of social stigma. My parents told me that reading the Bible and learning from Jesus was fine, but they did not want me to get baptized or call myself a Christian. When my family came to visit me and lived with me for six months at a time, I experienced a lot of strife. They could not understand why I considered Hinduism an inferior religion or why I believed that Christianity was the only true religion and only path to God. We quarreled every day and could not have a meal together without my parents arguing or mocking my Christian faith. Most of the opposition came from my father, who was vocal and very angry. This turmoil lasted for over 23 years, until March 2016, when I led him to faith in Christ. When evangelizing Hindus, we need to keep in mind that they will need strong support from their Christian family after they come to faith in Jesus and that evangelizing Hindus is a long process.

Since community is very important, Hindus should be evangelized in the context of community, especially an Indian community of believers in Jesus. Our faith in Christ can be lived out in the context of Indian culture. This approach will make Christian teachings more understandable, while also demonstrating to Hindus that Christianity is not exclusively a religion of the Westerners. Moreover, it will show Hindus that converting to Christianity does not mean they have to abandon or reject the Indian community and culture, a fear and hindrance many Hindus have. It is common to view being a Hindu and living according to Indian culture as one and the same thing; thus, to leave Hinduism is seen as leaving one's culture. For this reason, evangelizing them in the context of a community where Indian culture is affirmed will be appealing to Hindus and could make the evangelism process easier. Learning about and affirming aspects of Indian and Hindu culture such as food, clothes, respect for elders, language, and movies will go a long way in building bridges, developing relationships, and creating space for sharing the gospel. Being critical or condemning Indian culture will do just the opposite!

Worship services that include elements of traditional Indian culture will resonate with some Hindus. An elderly woman came to Christ recently through a worship service that incorporated elements of Indian Hindu culture in a contextualized Christian worship service in Chicago. This group holds *Arti* (ceremony of lights) every morning at 9:30 and *Satsang* (truth gathering) every Thursday morning. During these hour-long services, people remove their shoes, enter the sacred space of the *Mandir* (name for church in the Hindu context), and sit on the floor. Incense is lit, portions of the Bible are chanted in Sanskrit, *Bhajans* (worship songs) are sung in Hindi, and the guru (teacher) narrates the story of the Lord *Shri* Jesus in Hindi. The honorific title *Shri* shows Jesus reverence in an Indian cultural manner.

These are all elements that comprise prayer services in Hindu temples, but in the United States, they are contextualized to a Hindu-community-oriented Christian context, which helps present the gospel to Hindus in a manner they find understandable, relatable, and appealing. An important aspect of teaching in this setting is that, instead of criticizing Hinduism, which would be offensive to Hindus, the focus is on the Lord *Shri* Jesus, talking about and glorifying Him. Over the years, I have learned that in personal evangelism, instead of throwing mud on Hindus—in doing so I not only lose ground but also get my hands dirty—glorifying Jesus is far more effective for developing relationships and creating the space in which I can share the gospel.

In order to build relationships with Hindus, one Indian Christian whom I know practices what he calls "personal" contextualization, which comprises doing life in "Hindu culture." Since Hinduism is "a religion, a civilization and a culture," he believes that Christians reaching Hindus ought to adhere to those cultural aspects of Hinduism that are neutral and do not go against the teachings of the Bible. For example, he wears Indian clothes that are yellow, orange, or red, all of which communicate spirituality to Hindus, and he eats only vegetarian food. He uses Hindi vocabulary: God is addressed as *Bhagavan*, the transcendent God as *Bhrama*, the Holy Spirit as *Parmatma*, Lord Jesus Son of God as *Sanatan Putra*, emphasizing His eternal aspect, and moksha as salvation. These terms are used in the context of biblical stories, thus giving them biblical meaning, which makes it easier for him to communicate Christ to Hindus. The contextual worship and personal lifestyle are outward ways of communicating Christian spirituality using Hindu cultural forms and terms.

Furthermore, with the expectation that God is going to give opportunity to communicate the gospel with Hindus, he visits Hindu temples in the Chicago area. Through these temple visits, he establishes friendship with Hindus and engages in dialogue with them about spiritual issues outside the temple. These visits also serve as learning opportunities for him—a chance to evaluate Hindu practices that can be inculcated in his life as a disciple of Jesus. He views himself as a student of religion, as a communicator of Christ, and as part of the Hindu community.

Conclusion

In sharing Jesus with Hindus and with people of a plethora of other cultural, religious, and ethnic backgrounds, it is my experience that there isn't any single proven way to evangelize a religious group. Also, evangelism must be sustained in a relational context, with a clear presentation of Jesus from the scriptures and from the life of the evangelist, who needs to be a serious follower of Jesus Christ.

Moreover, it is important that we take the posture of a *learner*, with an openness toward those we are trying to reach with the good news of Christ. In evangelizing Hindus, we cannot overestimate the significance of being part of the Hindu community, understanding Hindu culture, developing friendships, and expressing our Christian faith, both personally and corporately, in contextualized ways. Many Hindus who leave India for education, work, or business are turning to Christ in overseas locations. The displacement out of land and culture is bringing them one step closer to Jesus and putting their faith in Him rather than in karma or reincarnation for their true moksha.

Amit Bhatia (PhD, Trinity Evangelical Divinity School) was born and raised in Bombay, India, in a Hindu family. Since becoming a Christian, he has spent many years in pastoral ministry in multiethnic congregations, often engaging people from Hindu, Muslim, and Jewish backgrounds. He serves as an assistant professor and OSCI Program Director at Corban University's School of Arts and Sciences. He is the author of *Engaging Muslims and Islam: Lessons for 21st Century American Evangelicals.*

12

Jainism

Leonard Thompson

Jainism is a relatively small religion, with just about six or seven million members worldwide, and is largely unknown by most peoples in our world. Yet it has a long and rich history and is still a very active and live religion. Though it has its origin in India and most Jains are still in India, it has spread to other areas of the world due to its followers moving for business or other purposes.

In order to better understand Jains, you should have a grasp of some basic facts about the religion, including the following:

1. Some Jains will call themselves Hindus rather than Jains.[1]
2. Jainism, like Buddhism, is an offshoot of the larger and even more ancient religion of Hinduism.
3. We can say that in origin, it is somewhat a contemporary of Buddhism.
4. The life of Mahavira, the founder of Jainism, parallels Buddha's life rather closely.

It is wise at the outset to remember that this chapter provides only a summary of Jainism. Within the religion is a wide variety of Jain teachings and practices. This is in large part because of the two large sects, the Digambara and the Svetambara, as well as subsects. The basic doctrines are the same among the sects, but there are dozens of variations in Jain lifestyle, worship, ceremonies, and so on.

History of Jainism

The word *Jainism* originates from the Sanskrit word *jina*. *Jina* means "conqueror" or "victor," and *jain* means "one who follows the conqueror."[2] *Jina* is a reference to the basic concept and aim of the religion, which is to be detached from the world, conquering all attachments of any kind, even that of family and friends. Specifically, the Jinas are revered and honored ancient prophets and teachers, more often known in Jainism as *Tirthankaras*. This word means "ford-maker" or "bridge-builders," with a special connection to building bridges over the vast expanse of the birth-to-death experience. There are 24 Tirthankaras in number, with the twenty-fourth being the final and most important *jina* in the current cycle of time. After the current cycle ends in decline (a period known as Dusama Dusama), another 24 Tirthankaras will appear to inform the next cycle of the way of Jainism.

Mahavira (ca. 599–527 BC)

Mahavira (*maha* means "great"; *vira* means "hero") is often referred to as the founder of Jainism. However, that is not technically correct, for the tenets of Jainism have filtered down through the previous 23 Tirthankaras. Mahavira is considered a historical person, and some facts about him help verify this. His real name was Nataputta Vardhamana, and he was a member of the Kshatriya caste. He was born of royalty in Northeast India (now Nepal). Keep in mind that there are slight variations within Jain tradition regarding his birthdate and birthplace, and some Jains claim that he was born in what is now the Bihar state of India.

The Tirthankara who preceded Mahavira was named Parshvanatha. He is said to have lived 250 years before Mahavira, living for 100 years. Like Mahavira, Parshvanatha is also said to have been of noble birth but was seeking enlightenment as to the meaning of life. At 30 years old, he left his wealthy home in his desire to find truth. After numerous and great difficulties, he was enlightened, and soon his doctrines spread, and many disciples followed him. Parshvanatha's life so closely resembles that of Mahavira himself that some feel there is an intermingling of stories, and hence some confusion does exist. His great contribution to Jainism is that he established the "fourfold restraint," which eventually evolved into the five great vows (with Mahavira adding the fifth):

12A. Statue of Mahavira at Ahinsa Sthal, a Jain temple in Delhi. Photo by Jain cloud (https://creativecommons.org/licenses/by-sa/4.0).

1. Abstain from any kind of violence.
2. Abstain from dishonesty.
3. Abstain from taking what belongs to others.
4. Abstain from any attachment, or abstain from owning anything yourself.
5. Abstain from sexual activity (added by Mahavira).

Interestingly, Mahavira has many similarities with Siddhartha Gautama, the Buddha, whose birth was also said to be in the sixth century BC. Like Mahavira, Buddha came from a noble family as well as from Northeast India. Also, just as Mahavira set about seeking truth about the realities of life, so did Buddha. Likewise, around the same time in distant China, both Lao Tzu, founder of Taoism, and Confucius, founder of Confucianism, were born. Certainly, it was an age of thinkers and reformers.

Mahavira grew up amid great wealth, and his early life was one of luxury and ease. He was married to a beautiful woman named Yashoda, who bore him a daughter named

Priyadarshana.[3] But he soon got restless and dissatisfied with his life, and after his parents died, he felt useless and unfulfilled. This restlessness, coupled with a great thirst for spiritual truth, motivated him at the young age of 30 to begin a quest for truth. He left behind his family and the comfortable life he had and embarked on his spiritual journey, seeking self-discovery and truth.

However, Mahavira did not gain peace of mind from any of the old rituals or ceremonies he discovered. He found that the only way to attain release from the cycle of births and rebirths was through self-discipline. So he tried to live an extremely austere life. He experienced severe hardships and deprivation, practicing penance and wandering around from place to place with no possessions whatsoever, not even a begging bowl.

> He walked about naked and accepted the alms in the hollow of his hand. For more than twelve years the Venerable Ascetic Mahavira neglected his body and abandoned the care of it; he with equanimity bore, underwent, and suffered all pleasant or unpleasant occurrences arising from divine powers, men, or animals.
>
> Henceforth the Venerable Ascetic Mahavira was houseless, circumspect in his walking, circumspect in his speaking, circumspect in his begging, circumspect in his accepting (anything), in the carrying of his outfit and drinking vessel; circumspect in evacuating excrements, urine, saliva, mucus, and uncleanliness of the body; circumspect in his thoughts, circumspect in his words, circumspect in his acts; guarding his thoughts, guarding his words, guarding his acts, guarding his senses, guarding his chastity; without wrath, without pride, without deceit, without greed; calm, tranquil, composed, liberated, free from temptations, without egoism, without property; he had cut off all earthly ties, and was not stained by any worldliness.[4]

He practiced this way of life for 12 or 13 years until he attained "Supreme Knowledge," known as *kaivalya*, around the age of 42 and became a *kevalin* (seeker of the absolute). Tradition says he attained this while sitting under a sal tree on the banks of the River *Rijupalika*. He then became known as "Mahavira Jain." Thus he attained the truth he sought—perfect knowledge.

After attaining Supreme Knowledge, Mahavira traveled widely, promoting his teachings. His travels took him all over India, and he influenced kings and rulers as well as common men and women. It is said that his strong personality, coupled with the simplicity of his teachings (in contrast to the complexity of the Hindu Vedas) were some of the reasons for Jainism's initial rapid spread. As a traveling teacher, Mahavira became one of the great reformers of ancient India. The emphasis on the need for nonviolence (*ahimsa*, the first great vow) automatically opposed any kind of animal or related sacrifices. His firm belief in karmic rebirth and final liberation led to a strong emphasis on right conduct and virtuous living. He traveled all over India, promoting his new philosophy, and died at 72.

Mahavira's life, at one point, seems to have been influenced by Makkhali Gosala, the founder of an ancient Indian sect called "Ajivika." They promoted extreme ascetic living, including the belief that its devotees did not need to wear clothing. They also believed in fatalism and karma. It is beyond the scope of this chapter to dwell much on the life and teachings of Gosala, but there were interactions between Mahavira and Gosala that, in the end, were not very cordial due to differences in teachings like fatalism. The Ajivika sect died out in about the fourteenth century AD.[5]

The Spread of Jainism

After the death of Mahavira, Jain monks continued their missionary efforts to spread Jainism, often aided by the patronage of prominent rulers like the Mauryas and Guptas. In the fourth century BC, a monk named Bhadrabahu traveled south and helped establish Jainism there, especially in what is now known as Karnataka in the southwestern region of India. Hence we find prominent temples and shrines there, among the most well-known being the location of the famous statue of Gommateshwara (also known as Bahubali, son of the first Tirthankara [Rishabhnatha]) in the city of Shravanabelagola. The Gommateshwara statue was built between AD 976 and 993 and is 57 feet tall, perhaps the tallest monolithic sculpture in the world.

12B. The 57-foot-tall Gommateshwara statue is anointed during the twelfth-year celebration known as Mahamastakabhisheka. Photo by Florian Maier (https://creativecommons.org/licenses/by-sa/4.0).

One famous convert to Jainism was Chandragupta Maurya, founder of the powerful Maurya Empire (322–187 BC). He renounced everything and became a Jain monk and an ascetic, and he died while in South India at the Gommateswara shrine.

Soon Jainism entered Sri Lanka, where many early kings and rulers were said to have practiced its teachings. But unlike Buddhism, which had protracted missions and missionaries to promote Buddha's teachings, Jainism did not do so in any planned or organized way. Jain monks and teachers traveled widely in India, but its movement abroad depended mostly on the migration of its adherents. For example, when Indian workers were taken by the British as midmanagement workers and laborers, they took their religion with them. So in addition to India, Jains are found in Kenya, Tanzania, the United Kingdom, the United States, Canada, Malaysia, Myanmar, and so on. Today, India holds the largest Jain population of over five million and is followed by the United States, with about 80,000. These are followed by Kenya, the United Kingdom, Canada, Tanzania, Nepal, Uganda, Myanmar, and Malaysia.[6]

Division

Around the year 80 BC, a sharp division arose in the Jain Sangha (the community of monks), the Svetambara and Digambara sects. The division was caused by a conflict concerning the application of the non-attachment concept. This conflict perhaps had its seeds even during the lifetime of Mahavira, but it deepened and developed over time. Some monks, perhaps following the teachings of Parshvanatha, wore clothes, in contrast to the teachings and practice of Mahavira and his followers, who taught that even clothes were a form of attachment. This led to a deep schism, which continues today and is cited as being a reason for Jainism's decline. The Digambaras get their name from being "sky-clad," clothed by the sky and not garments, while the Svetambaras are the "white-robed." Both groups, however, maintain the same foundational Jain beliefs.

The "white-robed" Svetambara are the more popular Jain sect. They are considered more liberal in their interpretation of the Jain Scriptures, a collection of sutras from Mahavira known as the *Agamas*. Women are allowed as nuns and can attain final liberation. Monks and nuns are allowed to collect food more than once a day and carry a begging bowl. The food is provided by Jain "householders" (laypeople). Once enlightened, monks continue to eat food. They also accept the traditional belief that Mahavira married and had a daughter.

The minority Digambara are found mostly in South India. They read the *Agamas* very conservatively. Monks wear no clothing at all. With this practice being considered unacceptable for women, women are generally seen as unable to attain final liberation. However, there is the hope of rebirth as a male. Monks are to collect food only once a day from householders. Rather than carry a bowl, they must receive the food in their hands alone. Once a monk attains enlightenment and becomes omniscient, he no longer needs food. They also believe that Mahavira never married and remained celibate throughout his lifetime.

Beliefs and Ethics of Jainism

As we look further into Mahavira's teachings, we find several differences between Jain beliefs and practices of classical Hinduism. We find in the concepts and practices of Jainism a renunciation of the supremacy of Brahmanism (the priesthood of Hinduism), the caste system, and the emphasis on images and idols. In fact, it might surprise many that Mahavira, like Buddha, placed no emphasis on the centrality of an Absolute God, who is also Creator of all things.

The Three Jewels

Mahavira taught that there were three absolute conditions for right living, called the *Triratna* (Three Jewels). These were Right Faith, Right Knowledge, and Right Action. These can cleanse a person for enlightenment. Right Faith, also known as Right Perception, involves seeking truth in the teachings of the Tirthankaras and cultivating a correct perception of reality. Right Knowledge means viewing the universe correctly. Right Action involves the dos and don'ts of Jain ethics.

Ahimsa

The five vows are compulsory for all monks and nuns, but the laity are also expected to follow them within their ability to do so. As mentioned above, Jains strictly forbid violence, dishonesty, theft, attachment, and sexual immorality (which, for monks and nuns, rules out sexual activity altogether).

Of these, perhaps the most distinctive ethical teaching of Jainism is nonviolence, known as *ahimsa*. A classic Jain statement puts it this way: "Do not injure, abuse, oppress, enslave, insult, torment, torture, or kill any creature or any living being."[7] "Any living being" is broad, and to practice this seems impractical, as living creatures can be killed by drinking liquids or even breathing. So there are five senses that determine the level of living creatures: touch, taste, smell, sight, and hearing. According to Pravin K. Shah of the Jainism Literature Center, their order is as follows:

- living beings with five senses: humans, animals, birds, heavenly and hellish beings
- living beings with four senses: flies, bees, and so on
- living beings with three senses: ants, lice, and so on
- living beings with two senses: worms, leaches, and so on
- living beings with one sense: plants, water, air, earth, fire,[8] and so on

Hence laypersons are allowed to eat vegetables for food, and in general, Jains are strict vegetarians.

> Humanity is the most developed class of living beings, but according to Jainism, is not a privileged species in any sense. Human reality is not the center of things, with the right to conquer and subdue nature, just as in modern astronomy the earth is not the center of the universe with the planets, the stars, and the sun all circling around it...In Jainism raw soil, raw minerals, snow, ice, vegetation, and so on are considered living organisms that are a class of immobile beings, though we do not find any concept of the entire biosphere as a living body.[9]

It is of interest that Mahatma Gandhi promoted and practiced nonviolence, especially in gaining independence for India from British colonial rule and was said to have been influenced by the Jain concept of *ahimsa*. In turn, it is said that Martin Luther King Jr. was influenced by the nonviolence of Mahatma Gandhi, which led to his great movements to enhance equality for his people.

Liberation

Why do Jains follow such a strict lifestyle? Simply put, it is because they firmly believe in karma and rebirth. Living things (*jiva*) exist and would flourish; however, they accumulate nonlife (*ajiva*) because of karma. It's because of this karmic accumulation that they are unable to escape the cycle of rebirth: "Jains believe that karma is a material substance, which binds to the soul whenever the soul becomes sticky with passion or other stronger emotions or attachments."[10] This "karmic matter" must be shed through a long process of self-denial. Here is an example of how this shedding works:

> To illustrate, we wish evil to our neighbour A: the thought activity invites the karmic matter into the soul...the matter comes and binds the soul...This karma may take two months to bear its full fruits; in the meantime it is an evil load for the soul. To get lightness and to get rid of the karma, the soul may deliberately feel an opposite kind of feeling towards other neighbours B, C, and D, or towards A himself. A still surer way is to practise austerity. By removing the mind from the demands and impulses of the body, and by mortifying the physical man through not listening to its greed and temptations, matter

> may be overcome and the soul freed from the bondage.[11]

In completely shedding their karmic matter through lifetimes of effort, Jains desire to eventually follow Mahavira into liberation, often called *moksha* or *nirvana*. Here is a description of Mahavira's passage into freedom:

> In the fourth month of that rainy season, in the seventh fortnight, in the dark [fortnight] of Karttika, on its fifteenth day, in the last night, in the town of Papa in king Hastipala's office of the writers, the Venerable Ascetic Mahavira died, went off, quitted the world, cut asunder the ties of birth, old age, and death; became a Siddha, a Buddha, a Mukta, a maker of the end (to all misery), finally liberated, freed from all pains.[12]

The Jain Way of Life

In general, most Jains are quite religious, and whether nuns or monks, all look for the same goal of spiritual purity and release from the cycle of birth and rebirth. Monks and nuns are extremely strict in following the required regulations of multifold abstinences and nonattachment practices. Mahavira's emphasis on right conduct pervades Jain life. Of course, as in any religion, there are those who stray from the orthodox paths, violating Jain principles and indulging in numerous non-Jain habits. Also, as in many faiths, women are often more conscious of following the rules. Incidentally, despite the ancient controversy as to whether women qualify for liberation or not, nuns far outnumber monks.[13]

Jains usually have six daily practices to follow: prayer, honoring Tirthankaras, showing respect to monks, self-punishment for sinning, meditating for 48 minutes, and abstaining from at least one item of pleasure. Of course, how strictly this is followed cannot be truly ascertained.

As mentioned above, Jain householders (laypersons) are mostly strict vegetarians, but with special care taken to avoid vegetables grown underground. It is not uncommon to go to a high-class Indian restaurant and find its menu stating that no onion or garlic was used in preparation of their dishes. Fruits, nuts, and even milk are consumed with the claim that these are by-products of living things and not life itself.

Fasting is common among Jains and is not limited to monks and nuns. This is more popular during festivals and auspicious occasions.

The adherence to nonviolence makes Jains shun certain professions in order to avoid destroying life unintentionally. Thus, farming and carpentry are typically shunned, and military careers are naturally avoided. On the other hand, Jains excel, and to some extent even dominate, professions involving finance and banking. This aptitude is aided by their vow to not take what does not belong to them.[14] In recent years, there has been a popular trend among Jain youth to abandon the householder way of living and remove themselves from society and take the vows of mendicancy leading to monkhood and nunnery. Many of these have come from prominent Jain families, creating temporal concerns not only within the families involved but in Jain society as a whole. Withdrawal from the householder life is painful not only for the mendicant:

> "I will never be able to hug my daughter again," says Indravadan Singhi, his voice breaking. He looks away,

> determined not to reveal emotion as he says, "I can never meet her eye again"... On the morning of Dhruvi's renunciation ceremony, her father hugged her for the last time before she donned the dress of a nun, grief etched on his face.[15]

Jain Worship

Worship is an important part of Jain life. Although worship is typically conducted in the temple, it can also be done by laypeople at a small shrine in the home. In a perhaps enigmatic way, Jains are not meant to worship the Tirthankaras but rather to concentrate their homage on the perfection that these saints have attained. The purpose of worship is to improve a person's spiritual growth and status, to help purify the material body, thus destroying the bad karma that can stick to the soul. Jains also try to meditate for 48 minutes at some point during the day. Many also follow a daily prayer routine. One prominent prayer they practice before dawn is the Namaskara Mantra: "I bow to the enlightened souls, I bow to the liberated soul. I bow to religious leaders, I bow to the religious teachers, I bow to all the monks in the world."[16]

Generally, all Jains strive to make temple worship a regular event. Inside Jain temples, there are images of the Tirthankaras, mostly in very large proportions, some being mammoth in size. Though they all look similar, Jains can find them identified by the caretakers in some way. In Svetambara temples, the Tirthankaras are decorated, especially during festivals and special days. Sandalwood paste, gold jewelry, flowers, and camphor are commonly used in decorating images. The statues in Digambara temples are always simple and undecorated.

The person going to the temple to worship is required to have bathed and cleansed himself and to wear fresh simple clothing (usually white), with some wearing masks over their mouths. Menstruating women and those in contact with the dead do not normally enter the temples. Footwear is left outside, and feet and mouths are rinsed. Leather items are often not allowed.

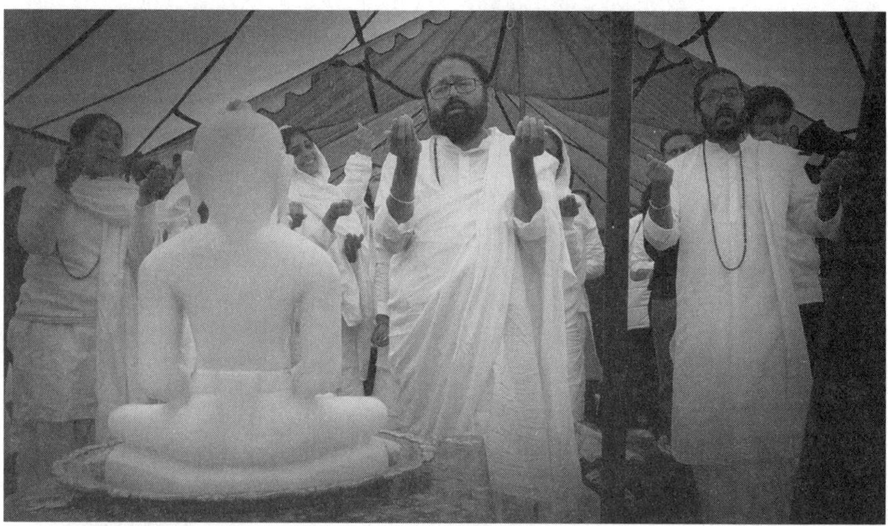

12C. Worshipers before a statue of Rishabhanatha, the first Tirthankara. Photo by Kailadgn (https://creativecommons.org/licenses/by-sa/3.0).

The *puja* (devotional offering) in the temple can only be done after several rituals are performed, such as salutations, going around the image clockwise three times, and prostration. The *puja* typically consists of substances symbolic of cleansing, including sandalwood paste, water, incense, coconut, dehusked rice, fruit, and flowers. There is also a more intense *puja*, which is internal: the offering made by developing the proper emotional state and meditation.

There are many Jain temples all over India, especially in the regions of Madhya Pradesh (with prominent ones in the city of Khajuraho) and Karnataka. There are also Jain temples spread throughout the world in many countries, including the United States.

Voluntary Death Fast

A curious custom among Jain monks and nuns seems to be slowly reviving itself today, with not much opposition. On the contrary, it appears, at least to some inquirers, that those monks and nuns who have followed this practice are praised and venerated. In fact, the voluntary fast unto death (*Sallekhana* or *Santhara*) is referred to optimistically as the "Celebration of Death." Further, Jains note boastingly that while other religions celebrate life, they celebrate death. In order to attain total detachment from all things and to prevent further bad karma, a monk or nun may achieve this by the ultimate means of voluntary fasting to death. Throughout this act, the person choosing to die often does so with joy, anticipating ultimate release. Commenting on the completed death fast of a 76-year-old Jain scholar and author of more than 76 books, one commentator explained,

> A Jain's approach to death by observing the ritual provides him an alternative, nonviolent approach to the ultimate rite of passage. Santhara is a highly respected practice in Jainism, one the community believes leads an individual to a world of nonviolence after rejecting all desires in the material world.[17]

Is this suicide? Many ideologists and others feel it is, but the Indian Supreme Court ruled, in August 2015, that it is permissible for those who are seeking complete separation from this world. This was after the High Court in the Indian state of Rajasthan put a ban on the practice that only lasted 20 days.[18] So the centuries-old custom continues today. The argument that Jains often make for allowing this practice is that it is undertaken not because of negative reasons, as is often the case in suicide, but is practiced joyfully and willingly, and hence it is a celebration.

Festivals

Jains often celebrate Hindu festivals as part of Indian tradition. Most notably, Jains regularly celebrate Diwali, a prominent Hindu festival. However, this should not be mistaken for religious syncretism. Diwali has its own unique meaningfulness to Jains, as it is considered the date that Mahavira attained nirvana/moksha.

Perhaps the most important Jain festival is Paryushana (Svetambara) or Das Lakshana (Digambara). This festival takes place at the end of the rainy season (August–September), which also marks the end of the Jain year. The word *Paryushana* means "abiding together" and refers to the close and sustained relationship between the renouncers (monks) and the householders. During the monsoon season (about four months), the renouncers do not move around and are dependent on the same laity for their food and other needs. There is, therefore, much interaction and sharing between the two groups. The festival lasts for eight days (ten days for the Digambara) and is enthusiastically celebrated by Jains, even though, like most Jain festivals, there is much restraint. Following the festival, the monks resume their normal moving around for their sustenance and to cultivate nonattachment to one place.

Another important festival is the celebration of Mahavira's birth, called *Mahavir Jayanti,* occurring between March and April. It is celebrated with great pomp and pageantry. The streets are highly decorated. Dramas are staged with actors playing gods and goddesses who have come to honor the baby Mahavira. At the same time, Jains pursue increased spiritual growth, making pilgrimages, taking part in special devotional rituals, doing pujas, and so on.

A massive celebration takes place every 12 years. The vast time gap, therefore, enhances the festival's importance. Its name is Mahamastakabhisheka, made up of three words: *Maha* (great), *mastaka* (head), and *abhisheka* ("anointing" or "crowning"). Hence it is a "head anointing festival." Devotees sprinkle water on all those participating, and they "anoint" statues with milk and sugarcane juice, showering them with flowers, turmeric, and sandalwood powders. Precious items including gold and jewelry are also offered. The entire festival serves to increase the spirituality of the worshiper. The festival takes place all over India, but the most famous and well-attended site is at the 57-foot-tall Gommateshwara statue in Karnataka.

It must be noted that although Jain festivals do have elements of gaiety and festivity, with rejoicing and entertainment, they are also occasions for renunciation, study of scriptures, recitation of hymns, and meditation.

Present Trends

There appears to be a resurgence in Jainism worldwide. This is not necessarily strange, given the confused and conflicting state of the world today. Humanity is plagued and consumed with materialism, leading to greed, corruption, and deceit, with the consequent accompaniment of hatred, vengeance, and violence. In this conglomeration of evil, Jainism provides, if not a valid solution, at least a retreat from our world into a realm of peacefulness, order, and some kind of meaning. The tenets of *ahimsa* and austerity stand in opposition to the ever-increasing violence and bloodshed as well as to vulgar displays of wealth and affluence. Jainism appeals to those who long to get away from it all!

These trends are also seen in the increase of Jainism worldwide, not merely in India. Mostly due to migration but also because of attraction to its principles, Jainism is slowly spreading around the world. One prominent indicator of this is the ever-increasing study of the intricacies of Jainism, particularly in some of the world's most prestigious universities and colleges.

Jainism and Christianity

There are major differences between Christianity and Jainism. This chapter will conclude with two. First and foremost is in the concept of God. There is no real concept of the Creator God in Jainism, let alone a Redeemer God. These are decidedly absent in Mahavira's teachings. Although the gods can play a minor role in the religion (e.g., in the Mahavira stories), Jainism is basically nontheistic. On the other hand, Christian faith and practice is grounded in a foundational fact: There is a living God, who is the Creator, Redeemer, and Sustainer of all creation. Jain nonattachment and the conquest of desire would ultimately, and quite logically, mean nonattachment to God Himself. Contrast this with what the Hebrew psalmist says so beautifully, that he *longs* for the Lord, passionately, just as the deer longs for the water brooks (Psalm 42:1).

The other prominent contrast is that Jainism is almost completely a religion of works. The five vows, the three pearls, and other beliefs derived from them are pronouncedly works-oriented, as spiritual progress rises or falls on doing the right things and avoiding the wrong things. This is in contrast with the biblical concept of grace and the related attributes of mercy, compassion, and forgiveness. Various types of abstinence can characterize Christians too, but the practice of extreme austerity and the consequent hurting of the body (voluntary starvation, for example) contradicts the high value placed by the Lord God on the human body, said to be specially formed by God Himself (Genesis 2:7) and to be the temple of the Holy Spirit for believers (1 Corinthians 6:19).

It is heartbreaking to see pictures of people starving themselves to death in hopes that doing so will bring about liberation. Although they celebrate severe austerities as though this is the way to conquer evil, they are in reality mistreating the body that God created as good. Life, both the spiritual and physical, is a gift from God. Instead of seeing renunciation as the point of existence, may Jains come to find the joy of reconciliation with God, saying yes to His grace and experiencing the resulting peace.

Leonard Thompson (DMin, Fuller Theological Seminary) is a world-traveling pastor who was born and raised in India. Trained at both Fuller and Wheaton, Leonard has taught at numerous colleges, including Lakeview Bible College and Seminary, Eastern Bible Institute, and Chiang Mai Bible Institute. He taught as an adjunct professor at Ozark Christian College for ten years. He is the author of *Demons*.

13

Sikhism

Natun Bhattacharya and C. Wayne Mayhall

"You should cut your turban off and you'll look like a Canadian," a Canadian man told a politician during a recent campaign stop at a shopping center in Montreal, Quebec. The politician's name was Jagmeet Singh, a practicing Sikh and the leader of a major political party in Canada. This strange incident happened in the province of Quebec, which enacted a law in 2019 banning government workers on duty from wearing religious attire such as a turban.[1] Although this encounter ended peacefully, the distinctive turban of the male Sikh population has raised curiosity and sometimes unease among Westerners unfamiliar with Sikhism.

In Canada alone, there are almost 500,000 Sikhs,[2] and there are roughly 430,000 Sikhs in the United Kingdom and 250,000 in the United States.[3] Some people not being familiar with Sikhs and their unique religion have assumed them to be Muslims because some Muslims also wear turbans, although not exactly the same way. This confusion has resulted in several violent incidences toward Sikh males over the years, especially since the 9/11 terrorist attacks on the United States.[4]

When many Americans come across turbaned, bearded Sikhs, they may wonder what national or ethnic origin these people come from. Originally from the Indian subcontinent, there are now two subsequent generations of Sikhs who have integrated into American society, especially in California and New York. Punjab, the state in northern India from which Sikhs originated, is considered the breadbasket of India and has thrived as an agricultural society. Having come from an agricultural society, Sikhs have naturally engaged in farming in California since their early arrival. Today, Sikhs have integrated into numerous occupations, for example, as convenience shopkeepers, in high tech jobs, on college faculties, in

13A. A Sikh wedding in Norway. Photo by Anders Bettum, Oslo Museum (https://creativecommons.org/licenses/by-sa/4.0).

medicine, in the American military, and in practically all walks of life. In the United States, there were 246 Sikh places of worship (*Gurdwaras*) as of 2012.[5]

Sikh immigrants began to arrive at the US West Coast in the early 1900s and began to work on the Western Pacific Railway in Northern California. These new immigrants continued their arrival in California, seeking work in the farms, lumber mills, and mines. To be Sikh in the United States, however, did not limit oneself to a life of common labor. The first Asian American to be elected to the US Congress was Californian Sikh Dalip Singh Saund. A successful farmer with a PhD in mathematics from the University of California, Berkeley, Saund was elected representative in 1956.

The millennial Sikhs who were born in the United States have unique challenges in carrying on the Sikh Punjabi cultural heritage while also seeking to assimilate into mainstream American culture.[6] Nowhere is this struggle more obvious than in dating and marriage. It is common practice for Sikh parents to seek out a Punjabi Sikh spouse for their children. Thus their grown children are often afraid of breaking the news that they are dating a non-Sikh American and considering marrying outside their religion. Another area of struggle for the male Sikhs raised in America is whether to keep the beard and wear a turban or to go clean-shaven and without a turban. In addition to the issue of arranged marriage, female Sikhs can also face family pressure to choose careers that seem appropriate to the family. Based on a fictional Sikh family in the United Kingdom, the hit movie *Bend It like Beckham* tells the story of a young 18-year-old woman who wants to play organized soccer but finds herself in great conflict with her family.[7] Given the strong family involvement that Sikh families have in their children's lives even when they are teenagers or adults, the story in the film would likely portray challenges in any Sikh diaspora. Keeping family honor (*Izzat* in Punjabi) is very important for all family members. Individual goals and aspirations may have to be sacrificed, since the priority here is not personal fulfillment but rather what makes the family look good in the community.

This chapter will seek to answer questions we may have as to the religious origins, beliefs, and culture of our Sikh neighbors, all leading us to a greater understanding of their faith in order to build a bridge to Christ.

Sikh History

Of the 27 million Sikhs in the world, 76 percent live in the Indian state of Punjab, where the religion originated. A relatively recent world religion, Sikhism began with its founder Guru Nanak, who lived from 1469 to 1539. Nanak was born into a Hindu family, and his father was an accountant. He was schooled in both Hindu and Muslim studies and had friends from both religions. He was notably brilliant in spiritual matters and even when doing mundane chores, he would spend hours dialoguing and meditating about such matters. At the age of 16, he married Sulakhani, a merchant's daughter, and the couple had two sons.[8] Though happy in marriage, Nanak grew increasingly discontent with the two main religions of the area—Hinduism, which held religious sway through the caste of priests (Brahmins), and Islam, which had long ruled the area through Muslim kings. At the age of 30, it was revealed to Nanak that he was to start a new religion: "Nanak experienced the ultimate reality as without form and transcendent, above all things. He did not actually see the ultimate reality in any concrete form. He heard the divine words, the cup of nectar appeared before him, and he drank from it… Thus began the Sikh religion."[9]

According to Sikh tradition, Guru Nanak traveled widely throughout both South Asia and Arabia to spread his teachings. The religion Nanak preached seems to have been influenced by both Hinduism and Islam but sought to transcend both. For example, from Hinduism, Nanak retained belief in karma and reincarnation. Like Muslims, however, Nanak was monotheistic. Nanak's monotheism was possibly influenced by Islam, although the deity of Sikhism shares many similarities with the Hindu concept of Brahman, the pantheistic Supreme Spirit.

After a lifetime of traveling, preaching, and gathering a following of Sikhs (Punjabi for "disciples"), Guru Nanak chose a successor to become the second guru. Shortly thereafter, he died. One account of his death well illustrates Sikhism's unique position between the two religions. Knowing his time to die was near, Nanak was presented with two options. The Hindus wanted to cremate his remains, while the Muslims wanted to bury his body. Thus he arranged that, at his death, Hindus would place flowers to his right, and Muslims would place flowers to his left. Whichever flowers remained fresh the next day would determine which side got to choose what to do with Nanak's body. We are told that in the morning, however, the body was gone, and both sides' flowers were fresh, for Nanak had "merged with the eternal light of the Creator."[10]

Sikhism continued to spread after Nanak's death. The growth and set-apartness of the Sikh community led to the founding of the city of Amritsar in the Punjab; the building of its Golden Temple by the fourth Guru, Ram Das; and eventually, conflict with the Mughal emperors, war, and martyrdom. The

13B. India's Golden Temple, or Hamandir Sahib, is among the holiest sites for Sikhs. Photo by Oleg Yunakov (https://creativecommons.org/licenses/by-sa/3.0).

history of the later gurus is closely connected with military and political struggles in northern India, and it is almost entirely a painful story. Though persecuted, Sikhism continued to grow under the leadership of its gurus.

Including Nanak, there are 10 men who have led the Sikhs as gurus. However, each complete list of gurus totals 11. How can it be that there were 10 men but 11 gurus? The answer is not that the eleventh is a woman. Rather, the eleventh guru is a book. The tenth guru, Gobind Singh (1675–1708), did not name a human successor. It was typical for a Guru to name his son as successor, but all four of his sons had died, two in battle and two from execution. Thus Singh named the eleventh and final successor to be the Sikh holy book, the *Adi Granth*. Compiled by the gurus, the Adi Granth is a collection of almost 6,000 hymns, written by multiple authors of various traditions, including Sikh gurus, Hindu poets, and Muslim Sufis (mystics). Thus the Adi Granth became the Guru Granth Sahib (the "Book of the Gurus"). The word *gurdwara*, designating a Sikh place of worship, means in Punjabi "residence of the guru" or "door that leads to the guru." Thus it is appropriate that during the daily congregational worship, every Gurdwara displays the Guru Granth Sahib on a raised platform. When not read, it is covered with expensive cloth. At night, the book is put away in its own room, ready to be brought back out in the morning in procession to its platform.[11]

In Hinduism, the Sanskrit word *guru* can mean any spiritual teacher. However, with only 11 total gurus in Sikhism since the 1500s, it would stand to reason that a Sikh guru must be a more exalted figure than in Hinduism. Indeed, "guru" in Sikhism

THE 11 GURUS

Guru	Years	Contribution
Nanak	1469–1539	Founder of Sikhism
Angad Dev	1539–52	Developed the Punjabi alphabet; built the langar kitchen
Amar Das	1552–74	Organized and expanded Sikh institutions, including the training of clergy
Ram Das	1574–81	Established the city of Amritsar as the base of Sikhism; named his son as successor, which began a line of physically related gurus
Arjan Dev	1581–1606	Built the Golden Temple in Amritsar; collected almost 6,000 hymns into the Adi Granth
Har Gobind	1606–44	Introduced militaristic tendencies into Sikhism, such as carrying swords and establishing an army
Har Rai	1644–61	Passed over his eldest son because his son distorted Sikh scriptures, naming the younger son Guru at the age of five
Har Kishan	1661–64	Began ruling at age five; died three years later of smallpox
Tegh Bahadur	1664–75	Beheaded by the emperor because he refused to become a Muslim
Gobind Singh	1675–1708	Named his successor as the Guru Granth Sahib; formed the Khalsa order
Granth Sahib	1708–	The holy book of Sikhism

is considered the "embodiment of Divine Light."[12] Sikhs use the term for God himself (the all-Pervading Divine Spirit, the Divine Light), for the Sikh gurus beginning with Guru Nanak, and for the Divine Word.[13]

In addition to making the Adi Granth the perpetual guru, Guru Gobind Singh is also credited with forming the "Khalsa." The reason Singh became guru at age nine was that his father had been beheaded by the emperor for refusing to convert to Islam. It was becoming clear to Singh that the Sikhs needed to establish a presence not so easily persecuted. It was necessary to be more intentional in militarizing themselves. Thus Singh established the Khalsa order. A Khalsa Sikh's appearance is distinguished by the "Five Ks": Kesh (uncut hair and beard), Kangha (comb), Kara (iron bracelet), Kachera (cotton undergarment), and Kirpan (steel dagger).

Male and female Sikhs who belong to the Khalsa order have been "baptized" into the order (a ceremony called *amrit*, which involves drinking sacred water) and have made vows to live according to the Khalsa Code of Conduct. The word *khalsa* is Punjabi for "pure ones." The first five Sikhs to undergo this commitment were given the last name of Singh (lion), which is now used almost universally as the last name of a Sikh male. Similarly, Sikh women who underwent *amrit* were given the last name of Kaur (daughter of kings), which became the common last name of Sikh females. This practice of sharing the same last name demonstrates an equality that contrasts with the caste divisions of Hinduism.

In northern India, Sikhs continued to experience periods of persecution and periods of peace, including its own independent reign in the Punjab during the first half of the 1800s. Although British rule in India was not met with passivity, eventually Sikhs became trusted soldiers and bodyguards for the British in India and all throughout the British Empire. The 1947 India-Pakistan division has proved problematic for many Sikhs who have felt caught in the middle. Some Sikhs have advocated for a separate Sikh nation, called Khalistan, in the Punjab. Some Sikh extremists have perpetrated terrorist acts toward this end. However, it is a mistake to assume from periodic Sikh violence that Sikhism is an extremist religion. The vast majority of Sikhs are peaceable.

God and Humans

The foundational gurus of Sikhism in the sixteenth century drew from the depths of all Indian religious experience, especially from the devotional traditions in North India, which transcended the religious boundaries of Hindu *bhakti* (devotion to God) or Sufism (Islamic mysticism). The gurus were also influenced by the traditions of devotional religious poets called Sants and by *yogic* groups called Naths, who seem to go beyond any sort of explicit religious affiliation. A sense of going beyond, or even of breaking down, traditional religious boundaries is at the heart of Sikhism. Thus the Sikh scriptures include "non-Sikh" Sants and poets, individuals traditionally identified as Hindu or Muslim. Nevertheless, the Sikh path remains distinct from both Hinduism and Islam as a new creative focus of the religious energies of India. The vitality of the Sikh path illustrates the power of religious creativity to transform individual lives and to establish a new social structure.

Sikhism is, first of all, the community of those who are Sikhs, disciples of the line of ten gurus, beginning with Guru Nanak. Sikhism arose from Guru Nanak's transformative religious experience, which led him to affirm surrender to the One, the formless and transcendent God, and so to reject both caste divisions and the competing religious identities of Hindu and Muslim. His devotional songs, compiled by Arjun Dev, the fifth Guru, in the Adi Granth (which later became the Guru Granth Sahib), along with poems of the other gurus and various other saints, affirm the singularity of God as the One, who, though without form, pervades and supports all. One owes God absolute submission in love. These feelings of love are fostered and expressed in communal singing of devotional songs (*kirtan*) more than through temple ritual or asceticism.

Guru Nanak's religious experience was first a repudiation of other religious traditions—their shrines, asceticism, prophets, incarnations, practices, and scriptures. After his transformation, he is reported to have said, "There is no Hindu; there is no Muslim."[14] His fundamental experience of God is found in the opening verses of his composition *Japji*, with which the *Adi Granth* begins:

> There is one God, Eternal truth is His Name, Maker of all things, Fearing nothing and at enmity with nothing; Timeless is His Image; Not begotten, being of His own Being: By the grace of the Guru, made known to men. As he was in the beginning: The Truth, So throughout the ages, He has ever been: The Truth, So even now He is Truth immanent, So for ever and ever he shall be truth eternal.[15]

In Sikhism, God is the "one and only one." Thus a common Sikh name for God is *Ekankar*, which is composed of three words: (1) *ek*, "the one"; (2) *aum* or *om*, the Sanskrit meditative syllable that is said to reflect God's essence; and (3) *kar*, "the only one."[16] Another Sikh designation for God is *Sat Nam*, which simply means "the true name." God is without form of image or incarnation. God is the Truth, residing in all creation but especially in the depths of the human heart. It is by loving surrender and self-forgetting *bhakti* (devotion to God) that the disciple achieves the goal of realizing God. The mystical encounter with the formless God takes place in community, in the congregational singing of devotional songs from the Guru Granth Sahib that bring the experience of the divine Name.

Various Sikh gurus in foundational decades rejected the Hindu caste system. Thus an outward characteristic of the Sikh community is the rejection of caste hierarchy and social separation on religious grounds. This fellowship of all people is symbolized by the shared kitchen (*langar*) in the Gurdwara, from which all eat together on the floor, thus expressing unity and equality among Sikhs through the "common table." In the United States, where fast food characterizes much social interaction, the great significance given to sharing food may seem obscure. In Indian society, however, sharing food reflects a relationship of intimacy that is generally impossible because of caste and religious divisions. Thus in Sikhism, the experience of a formless God who transcends all images and rituals becomes the foundation for a community that goes beyond the usual social boundaries. Eating together means that all social, class, and religious divisions have been put aside because of the transcending character of devotion to the One God who is beyond all forms of society and religion.

However, beyond the outward practice and perception of Sikh social equality, there are issues that show divides in caste relationships between Sikhs. Among Sikhs, there are various castes that comprise the Sikh population both in India and among immigrants

13C. An eighteenth-century painting of Guru Gobind Singh meeting Guru Nanak Dev. Public domain.

settled overseas: Jats (farmers), Rajputs (soldiers and warriors), Ramgarhias (blacksmiths, bricklayers, and other tradesmen), Ravidassias (tanners and animal skinners), Bhatras (fortune-tellers), and Valmikis (street sweepers). Punjabis, the people group from which Sikhs belong, adhere to the Hindu stratification of class or hierarchical occupational groups. Some of the examples of caste practices would be that intermarriages between higher and lower castes are not encouraged by many parents. Some groups also decided to open their own Gurdwaras based on caste identity. Lower caste Sikhs, such as Ravidassias, were discriminated at times by the higher castes, such as Jats.[17] Some Sikhs also add caste names after the common names Singh or Kaur as their last names. Thus the sociocultural realities of the Indian context and historical backdrop may come in the way of the scriptural ideal when it comes to caste issues in Sikhism.

Salvation and Congregational Life

The point of Sikhism is the eventual union with God, and Guru Nanak taught five stages on the path to this union. The first stage is a commitment to honor God and serve others. The second stage is a growth in knowledge of God, which transforms the adherent from self-absorption to love of God. The third stage is the effort to humble oneself before God and listen to his word. The fourth stage is being filled with spiritual power and peace. The fifth stage is to experience Truth and achieve union with God.[18]

Since Sikhism centers on surrender and commitment to God, a crucial practice is participation in the communal singing (*kirtan*) of sacred songs from the Guru Granth Sahib. Loving attention to the Name of God overcomes worldly desire and enters the depths of the heart where it becomes the principle of life.

Sikhs not only orient their piety toward God, but they also practice the principles of their religion to each other. The sharing of food together, for example, reflects the deep sense of fellowship that is the basis of Sikh life. As already mentioned, everyone sits together and eats on the floor, without regard to status, in the free langar meal.

The congregational encounter with the One God who is Truth becomes the norm for all behavior: living in accord with the Truth in surrender to God, in the depths of one's heart, and in all one's relations with others. This dynamic observance of Truth—a life of truthfulness—becomes the foundation for all right living. To be other than truthful in all one's dealings would betray the religious and communal experience of Sikhism. Obviously, then, this faithful observance of the Truth is not primarily a solitary activity.

Guru Nanak and the other Sikh gurus rejected the path of renunciation central to other Indian religions. Sikhism is thus not a religion for the *sannyasin*, or world renouncer, but for the householder, for those involved in family life and the world of commerce and government. The Sikh role in the world is one of activism, perhaps even a militant quest for social change. This world-transforming attitude is partly responsible for the fact that Sikhs have played a disproportionate role in the Indian circles of business, finance, defense, and government. The distinctive appearance of Sikh men—especially their wearing the turban and unshorn hair—ensures that they are a visible presence both in Indian society and throughout the Indian diaspora.

Contemporary Sikhism

Sikhs make up about 2 percent of the Indian population, but they also play a significant role in the Indian diaspora throughout Europe and the United States. Nevertheless, Sikhism is in many ways identified with the regional culture of the Punjab, where the Sikh population is concentrated.

The Punjab was divided in the 1947 partition that produced the nations of India and Pakistan, and Sikhs have struggled to find a cultural and religious identity within independent India. As mentioned earlier, agitation for Sikh regional autonomy within the Punjab or for an independent Khalistan, a separate Sikh state, continues to fan flames of violence in this region. Many Sikh political leaders have been slain on all sides, while the Indian government has sought an advantageous political solution. Political maneuvers seem only to have increased regional separatism and the internal death toll among various Sikh factions.

Even the Golden Temple in Amritsar, the most sacred Sikh shrine, became a pawn in the battle when it was occupied in 1984 by Sikh nationalists who turned the complex into a fortification. The Indian Army's subsequent invasion of the Golden Temple, which caused more than 1,000 deaths and widespread destruction in the shrine, brought on the assassination of Indian prime minister Indira Gandhi by her Sikh bodyguards and, in turn, the slaughter of thousands of Sikhs in Delhi and throughout northern India. In its founding, the Sikh tradition addressed its audience by drawing on all the available resources within Indian culture, adopting a wide spectrum of poets, Sants, religious vocabulary, shared cultural assumptions, and attitudes. However, present ethnic and nationalist pressures and resistant repression make the realization of the Sikh ideal of a universal community of disciples under a single transcendent God much harder to achieve.

American Sikhs have also found themselves caught in the middle of post–September

11, 2001, hostility against Muslims. Some time ago, I (Wayne) was able to speak with Valarie Kaur, from a family of Sikh farmers in Clovis, California. Her grandfather immigrated to California from India, traveling by steamship in the early 1900s. After 9/11, it was not uncommon for anyone who looked potentially Arabic to be the targets of revenge, as grief and fear gave way to prejudice and violence. "Sikhs who wore turbans became immediate targets," Kaur explained. "Temples were burned, homes vandalized, people threatened, shot, stabbed." She decided to travel the United States and document their stories on film. "Nearly every person you see in America who wears a turban is a Sikh," Kaur said. "We heard stories from Muslims, Arabs, and even Latinos who were placed in the 'Muslim-looking' category, until at one point the camera turned 180 degrees on us and people started yelling at us, telling us to go back to our country."[19]

Even when assimilation into the West goes smoothly, Sikhs can face another difficulty. Even though pride in Sikh heritage is strong, both North American–born Sikhs and newly immigrated Sikhs can struggle to preserve their identity while striving to succeed in their new homeland. For this reason, efforts are made to train young Sikhs in their heritage. For example, it is not uncommon for Gurdwaras to feature a "Punjabi school" on Sundays for teaching Sikh history, language, and philosophy.[20]

Contextualizing the Gospel for Sikh People

The word *contextualization* emerged in missionary circles in the 1970s. It was coined by Shokie Coe, a Taiwanese Chinese ecumenical leader.[21] The idea that cultural context should be taken into serious consideration in order to effectively communicate the gospel continued to gain ground in the following years with Lausanne Congress on Evangelism initiatives. It was not just an academic term with no practical relevance. The concept of contextualization had a deep impact on how the gospel was communicated to those who belong to the majority or two-thirds world whether they live in their original context or a diaspora.

In the 1980s and '90s, more awareness of the sociocultural context of people groups emerged. The words *enculturation* and *indigenization* were also used over the years to relate the message of the gospel to the local context of the people that were being reached. Catholic and Evangelical missionaries and theologians alike made efforts to reach out to their audience in culturally relevant ways. It was clear that one approach did not fit all. The Western approach of linear, systematic communication did not connect well with the people of the East who did not have the same constructs for communication. Likewise, traditional Christian apologetics can be presented in ways that wrongly assume that all people think and process the same way.[22] The truth of the gospel is universal, but the methods by which it is communicated are not.

Contextualization is crucial when it comes to presenting the gospel to Sikh people. We ought to be aware of the social, religious, and cultural constructs in Sikh culture.

Who are the Sikh people socioculturally and religiously? Sikhs come from the larger context of India. Thus Indian cultural and social values often play an integral part of their identity. My (Natun's) first encounters with the Sikhs were in the city of Kolkata when I was in my late teens attending college. In India, languages, communication patterns, and social customs may be vastly different from state to state. Having met hardly any Sikhs in my village in north Bengal, I was fascinated with the distinctive features of Sikhs, with their turbans and typically taller stature than Bengali people.

Many of these young Sikhs had moved to Kolkata from the villages and cities of the Punjab either to work to support families back home or to get their college education. I found them to be hardworking, honest, and family-oriented. Although we came from two distinctively different regions, religions, and food preferences, I discovered common threads of Indian culture among the Sikhs. For example, there was the collectivistic orientation, whereby it was not enough to succeed alone in Kolkata but important to honor one's parents by supporting the family back home. Then there was hospitality. One could not visit someone's home without being offered a meal or snacks at any time of day or night. There was an openness to arranged marriages by parents and to fulfilling family obligations, such as helping sisters to get married with an adequate dowry. At the same time, they were very focused on practicing their faith in the Gurdwara and preserving their Punjabi and Sikh heritage at all levels. These deeply ingrained cultural values may be put to the test if one steps out to accept Christ as it can be seen as rejecting one's heritage and people.

Years later, I (Natun) now live in the United States and have met Sikhs from diverse backgrounds over the years. Despite the pressure of Westernization and globalization, I have observed that some of the key Punjabi values have not altered. For example, community orientation, respect for the elderly, and deference to parents are still very much a part of Sikh culture even in diaspora. As mentioned earlier, it remains an honor-shame culture, in which the family honor needs to be preserved and the abiding expectation is to fulfill one's familial duties.

These strong values can make it difficult for a Sikh to be open to the gospel, for he or she might be confronted with an extended family and community that will not accept one of their own coming to Christ. Once someone comes to Christ in a South Asian community, that person is often alone, cut off from nuclear family, or one's nuclear family becomes cut off from extended family. Coming to Christ can seem like a betrayal to one's family and the collective Sikh community. The bridge back to the family and community is often no longer open.

Seeking the lone convert has been a general model of evangelism in the Punjab and elsewhere in India throughout the history of modern missions (with the exception of mass conversions from numerous Dalit and tribal people groups). However, this approach does not conform well in a collectivistic culture because it can isolate the new believer from his own community. In a recent thought-provoking publication called *Insider Jesus: Theological Reflections on New Christian Movements*, William Dyrness discusses a research and field study in the Punjab by Darren Duerksen from Fresno Pacific University.[23] Because of the Punjabi and Sikh communities' perception of Christianity being a foreign religion brought to India by Westerners to Punjab, a new group of Punjabi Christians has initiated a Punjabi Sikh style of worship, including an Indian style of music (*bhajan*). The house of worship resembles a Gurdwara, with the Bible in a prominent place in the front. Participants leave their shoes outside, men come in turbans, and women dress in the traditional *shalwar kameez*. All these adaptations show that, although they are followers of Christ, they have not abandoned their Sikh or Punjabi identity.

Duerksen emphasizes that these believers want to convey a message that social identity need not be changed in order to follow Christ, emphasizing instead the need for internal change.[24] This seems to be an effective strategy to make Christ known and followed in the Sikh community. Traditional values and practices—such as cultural expressions and connectivity to family—that do not conflict with one's loyalty and commitment to Christ ought to be upheld as much as possible. As one former Sikh, now a Baptist minister in the Punjab, advises,

> Don't use particulars about their religion or culture as a launching point for a gospel presentation. That would turn things they are proud of (their uncut

BELIEFS IN SIKHISM AND CHRISTIANITY		
	Sikhism	**Christianity**
God	God is the eternal one and only (*Ekankar*), an all-pervading spirit, formless and transcendent. He is Truth and eternal light.	Christianity, too, is monotheistic, but its God is less pantheistic and more personal than the Sikh God. He is the eternally relational Trinity (Father, Son, and Holy Spirit) who acts decisively in human history.
Salvation	The seemingly endless cycle of karma, death, and rebirth comes to an end with the soul's merger with its creator. This is accomplished through God's grace and through the devotedness of the adherent to God.	Sinful humanity can be restored to their original created purpose by the grace of God and through their faith in Jesus, the Son of God. Jesus died for humanity's sins, rose from the dead, has begun to reign as King, and will return to restore creation into the new heavens and new earth.
Scripture	The Guru Granth Sahib is the revered compilation of hymns and poems by various Sikh gurus and mystics of other traditions that provide the content for congregational worship in the Gurdwara.	The Bible is composed of Old Testament and New Testament. The former tells the story of how God delivered and established the nation of Israel. The latter tells the story of Israel's long-awaited Messiah (Jesus) who came into the world to seek and save the lost.
Afterlife	An individual experiences innumerable lifetimes because of karmic rebirth. In the fortunate event of a human rebirth, the Sikh devotee can experience liberation, merging with God at death.	A person's lifetime is infinitely consequential. For it is destined for each person to die once, and after that to face judgment (Hebrews 9:27). Those who respond to God's gift of salvation by putting their trust in God's sacrifice for their sins (i.e., Jesus) will live eternally in heaven. "Whoever does not believe is condemned already, because he has not believed in the name of the only Son of God" (John 3:18).

> hair, their dagger, their book) into objects of shame...Christians where I live often tell Sikhs that if they accept Jesus, they have to get rid of all their gods, cut their hair, and stop going to the *gurdwara*. Please don't make that a point of emphasis when you share with them. Wait for the right time, explain relevant Scripture to them, and let the Bible speak for itself. As they're being renewed in their faith, they will be able to make some strong decisions for Jesus.[25]

The message of Christ and His salvation is universally relevant. But the presentation of this life-changing message needs to be contextual. The expression of the new faith of the new community also needs to be framed by them because they best know their socioreligious identity. Cultural values should be preserved as long as they are not contrary to the biblical standards of truth and morality. Yet determining the distinction between culture and religion can be tricky because culture and religion are often intermingled in Sikhism.

Even after cultural and social values are taken into considerable and thoughtful consideration, there will still be elements within Christianity that may not sit right with a Sikh. The former Sikh mentioned above described his pre-Christian reaction against Christianity: "Jesus isn't the only way to God, and it's offensive to tell me that. There were plenty of gurus who taught what Jesus taught. You can follow any of their examples and be just as good a person as Jesus tells you to be."[26]

Although the exclusivity of Christianity can be off-putting to the Sikh, it is helpful to focus on Jesus as uniquely divine. His life on the earth was like no other. The truth is that Jesus viewed Himself not as just an embodiment of God's truth, like the gurus, but as the unique Son of God (Matthew 21:33-42) able to save us from our sins (26:28). W. Owen Cole and Piara Singh Sambhi, who have explored Sikhism in depth for many years and published substantive works on the subject, maintain that Sikhs find the Hindu concept of "avatars" (gods taking physical form and entering history, such as Rama and Krishna) problematic.[27] For one thing, why would an all-powerful God allow the world to get so out of control that there would need to be such an intervention? For another, Hindu avatars, such as the flirtatious Rama, displayed all-too-human tendencies, not least of which was their own death. Jesus Christ, however, is different:

> Christianity does not, of course, teach that Jesus should be regarded as a sudden intervention into history. He came "in the fullness of time" (Galatians 4:4) and was "the lamb of God slain from the foundation of the world" (Revelation 13:8). The Incarnation is part of the eternal plan of God for the redemption of humanity, not an after thought or a desperate rescue bid.[28]

In my (Natun's) years of ministry to South Asians and having been raised in the mainstream Indian context, I have found that a confrontational approach ("You're wrong; I'm right") does not seem to make any impact on a Sikh audience. It is best not to focus on how wrong they are. Christ's uniqueness is definitely scriptural, yet it should be a topic of continuing dialogue embedded in solid relationship and demonstrated in life as we build a truly incarnational relationship. We need to sense the freedom and willingness of the other person to delve deep into discussions on Christianity. Our right of such a conversation is earned by an incarnational witness, which opens the door for a more direct discussion of truth.

All the while, as we build bridges and cultivate relationships, the Holy Spirit draws the heart, convicting of sin (John 16:7-9). In the words of the Sikh-turned-pastor, "The faith I had in my gurus' teachings unraveled when I was overwhelmed by my sin. The Holy Spirit got my attention when I heard that the reason behind Jesus's death and resurrection was the sin I couldn't shake or fix by being a devoted, religious person."[29]

Sadhu Sundar Singh lived in the early 1900s in the Punjab. When his mother died, he retaliated against the Christian God he didn't believe in by persecuting Christian missionaries. After all, the Christian God claimed to be a God of love, and as such, shouldn't this God have prevented his mother from dying? He finished one evening by burning a Bible, page by page, to the sound of his friends' laughter. That night, he contemplated suicide. However, the next morning, he received a vision of the risen Jesus. Like the Apostle Paul before him, Sadhu became a Christian evangelist, undergoing severe persecution, including stoning, for the Jesus he had once persecuted.[30]

Sadhu never repudiated his Punjabi culture but kept the turban and robe, insisting there was no contradiction between being an Indian and a Christian. And he is right.

Natun Bhattacharya (DMiss, New Geneva Theological Seminary) was born and raised in India in a Hindu priest caste family. After becoming a Christian, he ministered in India in both evangelism and training. Now in the United States, he has served Asian Indian communities, international students, and a missionary training ministry agency equipping missionaries reaching the world. Currently Natun's interests include equipping others to understand the Hindu worldview as well as research and writing on issues related to culture and communication.

C. Wayne Mayhall (MACT, Bethel University) has taught philosophy, religious studies, and ethics at numerous colleges, including Liberty University, North Carolina A & T State University, and Newberry College. He is a contributing editor to the *Christian Research Journal* and the author or coauthor of six books, including *Patterns of Religion*, *Religious Autobiographies*, and *On Martin Buber*, and is EdD (ABD) at Liberty University in curriculum and instruction.

14

The East Asian Complex

Aaron Wheeler and Mike Ackerman

As in many places, religion in East Asia is complicated. Thousands of years of continuous cultural history makes the situation in East Asia especially difficult to describe. Yet these nations contain billions of precious people who matter to God. So let's begin to understand three major religions in the area: Confucianism and Taoism, which are native to China, and Shinto, which is native to Japan.

Confucianism

The Chinese Communist Party, the official governing body of China, lists five religions as protected by the constitution and legal to practice within the country: Buddhism, Taoism, Islam, Catholicism, and Protestantism.[1] But do you know what is not listed? It is one of the oldest and arguably the most influential of all. It is currently endorsed by the Chinese government through official party statements and propagated through the government-backed creation of institutions all over the world. It's Confucianism. Which isn't even a religion. Except when it is.

See what I mean? It's complicated.

If you ask the average Chinese person what religion he or she follows, the person would likely respond by saying, "I don't have a belief." Yet during an important occasion, such as preparing for a big exam, or waiting on a promotion at work, or before getting married, or when a child is to be born, he or she is likely to wear a piece of jade as a necklace or bracelet hung from a red string. And he or she most likely went to a temple recently to pray.

Is this religious activity? Most Chinese wouldn't see it as such. It's simply being Chinese. The particular activity of gaining fortune through wearing a religious token isn't necessarily rooted in any particular religion. It could be traced to elements of Taoism, it could be a symbol of Buddhism, or it could have just been something their grandparent made them put on. It really doesn't matter. It's just the Chinese way. It's tradition.

And thousands of years of tradition is a lot. Thus, religion in China is quite the task to cover in one chapter, and we won't be able to get to all of it. Instead, we will cover two religions native to China: Confucianism and Taoism. The third majorly influential religion in China, Buddhism, was covered in chapter 7.

14A. A painting depicting Confucius presenting the infant Buddha to Laozi. June 11, 2006. Public domain.

Religious understanding in China today can mostly be traced to the intertwining of Taoism, Confucianism, and Buddhism. They've all been practiced for thousands of years within the country, and because none of them claim to be exclusive, they often overlap with one another in thought, vocabulary, practice, and doctrine. Today, many Chinese pick and choose which elements of each are necessary for any given moment. As one writer put it, "Chinese wear a Confucianist hat for everyday life, Taoist robes for religious ceremonies, and Buddhist sandals for stepping into the next life."[2]

These ancient ways of thinking have become so integrated into the proper and correct way of life that they comprise their own worldview more than suggest specific religious practices. Respecting your family, burning incense, being loyal to your government, following your teacher's instruction, performing rituals for good luck—these aren't doctrines to believe or religious practices to adopt. For the Chinese, they're simply what's right, good, and the proper way to live. They're just true. But whether recognized or not, these practices do have religious origins, and understanding the impact of China's original religions is important to understanding China today.

So what is Confucianism anyway? It is many things. For example, it's a philosophy with religious elements. It's a religion that focuses on human systems instead of the supernatural. It's a political tool used by those in power to maintain social order. It's a tradition so foundational that it silently guides the largest country in the world. It's all those things and yet sometimes none. Can that even be true? How is that possible?

It's confusing. Of course it is. Part of that comes from its long history. After all, 2,500 years of Confucianism is a very, very long time, and in a country as old and diverse in culture and history as China, Confucianism has been a lot of things to a lot of people at various places and times. But don't worry; I'll do my best to walk you through all of it and try to explain in a way that makes sense.

The History and Beliefs of Confucianism

Confucianism begins, naturally, with Confucius himself. Or at least that's the name we give him today. His actual name was Kong Qui, with Kong being his clan's name and Qui the name given to him by his parents. But once he became an established figure, he was known as Kong Fuzi, which means "master Kong." Can you see it? The sounds of Kong Fuzi, if you say them really fast, can sound a lot like Confucius. Officially, it was Western missionaries to China who tried their best to sound out his name in Chinese in a way that people back home could understand and pronounce.[3] Hence we have Confucius.

Confucius lived from somewhere around 551–479 BC, about 500 years before Jesus. He lived during the Zhou dynasty and was a local official, meaning he was part of a class of society that dedicated itself to scholarship and politics, overseeing local towns and states and making the edicts of the ruling class a reality for everyone else. He wasn't especially famous during or immediately after his lifetime. It was the way in which his teachings were written, explained, and spread by his students many years later that led to him becoming such a powerful figure. So much of what he did in life is unknown or lost to history, mostly because it didn't seem that important at the time.

While living his life as an official, Confucius spent a lot of time teaching and writing. Hundreds of years later, these ideas were edited and compiled into a number of books spanning multiple genres and styles generally referred to as the Confucian classics. These would form the foundation of Confucius's ideas on how both the group and the individual should order themselves to create the best and most successful society.

In its most basic form, Confucianism is a philosophy about how people should live. It's essentially humanistic, which means that it cares most about how human beings function together and the manner in which they can best work together. This dutifulness is encapsulated in the Chinese word *li*. Pronounced "lee," this word means the standard in which people act, based on their behaviors, etiquette, and rituals. It's a bit like a report card in school. Every person is required to do certain things, and each person is judged based on how well they have met the standards expected of them.

Li is mostly lived out in relationships. Those relationships are based on a hierarchy, and in every relationship, there is someone with more power and someone with less power. Each group is expected to behave in a certain way. If both sides of the relationship succeed in doing that, then a society can be successful.

Confucius taught that there are five basic power relationships: ruler to subject,

14B. Temple of Confucius in Liuzhou, Guangxi. 李海斌 (https://creativecommons.org/licenses/by-sa/2.0).

husband to wife, father to son, older brother to younger brother, and friend to friend. For the ruler-to-subject relationship, the ruler is expected to act with compassion and generosity, while the subjects are supposed to act with loyalty and submission. For the husband-to-wife relationship, the husband is supposed to act with virtue and honesty, while the wife is required to be obedient and respectful. In the father-to-son relationship, the father is to be kind and generous, while the son is to show deference and reverence. For the older-brother-to-younger-brother relationship, the elder is required to be gracious, while the younger must be humble. For the friend-to-friend, the greater is supposed to be considerate, and the lesser is to be respectful.

The basic, most fundamental understanding of Confucianism, then, is this: If each of those people behaves according to the rules, society will be great. For example, if a husband behaves in a way that a husband should, and a wife behaves in a way that a wife should, then they will have a great marriage.

This concept of great, in Confucian terms, is called "harmony." The goal of all Confucian teaching is to help people understand the way harmony can best be achieved. Much of Confucian teaching, then, is an explanation of how each of these categories of people should behave.

Yet while Confucius's focus on hierarchical relationships is key to his philosophy, he also explained more general teachings about moral behavior in all relationships. For example, he believed strongly in reciprocity, which is the idea that relationships must maintain a balance of giving and receiving to be beneficial. He also encouraged familial piety, which is the deference to the needs of the family above oneself. And perhaps his most famous quoted saying is his version of the golden rule: "[Virtue] is, when you go abroad, to behave to every one as if you were receiving a great guest: to employ the people as if you were assisting at a great sacrifice; not to do to others as you would not wish done to yourself."[4]

Confucius's teachings are given, debated, explained, and codified in several important texts, but the most foundational to Confucianism are the *Five Classics* and the *Four Books*. Confucius believed that a major part of his purpose was not just to create new teachings but also to be a translator of traditional Chinese thought into the modern age of his time. He mostly accomplished this through *Five Classics*, a collection of five books of various genres of traditional Chinese philosophy and practice. His own teachings were compiled and explained in the *Four Books*. Chief among them is the *Analects*, a collection of Confucian teachings collected by his followers on how a noble person should behave in each of the five relational dynamics. The other three books are compilations of commentaries, speeches, and teachings by his followers. The *Four Books* were officially collected and set as central Confucian doctrine during the Song Dynasty (AD 960–1279), more than 1,000 years after Confucius's death.

While most of Confucius's teachings are concerned with the proper order of society through human relationships, he incorporated certain religious elements into his instructions and seemed to believe in the existence of God.[5] He spoke about a significant, if somewhat unclear, concept of God, referred to as *Tian*, or "Heaven." Tian is an unseen spiritual power that is only loosely related to humanity. Despite being the supreme power, ruler, and judge over all the earth, Tian only rarely chooses to involve himself with the affairs of humanity. This primarily takes place when a government, or in this context a dynasty, is removed from power because of their inability to govern their people in a noble and selfless way and is replaced by a superior leader. This right of an emperor or bloodline to rule over people is called the "Mandate of Heaven" and can be given or taken away by Tian based on the ruler's behavior. Ultimately, though, Confucianism has mostly concerned itself with how people should behave in an ordered society to be able to achieve collective harmony.

Confucius also taught on the correct forms of religious ritual. These instructions covered everything from how a leader can correctly make offerings and sacrifices to God to how ancestors are correctly enshrined and venerated within the home. The way these religious elements were highlighted and enforced often came down to the religious views of the dynasty in power at the time. At various points in Chinese history, these teachings were mixed with traditional Chinese folk religion and practices of Buddhism and Taoism. But again, while Confucianism does maintain religious elements and Confucius believed in the supernatural, his main focus was on human behavior and relationships. As one historian concludes, "[Confucius] asserted that human beings are to respect the gods and spirits, but to keep a distance from them."[6]

While starting small, Confucianism began emerging as a major influence on Chinese society when it was adopted as political ideology during the Han dynasty (206 BC–AD 220). It was during the time of Emperor Wu (141–87 BC) that it was standardized as the official philosophy of the government, and Confucian schools and academies began to spread their teaching across China and Asia at large. Eventually, a person's ability to memorize and pass tests on Confucian teaching became the main way career politicians were recognized and promoted. This system of imperial examinations began during the Han dynasty but wasn't fully integrated until the Tang dynasty (AD 618–907). This system would remain in place until the fall of the final imperial Chinese dynasty in the early twentieth century. Thus for nearly 2,000 years, the teachings of Confucius were the standard by which leaders in China were measured.

Once the Qing dynasty fell in 1911, many Chinese people perceived Confucianism as a relic of old thinking that was the very antithesis of the modern revolution they were trying to build. Thus it fell out of favor for two generations as the Republic of China, led by the Nationalist Party and its nationalist-democratic philosophy, was eventually replaced by the People's Republic of China and the Communist Party in 1949. Communist teachings were seen as foundationally different from Confucian principles. Both had a goal of a utopian society, but while Confucianism teaches that this is achieved through benevolence from the powerful and submission from the weak, communism teaches that a society can only advance when all power structures are eliminated and one class of equals remains.

Anti-Confucian thought reached a peak during the chaos of the Cultural Revolution of the 1960s and 1970s, where youth groups supported by Mao Zedong sought to rid China of all traditional elements in a bid to bring about a true revolution. But as the country has since attempted to modernize and maintain a stable social order while also having the world's largest population, the Communist Party has seen an opportunity to use the tradition and teachings of Confucianism once again.

As communism is officially a nonreligious

political system, this utilization of Confucianism is done with nearly all religious elements of Confucianism removed. But the foundational teachings of a traditional Chinese worldview based around order, harmony, and submission to authority remain.

This politicized propaganda is demonstrated on several fronts. In 2005, then Chinese President Hu Jintao said that "building a harmonious society" would be the principal goal of his administration.[7] In 2006, at the 16th Central Committee of the Communist Party, the "Chinese Communist Party Central Committee's Resolution on Major Issues of Building a Socialist Harmonious Society" was ratified, overseeing large areas of economic, social, and political reform. Observers stated,

> People from all walks of life—party leaders, public officials, college professors, students, China's new economic elites, workers, farmers, school teachers—suddenly found themselves in the middle of a propaganda campaign for a socialist harmonious society.[8]

This favoring of Confucianism is also seen when China shows itself to the world. During the 2008 Olympic opening ceremonies in Beijing, the *Analects* of Confucius were quoted. A newly built Communist Party school in Shanghai was modeled after Confucian architecture, and Confucian institutes have been created overseas in France and Germany, at the behest of the government.[9] These examples show how the Communist Party has come a long way in embracing an ideology that it once soundly rejected.

The political opportunity that Confucianism offers the government is easily identified. Central to the five core hierarchal relationships is the idea that an ordered and harmonic society can be achieved only if those in the lower power position are willing to submit to those in high power positions. Thus, a government that wants to maintain social order among a populous, crowded, and diverse people can be helped by pushing submission in the form of a traditional philosophy so deeply intertwined in its history that it is inseparable from Chinese identity itself.

The Lifestyle and Culture of Confucianism Today

The ingrained influence of Confucianism is demonstrated today in how Chinese people practice these principles. But in many ways, "practice" is the wrong word. Confucianism isn't practiced; it's lived.

Chinese people today have a strong sense of familial responsibility. When choosing a major in college, or a career after graduating, or which city to live in, or what to do with aging parents, it is the needs of the family that come before the individual. This sense of piety toward the family collective is a strong Confucian ideal, even if the individual Chinese person wouldn't necessarily attribute it to Confucianism.

Annual holidays also often have Confucian origins. The Qingming festival, for example, is devoted to visiting the graves of relatives to preserve their memory. Some people purchase paper goods in the shape of cars, houses, or fake money to burn at the graves alongside food and incense. Family members are expected to gather, regardless of how long the journey may be, to show respect to ancestors as Confucianism teaches.

Within relationships, there is a clear expectation that people will act according to the rules of hierarchy and reciprocity. This is seen in a number of ways. Within the education system, teachers are shown significant respect, and classroom management is a minimal task. When a group of people get together for a meal, issues such as placement around the table and who pays for the bill are decided according to titles and power structures. When guests come to a house, whether foreigners from another country or friends from another city, great expense is often invested, and individual needs are pushed aside so that a great show can be made of hospitality. And even among the best of friends, careful attention is paid toward all acts of service, gifts, and favors so that no one remains in any kind of debt to another. All these actions are based in repeated teachings of Confucius.

Confucianism and Christianity

Confucianism is a foundational way of thought and practice among the Chinese, regardless of whether it is recognized as such. Confucius's teachings "created the ruts for the Chinese to follow for untold centuries,"[10] ruts that still exist today. Thus it is critical for anyone who wishes to bring the gospel of Jesus to these people to consider the potential barriers and bridges to Christ and His teachings.

Barrier: The nature of humanity. One of the most conspicuous contrasts between Confucianism and Christianity concerns the nature of humanity, especially regarding sin and depravity. Is man essentially good or evil? Confucius did not give a clear teaching on this, and so it was up to two of his most influential followers to decide the direction of the ideology moving forward.

On one end was Menzi, who argued that humanity was essentially good and that the choices a person makes flow toward goodness like water down a stream.[11] He believed that bad choices arose from a person's bad habits or a corruption of their natural goodness. While he didn't deny that evil existed or that humanity had a penchant for harm and destruction, he claimed that this was not how humans naturally functioned and that these actions were devious breaks from our original essence.[12]

Xunzi, arriving later, rejected this premise and argued that humanity was basically selfish and tended toward evil choices. The only solution was to provide a strict environment of training and teaching to correct it and rise above uncivilized basic instincts. His teachings led to a focus on the importance of moral standards and the need of society to teach these standards and hold one another accountable to them.[13]

Eventually, Menzi's philosophies would be largely accepted over Xunzi's and would become the dominant teaching of Confucianism. Consequently, most Chinese people believe that humans are essentially good, an ideology reinforced by communist principles, as well. When encountering an individual who acts with selfish or destructive motives, education and behavior reforms are seen as the way to help humanity reach its full potential.

This belief clashes with Christianity's fundamental doctrine of sin and the fall of humanity as taught in Genesis 3. Humanity's fallen nature and inability to save itself is found in many places in Scripture, such as Romans 3:23; Isaiah 53:6; and 1 John 1:8-10. When attempting to share the gospel with a Chinese person, then, it is important to contextualize the concept of sin in light of its original Greek meaning of *hamartia*, which means "to miss the mark." While most Chinese people believe that humans are good, they know they are far from perfect. The New Testament explanation of sin as "missing the mark," like an archer missing the center of the target, can help render the concept of sin more understandable to a culture that isn't accustomed to thinking in terms of human depravity.

Barrier: The punishment of hell. As familial responsibility is so central to Chinese values, one must be careful when explaining the eternal separation of hell to an individual who likely doesn't have any Christian family members. Chinese people tend to consider the needs of the group above themselves, and so hearing that anyone who doesn't accept Christ will be eternally separated from those who do is quite a shocking concept. I'll never forget the moment I (Aaron) was listening to a gospel presentation that taught about hell when a Chinese woman stood up and said, "I'd rather go to hell with my parents than go to heaven without them."

This difficulty can be handled on two fronts. First, when sharing the gospel, it is important to bring in a person's group to be able to listen and respond together. Westerners tend to think of conversion as an individualized choice of personal faith, but the book of Acts gives many examples of entire households coming to Christ together. A return to this first-century strategy is an appropriate plan for a Confucian society. Second, if the family members aren't available, it's important to prayerfully consider when hell should be discussed. Some have concluded that a person can teach heaven without mentioning hell and saving that for a deeper discipleship topic. While I am not necessarily endorsing that tactic, it is worth considering.

Bridge: Family instructions and moral teaching in the Bible. Much of the New Testament is focused on how Christians are to live lives of peace, harmony, and selflessness in the world. These teachings, especially when they concern the family and genders as in Ephesians 5, 1 Timothy 3, Titus 2, and 1 Peter 3, would hold an instant ring of truth to the Confucian ear. Look especially for the many "one another" passages in Paul's writings, along with the emphasis on the body of Christ working together in Romans 12, 1 Corinthians 12, and Ephesians 4. These ideas would complement the Confucian values of group harmony and selfless morality that gives the listener a solid foundation for deeper Christian teachings. In addition, Jesus's Sermon on the Mount in Matthew 5–7 carries a similar tone and style to some of Confucius's speeches.

Bridge: Doctrine of sanctification. The Confucian concept that humanity can reach greatness through gradual training has some overlap with the doctrine of sanctification. The main difference, of course, is that Christians believe that this "process of being made holy" is powered by the Holy Spirit in the heart of those who have faith in Jesus. But the concept that people can be made better through obedience and submission to Christ would be a common ground that Confucianists would find appealing.

Regardless of the barriers or bridges anyone working with the Chinese might face, the task remains to stay in step with the guidance of the Holy Spirit. All our knowledge, learning, and strategies will only ultimately bear fruit in His time.

Taoism

As difficult as Confucianism can be to explain because of its blurred lines between philosophy and religion, its long and winding history, and its contrast with Abrahamic structures, Taoism isn't much easier for Western minds to grasp. Like its fellow Chinese native thought, Taoism has a number of confusing elements that are difficult to nail down as exclusively one thing or another.

To begin with, even the name of the

religion itself is muddled with the potential for misunderstanding. *Taoism*, the most widely used name, comes from attempts in the nineteenth century to make Roman letters from Chinese sounds. But for modern Chinese speakers using the standard Mandarin dialect, the name *Daoism* is much closer to the actual pronunciation. So while Taoism is more widely used, Daoism is more correct, and both are used interchangeably and mean the same thing, having come from the same word in Chinese.

The History and Beliefs of Taoism

The root word and central concept of Taoism is *dao* (pronounced "dow"), which can be translated roughly as "the way." To put it as simply as possible, Taoism teaches that there is a grand flow of energy, a balance of both light and dark, that flows through all things. The responsibility of everyone is to be aware of how this energy is flowing internally and externally throughout his or her experience and allow oneself to be carried with this flow. If done correctly, the result will be mental and physical wellness. A common metaphor for this is that each of our existences is like a person standing within a flowing river. We can choose to fight against that current and experience friction, or we can submit ourselves to its winding and unknowable path, release our will, and find wholeness by allowing the stream to carry us wherever it may.

The energy itself is called *qi* (pronounced "chee") and is made up of a balance of both light and dark, hot and cold, energies called *yin* and *yang*. These complementary opposites are graphically represented in one of Taoism's most recognizable images, the yin-yang circle of balanced black and white.

Over its thousands of years of history, Taoism has emerged in hundreds of variations ranging from formalized religious structures to secular philosophy to tips for interior design. Taoism itself isn't overly concerned with labels or rules, and as such, it is ripe for interpretation and individualized application. After all, it's not about fighting for clarity; it's about letting "the way" flow over you and take you wherever it may go.

One way that Westerners can most easily grasp basic Taoist ideas is to see their overlapping elements in *Star Wars*. Even though George Lucas claimed his ideas were based on a number of religions and meant to be universal, he undoubtedly borrowed heavily from Taoism when creating the idea of "the force," a central energy that runs through all things, balanced by both the "light side" and the "dark side."[14] Even his choices of wardrobe for Jedi masters and apprentices have a noticeable resemblance to Taoist monks, especially the warrior line known for practicing Taoist martial arts.

Others may recognize Taoism as having many similarities with the vague religious concept called "New Spirituality" (discussed

14C. The Taijitu, or yin yang, is a symbol of Taoism. Photo by Nyo. Public domain.

in chapter 20) that peaked in the West during the 1970s. This eclectic mix of religious and philosophical ideas borrowed heavily from several Eastern religions, and its focus on the passive acceptance of energy, the union of body and spirit, and even some of its exercises were inspired by Taoism.

Taoist ideas are said to have originated from Lao Zi, a possibly legendary figure said to have written the *Dao De Jing* (or *Tao Te Ching*, meaning "book of the way"), the closest thing to a sacred text within Taoism. The name Lao Zi literally translates to "old master." This ambiguous title, along with an unknown date of writing, has helped bolster the view that *Dao De Jing* came from multiple sources over a period of time.

Lao Zi is believed to have lived anywhere from roughly 600 to 400 BC. His writings were a direct response to Confucianism, which he believed was too rigid. Lao Zi placed much more emphasis on the experience of the individual over the harmony of the group. He did not believe that our desires would be met through conforming to the expectations of others, but rather through connecting to our feelings and releasing ourselves to experience what greater things are happening within.

Ironically, one of the core teachings within *Dao De Jing* is that "the way" cannot be explained. This style of teaching a concept through contrast is employed throughout the book, such as teaching that strength can only be found in weakness and that the best action is to be passive. This passivity is called *wu-wei*, a "nonstriving," wherein ambition is abandoned, and activity is minimalized so that focus is given to knowing the flow of energy around you and finding peace through humility and contentedness.

Over time, the vague supernatural concepts of philosophical Taoism began to splinter into a more religious form of Taoism. This smaller and more formal branch began to take noticeable shape in the second century AD. Being primarily concerned with immortality or the afterlife, this more religious Taoism began to develop a hierarchy of gods, demons, spirits, and ghosts; godlike heroes of faith; and the creation of rituals needed to help in this life and the next.

It is important to note that these two forms of Taoism are sometimes wildly divergent. For example, when I (Aaron) was living in China, I studied some of the teachings of philosophical Taoism and felt familiar with the central concepts. Then during the Chinese New Year, a friend invited me to visit a Taoist temple to see some of the rituals that take place during the holiday. I was shocked to see a section of the temple devoted to statues that demonstrate how certain sinful actions will be punished by demonic torturing in the afterlife, meant as a warning to followers to abstain from such actions or face future consequences. These statues were grotesque and their images appallingly violent. This seemed as far away from the peaceful and passive Taoism that I had read about, but it shows the way in which different types of Taoism can be in strong contrast with one another.

The Lifestyle and Culture of Taoism Today

Similar to Confucianism, the reality of Taoism is typically interwoven into the lifestyle more than focused on a deliberate set of religious practices. Taoism is a mindset of how to function within the experience of one's existence. Or said more plainly, how to handle life when both good and bad things occur.

There are a number of ways that the teachings of Taoism have become daily realities of Chinese life. One of the most concrete examples is in the practice of Chinese medicine.

As mentioned in the introduction to this chapter, the traditional Chinese worldview is a synthesis of Confucianism, Taoism, and Buddhism, which themselves have elements that derive from ancient folk religions. Thus it is difficult to distinguish which concepts behind traditional Chinese medicine come from which source. But fundamental to Chinese medicine is the idea that within the body are hot and cold energies. When someone experiences an illness, it's because one of these energies is out of balance with the other. The solution, then, would be to ingest a substance or interact with an external stimulus, which comes from the other energy in order to restore the needed balance.

For example, if a person is experiencing stomach pain, the doctor may conclude that his stomach has too much cold energy and would prescribe a pill form of a root that is known to have hot energy. The hope is that once balance is restored, the pain will subside. Much of this idea is rooted in the balancing concept of Taoism, specifically the force of qi and the way in which yin and yang must counter one another.

Another common practice of Taoist origin is *feng shui*, which translates to "wind-water." This idea teaches that every physical space, based on how it is arranged or how elements are spaced together, interacts with qi. Each type of element within a space has a certain characteristic, so it is important to arrange the elements of that space in such a way that the energy can flow best. If this is done, fortune and wellness will result. Spaces can be intentionally designed for the optimal feng shui in controlled spaces like the interior of a home, business, or temple. In natural spaces, such as the location of a major city or for the exterior of a home, business, or temple, practitioners of feng shui must seek the best arrangement based on natural characteristics. For example, Beijing was determined as the capital city of China because of the way the mountains to the northwest and the sea to the southeast, with low plains in between, are a strong balance of energies and would allow for the best flow of qi. Based on Taoist teaching, it was believed that this location would allow China to flourish.

Within the more formalized religious aspects of Taoism are several practices. One is fortune-telling. Often taking place at temples, the act of taking sticks, wooden blocks, or even rocks to divine a person's fortune is a common practice in important events or stressful life ventures. Another ritual is the funeral rites. These can include singing songs or telling stories during the funeral event, all with the goal of creating the most harmonious environment for the soul to depart and not remain behind to disturb the living family. A final example is the worship of gods. Taoist polytheism can take many forms, especially in the form of lesser gods who oversee a particular city or village. These gods are worshiped in the form of statues, usually found in temples, and can be the focus of a local festival.

Taoism and Christianity

When attempting to share the gospel with Taoists, there are barriers and bridges to consider.

Barrier: Basic Christian doctrine. A barrier a Taoist might face is the perceived strangeness of Christian doctrines. For example, the concept of a personal, knowable God who is actively involved with the affairs of humanity greatly contrasts with the vague spiritual presence of Taoism. To then think that God became flesh and dwelt among humanity would seem unrealistic and strange. When talking with a Taoist, it may be best to begin with a philosophical approach, emphasizing how our strivings and efforts to make life favorable are lost without a spiritual connection to a greater source.

However, not all Christian doctrine is unfavorable. Some Taoist teaching emphasizes the concept of a central divine trinity,[15] which would have obvious parallels to Christianity. Also, the role and action of the Holy Spirit can have some connecting ideas to Taoism, as will be addressed later.

Barrier: Christian exclusivity. I (Aaron) will never forget the first Taoist I encountered in China. He was a self-proclaimed Christian and actively involved in his church, and yet his profession as a doctor that mixed both Chinese and Western medicine led him to fully embrace the Taoist concepts of qi, yin yang, and the need to balance energies within a person to achieve full health. While not directly stating they came from Taoism, he believed these ideas were the way to better understand how God's creation worked.

This example illustrates how Taoists may push back against the idea that Christianity is an exclusive religion that cannot be meshed with other religions. The Chinese worldview can be pragmatic, looking to take the good of whatever is available to achieve the desired outcome. When working with a Taoist, then, it is important to carefully consider when to begin sharing the ways that Jesus must take an exclusive place in a person's life.

Bridge: Teaching style of Christ. A helpful bridge to consider is to highlight the teachings of Jesus that use ironic contrasts. Much of Jesus's teaching used this tactic on topics such as blindness and sight, light and dark, and weakness and strength. This concept of an upside-down kingdom was central to His way of explaining the kingdom of God and isn't unlike teaching methodology found in Taoist literature. For particular passages, the beatitudes of Matthew 5, the conversation with Nicodemus in John 3, and many parables (e.g., Matthew 13) are helpful points at which to begin introducing Jesus.

Bridge: The role of the Holy Spirit. The way the Bible describes the role and work of the Holy Spirit may serve as a bridge to Taoist thought. The idea that there is a powerful spiritual force at work in the world around us that flows through the life of a believer can be an attractive concept. Even the mysterious nature of the Spirit, which Jesus describes in John 3 like a wind that flows where it wants but no one can trace, is something a Taoist can begin to understand. Even more important, the requirement that a Christian submit to the Holy Spirit and live a life against personal desires, such as Jesus taught in Matthew 16:25, can be a foundation to begin a deeper conversation.

Shinto

Chinese culture, language, and religion had a deep impact on its geographical neighbor Japan. The two civilizations met as early as AD 200, with China at the time being the more culturally advanced. Chinese culture brought Buddhism to the island, which has become one of Japan's most persistent religious identities. In addition, Chinese influence brought elements of Confucianism, which manifested in the structures of Japan's government and society.[16]

Despite the influence of Chinese religion, Japan is not without its own homegrown religion called Shinto. One can recognize Taoist elements in Shinto, but Shinto remains a distinctively Japanese religion.

So what absolute truths does Shinto claim? What path to heaven does Shinto prescribe? Who is the savior in Shinto who rescues us from our sins?

Hold on. Those questions are asked from much more of a Western mindset than an East Asian one. Consider the following anecdotes.

I (Mike) was at the Atsuta Shrine in Nagoya, Japan, when I met an elderly man. He told me he comes to the shrine around a hundred times a year. I asked him why. He responded that it helps him to feel "clear."

I met a young lady in her twenties who was new to the area. She regularly visits the local Shinto shrine. Why? She told me that it's because she has found the shrine to be a "power spot" where she can greet the god and have good favor with it. She gives her name and address to the god for the god to bless her with good fortune in turn.

In Japan, I met a young man training to be a Christian pastor. He had grown up with a grandpa who was a Nichiren Buddhist monk. He once asked his mother why they practiced Buddhism in syncretism with Shinto. She simply answered, "This is what we do." He explained to me that when it comes to religion in Japan, "ambiguity is the only thing that is specific."

I met a young man at a Shinto shrine who described to me how the strength and beauty of the trees in the shrine complex gave him evidence that a god was present there. While there, he purchased a paper that predicted something negative coming for him, so he determined to be on his guard about whatever might be on the horizon.

Yet a Westerner might wonder, Do these people believe that Shinto is *true*? Do they believe that Shinto will *save* them? There are numerous challenges in defining Japanese religion, not the least of which is a common confusion of categories. That is, the fundamental categories for understanding other religions such as Christianity are often a mismatch for the more pragmatic concerns of the adherent of Shinto.

And "adherent" is probably too strong a term for the majority of Japanese who participate in various Shinto activities. Many Japanese consider themselves nonreligious; roughly 70 percent claim not to have any personal religious faith.[17] Yet even nonreligious Japanese will often visit a Shinto shrine when it comes to making a key life decision.

14D. The Uda Mikumari Shrine is dedicated to Mikumari, a female kami. Photo by Tawashi2006, April 8, 2007 (http://creativecommons.org/licenses/by-sa/3.0/).

Nonreligious Japanese still regularly get married in a Shinto shrine and will visit the shrine to celebrate Shinto festivals. Since so many Japanese claim no personal religious faith, yet 90 percent of Japanese funerals are Buddhist,[18] it is clear that many nonreligious Japanese are participants in Buddhist rituals too.

Why then would a largely secular nation not feel the nagging contradiction of holding little to no religious faith, and yet visiting Shinto shrines for a better life and undergoing Buddhist funerals for a better afterlife? One answer that might help is that many Japanese do not actually consider Shinto as "religion" but merely as Japanese tradition. Still, the religious rites participated in are not unspiritual. This mingling of secular outlook with spiritual techniques suggests a worldview of pragmatism: You do what works.

Logical contradictions between worldviews seem to be a nonissue, as Japanese lifestyles can contain a mixture of Shinto, Buddhist, and any number of superstitious or life-coaching techniques that could be seen as religious. The essence of Japanese religious life can be described as ambiguous utilitarianism. It's a pursuit of the good life minus the anxiety that comes from needing to know the exact truth. From a Christian perspective, truth is a value that ought to be doggedly pursued. Jesus said, "If you abide in my word, you are truly my disciples, and you will know the truth, and the truth will set you free" (John 8:31-32). Yet ambiguity in the area of truth is not thought of as problematic to the Japanese mind. Utility is supreme.

Moreover, pragmatically participating in Shinto seems appropriate for a religion whose sacred texts were created for pragmatic, political purposes.

Shinto History and Beliefs

Chinese inroads into Japanese culture cut deep, such that Buddhism in its many

14E. Wedding procession at the Shimogamo Shinto shrine. Photo by Nekosuki, February 19, 2011 (https://creativecommons.org/licenses/by-sa/4.0).

forms continues to be a highly influential religion in Japan today. Buddhism provided Japanese culture with more distinct truth claims, more developed views about the afterlife, and clearer articulation of good and bad. By the eighth century AD, the Japanese emperor decided it was time to clarify Japanese religion and to legitimize his reign at the same time. So the emperor commissioned the creation of two books: the *Kojiki* and the *Nihon Shoki* (*Nihongi*). Both were compiled from the available ancient Japanese myths that could be found. The *Kojiki* tells one continuous story, while the *Nihongi* features various versions of more stories.

Both books begin with the emergence of the gods (*kami*) and go on to narrate tales of kami feuds, which led to disasters on earth, kami who created the Japanese islands, and kami whose descendants were the line of Japanese emperors. Eventually, the myths merge into historically recognizable chronicles of imperial history, with the result that the divine lineage of the current emperor was able to be traced, specifically to Amaterasu, the sun goddess.

Thus Shinto has consistently provided an element of Japanese patriotism, even at times when Buddhism clearly had the cultural upper hand. This is not to say that Buddhism and Shinto have always been rivals. There is constant interplay, and at times, there have been conscious syntheses of the two, such as the Ryobu school, which equated various Buddhas with various kamis. Even in the Ryobu school, however, Buddhism emerged as the dominant force.

> Ryobu Shinto was not a merger of the two organizations such as that which usually characterizes the amalgamation of two groups. It was a subtle ideological coalescence of a deeper nature which enabled the two to exist together. As we have seen, Shinto accepted Buddhism by adding to its pantheon the foreign deities from China and India. Buddhism, however, approached the matter from a different angle. It declared that Shinto deities were derivative manifestations of the Buddhist deities which were regarded as original entities. The boundaries in this fusion became more and more obliterated. Buddhist priests took charge of Shinto sanctuaries, and Shinto priests began to play only minor parts in the ceremonies.[19]

Shinto enjoyed a period of ascendancy during the Meiji Restoration, from 1868 through the end of World War II, as the nationalistic Japanese imperial government made State Shinto the nation's official religion. This period ended, however, with the defeated Emperor Hirohito officially renouncing the claim to be divine. No longer the state religion, Shinto reestablished itself as Shrine Shinto, now dependent upon private, rather than government, funding.

The word *Shinto* comes from two Chinese words, *shen dao*. As we have already seen, *dao* (as in daoism) means "the way." The word *shen* is Chinese for "god." Thus Shinto is the "way of the gods." Since *michi* means "way" in Japanese, *kami-no-michi*, also meaning "way of the gods," is the common title for Shinto in Japan.

There are many kami to choose from. In fact, they are said to number eight million, a number traditionally used to suggest infinity.[20] As described in the *Kijoki* and the *Nihongi*, kami are often associated with various places. There can be numerous kami located in a particular space or object, such as a tree or mountain. And while kami often describes what we would conceptualize as gods invested with personality, kami can also denote inanimate forces and even be a word for the sacred in general.

What do Japanese people believe about the kami? While there are implied truth claims about the gods in the traditions and practices of Shinto, there are no agreed-upon central beliefs that practitioners must hold. It's not a matter of right belief but of expedient practice. This explains why someone at a shrine, purchasing a fortune, throwing coins into the collection bin, ringing a bell at the main hall, clapping to alert the deity of their presence, and bowing in the direction of the deity could still consider himself nonreligious.

Shinto Practice

Shinto is practiced both in the local shrine and in the home. The local shrine is typically thought to be the dwelling of a local kami. The shrine regularly hosts wedding ceremonies and baby dedications (but not funerals, as this is Buddhism's jurisdiction). In addition, various festivals are held at the shrine. For example, there are annual festivals for welcoming in the new year (*shogatsu*), for petitioning the kami for health and success for children (*shichigosan*), and for chasing away evil spirits (*setsubun*). In addition, someone might visit a shrine at any time during the year in order to venerate the kami and pray for blessings.

14F. A *torii* is a gate marking the entrance to a Shinto shrine. Photo by Chi King, December 14, 2016 (https://creativecommons.org/licenses/by/3.0).

The entrance to a Shinto shrine is marked by a *torii*, a gate with two vertical beams intersected at the top with two horizontal beams. Often the entrance is flanked by a pair of guardian statues, often of dogs or lions. Also near the entrance is a basin of water for cleansing the hands and mouth before entering. The shrine itself will contain two main structures: the *honden* and the *haiden*. The honden is the sacred inner area, which worshipers do not regularly enter. It contains sacred artifacts known as *shintai*, which are in some way connected to the shrine's kami. Unlike the honden, the haiden is accessible to the visitor. The haiden is known as the "offering hall" because it is where offerings of food and money are presented. There is also a written exchange of sorts that can take place in a Shinto shrine. As for communicating to the kami, there are wooden plates (*ema*) on which wishes can be written and left in the shrine for the kami to fulfill. As for receiving communication, some shrines contain papers predicting good or ill fortune, called *omikuji*, which can be drawn and used to welcome or ward off events.[21]

It is not uncommon for Japanese to also have a miniature shrine in the home called a *kamidana*. It is usually a shelf on which a daily offering of water or food can be made. There are also sacred objects on the shelf, such as amulets for good luck. There also might be an inscribed wooden tablet from the Ise Grand Shrine in Ise, Japan, a supremely sacred Shinto site dedicated to the sun goddess Amaterasu.

Shinto and Christianity

Here are some barriers and bridges to consider when interacting with somebody of a Shinto mindset.

Barrier: Basic Christian doctrine. As with Taoism, there is a noticeable mismatch of categories when it comes to the basic worldviews of Shinto and Christianity. The monotheistic idea of a single, nonspatially bound God is utterly foreign to the Japanese mind. As for creation, Christianity presents a purposefully created universe, not the product of spontaneous emanations. As for sin, although Shinto makes room for negative forces in the world, the Christian belief in humanity's fundamental proneness to sin is absent. Although every human feels guilt and alienation at some point, Shinto's kami are not capable of absolution or desirous of reconciliation. In Shinto, there is no resurrection or new heavens and earth, and so naturally no means to get there.

Barrier: Genuine worship and pragmatic petition. Another major incongruity is how Shinto and Christianity approach God. One approaches the kami for benefits. A small offering in petition for a day's favor. A visit to a place of localized spiritual power in hopes of boosting one's fortune. In return, there is relatively little asked of the adherent. Certainly not the internalizing of truth claims or the offering of wholehearted worship. Hence Japanese people who investigate Christianity (or who even make a profession of faith in Jesus) often do not realize there would be any conflict between faith in Jesus and Shinto practices. The conflict is essentially one-way, with Christianity demanding exclusive devotion.

The Christian idea of worship is completely foreign to the Japanese religious norms. While adherents of Buddhism or Shinto can be observed reverently praying at a temple or shrine, the aim of the activity is quite different than the biblical description of glorifying God with all of one's life. The joyful acknowledgment of the greatness of God that characterizes Christian worship simply has no corresponding attitude or practice in the Japanese system. Psalm 16:11 acknowledges that in God's presence there is fullness of joy. Jesus said in John 10:10 that He gives life to the full. But the root of this blossoming fullness is the acknowledgment of the worthiness of God. For Japanese people to understand Christianity, the personal and almighty nature of God must be highlighted as totally unique and distinct from their conception of the kami. An all-powerful, all-good God demands far more, but the trade-off is that you place your trust in something that you can truly trust.

Bridge: Community. Paradoxically, Japan is both densely populated and yet filled with lonely people. Consider three types of death that are not uncommon in Japan: overworking oneself to death (*karoshi*), dying alone and often undiscovered for some time (*kodokushi*), and suicide. Karoshi is symptomatic of an overworked society. Kodokushi bespeaks an aging population that, because of low marriage and birth rates, is not replenishing itself. And suicide has become, for some unemployed people in an honor-shame culture, a way to remove the family's dishonor. Add to this that over a half million young people who feel bullied or overwhelmed—usually young men—have retreated to their rooms. Known as *hikikomori*, these young people live in their rooms for months, years, and even decades on end out from under the burden of societal expectations.[22]

Into an isolated, overburdened culture, the church invites precious people into its community of grace. Shame? The church is a community that forgives each other, just as the Lord has forgiven us (Colossians 3:13). Burdens? The church is a community that bears each other's burdens (Galatians 6:2). Loneliness? The church is a community that welcomes one another (Romans 15:7), loves one another (John 13:34), and encourages one another (1 Thessalonians 4:18).

Conclusion

Religion in East Asia is complex and varied. What is important to remember when working with a person from one of these religious backgrounds is to gauge the level at which their beliefs are either a traditional thought system or more of an organized religious faith. Hopefully, this chapter has encouraged you to enter into conversations that lead people to find peace (not merely fortune) and harmony (not merely social dutifulness) in the One who reconciled us to God (2 Corinthians 5:18-20) and who reconciles us to each other (Ephesians 2:15-16).

Aaron Wheeler (PhD, Biola University) served for a number of years as a disciple-maker in Asia. Trained at both Wheaton and Biola, he has served as a professor in the intercultural studies department at Ozark Christian College. He is currently a small groups minister at College Heights Christian Church, where he works to build and multiply dynamic disciple-making communities.

Mike Ackerman (MA, Midwestern Baptist Theological Seminary) was a missionary in Japan and was one of the founding members of Mustard Seed Network, which continues to plant churches in the major cities of Japan. He currently serves as a professor of church planting and New Testament at Ozark Christian College.

Part 4

MODERN RELIGIONS

15

Baha'i

John Ferrer

The Baha'i faith is one of the youngest world religions, yet it is already a global phenomenon. Baha'i scriptures have been translated into over 800 languages.[1] There are more than five million Baha'is worldwide and 100,000 Baha'i communities peppered across almost every country on the planet.[2] How should Christians understand and relate to the Baha'i faith? To answer this question, there is no better place to start than at the beginning.

History of the Baha'i Faith

The Baha'i faith began with a Muslim merchant in Persia in the mid-nineteenth century. His name was Mirza Ali Muhammad, and along with his fellow Muslims at the time, he eagerly awaited the twelfth imam, the Imam Madhi, a messianic end-times character prophesied in Shia Islamic theology.[3] But when he was just 24 years old, he did something that shocked his Muslim community and eventually cost him his life.

The Bab: The Founder of the Babi Faith (1819–50)

On May 23, 1844, in Shiraz, Persia (modern-day Iran), Mirza Ali Muhammad declared that he is the twelfth imam, the Imam Madhi, a direct descendent of Muhammad, and the most recent manifestation of God.[4] He also adopted the honorific name "the Bab," meaning "the gate," as in a gateway between the former era of prophecies and their new fulfillment.[5] This bold move set him at odds with the Muslim world, since anyone claiming to be a later or greater prophet than Muhammad might be killed for blasphemy.

The more opposition he withstood, however, the more he drew followers with his message of a new era of prosperity and peace, where mankind will unite under an inspired prophet known as, "He-Whom-God-Will-Manifest."[6] His collected enigmatic scriptures are known as the *Bayan*, meaning "utterance" or "expression."[7] His followers are "Babis" (pronounced "Bobby's") and the religion is "Babism" (Bobbism).[8]

Within six years of the movement, the Bab was martyred.[9] Persian authorities ordered a public execution by firing squad. Baha'is teach that after three volleys of shots, from 750 riflemen, he was miraculously unhurt, only to be found later in his prison cell, finishing a conversation. After that conversation, he kindly cooperated with authorities and was executed on July 9, 1850.

Subh-I-Azal: The First Successor to the Bab (1831–1912)

The Babis were left with a leadership void. A feud soon formed over who would fill it. Two Babis had competing claims and were brothers no less: Mirza Yahya and Mirza Husayn Ali.

Mirza Yahya was the Bab's appointed successor and came to be known by the honorific name Subh-I-Azal (Morning of Eternity).[10] Official Baha'i records claim that his brother, conspiring earlier with the Bab, appointed Yahya as a temporary successor to divert attention from himself until a better time for him to take over.[11] In the unofficial account, only the Bab appointed Yahya, intending him to be the successor indefinitely.[12] Either way, Yahya was a reclusive and private successor, administrating from behind the scenes.[13] He had a small following known as Azali Babists. Many years later when he died in 1912, he had few followers, no successor, and came to be villainized by Baha'is.[14] What happened?

Between the brothers' competing claims, Yahya faded over time while Mirza Husayn Ali rose in prominence.[15] Even though Yahya was the appointed successor, he was also the younger brother by 13 years.[16] Husayn Ali served as the spokesman for his bashful sibling.[17] Husayn Ali was, for all practical purposes, the unofficial successor because he was a bold, outgoing leader and popular public figure compared to his brother, a secretive private figure.[18] After about 13 years of this arrangement, Yahya's successorship had grown controversial with Husayn Ali having the greater following.[19] Out of sight, out of mind. The time was ripe for Husayn Ali to make a declaration that would radically change the course of the Babi Faith.

Baha'u'llah: The Founder of the Baha'i Faith (1817–92)

Just nine years after the Bab's passing, on April 22, 1863, Husayn Ali announced to a small group of his followers that he was the prophesied Messiah, "He-Whom-God-Will-Manifest."[20] He was a manifestation of God, on par with Jesus, Muhammad, and the Bab, and he was God's voice to mankind.[21] Donning the honorific title of Baha'u'llah (Glory of God), or "Baha" for short, his followers were known as Baha'is (followers of Baha).[22]

His message was one of unity and cooperation, interpreting the world's religions as a single narrative of God's progressive revelation to humankind.[23] The major world religions each arose by God's revelation through manifestations, including Abraham, Jesus, Muhammad, and others.[24] According to Baha'is, these "God-men" are not incarnations, since they lack a divine nature/essence, but they are still perfect reflections of God.[25] Baha'u'llah could even call himself "God" in the same way that someone looking at a reflection of the sun can point at the mirror and say, "That's the sun"; so Baha'u'llah *is* God.[26] Reinforcing his exalted status, Baha'u'llah's writings depict him fulfilling dozens of messianic and "last days" prophecies and gathering a host of titles for himself, including the "Second Coming of Christ," the "Holy Spirit," the Day of God, "Maitreya" (Buddhism), Krishna (Hinduism), and others.[27] Perhaps the most celebrated scriptures from Baha'u'llah's pen are the *Kitab-i-Aqdas* (Most Holy Book), and *Kitab-i-Iqan* (Book of Certitude).

Eventually, Azali Babism, following the brother Yahya, dwindled to obscurity.[28] It never died out entirely, however, in part because Azalis claim Baha'u'llah arrived between 1,500 and 2,000 years too early to be "He-Whom-God-Will-Manifest."[29] Baha'is today maintain that Azalis are mistaken and consider Yahya a heretic and enemy of the faith.[30] Given the decline of Babism and the growth of the Baha'i faith, most Babis seem to have died off, returned to Islam (escaping persecution), or switched allegiance to Baha'u'llah.

Those Babis who converted to the Baha'i faith believe this transition did not betray but rather fulfilled Babism in the same way John the Baptist's ministry was fulfilled by Jesus.[31] John the Baptist's ministry drove people to Christ, just as the Bab's ministry drove people to Baha'u'llah (Matthew 3:1-12).

His brother Yahya was not Baha'u'llah's only antagonist. The Baha'i leader spent most of his 40-year ministry as a prisoner of conscience, escorted in and out of prisons in Persia (modern-day Iran), Iraq, Egypt, and the Ottoman Empire (modern-day Turkey and Israel).[32] The religious persecution that plagued the Babis loomed over Baha'u'llah as well. Somewhere between his writing, teaching, and incarceration, he managed to start a family, taking for himself three wives and fathering at least 14 children.[33]

In the course of his teaching, Baha'u'llah grew the Baha'i faith from a small offshoot of Islam to a moderately large independent world religion.[34] He never traveled farther west than Adrianople (Edirne, Turkey), but he ministered to pilgrims from around the world who traveled to see him.[35] During his exile in the prison city of Akka (Israel) in 1868, he reached out to the world by writing to key world leaders, petitioning them to acknowledge his authority and lead righteously, but he received only a collective yawn.[36] Under Baha'u'llah's leadership, the Baha'i faith was a local Middle-Eastern religion poised for international growth. However, not until his son and grandson took the helm did the Baha'i faith truly arrive on the world stage.

Abdu'l-Baha (1844–1921)

Before Baha'u'llah died of fever in 1892, he appointed his eldest son, Abbas Effendi, as his executive successor.[37] Effendi took the name Abdu'l-Baha (Servant of Baha) and is also known as "the Master."[38] He was a handsome and eloquent man of letters whose prolific writing (27,000 tablets) and sharp wit were all the more impressive as he had almost no formal education.[39]

Like his father, he endured constant harassment and house arrest as a political prisoner in the Islamic theocracy of the Ottoman Empire.[40] Religious persecution was limiting Baha'i's spread primarily to the Middle East, but a new opportunity bloomed in 1908 when the Ottoman Empire experienced the Young Turk Revolution.[41] The land was renamed "Turkey" for ethnic Turks, and all political prisoners from the Ottoman era were released, including the 64-year-old Abdu'l-Baha.[42] With his newfound freedom, Abdu'l-Baha traveled west, personally bringing the faith to Europe (1910–13) and to North America (1912).[43] Having spent 64 years of his life under the boot of religious discrimination, he saw the religious freedom in America as one of the greatest hopes in fulfilling the Baha'i prophecy of "organic global unity" and a "golden age of peace."[44]

Shoghi Effendi (1897–1957)

Abdu'l-Baha died in 1921 at the ripe age of 78, but not before designating his grandson, Shoghi Effendi, as his successor.[45] Shoghi Effendi, known as "The Guardian," was an Oxford don and fluent in English.[46] An academic, enculturated in the East and West, his leadership style was more administrative than his predecessors.[47] He appointed and mobilized 32 members of the leadership council, known as "Hands of the Cause."[48] He helped set the precedent of seven-year and ten-year plans for the Baha'i faith.[49] In many ways, he transitioned the Baha'i faith from a Middle-Eastern patriarchy to a western democratic republic. Under his leadership, the Baha'i faith became a truly international phenomenon, quadrupling in size.[50]

He was not without controversy, however, with disputes over successorship before and after his time. Some believed Abdu'l-Baha should not have appointed his grandson but instead Abdu'l-Baha's half brother, Mirza Muhammad Ali, whom Baha'u'llah had praised as the "greater branch" (Arabic: *Ghusn-i-Akbar*).[51] However, a long-standing feud between the two brothers marginalized the half brother, reassuring that leadership would fall to Shoghi Effendi.[52] Shoghi Effendi also ended his career with a dispute.

Shoghi Effendi died unexpectedly of the flu in 1957 without explicitly designating a successor and without fathering any children.[53] Yet Abdu'l-Baha had instructed in his *Will and Testament* that after Shoghi Effendi, the role of Guardian was to follow the rule of primogeniture, passing to the "first-born of his lineal descendants."[54] Baha'is were left in dispute without a clear path forward.

The Universal House of Justice (1963–Present)

Shoghi Effendi did not identify a successor, but he did clarify the ideas of Baha'u'llah and Abdu'l-Baha regarding a "Universal House of Justice" (UHJ).[55] Within six years, the dispute would be settled, with the UHJ taking over international leadership of the Baha'i faith.[56]

Abdu'l-Baha's descriptions of the UHJ make it sounds like it was to serve as a legislative branch of government working alongside the executive branch, the Guardian(s).[57] That would mean, though, working with a successor, and there was no successor. Plus, the Baha'i faith had always been autocratic with a divinely ordained leader. Even with dozens of appointed regents (Hands of the Cause), the Baha'i faith did not yet have a democracy in place, or anything resembling the UHJ of today.

At Shoghi Effendi's death in 1957, the "Hands of the Cause" gathered and appointed

15A. The Universal House of Justice in Haifa, Israel. Photo by Alexey Mokeev, Wikicommons. Public domain.

nine leaders to serve as "Custodians of the Faith."[58] The Custodians had a lot to work with because of Shoghi Effendi's meticulous work.[59] He had expanded the number and powers of the Hands of the Cause. Moreover, at the time of his death, Baha'is were four years into a ten-year crusade Shoghi Effendi had launched to grow the Baha'i faith internationally.[60] This meant his leadership still had six years of momentum left before a new leader would be needed. With several years of "marching orders" still in place, the Custodians had a deadline for organizing the UHJ.

But six years is a long time. Just three years later in 1960, one Custodian of the Faith—Charles Mason Remey—sought a quicker solution by declaring himself Shoghi Effendi's successor.[61] This idea made sense because he was already one of the highest ranking authorities at that time, and because Shoghi Effendi had appointed him President of the International Baha'i Council. But Remey still lacked the credentials of his predecessors.[62] Plus, Remey never held majority approval.[63] The only way he could clearly qualify as the next Guardian would be as Shoghi Effendi's eldest son, and he was not that either. It was no surprise when the rest of the Hands of the Cause denied Remey's claim and excommunicated him and his followers as "covenant breakers."[64] He commanded an unsanctioned following for many years, known as "Orthodox Baha'is" or the "Baha'is under the Hereditary Guardianship."[65]

In 1963, with Remey's power grab squelched, the Custodians of the Faith could move forward with plans to elect the first members of the UHJ.[66] That first election set the standard still used today. Elections for the members of the UHJ are held every five years, with no campaigning or lobbying, and only a secret ballot at the convention of the National Spiritual Assemblies (where Baha'i representatives gather from around the world). While Baha'is otherwise teach full equality between men and women, no women are allowed on the election ballot. Each elected member resides in Haifa, Israel, on Mount Carmel at the Seat of the Universal House of Justice—a neoclassical colonnade reminiscent of the US Supreme Court.

When they convene as the UHJ, their declarations carry full authority to direct Baha'is worldwide, but only when they convene as the UHJ. The nine members do not have authority individually or when they speak "off the record." Nor do they have authority to speak new scripture or change revelation from the Bab or Baha'u'llah. They are authoritative, however, when issuing official interpretations of scripture, laws, and practices. From 1963 through today, the UHJ has been the supreme ruling body for the Baha'i faith.

Teachings of the Baha'i Faith

God Is One and Unknowable

Baha'is believe in only one God, but stress that God is "unseen, inaccessible, and unknowable."[67] In the words of Abdu'l-Baha, "The Reality of the Divinity is hidden from all comprehension, and concealed from the minds of all men."[68] They maintain a "mystical faith," since God cannot be rationally or directly known.[69] People can know about God and understand him indirectly by identifying what he is *not*. This is called the *via negativa* (negative way), or negative/apophatic theology, since God is understood through negation (apophatic) language.[70] For example, God is *not* mortal, so he is immortal; he is *not* finite (limited), so he is infinite, and so on. This doctrine can sustain a sense of reverence treating God as holy and set apart. This doctrine also helps explain why many different world religions might be needed

Ancestry of the Baha'i Faith with Schisms

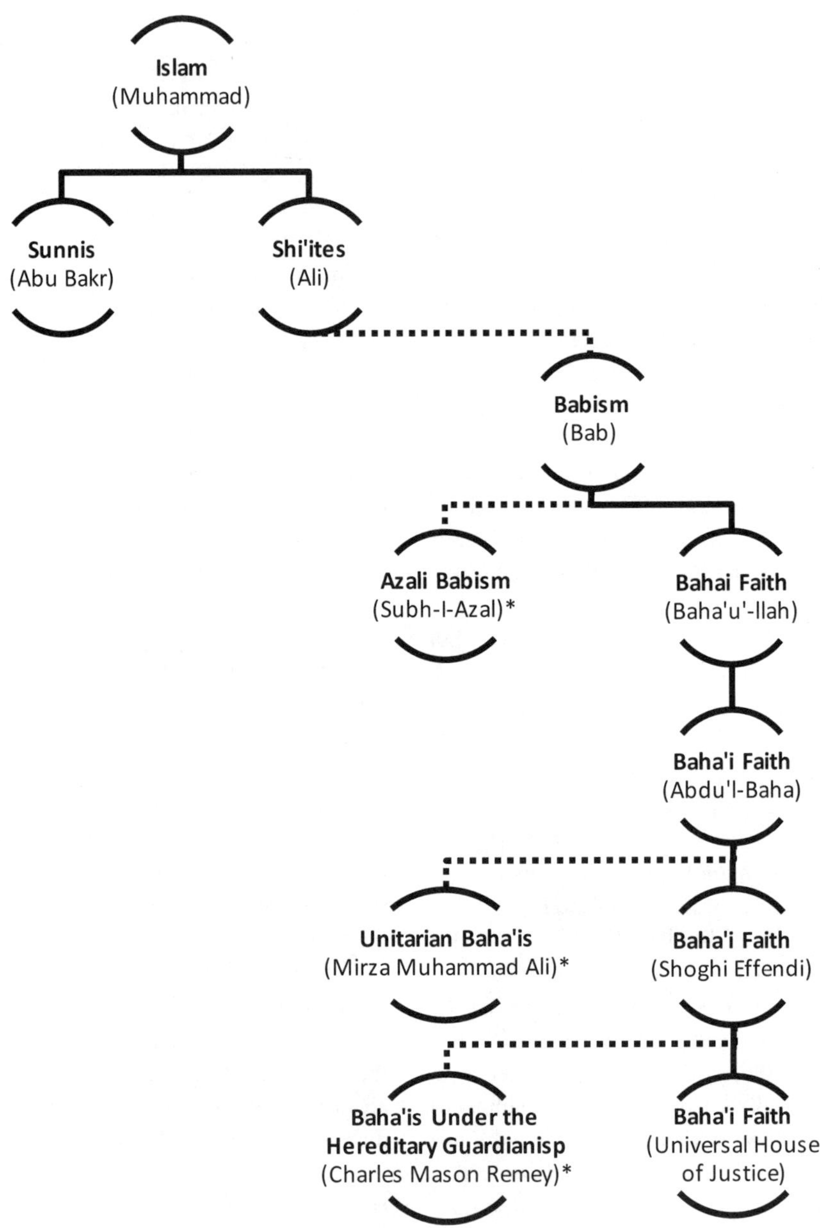

* Covenant Breaker/Excommunicated.

** Dotted lines represent unsanctioned schisms/heterodoxy.

to "reveal" God to mankind. According to the Baha'i faith, God is too mysterious to fit inside a single doctrinal box or one religious tradition.

Unity of the Religions

Perhaps the most prominent feature of Baha'i teaching, however, is their emphasis on unity, especially their acceptance of different world religions.[71] Baha'is affirm the "essential unity of all religions."[72] On the surface, this may seem like a contradiction. Muslims deny Christ's deity, while Christians affirm it. Christianity teaches the Trinity, but most religions deny it. For Baha'is, however, the different world religions can be affirmed as partially true, stemming from one common faith, even if they are layered in cultural trappings and misinterpretations.[73] So long as the original teachings from those religions agree, then any differences can be explained as the following:

- social law superseded by spiritual law
- early revelation superseded by later revelation
- corrupted teaching corrected by pure teaching
- misinterpretation corrected by right interpretation
- literal interpretation superseded by mystical-symbolic interpretation[74]

Progressive Revelation

Baha'is also believe that the religions line up as God's progressive revelation to man. Each of the major world religions, in each one's original state, is thought to be the purest divine revelation in its particular era.[75] Over time, however, cultural laws become outdated and teachings are misinterpreted and calcified until that religion loses step with evolving society or it just veers away from the intent of its founders. Shoghi Effendi summarized this progression:

> The fundamental principle enunciated by Baha'u'llah, the followers of His Faith firmly believe, is that religious truth is not absolute but relative, that Divine Revelation is a continuous and progressive process, that all the great religions of the world are divine in origin, that their basic principles are in complete harmony, that their aims and purposes are one and the same, that their teachings are but facets of one truth, that their functions are complementary, that they differ only in the non-essential aspects of their doctrines, and that their missions represent successive stages in the spiritual evolution of human society.[76]

In Baha'i thought, religions get stale over time as followers eventually treat their religion as an unchanging focal point instead of as a chapter in God's developing story. While Baha'is are exploring the most recent chapter, Christians, Muslims, Buddhists, and so on are treating their earlier chapter like it is the end of the book. The world's religions are not competitors, so to speak, but a family heritage, spanning many generations, each of them adding to the same legacy.

Not every world religion is included.[77] Yet the Baha'i faith is still considered pluralistic for embracing the world's religions generally and as inclusive for including followers of different religions as implicit Baha'is.[78] In that way, the Baha'i faith is also evolutionary, framing most everything within a continuum of gradual change over time: people, cultures, government, religion, and so on. Abdu'l-Baha likened this evolution to a growing person saying, "That which was applicable to human needs during the early history of the race can neither meet nor satisfy the demands of this day, this period of newness and consummation."[79] He goes on to say,

> Man must now become imbued with new virtues and powers, new moral standards, new capacities...The gifts and blessings of the period of youth, although timely and sufficient during the adolescence of mankind, are now incapable of meeting the requirements of its maturity.[80]

As civilization matures through this age of "turbulent adolescence," we outgrow past religions, needing a whole new wardrobe, so to speak, with new teachings, new social standards, and so on.[81] Each new religious dispensation can lead mankind toward greater enlightenment. Since the Baha'i faith is the most recent, "evolved," and complete revelation, Baha'is understand their religion to be superior to Christianity. In this way, Baha'is are still motivated to win people to the Baha'i faith. Yet that motivation is balanced against the Baha'i belief that people will have eternity to get right with God, since there is no physical hell or inescapable suffering for the lost.[82]

Baha'is clearly teach that all the major world religions can be reconciled. Baha'is follow through on this pluralistic idea by promoting diversity, trying to eliminate all prejudice, including sexism, racism, and ethnocentrism.[83] They teach that world peace is imminent in the form of a "lesser peace" (international cease-fire) and the "most great peace" (akin to utopia).[84]

World peace is an ambitious goal, but Baha'is are shameless optimists. They view human nature in a humanitarian light, seeing mankind as essentially good.[85] That optimism combines well with another Baha'i teaching, the harmony of science and religion. Baha'is believe that science and religion are not enemies; rather they complement and reinforce each other so mankind can benefit from the best of both worlds: scientific advances and spiritual enlightenment.

Unified Government, Language, and Education

This goal of universal peace is also made possible, they believe, through shared governance under a single political head—namely, the UHJ.[86] Baha'is see the UHJ as a growing influence, which will eventually become the universal arbiter of justice in a future era of peace and harmony.

Nevertheless, pride and ignorance tend to interfere with peaceful plans. Baha'is seek to overcome those obstacles by promoting an auxiliary language, a single language that works for everyone in the world.[87] People can still have their native tongue, but would have an additional shared language so they can communicate across cultural and ethnic borders, aiding cooperation and fostering global community. Baha'is also promote universal education, which is a kind of public schooling, except rooted in the UHJ.[88] To cap it all off, Baha'is fortify their proeducation stance by placing a premium on individual study. Abdu'l-Baha explained this tenet saying:

> Discover for yourselves the reality of things...No man should follow blindly his ancestors and forefathers. Nay, each must see with his own eyes, hear with his own ears, and investigate independently in order that he may find the truth. The religion of forefathers and ancestors is based upon blind imitation. Man should investigate reality.[89]

The Baha'i faith is not blind faith. A sincere

intellectual tradition runs through the heart of this vigorous young religion.

Lifestyle and Culture

Peacemaking

Their history and teachings give some indication of what life is like for Baha'is. Baha'i life is forward-looking, hopeful, intellectual, and above all, peacemaking. They aim at uniting nations, religions, and cultures into a single family. Baha'i life is largely characterized by qualities that stimulate spiritual growth together.

Visitors to a Baha'i meeting can expect hospitality, diversity, eclectic studies, and a blend of intellectualism and mysticism. In my experience, Baha'is are humble, prayerful, intelligent, and spiritually sensitive people. They avoid "proselytizing" (trying to "convert" people) but love to discuss theology and worldviews or help any seekers who are interested.[90] One can often find an eager discussion about religion and politics, but be careful about politics because they are not supposed to engage in divisive political arguments.[91] I have also found Baha'is to be cosmopolitan for their savvy interaction across different cultures.

Baha'is also prize humility, prayerfulness, and purity.[92] They are instructed to pray daily, using spontaneous prayers and prescribed (obligatory) prayers.[93] Similar to Islam, the obligatory prayers are to be said at specific times and facing a specific direction.[94] Regarding purity, Baha'is are instructed to avoid alcohol, recreational drugs, and gambling.[95]

Baha'is also blend conservativism and liberalism. Along with their views on alcohol and drugs, Baha'is emphasize traditional sexual ethics, traditional marriage, and a pro-life view on abortion, so they can be quite conservative socially.[96] But with their emphasis on global unity, one-world government (UHJ), and their progressive (evolutionary) worldview, they could also qualify as political liberals.

Overall, it is impossible to navigate long within Baha'i culture without encountering feast days, the Baha'i calendar, and the administrative order.

Feast Days

Feast days are the "bedrock of community life" for Baha'is.[97] Feast days are the closest thing to "Sunday services" that Baha'is practice. These feasts are more like a small group Bible study than a church, mosque, or synagogue meeting. Baha'is may own dedicated buildings in some cities, but most Baha'is have no access to them. Baha'is have worship centers called "Houses of Worship," but these are rare, with only about ten in the world.[98] As such, Houses of Worship are not regular fixtures in Baha'i life either.

The primary setting for Baha'i life is in the home. Every month, Baha'is gather for a feast, mostly in homes.[99] On feast day, Baha'is and any non-Baha'i guests can expect food and drinks reflecting an array of

KEY BELIEFS & PRACTICES

1. Independent investigation of reality.
2. Banish all prejudice.
3. Unity of the world of humanity.
4. Unity of the foundation of all religions.
5. Unity of science and religion.
6. Universal auxiliary language.
7. Universal education.
8. Equality of the sexes.
9. Parliament of man (one supreme government).
10. World peace.

Abridged from Abdu'l Baha, *Abdu'l-Baha on Divine Philosophy*, 24 cultures. Besides the meal, feast day includes prayer and scripture readings, news and updates on the local community, and time for discussion and fellowship.[100] Baha'is are not limited to those elements, however. Feast days can also incorporate music, visual art, children's activities, a lesson or testimony, or even a service project.

Feast days are fairly informal, since Baha'is have no clergy and no sacraments and generally avoid liturgy and tradition.[101] This informality is partly because "Baha'i teachings emphasize that each person is in charge of his or her own spiritual development."[102] "The responsibility for spiritual growth ultimately rests with each individual," instead of on a priest, sacrament, or tradition.[103] Baha'is also reject the notion of clergy because they prefer to emphasize equality, without class distinction between priest and laity.[104]

Another reason for informality is that Baha'is see the world through a lens of evolutionary progress. Baha'is prefer to keep their religious expressions adaptable so that, as civilization evolves, the physical expressions of the Baha'i faith will be agile enough to adjust to the changing spiritual landscape. Rigorous tradition, on the other hand, tends to cage religion into archaic formulas.[105] In other words, formal trappings calcify religion, replacing vital growth with dead routines.

Baha'i Administrative Order

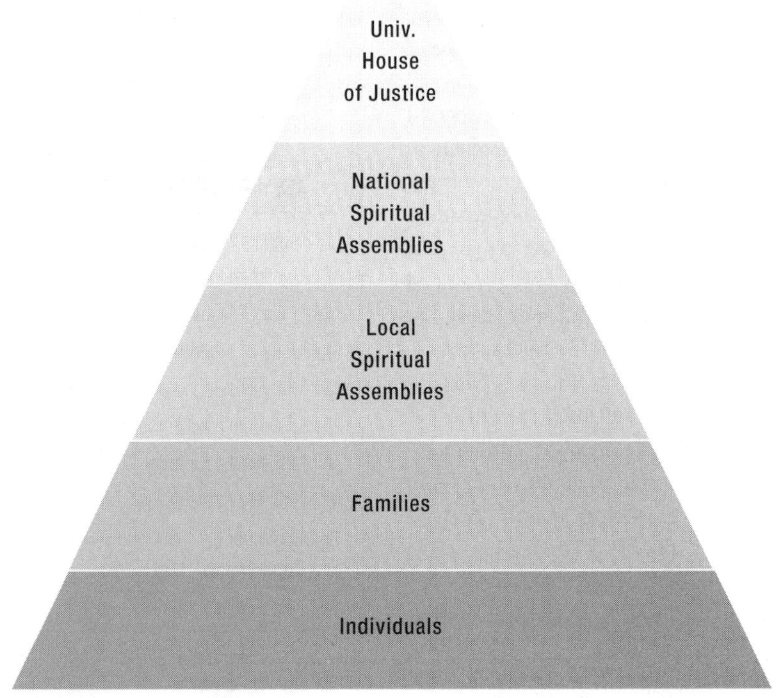

The closest thing Baha'is have to liturgy are obligatory prayers, where Baha'is are required to pray at least one of three specific prayers every day.[106] Another big difference between feast day and church services is that they are not weekly, but monthly, which is every 19 days according to the Baha'i calendar.[107]

Administrative Order

Another organizing principle for Baha'is is their method of government. Baha'is typically cooperate well under the rule of civil government, especially if they are not facing persecution.[108] In addition to civil government, Baha'is also recognize a religious democratic hierarchy known as the "Administrative Order," where "all decisions rest in the hands of democratically elected bodies at the local, regional, national, and international levels."[109]

At the simplest level, each individual has self-governance through one's personal search for truth.[110] Everyone is fit to scour reality for enlightenment with no need for clergy to mediate for them. Besides self-government, Baha'is acknowledge the dignity and value of family, implicitly affirming family-level governance by managing their own households. Above one's self and one's family is the Local Spiritual Assembly (LSA), made up of nine elected members, each serving one-year terms.[111] They meet with Baha'i communities on feast days to discuss local matters in a frank but gracious manner, which they call "consultation."[112]

Above the LSAs are the National Spiritual Assembly (NSA).[113] This nine-member elected council offers guidance and consultation for their respective nation, and they represent their nation at international assemblies. The NSA's in turn elect the nine members of the supreme head of the Baha'i faith, the Universal House of Justice (UHJ).

Baha'i Faith and Christianity

Baha'is prize unity and tolerance, so they normally treat Christians and Christianity with an affirming and positive attitude. Indeed, the two faiths have a lot in common. Both are monotheistic religions that hold the Bible in high esteem and consider Jesus Christ a great teacher and prophet. They can readily affirm biblical values like faith, hope, love, humility, and self-sacrifice. Baha'is can stand with historic Christianity, affirming the value of family, community involvement, and conservative sexual ethics (i.e., traditional marriage, monogamy, sex reserved for marriage, and no adultery). Christians can also applaud Baha'is for their efforts to promote peace and combat prejudice. Further, most Baha'i gatherings are open to visitors, and Baha'is themselves can visit Christian churches.[114] So Baha'is and Christians can enjoy a wealth of opportunities for engagement and fruitful spiritual discussions.

The Baha'i faith is a bridge-building religion that actively promotes "independent investigation of truth."[115] Christians can honor and share those commitments by building sincere relationships and earning trust before attempting to wade through theological disagreements.

How Do These Religions Compare?

When comparing Christianity and the Baha'i faith, respectful disagreement is in order. Even while admitting some points of agreement, historic Christianity and the Baha'i faith, ultimately, cannot both be true. Shoghi Effendi explained this in no uncertain terms:

> We, as Baha'is...cannot subscribe to both the Faith of Bahá'u'lláh and ordinary church dogma. The churches are waiting for the coming of Jesus Christ; we believe He has come again in the

> Glory of the Father [Baha'u'llah]. The churches teach doctrines—various ones in various creeds—which we as Baha'is do not accept; such as the bodily Resurrection, confession, or, in some creeds, the denial of the Immaculate Conception. In other words, there is no Christian church today whose dogmas we, as Baha'is, can truthfully say we accept in their entirety—therefore to remain a member of the Church is not proper for us, for we do so under false pretences [sic]. We should, therefore, withdraw from our churches but continue to associate, if we wish to, with the church members and ministers.[116]

Baha'is believe that Christianity and all the major religions can be reconciled to each other but only within a Baha'i framework, at the expense of Christian orthodoxy. From a Christian standpoint, "unity" with the Baha'i faith means disavowing historic Christianity. Critical differences persist.

Baha'is promote religious pluralism and one-world government, but to Christians, these seem uncomfortably close to the Tower of Babel (Genesis 11:1-9; Revelation 14:8) and the Beast in Revelation to whom "authority was given...over every tribe and people and language and nation" (Revelation 13:7). Even if those concerns were unwarranted, the Baha'i faith still cuts at the heart of Christian orthodoxy. Baha'is deny original sin, the Trinity, the deity of Christ, Jesus's bodily resurrection, the existence of Satan and other demons, and the physical existence of heaven and hell.[117] Fortunately, there are many open doors for Christians and Baha'is to graciously engage with each other about these disagreements.

Doctrine of God

At the heart of the Baha'i faith is one God, who is unknowable in essence. God "is invisible, incomprehensible, inaccessible, a pure essence which cannot be described."[118] This teaching, however, risks self-defeat because if God is essentially unknowable, then not even the idea that "God is unknowable" could be known about him. This doctrine might also be unverifiable, since there would be no

QUICK TIPS FOR TALKING WITH BAHA'IS

- Be respectful and gracious. Remember the Golden Rule (Mark 12:31).
- Baha'u'llah is pronounced "Buh-HA-oo-la." Bab is pronounced "Bob."
- A follower of Baha'u'llah is called a "Baha'i" (Bah-HIGH). The plural is "Baha'is" (Bah-HIGHs).
- The religion is "The Baha'i Faith," not "Baha'ism."
- The apostrophe in "Baha'i" matters. Do not leave it out unless print limitations require it.
- Baha'is are often eager to discuss religion, but no one likes to be lectured or talked down to.
- The deeper your friendship is, the more freedom you have to explore your differences together.
- Baha'is do not think their religion commits syncretism. They do not see it as mixing and matching other religions, but rather as a distinct and independent religion.
- Baha'is often blend libertarian, progressive, socially conservative, and theologically liberal ideals, although they shun partisan politics, and any Baha'i or Baha'i community is liable to surprise you.

divine reference point in reach to verify or falsify claims about God, even claims made by the manifestations or the claim that "God is unknowable."

Christians have a similar doctrine called "ineffability," as Christians believe God is transcendent and cannot be comprehensively understood or fully expressed in human language. However, Christians do not emphasize God's unknowability to the same extent as Baha'is. For Christians, ineffability is hedged in by the doctrine of God's immanence (Psalm 139:7-12; John 1:14; Acts 17:27; Colossians 1:17), and by the doctrine of incarnation where Jesus is the perfect expression of the Godhead, equal to and identical with God (John 1:1-3; Philippians 2:5-10; Colossians 1:15-20; Hebrews 1:3).

The Baha'i doctrine of "manifestation" might help Baha'is respond to the predicament of God's unknowability. "Manifestation" is similar to "incarnation," but it is critically different in that manifestations are not *literally* divine. Manifestations are reflections of God, like mirrors, but not *themselves* God. However, the doctrine of manifestation raises an additional logical problem: How can an unknowable God be known to reflect himself in a knowable way? Perhaps God is reflected not in his essence but in some secondary or external way—but then, we would still be knowing something fundamental about God—namely, that he has essential and nonessential aspects. It seems that even the doctrine of "manifestation" cannot solve the problem without showing that God is directly knowable, at least in part.

Now, Baha'i theology can get complicated at this point, delving into philosophical theology. Plus, Baha'is can always appeal to mystery and mysticism, allowing apparent contradictions to resolve nonrationally or by appealing to future revelation.[119] Nevertheless, Christians have the benefit of complementary doctrines of transcendence and immanence, so God's unapproachable holiness can be maintained without sacrificing His personable closeness. Moreover, Christians can appeal to the doctrine of "analogy" to help explain how theological language works.[120]

Oneness of Religion

Baha'is are also distinguished by their bold claim about the oneness of religion. If all the major religions of the world, at their core, align within the same progressive revelation, then that means most practitioners in other religions are radically mistaken about their own belief system. Christians who believe Jesus is the only way of salvation would be fundamentally wrong about the cornerstone of their faith (Acts 4:12).

Christianity has no strong parallel to the Baha'i notion of "one religion" (hereafter, "oneness"). Baha'is understand the major religions to be true at their core even if they errantly differ at the periphery. Christians teach the opposite: The major religions are primarily mistaken, even if they have goodness, truth, and beauty at peripheral levels.[121] From a Christian perspective, any religion that denies the literal deity and humanity of Christ, His bodily resurrection, mankind's need for salvation, or the suggestion that adults can be saved without even implicit faith in Christ runs contrary to Scripture (Acts 4:12; John 3:16-18; 14:6; Romans 1-10; 1 Corinthians 15; 1 John 4:1-3; etc.).[122]

Compared to Baha'i "oneness," the closest parallel in Christianity is probably "natural revelation," where God reveals Himself, not explicitly in another religion, but still in a genuine mode of revelation, such as natural moral laws (natural law theory), an innate sense of the divine (*sensus divinitatis*), or by inference from nature (natural theology).[123]

While "oneness" is a bold claim, it is theoretically possible. Religions are staffed by people, and people make mistakes. So it's logically *possible* that all the world's religions, except Baha'i, are fundamentally mistaken about their own religion and, instead, they all should embrace the Baha'i account of those religions. Perhaps Christian Scriptures have been so corrupted that a Baha'i revision is needed in order to understand the true message of Jesus Christ.[124] Radical claims cannot be judged "false" just because they are radical, but neither should they be accepted without sufficient reason.

The "oneness" doctrine risks explaining away the differences dismissively, instead of giving religious adherents the benefit of the doubt regarding their interpretation of their own religion. Baha'is interpret the world's religions according to the Baha'i worldview. Unity, oneness, and harmony are appealing, but they are offered only on Baha'i terms. This one-way mode of explanation risks presumptuous condescension.

Additionally, Christian philosopher Francis Beckwith points out,

> By calling all significant differences "unimportant" [the Baha'i faith] has not only preserved itself from criticism, but also from proof. Without being liable to falsification, it has not entered the ring of testability. It's like proclaiming oneself "heavyweight champion of the world" because no boxer qualifies to fight you. It is not the self-proclamation but the objective testing that reveals who is the champion.[125]

Lastly, Baha'i "oneness" amounts to a substantial doctrinal attack on all the world's religions, claiming that all those other religious adherents failed to preserve their religion with integrity. With a big accusation like this, they carry a heavy burden of proof.

Baha'is can go a long way to assuage these issues at an interpersonal level, by avoiding any condescending tone or dismissive attitude. But these are not just interpersonal issues. Oneness poses a rational problem too. The Baha'i faith did not launch until the mid-nineteenth century, over 1,000 years since the next youngest world religion, Islam, and over 1,800 years since the day of Jesus. A fairly small number of Baha'i authorities, beginning less than 200 years ago, are claiming to understand Christianity better than the combined efforts of millions of scholars, church fathers, clerics, and devotees who have been studying, applying, and exploring the Christian faith for almost 2,000 years. At face value, the chances of the Baha'i revision being superior seems unlikely.

Combine the other major world religions—Islam, Buddhism, and so on—and the likelihood plummets. Baha'is are claiming to understand all the world's religions better than the combined efforts of all those religious adherents in knowing their own religion, which seems unlikely.

To be clear, however, Baha'i "oneness" readily admits substantial differences between these religions. Baha'is have the difficult task of explaining religious differences without damaging any underlying unity. For this task there are five distinctions, which were mentioned earlier: (1) social law versus spiritual law, (2) early revelation versus later revelation, (3) pure teaching versus corrupted teaching, (4) correct interpretation versus misinterpretation, and (5) literal versus mystical-symbolic meaning.

Mysticism

So long as these distinctions are not abused, they are valid tools in navigating the messy terrain of religious studies. The last distinction, however, between literal versus mystical-symbolic meaning, deserves a special note. The Bible has literal *and* symbolic aspects. And fair-minded readers should take measures to treat the literal parts literally and the symbolic parts symbolically. But the practice of Baha'u'llah and others after him has been to allegorize liberally, reading the Bible and other sacred texts through a mystical-symbolic lens that always seems to cast Baha'u'llah in a good light.[126] Baha'is often make lavish claims about how Baha'u'llah fulfills prophecies across the world's religions, yet those "fulfillments" lean heavily on a mystical-symbolic interpretation of the text.[127]

For example, in the *Book of Certitude*, Baha'u'llah looks over the "Son of Man" prophecy in Matthew 24:29-30 and proceeds to interpret the darkened sun, lightless moon, and falling stars, saying,

> By these words is meant that when the sun of the heavenly teachings hath been eclipsed, the stars of the divinely established laws have fallen, and the moon of true knowledge—the educator of mankind—hath been obscured; when the standards of guidance and felicity have been reversed, and the morn of truth and righteousness hath sunk in night, then shall the sign of the Son of man appear in heaven.[128]

Baha'u'llah claims to be the "Son of Man" and the "Second Coming of Christ," using Matthew 24:29-30 as evidence. But those claims are not impressive, since a person could just as easily use the same subjective methods to interpret the sun, moon, and stars as certain people who died, or institutions that collapsed, or defunct countries, or debunked theories, and so on.[129]

This mystical penchant also generates a circularity problem. Across the *Book of Certitude*, for example, Baha'u'llah wields his divine authority to justify using a mystical interpretation of Bible verses, which, to no surprise, reinforce Baha'u'llah's divine authority. He is presuming to have the supernatural authority for perfect mystical interpretations that demonstrate his supernatural authority. It is a circular argument.

Additionally, turnabout is fair play. Just as Baha'u'llah interpreted the Bible in a mystical way, betraying historic Christianity, the same mystical method could be used to interpret Baha'i writings in a way that betrays the Baha'i faith. As long as the literal, contextual, and objective meaning of the text can be dismissed, then the text can mean whatever the reader wants.

It ought to be noted that Baha'u'llah and his advocates do not rely exclusively on mystical-symbolic interpretations of prophecy. Baha'i use of prophecy merits more discussion than can be offered here. The modest point is that it is problematic to rely heavily on mystical-symbolic interpretation especially on matters of ultimate importance.

Reinterpreting Jesus

For Baha'is, Baha'u'llah is the central character, and Jesus is one among many other manifestations, an inspired and anointed human being, but not literally God. According to the UHJ, Jesus's bodily resurrection is "not reasonable" in light of modern science.[130] Instead, they say that Jesus's "Spirit, released from the body, ascended to the presence of God and continued to inspire and guide His followers."[131]

For Christians, however, everything revolves around Jesus (Colossians 1:15-20). The Christian church has circled the wagons on the deity and resurrection of Christ.[132]

Deifying Christ was not some late legendary development either: "Giving Jesus divine honors...was an established, characteristic feature of the Christian movement within the first two decades of its existence."[133] The bodily resurrection of Christ was the standard Christian teaching among the church fathers, dating back as early as the apostles themselves.[134] The Apostle Paul says bluntly, "If Christ has not been raised, your faith is futile and you are still in your sins," and if Christ did not rise from the dead, "we are of all people most to be pitied" (1 Corinthians 15:17,19).

If Jesus physically rose from the dead, and if He was and is God (literally), then Baha'is need to rethink all the issues just raised. If Jesus is who Christians say He is, then Baha'is are deeply mistaken about

- their doctrine of God's unknowability, since God is known in the divine person of Jesus;
- their doctrine of manifestations, since Jesus would instead be the actual incarnation; and
- their mystical interpretations of the Bible, since the resurrection passages present physical resurrection.

Conclusion

As long as the Baha'i faith continues to affirm unity, respectful dialogue, and individual study of reality, the doors are open for fruitful interfaith dialogue. And there is no more important character to focus our conversation on than Jesus Christ, who conclusively demonstrated the glory of God: "And the Word became flesh and dwelt among us, and we have seen his glory, glory as of the only Son from the Father, full of grace and truth" (John 1:14).

John Ferrer (PhD, Southwestern Baptist Theological Seminary) has experience as a teacher, minister, curriculum writer, and campus minister. In public debates, he has advocated for the existence of God and the pro-life position. He founded Intelligent Christian Faith, where he publishes articles at the intersection of Christianity and culture.

16

Church of Jesus Christ of Latter-day Saints

Ross Anderson

History of the Church of Jesus Christ of Latter-day Saints

The Church of Jesus Christ of Latter-day Saints[1] has a growing worldwide presence, with 9.6 million of its 16.3 million members living outside the United States.[2] But Mormonism's origins are firmly rooted in America. The church was started by Joseph Smith in 1830 in New York—although Mormons claim their church is the restoration of the church Jesus originally organized in the New Testament.

Joseph Smith and the Restoration

Joseph Smith was born in 1805. During his teen years, his family lived near Palmyra, New York. With parents known as spiritual seekers, Joseph grew up with an interest in spiritual truth.[3] Members of the family considered joining the various Protestant denominations found in Palmyra, but Joseph reported that, at age 14, he was confused about which church to join.[4] One day, he went to a grove near the family farm to ask God for wisdom. There a bright light shone from above, and two persons appeared in the air above him. They identified themselves as God the Father and Jesus Christ.[5] God the Father gave Joseph instructions to join none of the churches, for "all their creeds were an abomination in his sight."[6] Called the "First Vision," this event establishes an important principle in the LDS story. The true church, established by Jesus and handed off to the first apostles, had been lost from the earth. In the early centuries of Christianity, apostasy had crept into the church.[7] Priesthood authority, required to act for God, had disappeared. The Bible was corrupted, and the heavens fell silent. Latter-day Saints believe that God chose Joseph Smith to restore the true church.[8] In order for the church to be restored, there would have to be a restoration of the priesthood. Thus Smith and his friend Oliver Cowdery were visited on two occasions for the receiving of priesthood—first by John the Baptist, who conferred upon them the Aaronic Priesthood, and second by Peter, James, and John, who conferred upon them the Melchizedek Priesthood.[9]

16A. Joseph Smith Jr. in 1843. Photo by Lucian Foster (November 12, 1806–December 12, 1845). Public domain.

16B. John the Baptist bestows the Aaronic Priesthood on Joseph Smith and Oliver Cowdery. Photo by George Washington Crocheron, copyright claimant. Public domain.

Over the next few years, Joseph was prepared for this calling. He told how an angel named Moroni appeared to him to reveal the location of a lost, ancient work of scripture. Moroni showed Joseph a set of golden plates buried in the ground.[10] On these plates was inscribed a record of the people of ancient America. When Joseph was allowed to take possession of the plates, he began the process of translating this ancient record, known as the Book of Mormon.[11] As word spread about Joseph Smith's activities, persecution arose. But Joseph also began to gather a number of followers, starting with family members and some of their friends. Joseph raised the money to have the Book of Mormon published, and his followers began distributing it to anyone interested.[12]

Shortly after completing the Book of Mormon, Joseph officially started a church and began receiving new members.[13] As the group grew, Joseph's vision was to gather them into a faith community. He moved the group to Kirtland, Ohio, which became the epicenter of Mormonism.[14] But Joseph foresaw that the future of the LDS Church lay westward. He sent leaders to secure land in western Missouri.[15] By the time the Latter-day Saints ran into trouble in Kirtland, they had already relocated a large number of their members to Missouri.[16] Wherever the Saints settled, trouble followed. Their neighbors were often threatened by how the Mormons stuck together and how different they were. They endured persecution, and sometimes they fought back.[17] After a few years in Missouri, they were forced to flee to Illinois, where they built the city of Nauvoo along the Mississippi River.[18]

Ever since Joseph published the Book of Mormon, he was acknowledged by his followers as a prophet and seer.[19] The revelations he produced included many new doctrines and practices that were foreign to traditional Christianity. For example, Joseph taught that husbands and wives could be united in marriage for eternity. He introduced plural marriage, where one man could be married to several women at once, both in this life and in heaven. Joseph taught that there are multiple levels of heaven, that God is an exalted human being, and that men and women can become like God themselves in the next life.[20] Many of these innovative doctrines and practices were introduced during the Mormons' time in Nauvoo.

In many ways, Nauvoo was a great success. The Latter-day Saints had been sending missionaries around the United States and to England for several years, and converts were now pouring in.[21] Joseph Smith became not only the president of the church but also the city's mayor and commander of its militia. The Mormons started to build a new temple in which the ordinances for eternal marriage could be practiced.[22] But as in Ohio and Missouri, citizens of neighboring towns feared the growing economic and political power of the Latter-day Saints. Opposition also arose from within.[23] Some people were alarmed at all the power Joseph held. Word began to leak out about his secret practice of polygamy. When the city council ordered the destruction of an opposition newspaper, the state issued a warrant for Joseph's arrest. He was taken by an armed guard to the nearby town of Carthage, where the local militia assigned to protect him turned against him. Joseph and his brother Hyrum were attacked and killed in the Carthage jail.[24]

The Shaping of Modern Mormonism

After Joseph Smith's death, Brigham Young assumed leadership of the Latter-day Saints.[25] Young mobilized the people for the challenging westward exodus across the Great Plains to find a new home in what is now Utah. The first wave of around 2,000 people arrived in 1847. Over the next 20 years, a total of 70,000 Saints came across the plains in covered wagons or pushing handcarts.[26] The Mormons established a thriving new community far from outside influence and opposition. Young was the president of the LDS Church until his death in 1877. He also served as the governor of the Utah Territory.[27]

Once the Latter-day Saints were established in Utah, the doctrine of plural marriage was made public. The practice of polygamy, along with the desire to be free from outside control, created tension between the Mormons and the United States. In the 1880s, a series of federal laws outlawed plural marriage, assigned stiff jail penalties, and revoked the church's incorporation.[28] With the church's existence at risk, in 1890, church president Wilford Woodruff issued an official statement advising members of the church to stop entering into polygamous marriages.[29] Many Mormon leaders continued to secretly live in polygamy until finally, in 1905, the church completely disavowed the practice.[30] From that point on, Mormonism became increasingly mainstream. In fact, by the 1950s it became a shining example of America's prevailing values, such as good families, conservative morality, patriotism, and a strong work ethic.[31]

The Mormon movement has generated many different splinter groups, each claiming to be the best expression of Joseph Smith's teaching.[32] Some arose when Brigham Young came to power and led the Saints west. Groups formed at that time rejected polygamy and stayed in the eastern United States. More recent splinter groups believe that the LDS Church was wrong to renounce plural marriage. Known as "fundamentalists," they look back to Smith to give sanction to their practice of polygamy.[33] All the splinter groups are small compared to the mainstream Church of Jesus Christ of Latter-day Saints.

Beliefs of the Church of Jesus Christ of Latter-day Saints

God and Humanity

In the LDS story, human beings are the same species as God. Every person existed as a spirit before being born physically into this world. God is our Heavenly Father because he is the literal father of our spirits.[34] In fact, God himself was once a man who lived in a world like ours[35] and presumably has a heavenly father of his own. God attained deity by obeying the laws and principles that govern the universe. It follows that human beings can become like God is now. We have the capacity to gain exaltation—that is, to develop all the qualities of divinity.[36] Then, like God, we can create our own eternal families, provide for their salvation, and guide their development toward becoming gods themselves.[37] In this view, it is likely that there are also many other divine beings besides the God we worship as our Father.

As an exalted human being, God the Father has a physical body of flesh and bones.[38] He lives in great glory and possesses all knowledge and wisdom. He has power and dominion over all things.[39] As our creator, God did not make anything from nothing. Joseph Smith taught that matter and energy are uncreated and eternal.[40] God's creative act was to take the existing materials of the universe and organize them into their current state.[41]

Latter-day Saints believe that Jesus and the Holy Ghost are also divine beings. Along with God the Father, they constitute the Godhead. They are not seen as one being, as the traditional doctrine of the Trinity asserts, but are nonetheless one in purpose.[42] Jesus is preeminent as the literal firstborn of God's family. This makes Jesus the older brother of every human person.[43] At what point Jesus became divine is uncertain. The Holy Ghost's path to deity is an even greater mystery.[44] Latter-day Saints are comfortable with ambiguity on such questions. There will always be private speculation among them about doctrine, but they tend to be less concerned with doctrinal details than with how to live.

The Plan of Salvation

The grand story that defines life for Latter-day Saints is called the Plan of Salvation. It begins before anyone was born into this life. We all lived with our Heavenly Father as his spirit children in "the preexistence." As wonderful as this life was, we could not advance toward exaltation without gaining physical bodies and being tested in the mortal world. So God the Father gathered his countless spirit children to explain that we would need a Savior in order to return to him.[45] Two of God's spirit sons offered themselves. The first, Lucifer, promised to bring all of God's children back to him again, but he would receive the honor. The second, Jesus, promised to give God's children free agency. While many would not return to Heavenly Father, the choice would be theirs, and all the honor would go to the Father. God chose Jesus to be our Savior. Lucifer rebelled and convinced one third of God's children to join him in war against the Father.[46] His forces were defeated. Those who rebelled were denied the privilege of gaining a body. Lucifer became Satan, and his followers became the evil spirits of the Bible.

When a person leaves the preexistence to be born into this world, everything about that former realm is forgotten. Life on this earth is a test of whether or not we will prove worthy of returning to our Father and achieving godhood ourselves.[47] A person proves worthy by keeping all the commandments, including baptism, church attendance, loving God and neighbors, prayer, scripture study, following the LDS prophets, and much more. To gain exaltation, a person must also perform certain ordinances, including baptism, a ritual called "the endowment," and temple marriage.[48]

Mormonism teaches that God created Adam and Eve in a state of innocence. But in their innocence, they could not fulfill God's command to "be fruitful and multiply."[49] Yet God also told them not to eat of the fruit of the tree of knowledge.[50] In Mormonism, these two commands are contradictory, because the tree of knowledge would include knowledge about how to procreate. Eve courageously chose the greater commandment. Without her transgression, our first parents would have had no posterity.[51] Because of their act, death entered the world and human beings were expelled from Eden, but they could now fulfill their higher calling to create families.

Latter-day Saints talk about different levels of salvation. Jesus's atonement provides salvation from physical death for everyone. All people will be resurrected, regardless of how they lived their lives or whether they had faith. Yet to be saved from sin, a person must exercise faith, repent, be baptized, and receive the gift of the Holy Ghost. The highest form of salvation is exaltation. Jesus's atonement provides that all people have the opportunity, by keeping the commandments and ordinances, to achieve the highest level of heaven.[52] Mormonism is a system of grace plus good works. The Book of Mormon says, "We know that it is by grace that we are saved, after all we can do."[53] Because of Jesus's atonement, our good works and moral performance can count before God. Latter-day Saints believe that Jesus's atoning work began as he suffered in the Garden of Gethsemane and was completed on the cross.[54] They believe that after His death, He rose again from the dead and lives today.

Upon death, but before the resurrection and final judgment, every person enters the spirit world.[55] The spirit world has two parts: paradise and spirit prison. The righteous enter paradise, while those who never heard the LDS message or rejected it enter spirit prison. Mormons believe that people in paradise will share the gospel with people in spirit prison,[56] giving them an opportunity to respond even after their death. However, the ordinances required for exaltation can only be performed by living people on this earth. People in spirit prison, having accepted the truth, are waiting for those ordinances to be done on their behalf.[57] These proxy ordinances include baptism, the temple endowment, and marriage. Mormons do genealogy to collect the names of their ancestors in order to complete the necessary saving rites in their place.[58]

Latter-day Saints believe that Jesus will one day return to this earth and usher in 1,000 years of peace. This will provide time for all the ordinances to be completed for everyone who has lived.[59] At the end of that time, all humanity will be resurrected and will stand before God for final judgment.[60] Each person will be assigned to one of three levels of heaven.[61] The lowest level of heavenly glory is called the Telestial Kingdom. It is reserved for most of humanity, including the worst members of humanity and everyone who rejected the LDS gospel. The middle level, called the Terrestrial Kingdom, belongs to honorable people who were blinded from receiving the LDS gospel along with those who embraced it but were not valiant in living it. Only those who keep all the commandments and fulfill all the ordinances will be permitted into the highest level of heaven, the Celestial Kingdom. These people live with Heavenly Father forever. Within the Celestial Kingdom, those who attain the highest level can become gods.[62]

The only people who will not inherit some degree of heavenly glory are those who had a divinely revealed knowledge of Jesus but denied the truth. These people will live in eternal torment in "outer darkness" along with Satan and the demons.[63]

For Latter-day Saints, exaltation cannot occur individually, but only in families.[64] Worthy Saints are married in their temples "for time and eternity" so that families can be together forever in the Celestial Kingdom. The ultimate idea of exaltation is to create an eternal family, just as God the Father has done.

Holy Books

Latter-day Saints regard four books as their scriptural "standard works." First, they consider the Bible to be divinely inspired.[65] Yet they believe the Bible as we have it now has been corrupted over time, so important truths have been lost.[66]

In 1833, Joseph Smith completed a revision of the Bible, called the Joseph Smith Translation. He sought to resolve contradictions and correct errors. Smith's revisions were based on direct revelation he claimed to receive from God. The LDS Church has never published an edition of the Joseph Smith Translation, but it is frequently cited in cross-references found in official LDS scriptures.[67] The official Bible version of the LDS Church is the King James Version.

As a prophet, Smith also gave numerous revelations that were published in 1835 as *The Doctrine and Covenants*.[68] Of the 138 chapters—or "sections"—135 are from him. Three of his successors contributed one apiece, and more may be added in the future. The work also includes two official declarations, from 1878 and 1890, which give direction for important issues of LDS practice. Many sections of *The Doctrine and Covenants* deal with ordinary matters that arose in governing the LDS Church in its early years. Some sections expand on biblical themes, while others contain prophecies of the future. The book also contains a number of Mormonism's unique teachings that are not found in the Book of Mormon, including eternal marriage,[69] the three levels of heaven,[70] polygamy,[71] salvation for the dead,[72] and the LDS priesthood.[73]

The third volume of LDS scripture, the Pearl of Great Price, is a collection of three shorter works, beginning with the Book of Moses. In 1830, Smith claimed to receive an inspired amplification of the Bible's book of Genesis. This included a vision of the Prophet Moses and an expansion of Genesis 1–6. The book of Moses introduces the story of how Jesus, instead of Lucifer, became the Savior.[74]

In 1835, Smith bought some papyrus scrolls from a traveling exhibitor. One of the scrolls, he said, contained the writings of Abraham while he was in Egypt. Smith translated this as the Book of Abraham. Several unique LDS doctrines come from the Book of Abraham, including the notion that human spirits are eternal and uncreated.[75]

The final part of the Pearl of Great Price consists of Smith's revision of Matthew 24, a brief retelling of how Mormonism was founded, and a short explanation of a few basic Mormon beliefs, called the Articles of Faith.

In many ways, the most significant LDS scripture is the Book of Mormon. The Book of Mormon presents itself as the record of ancient inhabitants of America. Descended from the Israelites, these people are said to be the ancestors of today's Native Americans.[76] This record was engraved on plates of gold and hidden in the ground. Smith began translating the plates by divine inspiration and published the Book of Mormon in 1830.[77] To Latter-day Saints, the Book of Mormon is a spiritual history comparable to the Bible, which recounts the cycles of wickedness and repentance of God's people. The highlight of the book is the appearance of Jesus himself in America. Faithful Latter-day Saints read the Book of Mormon diligently. The book shapes Mormon culture by reinforcing key values and ideals.[78] It invites readers to seek a spiritual experience that will convince them of the truth of its message and thus validate Joseph Smith as a prophet of God.[79] This spiritual witness is an important experience that shapes those raised in Mormonism and those who join it.[80]

Additional holy books can be added to the LDS scriptures at any time. Latter-day Saints expect that ancient books of scripture unknown to us now will one day be restored.[81] A current prophet could also receive new revelation. This is why no holy book carries final authority in Mormonism. In the end, the word of a living prophet stands above any written scripture.[82]

Lifestyle and Culture

Mormonism as a Cultural Identity

Being a Latter-day Saint is far more than being a member of a particular church. Mormonism is a complete cultural identity[83] involving shared worldview, customs, and values integrated into a whole life experience.[84] Mormon culture—like any other—reflects its own language, folklore, ways of organizing, buildings, artwork, ritual and other shared experiences, and expectations of how to act.[85]

16C. The Salt Lake Temple in Salt Lake City, Utah. Photo by Farragutful (https://creativecommons.org/licenses/by-sa/4.0).

The LDS cultural identity has been powerfully formed by shared historical experiences. The journey of the Mormon pioneers to Utah in 1847 helped create a sense of "peoplehood," like the exodus of Israel in the Bible.[86] The experience of past persecution also shapes LDS culture. Because they remember the wrongs committed against their forebears, Mormons see themselves as a persecuted minority and are often sensitive to criticism.[87]

People enter the LDS cultural community in two ways: by birth or by conversion. Converts take on their new identity by first embracing the LDS message and then by adopting the Mormon lifestyle and values.[88] By contrast, those born into the church move through a series of stages or events that reinforce who they are as a unique people.[89] These include baptism at age 8, initiation into the LDS priesthood (for males) at age 12, a special patriarchal blessing as a teenager, serving a mission as a young adult, and eventually, temple marriage.

All Latter-day Saints are urged to seek an individual conversion experience, called "gaining a testimony." This is the moment when a person comes to know with divinely inspired certainty that Joseph Smith is a prophet of God, the Book of Mormon is true, and the Church of Jesus Christ of Latter-day Saints is the only true church.[90] Church membership is important, but the real faith journey begins when a member or potential member gains this assurance that the LDS Church and its claims are true.

Even though Latter-day Saints are a tight-knit group sharing a common culture, there is a great deal of variation among them.[91] For example, a member of the church might be "active" or "inactive." Among active Mormons, some are "true believers" and others are closet doubters. Members born into the church are different in many ways from converts.[92] Those living in the LDS heartland are different from those who live where Mormons are a minority. Younger members experience Mormon beliefs and practices differently than older members.[93] Despite the shared elements of a common culture, different segments of the LDS population define the meaning of their church membership in different ways.[94]

Church Organization

Latter-day Saints don't just "go to church." For those who are active, the church is central to every aspect of their lives, and they give to it a great deal of time, money, energy, and loyalty. Faithful Mormons believe that their church is the only true church on earth.[95] As such, no one can reach exaltation without its teachings, ordinances, and authority.

The church's basic unit of organization is the "ward"—a local congregation comprising 300 people or so.[96] A "stake" consists of between 5 and 12 wards, while a group of stakes make up an "area."[97] At the top of this hierarchy are the "General Authorities," who oversee a large staff of professional administrators.[98] Preeminent among the General Authorities is the "First Presidency," consisting of the church's president and his two most trusted counselors. Policy is set by the Quorum of the Twelve Apostles, also numbered among the General Authorities.[99] General Authorities are revered by church members and hold their positions for life. This reverence is understandable given that Latter-day Saints believe the church is led by living prophets who speak and act for God.

Ultimately, the LDS Church is administered by the power of the priesthood, which Mormons consider to be the authority to act in God's name. Every worthy male is eligible to receive some level of priesthood authority. Without the priesthood, the keys to governing the church are absent, and the ordinances required for salvation are not valid.[100]

Much of a Mormon's life connects with the church as a whole. For example, the church holds General Conference every spring and fall, which members are encouraged to watch on a satellite feed. Many LDS young adults will attend one of the church's four colleges, such as Brigham Young University. The Church Education System runs classes for high school and college students, typically at buildings next door to schools. Faithful church members will likely subscribe to the church's magazines for adults, teens, and children. They will use the resources on one of the church's websites. Many church members will interact with LDS Welfare Services[101] either as a volunteer or as a recipient of material help in times of need.

Yet a member's church relationships and activities primarily revolve around their ward. Members are required to attend the ward nearest their home. In many ways, an LDS ward is similar to any local church. It has weekly meetings and programs for various age groups, and it provides a close-knit community.[102] Each ward is led by a bishop and two counselors. The bishop manages an extensive volunteer force as the primary administrator and spiritual overseer of the congregation. Bishops serve about five years but do not receive any professional training or financial compensation for the task.[103]

Adult men who hold the Priesthood meet regularly in a priesthood "quorum." Adult women belong to the women's agency called the Relief Society.[104] Young Men's and Young Women's organizations give teens a peer group and prepare them for the duties of adulthood. Sunday School classes provide age-specific religious training for ward members aged 12 and older. Younger children attend Primary.[105] Adult members serve, strengthen, and teach each other through a program of informal visits called "ministering."

A ward's Sunday schedule is about two hours long. One hour is called Sacrament meeting. It includes hymns, talks by laypersons, congregational business, and "the sacrament"—the LDS version of Communion. People come dressed in their Sunday best—dresses for women and ties for men.[106] The mood of Sacrament meeting is reverence. The other hour of the Sunday block alternates between Sunday school for all ages on one week and Priesthood Meeting and Relief Society on the opposite week.[107]

Family Life

All families are unique, but compared to the general population, LDS families share certain common features.[108] First, Mormons are more conservative about sexual activity before marriage. Procreation is seen as the way God brings spirits out of the preexistence and creates eternal families.[109] Second, Mormons are more likely to marry and less likely to divorce. Third, LDS families tend to be larger than the norm. Fourth, their families are marked by more male authority and traditional gender roles. Wives are less likely to work outside the home. The father is the patriarch and priesthood leader.[110] He will baptize the children, give family blessings, and ordain his sons to priesthood offices.

Several LDS practices reflect the value of families. Each week, families are encouraged to do Family Home Evening, using lessons and activities provided by the Church.[111] Family reunions are common.[112] Mormons place a great emphasis on family history, compiling records and journals from their forebears. Families often do genealogy together and share the results.

Mormonism teaches that the universe is organized along family lines and that heaven is an extension of home life on this earth.[113]

Temples

In 1975, the LDS Church had 16 temples worldwide; in 2019, they had 164. That number is rapidly increasing, with 45 more either planned or under construction.[114] More than any other aspect of Mormon life, the temple represents the unique elements of the LDS worldview. By contrast to the local ward, which is public, the temple is private. If the ward experience is about how to live in this world, the temple focuses on how to prepare for the world to come.[115] Temples are required for saving ordinances considered too sacred for the general public, including those rituals performed for the dead. Because these rites are sacred, Latter-day Saints don't talk about what goes on there even among themselves.

Once a person has been initiated into the basic temple ritual, he or she wears a special form of underclothing called the "garment." The temple garment is a daily reminder of the covenants made in the temple, and a protection against temptation and evil.[116] Latter-day Saints view the garment as sacred. It is not to be exposed to the uninitiated or adjusted to accommodate fashion styles.[117]

Only the worthiest church members can attend the temple.[118] Because of this, the temple experience creates a sort of church within a church.[119] Temple-worthy Mormons are typically more serious about their faith. This is one reason the church urges members to become temple-worthy and to attend the temple often.

Worthiness

The LDS story of progression toward exaltation creates a drive for achievement and advancement.[120] This is coupled with a "can-do" attitude and strong work ethic forged in the pioneer experience. This drive to achieve shows up in educational advancement,[121] economic prosperity,[122] self-reliant living,[123] and personal righteousness, or "worthiness."

Worthiness is the strongest motive driving the daily life of active Mormons.[124] It can be defined as living up to the church's standards.[125] For example, active Latter-day Saints are expected to give 10 percent of their income to the church.[126] They are expected to give generously of their time and energy in service. They are urged to do genealogy and to perform the temple work for their ancestors. They help their neighbors in times of need, and they do much more. To be worthy, members are expected to obey the Law of Chastity.[127] Any sexual relations or practices outside of marriage are taboo. Faithful Mormons also follow the Word of Wisdom, a unique health code that forbids alcohol, tobacco, coffee, and tea.[128] Mormons are held accountable for all of these standards by regular interviews with church leaders.

Outward worthiness is cultivated by several personal spiritual practices. Mormons are regularly challenged to read through the Book of Mormon. Most Mormons pray daily.[129] Fasting and journal-keeping are common. Active Latter-day Saints are expected to honor Sunday as the Sabbath by avoiding work and frivolous activities in order to focus on family time and church attendance.[130]

Latter-day Saints often report personal spiritual experiences where they "feel the Spirit." These tender emotions are understood to be the activity of God's Spirit affirming the truth.[131] Such moments are most likely to happen in private settings and are not widely shared with others. Mormons believe members can receive divine revelation for their own lives and for those under their leadership.[132] Such inspiration comes as a warm, peaceful feeling or a sense of insight and clarity.

Growth and Decline

Serving a mission is a vital rite of passage that strengthens the commitment of young Mormons. In 2019, the LDS Church had 65,000 proselytizing missionaries serving in 407 "mission fields" around the world.[133] Young men are expected to serve a mission for the church, while young women are invited to serve.[134] Men typically serve for two years, while women serve 18 months. Candidates for missionary service must meet high standards of worthiness, including the Law of Chastity, the Word of Wisdom, tithing, and church attendance. They are encouraged to prepare throughout their lives by learning LDS doctrine, becoming self-reliant, and saving their money.[135] Most missions are primarily self-funded.

The main purpose of missionary service

is to spread the LDS gospel to the world.[136] But a mission also reinforces a young adult's LDS testimony and identity, preparing him or her for a lifetime of service to the church.[137]

The LDS church has roughly doubled in the past 25 years—although the growth rate has decreased a great deal in recent years.[138] The church grows by the birth of children and by the baptism of converts. About 30 percent of church members are converts.[139] Yet in spite of this growth, people are leaving Mormonism in unprecedented numbers. One LDS scholar claims that 50 percent of converts in the United States drop out after a year.[140] One third of those raised LDS will leave the church.[141] Many factors contribute to people leaving the church: the stress of demanding expectations, questionable issues in Mormon history, the authoritarian approach of the church's leadership and its conservative stance on social issues, and comparison with the Bible. A growing number of Latter-day Saints reject LDS claims and teachings but stay in the church as closet doubters. They may stay for marital and family stability or job security or to try to influence change.[142]

For those raised LDS, leaving Mormonism is hard. It goes against their deep roots and group identity.[143] They are considered apostate by church members and may be slandered and shunned.[144] Thus doubting Mormons may go through insecurity, alienation, anger, and confusion before ultimately deciding to leave the church.[145]

The Church of Jesus Christ of Latter-day Saints and Historic Christianity

One reason to understand the history, beliefs, culture, and experience of Latter-day Saints is to be wise about sharing the good news of God's grace with them. Having faith conversations with Mormons is easy in some ways but challenging in others. Consider these insights to help you engage your LDS neighbors.

Common Ground

First, traditional Christians can find common ground for engaging Latter-day Saints in our shared concerns as human beings. Mormons have relational and emotional needs like everyone. They value their marriages, love their children, and want the best for their lives. We can connect with them through these common human aspirations.

We also share with Latter-day Saints a Judeo-Christian moral framework. Mormons have many of the same values we do about family, sexual ethics, personal responsibility, sobriety, and more. They typically share many of the same concerns we may have about the moral and spiritual condition of society.

The Bible is another area of common ground. As we have seen, Mormons consider the Bible to be scripture. Even though they see it as inferior to their other scriptures, they still have a respectful attitude toward the Bible. Latter-day Saints are open to what the Bible says and are often willing to read and study the Bible with Christian friends.

The most significant area of affinity between traditional Christians and Mormons is Jesus—especially the historical person of Jesus revealed in the four Gospels. Their ideas about Jesus before his birth and after his ascension come largely from their unique scriptures. But Mormonism draws its picture of Jesus's earthly life almost exclusively from the Bible. By and large, Mormons love Jesus. They are not reluctant to talk about Jesus or to read about Him and His words in the Bible. This interest and affection toward Jesus provide what is likely the best avenue of discussion with Latter-day Saints about the gospel and what it means.

Finally, Mormons are interested in matters of faith. It's usually fairly easy to have faith conversations with them, because faith is such an important part of their lives. They like to talk about their beliefs and may be very interested in comparing the beliefs of others.

Crucial Contrasts

Traditional Christianity also differs from Mormonism in several important ways. First, Mormons and traditional Christians see the universe differently. The LDS view the universe as eternal and uncreated. By contrast, biblical Christianity teaches that the universe was created by God out of nothing.[146] Only God is eternal and uncreated.[147] Everything else that exists depends on Him, not just for its present form, but for its very existence.

We saw that Latter-day Saints believe that God is an exalted human with a physical body. By contrast, Christianity teaches that God is not a physical being but an infinite spirit[148] who has always been God.[149] He is not the same species as humanity.[150] He is not subject to the limitations of time or space.[151] Biblical passages that speak of God as having physical attributes are metaphorical, not literal.[152] Like Mormonism, traditional Christianity identifies Jesus Christ and the Holy Spirit as divine persons. But unlike Mormons, Christians hold that there is only one God,[153] who exists eternally in three distinct persons.[154] Thus Jesus has always been God.[155]

While the LDS Church views human beings as literal spirit children of God the Father, with the potential to become gods themselves one day, biblical Christianity teaches that humans are creatures of God.[156] We can become adopted as God's children by faith,[157] but we are a completely different kind of being compared to God.[158] We did not live with God in some preexistent world. In fact, we do not exist until God forms us in our mothers' wombs.[159] Human beings have incredible value, not because we are potentially divine, but because we are the only creatures made to reflect the attributes and purpose of God.[160]

Beneath these opposing ideas about God and humanity lie two different views of truth and authority. In LDS culture, the primary way of validating truth is through experience. We noted earlier that Mormons are urged to seek a spiritual and emotional experience to gain assurance about the core claims of Mormonism. By contrast, the Bible warns us to test all things. The test is not a warm, peaceful feeling, but a reasoned evaluation of doctrinal truth.[161] For Christians, the Bible itself is the final test of what is true.

Compared to LDS claims of continuing revelation and additional scripture, Christians see the Bible as God's final authority for what we believe and how we live.[162] The Bible has not been corrupted over the centuries but has been handed down with incredible accuracy.[163] By contrast, the additional LDS scriptures lack credibility. Unlike the Bible, there is no historical or archaeological evidence to support the Book of Mormon.[164] The Book of Mormon shows signs of being a nineteenth-century work rather than an ancient book.[165] The Joseph Smith Translation of the Bible is filled with errors.[166] The claim that the book of Abraham translates ancient Egyptian writings by Abraham has been proven to be unfounded.[167]

While the LDS Church claims to be led by living prophets, the Bible teaches that the coming of Jesus as God's final revelation makes that kind of prophets obsolete.[168] But even if we were to allow that prophets like those in the Bible might be possible, the Bible outlines how to test any prophetic claim. First, do the prophet's predictions come true?[169] On this count, many of Joseph Smith's prophecies fall short.[170] Second, do the prophet's teachings line up with what God has already revealed about himself?[171] As we have seen, Joseph Smith's teachings about God contradict biblical truth.

The Bible describes priesthood,[172] the role of temples,[173] and the nature of the church[174] very differently from Mormonism. The LDS claim that Jesus's original church was lost cannot be proven.[175] But let's conclude this section by contrasting how Mormonism and historic Christianity look at sin and salvation. Latter-day Saints see Adam and Eve's sin in Eden as a good thing because it allowed human beings to fulfill their larger destiny. Yet the Bible portrays their sin as an utter disaster for humanity.[176] It resulted in all people being alienated from God.[177] It ushered in spiritual and physical death. It introduced a deep corruption into human nature so that human beings are totally unable to please God or contribute anything toward knowing God.[178] Instead of the potential of divinity, human beings are hopelessly lost and fallen, in desperate need of deliverance and new life.

The Bible consistently presents the cross, not the Garden of Gethsemane, as the place where Jesus secured our salvation.[179] He died there not only to deliver us from physical death but also to pay the entire penalty of our sin—for those who trust in His provision. Jesus did everything required for us to be forgiven. His sacrifice is enough for anyone to be right with God. We don't need to add church, good works, commandments, or ordinances.[180] God offers this to us as a free gift, not a reward for worthiness or achievement.[181] In fact, all the benefits of Jesus's atonement, including forgiveness, new life, righteousness, resurrection, and heaven, are ours by God's grace alone, to be received by faith alone.[182]

Those who trust in Jesus alone receive eternal life—the privilege of living with God forever, in the presence of Father, Son, and Holy Spirit in heaven.[183] There we will fulfill all the purposes God originally gave the human race. There is no second chance for salvation after this life is over,[184] just as there are no secondary heavens for the rest of humanity. Sadly, those who reject Jesus will face God's righteous judgment for their sin and will be eternally separated from God in hell.[185]

Communicating with Latter-day Saints

Challenges

With these contrasts in mind, it is possible to have meaningful faith conversations with Latter-day Saints. But there are challenges.

First, personal relationships can be difficult. Mormons don't always have room for or interest in relationships with non-Mormons. When I was growing up LDS, our family had no real friends outside of our LDS ward. Our lives were complete within the LDS community. Likewise, Mormons are not always aware of nonmembers and how they live.

Second, Latter-day Saints typically want to convert you to their faith. They may invite you to LDS Church events, to read LDS literature, or to meet with their missionaries. But in conversations with non-Mormons, they tend to minimize beliefs that might be hard to swallow. For example, they are not always eager to say that God was once a man, to talk about people becoming gods, or to discuss Joseph Smith's polygamy.[186] Because we both may be interested in converting each other, relationships can feel like they count only if we get the outcome we want. Those expectations can get in the way of real friendship.

Third, Latter-day Saints and Christians use the same words, but with different meanings. Mormonism has reinterpreted many common Bible terms, like "grace," "salvation," and "eternal life." You might think that your LDS friend agrees with you when in fact the ideas beneath the words you are using are very different. Misunderstanding happens easily unless words are carefully defined.

Fourth, traditional Christians have a history of interacting with Mormonism in a way that feels to them like an attack. Christians have often sought to prove Mormonism wrong. This approach makes Latter-day Saints believe that we are trying to tear down their church. While there is a place for comparisons between LDS doctrine and the Bible, this feels to Mormons like our message is little more than, "We're right and you're wrong." As we saw, Latter-day Saints are very sensitive to persecution. They are wary about anything that might be labeled as "anti-Mormon." They are also wary about "contention."[187] If they sense you are becoming argumentative, you will lose their trust and the conversation will end.

Cult or Culture?

In the past, Christians have typically engaged Mormonism as a cult. While it's true that there are major contradictions between Mormonism and the Bible, talking about Mormonism as a cult doesn't help us share God's good news. The word *cult* brings to mind many negative stereotypes. It's not surprising that LDS people are offended by that label. Calling our Mormon neighbors cultists will shut the door to any real communication and thus to any real change.

Instead, let's think about how to approach Mormonism as a *culture*. This is how missionaries interact with other faith groups around the world. The Apostle Paul is the best biblical example of this. Speaking to a Jewish audience,[188] Paul started his message by quoting the Jewish scriptures and referring to their history. He then proclaimed Jesus as the fulfillment of Jewish scripture and history. Speaking to a rural pagan audience,[189] he began by describing the goodness of the Creator as revealed in nature. Addressing sophisticated urban pagans,[190] Paul started with their speculations about God. He quoted their own writers, eventually introducing Jesus as the fulfillment of their spiritual search. In each situation, the Apostle used a different starting point to communicate in ways that would speak to each different audience. But the message always came around to Jesus.

With Paul's example in mind, it's not enough just to debate contrasting belief systems. We should adopt methods of sharing the unchanging message of Jesus that take into account the unique elements of Mormon culture. There is a time and place to defend historic Christian beliefs and to point out the fallacies of Mormonism. But we need to speak to the whole person, not just his or her mind. And we need to think about elements of LDS culture that influence issues like how Mormons experience faith, how they think about truth, whom they are willing to listen to, and how they make spiritual decisions.

Being Wise Communicators

Keeping the unique culture of Mormonism in mind, let's consider some basic principles for communicating God's good news to our LDS neighbors.

First, your attitude matters. Ask God to give you genuine care for Latter-day Saints. Listen humbly. If you adopt the attitude of a learner (rather than just a teller), you create space for true understanding, as people can express their unique beliefs and attitudes in their own words. Above all, don't be combative.[191] If you attack their beliefs or insult things they hold sacred, it will trigger the LDS persecution complex. You will lose credibility and they will stop listening.

Second, be open to real relationships with Mormons. Invite them into your life, and be willing to accept their invitations. Value each of them as a person, not a project. Be willing to serve them in practical ways, and be willing to let them serve you.

Third, be ready to answer the question, "Are Mormons Christians?"[192] Mormons are confused about why traditional Christians deny that Mormons are also Christians. After all, they love and follow Jesus. Jesus is in the very name of their church. The problem is that we use a different definition of "Christian" than they do. To Latter-day Saints, if you try to follow Jesus's example, you are a Christian. Instead, historic Christianity focuses on having a transforming experience of trust in Jesus alone. Don't get bogged down in this debate. It can be fruitful to talk about what a Christian actually is but not if it becomes an argument about mere labels. When I had this conversation with a very loyal LDS man, he said, "I now understand what you mean by 'Christian.' I realize that's not what I want to be."

Fourth, learn to speak the language of experience. Since LDS people validate truth by emotional and spiritual experiences, let's take this into account as we share biblical truth. One way to do that is to tell your story about how God has changed your life through Jesus. Talk about how God has guided you and answered prayer. Another tactic is to talk about doctrinal truth in experiential terms. In other words, as you share the truth, include how it impacts you personally. For example, when I talk to a Mormon about the Trinity, I can make my case from the Bible, and he will disagree with me. But at some point, I also want to share how amazed and in awe I am at a God who is infinitely beyond my limited understanding. When I talk to a Mormon friend, we will disagree about whether God has a physical body. We will interpret the Bible passages differently. But before we're done, I also want to let him know the confidence I have, knowing that wherever I am, God is always there with me. Don't just leave the conversation with a rational argument for the truth. Weave in your experiences in response to the truth. Ask the Holy Spirit to use those experiences to give your LDS friend a greater thirst for a living relationship with God.

Fifth, major on the majors. Mormonism provides plenty of topics that invite debate. Yet most of these topics aren't likely to lead an LDS person toward faith in Christ. For example, pointing out the problems with Joseph Smith's polygamy isn't going to make a Mormon want to hear the gospel. Focus your conversations as much as possible on Jesus, using the Bible to share about who He is and what He has done.

Sixth, focus on what the gospel has to offer to a Latter-day Saint's felt needs. Mormons are very confident in what they have to offer traditional Christians: a restored priesthood, continuing revelation, and more. But they don't think historic Christianity has anything to offer them. In part, that's because Christians keep trying to engage Mormons with topics that they don't find compelling. Most of them aren't very interested in debating the nature of God or the reliability of the Bible. But life in a perfectionist religion has several stress points. So let's think about three positive gifts the Christian gospel has to offer to Mormons who are struggling to be worthy.

First, we can share the delight of an intimate relationship with God. Even though LDS see themselves as literal children of Heavenly Father, their relationship with God is more like that of a servant than a child. Servants do what they're supposed to do, out of duty and obligation. Sons and daughters obey their father, but they also have a delight in him, which leads to intimacy. We can also point to a life with our Heavenly Father that is energizing and alive, where it is a joy, not merely an obligation, to serve God, and where we have direct access to Him without human authorities and rituals standing between.

We can share the gift of security before God. Latter-day Saints have a grand vision of what they might become in eternity, but no one can know in this life where they really stand with God. They can never know whether they have done enough to merit the Celestial Kingdom. In light of that, we can bear witness to the assurance that comes, not from our efforts or merit, but from the mercy and the promises of God.

We can point our LDS friends to the good news of God's grace lavished on us in Christ. When the pressure to perform becomes overwhelming, we can offer hope. When Mormons realize that they can never be worthy enough, we can point them to God's unconditional acceptance. When they are crushed from trying to be good enough to achieve eternal rewards, we can invite them to simply receive God's free gift.

As we wisely engage with Latter-day Saints, our prayer is not merely that they leave the LDS Church. Many people are leaving Mormonism for atheism. They are no closer to Christ than they were as church members. Our prayer is that our Mormon friends embrace the reality that Jesus is enough. Through our caring witness, we pray that they become aware of their spiritual need and God's gracious provision. Be patient! It won't come overnight. You may never see a hint of it at all. But don't give up. Many Latter-day Saints are finding a new faith in Christ. There is hope that everything you have shared and modeled about God's grace will one day win their hearts.

Ross Anderson (DMin, Salt Lake Theological Seminary) was raised in an active Latter-day Saint family and has served as a pastor in Utah since 1983. As Director of Utah Advance Ministries, Ross helps leaders contextualize ministry in Utah's unique cultural climate and directs the annual Faith After Mormonism Conference. He is the author of *Understanding the Book of Mormon, Understanding Your Mormon Neighbor*, and *Jesus Without Joseph: Following Christ After Leaving Mormonism.*

17

Jehovah's Witnesses

Lindsey Medenwaldt

Imagine you are at home after a long day at work or school, and you are just getting ready to sit down to watch your favorite television show. Just as you settle in, you hear a knock on your door. You get up, answer it, and find two well-dressed people holding Bibles whom you identify as Jehovah's Witnesses.[1] They might introduce themselves to you by asking you if they can share a positive view of the future with you. What would your first reaction be? Nowadays, you will not just find JWs at your doorstep—you will find them at the mall or the local art museum. My family was at Mount Rushmore in South Dakota recently, and Witnesses were there too. My hope is that after you read this chapter, you'll feel confident to engage in a conversation with them and show them the true hope found in Christ (1 Peter 1:3-6).

History of the Jehovah's Witnesses

In order to understand the Witnesses, you need to have a basic understanding of their history because their roots provide the basis for everything they do. By knowing their history, you can have a greater connection with them, which will hopefully help lead to fruitful conversations and meaningful relationships. Their story begins with a teenager who is overwhelmed by denominations and ends with the Armageddon. In addition to their founder, Charles Taze Russell, there are several other people who played a key role in the fundamental JW beliefs, which we will cover below.

Charles Taze Russell (1852–1916)

Russell was born in Pennsylvania in 1852. He began questioning his faith at a young age, and by 16, he was ready to leave his Presbyterian and Congregational religious background because he could not accept the doctrines of eternal punishment in hell or the Trinity.[2] He avoided organized religion, but he was drawn to Adventist beliefs, particularly because of their view that there is no eternal punishment for the wicked.[3] Eventually, Russell developed his own theology and formed a group that got together regularly to study the Bible. This group became the Watchtower Bible and Tract Society (WTBTS). They focused heavily on the second coming of Christ, which Adventists predicted would happen in 1874.[4] When 1874 came and went with no physical evidence of Christ's return, the Adventists and Russell's group adopted the idea that Christ did, in fact, return—but not in the physical way they thought it would happen.[5]

In 1879, Russell launched the *Watchtower* magazine, which is still in publication today.[6] This was considered his official split from the Adventists, even though he carried over some of their beliefs into his own theology. In 1908, he moved the Watchtower headquarters from Allegheny, Pennsylvania, to Brooklyn, New York. The headquarters remained in Brooklyn until 2009, when they relocated to Warwick, New York.[7]

Although Russell had several followers, he wasn't free from controversy. In June 1912, Baptist pastor J.J. Ross wrote a scathing pamphlet alleging that Russell was not qualified to be a minister because he hadn't received proper training in philosophy, theology, or ancient languages.[8] Russell responded by suing Ross for libel. The only evidence Russell offered to give, though, was his own testimony. While under oath, he was forced to admit that he left school at age 14, and he was not actually familiar with the Greek language, which contradicted his previous testimony.[9] The court subsequently threw out the case because he lied under oath.[10]

17A. Charles Taze Russell (1852–1916). Photo by Rursus. Public domain.

It is important to note the modern-day JW view of Russell. Although Witnesses once considered him a "wise and faithful servant," that phrase is now used to describe only a group of "anointed" Governing Body members.[11] Further, it seems as though the JWs have tried to separate themselves from their founder, noting on their website that "while Russell took the lead in the Bible education work at [the beginning] and was the first editor of the *Watchtower*, he was not the founder of a new religion."[12] Instead, they credit Jesus Christ as their founder. Although there have been attempts to minimize Russell's influence on JW theology, other various writings since his death have elevated him to near sainthood. For example, more than ten years after Russell's death, his successor, Joseph F. Rutherford, wrote:

> As William Tyndale was used to bring the Bible to the attention of the people, so the Lord used [Russell] to bring to the attention of the people an understanding of the Bible, particularly of those truths that had been taken away by the machinations of the Devil and his agencies. Because it was the Lord's due time to restore these truths, he used [Russell] to write and publish books known as *Studies in the Scriptures* by which the great fundamental truths of the divine plan are clarified. Satan has done his best to destroy these books because they explain the Scriptures.[13]

There are still separate Russellite groups who follow Russell's teachings.[14] Regardless of how he is viewed, though, Russell certainly influenced the legacy of the Witnesses and the WTBTS.

Joseph F. Rutherford (1869–1942)

Following Russell's death, attorney Joseph F. Rutherford became president of the WTBTS. In addition to setting a new date for the Armageddon (1925), Rutherford changed the name of the organization to the Jehovah's Witnesses in 1931.[15] Rutherford started the JW tradition of evangelizing door-to-door.[16] He also said that those who became a Witness before 1935 would be part of the *little flock*; that is, they would reign with Christ in heaven. All other true believers, the *great crowd*, would live in earthly paradise after the Armageddon.[17]

Nathan Knorr (1905–77)

Nathan Knorr succeeded Rutherford, and under his leadership, a change was made to future Watchtower publications: They would all be published anonymously.[18] It was also under Knorr that the church began to say that Jesus had returned invisibly in 1914, and a new date was set for the Armageddon: 1975.[19] While Knorr was president, the Witnesses also published their version of the Bible, *New World Translation of the Holy Scriptures.*

Frederick Franz (1893–1992)

Frederick Franz replaced Knorr, and his job was to regain the trust of the Witnesses, especially after another failed Armageddon prediction. No dates for the Armageddon were set under Franz, but he "steadfastly taught that persons alive during 1914 would definitely experience Armageddon."[20]

Milton G. Henschel (1920–2003)

Franz's successor, Milton G. Henschel, revealed that there had been "new light" regarding the Armageddon and threw out Franz's prophecy about the 1914 generation.[21] "Generation" meant anyone who lived in today's wicked world, including anyone at any time and any place, not just those alive in 1914.[22]

The Governing Body

Henschel was replaced by Don A. Adams (1925–), and in 2014 Robert Ciranko (1947–) took the helm. Starting with Adams, though, the presidency has been a primarily administrative role. Instead, the Witnesses are led by the Governing Body, a group of men who set the rules for the religion. They are located at JW headquarters in New York and "meet each week to consider the needs of the organization. In these meetings, the members discuss what the Scriptures say, and they yield to the influence of God's Holy Spirit, striving for unanimous decisions."[23]

Teachings of the Jehovah's Witnesses

Whole books have been written to discuss the beliefs of the Witnesses, but we'll limit the discussion to their literature and Bible translation as well as their teachings about Jehovah, the Trinity, Jesus, and salvation. If you have a basic understanding of these four tenets, you'll be in a good position to have a conversation with Witnesses you meet. Keep in mind that the terminology will sound very similar to Christianity, which is why I always emphasize that people ask others what they mean when they say certain things. This way, we can see what is truly similar and what is distinguishable from fundamental Christian beliefs.[24]

Literature

From the outset, it is important to note why Witnesses believe what they believe. My friend and former JW, Cynthia Hampton, has told me several times that they believe whatever the Governing Body tells them to believe. They are not encouraged to think for themselves. If something is published in the *Watchtower* or other Witness literature, it is to be considered true. In fact, it has been said time and again that the JW organization is the arbiter of truth for God's people. For example, a 1957 edition of the *Watchtower* magazine said, "God has not arranged for [His] Word to speak independently or to shine forth life-giving truths by itself. It is through His organization God provides this light."[25] The risk is high for those who seek truth outside of the religion: The punishment is disfellowship from the church and all Witnesses, including family and friends.[26]

New World Translation of the Holy Scriptures (NWT)

In 1950, the Witnesses published their own version of the Bible because they wanted to "restore the name *Jehovah* in the Old Testament where the Hebrew consonants 'YHWH' appear."[27] They also inserted the name *Jehovah* in the New Testament 237 times.[28] The translators of the NWT remained anonymous because "they were not seeking prominence for themselves but only to honor the Divine Author of the Holy Scriptures."[29] The Watchtower Organization considers the NWT the most accurate version of the Bible today.[30]

Jehovah

Witnesses believe that God's true name is *Jehovah* (Psalm 83:18), and they believe that their salvation *depends* on using the name *Jehovah*.[31]

The Trinity

Witnesses reject the doctrine of the Trinity outright. They assert that belief in the Trinity

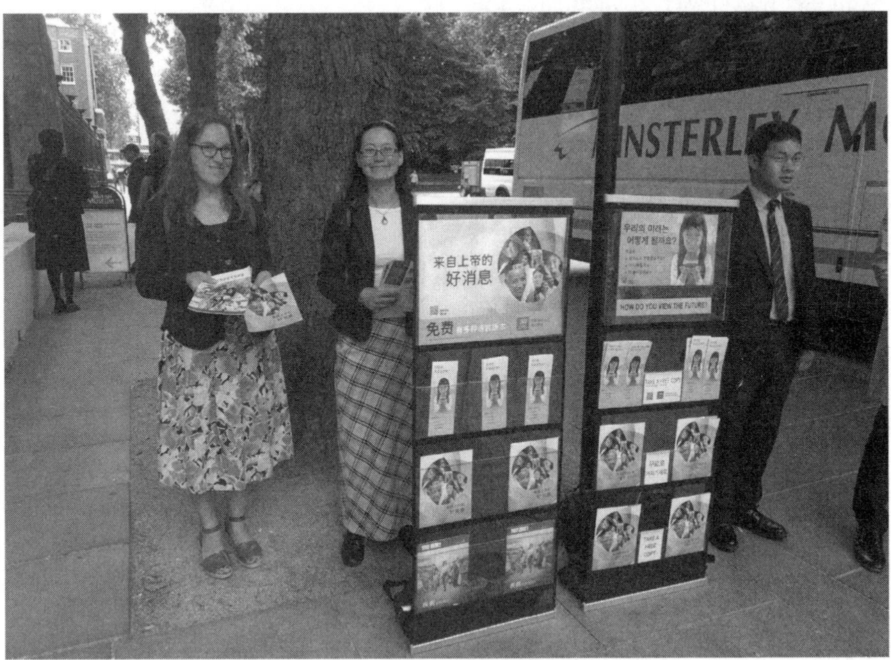

17B. Jehovah's Witnesses offer literature to visitors to a museum. Photo by Philafrenzy (https://creativecommons.org/licenses/by-sa/4.0).

"is a barrier to knowing and loving God."[32] They also argue that because the word *trinity* does not appear in Scripture, the concept must not be true.[33] Thus although they believe in one God, for Witnesses, God the Father is Jehovah, Jesus is God's first creation, and the Holy Spirit is the active force of God.[34]

Jesus

Witnesses believe that Jesus was God's first creation and that he lived on heaven before he lived on earth.[35] They believe that Jesus is actually the archangel Michael, and following his ascension to heaven after his resurrection, he resumed his role as Michael.[36] Although they will say Jesus and the Father are one, they are quick to clarify that God is Jehovah the almighty, while Jesus is only a "mighty god."[37] They use passages like John 17:3 (where Jesus said that God the Father was the only true God) and Isaiah 44:6 (where God said there was no other God besides Him) to support their conclusions. Ultimately, Witnesses believe Jesus was created by God just like everything and everyone else. Jesus is still God's son, but only as far as *we* are also God's sons and daughters.

Although the Witnesses believe that Jesus was impaled on an upright stake and died for the sins of mankind, they wholly reject the cross as the means of his death and think the cross is a pagan symbol.[38] They believe Jesus's body disintegrated into gases in the grave, and he was then resurrected as an imperishable spirit body and temporarily took on a human body. He could appear and disappear at will.[39] This is a significant distinction between Jesus's resurrection and other resurrections that took place prior to his, like the little girl in Luke 7:11 and Lazarus in John 11:1-44. At his ascension, Jesus disintegrated into gases and began to sit at the right hand of his Father, but he is no longer at the Father's right hand. JWs believe that since 1914, Jesus has been ruling as Heavenly King.

Salvation

If you ask Witnesses if they are saved, they will likely say, "Thus far, yes."[40] That's because they believe that even though they are saved through Jesus's death, no one is automatically declared worthy to receive everlasting life. Rather, Christ's death allowed us to begin working for our salvation.

Only 144,000, the "little flock," will spend eternity in heaven ruling earth with Jehovah. All other faithful followers, the "great crowd," will spend eternity on the new earth with Jesus but will never enter heaven. The 144,000 have already been determined (those who joined the JWs before 1935). Witnesses believe they can lose their salvation if they are not faithful and obedient to the Watchtower Organization.[41]

JWs believe in hell but not eternal punishment. They consider hell a common grave, a place of eternal unconsciousness and nonexistence.[42] Witnesses believe that the spirit is simply the life force of a human. When the person dies, the life force leaves the body and either goes to the common grave or continues to exist in a sleep state until resurrected by God after the Armageddon.[43] God can resurrect anyone who is in hell, except for unrepentant apostates and dedicated Christians who "persist in willful sin."[44]

Lifestyle and Culture

The Kingdom Hall

The Kingdom Hall is where the Witnesses gather twice per week to pray, study Scripture and church doctrine, and work on strategies for evangelism. JWs do not use the word *church* because they believe it refers to God's people, not the building where his people gather.[45] There are no paid clergy, and all local congregations submit to the authority of their local elders, district overseers, and the Governing Body.[46] There are more than 110,000 Kingdom Halls worldwide, and between 100 and 300 people attend services at each one.[47]

Weekend meetings consist of a 30-minute Bible discourse, followed by a 1-hour Watchtower study. Midweek meetings are 1 hour and 45 minutes long and have three parts geared toward helping members hone their evangelism skills. Every Kingdom Hall studies the same material each week, and all meetings are open to the public.[48]

Evangelism

Evangelism is a key part of a JW's life. All Witnesses are required to do at least 10 hours every month of door-to-door evangelism.[49] Some even evangelize 130 hours or more each month![50] For them, salvation is works based, and evangelism is part of the work they need to complete in order to earn their salvation.

Holidays

Witnesses do not celebrate birthdays, Christmas, Easter, or any other holiday typically listed on a standard calendar. This is primarily because they consider most holidays pagan or a distraction.[51] For example, I once spoke to a JW convert who told me that she left Christianity because she didn't like that so many Christian churches host Easter egg hunts. She thought the emphasis should be solely on Christ's death and resurrection.[52]

The only holiday Witnesses recognize is the Memorial of Christ's Death (which is on Good Friday each year). In 2019, I had the opportunity to attend the service hosted by one of our local Kingdom Halls.[53] The tone at the Memorial was somber. Of course, they were "celebrating" Christ's death, so a subdued atmosphere was probably appropriate,

17C. A Kingdom Hall in Omotepe, Nicaragua. Photo by Milei.vencel. (https://creativecommons.org/licenses/by-sa/3.0).

but at times, the service was downright depressing. For example, the difference between the JW Memorial and a Good Friday service at a Christian church is that they don't really have a "Sunday is coming!" attitude. Instead, it is just a "Christ has died" attitude. Further, communion is offered, but very few people partake.[54] This is because they believe that unless they are part of the little flock, the chosen 144,000, they cannot partake of communion. Instead, they simply pass the plate and cup to the next person. At the service I attended, I didn't see a single person partake in communion.

This is a strikingly different experience than at my church, where we partake in communion weekly, and all who believe are welcome at the Lord's table. Christians throughout the world experience something similar, where even if communion is offered only a few times a year, all believers are welcome to partake. In the end, Witnesses believe those who can partake "includes, not all Christians, but only 'those who have been called' in a special way by God...These ones will rule in heaven with Christ, and the Bible says that just 144,000 people receive that privilege."[55]

The message at the Memorial was not particularly uplifting either. It mirrored the information found in the Watchtower publication *You Can Live Forever in Paradise on Earth*, which is supposed to give hope to those Witnesses who are not part of the little flock.[56] After being told that only 144,000 people will go to heaven to rule with Christ, the congregation at the Memorial was reminded that after the Armageddon, there will be a Paradise Earth, which will mean that all of humanity will live in peace; there will be no more war, no more sickness or old age, or hostility between people and animals. At the Memorial I attended, an image of a child hugging a bear and sharing raspberries with it was described to illustrate what we can look forward to.

Additional JW Practices

- *Blood transfusions and organ transplants.* Witnesses are not allowed to get whole blood transfusions, which are often required during surgery, and most will not receive organ transplants. Bloodless surgery is encouraged.[57]
- *Military service and voting.* Witnesses are dedicated to civic neutrality and avoid any kind of nationalism, including military service, recitation of a national pledge, and voting.[58]
- *Divorce.* Witnesses can get divorced, but only when there is sexual immorality. Even then, though, it is discouraged.[59] Remarriage is typically not allowed except when there is a scriptural divorce or one of the spouses dies.[60]
- *Drugs, alcohol, and dancing.* Witnesses are encouraged to avoid explicit music, suggestive dancing, and intoxication, and to avoid any place that features such behavior, like dance clubs.[61]

Prophecy and the Witnesses

Much can be, and has been, said about the prophecies of the Jehovah's Witnesses, and you need to understand what it is you are getting into when you begin to talk about prophecy with JWs. It is also a topic that Christians like to discuss with each other, so it is important to be well versed in what really happened rather than what some people claim happened. When you speak with

Witnesses about their history, remember that they may not even know the ins and outs of their religion's prophetic history, so be gentle, loving, and respectful.

Most of the prophecies within the JW religion have to do with the Armageddon, and they go all the way back to their founder, Charles Taze Russell. For example, Russell never recanted the Adventist view regarding Christ's return in 1874, and he doubled down on the prediction in his book *The Battle of Armageddon*, where he wrote that Christ returned invisibly:

> By now we are in the end of this Gospel age, and the Kingdom is being established or set up. Our Lord, the appointed King, is now present, since October 1874, AD, according to the testimony of the prophets to those who have ears to hear it: and the formal inauguration of His kingly office dates from April 1878, AD: and the first work of the Kingdom, as shown by our Lord, in His parables and prophecy (the gathering of "His elect"), is now in progress.[62]

In another book, *The Time Is at Hand*, Russell boldly proclaims that "the lease of power to the Gentile kingdoms must terminate with the year 1914."[63] Other publications also predicted the end of the world as 1914, including an 1892 issue of the *Watchtower* magazine, which said, "The date of the close of that 'battle' is definitely marked in Scripture as October, 1914. It is already in progress, its beginning dating from October, 1874."[64] Even when followers of the faith suggested that the prediction may be wrong (thinking it might come sooner rather than later because of the state of the world), the *Watchtower* continued to stand by the prediction, saying,

> We see no reason for changing the figures—nor could we change them if we would. They are, we believe, God's dates, not ours. But bear in mind that the end of 1914 is not the date for the *beginning*, but for the *end* of the time of trouble. We see no reason for changing from our opinion expressed in the view presented in the *Watchtower* on Jan. 15, '92. We advise that it be read again.[65]

As history now shows, 1914 came and went with no apparent Armageddon, though many Witnesses, including Russell, did think that World War I was the end.[66] Despite the failed prophecy, other church leaders continued to make prophetic claims, like Russell's successor, Rutherford, who said Armageddon would come in 1925, evidenced by the end of earthly governments, the resurrection of Old Testament saints like Abraham, and the beginning of God's kingdom on earth.[67]

As 1925 approached, the *Watchtower* magazine seemed to be unsure about Rutherford's prediction, writing that "the year 1925 is a date definitely and clearly marked in the scriptures, even more clearly than that of 1914; but it would be presumptuous on the part of any faithful follower of the Lord to assume just what the Lord is going to do during that year."[68] The year came and went with no evidence of the Armageddon, and the church has been trying to downplay Rutherford's prophecy ever since.[69]

Despite the previously failed prophecies, Knorr also predicted the Armageddon during his tenure as president of the Witnesses. He proclaimed that the end would come in 1975.[70] Knorr's successor, Franz, never suggested a specific date but said that anyone who was living in 1914 would experience the Armageddon.[71] By 1995, most of that generation had passed away, leaving the society no other option but to come up with a believable explanation for all the past prophecies, which were now considered false. Henschel explained that "new light" confirmed that Armageddon could be seen by any generation of "wicked mankind," not just those related to the year 1914.[72]

The term "new light" is used to help explain the changing doctrines and prophecies throughout the Witnesses' history. Using Proverbs 4:18 as their support, the Witnesses believe that

> "the path of the righteous ones" is like a light shining ever more brightly. If at times there is a measure of adjustment, invariably an improved position results. The refinement has not been in vain. With Christ now reigning, the enlightenment enjoyed by Jehovah's people "is as the light of morning, when the sun shines forth."[73]

In other words, doctrine and prophecies may change over time, but only because that is the path of illumination that results in a closer connection with God.

Jehovah's Witnesses and Christianity

Unfortunately, as I've researched the Witnesses in preparation for this chapter, I have discovered material by Christians written in hostile or sarcastic tones against the Witnesses. This is not necessary, and it is my hope that I have avoided such a tone in this chapter. When we are talking *with* Witnesses or *about* them, we should do so in a gentle and respectful way. This goes for anyone from any religion. Being rude is just a way to turn them away from the message you are trying to convey. Rudeness is also not biblical because we are supposed to share our faith with gentleness and respect (1 Peter 3:15). Further, I always aim to be as accurate as possible in my writings, and you should be the same way when you write or speak about another world religion.[74] With that in mind, here are some Christian responses to the key JW beliefs: Jehovah, the Trinity, Jesus, and salvation.

Jehovah

Yes, there are other names we can use for God besides Jehovah, but it is not incorrect to use the name Jehovah, so this could be a place to find common ground. There are more important things you could discuss with them besides their use of the name Jehovah.[75]

The Trinity

One of the main reasons the Witnesses reject the Trinity is because they find Trinitarian theology confusing. The concept may well be confusing, but "confusing" does not automatically mean something is not true. In fact, in their own literature, they say just the opposite. *Reasoning from the Scriptures* says:

> Our minds cannot fully comprehend [Psalm 90:2]. But that is not a sound reason for rejecting it. *Consider examples*: (1) *Time*. No one can point to a certain moment as the beginning of time. And it is a fact that, even though our lives end, time does not. We do not reject the idea of time because there are aspects of it that we do not fully comprehend. Rather, we regulate our lives by it. (2) *Space*. Astronomers find no beginning or end to space. The farther they probe into the universe, the more there is. They do not reject what the evidence shows; many refer to space

> as being infinite. The same principle applies to the existence of God... *Should we really expect to understand everything about a Person who is so great that He could bring into the existence the universe, with all its intricate design and stupendous size?*[76]

I am not a scientist, and honestly, most of what I read about space and time goes right over my head, but just as the JWs note above, I do not disregard the truth of how space and time function, even if I do not understand it. There are certainly things in Christianity that I do not fully understand, but that does not mean it is not true. We have a responsibility to know why we believe what we believe and to be able to defend our beliefs to anyone who asks for the hope within us (1 Peter 3:15). The Trinity is a topic that is very tough to discuss with JWs, and it should probably be brought up only after you have an established and meaningful relationship set in place.[77]

Jesus

Was Jesus really the archangel Michael as the Witnesses contend? Witnesses cite Daniel 10:13 to support their view ("The prince of the kingdom of Persia withstood me twenty-one days, but Michael, one of the chief princes, came to help me, for I was left there with the kings of Persia"). Although Michael is called *one* of the chief princes, he is not *the* chief prince. Jesus is never explicitly mentioned in Daniel 10, and later in Scripture, Jesus is called the "King of kings" (Revelation 19:16). Based on this, it seems that Michael and Jesus are two different people.

Regarding Jesus's death on the cross, there is debate among scholars as to the actual shape of the device Jesus died on, especially since Romans used several different shapes for crucifixion.[78] Although Witnesses like to bring this up in conversations with Christians, it is not a necessary place to dwell. The important point is that Jesus *died*, not the shape of the cross the Romans used.

As far as the resurrection of Christ, Witnesses will use 1 Corinthians 15:44-50 to support their view that Christ returned from the grave spiritually, but not physically (v. 44 says, "It is sown a natural body; it is raised a spiritual body"). However, the word *spiritual* in that text likely means "supernatural" and "spirit-dominated," rather than "nonphysical." Similarly, Paul uses the phrase "spiritual person" in 1 Corinthians 2:15 to refer to an in-the-flesh human infused with God's power, not to a nonphysical, invisible person.[79]

Salvation

Witnesses believe we need to earn our salvation through works, but the Bible does not support this. In fact, the New Testament emphasizes nearly 200 times that our salvation comes by placing our faith in Jesus.[80] Once a person has been saved, good works should necessarily follow as a natural outpouring of our faith, but good works are not required to earn one's salvation (Romans 4:1-25; Matthew 7:15-23; James 2:14-16).

Witnesses at Your Doorstep

One of the most common questions I hear is how to talk with JWs when they arrive at your door. *First, before they even knock, pray and read your Bible.* The Bible tells us to pray without ceasing (1 Thessalonians 5:17), and I truly believe this is a fundamental task we must undertake when engaging with people from other worldviews. Ask God to give you wisdom and guidance in any conversations you might have with people from different religions. Reading and studying Scripture is crucial because if you are not familiar with your Bible, how will you be able to know truth from falsehood?

Second, ask questions. Ask them how they became a Witness and about their life. Take an interest in who they are. As a former pastor of mine recently wrote, "You don't have to be professionally involved in ministry to practice the art of really seeing someone. You can start by asking people to share their stories. Ask simple questions."[81] Find common ground, which could be something as simple as the schools your children attend or your favorite ice cream shop. This is your chance to build a relationship, which is one of the best ways to bring people to Christ.

Third, listen. Once you have asked a question, truly take an interest in what they are saying. Take notes to help you remember what you talked about. My friend Cynthia says that many of the people she knows who have left the Witnesses have become atheists. That should be further motivation for you to work diligently to listen respectfully in order to have meaningful relationships with Witnesses you meet.

Finally, do not wield your knowledge about their beliefs as a weapon. Instead, use what you know to support your well-reasoned discussions, discussions that are based in *love*. Our goal should be to plant seeds, not weeds. We're paving the way for the Holy Spirit to transform their lives. Witnesses are members of humanity, created by God and loved by Him. We must not forget this when we engage with them. The Spirit of truth abides in us (John 14:17). Let our actions and our words exude His truth, His hope, and His love.

Lindsey Medenwaldt (MA, Denver Seminary) holds a Juris Doctor degree as well as a master's in public administration. Her master's at Denver Seminary was in apologetics and ethics. As a Christian apologist, she is the Executive Director of Mama Bear Apologetics and also helps manage Apologetics Awareness.

18

Unitarian Universalism

Alan Gomes

The Unitarian Universalist Association (UUA) is an association of fellowships, congregations, churches, or societies that often vary widely from one another in belief but subscribe to certain broad, liberally understood principles of freedom, tolerance, and religious pluralism. This diverse group maintains an official, organizational connection with the Unitarian Universalist Association, headquartered in Boston, Massachusetts. The association takes its name from the 1961 merger of the Unitarians and the Universalists, historic religious bodies that had been formerly distinct. The Unitarians derived their name from their denial of the Trinity, and the Universalists were so called because they taught that God would ultimately bring about the salvation of all human beings.

Throughout most of their history, the Unitarians and the Universalists considered themselves to be Christians, though certainly not in terms of mainstream, orthodox Christian belief. Today's UUA, however, does not consider itself "Christian" in any official sense, though a small minority of individual Unitarian Universalists (UUs) consider themselves liberal Christians. In contrast to a typical denomination or religious body, the UUA is more of a service organization supporting congregations with a variety of faith positions, including not only a small number of liberal "Christian" congregations but also various flavors of non-Christian theism, atheism, neo-paganism, humanism (both secular and religious), the New Spirituality, and a host of other stances.

In 2019, there were 192,820 UUs in 1,029 congregations worldwide.[1] (This number includes "Religious Education Enrollments" as well as formal members.) However, one important, albeit now dated, study of religious demographics indicated that there were around twice as many who considered themselves to be UUs than appeared in the official UUA-published statistics.[2] This same demographic study placed UUs at the top of the heap, sociologically speaking. For example, at the time of this study, UUs had the highest percentage of college-educated adherents among any religious denomination (with approximately half holding a college degree), and they were close to the top in other important measures, such as median family income and home ownership.

Unlike most other liberal religious groups, the UUA experienced steady growth from 1982 through 2003, turning around over a decade of decline.[3] This appeared to be due, at least in part, to aggressive proselytizing and advertising efforts, activities eschewed in the past. The UUA made particular inroads with the baby boom generation, with many congregations tailoring church services to incorporate upbeat music and more spiritual messages. In some cases, these churches explicitly sought to mimic the approach of some evangelical "seeker sensitive" megachurches, such as Saddleback Community Church in Lake Forest, California, and Willow Creek Community Church in South Barrington, Illinois, replacing the conservative, evangelical theology with their own liberal "good news." From 2003 to 2008, UUA membership remained more or less flat, and has seen a slight but steady decline since 2009.

The History of Unitarian Universalism

The origins of the modern Unitarian Universalist movement are traced, on the Unitarian side, to the anti-Trinitarians of the sixteenth century—that is, during the period of the Protestant Reformation. Unitarian teachings were particularly active in Poland and Transylvania and then spread to England and finally to the United States. The Universalists, who opposed the doctrine of eternal punishment and taught the salvation of all people, gained popularity in eighteenth-century England, and from there spread to the United States. As UU author George N. Marshall notes, around the time of the Revolutionary War, "Unitarianism emerged first and most conspicuously from the Calvinistic First Parishes of the Congregational order, whereas Universalism emerged from the Methodist and Baptist churches."[4]

Unitarianism

Considering the Unitarians first, many see the Spanish physician Michael Servetus (ca. 1511–53) as the founder of their movement. He became notorious for his seven controversial and inflammatory books attacking the doctrine of the Trinity. Servetus

18A. Monument to the Unitarian Michael Servetus in Geneva, France. Photo by Iantomferry (https://creativecommons.org/licenses/by-sa/4.0).

was elevated to martyr status in the eyes of his followers when he was burned alive, together with his writings, on October 27, 1553.

If Servetus was the founder of the Unitarian movement, then Faustus Socinus (1539–1604) was its organizer. An Italian who migrated to Poland, Socinus took the reins of the "Minor Reformed Church," defending their teachings in writing and in oral debate. Besides his denial of the Trinity, Socinus wrote a famous work denying that Christ paid for our sins on the cross in order to satisfy the demands of God's justice.

The Jesuits, through persecution, essentially eradicated the Unitarians from Poland. Some merged with fellow Unitarian bodies in nearby Transylvania and Hungary, while others sought refuge in the Remonstrant (Arminian) and Mennonite congregations in the Netherlands. Significant Unitarian congregations remain in Hungary and Transylvania today.

In England, many regard John Biddle (1615–62) to be the father of English Unitarianism. Because of his anti-Trinitarian writings and teachings, Oliver Cromwell sent him into exile on the Isles of Scilly in southwest England, and eventually he died in prison in 1662. Theophilus Lindsey (1723–1808) was another famous English Unitarian. Lindsey was formerly an Anglican clergyman who left the Church of England over doctrinal differences, including his refusal to give worship to Christ and to the Holy Spirit. Lindsey joined forces with Joseph Priestley (1733–1804), and with Priestley's support, opened the Essex Street Chapel in 1774, which was the first real, overtly Unitarian congregation in England of any significance.[5] Priestley left England for America in 1794 due to persecution for his political views. He was on friendly and familiar terms with Benjamin Franklin, George Washington, Thomas Jefferson, and John Adams. With Franklin's encouragement, Priestley founded a Unitarian church in Northumberland, Pennsylvania, in 1794. Although King's Chapel in Boston had adopted a Unitarian theology nearly ten years earlier, as Earl Morse Wilbur notes, it was Priestley's church that first applied explicitly the title "Unitarian" to itself.[6]

Unitarianism spread its influence primarily within the orbit of the Congregational churches, facilitated in part by the autonomy of the local congregation within the Congregationalist church structure. The influence of Harvard University, which had become liberal by this time, played a significant role in this defection. By the early nineteenth century, the First Parish Church in Plymouth, founded by the Pilgrims, had become Unitarian. In 1819, William Ellery Channing, known as the "apostle of Unitarianism," gave his epochal sermon titled "Unitarian Christianity," which is among the most influential sermons ever given in defense of the Unitarian cause.[7]

Throughout the nineteenth century, the Unitarian movement continued to slide away from its Christian roots. This was seen in the rise of transcendentalism, typified by the famous Unitarian author Ralph Waldo Emerson (1803–82). The transcendentalist movement drew heavily from the Unitarians, many of whom felt that their movement remained too conservative. For the transcendentalists, religious experience and intuition became the touchstones of truth. According to them, God reveals Himself directly to our souls and not through some external "revelation," such as the Bible. In this shift, Emerson was influenced by Hindu and Eastern mystical beliefs.

Emerson's disciple Theodore Parker was even more radical than his teacher. In his famous sermon "The Transient and the Permanent in Christianity," Parker went so far as to proclaim that Christianity would be just as true even if Jesus had not lived, for the truths that Jesus taught transcend Him and do not require Him for their value or validation.

In 1867, the more radical among the Unitarians founded the Free Religious Association (FRA). At the Unitarian's National Conference in 1868, members of the FRA pushed through an amendment to their organization's constitution, allowing for complete freedom of belief, whether or not it included Jesus or the Christian faith. This is significant because earlier the Unitarians had always considered themselves to be, in some sense, "Christian"; now, the Unitarians made even *nominal* Christian allegiance optional.

Universalism

As for the early Universalist movement, one of the first and most influential proponents in the United States was John Murray (1741–1815). In 1779, Murray founded the first Universalist church on American soil, the Independent Christian Church of Gloucester, Massachusetts. An important nineteenth-century Universalist was Hosea Ballou (1771–1852), who served as pastor of the Second Universalist Church in Boston from 1817 until his death. In addition to his denial of the doctrine of eternal, conscious punishment, he also rejected the orthodox teachings on original sin, the Trinity, and Christ's substitutionary atonement.

18B. John Murray, founder of the first Universalist church in the United States. Public domain.

It is important to note that early on, certain doctrinal differences separated the Unitarians from the Universalists. The earliest Universalists were Trinitarians, though eventually they largely abandoned the doctrine. Conversely, some of the earliest Unitarians believed in eternal punishment, but they eventually came to deny it. As each group shifted its theological position in a liberalizing direction, they came to have more in common with one another, ultimately becoming "closely alike in thought."[8] As the famous Universalist Thomas Starr King, who was also pastor of the First Unitarian Church of San Francisco, quipped, "The Universalists believe that God is too good to damn them, and the Unitarians believe they are too good to be damned!"[9] The strong doctrinal affinity between these two groups yielded many instances of fraternal cooperation, even though they remained organizationally separate.

Humanism

Moving into the twentieth century, a new system called "humanism" began to sweep through the Unitarian ranks, creating dissention among the adherents of this new, man-centered teaching and the old-guard Unitarian theists. The main thrust of humanism is that religion must focus on human beings and not on God. Human beings create their own destinies and must solve their own problems rather than look to some kind of divine assistance from beyond themselves. All one's energies should concentrate on the concerns of this present life, not on a future age. Whether or not there is a God is of no particular concern to humanists; human beings must fend for themselves in any case.

The humanist position was codified in the *Humanist Manifesto I* (1933). Half of the *Manifesto*'s signers were Unitarian ministers. Paul Kurtz and Vern Bullough summarize the *Manifesto* as follows:

> The *Manifesto* called for a new statement of the purposes of religion. It held that the universe was self-existing rather than created, and that humans are a part of nature and a product of evolution. It urged the use of science and reason, rather than supernatural beliefs, to explain natural phenomena. It maintained that human values could not be derived from theistic doctrines or expectations of salvation. Values arise from human communities, and the highest value is the complete realization of human personality and the quest for the good life here and now.[10]

Eventually, the humanists and theists managed to coexist within the Unitarian movement.

The Modern Unitarian Universalist Movement

In 1961, the American Unitarian Association (AUA) merged with the Universalist Church of America (UCA), forming today's Unitarian Universalist Association (UUA), with its headquarters in Boston.

Trajectories

The UUA has continued its move to the left, both politically and religiously, especially in the latter part of the twentieth century. The UUA was among the first religious bodies to ordain openly practicing homosexuals beginning in 1970, and in 1984, it became the first group to perform gay "ceremonies of union." Under the influence of radical feminism, they removed "patriarchal" and "sexist" references from their hymnbook, adopted a "right to die" resolution at their 1988 General Assembly, and in 1996, became the first denomination to advocate the legalization of same-sex marriages.

According to a 1987 resolution of the UUA, "Unitarian Universalists believe that the inherent worth and dignity of every person, the right of individual conscience, and respect for human life are inalienable rights due every person." One might figure that the language of inherent worth and dignity suggests an antiabortion stance. However, the resolution continues that it is *because* of each individual's inherent worth and dignity that "Unitarian Universalists actively oppose all legislation, regulation and administrative action, at any level of government, intended to undermine or circumvent the Roe v. Wade decision."[11] The UUA is decidedly proabortion.

Though humanism has had a strong following in the UUA, its influence may be on the decline. As researcher Gustav Niebuhr pointed out, the earlier "cool, cerebral sermons on the greatness of human reason" have in many instances given way to more "spiritual" messages instead.[12] New Spirituality beliefs and neo-paganism are among the more "spiritual" positions to find a home in the UUA.

A Typical UU Church Service

Because of the religious pluralism and diversity within the UUA, not all their church services look the same. The organization's website says, "Our worship styles vary by congregation, and even within congregations. Some congregations' worship is contemporary and high tech. Some congregations' worship is traditional and formal. Some features exuberant music, while some includes long periods of silent reflection." For example, worship may be "led by Jewish, Christian, or Pagan members of the congregation." Sunday morning worship meetings are the norm.[13]

UU worship services commonly include the following:

- the lighting of a flaming chalice (the UU symbol of faith)
- a "multigenerational segment, such as a 'story for all ages'"
- music, which may vary in style
- sharing
- a time of meditation and/or prayer
- inspirational readings
- a sermon
- an offering

18C. The flaming chalice has become the official symbol of the Unitarian Universalist Association. Photo by ErinMRen (https://creativecommons.org/licenses/by-sa/4.0).

Unitarian Universalism and Christianity

Approaching Dialogue Through Appreciating Values

The earliest Christians taught that "there is salvation in no one else," for there is no other name than Jesus "by which we must be saved" (Acts 4:12). Followers of Jesus ought to recognize that other religions cannot present us with the path to salvation. Still, this recognition should not make us hostile in our attitudes toward people of other religions. And when we see something worth appreciating in another religion, we ought to acknowledge it. That being said, something UUs have shown themselves adept at is unity. It is true that values can go too far and trample other important values (e.g., unity at the expense of fidelity to Jesus and His teachings). Nevertheless, unity is a valuable thing and is something UUs have historically exhibited.

For one thing, Unitarianism can be a unifying belief. If Jesus was not actually God, then that means the impeccable morals of this man are in reach of the rest of us humans—without resort to any kind of supernatural infusion of grace through faith. Human potential is therefore exalted as we find ourselves no longer in need of the "one true religion." We can see the unifying nature of Unitarianism when we look back at a Unitarian-type offshoot of Christianity called "Arianism." We have all heard of Constantine, the emperor who made Christianity legal in the Roman Empire. After Constantine, his son Constantius embraced a non-Trinitarian belief about Jesus called "Arianism." According to Arianism, Jesus was not of the same nature as God, but was only of "like nature" with God. Though ultimately unsuccessful, Constantius was insistent on making Arianism the official religion of the empire. And although Arianism was not in favor among the majority of the church's bishops, it played much better with the other religions of the time, being much more syncretistic than orthodox Christianity.[14] The idea of Jesus being something of a lesser god fit much better with the polytheistic Roman Empire than did the doctrine of the full divinity and eternality of Jesus.

For another thing, Universalism is a very unifying belief. The belief that all people, regardless of their faith tradition, will eventually end up saved is an all-embracing view. As UU author Phillip Hewett states, "No one person, no one faith, no one book, no one institution has all the answers, nor even any patent on the way of finding answers."[15] Likewise, Karl Chworowsky and Christopher Raible state, "The following of almost any religion can help a dedicated individual find a better and more meaningful life."[16] In their search for religious meaning, some UUs draw on Christian tradition (understood liberally, of course), while others look elsewhere. Some mix and match different faith positions into a religion that suits them. As they see it, no one religion can have an entire corner on the truth because truth itself is not absolute but relative and changing. As UU John Sais describes, "All people should be tolerant of the religious ideas of others. Truth is not absolute; it changes over time."[17]

With both Unitarians and Universalists making use of unity as a high, even overriding, value, it is appropriate that the two would historically join together in a notable display of religious unity. As they focus on "deeds, not creeds," UUs roll out the welcome mat for people of various religions and no religion at all. Although UU can accommodate differing beliefs, they are united in embracing particular values. Past UUA president William F. Schulz stated, "It is *not* true that one can subscribe to views at variance with our most basic values. Clearly, one could never advocate racism or genocide, for example, and still in any meaningful sense call oneself a Unitarian Universalist."[18] The most basic values of the UUA are expressed in their statement of *Principles and Purposes*, adopted as bylaws at the 1984 and 1985 UUA General Assemblies. These seven *Principles*, which are still adhered to today, are as follows:

- the inherent worth and dignity of every person
- justice, equity, and compassion in human relations
- acceptance of one another and encouragement to spiritual growth in our congregations
- a free and responsible search for truth and meaning
- the right of conscience and the use of the democratic process within our congregations and in society at large
- the goal of world community with peace, liberty, and justice for all
- respect for the interdependent web of all existence, of which we are a part[19]

When it comes to fruitful dialogue between Bible-believing Christians and UUs, it can be difficult to know where to begin in finding doctrinal common ground. Even monotheism is not a "given" for all UUs. It makes dialogue challenging when UUs have historically drifted ever farther from their roots in Christian doctrine. Likewise, much of modern UU seems to be a reaction against what it perceives as dogmatism within Christianity.

Nonetheless, it is possible to approach dialogue by appreciating some of the values that UU teaches and shares with Christianity, such as "the inherent worth and dignity of every person." True, there will tend to be differences in how these values are taught. For example, does "accepting of one another" mean affirming sinful decisions? Does "search for truth and meaning" exclude God's revelation from the discussion? Regardless of the obstacles, it is possible to find common values to fuel fruitful conversation. And with many UUs convinced that the "search for truth and meaning" leads logically *away from* historic Christianity, it will do them well to meet articulate and intelligent Christians who are able to explain and defend what Christianity teaches, always "with gentleness and respect" (1 Peter 3:15).

Divine Revelation and the Bible

From the foregoing, it should be obvious that UUs do not regard the Bible to be the authoritative word of God, as evangelical Christians believe. For UUs, it is typically reason, conscience, and personal experience that serve as the final arbiters of religious truth and value. As a pamphlet published by the UUA puts it, "We believe that personal experience, conscience and reason should be the final authorities in religion. In the end religious authority lies not in a book or person or institution, but in ourselves."[20] Accordingly, UUs generally reject whatever does not conform to reason or personal experience. For example, the doctrines of historic Christian orthodoxy, such as the bodily resurrection, the virgin birth, and the deity of Christ, are all rejected as unreasonable.

Some UUs, though certainly not all, do allow that the Bible contains helpful, inspiring truths. Often the Bible is placed alongside the spiritual literature of other religions. In any event, the Bible is not considered exclusively true, nor is it thought to be without error. It is a human book, subject to the limitations and shortcomings of any other human book. Those who draw inspiration from the Bible tend to interpret it figuratively, not literally. A view most common among UUs who find benefit in the Bible is to interpret it as religious myth.

The Doctrine of God

Because of the pluralism within the UUA, there is not a single doctrine of God. Thus one must speak of the *doctrines* of God found within the UUA.[21]

The following are some representative views of God that one could find in the UUA:

1. God does not exist (i.e., atheism).
2. God is a higher power or a "divine spark" within a person.
3. God-language is used to describe some naturalistic process, such as evolution or an ordering principle in nature. (This is the typical approach taken by religious humanist UUs.)
4. God is a personal being (e.g., held by UU theists). This would include both "Christian" theist UUs as well as UU theists who claim no particular Christian allegiance.
5. Neo-pagan views of God (or the goddess) are embraced by a neo-pagan contingent within the UUA (e.g., the Covenant of Unitarian Universalist Pagans).[22]
6. Pantheism is held by some UUs, particularly among those who embrace the New Spirituality.
7. Process theology—the idea of a finite, mutable God who is growing and

evolving along with his universe—also has UU adherents.

Regardless of what view of God is held (if any), all UUs reject the biblical, orthodox doctrine of the Trinity.

The Doctrine of Christ

As with the doctrine of God, there are a wide range of opinions on the person of Christ within the UUA. The only commonality is that UUs consistently reject the orthodox doctrine of Christ—namely, that He is both fully God and fully man, virgin born, and the unique Son of God, the second Person of the Trinity. They also typically deny that He performed miracles and rose from the dead.

UUs do not believe that Jesus was divine—at least not in any special, unique sense. Chworowsky and Raible ask, "Do Unitarian Universalists think that Jesus Christ was divine?...In a sense they think that every person is divine—that is, that there is goodness and worth in everyone...Unitarian Universalists see no need for the concept of a special divinity in Christ."[23] Others can attain, and have attained, the same spiritual heights that Jesus did.

Some UUs regard Jesus as a great moral teacher who taught important spiritual and ethical truths. However, even here Jesus was not infallible, and His teaching is to be rejected where it contradicts our moral intuitions. Again, Chworowsky and Raible state, "In general, Unitarian Universalists... honor the ethical leadership of Jesus without considering him to be their final religious authority."[24] Some UUs have expressed open hostility toward Jesus and His teaching to varying degrees. For example, UU minister Tony Larsen stated, "If I had been around in Jesus' time...I'm not so sure I would have become a disciple. I think he had some very mistaken ideas about himself and the world."[25] UU humanist Delos B. McKown was even more critical: "The better we get to know the historical Jesus, the less we shall admire him."[26]

As for Christ's miracles and virgin birth, UUs reject these completely. Barbara Marshman tells us these are "embellishments to heighten interest in the life of a good man."[27]

Much could be said in response to the UU views of Jesus, but C.S. Lewis's oft-quoted statement from *Mere Christianity* is certainly appropriate here and has relevance at least for those UUs who wish to regard Jesus as a great moral teacher but nothing more:

> I am trying here to prevent anyone saying the really foolish thing that people often say about Him: "I'm ready to accept Jesus as a great moral teacher, but I don't accept his claim to be God." That is the one thing we must not say. A man who was merely a man and said the sort of things Jesus said would not be a great moral teacher. He would either be a lunatic—on the level with the man who says he is a poached egg—or else he would be the Devil of Hell. You must make your choice. Either this man was, and is, the son of God: or else a madman or something worse. You can shut Him up for a fool, you can spit at Him and kill Him as a demon; or you can fall at His feet and call Him Lord and God. But let us not come with any patronising nonsense about His being a great human teacher. He has not left that open to us. He did not intend to.[28]

Human Beings and Sin

According to the UUA's *Principles*, UUs affirm the dignity and worth of all human beings. At the same time, most UUs believe that human beings are the products of evolution.

UUs focus on human potential and the ability of people to do good, teaching that people are not sinful by nature but are basically good, as UU author John Sias stated, "Rather than feel bound by human weaknesses and frailties, we emphasize human strengths. We believe people have the strength, power and intelligence to make good things happen. You might call [Unitarian Universalism] a 'can do' religion."[29] They completely reject the biblical doctrine of original sin—namely, that due to Adam's sin, people are born guilty for his transgression and possess a bias or propensity toward sin. As UU minister Leonard Mason quipped, "Come return to your place in the pews, and hear our heretical views: You were not born in sin so lift up your chin, you have only your dogmas to lose."[30] Indeed, Sias stated that one "could attend a UU church for years and seldom hear the word sin."[31]

While UUs are correct in asserting that human beings have dignity and worth, this conviction actually cuts against various UU teachings. Darwinian evolution logically devalues human worth because it makes human beings the result of blind chance rather than as beings created in the image of God. The UUA's support of abortion rights also devalues human worth, granting that they are willing to annihilate unborn human persons in the name of "choice." Their denial of hell actually devalues human worth, since punishment acknowledges the dignity of human persons as free moral agents who choose freely to sin despite its just consequences. Furthermore, the biblical doctrine of hell respects a person's own moral choice to live apart from God for all eternity.

As for original sin, this is a fact not only of revelation (e.g., Romans 5:12,16-19) but of universal experience. Though human beings are indeed good "by nature" in the sense that human nature is good, per se, insofar as God is the author of our nature, sin has resulted in a pervasive corruption of it, with a corresponding bias toward evil.

UUs hold a variety of views on salvation, though they all reject salvation from sin in the orthodox, biblical Christian sense. According to George N. Marshall, "Unitarian Universalism is not a salvation religion."[32] According to Sias, "Since we believe in neither original sin nor hell, we do not feel a need to be saved from either."[33] Rather, all people are God's children, quite apart from Jesus "saving" them. As well-known UU minister and bestselling author Robert Fulghum put it, "We're all sons of God."[34]

While UUs generally do not speak about salvation, when they do, they typically mean making this present world a better place through transforming the political structures of oppression, saving the planet ecologically, working to eradicate racism and injustice, and so forth. Charles A. Gaines, director of the UUA Department of Extension, defined UU "salvation" in these terms:

> We need more governors in state houses, more legislators in Washington, and more judges on the benches who represent the ideals and principles of Unitarian Universalism. We need more people thinking about saving our environment, guaranteeing individual free choice, promoting justice and compassion...All this is what might be meant by the word "salvation."[35]

In terms of Jesus, some speak of Him as

a "savior" in a loose sense (e.g., as an enlightened spiritual leader who sought to help his fellow man and woman). They reject, however, any notion of Jesus as savior in an exclusivist sense, claiming that it is arrogant and narrow-minded to limit salvation only to Jesus. Tony Larsen, in answering "narrow-minded Christians," countered that "the world has many saviors [besides Jesus] and I revere all who have tried to help their fellow man and woman."[36] Obviously, the UU conception of salvation—or more accurately, its denial—is contrary to the biblical view. Regarding the charge that Christians are narrow-minded or arrogant for declaring Christ to be the only way of salvation, UUs misunderstand what motivates Christians to say this. Jesus Christ Himself taught that He was the only way to salvation (John 10:1,7; 14:6), as did His apostles (e.g., Acts 4:12). Thus when Christians say the same thing, they are "guilty" merely of believing that Jesus and His apostles were trustworthy witnesses. Christians are not being arrogant but are merely being faithful to what they believe Christ revealed. If, hypothetically speaking, the claims of Christ and His apostles should turn out to be incorrect, then the Christian would have been duped into believing a lie but not guilty of arrogance.

Heaven, Hell, and the Afterlife

Historically, the Unitarians and the Universalists believed in an afterlife. Indeed, the main issue animating the Universalists was their affirmation that God would ultimately bring everyone to salvation. However, most modern UUs do not believe in an afterlife, which includes a literal heaven or hell.

Whatever their view of the afterlife, UUs deny the bodily resurrection as unscientific and unreasonable. Jay Johnson and Marsha McGee stated, "Because bodily decay occurs rapidly following death, from the scientific point of view, bodily resurrection is not possible. The spirit may continue somehow or in some form."[37] Furthermore, all UUs deny that a loving God would send anyone to hell. As Larsen put it, "When it comes to a god who would condemn souls to hell, I'm an atheist. I can't believe in that kind of deity."[38]

The focus for almost all UUs, then, is entirely on this present life. People must work to make this present world a better place, as noted above in the UU doctrine of salvation. Although there is no future judgment in the biblical sense of hell, UUs often believe in "compensation"—namely, that people are compensated for their deeds in this present life. As Johnson and McGee stated, "No one 'goes' to hell; people create their own hells here on earth…As with the good, what evil people do is compensated for in this life. 'Compensation' is the U.U. position."[39]

In contrast, Christians accept the truth of the afterlife, including both heaven and hell, because the afterlife is clearly taught in Scripture, most particularly by Jesus Christ. As for the bodily resurrection, Christ not only taught this doctrine; He Himself rose just as He said He would. As for a belief in the afterlife blunting motivation for doing good in the present life, such a notion is contrary to the express commands of the Bible, which enjoins us to do good to all people (Galatians 6:10). It is precisely *because* God has given us eternal life that we are able to show our thankfulness to Him by doing good to others. Certainly Christians have historically understood this, as even a cursory glance at Christian philanthropy thorough the ages readily attests.[40] Finally, contrary to the UU position, compensation does not always take place in this present life. To cite but one example, Adolf Hitler never received adequate compensation in this life for murdering six million innocent Jews. However, as Christians, we know that he has received his due in the life to come (Colossians 3:25; Revelation 20:12).

Alan Gomes (PhD, Fuller Theological Seminary) is professor of historical and systematic theology at Biola University. He has edited, contributed to, and authored numerous books, including *40 Questions About Heaven and Hell* and *Unitarian Universalism*. He has published articles in a variety of journals, including *Harvard Theological Review*, *Reformation and Renaissance Review*, and *Westminster Theological Journal*. He has also spoken at churches throughout Southern California and has been a featured guest on radio shows across the United States.

Part 5

RELIGIOUS MOODS

19

Religious Pluralism

Paul Copan and Benjamin B. DeVan

How do Evangelical Christians approach religious diversity—also known as "descriptive pluralism"—as we love God and God's world together? Jesus taught us His greatest commandment: "Love the Lord your God with all your heart and with all your soul and with all your mind and with all your strength. The second is this: 'You shall love your neighbor as yourself.'"[1] Jesus extended His Great Commission in the same spirit: "Go therefore and make disciples of all nations, baptizing them in the name of the Father and of the Son and of the Holy Spirit, teaching them to observe all that I have commanded you. And behold, I am with you always, to the end of the age."[2]

At least three intersecting issues are relevant for Jesus's followers who labor to fulfill His great commandment and Great Commission in religiously diverse contexts. The first pertains to personal, social, national, and global relationships with our neighbors who identify as Buddhist, Hindu, Jewish, Muslim, Sikh, and so forth. How do we proceed in light of "descriptive" pluralism—the *fact* or *reality* of pluralism, which involves religiously diverse people living and working together?

A second concern is truth. Are Evangelicals who love God and their neighbors required to affirm that all, some, one, or no "religions" are true or teach significant truths? "Prescriptive" pluralism claims that all religions are *equally* true.

A third question is whether all, some, one, or no religions facilitate "salvation," enabling their practitioners to experience everlasting joy. Do various world religions play a role in preparing or disqualifying people for eternal bliss? If the Happy Hunting Ground, Islamic Paradise, the New Heaven, Nirvana, the Pure Land, Utopia, or some variant of these exists (or will exist), will proportionally few, many, or every person participate?

These categories may not correspond as some would initially expect. For example, we need not celebrate every opinion about God as equally valid to live peaceably with people who disagree. Declaring that Mahayana Buddhism is true or that Vaishnavite Hinduism leads to salvation is not a precondition for fostering productive relationships with people in those faiths.

Whether all or some or one or no religion teaches truth is also partially distinct from who receives salvation and why. For example, Evangelicals might appreciate Buddhist or Hindu insights into psychology and spiritual discipline but proclaim that no one can be saved until she verbally confesses and believes in her heart that Jesus is Lord.[3]

We discern parallel sentiments among exemplars from other world religions. For example, Muslims announce that Islam is the truest faith yet anticipate that Allah will reward righteous Jews and Christians with paradise even while barring some Muslims from entering.[4] Gandhi (AD 1869–1948) upheld Hinduism and the Dalai Lama Tibetan Buddhism as the *best* account of ultimate reality or the most *efficient* path to nirvana, but they could also presume that Jews, Christians, and Muslims would eventually achieve enlightenment, even if it takes more lifetimes to do so.[5]

Keeping this in mind, we will set forth principles for engaging with descriptive pluralism—the face of religious diversity—before transitioning to prescriptive pluralism relating to truth and salvation. First, however, we will provide a picture of pluralism in the form of an interview with Diana L. Eck, the founder and director of the Pluralism Project at Harvard University.

Snapshot of Religious Pluralism: Interview with Diana L. Eck[6]

Q1: How do you define (or we might ask, how does the Pluralism Project at Harvard University define) religious pluralism?

Eck: Religious pluralism is, to begin with, recognizing the reality of religious difference and engaging one's own religious community, or one's own religious self, with the religious other. It doesn't mean finding a lowest common denominator. It doesn't mean blanket tolerance. It does mean engagement across lines of difference. And since that's part of the reality of the society that we live in today, religious pluralism is critical for our common life.

I might go on to say that there are two ways in which one engages religious pluralism. One is as a citizen. As a citizen of a multireligious democracy like the United States, we engage religious pluralism along the lines of our Constitution that guarantees the free exercise of religion and the nonestablishment of one religion as a religion of the state. So in other words, religious pluralism is about recognizing that our lives as co-citizens in the United States depend on our ability to engage with one another toward the creation of a common society.

Religious pluralism is also an issue for people of particular religious traditions, whether Christian or Muslim or Jewish or Hindu. This raises the question of how we think about the religious other, not simply along the lines of our civic relationships but in relation to our own religious community. In that case, we're referring not simply to the Constitution but to our own scriptures and the many ways in which they are interpreted. We think about our neighbors of other faiths from the religious resources of our own faith. And that can be very different. Within the Christian tradition, people engage many scriptural sources and roots to think about who their neighbors of other faiths are and how they think about their relationship to them.

Q2: How might someone who is committed to religious pluralism perceive or take into account people who identify as agnostic, atheist, nonreligious, irreligious, or secular?

Eck: Our ways of engaging the world, and our lives, and the reality of our creation are many. They are not simply different religious traditions but also people who are questioning, who are agnostic, who are not theists, and who think of themselves as nonreligious or secular. Our society depends on all of us. There are many people who are atheists, for example, who want to be in relationship with—who are always in relationship, really—with theists of various sorts. There is even the gentlemen who wrote the book called *Faitheist* who insisted on a place at the interreligious table for those who are atheists, partly because their lives as citizens in a common society depend on being engaged with everyone, as do ours as religious people.[7]

So, of course, agnostics, atheists, and secular people have a seat at the "table," wherever that table is in our society. We can't eliminate their views or their positions simply because they're different from our own. After all, religious pluralism begins not with our commonalities, but it begins with the fact of our difference.

Q3: What do you see as humanity's biggest problems and greatest assets from a religious pluralist perspective?

Eck: The biggest problem is lack of connection. Connection is one of the things that we depend on in order to inhabit a common world. We need connection with one another that is as firm and as dialogical as the connection that banks make around the world or the connection that people make in the many ways that globalization is the engine of our world economy. One of our biggest problems is the lack of connection and the misunderstanding of one another within societies and across the world because we don't have relationships. That really is one of the most important assets of religious pluralism: that we build relationships. It's not really about coming to a common ideology but about finding in our lives and in the lives of our communities the resources for positive and sometimes critical but important relationships.

Q4: What resources does a commitment to religious pluralism offer to address these problems and to help people live more fulfilling lives?

Eck: One of the things that we find as we recognize religious others—as we come into dialogue with them or as we work with them on the issues of our society, whether that's the infrastructure of our cities, whether it's Habitat for Humanity, whether it's building coalitions to address education and the future that we hope to offer young people—is that as we come into these relationships and work with one another, we also discover a great deal about the energies of faith that each community has. These discoveries may actually begin to alter our own understanding. We are, after all, complex human beings, and we discover things that are beautiful and inspiring in the religious lives of others: of people who have not grown up in our community, of people who have different resources for their social lives.

Q5: Does religious pluralism have anything to say or contribute to philosophical or theological questions about what is objectively true?

Eck: Well, yes, it certainly does! Because truth is really an aspiration; it's not a possession. It's not a possession of any one religious community, to be sure.

As we think of ourselves as pilgrims along the path of our lives and of our communities, as we raise children, as we grow, as we grow old and face illness and death, this is a way in which we discover the truths of our own tradition. But this is also a way in which we might discover things that are true and inspiring in the journeys and traditions of our neighbors.

So the first thing I would say is what is objectively true theologically is something that we human beings really don't have access to. We all are sort of looking through the lens of our own religious commitments. And the things that we see can come into clear focus or sometimes fall out of focus as we live our lives, as we encounter new forms of being. This includes everything from technology and science to the things that we discover when we encounter people who are inspiring but who are inspiring from another religious standpoint.

Q6: What do you think will happen when we die?

Eck: We'll find out. This is a question that people in every religious community raise. So far, no one has conclusive proof about this. And frankly, our religious traditions are mostly about what happens as we live. What happens right here. What happens in the world that we know and in which we live, day by day.

Q7: What do you think of Jesus?

Eck: As a Christian, I think Jesus had two major plumb lines of his own teaching and message. One of them was love and the kind of relationship that love creates among human beings. The other was justice—the form of economic and political community that yields a sense of flourishing, of justice in life for everyone. Those are the things that Jesus spoke most about, love and justice. This was not anything that was exclusive to his own followers. When he talks about the end times of separating the sheep from the goats etc. in Matthew 25, it's not really about who is saved according to some sort of ideological confession of faith. It really is about, Whom have you served and how? Whom did you visit in prison? Whom did you feed who was hungry? Whom were you kind to? And those are the things that finally matter in the issue of our salvation.

Descriptive Pluralism: Pursuing Fruitful Relationships with Religiously Diverse People

How do Christians cultivate meaningful relationships with religiously diverse people? We suggest seven principles, reinforcing them with matching sympathies from other world religions.

Human Dignity

A biblical approach to relationships begins with distinguishing every person as God's immeasurably valuable image bearer who possesses inherent dignity. In Genesis 1, God pronounces animals and plants "good" (*tob*). After creating humans in God's image, God calls creation good "exceedingly" (*meod*).[8] Irenaeus (ca. 130–ca. 202) consequently exulted, "The glory of God is humanity fully alive and the life of humanity is the vision of God."[9] Jewish readers of Genesis concur. In the words of Rabbi Lord Jonathan Sacks, the challenge is "to see God's image in one who is not in our [religious] image."[10]

Noteworthy Muslims agree, perhaps due to biblical influences on them and despite traditional Muslim objections to the idea of divine imagery. The "Great Shaykh" Ibn 'Arabi (1165–1240) hailed humanity as created with God's form and attributes.[11] Al-Ghazali (1058–1111) analogized that whenever humans distort their God-intended goodness, the effect was like grime on a mirror.[12] Riffat Hassan referred twenty-first-century Evangelicals to the Qur'an, Surah 95:4-6, which states that God made humanity in the best of molds, even though humans intermittently act like the "lowest of the low."[13]

Universal Rights

Second, universal dignity implies universal rights. The United Nations Universal Declaration on Human Rights (1948), drafted in part by Lebanese Christian Charles Malik (1906–1987), was ratified by numerous countries representing religiously diverse populations.[14]

At the same time, Princeton's Max Stackhouse (1935–2016) noted that the UN declaration emerged "out of key strands of the biblically-rooted religion."[15] Harvard Law School's Mary Ann Glendon cites the declaration's chief initiators as Christian leaders, church coalitions, and Jewish rabbis.[16] Articles 2, 16, and 18 address religion, uniting freedom of worship, thought, practice, opinion, observance, expression, and conscience "without distinction of any kind."[17]

It is shameful that, when church and state became closely intertwined, Christians were not always champions of the rights of followers of other religions. The reformer Martin Luther (1483–1546), for example, penned an inflammatory pamphlet that advocated, among other things, setting "fire to [Jewish] synagogues or schools" and razing and destroying their houses.[18] Yet albeit hypocritically, Luther was also aware that persecution of religious dissenters was unfortunate and that religious liberty was preferable: "I am really distressed that these poor people should be so pitifully murdered, burned, and horribly put to death. Everyone should be allowed to believe what he likes. If he is wrong, he will be punished enough in hell fire."[19] While many readers will chafe at applying hellfire (which Luther interpreted as metaphorical) simply for holding mistaken beliefs, Luther's corollary is to refrain from persecuting anyone *before they die*.[20]

One of Luther's contemporaries, the Anabaptist Balthasar Hubmaier (1480–1528), wrote with a like-minded disposition. Hubmaier saw the inquisitors of his day as "the biggest heretics of all since against the teaching and example of Christ they have condemned heretics to the flames, and before the time of harvest root up the wheat together with the tares."[21]

Hubmaier alluded to Matthew 13:24-30, where tares or weeds (the wicked) can mimic or intertwine with similar-looking wheat (the righteous). God appoints final judgment as a time for harvest when God, rather than any earthly power, will disentangle weeds with minimal harm to the wheat. American Baptist John Leland (1754–1841) inferred, "Let every man speak freely without fear—maintain the principles he believes—worship according to his own faith, either one God, three Gods, no God, or twenty Gods; and let government protect him in so doing."[22]

The founder of Methodism, John Wesley (1703–1791), bequeathed further precedents for religious liberty. Wesley, who also partly inspired global Pentecostalism, commended North America, for he observed, "Total indifference to the government there whether there be any religion or none leaves room for the propagation of true scriptural religion without the least let or hindrance."[23]

According to Wesley, Christians must extend even to bigots the same rights Christians desire for themselves. "At least allow *them* the liberty which they ought to allow *you*."[24]

The Qur'an appears to contain a number of verses that endorse such liberty:

> There is no compulsion in religion: true guidance has become distinct from error, so whoever rejects false gods and believes in God has grasped the firmest hand-hold, one that will never break.

> Turn away from those who join other gods with Him. If it had been God's will they would not have done so, but We have not made you their guardian, nor are you their keeper.
>
> Had your Lord willed, all...would have believed. So can you [Prophet] compel people to believe?
>
> But if they turn away [Prophet], your only duty is to deliver the message clearly...Say, "Now the truth has come...let those who wish to believe in it do so."
>
> Say [Prophet], "Disbelievers: I do not worship what you worship, you do not worship what I worship, I will never worship what you worship, you will never worship what I worship: you have your religion and I have mine."[25]

Contemporary literature documents a resurgence of threats to freedom of conscience, expression, and religion due to blasphemy laws, "honor" killings, "hate speech," and the indicting or degrading of dissidents throughout the world.[26] Some practices and policies violate not only freedom of religious conviction or affiliation but freedom *within* a religious identity or for some religions to be recognized as approved religions. For example, Indonesia has at times restricted what constitutes "true" belief in state-sanctioned religions and inflicted punishment for dissent.[27]

Open Marketplace of Ideas

Religious liberty guarding free exercise of religion and lack of government establishment thereof leads to a third principle for interactions between religiously diverse people: a free and open marketplace of ideas. Participating in the marketplace of ideas dictates the initiative to represent one's convictions, defend them, and recruit others to participate. The apathetic or the isolationist may abstain, but Jesus directed His followers to preach the gospel to all nations.

Seeking to fulfill Jesus's commission, the Apostle Paul in Acts 17 spoke in synagogues and marketplaces, where he was vulnerable to misinterpretation and scorn. These risks apply to anyone in the public square.[28] Christians can look to Paul's example in not trying to coerce his audience to believe, or they can resort not to mean-spirited misrepresentation, intimidation, bribery, or second-order benefits but rather to trusting the gospel to "carry its own weight" in deliberation.[29]

Puritan poet John Milton (1608–1674) reiterated in his classic tract named after Paul's Areopagus in Acts 17,

> Give me the liberty to know, to utter, and to argue freely according to conscience...Though all the winds of doctrine were let loose to play upon the earth, so Truth be in the field, we do injuriously, by licensing and prohibiting, to misdoubt her strength. Let her and Falsehood grapple; who ever knew Truth put to the worse, in a free and open encounter?[30]

William J. Abraham utilizes philosophical vocabulary to advocate for this type of exchange: "The best way forward in adjudicating claims is to allow particular, positive claims and their particular appropriate defeaters to proceed without prejudice or restriction."[31]

Multireligious precedents from Asia are sympathetic in principle if not always in practice. In AD 1856, the Ottoman Empire's Tanzimat and Hatt-i-Humayaun reforms ruled that Muslim and non-Muslim subjects deserve to be treated as "equals, with equal rights and responsibilities in the Ottoman State," including "freedom to build places of worship."[32] Sudipta Kaviraj praises postcolonial India (prior to the rise of recent Hindu-nationalist governments) for permitting cultural and religious multiplicity.[33] Twentieth-century Indonesian Pancasila politically constitutionalized humanitarianism, democratic consensus, and social justice for all.[34]

Shaming, stifling, or criminalizing free expression compels believers to choose between political or social conformity and bearing witness to what is often most significant to them.[35] The resulting inquisitions, gulags, religiously based subjugation, discrimination, prosecution, and—to a lesser degree—cultural relativism that forbids believers to cross-examine or critique those from other backgrounds are "ways that lead to death" that are hardly preferable.[36]

Mutual Enrichment Through Critique

A dynamic marketplace of ideas facilitates a fourth principle: mutual enrichment through critique. According to Owen C. Thomas, when the church throughout history faced attacks from other religions, philosophies, and worldviews such as Judaism, Middle Platonism, Gnosticism, Roman paganism, Islam, Deism, skepticism, rationalism, naturalism, and positivism, Christians frequently inquired whether there was any truth to their critics' salvos.[37] John Wesley counseled conversing in the following manner:

> My mind is open to conviction. I sincerely desire to be better informed... Are you persuaded you see more clearly than me?...Point out to me a better way than I have known...If I linger in the path I have been accustomed to tread, and am therefore unwilling to leave, labour with me a little...But be not displeased if I entreat you not to beat me down in order to quicken my pace...May I not request of you, farther, not to give me hard names in order to bring me into the right way? Suppose I was ever so much in the wrong. I doubt this would not set me right. Rather it would make me run so much the farther from you—and so get more and more out of the way. Nay, perhaps, if you are angry so shall I be too, and then there will be small hopes of finding the truth.[38]

Precedents from other world religions convey a kindred posture of receptiveness. The Hindu Rig Veda encourages learning from noble thoughts or auspicious powers from any and every direction.[39] A Confucian aphorism teaches that where three or more walk together, one follows whatever is excellent among them.[40] The Qur'an, Surah 5:82, includes this assessment of certain Christians whose attitudes—though not necessarily their decisions—are sensible to emulate: "Closest in affection to the believers are those who say, 'We are Christians,' for there are among them people devoted to learning and ascetics...not given to arrogance."

Common Priorities

A fifth principle concerns collaborating around common priorities. Diverse religious believers can cooperate in some matters without denying disagreements in others. The Catholic Pontifical Council for Interreligious Dialogue christens this "Dialogue of Action."[41]

Causes on the "left" and "right" supply opportunities for justice, peacemaking, care for the creation, and more. John Wesley paraphrased 2 Kings 10:15: "If your heart is as my heart, then take my hand." And "Though we can't think alike, may we not love alike?" And again, "So far as in conscience thou canst... join me in the work of God, and let us go on hand in hand."[42]

Evangelist Billy Graham (1918–2018) references the biblical Daniel's example of working with pagan Babylon officials.[43] Pentecostal Amos Yong esteems Mahayana Buddhism's ideals of compassion for those who suffer.[44] Nobel laureate Leymah Gbowee records Christian and Muslim women praying and protesting together nonviolently against ruling warlords in Liberia.[45]

Muslims might contemplate fulfilling charity or Zakat—Islam's fourth pillar—by pooling resources and practicing a friendly competition in "good works" with Jews and Christians whom Surah 3:114 presents as hastening "to do good deeds as if competing with one another." Surah 2:177 exhorts, "The truly good are those who believe in God and the Last Day, in the angels, the Scripture, and the prophets; who give away some of their wealth, however much they cherish it, to their relatives, to orphans, the needy, travelers and beggars, and to liberate those in bondage...who keep pledges...who are steadfast in misfortune, adversity, and times of danger."

Diana Eck in her interview for this chapter alludes to Jesus's words in Matthew 25, which correspond to a Jewish Midrash on Psalm 118.[46] *Sahih Muslim* 32:6232 rephrases Jesus like this:

> Allah will say on the Day of Judgment, "O son of Adam, I was sick and you did not visit me." He will say, "O my Lord, how could I visit you, when you are the Lord of the worlds?" Allah will say, "Did you not know that My servant so-and-so was sick and you did not visit him? Did you not know that if you had visited him, you would have found Me there?" Allah will say, "O son of Adam, I asked you for food and you fed Me not." He shall say, "O my Lord, how could I feed you...?" And Allah will say, "Did you not know that My servant so-and-so was in need of food and you did not feed him...?" "O son of Adam, I asked you for water and you did not give Me to drink." The man shall say, "O my Lord, how could I give You water...?" Allah will say, "My servant so-and-so asked you for water and you did not give him to drink water. Did you not know that if you had given him to drink, you would have found that to have been for Me?"[47]

Across the Red Sea in Africa, Joe Gorman, executive director of Compassion for Africa, champions serving "the poor of other religions," where churches supply bedding, furniture, and food.[48] Pastor Frank Mills in Ghana leverages Jesus's imagery of "living water" to share his church well water with African animists and Muslims: "As God's grace is free to all, so is [our] access to clean water."[49]

We pray that religiously diverse people in the future will express gratitude to Christians as the pagan Roman emperor Julian, the Apostate (331–361), inadvertently heralded Christians of his era: "The...Galileans support not only their poor but ours as well."[50]

Motivations for solidarity will vary. Catholic professor Terrence W. Tilley explains, "We can talk about what is true, beautiful, good, and just across traditions even if we might dispute just what better or best satisfies these criteria."[51] Yet even if motives conceal selfish ambition, insincerity, or jealousy, Christians can celebrate any and all cooperative "moves against destructiveness."[52]

Discernment

A sixth principle for relationships in religiously diverse contexts is the importance of praying for discernment in how to respond to circumstances where collaboration is impracticable and conflict seems inevitable. The great cloud of witnesses in Hebrews 11 showcases saints who stood with integrity against all sorts of adversity.

The Reverend Dr. Martin Luther King Jr. (1929–1968) demonstrated a kind of principled antagonism toward those who advised waiting and being patient in hopes that civil rights would come to pass on their own. King responded, "The time is always ripe to do right."[53] Further, "Justice too long delayed is justice denied."[54] Finally, "When evil men plot, good men must plan. When evil men burn and bomb, good men must build and bind. When evil men shout ugly words of hatred, good men must commit themselves to the glories of love."[55]

Nonnegotiable flashpoints between people of different persuasions will continue to be a reality. Deciding whom to defend, what to oppose, and which methods to use are matters to debate. Still, a common commitment to universal dignity, rights, cooperation where feasible, and an open marketplace of ideas will decrease less charitable forms of interaction.

Christians who confront injustices and other ills should advance as Martin Luther King Jr. did—by endeavoring not to humiliate their opponents but to win their friendship, understanding, and acknowledgment of what is right.[56] Pope Pius II (1405–1464) wrote to Ottoman sultan Mehmet II (1432–1481) amid interreligious conflict in AD 1461, "We are hostile to your actions. Not to you. As God commands, we love our enemies and pray for our persecutors."[57]

Muslims from the opposing side could consider Surah 41:34: "Repel evil with what is better and your enemy will become as close as an old and valued friend."

Love

The previous six injunctions lead to a seventh principle mentioned by Jesus at the beginning of this chapter: "Love your neighbor as yourself." The Apostle Paul famously elaborated on love in Romans 12:14-15 and 1 Corinthians 13. Perhaps one reason God permits religious diversity is to give us opportunities to love people with whom we deeply disagree.

Christians pay lip service to love as the greatest commandment, but do we apply it across religious boundaries? One apparently well-meaning theologian urges Evangelicals to hate people whom he accuses of hating God![58] Some furious Muslims brandish Surah 5:51 and 48:29 from the Qur'an: "Do not take the Jews and Christians as allies: they are allies only to each other" and "Muhammad is the Messenger of God. Those who follow him are harsh towards the disbelievers and compassionate towards each other."

Old Testament characters provide three poignant previews of Jesus's love for his adversaries. Behold the examples of King David with Saul, the Prophet Elisha and an anonymous Israelite slave girl toward the enemy military general Naaman the Syrian, and Elisha's hospitality for an army of invading Arameans.[59]

We can also discover exemplars among the world's religions. Martin Luther King Jr. praised the Hindu Gandhi for applying Jesus's ethics on a national scale,[60] even if Gandhi did not always apply those ethics consistently.[61] John Wesley wrote that some of his Jewish parishioners seemed to be "nearer the mind that was in Christ than many of those who call him Lord."[62] Surah 60:7

impels, "God may still bring about affection between you and your present enemies."

Jewish convert to Christianity Joel Rosenberg recounts his reconciliation with former Muslim Fatah fighter Tass Saada. Both had reoriented their lives around Jesus and were deeply moved when they met to organize humanitarian initiatives in Gaza and the West Bank: "Here we were, a former aide to PLO Chairman Yasser Arafat and a former aide to Prime Minister Netanyahu, hugging each other—not trying to kill each other—in the heart of Jerusalem. All because of the work Jesus had done to give us hearts of love rather than hatred."[63]

Carl Medearis, an expert on Muslim-Christian relations, narrates one exchange in the Lebanese parliament where religiously diverse members pondered how Christians, Druze, and Muslims could pray and study the life of someone they admired together. One parliamentarian pounded the table and yelled, "I've got it. It's Jesus! Muslims like Jesus. Druze like Jesus. Even Christians like Jesus...We would all love to meet and discuss Jesus." So they read through the Gospel of Luke.[64]

Although not always recognized as such, Jesus's parable of the good Samaritan in Luke 10:25-37 is a model of love between religious rivals, since Jews and Samaritans in the ancient Near East harbored historic ethnic and religious contempt for each other.[65] We might speculate whom Jesus would specify as players in His parable if He were telling it to us. Would He cast a Christian pastor and politician passing by the wounded victim and a Muslim imam taking pity?

Martin Luther King Jr. preached an imperative that is as pertinent to future religiously diverse relationships as it was to King's original audience: "We must all learn to live together as brothers or we will all perish together as fools."[66] If such perishing transpires, it will be despite rather than because of these seven principles for engaging descriptive pluralism.

Prescriptive Pluralism and Truth

Pursuing fruitful relationships with religiously diverse people should not require anyone to profess that every religion is equally true. Each of the following prescriptive pluralisms is driven by the "normative" or "absolute" assertion that all religions are roughly on a par with regard to truth.[67] We critique a variety of prescriptive pluralisms and their alternatives. Prescriptive "cafeteria" pluralism supposes that the best way to discern truth is by mixing and matching ideas from multiple religions. This begs questions about how to determine what is true. "Core," "essence," or "fundamental teachings" pluralism presents essential teachings of all or at least the "major" religions as equally true, however "true" and "major" are defined. "Epistemic" pluralism claims that all religions equally *have* or *lack* access to the truth due to their conceptual limitations and worldviews. "Ethical" pluralism casts all religions as equally valid or divine ethical systems. "Transcendental" pluralism teaches that all religions mediate contact with the same ultimate reality while employing different vocabularies for that reality. "Extreme" or "naive" pluralism supposes that every religious belief is somehow equally true.

Probably the most popular tale epitomizing prescriptive pluralism is the parable of the blind men and the elephant.[68] In this fable, a king brings seven blind men to an elephant. They each touch a part of the pachyderm. The king then asks them to describe what the elephant is like:

"A thin vine, rope, snake, or brush," says the first, tugging the elephant's tail.

"No! The elephant is like a tube with two holes," retorts a second, squeezing the trunk.

A third clasped the elephant's leg: "It's like a tree!"

A fourth tickled the elephant's ear. "No, a fan!"

A fifth man pressed against the elephant's side: "I feel a rough wall."

A sixth grasping the tusk interjected: "An elephant is like a spear or a plowshare."

Shouted a seventh who perched atop the elephant's back: "You are all mistaken! An elephant obviously resembles a moving mountain!"

The king smiles as he concludes the tale. Each blind man has communicated part of the truth but is equally wrong about the greater reality. The moral? God—or whatever you want to call the transcendent—is too big for the partly perceptive explanations of any one religion![69]

There is a little wisdom to this adage in that no Christian should pretend to comprehend God comprehensively.[70] All creatures great and small look at reality incompletely and imperfectly, like gazing at a dark glass or a dim reflection in a mirror.[71]

Otherwise, the oft-cited parable of the blind men and the elephant faces some hairy problems, metaphysically speaking. Prescriptive pluralists represented by the king contend that all the religions (blind men) aspire to tell the whole truth but can do so only in part while the pluralist somehow sees the big picture. It is unclear how, why, or on what basis pluralists obtain this vantage. How do *they* know the elephant (God) exists at all or whether each blind man encounters the same animal? Persistent disagreement does not mean that every viewpoint is equally murky.

We submit that the best way to adjudicate disputes about the "elephant" would be for the elephant to appear authentically on her own behalf. The Bible teaches that Jesus did this when He became a human who testified, "Whoever has seen me has seen the Father."[72]

To insist that no religion is truer than any others is to plunge oneself into a rabbit hole leading to subjectivism, relativism, and incoherence. For subjectivists, any perspective can be right for the person believing it.[73] Relativists suggest the same for communities instead of individuals.[74]

Concerning incoherence, both subjectivism and relativism are self-undermining and self-contradictory. If a subjectivist portrays all truth claims as subjective except for subjectivism, he commits a "self-excepting" fallacy. The relativist does so as well if she says that it is universally true that there are no universal truths, or that universal objective truth does not exist (alethic skepticism), or that it cannot be known (epistemological skepticism). If everything is a matter of opinion, then so are relativism and subjectivism. Why should anyone believe either of them?

Furthermore, just because no one other than God is infallible or enjoys omniscience does not mean that we cannot know whether anything is true at all, even if our knowledge about truth is limited. We are born into cultural-historical milieus where we can think about, embrace, or disavow our assumptions in favor of competing options. We are influenced by our cultures and perceptions, but we can reflect, rise above, and even resist them.

"Logical religious exclusivism"—the belief that particular religious beliefs are true to the exclusion of others—is unavoidable as a conceptual alternative to prescriptive pluralism. Holding any position to be true necessarily excludes incompatible positions, whether or not they are rendered metaphorically. For even metaphorical truth claims that make sense will correspond at some level to the literal truths that they illuminate.

I (Ben) recall hearing at Berry College the philosopher Norman L. Geisler (1932–2019) revisit his debate with a secular humanist who commenced their dialogue in this way: "These Christians are so narrow minded! They think they are right and anyone who disagrees with them is wrong!" Geisler's reply? "These secular humanists are so narrow minded! They think that they are right and anyone who disagrees with them is wrong!"

Prescriptive pluralists, subjectivists, and relativists treat religions as though they were merely metaphors or matters of taste whose disparities can be reduced to personal preferences. They hypothesize that just as certain people like chocolate versus vanilla, basketball over baseball, or winter more than summer, so do Buddhists practice Buddhism rather than Hinduism and Hindus Hinduism instead of Buddhism due to their aesthetic or psychological preferences.

We (Paul and Ben) believe that the gospel is uplifting, fulfilling, and beautiful. Even so, we would not have a wholehearted faith in it if we were not convinced that it is also true.

First Corinthians 15:19-20 construes Jesus's resurrection as an actual event with cosmic ramifications: "If in Christ we have hope in this life only, we are of all people most to be pitied. But in fact Christ has been raised from the dead, the firstfruits of those who have fallen asleep." Jesus's resurrection has metaphorical applications too. But the *fact* that God raised Jesus from the dead anchors our hope that God will resurrect us as well at just the right time.

Standard Christian doctrines are better classified as matters of truth. For example, the law of noncontradiction necessitates that either the Triune God exists or He does not and that Jesus is or is not God the Son who died for the sins of the world. These statements and those opposing them cannot be true at the same time in the same sense. This is not to discount that truth can be complex or that subtle scrutiny regularly resolves superficial squabbles.

We concede that there are three "attitudes" or "sympathies" Christians can have that sometimes invite naive logical religious exclusivism and that these are misguided and unjustifiable. First is arguing in a nasty manner or haughty spirit. First Peter 3:15 rebukes conceit and insolence: "In your hearts honor Christ the Lord as holy, always being prepared to make a defense to anyone who asks you for a reason for the hope that is in you; yet do it with gentleness and respect."

Second, if a Christian insists that there is no truth in any religion besides Christianity or that every other formulation of religion is false, then the shared principles documented in the previous section contravene this notion.[75] As a further example, if Christians are right when they proclaim that only one God is worthy of worship, then Jews and Muslims are also right to affirm this. Preaching the gospel does not mean being deaf or dismissive to every other outlook.

St. Augustine (354–430) wanted every Christian to understand that wherever she finds truth, it is her Lord's.[76] Augustine wrote elsewhere, "Pagan learning contains not only false and superstitious fictions...but also liberal disciplines better suited to arriving at the truth, as well as some most useful moral precepts, and...some truths having to do with the worship of the one God."[77] C.S. Lewis (1898–1963) penned similar thoughts in *Mere Christianity*:

> If you are a Christian you do not have to believe that all the other religions are simply wrong through and through...You are free to think that all these religions, even the queerest ones, contain at least some hint of the truth. When I was an atheist I had to try to persuade myself that most of the human race have always been wrong about the question that mattered to them most; when I became a Christian I was able to take a more liberal view. But, of course, being a Christian does mean thinking that where Christianity differs from other religions, Christianity is right and they are wrong. As in arithmetic—there is only one right answer to a sum, and all other answers are wrong: but some of the wrong answers are much nearer being right than others.[78]

We would modify Lewis that Christianity's truth is not in itself as a religion but in its biblical basis that bears the *fullest witness to Jesus Christ.*[79] Jesus rather than any religious or ideological system is the way, the truth, and the life.[80] Missionary to India E. Stanley Jones (1884–1973) stressed, "The *final* issue is not between the systems of Christianity and Hinduism or Buddhism or Mohammedanism, but between Christlikeness and un-Christlikeness."[81]

A third hazard is yoking salvation with espousing correct theology. Anabaptists and Lutherans cannot both be right about infant baptism.[82] Do those who are incorrect on this issue forfeit their redemption? We stand with John Wesley: "God will not cast him into everlasting fire prepared for the devil and his angels because his ideas are not clear, or because his conception is confused. Without holiness, I own, no man shall see the Lord; but I dare not add, or clear ideas."[83]

Asbury Seminary president Timothy C. Tennent suggests the phrase "engaged exclusivism" for commitment to biblical revelation that also welcomes wisdom from other sources.[84] Gerald R. McDermott is the author of *Can Evangelicals Learn from World Religions?*[85] McDermott uses the following analogy in a companion volume: Geocentrists taught heliocentrists certain things even though the former were wrong in their overall interpretation of the data.[86]

Catholic theologian Paul J. Griffiths prefers the moniker "open inclusivism" as a reminder to Christians that they also "might have something important to learn" as well as to teach practitioners of other religions.[87] We catch a glimpse of this openness in a Buddhist anecdote. When the Buddha was at Kosambi in the Sinsapa forest, he took a few leaves in his hand: "What do you think, my disciples: which is more, these few leaves I hold, or the other leaves in the wood and the trees above and around us? As the leaves of the forest are more numerous than those in my hand, so are the leaves of truth I have not communicated to you in proportion with those I have communicated."[88] Process theologian John B. Cobb declares that nurturing such awareness can be transformative:

> Lack of faith expresses itself in fear of being affected by the wisdom of other communities. If we trust Jesus Christ as our Lord and Savior, we have no reason to fear that truth from any source will undercut our faith. Indeed, we have

> every reason to believe that all truth, wisdom and reality cohere in him... Faith in Jesus Christ encourages and even requires us to assimilate into our tradition what others have learned...It is incumbent upon us as Christians to transform ourselves by being open to this wisdom and goodness and learning all we can from it. It is also incumbent upon Christians to share the saving wisdom that we have derived from our own tradition. Listening to others and witnessing to them are not in conflict; in fact, as we are transformed by what we learn from others, our witnessing may become far more convincing to them.[89]

McDermott is again worth quoting at length. He outlines specific instances where Christians can benefit from Buddhist, Confucian, Daoist, Greek philosophical, Hindu, and Islamic intelligence:

> God uses the religions to teach the church deeper insight into the meaning of Christ...We saw this even in the Bible...It may be that some of today's religions portray aspects of the Divine mystery that the Bible does not equally emphasize: for example, the Qur'an's sense of the divine majesty and transcendence... Hindu traditions...remind Christians of God's immanence when deistic tendencies have obscured it. Theravadin Buddhists may be able to show...dimensions of the fallen ego that will shed greater light on what Paul meant by "the old man." Philosophical Daoists may have insights into nonaction that can help Christians better understand "waiting on God." Confucius's portrayal of virtue may open new understandings of radical discipleship...I am not saying these...[are not taught] in the Bible... But many of us...see them less clearly than we could...God used Aristotle to shed light for Thomas Aquinas on certain aspects of Christ and life with him...Peter learned from Cornelius's religious experience and heard God's word through him.[90]

God's chosen people in the Old and New Testaments were spiritually enriched by some of their contacts with people from other backgrounds. Job was a righteous man from "Uz."[91] Abraham donated a tithe to Melchizedek, the priest of Salem.[92] Abimelech of Gerar reverenced God, acted with integrity in his heart, and received God's partial vindication despite Abraham assuming "no fear of God" among Abimelech's people.[93] Ishmael's mother, Hagar, recognized God as the one who sees.[94] Moses's father-in-law, Jethro, a priest of Midian, instructed Moses in governing Israel and offered sacrifices at Israel's tent of meeting.[95] C.S. Lewis said of Moses, "Whatever was true in Akhenaten's creed came to him, in some mode or other, as all truth comes...from God. There is no reason why traditions descending from Akhenaten should not have been among the instruments which God used in making himself known."[96]

Furthermore, the faithful Ruth was from Moab. The queen of Sheba tested King Solomon with hard questions.[97] Pharaoh Necho reportedly rebuked Judah's good King Josiah with words from God's mouth, and Josiah died for not heeding them.[98] Non-Israelite sailors trying to spare Jonah's life behaved more righteously than Jonah.[99] Divinely guided magi or wise men—perhaps Persians or, more likely, Arabians—were among Jesus's earliest worshipers.[100]

Jesus acclaimed a Canaanite or Syro-Phoenician woman's faith and the faith or actions of a Samaritan over a priest and a Levite.[101] He commended a Samaritan woman's thirst for "living water." And though He classified Samaritans as less knowledgeable in their worship than Jews, He foretold a time when Jews and Samaritans would worship God together in Spirit and in truth.[102] Jesus spoke of outcasts and Samaritans entering God's kingdom ahead of Israelite religious leaders and praised a Roman centurion for having greater faith than any Jesus found in Israel.[103]

In the same spirit of learning, Martin Luther King Jr. went so far as to highlight the importance of listening carefully even to "the enemy's point of view, to hear his questions, to know his assessment of ourselves. For from his view we may indeed see the basic weaknesses of our own condition, and if we are mature, we may learn and grow and profit."[104]

One of Gerald McDermott's childhood friends was the Jesuit priest Francis X. Clooney, who served as the Center for the Study of World Religions director at Harvard Divinity School when I (Ben) was a ThM student. I had the pleasure of meeting Clooney and contributing to the first issue of *Journal of Comparative Theology*, which Clooney advised.[105]

We suggest that "engaged exclusivism" or "open inclusivism" are both more responsible modes of thinking about truth and religious diversity in place of prescriptive pluralism, relativism, or subjectivism. (Recall that this is inclusivism in the sense of appreciating the truthfulness found in other religions, not inclusivism in the sense of the ability to be saved in other religions.) We abbreviate one passage from Clooney that gets at the crux of engaged exclusivism/open inclusivism. Clooney deliberates in *Comparative Theology: Deep Learning Across Religious Borders*,

> Deep learning across religious borders...will always be a journey in faith. It will be from, for, and about God, whose grace keeps making room for all of us as we find our way faithfully in a world of religious diversity. That for me the work of comparative theology finally discloses a still deeper encounter with Jesus Christ only intensifies the commitment to learn from...religious diversity...In Christ there need not be any fear of what we might learn, there is only the Truth that sets us free.[106]

Prescriptive Pluralism on Salvation

Can We Answer the Question?

For our third section, we turn to whether all, some, one, or no religions facilitate eternal happiness. This is arguably the chief question behind whether one or more religions is true.

Not everyone believes the question can be answered definitively or affirmatively. Proponents of "religious antipathy" claim that no religion permits limitless joy since there is no such thing as salvation, and all religions are mistaken in their core beliefs.[107] From another direction, Gotthold Ephraim Lessing (1729–1781) in *Nathan the Wise* illustrates a negative "epistemic pluralism" where it is futile to try to fathom which if any religion qualifies its adherents for eternal life.

In Lessing's story, a father retained a priceless ring that rendered its wearer pleasing to God. The father pledged the ring to three sons, but instead of keeping his promise, he fashioned what appeared to be indistinguishable replicas of the true ring. It is unclear whether the father intended to give the true ring to any son or if the true ring was lost and only replicas remained.

Before the father died, he beckoned each son separately to his side and presented him with one of the rings, accompanied by a blessing. Each son assumed that he—and not the others—had the true ring. The father thought that all his sons would behave virtuously due to their assumptions. The moral? "Vainly they search, strive, argue. / The true ring was not proved or provable—/ Almost as hard to prove as to us now / What the true creed is."[108]

Nathan the Wise is partly incisive. Everyone faces intellectual uncertainty about ultimate concerns. This is one reason Christians look forward to "eschatological vindication" or "verification." We wait for "our blessed hope, the appearing of the glory of our great God and Savior Jesus Christ," when we will know fully even as we are fully known.[109]

We (Paul and Ben) are confident there are powerful reasons to trust in Jesus rather than anyone (or anything) else for salvation. Yet after weighing the available evidence, we must still take a stance or make a choice of faith or trust (John 7:17). Kierkegaard referred to this as a "leap of faith"—to place our "wager," as Blaise Pascal portended.[110] Not to wager is itself a wager. As Bob Dylan sang, "You've gotta serve somebody." Until the time when our faith is sight, we must choose wisely with whatever acumen we have.[111] Beyond this, we must take into account that certain negative childhood experiences, deep losses (e.g., of a parent or parent substitute), or disturbing encounters with evil may radically color or distort our perception of God. We may end up privileging our own negative experience over against a biblical—and thus accurate—portrayal of a loving God.[112]

Avoiding ultimate questions is fraught with risks resting on assumptions that we can put them off without serious consequences.[113] Such "religious indifferentism" is an opiate for the spiritual slothful and the hectically busy alike. We instead recommend sifting the evidence with an *ESV* or *NIV Study Bible* or the *Apologetics Study Bible*, plus Presbyterian pastor Timothy Keller's bestseller *The Reason for God*, along with published correspondence between atheist Edward K. Boyd and theologian Gregory A. Boyd in *Letters from a Skeptic: A Son Wrestles with His Father's Questions About Christianity*.[114]

Nathan the Wise has several additional shortcomings. The deceptive dad, of whom God supposedly approves due to his ring, is of dubious character. The father misleads his children by guaranteeing each of them salvation but supplies most or all of them with placebos. The father expects his sons to live honorably, but they may slide into inactivity if they imagine that their heavenly dwellings are mechanically secure by virtue of their rings. Whatever the father's motives, he bamboozles his children about the topic that matters most to them.

Second, the parable presumes but does not "prove" that determining the sure way to salvation is impossible. Once again, ongoing disagreement does not in itself demonstrate that all disputing parties are equally wrong or equally right.

Third, it requires a logical leap to harness *Nathan the Wise* as an allegory to not only suspend judgment but insist that all religions expedite salvation. How does contending that no one knows which if any religion is true lead to all religions being effectual? There are more consistent ways to proceed, but first we sketch prescriptive pluralist perspectives on eternal joy.

Pluralism and the Bible

"Transformational" pluralism presents world religions as equally capable of transforming their adherents so that they bear spiritual fruit, live righteous lives, and please God. "Unitary," "unitive," or "soteriological" pluralism classifies all world religions as equally trustworthy programs for bringing us to salvation. According to these views, all religions—or at least the good or major religions, however these are qualified—arbitrate liberation, endless bliss, or union with the divine. Each is said to chart a map to scale the mountain of holiness. Just as multiple rivers feed into one ocean, so do all religions lead to one God. To quote the Hindu deity Krishna's advice to Arjuna in the Bhagavad Gita 4:11, "For many are the paths of men, but they all in the end come to me."[115]

Christian "particularists," those who believe that Jesus is the source of all redemption, can still detect some truth in these path and mountain metaphors. After all, Jesus invites pilgrims from every nation, tribe, and tongue to follow Him.[116] This includes those who traveled Buddhist, Hindu, Muslim, and other thoroughfares, who in various ways were providentially prodded to follow Jesus through contact with these religions.[117] We predict that God's kingdom will also include citizens who at one time or another identified as agnostics, atheists, or antitheists but who eventually responded to Jesus's call to follow Him. God works all things together—including the world's religions and ideologies—for the good of those who love Him, who are called according to His purpose.[118]

At the same time, it is perilous to certify every conceivable itinerary as a dependable guide to the same destination. Contrary to ancient Rome, some roads also lead away from or without reference to the Eternal City. The Bible repeatedly repudiates diabolical, hypocritical, and wicked idolatries, confronting pretensions that all religions are auspicious or that myriad deities are worthy of worship. God judged Egypt's gods so that the Israelites and Egyptians would know there is no one like God.[119] God disciplined Israel for venerating metal calves and crediting other gods for bringing them out of Egypt.[120] The first three of the Ten Commandments forbade Israel to worship other gods, to make idols, or to use God's name in vain.[121]

To anticipate objections that these restrictions applied only to Israel, it is important to note that the Bible censures other nations for reprehensible religious practices as well. Canaanites performed abhorrent actions for their gods, which God hated.[122] The Bible condemns cultic rituals paired with prostitution, child sacrifice, and oppressing the foreigner, orphan, poor, and widow.[123] The Bible denigrates the Ba'als and other entities as "no gods."[124] The statue of the Philistine god Dagon fell on its face before God's Ark of the Covenant.[125] Angelic rulers or mighty ones in Psalms 29:1 and 97:7 are not divine in the same way God is but are invited to worship and glorify God. God vindicates Shadrach, Meschach, and Abednego for not bowing to Nebuchadnezzar's statue.[126] Daniel—despite being given a Babylonian name ("Belteshazzar," after Nebuchadnezzar's "god") and being placed in supervision over Babylon's magicians or wise men—drew a line in the Persian sand by praying to God alone.[127]

The New Testament likewise reproaches rival gods, powers, corruption, false gospels, and misdirected zeal. Jesus rebuked Jewish leaders who hankered after honorific titles, external regulations, and legal niceties as "blind leaders of the blind."[128] Jesus denounced false prophets who pretended to be His disciples: "Not everyone who says to me, 'Lord, Lord,' will enter the kingdom of heaven, but only he who does the will of my Father in heaven."[129]

The Apostle Paul confronted diabolical opposition and idol worship.[130] Paul and Barnabas rebuffed the Lystrans for wanting to worship them as Zeus and Hermes, informing the Lystrans instead that they were "friends" who brought good news so that the Lystrans could forsake their worthless idols and turn to the living God.[131] Moreover, "Satan disguises himself as an angel of light. So it is no surprise if his servants, also, disguise themselves as servants of righteousness."[132] First John 4:1 instructs, "Do not believe every spirit, but test the spirits to see whether they are from God, for many false prophets have gone out into the world."[133]

These examples are incompatible with decreeing that all things "religious" please God. "Truly in vain is salvation hoped for from the hills," but truly in the Lord salvation is found.[134]

Before moving to Christian particularism, we mention a more nuanced "orientational" or "pluriform pluralism" that takes seriously diverse religious goals and ideals. Even while pluriform pluralism prescribes countless *avenues* to flourishing, it also recognizes assorted *goals* or *destinations*. Islam propels Muslims toward the Muslim Prophet Muhammad's paradise. Disciplined Buddhists in time achieve Buddhist nirvana and Hindus nirvana of another sort. Christians go to the new heaven and new earth—with transformed, immortal, physical resurrection bodies—and others attain their own aspirations of what is optimally good.

S. Mark Heim offers an intriguing version of orientational pluralism, but it is highly speculative and lacks substantial biblical support.[135] However, pluriform or orientational pluralism, more so than unitary pluralism, does helpfully acknowledge that world religions offer diverse objectives. Without claiming that God ordains all religions as structures for obtaining salvation, Christians can still appreciate some of the practices, purposes, or penultimate goals in other faiths. For example, the Apostle Paul was able to compliment the Athenians for their religious zeal (Acts 17:22), even if, as he explained, "we ought not to think that the divine being is like gold or silver or stone" (17:29).

Exclusivism, Inclusivism, and Universalism

Christian particularism attests to the one source for eternal life who is not bound by any ethical theory or ideology. Jesus is the one and only Savior; the way, the truth, and the life; and the Mediator between God and humanity in whose name salvation is accomplished.[136]

I (Ben) remember reading as a teenager a striking illustration of Christian particularism. A traveler became lost and fell into a bed of quicksand. Confucius noticed the sojourner's plight and warned, "People should stay away from places like this." Buddha observed, "Let this suffering be a lesson to the rest of the world." Muhammad lamented, "Alas, it is God's will." Finally, Jesus reached down and said, "Take my hand, friend, I will save you!"[137] R.C. Sproul elaborates, "Moses could mediate on the law; Muhammad could brandish a sword; Buddha could give personal counsel; Confucius could offer wise sayings; but none...was qualified to offer an atonement for the sins of the world...Christ alone is worthy of unlimited devotion."[138]

Jesus is *the* way, *the* truth, and *the* life, not just *a* way, *a* truth, or *a* life, no better or worse than other ways. Christian particularists concur that Jesus is the *source* of salvation. We next survey a gamut of possibilities within particularism regarding the *scope* of salvation.

I (Paul) went to college in South Carolina, whose state motto is *dum spiro spero*, "While I breathe, I hope." Placing hope in Jesus in one's lifetime is at the heart of soteriological "exclusivism" or "restrictivism," where responsible adults who desire to receive eternal life must believe in Jesus before they die.[139]

Soteriological exclusivists might make exceptions for people who die very young or who have mental disabilities.[140] Regarding the young or disabled, some will say that Jesus saves only those who are the elect or that God grants a time of decision after death for any who lack mental acuity now.[141]

"Ecclesiocentrism" or "church exclusivism" asserts that to be saved, one must belong to the one true church, or to a continuum of favored denominations, or to the spiritual communion of saints where only God knows who believes sincerely.[142] "Gospel exclusivism" emphasizes not the church per se but hearing or reading the gospel from a human messenger and then responding receptively.[143] "Special revelation exclusivism" suggests that people can also be reconciled to God through Jesus via "special" revelations such as miracles, dreams, visions, or angels.[144]

Calvinist exclusivists praise God for predestining anyone to be saved, since all deserve condemnation. Arminian or Molinist "accessibilists" hypothesize that everyone has an opportunity to believe the gospel in this life or that God knows and ensures that anyone who under optimally balanced circumstances *would* receive the gospel is able to do so. "Final option theory" conjectures that whoever has not yet made a decision will have a chance at the moment of death.

The parable of the wedding garment in Matthew 22:1-13, the parable of the virgins in Matthew 25:1-13, the parable of the rich fool in Luke 12:13-20, and Hebrews 9:27 (which affirms that people are appointed "to die once, and after that comes judgment") support exclusivist urgency. We (Paul and Ben) agree that the only way to be *sure* of salvation is to repent of our sins, confess with our mouth, and believe in our heart that Jesus is Lord and to do so in this life.[145] Today is the day of salvation.[146] The stakes are too high to delay.

What about people who have never heard of the gospel, or who misunderstood it, or who listened to it inadequately articulated? "Inclusivism" proposes a "wider hope" where God extends mercy not only to the young, to the disabled, and to righteous believers who lived before Jesus but to those who lived later but did not definitively accept or renounce the gospel. In this case, Jesus is *ontologically* necessary for salvation though not *epistemologically* necessary; that is, recognizing one's sin, one can by faith cast himself upon God's mercy and find salvation, even without knowing *in this life* about Jesus of Nazareth, who is ultimately and actually their Savior.

In *The Great Divorce*, C.S. Lewis whimsically portrayed a "postmortem" or "eschatological evangelism" by Jesus or other preachers based on 1 Peter 3:19 and 4:6.[147] In this scenario, Jesus judges everyone after death per Hebrews 9:27, but there could be an interim between death and final judgment where people may still repent and believe. First Corinthians 15:29 recounts a "baptism for the dead," some interpretations of which portray early Christians interceding on behalf of deceased loved ones. A literal reading of the rich man and Lazarus in Luke 16:19-31 adds tension or complexity to either of these prospects.

Evangelist Billy Graham is among those who advocated a "general revelation inclusivism" that appeals to Luke 12:47-48; John 1:9; 8:12; Acts 10:34-35; 17:26-27; Romans 1–2;

and other verses.[148] Jesus in this view saves people according to their intent, character, or response to the grace that they received or the light they had through God's *natural* or *general* revelation to all people via reason, conscience, intuition, yearning for a redeemer, and awe at the natural world.

C.S. Lewis in *The Chronicles of Narnia* and elsewhere tilted toward a "world religions inclusivism" or "structural inclusivism," which ranks world religions hierarchically. Appealing to Deuteronomy 4:19, this view ventures that God ordains even defective religions as mechanisms to bring about salvation.[149] In our opinion, this treks too close to a prescriptive pluralism that endorses all religions as effective. A "cautious" or "modal inclusivism" can remain open to God's grace through general revelation, truth, virtue, and beauty in the world's religions without upholding or certifying any number of them as surefire conduits for salvation.[150]

"Christian universalism" proceeds even further. "Hopeful universalists" pray that Jesus will save all *people*, or even all *creatures* (including fallen angels), whether in this life or the next. "Convinced" or "necessary universalists" are confident that Jesus will finish this work.

Universalists point to the cycle of discipline and restoration for Israel and the nations in the Old Testament, Romans 11, and Revelation 22:2. They read universal reconciliation as the mystery of the ages in Ephesians 3. Every knee will bow and every tongue confess that Jesus is Lord to the glory of God the Father.[151] John 12:32,47; Romans 3:23-24; 5; 11; 1 Corinthians 15:22; Colossians 1; 1 Timothy 4:10; and Revelation 5:13 can all be read to indicate that all will be saved. The Dead Sea, associated with the lake of fire or Gehenna, where the wicked Sodom resided, is destined for healing waters from the New Jerusalem's tree of life.[152]

We offer three critiques of universalism. First, universalists must account for everlasting destruction or the second death in Matthew 5:22; 10:28; 25:41; Mark 9:43-48; 2 Thessalonians 1:9; Jude 1:6-13; and Revelation 14:11; 19:20; 20:14; and 21:8.[153] These mention a fire or hell prepared for the devil and his angels.[154] If this penalty goes on forever as "eternal conscious torment" or if it has consequences that are forever because the wicked eventually cease to exist according to "annihilationism," then, likewise, the "all" who are saved in the verses previously cited is better interpreted as hyperbole or as representing all *types* of people from all *nations* who believe in Jesus.

A second objection is that universalism gives the impression of undermining free will for God, for people, or both. Is God obliged to save all people, or are all people obliged to turn to God? For atheist Christopher Hitchens, God, according to universalism, is worse than any human dictator because "you can't defect from North Korea, but at least you can die."[155]

Third, as with *Nathan the Wise*, where the sons are deceptively certain about salvation, universalism could promote passivity, presumption, or flippancy toward God's judgment if Jesus rescues all in the end.[156] If universalism is true, then why is it vital to repent and believe now?

In the final analysis, we are "modest agnostics" regarding what will happen after death for those who have never heard the gospel or who lacked a definitive understanding of it. Indeed, God has given sufficient light to all without exception so that they are "without excuse" (Romans 1:20). God is not far from each one of us (Acts 17:27). And the fact that God commands every person to repent implies that His grace is available in order to enable this command to be fulfilled.

No one is condemned by God because she has been "born at the wrong place and time." One can go further by saying that it could well be the case that God, who knows the bounds of our habitation (Acts 17:26), could ensure that everyone who would respond to the gospel would have a chance to hear it, as the Molinist view affirms.

I (Paul) once served in Ravi Zacharias International Ministries. In one interview, Ravi reminded journalist Lee Strobel how Abraham asked God in the case of Sodom and Gomorrah, "Will not the Judge of all the earth do right?" Ravi concluded, "This means we can be absolutely confident that whatever God does in the case of...any... person, he will do what is right."[157]

At the same time, we are persuaded that Jesus commands us to make disciples of all nations so that whoever believes in Him experiences the joy of knowing Jesus now and the assurance of their heavenly adoption in this life and the next.

The Gospel for Pluralists?

The final section of our chapter on atheism and agnosticism (chapter 21) gives a glimpse of Christian hope. We urge comparison with visions of hope offered by other religions and refer readers to what we write there. Next, we invite readers to reflect on what manner of life following Jesus before all others evokes: "Oh, taste and see that the Lord is good!"[158] Is it a flourishing life that defends the dignity of all people, including the weak and the oppressed, whom Professor Eck discusses in her interview?[159]

Third, Dorothy Day characterized citizens of Christ's kingdom as giving shelter, food, and succor to anyone who needs it.[160] Yet something is amiss if we think to earn eternal life by our own efforts. When can we be confident that we have accomplished or sacrificed enough?[161]

We choose to trust not in ourselves but in Jesus:[162] "I write these things to you who believe in the name of the Son of God, that you may *know* that you have eternal life."[163]

I (Ben) recollect how one of my pastors, J.D. Greear at the Summit Church in Durham, North Carolina, presented Jesus to Muslims who were fearful about whether God would finally approve of them. J.D. confided that all prophets teach truth but that Jesus actually *reveals* the truth about salvation.

A heckler once scolded the missionary and children's author Patricia St. John, "People have their own religion, and by trying to impose your views upon them, you're forcing them into a different culture, dividing them, and introducing unnecessary problems. Why can't you just leave them alone?" St. John's reply? "Do we really believe that Christ is so eternally precious that he is worth infinitely more to them than all that they may lose, even life itself—whom to know is life eternal?...If we do, let us press on; if not, by all means, let us leave them alone."[164]

Paul Copan (PhD, Marquette University) is a Christian theologian, analytic philosopher, and apologist. He is a professor at Palm Beach Atlantic University and holds the Pledger Family Chair of Philosophy and Ethics. His numerous books include *"True for You, but Not for Me": Overcoming Common Objections to Christian Faith*; *Is God a Moral Monster? Making Sense of the Old Testament God*; *Contending with Christianity's Critics: Answering the New Atheists and Other Objectors* (coedited); and *Loving Wisdom: A Guide to Philosophy and Christian Faith*.

Benjamin B. DeVan (PhD, Durham University) has taught numerous courses at North Carolina Central University, Peace College, and Palm Beach Atlantic University, including a January-term minicourse at MIT: "Religion: Bringing the World Together, or Tearing the World Apart?" He has published more than 60 articles, book chapters, and book reviews. He earned his MA in counseling from Asbury Seminary, MDiv from Duke, and ThM from Harvard (with a thesis on Evangelical Christians and Muslims) and penned his PhD dissertation on the New Atheists.

New Spirituality

Douglas Groothuis

Talking about deep suffering can bring out people's deepest beliefs about life, true or false. Someone I once knew asked me how I was coping with my wife's dementia.[1] After I said a few things, Eve (not her name) told me that in a previous life, my wife had chosen to come to earth and experience all of her suffering because she wanted to learn from it. Eve went on to say that her daughter had been Eve's mother in a previous lifetime.

Eve was talking to someone who had written about 1,000 pages over many years refuting her New Spirituality worldview. She was trying to comfort me. I could have lectured her about reincarnation, karma, and New Spirituality ideas for hours. Instead, I said, "Eve, Becky and I don't believe that about the afterlife. We believe that we will both be with God in a new world. If you want to know what we believe, you can read Revelation chapters 21 and 22." She wrote down the references and went back to work. I hope to talk to her again, and I continue to pray for her.

What Is the New Spirituality?

Although I didn't ask Eve about her whole view of life, her comments about reincarnation told me she had been influenced by the New Spirituality (also known as the New Age movement). While the movement is no longer in the headlines as a new cultural force as often as it was in the 1980s, its worldview has become mainstream for many Americans and those around the world. The New Spirituality perspective is no longer *new* and has lost its panache as a messianic movement making grand claims about bringing about a spiritual utopia. Nevertheless, many mere mortals deem themselves divine and seek salvation in the depths of their own being. They take this quest to be the only way to solve the world's problems. A prominent New Spirituality author and speaker, Marianne Williamson, ran as a Democratic candidate for US president in the 2020 election.[2] While her emphasis is on love, her concept of God is that of an impersonal and loveless something. She is a pantheist, not a Christian.

Religious historian J. Gordon Melton defines the New Age as "a movement that spread through the occult and metaphysical communities in the 1970s and '80s. It looked forward to a 'New Age' of love and light and offered a foretaste of the coming era through personal transformation and healing."[3] The New Spirituality movement has never been a unified movement; rather, it is a collection of organizations, ideas, and goals all based on the false hope that humanity can raise itself up by tapping into the God within.[4]

As a young man in the 1970s, I was interested in New Age ideas and practices. Some of my favorite musicians had gurus and followed Eastern philosophies, which influenced their song titles, styles of music, and liner notes. This led me to read about Hinduism, Buddhism, and other non-Christian perspectives, such as the esoteric Gurdjieff-Ouspensky teachings and out-of-the-body travels. God had other plans for me, though, and I became a Christian and was baptized in the summer of 1976. After that, I extensively researched and evaluated the movement, writing several books and many articles. I also participated in public debates, handed out tracts at New Age events, and witnessed to New Agers.[5]

There is no one creed or holy book or pope for those involved in New Spirituality thinking; however, we can summarize the general worldview before comparing it with biblical Christianity. We aim to understand those enmeshed in a deceptive worldview and to help them find the light of Jesus who dispels the darkness.

First, all is one. All of reality is a seamless whole. There is no real difference between humans, nature, and God. Think of taking a mystical eraser and erasing the distinctions between you and others, you and the planet, and you and God. All is one without a second. Philosophically, this is called "monism" or "nondualism." All supposed dualities such as body and soul, subject and object, even good and evil are denied in favor of an all-comprehensive oneness. We are all just waves in the ocean.

Second, all is divine. This great oneness is a oneness of spirit or divinity. God is not a being separate from creation but is the only reality. This concept of God is not of a personal and relational being but of an

20A. Helena Blavatsky, occultist and spirit medium, and Henry Steel Olcott, theosophist and Buddhist, pioneered an esoteric approach to religion that New Age thought utilizes. Public domain.

impersonal, amoral force, principle, substance, or consciousness. God is more of an *It* than a *He* or *She*. This is known as *pantheism*. As Christian philosopher Francis Schaeffer pointed out, the word *pantheism* can deceive people into thinking that it refers to a *personal* God (or *theos*), but it does not. The word only gives a false *connotation* of a personal God. A better term is "pan-everything-ism," since everything is lumped together and called "God."[6] This is not a God who can create, speak, or love—or even exist. No one summarized the perennial temptation of pantheism better than C.S. Lewis:

> Pantheism is congenial to our minds not because it is the final stage in a slow process of enlightenment, but because it is almost as old as we are...It is immemorial in India. The Greeks rose above it only at their peak, in the thought of Plato and Aristotle; their successors relapsed into the great Pantheistic system of the Stoics. Modern Europe escaped it only while she remained predominantly Christian; with Giordano Bruno and Spinoza it returned. With Hegel it became almost the agreed philosophy of highly educated people, while the more popular Pantheism of Wordsworth, Carlyle and Emerson conveyed the same doctrine to those on a slightly lower cultural level. So far from being the final religious refinement, Pantheism is in fact the permanent natural bent of the human mind.[7]

The New Spirituality trades on this ancient, perennial, and egregious error, that of denying the Creator/creation distinction. While claiming that everything is divine, it demotes God to less than who He is by identifying Him with all that is.

Third, we are divine. If all is one and all is God, then we are God. The story is told of a popular New Spirituality guru who was once asked, "Do you think you are God?" He answered, "Yes, but only if you are too." So when a New Spirituality practitioner claims to be divine, she does not mean that she is any more or less divine than anyone else. The issue is whether or not you realize that you are divine. In the popular television series and book *The Power of Myth*, professor Joseph Campbell proclaimed that "each of us is the incarnation of God," not Jesus only.[8] "We are all manifestations of the Buddha consciousness or Christ consciousness, only we don't know it," he asserted.[9] Or consider the popular statement, "You are not a human being having a spiritual experience but a spiritual being having a human experience." I heard this read at a Christian funeral, sadly. We are human beings who are finite, spiritual beings. The quote above intimates that we are more than human and perhaps even divine.

Fourth, we have unlimited potential, since we are divine. As the old counterculture almanac *Whole Earth Catalog* put it, "We are as gods and might as well get used to it."[10] Only ignorance of our divinity drags us down. As divine beings, the paranormal beckons us: ESP, telepathy, contact with "spirit guides" (channeling or mediumship), and out-of-the-body experiences become desirable. We are miracles waiting to happen.

Shirley MacLaine, an original leader of the New Age movement, taught, "*You* are unlimited. You just don't *realize* it."[11] (We are gods who somehow forgot that we are gods—a problem of divine amnesia.) And if we don't "master the possibilities" of godhood in this life, reincarnation assures us that we will have endless other opportunities for advancement. The idea of a final judgment before a holy and just God is deemed old fashioned and just too judgmental. So is the idea of sin, which is viewed as an outmoded notion that causes guilty feelings that are unbecoming of divine beings. As Hindu guru Vivekananda said, "Ye divinities on earth—sinners! It is a sin to call a man so; it is a standing libel on human nature."[12] It is also a self-refuting statement and thus is false.

Fifth, we can tap into our unlimited divine power through meditation, visualization, chanting, or yoga in order to attain a higher level of consciousness. The New Spirituality challenges us to awaken our "God consciousness" through various mystical methods, such as transcendental meditation (TM), Silva Mind Control, yoga, self-hypnosis, visualization, or participation in consciousness-raising programs, such as EST (Erhard Seminars Training), Lifespring, or the Forum. We all have divine potential, but few have tapped into it successfully. So we find thousands of New Spirituality self-help books and programs to summon the sleeping savior within.

For many practitioners, being divine also means "creating your own reality" through thought and "creative visualization." This is the premise of Rhonda Byrne's best-selling book *The Secret*.[13] Far from being a secret, she is repeating an old principle of occult magic. Instead of asking God for something, we can conjure up the reality ourselves through the strength of our own consciousness. While teaching a philosophy course at a secular school, I met a young woman with a terminal illness whose Christian faith had been rocked by *The Secret*. After several conversations with me and by looking at a video against the New Spirituality, she returned to trusting in Christ, not in her own powers of mind.

Sixth, New Spirituality philosophy teaches that all religions teach pantheism at their core. While Christianity seems to separate the

20B. Swami Vivekananda (fourth from the right), who popularized pantheism at Chicago's Parliament of Religion in 1893. Public domain.

Creator from the creation, the esoteric and supposedly truest teaching is that all is one and all is God. Biblical texts are taken out of context and become a pretext for this error. For example, practitioners of New Spirituality contend that when Jesus said "The kingdom of God is within you" (Luke 17:21 KJV), He really meant that we are all God. The fact, however, is that Jesus was speaking of a new order of history in which God's ways will be brought to bear on history with great glory and power.[14] While certain schools of Hinduism and Buddhism teach pantheism, this is not the essence of all religions. Even more, Christianity, Judaism, and Islam teach that the dead shall be raised at the end of history, while New Spirituality adherents typically believe in karma and reincarnation.

20C. Maharishi Mahesh Yogi created and popularized transcendental meditation, one among numerous techniques that New Agers have used to awaken spirituality. Photo by Ben Pirard (https://creativecommons.org/licenses/by-sa/3.0).

Snapshot of the New Spirituality: Interview with Neale Donald Walsch[15]

Neale Donald Walsch is the author of 29 books, including the bestselling *Conversations with God* series, which teaches New Spirituality. Seven of the books in the *Conversations with God* series made it on the *New York Times* Best Seller List, one of them remaining on the list for two and a half years. In the series, Walsch gives messages he believes he received from God.

Q1: Let's say that there's a map of all the world religions with an arrow that says, "You are here." Is there a place on the map of world religions where you would say, "Yep, I'm here"?

Walsch: I would say that my place on that map would be in a city called "Nondenominational Spirituality," as in nondefined and nonaligned spiritual experience. And in that place, one is referred to one's innermost spiritual reality. And that means that it could be, depending on the individual, a spiritual reality that does align doctrinally or philosophically or theologically with a faith tradition, or it could not. So it's a place where one lives in the ultimate experience of spiritual freedom. Then what one believes and experiences within oneself becomes one's guideline, one's doctrine, one's dogma, and one's spiritual expression. In my own experience, I find that all of the world's great faith traditions have offered me something powerful. But I have not found any particular spiritual tradition or faith tradition that has offered me all or everything that I have found my innermost being to be seeking. So therefore, in my own personal experience, I have turned to my own understanding, my own awareness, my own truth with regard to what we call God and life. I think that the world's religions have a great deal to offer. But I think that the world's religious are simply incomplete.

Q2: What are some of the key truths that your personal conversations with God have led you to?

Walsch: The first and most important truth is that all things are one thing. Our idea of separation is a myth. There is only one thing, and all things are part of the one thing there is. This means that we are all a part of each other, that we are not separate from each other. We are all a part of life in every one of its manifestations. There is no true, ultimate, and complete separation between us and the world around us. This means that we are, in fact, not separate from that aspect of life that we call "Divinity" or, if you please, "God." It means that God and we are one. And I don't mean one philosophically. I mean one *actually*. We are, in fact, an expression of Divinity Itself. Humanity's pathological behaviors of self-destruction are produced by our belief that we are separate from God and from each other.

The second most important principle that came from my conversations with God is that there's enough. The idea of insufficiency is likewise an illusion, as is the idea of separation. And so we don't have to compete with each other for what we think of as "the stuff of which there's not enough," because there is enough for all of us to be happy and to survive joyfully. All we need to do is simply share.

The third fundamental principle is that there's nothing you have to *do*. We think that we're going to change the world through doing this or doing that. But we are, in fact, human *beings*, not human *doings*. It is what we are *being* that will set the course of human history and direct the experience of our entire lives, individually and collectively, on this planet.

Q3: How would you describe humanity's basic instinct?

Walsch: Survival is not the basic instinct. Our fundamental instinct is the expression of what I refer to as our True Nature. And that is the expression of Divinity, of which we are individual expressions. If survival was the basic instinct, you wouldn't run into the burning building to save the crying baby. When we mistakenly think that survival is our fundamental instinct, we end up only doing what we think is necessary for us to survive.

Q4: What is the soul's ultimate purpose?

Walsch: The soul's ultimate purpose is to announce, to declare, to express, to fulfill, to become, and to experience its True Nature. I do not believe that life begins and ends with our physical experience on the earth in what we call this particular lifetime. But I believe that the soul is on an eternal journey that never ends and that the purpose of the journey—as opposed to the destination—is to use every moment of every expression of every lifetime to announce, declare, express, and fulfill our True Nature. That is, to be Divinity Expressed, in every way that life in the physical realm affords us an opportunity to be. In short, our purpose is to experience Divinity in, as, and through us.

Q5: What would you say is the biggest problem on the planet?

Walsch: The biggest problem on our planet is that we don't know what the biggest problem on our planet is. You know you've got a problem when you can see fallout from the problem everywhere you look, but you can't figure out what's causing it. That's a real problem. The fallout from the world's biggest problem is called alienation. We are becoming a society, a culture, a civilization of alienated beings who separate from each other, often disdainfully. The underlying problem is our insistence on separation as the fundamental construction and reality of life. Once we move into a full awareness of and a full implementation regarding our oneness, alienation will become not only obsolete but impossible. We will see each other as different fingers on the same hand.

Q6: Do you have spiritual practices that help you to realize the oneness of all life?

Walsch: It starts by seeing myself across the room. It starts in my own kitchen. If I'm having a difficult moment with a loved one, let's say a beloved member of my own family, and we're just having a bit of a conflict, I can allow myself to fall into defensiveness, into survival mode, or I can ask myself two important questions. First, "Is there any part of me that I am seeing over there, on the other side of the room?" Can I own the part of me that has behaved in exactly the same way as I am seeing the other person behave now? If so, then I can embrace both that other person and myself in a place of unconditional love. I may not approve, condone, or agree with the person, but I can still understand where the other person is coming from. The second question I can ask is "What does this have to do with the agenda of my soul?" If I really am a spiritual entity—a soul that *has* a body and a mind—then I need to be clear about what the agenda of my soul is. Again, the soul's agenda is to announce, declare, fulfill, become, and experience Who I Really Am. It is my True Nature to become the living expression of Divinity Itself.

Q7: What do you think of the historical Jesus?

Walsch: I think the same thing of the historical Jesus that I think of the historical Muhammad, the historical Buddha, the historical Lao Tzu, and all of the wonderful messengers and teachers, both male and female, throughout human history who have understood at a deep level who they really are and have chosen to use their life to bring us an awareness of who we really are as well. So my understanding of the historical Jesus is that he was the Son of God exactly, as he declared himself to be. And so are we. And he used his whole life to convince us of that. He would walk around the streets saying things like, "Why are you so amazed? These things, and more, shall you do also." As well, every word that he uttered was a word of unconditional love and acceptance of us as being on his plane—his equal in God's eyes.

New Spirituality Influences on Christians

New Spirituality influence can corrupt the thinking of Christians. For instance, the Pew Research Center reports that 22 percent of those who identify as Christians believe in reincarnation, although Scripture teaches no such thing.[16] Further, many Christians practice and support yoga without knowing its Hindu roots and assumptions.[17]

While in a Christian bookstore, I met a woman who called herself a "New Age Christian." She told me that Jesus taught reincarnation because He said that John the Baptist was really the Old Testament Prophet Elijah. I mentioned that Jesus wasn't speaking literally because Elijah never died but was taken directly to heaven (2 Kings 3). Thus he never gave over his soul to be reincarnated as John the Baptist. I added that John the Baptist denied being the literal Elijah (John 1:21). Jesus never taught reincarnation but affirmed that the dead would be resurrected once and for all in physical bodies that would spend eternity in heaven or hell. She pondered this a bit before leaving the store.

Spiritual Error: Where Did It All Come From?

The roots of the New Spirituality movement—and all false philosophy and religion—ultimately trace back to a man, a woman, and a snake in a garden. God created Adam and Eve, placed them in a garden, and told them to tend the garden and to have dominion over the creation. He gave them one prohibition: to not eat of the tree of the knowledge of good and evil. God provided all that they needed and put a clear boundary before them. But the serpent tempted our first parents to disobey the one thing God forbade. A half-truth was his ploy. They would not die but would be like God, knowing good and evil.

In full truth, they were already like God, having been made in His image and likeness. God was the standard of good and evil, having created them "very good" and then commanding them in the way of life and goodness. When Eve ate the fruit from the tree and Adam joined her, their eyes were opened, and they died spiritually. God expelled and banished them from Eden and pronounced a punishment of pained work, strained relationships, physical ills, and ultimately death. The fall damaged four relationships: between God and humans, between humans and their own selves, between humans and each other, and between humans and the rest of creation.

At the heart of the fall was the lie that God's creatures could live apart from God's authority and direction. Though creatures dependent on God, they believed they could become the center of the universe and suffer no adverse consequences from their absurd rebellion. Rebellion is in the marrow of mere mortals.

The results of the fall cannot be reversed by repeating the lie that brought it about. Salvation cannot be found by looking within for a divine self that does not exist in mere mortals. This is bad news for pride but good news for salvation through the merits of Jesus Christ alone. Our alienation from God is rectified only through the finished and final work of Jesus Christ on the cross on our behalf. He alone is the mediator between a holy God and sinful people (1 Timothy 2:5; Acts 4:12). Let us contrast the New Spirituality worldview with Christianity in more detail.

The Christian Alternative to the New Spirituality

New Spirituality "open mindedness" notwithstanding, biblical teaching stands at odds with the New Spirituality mindset. Not everything billed as "spiritual" is of the same spirit. The differences make a difference.

From the first to the last book of the Bible, the Supreme Spirit is shown to be the personal and living Lord of the universe. When God revealed Himself to Moses in the burning bush, He declared, "I AM WHO I AM" (Exodus 3:14). God speaks as a personal being, a center of consciousness. The Bible never presents God as an impersonal abstraction such as a principle, essence, or force. God is not an *It* but rather a personal being.

The Bible reveals that God creates, God hears, God speaks, God judges, and God forgives. He is not to be identified with His creation. The Apostle Paul highlights this when he writes of those who deny God, "They exchanged the truth about God for a lie and worshiped and served the creature rather than the Creator, who is blessed forever!" (Romans 1:25). All is not God, but all should praise the Creator, who alone is God.

Alone among all religions, Christianity teaches that God is a Trinity. God has existed from eternity as Father, Son, and Holy Spirit. There are not three gods, but one God in three coequal and coeternal persons. Each person has His own part to play in creating and redeeming the universe, and these roles overlap. The subject is vast, but the Trinity is who God is, a personal being. The members of the Trinity love and glorify each other from eternity.[18]

As creatures, we do not possess the credentials of the triune Creator and Redeemer. Yet humans are more like God than anything else in the universe. We are "wonderfully made" (Psalm 139:14) in His image and likeness (Genesis 1:26). Yet we fall infinitely short of godhood. God spoke through the prophet Ezekiel to the king of Tyre, an ancient God imposter: "Because your heart is proud, and you have said, 'I am a god, I sit in the seat of the gods, in the heart of the seas,' yet you are but a man, and no god, though you make your heart like the heart of a god" (Ezekiel 28:2).

God pronounces His judgment on such foolish pride and asks this stubborn God player, "Will you still say, 'I am a god,' in the presence of those who kill you, though you are but a man, and no god, in the hands of those who slay you?" (Ezekiel 28:9). When any practitioner of New Spirituality proclaims or thinks, "I am God," the great I Am knows better. As He declared through His prophet Isaiah, "I am God, and there is no other; I am God, and there is none like me" (Isaiah 46:9).

God is everywhere simultaneously (without being everything), but we can only be one place at any given time. God is all-powerful; we are limited by our creaturehood. God knows everything; we know only in part. God is morally perfect and infinitely holy; we are less than true to our own consciences and so experience true moral guilt. We deserve a failing grade in divinity, and there are no retakes.

If God is holy and just, then our moral failings put us out of step with His character and purposes. Jesus never taught that humans suffered from a lack of knowledge of their true nature as divine. New Spirituality thinking to the contrary, we cannot become divine or "Christed." Rather, Christ accurately diagnosed the problem as one of ethical wrongdoing. He located the root of moral uncleanness squarely in the human heart. He said, "For from within, out of the heart of man, come evil thoughts, sexual immorality, theft, murder, adultery, coveting, wickedness, deceit, sensuality, envy, slander, pride, foolishness. All these evil things come from within, and they defile a person" (Mark 7:21-23).

Jesus also knew that this uncleanness was not an occasional problem but a general condition of humanity. He said, "Truly, truly, I say to you, everyone who practices sin is a slave to sin" (John 8:34). Those who are prone to view sin as only severe wrongdoings such as murder and theft should consider Jesus's standards. His rule of moral goodness was "love the Lord your God with all your heart and with all your soul and with all your mind" and "love your neighbor as yourself" (Matthew 22:37,39). Who can live up to God's perfect standard of goodness? As Ecclesiastes teaches, "God made man upright, but they have sought out many schemes" (7:29). The Apostle Paul did not tone this down but ramped it up.

> Both Jews and Greeks are under sin,
> as it is written:
>
> None is righteous, no, not one;
> no one understands;
> no one seeks for God.
> All have turned aside; together they
> have become worthless; no one
> does good, not even one.
> Their throat is an open grave;
> they use their tongues to deceive.
> The venom of asps is under their lips.
> Their mouth is full of curses and
> bitterness.
> Their feet are swift to shed blood;
> in their paths are ruin and misery,

> and the way of peace they have
> not known.
> There is no fear of God before their
> eyes (Romans 3:9-18).

Only the Jesus of space-time history and eternity can rescue us from this plight of sin against a holy God. Sadly, the New Spirituality Jesus can save no one.

Jesus: Guru or Lord?

Those in the New Spirituality movement highly esteem Jesus as a great teacher, master, guru, or yogi. Consider the comments Oprah Winfrey made on a special program dedicated to the New Spirituality ideas of popular author Eckhart Tolle:

> I believe that God is love and that God is in all things...What I believe is that Jesus came to show us Christ consciousness...Even as a Christian, I don't believe that Jesus came to start Christianity...I am a Christian who believes that there are certainly many more paths to God other than Christianity.[19]

The real Jesus does not echo the message of Oprah's New Spirituality vision. He did not claim to be an example of a self-realized guru but the unique and unrepeatable revelation of a personal God. He said about Himself, "The Son of Man came to seek and to save the lost" (Luke 19:10). Jesus was on a rescue mission to planet Earth to save those lost in sin, those who cannot live up to God's requirements. Jesus also proclaimed that "the Son of Man came not to be served but to serve, and to give his life as a ransom for many" (Mark 10:45).

While those involved in the New Spirituality claim to tap into their deity (with varying degrees of success), Jesus demonstrated His deity in ways never approached by any other historical figure. He performed countless miracles over nature, over sickness, and over death itself when He raised his friend Lazarus from the dead. The deaf heard, the blind saw, the crippled leaped for joy (Matthew 11:1-11). Jesus taught with an undeniable authority, which either commanded respect or fueled hatred from those who could not bear pure truth. He claimed to be no less than God in human form when He said He had the authority on earth to forgive sins (Mark 2:1-12) and that He was "Lord of the Sabbath" (Mark 2:23-28). Because God created the Sabbath, Jesus was claiming to be God. When Jesus declared, "Before Abraham was, I am" (John 8:58), He used the divine title "I AM" for Himself, and His audience knew it (Exodus 3:14). As a result, they tried to stone Him, but it was not His time to die.

Jesus was so bold as to divide all people in terms of their response to Him. He asserted, "Whoever is not with me is against me, and whoever does not gather with me scatters" (Matthew 12:30; see also Matthew 25:31-46). Jesus invited His hearers to place their faith in Him and to commit themselves to Him alone. He said, "For God so loved the world, that he gave his only Son, that whoever believes in him should not perish but have eternal life" (John 3:16). God has but one Son who alone can save us from perishing.

When His disciples asked Him the way to God the Father, Jesus uttered as clear a statement about His identity and mission as can be imagined. He said, "I am the way, and the truth, and the life. No one comes to the Father except through me" (John 14:6). Only Jesus had the credentials to make this claim stick. He laid down His life for those needing new life. "I am the good shepherd," He said. "The good shepherd lays down his life for the sheep" (John 10:11).

This is the meaning of Jesus's crucifixion. Although He had the authority to call down legions of angels to deliver Him from death, He chose to offer His life as a sacrifice for the sheep who had strayed. As the Apostle Paul put it, though Jesus Christ was rich in heaven before His incarnation, He left heaven for earth and became poor in order to make us rich (2 Corinthians 8:9).

In His death, He who was sinless and perfect paid the penalty for human sin. Paul makes this clear: God "made him to be sin who knew no sin, so that in him we might become the righteousness of God" (2 Corinthians 5:21).

Although practitioners of the New Spirituality think of the idea of sin as negative and limiting, we must take it seriously if we are to understand Jesus Christ. The life, teachings, and death of Jesus dissolve into nonsense without the true meaning of sin. Jesus came to die for our sins in order to set us right with God. This is the great divide between the New Spirituality and the message of Jesus.

The pantheistic deity of the New Spirituality is an impersonal and amorphous abstraction that loves nothing and feels nothing. A mere energy source can't show compassion. It can't die in order to save us. Being impersonal, it can't even relate to us person to person. But Jesus declared that He came into the world in love to rescue those enslaved to sin. God, the personal Lord, cared enough to make a provision for our sorry state. And a just God required no less than a perfect sacrifice for the forgiveness of sin. Jesus offered His life for ours and, in doing so, defeated the power of sin and Satan himself. As the Apostle John said, "The reason the Son of God appeared was to destroy the works of the devil" (1 John 3:8; see also Colossians 2:14). That is God's love in action.

To vindicate His claims, Jesus did what no one else has ever done. After three days in a tomb, He rose from the dead never to die again, just as He predicted. Even before His death, Jesus was certain of His victory over death, sin, and the devil. He proclaimed, "I am the resurrection and the life. Whoever believes in me, though he die, yet shall he live, and everyone who lives and believes in me shall never die" (John 11:25-26).

Jesus offered no hope in reincarnation as a way to find liberation. He pointed people to Himself for eternal life. To find Him was to find life, and to reject Him was to lose life. Christ affirms, "So everyone who acknowledges me before men, I also will acknowledge before my Father who is in heaven, but whoever denies me before men, I also will deny before my Father who is in heaven" (Matthew 10:32-33).

In Jesus and in Jesus alone can we find hope for new life, hope, and peace. His followers know the joy of being forgiven of their sins and welcomed into fellowship with God Himself. In light of the supremacy of Jesus Christ, the trappings of the New Spirituality fall into insignificance. They are dangerous diversions away from spiritual reality. Jesus Himself refers to those who do persist in practicing "magic arts" (the occult) as being lost in hell (Revelation 22:15 NIV; see also Deuteronomy 18:9-14). God warned His people against such "abominable practices" before they entered the Promised Land.

While the New Spirituality promises godhood and unlimited potential through self-discovery and occult experimentation, Jesus promises Himself as the final satisfaction:

> All things have been handed over to me by my Father, and no one knows the Son except the Father, and no one knows the Father except the Son and anyone to whom the Son chooses to reveal him. Come to me, all who labor

> and are heavy laden, and I will give you rest (Matthew 11:27-28).

Instead of looking within for unlimited power, we can look to Jesus for strength, wisdom, and direction. The Apostle Paul knew this well when he said that "we have this treasure in jars of clay, to show that the surpassing power belongs to God and not to us" (2 Corinthians 4:7). Those who know this power of God are impressed to make Jesus known and to live out His principles in service to a needy world.

The Way to Life

This life-giving, resurrected, and never-dying Jesus asks something from us—namely, everything. Mere mortals find their value and significance only by serving their Sovereign, not by pretending to be sovereign. This is what we were meant to do. So Jesus says, "Whoever finds his life will lose it, and whoever loses his life for my sake will find it" (Matthew 10:39). If we live for ourselves, we ultimately lose all. If we live for the One who created us and gives us life eternal, we gain all.

This salvation cannot be earned or found within the self. Human beings do not possess a divine self, since the finite is not the infinite. Salvation can only be received as a loving gift by having faith in what Jesus has done through His death and resurrection. As Jesus's close friend John wrote, "But to all who did receive him, who believed in his name, he gave the right to become children of God, who were born, not of blood nor of the will of the flesh nor of the will of man, but of God" (John 1:12-13).

The only way into God's New Age (the kingdom of God) is the new birth that is found in Jesus, the one and only Christ. So how might we lead those in spiritual error into the liberating truth of the gospel of Jesus Christ?

Principles for Witnessing to Practitioners of the New Spirituality

Every person involved in the New Spirituality has his or her own story and unique personality. Thus every apologetic or evangelistic opportunity will be different. Nevertheless, here are several general principles for fruitful interactions with those whose minds have been darkened by the New Spirituality.

First, the secret of all Christian witness is dependent on prayer for courage, confidence, and competence in commending the way of Jesus. All revivals are instigated by concerted prayer, and no evangelistic encounter will be effective without it. We should pray and have others pray for us. As Paul said,

> Continue steadfastly in prayer, being watchful in it with thanksgiving. At the same time, pray also for us, that God may open to us a door for the word, to declare the mystery of Christ, on account of which I am in prison—that I may make it clear, which is how I ought to speak. Walk in wisdom toward outsiders, making the best use of the time (Colossians 4:2-5).

Second, we need to be prepared for spiritual conflict, since an evangelistic or apologetic encounter involves a clash between the one true God and Satan, the father of lies. Both spiritual and intellectual weapons should be readied. Remember, though, that the enemy is Satan and his demons, *not* the New Ager. Be sure to put on "the whole armor of God" as you reach out (Ephesians 6:10-19).

Third, Christians should clearly define their terms concerning the Christian message. The great countercult apologist Walter Martin wrote of "scaling the language barrier" with those in non-Christian cults and religions.

> The average non-Christian cult owes its very existence to the fact that it has utilized the terminology of Christianity, has borrowed liberally from the Bible (almost always out of context), and sprinkled its format with evangelical clichés and terms wherever possible or advantageous. Up to now this has been a highly successful attempt to represent their respective systems of thought as "Christian."
>
> On encountering a cultist, then, always remember that you are dealing with a person who is familiar with Christian terminology, and who has carefully redefined it to fit the system of thought he or she now embraces. A concrete example of a redefinition of terms can be illustrated in the case of almost any of the Gnostic cult systems that emphasize healing and hold in common a pantheistic concept of God (Christian Science, New Thought, Unity, Christ Unity Science, Metaphysics, Religious Science, Divine Science).[20]

The practitioner of New Spirituality believes that at the core of all religions is pantheism. Therefore, you need to counter the New Spirituality tendency to read that worldview into Christianity. For example, when practitioners speak of "Christ consciousness," they refer to a mystical state of "enlightenment" wherein we realize that we are one with God. Jesus, they think, was a mere man who became "the Christ" and realized that He was divine. Luke 2:11 refutes this by saying that Jesus was "the Christ" even as an infant. Moreover, He was the only Christ who ever was, is, or will be.

Fourth, point out common ground or points of contact with practitioners of New Spirituality. This can open a door for evangelism (see Acts 17:16-34). We are free to recognize and honor truth wherever it appears (always taking God's Word as our authority). The New Spirituality adherent, for instance, has rightly rejected an atheistic worldview, wants to lead a spiritual life, and may rightly be concerned about ecological matters or other social issues.

Fifth, the New Spirituality worldview should be intellectually challenged, but in a loving spirit. Paul should be our model: "The weapons of our warfare are not of the flesh but have divine power to destroy strongholds. We destroy arguments and every lofty opinion raised against the knowledge of God, and take every thought captive to obey Christ" (2 Corinthians 10:4-5).

I have already compared Christianity with New Spirituality views but consider the following arguments against the New Spirituality worldview:

1. For practitioners of the New Spirituality, evil makes no sense, since they do not believe that we are sinners who have rebelled against God. The Christian account of humans as limited and morally corrupted explains better who we are.

2. The New Spirituality worldview opens a Pandora's box of demonic deceptions and dangers and leaves the New Spirituality person without defense. Satan himself disguises himself as "an angel of light" (2 Corinthians 11:14). Further, the "altered state of conscious" desires by these spiritual seekers are deemed

beyond reason. As such, irrationalism is welcomed and sanity is put at risk. Biblically, we are called to love God with all our minds, not to leave them behind in mystical experiences (Matthew 22:37-40; Romans 12:1-2).

3. Reincarnation, so loved by New Spirituality practitioners as giving spiritual potential, is unbiblical and illogical. We are given one life to live before God. Then we face judgment (Hebrews 9:27). Those who are forgiven by Christ will be resurrected for the new heaven and new earth (Revelation 21-22). Those whose sins are not forgiven will face a resurrection unto damnation (Daniel 12:2; John 3:16-17).

But practitioners say reincarnation is backed up by the evidence of "past life regressions" in which one is hypnotized and facts from previous lives are extracted through questions. But hypnosis is not a reliable guide to events in this life, let alone other lives! Testimony from "past life regressions" is better explained by other factors, including demonic intervention.

The morality of karma and reincarnation makes no sense either. Practitioners of the New Spirituality think we can learn from karma and reincarnation to become more spiritual. Although some claim that previous lives can be remembered through hypnotic regression (for which there is no evidence), the standard theories think that karma works fine without the knowledge of previous lives. But if we are punished or rewarded without any knowledge of why this is so, there is no way we can learn from these karmic experiences. If a child is punished for being Adolph Hitler in a previous life but never learns this fact, how could that be just? Even worse, how could Adolph Hitler and a female child *be the same person* when they are so different? It makes no sense.

New Spirituality, Old Lie

The New Spirituality movement should challenge us to reach out to those who are spiritually deceived. When we "test the spirits" (1 John 4:1-6), we find that the New Spirituality embodies the spirit of error, an ancient and perennial error of trying to find salvation apart from the one true God revealed in Christ and the Bible (Genesis 3:1-6). We must seek wisdom and courage from the Holy Spirit in order to witness to His saving truth to those in darkness.

Douglas Groothuis (PhD, University of Oregon) is professor of philosophy and heads the Apologetics and Ethics MA program at Denver Seminary. He is the author of numerous books, including *Unmasking the New Age*, *Confronting the New Age*, and *Christian Apologetics*. He has written for scholarly journals such as *Religious Studies*, *Sophia*, *Research in Philosophy and Technology*, and *Philosophia Christi* as well as for popular magazines such as *Christianity Today*, *Christian Counseling Today*, and *Philosophy Now*.

21

Atheism and Agnosticism

Paul Copan and Benjamin B. DeVan

In *Wishful Thinking: A Seeker's ABC*, Presbyterian minister and Pulitzer Prize finalist Frederick Buechner defines an agnostic as "someone who doesn't know for sure whether there really is a God. That is some people all of the time and all people some of the time."[1]

Another Presbyterian pastor, John Ortberg, concedes in his book *Know Doubt*, "After I die, if it all turns out to be true...death is defeated, the roll is called up yonder and there I am—there is a part of me that will be surprised. What do you know? It's all true after all."[2]

Mother Teresa, a Catholic saint who worked among the sick and poor in Calcutta, recurrently perceived God as absent.[3] Likewise, when an interviewer asked 74-year-old Billy Graham what he hoped people would say about him when he died, he replied that he mainly wanted to hear God say, "Well done, good and faithful servant." However, he followed up with, "But I'm not sure I'm going to hear it."[4]

Nearly everyone doubts and questions whether God is real. Emotions, intuitions, mood, circumstances, and relationships all play a role.[5] One may encounter friends, family, colleagues, and authority figures who disbelieve, raising troubling intellectual difficulties.

In the Bible, numerous people voiced hurt, perplexity, or probing inquiries to God. They include Abraham, Moses, Naomi, Hannah, Job, the psalmists, Jeremiah, Habakkuk, and Jesus's mother, Mary.[6] Jesus quoted Psalm 22 from the cross: "My God, my God, why have you forsaken me?"[7] The very name "Israel" means "wrestler with God."[8] Yet each of these biblical characters demonstrated faith in God that was deeper than his or her doubts.

By contrast, some people who are more settled in their uncertainty about God identify consistently as agnostics. Still others describe themselves as atheists who are confident that there is no God. This chapter explores agnosticism (not knowing) and atheism (without God). We confront definitions, probe history, and ask whether approaching atheism and/or agnosticism as a religion is productive. Suggesting principles for fruitful relationships, we uncover conflicts and surprising commonalities uniting Christians, atheists, and agnostics.

As statistics go, atheist sociologist Phil Zuckerman estimated in 2007 that there are between 500 and 750 million nonbelievers in God worldwide.[9] A 2008 International

Social Survey Programme omitted Asian countries such as China but calculated over 200 million atheists and agnostics in 40 countries in Europe, the Western Hemisphere, and Japan.[10] In 2013, *The Oxford Handbook of Atheism* projected 23 million atheists and 164 million nonreligious people in North America, combining Canada, the Caribbean, Mexico, and the United States.[11] By 2025, *The World Christian Database* predicts about 142 million atheists and 707 million agnostics globally.[12]

Definitions

One difficulty with quantifying the number of atheists and agnostics is the diverse ways that these are understood. Examples permeate *The Oxford Handbook of Atheism*, a nearly 800-page reference book with mostly atheist contributors. Its coeditors first define atheism as the absence of belief in a God or gods.[13] Then one of the editors, Catholic Stephen Bullivant, goes on to conflate atheism with skepticism, freethinking, and nonbelief generally, proposing strands of atheism in some major world religions. Bullivant later quotes Alister McGrath's stricter definition of atheism as a principled and informed decision to reject belief in God, adding philosophical claims that the word *God* is meaningless, an idea also known as "ignosticism," "igtheism," or "theological noncognitivism."[14] Bullivant amplifies these ambiguities by advising that "atheist" could encompass disbelievers in Christian or other concepts of God who believe in alternative gods or supernatural phenomena.[15]

Difficulties arise with each characterization. Is atheism synonymous with skepticism? A believer in God can be just as skeptical about many things as an atheist. What about the connection between atheism and freethinking? Jews, Christians, and other religious practitioners can freely follow the evidence where it leads. Humanism? Yet Christian, Renaissance, and other humanistic philosophies are not inherently atheist. Secularism? A person who is politically secular, is against theocracy, or identifies as religiously unaffiliated or spiritual but not religious might still believe in God.[16] Evangelical Christians are notorious for communicating their faith in God not as a "religion" but as a "relationship."[17]

In the same way, agnostics and atheists are not the only ones who rebuke what they see as ridiculous or reckless religious practices. The Hebrew prophets, Jesus, and Jesus's disciples were relentlessly critical of idolatries and injustices, as were in other ways Siddhartha Gautama (the Buddha), Confucius, Gandhi, the Muslim Prophet Muhammad, and countless others.

A second complication is defining atheism as "an *absence* of belief in the existence of a God or gods." This corrals agnostics into the atheist fold, potentially against their will. Must agnostics stand by default with atheists who actively reject God? The same dilemma is intrinsic to former atheist Antony Flew's conjoining of "negative" atheists, who lack a definite belief in God, with "positive" atheists, who intentionally deny God.[18] *The Oxford Handbook of Atheism* documents how American agnostics have been reluctant to identify as atheists.[19]

Third, if atheism involves the denial of some concepts about God while making room for others, or other gods, this appears to dilute the term "atheist" beyond recognition. It brings to mind Richard Dawkins's needling in *The God Delusion* that most of his audience was atheist with regard to "Zeus, Apollo, Amon Ra, Mithras, Baal, and Thor, Wotan, the Golden Calf, and the

Flying Spaghetti Monster. I just go one God further."[20]

On such a reckoning, one can fathom how ancient Romans charged early Christians with atheism for refusing to honor the Romans gods, but then the Romans would have been rival atheists repudiating the Christian God. Every skeptic, critic, or disbeliever in a veritable multitude of theologies, together with polytheists who believe in gods and goddesses but not one God, could all be atheists. The burgeoning prevalence of atheism would expand exponentially without any prevailing consensus about what atheists actually disbelieve.[21]

Pitfalls from this absence of clarity are not limited to academic reference books. A number of years ago, I (Paul) was speaking at an open forum at Worcester Polytechnic Institute in Massachusetts. After finishing my lecture, one student stood up and proclaimed, "The reason I'm an atheist is that there aren't any good reasons to believe in God." I told him, "You should be an agnostic then. It's possible that God exists even if no good reasons for His existence are available to us." I then proceeded to ask what kind of agnostic he was.

The *Popular Handbook of World Religions* attempts straightforward definitions while acknowledging authentic diversity among those who identify as atheists or agnostics. We define a "soft" or "weak" agnostic as someone who consistently contends that she or he is unsure whether God is real. The famous journalist Larry King once explained himself as this type of "I don't know" person.[22] King qualifies that he does not mean that he does not care whether God exists, nor does he insist that other people cannot know. His agnosticism is provisional, modest, and open.

Comedienne Sarah Silverman is more vehement as a "hard" or "strong" agnostic. She reproaches anyone she sees as overconfident in his belief for or against God: "Atheists have that same chip on their shoulder that people who feel like their religion is the only right thing have. It's to know something, to think you know something *definitively* that, I feel, we as mere mortal humans can't possibly know...I'm agnostic. I don't know, and neither do you!"[23]

Hard agnostics display further distinctions among themselves. One could conjecture that no one knows *for now* if God exists, but perhaps some or all sufficiently intelligent creatures in *the future* will know. Or one could offer that the hard agnostic should speak for herself: *She* may not know, but why demand that others cannot know? What is the justification for claiming that one cannot know God exists? Another could claim that it is impossible to know whether God exists or that it is *theoretically* possible to know, even if no one will *actually* know. Illustrating the first option is philosopher Bertrand Russell's self-assured "Not enough evidence," which he said in reply to how he would justify his earthly disbelief if he were to meet God after death.[24] Compatible with either of the remaining attitudes is Dawkins appealing to Mark Twain: "I do not fear death. I had been dead for billions and billions of years before I was born and had not suffered the slightest inconvenience."[25] Although one's previous nonexistence can't properly be called "death," we understand the point that, presumably, one cannot know whether God is real or not if one is not conscious to know.

Positive atheists closer to McGrath's definition also fluctuate in their intensity. Some say that nothing conceivable could change their minds about God, while others profess that they are open to fresh evidence.[26] Dawkins claims to be "6.9" on a scale of 1 to 7 in his certainty.[27] Antireligious or "antitheist" atheists also tend to exhibit more fury and fervor than apathetic atheists or agnostics—"apatheists"—who say that they are indifferent or passive in their unbelief.

One theory closely aligned with atheism is "philosophical naturalism." In the interview for this chapter, Graham Oppy identifies as both an atheist and a naturalist. Professor and media-savvy atheist Carl Sagan (1934–1996) put the thrust of philosophical naturalism this way: "The cosmos is all that is or ever was or ever will be."[28] For Sagan, there was no reality except *physical* or *material* reality. Sagan maintained that religious ideas simply propped up "a God of the Gaps" by fabricating explanations for physical marvels that we do not yet understand.[29]

Connected though not identical to philosophical naturalism is "scientism." A "soft" or "weak" scientism maintains that science is the *best* or *surest* path to true knowledge but permits the possibility of other sources.[30] "Hard" or "strong" scientism declares that science is "the only begetter of truth," to use Harvard biologist Richard Lewontin's phrase.[31] Hard scientism is frequently coupled with aspirations that science has no limits: It will comprehensively describe everything that exists and eventually solve every quandary. As we will see, imagining that science will enable the possibility of omniscience and omnipotence is not necessary to practicing science with excellence.

The next section expands on diversities among atheists and agnostics. *Misotheists* (*mis* means "ill, mistaken, wrong") and *dystheists* (*dys* means "bad, ill") admittedly hate God.[32] Other atheists or agnostics counterintuitively concede that belief in God is in certain respects desirable to disbelief.[33] Existentialist atheists have argued that consistent atheism equals despair, while New Atheists celebrate their atheism as liberating. Some atheists assault specific religions such as Christianity or Islam, while others aim to undermine anything that they identify as religious. Still others hold to atheism or agnosticism like a religion.[34]

Snapshot of Atheism: Interview with Graham Oppy[35]

To help give a picture of atheism, we interviewed Graham Oppy, professor of philosophy and director of the Philosophy Graduate Program at Monash University, Australia.

Q1: Can one identify as an atheist or agnostic while also identifying as religious in some sense?

Oppy: I take it that atheists believe that there are no gods and agnostics suspend judgment on the question of whether there are gods. Some religions maintain that there are no gods or suspend judgment on the question of whether there are gods. Full participants in those religions are either atheists or agnostics. For example, there are branches of Buddhism that are atheistic or agnostic, though, of course, there are other branches of Buddhism that are theistic.

Setting considerations about atheistic or agnostic religions to one side, it is also worth noting that one can make a cultural identification with a theistic religion even if one is an atheist or an agnostic. Thus there are atheists and agnostics who identify as Jews, Christians, Muslims, Hindus, Buddhists, and so forth.

Q2: What do you think are humanity's biggest problems and greatest assets?

Oppy: Our greatest assets—like our greatest weaknesses—are products of our biological and cultural evolution. We have significant general and emotional intelligence, we belong to long-standing social and cultural traditions, we are driven to lead collectively meaningful lives, and so on.

The biggest problems we face include global warming, global degradation of arable soils, global water pollution, global exhaustion of critical resources, global disappearance of insects, global disappearance of marine life, global agricultural failure, local and global war, failure of global financial markets, globally inequitable distribution of resources, failure to establish global governance, widespread failure of responsible governance, and so forth.

Q3: What resources do your beliefs and community offer to address these problems?

Oppy: I'm a naturalist. I believe that natural reality exhausts causal reality: The only causal things are natural things. Atheism is a consequence of my kind of naturalism: If there were gods, they would be nonnatural causal agents. Note that my naturalism, on its own, entails nothing about my evaluative views: my ethics, my politics, my aesthetics, etc. Nor does it entail anything about my views concerning abstract objects. One view that is close to a consequence of my naturalism is that minded things are late and local: The only things that think, and feel, and perceive, and so forth are relatively recently evolved biological organisms (and, perhaps, artifacts made by such organisms).

I'm a naturalist of a virtue ethical bent. I belong to a range of communities. One of the most important resources required for addressing the problems I listed above is the ability to recognize that these kinds of problems are the biggest problems that we face. Consider global warming. The window for effective action to minimize and mitigate the effects of global warming is rapidly closing. We need our political and industrial leaders to recognize the need for effective action right now. Communities to which I belong are working to try to get this message where it needs to go.

Q4: How do your beliefs about what ultimately matters help you live a fulfilling life?

Oppy: I believe, very roughly, (a) flourishing human beings are members of communities that aim to bring about the flourishing of their members, and (b) flourishing members of communities exercise virtue in pursuit of worthwhile individual and collective ends. What ultimately matters is that we live in ways that conduce to the flourishing of the members of the communities to which we belong, ourselves included.

Q5: What do you wish other people understood about your worldview?

Oppy: My book *Naturalism and Religion* opens with a discussion of common misconceptions about naturalism.[36] I do not really have anything to add to what I have already said there. It is probably worth saying that there are many kinds of "other people." Some understand my worldview as well as or better than I do. Others have no interest in understanding any worldview other than their own.

Q6: What do you think will happen when you die?

Oppy: When I am dead, I will no longer exist. I will be survived by family and friends. In turn, they, too, will die, to be survived by their families and friends. If all goes well, there will be many further iterations: many future generations that get to live flourishing human lives. But we will not be around forever; at some point in the future, the last human being will die. Much further in the future, the expanding universe will be very cold and empty except for an occasional blip of radiation. This is not something to be feared or mourned. The value of our lives is not in the least bit diminished by what happens in that very distant future.

Q7: What do you think of Jesus?

Oppy: I doubt that we know very much about the historical Jesus. What we do know is gleaned from a small number of not independent writings of uncertain genre produced between 30 and 80 years after his death. (We learn next to nothing about the historical Jesus from Paul's letters.) There are many conjectures about the sources for these writings; it is not at all clear which of those conjectures should be believed.

Perhaps the main contours of what we know are something like this: Jesus was a Jewish preacher who engaged in debates about how to follow God, taught parables, and gained followers; he was arrested by Jewish authorities, tried, and turned over to the Roman government for execution; after his death, his preaching was continued by his followers. Certainly, there is nothing in this account—or in any elaboration of these kinds of details—at which a naturalist must scruple.

A Short History of Atheists and Agnostics: People and Trends

We find themes related to atheism going back to ancient times. From one angle, atheists manifest a long trajectory of critique, disbelief, and dissent. Biblical prophets criticized hypocrisy, injustice, and what they denounced as false gods and false concepts of God. Elijah ridiculed the priests of Baal (1 Kings 18:27-29), vividly foreshadowing atheist disdain toward all deities.

Less sympathetically, the authors of Psalms 14:1, 53:1, and possibly 10:4 warn fools who say in their hearts, "There is no God." Atheists often express indignation at this statement, as though the biblical authors thought atheists were intellectually deficient. This interpretation is mistaken. Few would deny that intelligent atheists exist.

Evangelical professor of biblical interpretation at Eden Theological Seminary J. Clinton McCann argues that these psalms are less about rebuking philosophical or intellectual atheism and more about reproaching evildoers who say that no God keeps them accountable.[37] We add that the "fool" or "crass person" (*nabal*) acts as though God is removed, uninvolved, and uninterested. The fool is thinking, "God is not here." So this "scoundrel" thinks she can get away with committing injustice, since God won't do anything about it. In Psalm 10, the very one who says, "There is no God" (verse 4) claims, "God has forgotten, he has hidden his face, he will never see it" (verse 11). For him, to "renounce God" is to tell God, "You will not call to account" (verse 13).

As a consequence, to malign everyone as a "fool" who fears, doubts, or is persuaded that God does not exist risks freighting the psalms beyond their intent. Some people foolishly or viciously deny God's existence, but these need not exhaust the reasons atheists disbelieve. Since Jesus cautioned against slandering people as fools, His followers are wise neither to label every atheist a fool nor to ignore foolishness by atheists or anyone else, including themselves.[38]

Moving across the Mediterranean, we note that perhaps the earliest Greek uses of *atheos* are found in Plato's *Apology* § 26c and *Laws* § 12.967a.[39] Classical Greek atheists spurned the gods of the city-state or altogether denied deities of any sort. Plato recalls a charge of atheism against Socrates that he repudiated.[40]

The philosopher Epicurus (341–270 BC) was not necessarily atheist in either sense, but his *On Nature* § 12 resembles later atheists by associating "raving lunatics" with worship and belief in gods.[41] Epicurus's insanity rhetoric predates Dawkins's *The God Delusion* by over two millennia.

Christopher Hitchens's anthology, *The Portable Atheist: Essential Readings for the Nonbeliever*, hails Lucretius (ca. 98–55 BC) and his poem "On the Nature of Things" as a distillation of a materialist or naturalist philosophy, emphasizing physical reality over the supernatural. Hitchens reproduces selections from Lucretius's poem (books I–V), which also narrate repugnant religious rituals, such as a father killing his virgin daughters.[42]

A few decades after Lucretius, the Roman biographer Plutarch (ca. AD 45–120) positioned atheism as at least preferable to worshiping a malicious deity. One paraphrase renders Plutarch's *On Superstition* § 10 as "Better to admit no God than to grovel to an ogre."[43]

21A. Marble bust of Epicurus, author of an influential problem-of-evil argument. Photo by Interstate295. Revisited at English Wikipedia. Public domain.

Soon after Plutarch, Syrian satirist Lucian of Samosata (ca. AD 125–185) forecasted future debates between atheists and their critics. In Lucian's *Scholia*, one interlocutor, "Damis," reviles a brutal Scythian cult as epitomizing the human tendency toward superstition. Damis's foil, "Arethas," counters that conflating nobler forms of religion with cultic distortions was like mistaking an ignorant servant for a master or judging all paintings by an amateur's daub.[44]

Early Christians such as Ignatius of Antioch (AD 35–117) and Polycarp (AD 69–155) refused to honor Roman gods and were subsequently accused of atheism. Receiving the same charge prompted Justin Martyr (AD 100–165) to reply, "We are atheists, so far as gods of this sort are concerned, but not with respect to the most true God."[45] We could add that various modern philosophers of religion refer to this rendering of God in terms like "the maximally great Being" or "the greatest conceivable Being."

Jains and some Buddhists from South Asia are intermittently cast as atheists who reject a Creator God, though not necessarily all gods. Noted Buddhist philosopher Shantideva (ca. AD 600s–700s) assailed the very idea of God.[46] Around the same time, the Jain scripture *Mahapurana* 4:16 inverted the thrust of the aforementioned psalmists: "Foolish men declare that Creator made the world."[47]

In an Islamic context, medieval Syrian

poet Al-Ma'arri (AD 973–1057) depicted religious people as lacking intelligence and intelligent people as lacking religion.[48] Hitchens acclaims Persian poet Omar Khayyam (AD 1048–1131) from the same era. Reminiscent of the Sadducees in Matthew 22, Khayyam lyricized,

> Men talk of heaven,
> There is no heaven but here;
> Men talk of hell,
> There is no hell but here.[49]

Research into ancient atheism is ongoing.[50]

Moving toward the modern era, Sir John Cheke in his *On Superstition* (1540) probably coined the English term "atheism."[51] Rather than explicit disbelief or even unbelief in God, Cheke's definition more closely resembled deism with its distant God who does not interfere with nature.

Across the English Channel, the French priest (*abbé*) Jean Meslier (1694–1759) wrote piercingly about his private atheism centuries ahead of contemporary clergy and ex-clergy announcing their deconversions to atheism.[52] Meslier's writings were published posthumously.

Prior to the French Revolution, French *philosophe* Denis Diderot (1713–1784) abandoned his family's religious roots to later become Karl Marx's favorite prose author.[53] In addition to assailing clergy and the monarchy, Diderot savaged philosophical arguments for God from design, particularly those set forth a century earlier by his fellow countryman René Descartes.

Romantic philosopher Jean-Jacques Rousseau recounted how French atheists under Baron d'Holbach (1723–1789), a popularizer of Diderot, debated how the observable world owed its order to chance rather than to Providence.[54] Reminiscent of Muslims with Islam, d'Holbach decreed that atheism is every person's default from infancy: "All children are born Atheists; they have no idea of God."[55] D'Holbach paradoxically provided analogous metaphors to belittle belief in God, linking it to the childhood of the human race: "It was in the lap of ignorance, in the season of alarm and calamity that mankind ever formed his first notions of the Divinity."[56]

D'Holbach's colleague Jacques-André Naigeon (1738–1810) echoed Plutarch by portraying God as the ultimate tyrant and belief in God as hampering progress, happiness, peace, and reciprocity.[57] Another French materialist, Julien Offray de La Mettrie (1709–1751), described a similar view, which he heard in a conversation with a fellow skeptic: "'The universe will never be happy, unless it is atheistic'...No more theological wars, no more soldiers of religion—such terrible soldiers! Nature infected with sacred poison, would regain its rights and its purity."[58]

Historian Edward Gibbon (1737–1794) described d'Holbach's coterie of conversationalists: "With the bigotry of dogmatists," they pronounced everyone "must either be an atheist or a fool."[59] Gibbon himself attempted a scientific or secular study of religion, as did pantheist philosopher Baruch (or Benedict) Spinoza (1632–1677) with the Bible a century prior.[60] Weakly deistic David Hume (1711–1776), in his posthumous *Dialogues Concerning Natural Religion*, criticized arguments for God's existence and miracles in ways that later atheists emulated. Praised as the "prince of agnostics" by biologist Thomas Huxley, Hume marshaled natural disorders, pain, and suffering as evidence against an all-powerful, benevolent theistic God.[61]

Early twenty-first-century atheists have tried to co-opt for the atheist cause deists such as Thomas Jefferson (1743–1826) and

Thomas Paine (1733–1809).[62] They suggest that such thinkers *would* have been atheists if they lived long enough to read Charles Darwin (1809–1882). They also suggest that Einstein, who seemed to be a pantheist, was disgruntled by religion and held an affinity for atheism. Hitchens gathers enough quotes from Einstein to instigate debate.[63]

In nineteenth-century Germany, Ludwig Feuerbach (1804–1872), whom Sigmund Freud lauded as his favorite philosopher, went beyond Gibbon to rationalize away religion as a purely human creation.[64] Karl Marx (1813–1883) drew on Feuerbach to classify criticism of religion as prerequisite to all criticism. Marx would become a central pillar for twentieth-century militant atheism, interpreting religion as "the sigh of the oppressed" and "the *opium* of the people. The *abolition* of religion as the illusory happiness of the people is required for their *real* happiness."[65]

In Britain, "Darwin's bulldog" Thomas H. Huxley (1825–1895) pioneered the term "agnostic."[66] Huxley's "X Club" stirred up ideas of a war between religion and science. Across the Atlantic, New York University School of Medicine founder John William Draper prepared a popular salvo, *History of the Conflict Between Religion and Science* (1874), and Cornell University cofounder Andrew Dickson White wrote *A History of the Warfare of Science with Theology in Christendom* (1896).[67] Auguste Comte (1798–1857) and A.J. Ayer (1910–1989) also credited science coupled with logic as the sole arbiters of true, meaningful knowledge.[68]

Robert Ingersoll (1833–1899), whom American atheist and secularist Susan Jacoby memorializes in *The Great Agnostic*, was an outspoken orator who pitted natural selection against religion, especially Christianity.[69] Ingersoll challenges,

> Write the name of Charles Darwin on the one hand and the name of every theologian who ever lived on the other, and from that name has come more light to the world than from all of those. His doctrine of evolution, his doctrine of the survival of the fittest, his doctrine of the origin of the species, has removed in every thinking mind the last vestige of orthodox Christianity.[70]

Darwin himself saw belief in God and evolution as compatible. He added near the end of his life, "I have never been an atheist in the sense of denying the existence of a God—I think that generally...not always, that an agnostic would be the most correct description of my state."[71]

The late nineteenth through the early

21B. Thomas Henry Huxley, "Darwin's bulldog" and coiner of the word *agnosticism*. Photo by MMR. Public domain.

twenty-first centuries facilitated fresh forms of atheism. Psychoanalyst Sigmund Freud (1856–1939) demeaned belief in God as childish wishful thinking. Like d'Holbach, Freud cast religions as infantile neuroses that carried "the stamp of the times in which they originated, the ignorant childhood days of the human race."[72]

Bertrand Russell (1872–1970) was another public intellectual who leveraged illness as a metaphor for religion as "a disease born of fear" and "a source of untold misery."[73] Russell set the pattern for his life as a teenager: "My views on religion remain those that I acquired at the age of 16. I consider all forms of religion not only false but harmful."[74]

In contrast, existentialist atheists such as Albert Camus (1913–1960), Jean-Paul Sartre (1905–1980), and Friedrich Nietzsche (1843–1900) were deeply affected by atheism's nihilistic cost.[75] Sartre mourned that humanity is forlorn if God does not exist because

21C. Bertrand Russell, author of the influential *Why I Am Not a Christian*. Unknown, Mondadori Publishers. Public domain.

neither within nor without do we find "anything to cling to."[76] Nietzsche brooded on suicide, despite predicting that superhumans or *Übermenschen* would rise following God's demise.[77] For such existentialists, if God is dead, the proper reaction is to stare solemnly into the abyss. Even Russell foresaw that all human achievements would be buried in the debris of a ruined universe: "Only...on the firm foundation of unyielding despair, can the soul's habitation be safely built."[78]

Atheists might prefer that we omit the following, but a historical overview must mention militant atheism in twentieth-century Soviet, Maoist, and other communist states. Marx's heirs in Russia, such as Vladimir Lenin (1870–1924), Leon Trotsky (1879–1940), and Joseph Stalin (1878–1953), as well as Mao Zedong (1893–1976) in China, Pol Pot (1925–1998) in Cambodia (then Kampuchea), and the Democratic People's Republic of North Korea waged violent revolutions suppressing religion and killing millions. On this, we recommend as further resources *The Black Book of Communism*, David Aikman's brief *Delusion of Disbelief*, and Aleksandr Solzhenitsyn's (1918–2008) Nobel Prize–winning *Gulag Archipelago*.[79]

Sociologist and atheist activist Phil Zuckerman distinguishes coercive atheism with its freer forms, proliferating with less government interference in countries such as Sweden and the Netherlands. Zuckerman rebukes totalitarian atheism for poor economic development, censorship, corruption, and its correlation with depression. He prefers "organic atheism," proceeding without compulsion in healthier, wealthier, more educated societies.[80] We disagree that atheism naturally nurtures prosperity but heartily uphold the freedom of conscience where atheism and differing beliefs about God are both legally protected and civilly acceptable.[81]

Historians might highlight other twentieth-century streams feeding the atheist river. Madalyn Murray O'Hair's (1919–1995) nonprofit organization American Atheists, which was founded in 1963, supported *Abington School District v. Schempp* (1963) to the US Supreme Court, which ruled that mandatory prayer and Bible reading in American public schools was unconstitutional.

Rhetorically stimulated by Nietzsche, a second rivulet—sometimes called "Christian atheism," "theothanatology," or radical "Death of God" theology—descends from ancient Patripassianism, the Christian heresy that God the Father died on the cross. Theologian Thomas J.J. Altizer and others in the 1960s hypothesized that instead of raising Jesus to life, God died after being crucified as Jesus.[82] On Easter weekend, *Time* magazine posted this on the April 8, 1966, cover in red ink: "Is God Dead?" "Death of God" theology is not yet dead itself but continues as an intellectual niche.

A third tributary, "postmodernism," is not necessarily atheist in its questioning of grand narratives and worldviews—for example, the postmodern Jewish theist Emmanuel Levinas (1906–1995). At the same time, many prominent postmodern philosophers were atheists, such as Michel Foucault (1926–1984), Jean-François Lyotard (1924–1998), and Richard Rorty (1931–2007). Jacques Derrida (1930–2004) commented more coyly, "I quite rightly pass for an atheist."[83] Critics, including other atheists, have judged postmodern philosophy to be incoherent and impracticable due to its renouncing objective truth as well as undermining science and logic.[84]

Bernard Schweizer sheds light on a fourth source in *Hating God: The Untold Story of Misotheism* (2011). Though he overstates the distinction, Schweizer differentiates atheists from historic and literary personalities who believed in but hated God. Yet reviling God sincerely or in pretense is not inconsistent with atheism. Atheists do not inevitably hate God, though some do, even if as a deleterious phantom. Cambridge professor C.S. Lewis (1898–1963) recollected his atheist phase: "I was at this time living, like so many Atheists or Anti-theists, in a whirl of contradictions. I maintained God did not exist. I was also very angry at God for not existing."[85] The notorious libertine Marquis de Sade (1740–1814) also held forth in verse,

> Yes, vain illusion, my soul detests you.
> And I protest that, in order to further
> convince you,
> I wish that for a moment you
> could exist
> To have the pleasure to better
> insult you.[86]

Insulting God and people who believe in God continues with early twenty-first-century New Atheism, spearheaded by the "Four Horsemen"—Richard Dawkins, Daniel Dennett, Christopher Hitchens, and Sam Harris.[87] Although none of these men coined the phrase "New Atheism," galloping in their hoofprints advanced a horde of would-be rough riders who received, donned, or cloaked themselves in the New Atheist mantle.[88] Eloquent, educated, and provocative, the Four Horsemen and their followers have labored to revitalize atheism for the twenty-first century through their bestselling books, rallies, speeches, debates, and media.[89]

Unlike ivory tower academics, New Atheists take atheism to the masses by writing for the public as well as for scholars. They break with existentialist angst by marketing atheism as more rewarding and jubilant than other approaches to life. Yet neither do they take up the full-fledged libertinism of a Marquis de Sade or the selfishness of an Oscar Wilde's *Dorian Gray*.[90]

Against postmodern relativism, New Atheists try to commandeer the moral high ground by arguing that atheism motivates superior ethics over its competitors. Diverging from hard scientism, Dawkins and Hitchens commemorate art, music, literature, and other forms of human creativity as luminous qualities of a new Enlightenment. They extol all this and more for the sake of a thriving humanity, affecting righteous indignation against God as they do so.[91]

A charitable summary could construe the Four Horsemen as supporting Jesus's second greatest commandment absent the first: "Love your neighbor as yourself" without "Love the Lord your God with all your heart, soul, mind,

21D. Richard Dawkins at the 2012 Reason Rally in Washington, DC, where he encouraged this response to Catholics who believe in transubstantiation: "Mock them! Ridicule them! In public!" Photo by S. Pakhrin from DC, USA (https://creativecommons.org/licenses/by/2.0).

and strength."[92] Less charitably, one atheist scholar observed that such atheists who are indebted to religious ethics for their outrage supply not an alternative to religion "but rather a degenerate and unwitting version of it."[93]

Not every twenty-first-century atheist or agnostic is so belligerent. The next section surveys those who advocate for atheism as a religion or an expression of religious diversity.

Is Atheism Akin to a Religious Position? Can Atheists Be Religious?

Even though atheists reject belief in God, some yearn to partner in interreligious dialogue or projects. Paul Chaffee reports how atheist protesters at a post-9/11 interspiritual service complained to the San Francisco Interfaith Council, "Why didn't you invite us?...We're the atheists! We're the humanists. No one invited us."[94]

Including atheism as a religious conviction or a position oriented to religion is implied by previous academic literature such as *The Oxford Handbook of Religious Diversity*, reserving its final chapter for atheist Michael Ruse.[95] In *Science and Religion Around the World*, John Hedley Brooke and Ronald L. Numbers insert a chapter on "Unbelief" amid others on Buddhism, Judaism, Christianity, and Islam as well as Chinese, Indic, and African religions.[96] In the late twentieth century, William Lloyd Newell christened Marx, Freud, and Nietzsche "secular magi" whose philosophies interact constructively with Christian theology.[97] These are just a few examples of religious scholars welcoming atheists and agnostics to the roundtable.

So what does religion entail? Anthropologists and missiologists have articulated religion as core motivations and feelings, fundamental values and allegiances, overriding authorities, and frameworks for interpreting experiences and ideas.[98] We add that religions can stipulate behaviors, codes, creeds, individual or communal rituals, and beliefs connected with spiritual beings or forces. Moreover, religions often claim to mediate encounters with the transcendent.

While many atheists or agnostics repudiate nonphysical or spiritual forces, their belief parallels religion when it serves as a deeply held conviction, a chief allegiance or fundamental value, an organizing belief about reality, the basis for awe at the "infinite" universe, or a prevailing attitude for pursuing relationships and social activism. Atheists persuaded by atheism may become deconversion missionaries who recruit others.[99] Dawkins mentions several of the above incentives when he brands himself "a deeply religious non-believer."[100]

Atheists in the nineteenth, twentieth, and twenty-first centuries have struggled to harness what they consider to be pragmatic elements of religion for the sake of atheism. Realizing the power of ritual, August Comte in the nineteenth century strove to reinforce atheism by casting humanity in place of God as a "Great Being" worthy of worship. Comte anticipated atheist scriptures, dogmas, liturgies, saints, missionaries, priests, cathedrals, and metropolitans. He envisioned churches with thrice-daily devotions and no fewer than nine sacraments. Comte's mostly dormant chapels and temples still linger in France and Brazil.[101]

Soviet atheists in the twentieth century supplemented the Russian Orthodox Church with a winter festival, red stars atop trees, Grandfather Frost (*Dedushka Moroz*) giving children presents, replacement ceremonies for christenings and marriages, the postmortem apotheosis (exaltation) of Lenin reminiscent of an Orthodox saint, and pilgrimages to Lenin's tomb on which is inscribed "Savior of the World." Songs praised Lenin, who "did not die," paradoxically preaching that Soviet science would resurrect him.[102]

In the twenty-first century, humanistic atheists have sought to invest atheism with legal and social religious status. The British Humanist Association and United States Humanist Society accredit celebrants for naming babies, godparent liturgies, weddings, civil partnerships, funerals, and memorials.[103] Self-proclaimed atheist Gretta Vosper of Toronto's West Hill United Church pastors one congregation of humanists, nontheists, religious secularists, atheists, freethinkers, and different faith families. She says that what binds them is exploring life on a deeper level.[104]

In higher education, Stanford University atheists have located as "faith-based" groups in Stanford Associated Religions and the Religious Life Office.[105] The Harvard Humanist Community positions itself alongside Harvard religious life, retaining offices at the Harvard Memorial Church. One Harvard humanist titled his first book *Faitheist: How an Atheist Found Common Ground with the Religious.*[106] A second presented humanistic atheism as analogous to religion, with its shared values, fellowship, and coordinated ways of life.[107]

According to a third Harvard humanist, atheists face the same pastoral issues of death, illness, and meaning that overtly religious people do and benefit from talking to sympathetic nontheists.[108] One advocate for chaplains for atheists remembered her university years: "I could have benefited from a supervisor and group…who shared my worldview and would engage with my existential questions… They bring a sense of the sacred, of wonder and awe, to a secular context."[109]

One playfully agnostic author said atheism functions like a religion when it occupies the center of atheists' lives, governing "who they are, how they think, and with whom they associate."[110] Approximating Ninian Smart's seven dimensions of religion, atheism can undergird, underline, or orient beliefs, narratives, and stories about ultimate reality.[111] Atheists prescribe moral principles, inspire art, and conduct other initiatives. Atheists formulate ethical codes, creeds, and a "cultus," such as the Secular Seasons calendar. Explicitly atheist literature includes apologetics, polemics, de/conversion testimonies, philosophy, fiction, and film.[112] Each has its place in studying atheism and can draw on theory and methods previously applied to religion.[113]

It is also important to recognize that atheists occasionally adopt dual identities such as Buddhist-atheist or Jewish-atheist. Atheism, like a world religion, is globally distributed with competing factions, schools of thought, and quasi denominations.

Many of the practices that atheists modify have been heretofore associated with religion. This does not mean that atheism or agnosticism *must* be categorized as religious, yet neither does setting oneself in opposition to religion mean that one does not partake in something like it.[114]

In our chapter on religious pluralism in this volume (chapter 19), we suggest seven overarching principles for fruitful relationships among practitioners of the world's religions. Based on the perspectives above and below, we hope that sympathetic atheists and agnostics will joyfully collaborate in each of these ventures as well.

Cultivating Fruitful Relationships Among Christians, Atheists, and Agnostics

How ought Christians interact with atheists who are made in God's image yet who deny that God exists? Can principles from our chapter on pluralism for fostering meaningful relationships among religiously diverse people incorporate atheists and agnostics? Reviewing the guidelines we outline there, we discover atheists who resonate with each of them here.

First is universal dignity and worth. The *Humanist Manifesto III*, signed by Dawkins, is one atheist/agnostic statement that affirms universal human dignity.[115] Unfortunately, Christians have not reliably defended this for atheists. One historic example is the execution of "Lucilio" Vanini Cesare in 1619 by the Parliament of Toulouse, France, for the crimes of *lèse majesté* (speaking ill of royalty) and atheism.[116] The magistrate recalled cutting out Cesare's tongue, whereupon Cesare "let out a horrible cry that you could say resembles a cow bellowing...The shout proved him to be an animal in death."[117] Though we see the image of God rather than valueless naturalistic processes furnishing a more solid basis for human dignity and human rights, Christians must fight the dehumanization of anyone.

The second guideline is the support for universal rights such as the freedom of religion, speech, and conscience for everyone. Again, there are plenty of examples where this guideline has not been followed. In the past few centuries, both the US Constitution and European Convention have referred to religion and religious devotees without clearly specifying their freedoms to include atheists.[118] Oxford University expelled the poet Percy Bysshe Shelley in 1811 for publishing "The Necessity of Atheism." The British Parliament did the same to atheist Charles Bradlaugh in 1880 after his irregular oath swearing. Atheists as late as 2011 were pressing for the legalization of humanist weddings in Ireland, England, and Wales.[119]

Discrimination against atheists also persists in South Asia and the Middle East. Samuli Schielke mourns the 1965–1966 Indonesian genocide against communists—generally assumed to be atheists—where perhaps half a million people died.[120] In 2013, thousands of marchers in Bangladesh petitioned to arrest or hang 84 atheist bloggers.[121] In 2014, Saudi Arabia designated atheists as "terrorists," threatening them with up to 20 years in prison.[122]

There are numerous examples of atheist and agnostic endorsers of universal rights. The atheist Carl Sagan indicated his accord with human dignity and the freedom of conscience: "Every one of us is, in the cosmic perspective, precious. If a human disagrees with you, let him live. In 100 billion galaxies, you will not find another."[123]

Religious advocates for freedom of speech can affirm the sentiment frequently attributed to—and accurately describing the mindset of—the deist Voltaire (1694–1778), who is popular with atheists: "I disapprove of what you say, but I will defend to the death your right to say it."[124] As regards a free press, we can affirm the words of atheist George Orwell (1903–1950), author of popular novels *Animal Farm* and *1984*: "The journalist is unfree, and is conscious of unfreedom, when…forced to write lies or suppress what seems to him important."[125]

New Atheist A.C. Grayling is another potential ally who laments that campaigning for universal rights makes little difference in delinquent autocracies. Still, he says, stalwart defense of universal liberties will sometimes have an impact in the present and the future.[126]

The third overarching principle is the preservation of an open marketplace of ideas. If religious believers are free to share their beliefs when opportunities permit, atheists and agnostics can also be included. An open marketplace includes the right to remain silent, to decline to listen, or to listen and disagree. Yet agnostics, atheists, and Christians should all view attempts at convincing or converting each other with a spirit of love, goodwill, or genuine respect.[127] Atheist Penn Jillette goes so far as to portray evangelism as a moral imperative for anyone who believes in heaven and hell: "How much do you have to hate somebody to believe that everlasting life is possible and not tell them?"[128]

The fourth guideline for interaction is promoting constructive reciprocal critique for the sake of growth. Evangelical philosopher Merold Westphal advises Christians to read atheist books during Lent to stimulate self-examination, which leads to personal and corporate spiritual vitality.[129] Christians who strive to grow in faithfulness can benefit when atheist criticisms are partly right.[130]

Grayling is again an ally here. He invokes Plutarch's "Dinner of the Seven Wise Men" to endorse the conversational duties of keeping well informed, listening to comprehend others accurately, challenging and arguing with excellence where necessary, being open to revising one's views, and pursuing the truth with clarity.[131] These duties are valuable for interreligious dialogue as well as for productive discussions among Christians, agnostics, and atheists.

Fifth, Christians can cooperate with atheists and agnostics in common concerns without pretending that they agree on other matters. Causes on the political "right" and "left" provide opportunities for Christians and sympathetic atheists or agnostics to collaborate for the sake of justice, peacemaking, standing up for the vulnerable, and caring for the natural world. Rev. Dr. Martin Luther King Jr., for example, toiled for civil rights with secular activists such as A. Philip

Randolph, who signed the *Humanist Manifesto II*.[132] As an atheist chaplain at Harvard, Chris Stedman summoned Buddhists, Christians, Hindus, Jews, Muslims, pagans, and Sikhs: "We may not agree on the existence of God or an afterlife, but surely we can agree that life in the here and now requires that we create peaceful, collaborative ways to work and live together."[133]

The atheist Albert Camus petitioned the Jesuits, "Perhaps we cannot prevent this world from being a world in which children are tortured. But we can reduce the number of tortured children."[134] In the same spirit, Christians and atheists can also cooperate to reduce hunger, homelessness, ignorance, illness, loneliness, tribalism, tyranny, and myriad more miseries.

Yet when should Christians *not* collaborate with agnostics or atheists? Deciding what initiatives to prioritize or to oppose and with what methods are topics about which godly Christians will differ. Neither Christians nor atheists nor agnostics ought to lie back and play dead under venomous assaults, slander, or repression from any quarter. Whenever Christians and atheists clash, they can curtail uncharitable interactions by committing to universal dignity and rights, upholding an open marketplace of ideas, and supporting each other in areas of mutual concern.

A final ideal for pursuing fruitful relationships among Christians, atheists, and agnostics is "agape" love: giving devotion to others, desiring their welfare, and committing ourselves to their well-being.[135] Jesus directed His disciples to love their enemies and to pray for persecutors.[136] Not everyone approves. Hitchens thundered in protest, "Hatred, yes, I plead guilty to that...Go love your own enemies, don't be loving mine. I'll get on with the business of destroying, isolating, combatting the enemies of civilization."[137]

Must Hitchens rather than Jesus be normative for atheists? Sam Harris implicitly signals otherwise by his admiration for another rabbi, who displayed love after receiving threatening phone calls from a white supremacist. Instead of calling the police, the rabbi "heard the man out, every time he called, whatever the hour. Eventually they started having a real conversation... [and] became friends." Harris concludes, "One certainly likes to believe that such breakthroughs are possible."[138]

Agnostic Robert Ingersoll correspondingly praised Thomas Paine's example as an honorary French citizen who risked his life to fight King Louis XVI's execution: "You will find but few sublimer acts than that of Thomas Paine voting against the King's death. He, the hater of despotism, the abhorrer or monarchy...[tried] to save the life of a deposed tyrant—of a throneless king."[139]

Putting aside for the moment the sexual ethics that Chris Stedman defends, Christians and atheists can learn from the altercation he publicized below in which both sides appear to advance toward Jesus's agape love ideal for adversaries. Stedman relays that he felt at first smug and superior when self-styled missionaries accosted him by shouting, "Fags! Repent." Yet something prompted him to engage with their passion:

> Though we all remained relatively fixed in our convictions, we came to understand one another as fuller human beings instead of as mere caricatures of our sexualities or religious identities. I never saw them shout at gay people on that street corner again...There are times where personal safety is a higher priority than respectful discourse. Yet I will also always remember my night outside a gay bar, sharing stories...

with new friends who were supposed
to be enemies.[140]

How might Christians further demonstrate love for atheists or agnostics? Hitchens's answer is by leaving them alone when they ask to be.[141] Like Queen Gertrude in *Hamlet*,[142] however, Christians will object that some atheists protest too much about being left alone when the same atheists brazenly provoke disputes and confrontations.[143]

Detachment is not always the best approach. Might American atheist Madalyn Murray O'Hair have proceeded differently if Christians had been more perceptive in responding to the longing inscribed in her postdivorce diary, "Somebody, somewhere, love me"?[144]

One way Christians can show love to some agnostics or atheists is to help those who possess less economic, educational, political, or social clout than their celebrity atheist counterparts. In March 2012, Texas Christians financially assisted a local atheist firebrand, Patrick Green, after they learned that he might lose his eyesight. Flabbergasted at first, Green enthused that their generosity was so amazing that he may write a book about it: *The REAL Christians of Henderson County*.[145] Green briefly converted to Christianity, then reverted to atheism. One pastor who knew him elaborated, "I've struggled with exactly how to deal with him...[but] people nationwide saw how Christians ought to react to these situations."[146]

Al Truesdale and Keri Mitchell tell the story of a second atheist, Hitoshi (Paul) Fukue, from Japan. When Hitoshi's Tokyo school closed after an earthquake, an American professor encouraged him to enroll at Northwest Nazarene College. Hitoshi reflected on his reception there: "Never had I been in a setting where people cared so much for each other." Hitoshi was at first unable to discern any good reasons to believe in God but resolved to attend a church where the "same spirit of love greeted him." After a mystical experience, he accepted Jesus's offer of pardoning love and transforming grace. He recounted Jesus's invitation to follow Him: "This I have done, by His grace, from that day to this."[147]

Our chapter on religious pluralism (chapter 19) features the parable of the good Samaritan (Luke 10:25-37) as one example of agape love toward enemies of an opposing religious persuasion. If Jesus had spoken this parable to contemporary Christians, might He have specified an atheist taking pity, while a deacon and a bishop passed by on the other side? To atheists, would He have designated a naturalistic evolutionary biologist and a secular activist passing by the wounded traveler, while an Evangelical pastor took pity? Such scenarios are not purely hypothetical in light of Hitchens enduring a brutal beating in Beirut, just a few miles from the Jericho road in Jesus's parable.[148]

During the Cold War, the United States and many of its Christian-majority allies faced off against the officially atheist Soviet Union and its satellites in a policy of mutually assured destruction (MAD). With noticeable exceptions in Asia today, tensions among atheists, agnostics, and Christians are not at the time of this writing so noxious on the global stage. Even so, when adversaries in any conflict neglect or actively thwart universal dignity, rights, constructive critique, cooperation, and agape love, the world is worse off.

The Gospel for Agnostics and Atheists?

In her book *Nomad*, atheist Ayaan Hirsi Ali delivers a striking request. In distinction from her other bestsellers on Islamic reform and her journey to atheism, she urges Christians to love and evangelize Muslims to preempt future violence. She exhorts us to serve Muslims by building schools, hospitals, and community centers. Then she implores Christians active in interfaith dialogue to "redirect their efforts to converting as many Muslims as possible to Christianity, introducing them to a God who rejects Holy War and has sent His son to die for all sinners out of love for mankind."[149]

Though Hirsi Ali commends Christianity to Muslims, she has not, so far as we know, embraced it yet herself. How might Christians beckon agnostics and atheists such as Hirsi Ali closer to the God who loves them and sent His Son to die for them?

In one sense, the gospel is the same for everyone: "For God so loved the world, that he gave his only Son, that whoever believes in him should not perish but have eternal life" (John 3:16). In another, we commend the father's prayer in Mark 9:24 to anyone who teeters on the edge of belief, including ourselves, during seasons of doubt: "I believe, help my unbelief!"

Conversing with atheists and agnostics may dismantle their roadblocks for believing in Jesus and advance the process of discipleship. With regard to ethical or intellectual misgivings, we find that it helps to explore different perspectives and hint at how Christianity supplies satisfying answers. In this final section, we shed light on a few key controversies dividing Christians, agnostics, and atheists without presuming to pronounce the final word on them.

Who Made God?

An obvious dispute is whether God is real. Rather than rehearsing philosophical arguments for God's existence, we refer interested readers to Peter Kreeft and Ronald K. Tacelli's *Handbook of Christian Apologetics* and William Lane Craig's *Reasonable Faith*.[150] Nor will we sift evidence for Jesus as a unique historical figure as we do elsewhere.[151] We will reply briefly to Bertrand Russell, who quotes John Stuart Mill: "My father taught me that the question 'Who made me?' cannot be answered, since it immediately suggests the question, 'Who made God?' If everything must have a cause, then God must have a cause."[152]

Russell and Mill make a common mistake by supposing that everything must be dependent on something else, so there can be no uncaused entity like God. Yet if God is an eternal, necessary being who has no beginning, it makes no sense to ask who made God. God, by definition, is neither created nor caused. Only things that begin to exist need a cause or creator. Indeed, unless we believe that the finite universe simply popped into existence uncaused out of nothing, then we'll have to hold that something has always existed.[153]

Science

Second, atheistic scientism holds that only the physical world exists and that science alone can discover truth. This is self-refuting, since there is no way to verify scientifically that all truth must be scientifically verifiable—nor that the physical universe is all that exists![154] Scientism also fails to account for nonphysical realities such as mathematical formulas that exist independently of human brains or physical media that reveal them. It is better to say that science is the attempt to discover objective truth about the natural world. Agnostics, atheists, Christians, and other religious believers can enthusiastically practice science with this intention.

Many scientists see themselves as discovering and explaining how the God-created universe operates. John Simmons, in his whimsical *The Scientific 100: A Ranking of Influential Scientists, Past and Present* (1996), is one useful source. Among those he ranks in the top 20 are 15 religious scientists, including Isaac Newton, a committed but not a Trinitarian Christian; Catholic priests Claude Bernard and Nicolaus Copernicus; Catholics Galileo Galilei, Antoine Lavoisier, and Louis Pasteur; Lutherans Johannes Kepler and Werner Heisenberg; Presbyterian James Clerk Maxwell; Scottish Sandemanian Michael Faraday; Jewish Franz Boas; and deistically inclined Rudolph Virchow, Erwin Schrödinger, and Ernest Rutherford.[155] Sana Saaed concludes in her own supplemental catalog of multireligious scientists,

> This list could be multiplied many, many times...of scientists who were able to pursue their passion for science while practicing a religious faith. To be sure, there are many humanist and atheist scientists...but it is misleading to assume that all scientists lack a religious perspective or spiritual life, even though they might be in a field that is challenging popular religious assumptions.[156]

Alleging that "science" and "religion" are irreconcilable is disingenuous and harmful. It pits belief in God against scientific inquiry by insisting that scientists are duty-bound to reject God, forcing some to opt for "God" over "science," draining the pool of aspiring scientists and inhibiting public support for the subsidies on which modern science depends.[157]

Suffering and Life's Value

A third atheist objection to God is the persistence of suffering. I (Ben) dialogue in detail with atheists about this in my doctoral dissertation.[158] Without fully explaining or explaining away this vital issue, we gratefully trust that an all-wise God can utilize adversity to develop our character, to bring about goodness and joys that might not otherwise be possible or that we do not foresee.[159] The Bible teaches that God, in the person of Jesus, has suffered as we have.[160] God promises to be with and sustain anyone through life's difficulties if only she asks, and God will eventually heal and set the world right.[161] In the meantime, God gives us some responsibility in how we respond to and alleviate suffering.[162]

Skeptical atheists may holler "Wishful thinking!" but God's transforming grace is a deep reality, not the product of human pretending. Combined with the other evidence for God and Jesus we alluded to earlier, this grace is far more redeeming and restorative than attributing suffering to cosmic "pitiless indifference," as Dawkins does, or Russell's universe in ruins, where pain stops only when there is no one left to experience it.[163]

Oppy writes above that life's value is not diminished by its transience. Theologian Thomas Oden objects: "No happiness can be complete if constantly dogged by the awareness that it might soon end; hence perfect happiness must be eternal happiness."[164] Jerry L. Walls elaborates on Oden:

> The ultimate end of something casts its shadow over it and gives it final definition...Even wonderful goods may lose their meaning, or...have their meaning significantly diminished, if they come to a negative end...It may be exciting or wonderful at the time, but it finally comes to futility and frustration if death is the end...If these things are truly good things to be cherished, it is odd to say that it would be a triumph

> to be forever cut off from experiencing them...It might be better than to allow the prospect of death to rob one of all joy, but it is hardly for that reason an unqualified triumph.[165]

Crimes of Christianity

Relatedly, atheists sometimes rightly and sometimes mistakenly rebuke believers in God for perpetrating evils in God's name. Whenever an atheist or agnostic's "reverse prophetism" is on target, it should prompt Christians to reexamine their theologies, actions, and institutions with sober judgment.[166] Like anyone, atheists and agnostics are capable of sharing moral intuitions and living ethically. After all, they have been made in God's image, whether they acknowledge God or not. At the same time, Christians justifiably inquire, what is the objective basis for ethical principles atheists profess? How and why does objective or absolute morality exist if there is no ultimate source of morality? What is the final arbiter or authority for what is right and what is wrong if atheism is correct? If God does not exist, then human dignity, worth, and moral duty seem to emerge inexplicably from valueless processes. By contrast, if there is a truly objective or absolute standard of goodness from which evil deviates, it makes sense that something or someone like God acts as its ground and source.[167]

New Heaven and New Earth

Finally, a biblical theology of the new heaven and new earth completes and energizes numerous ethical imperatives that agnostics and atheists esteem. In the interview, Oppy discloses his concern for the environment, plants, animals, and human relationships.

One response is that Genesis 1, Romans 8, and 1 Corinthians 15 envision a glorious new heaven and new earth where physical existence is not ill-fated to freeze or fry in a doomed universe but is rather "very good" and ordained for purification and resurrection and permanency—a "transformed physicality," as one theologian has put it.[168] Anticipating this has ramifications from the quantum to the celestial levels.

Redemptive stewardship of God's creation incorporates every aspect of air, animal life, atoms, the climate, energy, minerals, outer space (and its inhabitants, if there are any), plants, soil, and water. In light of God's promised future where living and nonliving creatures interface with each other and God in harmony, to care for God's physical creation is to prepare for, look forward to, and conceivably participate in bringing about God's new creation.

Second, the opportunity to recommence at least some relationships with friends, children, colleagues, and other loved ones after death will surely be attractive to many atheists. Maybe, too, will possibilities to mend past relationships where one or more parties hurt the other. First Corinthians 13:12, in tandem with the other verses above, implies that relationships among God, people, and the created order will be enhanced by deeper knowledge and love. St. Jerome consequently counseled, "Learn on earth that knowledge which will continue with us in heaven."[169] Such knowing may involve not omniscience but perfect perception and intention.

What about meaningful work and leisure? Genesis 1–2, John 4:34, and John 5:17 declare that God the Creator and Jesus are gratified in their work and rest. God's image bearers can likewise enjoy pursuing creative enterprises with excellence now and later in the new heaven and new earth, without the inhibitions and irritations caused by sin.

Andy Crouch devises "culture making" as an activity that looks ahead to the New Jerusalem. This great city described in Isaiah 60 and Revelation 21 receives the glory and honor of nations and teems with cultural goods, "domesticated animals, ships, precious minerals and jewels, and timber."[170]

Crouch cites Richard Mouw's exegesis to point out that the new earth's dignitaries convey "the best of their nations—*even the cultural goods that had been deployed against God and his people*." The New Jerusalem is filled "not just with God's glory and presence, not just with his own stunningly beautiful architectural designs, not just with redeemed persons from every cultural background—but with redeemed human culture too."[171]

This raises the plumb line for every effort and its fruits. Will it contribute with integrity, continuing on in the new heaven and new earth? Culture making intimates not eternal tedium that some atheists or agnostics imagine but ongoing dynamism and endless delight as God's cocreators. To quote N.T. Wright, God's new creation will brilliantly integrate and augment every true ethic, every good endeavor "done very well, by those of other faiths and none."[172]

Atheists and agnostics who snub vexing religious doctrines or practices but who long to scale the peaks of beauty, truth, and innovation may be surprised at who their fellow prospective climbers are, not to mention the One who beckons on to perfection ever higher.[173]

The atheist alternative where all life, growth, ingenuity, reconciliation, and other pleasures cease is far less compelling, except to the metaphysical nihilist or the incorrigibly defiant. In place of cosmic emptiness, Jesus in the light of the New Jerusalem issues this invitation: "Let the one who is thirsty come; let the one who desires take the water of life without price" (Revelation 22:17). Let it be so.

Paul Copan (PhD, Marquette University) is a Christian theologian, analytic philosopher, and apologist. He is a professor at Palm Beach Atlantic University and holds the Pledger Family Chair of Philosophy and Ethics. His numerous books include *"True for You, but Not for Me": Overcoming Common Objections to Christian Faith*; *Is God a Moral Monster? Making Sense of the Old Testament God*; *Contending with Christianity's Critics: Answering the New Atheists and Other Objectors* (coedited); and *Loving Wisdom: A Guide to Philosophy and Christian Faith.*

Benjamin B. DeVan (PhD, Durham University) has taught numerous courses at North Carolina Central University, Peace College, and Palm Beach Atlantic University, including a January-term minicourse at MIT: "Religion: Bringing the World Together, or Tearing the World Apart?" He has published more than 60 articles, book chapters, and book reviews. He earned his MA in counseling from Asbury Seminary, MDiv from Duke, ThM from Harvard (with a thesis on Evangelical Christians and Muslims), and penned his PhD dissertation on the New Atheists.

Part 6

WHAT GOD IS DOING TODAY

22

Stories of Coming to Christ

Edited by Patrick Zukeran

As Christianity shifts to the global South and East, we can be encouraged by statistics that describe a global rise in Christianity. Today, there are more than a billion professed Christians in Latin America and Africa. Christianity continues to rise in Asia as well, especially in China.[1] Meanwhile, the Western world continues severing itself from its historic Christian roots. As we explore what God is doing in the world today, statistics can be helpful, but stories are transformational. May these stories of people coming to Christ from other religions encourage, motivate, and teach you as you join in God's mission of making disciples.

Seeking Allah, Finding Yahweh and Jesus

Padmé Lin

I remember sitting on my prayer mat, unable to hold my tears back any longer, feeling crushed and ashamed. I was convicted of my sins and felt utterly alone. Silently, in my anguish, I cried to God, "Am I not worthy, God? Where are you? Are you listening to me?" I rocked myself silently, tears flowing down my cheeks, trying to understand it all. It was the Muslim holy month of Ramadan, when Muslims around the world fast from dawn until dusk and abstain from sin. During Ramadan, Muslims are also encouraged to read the Qur'an.

One night after praying, I was on my prayer mat reading the English translation of the Qur'an. It suddenly struck me while reading Al-Baqarah, the first chapter of the Qur'an, "Why was it that in the Judaic and Christian traditions, it was *Isaac* who was supposed to be sacrificed by Abraham, but that in Islam, the boy was *Ishmael*?" To my mind, that was a historical discrepancy, and I wanted to dive in deeper. I decided to go back to the source and learn about the Old Testament.

I started petitioning God, asking to see the truth. I felt frustrated on the prayer mat every night when my prayers seemed to come to nothing. I constantly wondered, "God, are you listening to me?" I had Jewish friends, so it wasn't too difficult to get introduced to the rabbi and his wife at the local Chabad house.

The more I read the Old Testament, the more I felt that I had done the right thing. It seemed that Islam was a cut-and-paste job from the Old Testament, and at times, it felt incomplete and that the rationale for a command was often unclear. I thought Judaism was logical, rational, and well thought through, and I got to work reading about it—namely, learning about the Torah, the Old Testament, and the rabbinic teachings, such as the Midrash and Talmud. It was a joyous journey. I thoroughly enjoyed trying to learn Hebrew and trying to understand all the teachings and traditions.

While other Jewish people regarded me as an oddity because it is not often that one comes across an Asian in the synagogue, the rabbi's wife referred to me as a *ger tzedek*, meaning a "righteous convert." The Chabad house was literally an open house. The Chabad movement doesn't proselytize to non-Jewish people but is focused on reaching out to all Jewish people, including those who may have erred or lost their way. I found it welcoming and nonjudgmental. Jewish men and women in their twenties, usually on a backpacking trip, would traipse in with dreadlocks, grimy T-shirts, and even shorts and slippers. The rabbi and his wife would never bat an eyelid but would bid them welcome.

I followed the teachings of Judaism for a full year. This included celebrating their holidays, including Yom Kippur (the Day of Atonement), where one fasts for 25 hours. The afternoon before its commencement, I arrived at the Chabad house early, having brought two Jewish men with me so that we could reach the *minyan*, a quorum of ten men required for Orthodox Jewish worship. There were not many Jewish people in the city that I lived in.

That night, I stayed at the Chabad house, the home of the rabbi and his wife, Sarah, spending the night in an annex building with a girl in her late teens who was learning the ropes and assisting Sarah. Yom Kippur reminded me of Shabbat but was more special, as it was such a sacred holiday. I've always enjoyed observing Shabbat, where for 25 hours, from before sundown on a Friday to nightfall on Saturday, one engages in prayers and reflection and abstains from labor.

To the Jewish mind, Shabbat is the pinnacle of the creation of the universe. Its observance is a reminder of the role God created for humanity. Shabbat also serves as testimony to God's rescue of the Israelites from slavery in Egypt by setting aside a day, free of labor, for personal autonomy and freedom.

On Friday at lunchtime, I would slip out of work and drive over to help Sarah make the *challah*, the special braided bread eaten on Shabbat. I would return in the evening. I wasn't a strict observer of Shabbat because I would still drive and check my phone during dinner, taking care to do so under the table.

I had been reading Blu Greenberg's book *How to Run a Traditional Jewish Household*, and by the time Pesach (Passover) rolled around, I was feeling a little overwhelmed. The minutiae of details made me quite certain that a working Jewish wife with children would find it very difficult to do all that is demanded of her. She needed to clean her house of all *chametz* (leavened food forbidden during Pesach), including in school bags (think forgotten lunches); sell the chametz before Pesach as required by Jewish law; make her kitchen—including utensils, pots, and pans—kosher for Pesach; and search one last time for chametz 24 hours before Pesach. I felt it was too much and not what God would want for us.

As much as I admired my Jewish friends, Judaism began to feel a little forced, too focused on jurisprudence and legalism. For example, in Islam, a married couple cannot have sex while she is on her period. The couple must wait until her discharge has turned white. In Judaism, two additional "white days" are added after the end of a woman's period to be on the safe side. In the meantime, the husband and wife cannot touch, not even to hold hands. This time of separation is called *niddah*. A Jewish woman is only cleansed after immersing herself in a *mikveh*, a ritual bath. By contrast, in Islam, the woman can simply shower and be considered clean. Before the construction of a mikveh in my country's capital city, Jewish women drove for up to 13 hours to the only known mikveh in the country for ritual cleansing every month!

I grew increasingly despondent and searched for help. A coworker gave me a Bible in which the following piece of Scripture was inscribed: "Ask and it will be given to you; seek and you will find; knock and the door will be opened to you" (Matthew 7:7 NIV).

I was introduced to an American pastor, Phil, and his wife, Lee Ann. They were generous with their time. I felt it was necessary for me to learn because of the spirit of learning instilled within me by Jewish tradition. We would meet and talk and have dinner at their apartment every Wednesday.

One winter day, I fell ill with malaria. It was hard to get well where I was staying, as the place was infested with mosquitos and was not well heated. Pastor Phil and Lee Ann took me in for two months and nursed me back to health. It was during this time that Pastor Phil gave me a copy of Christian apologist Nabeel Qureshi's book *Seeking Allah, Finding Jesus*.

I read it in one sitting, and by that evening, the world as I had known it had changed. Happily, being a Christian meant that I could still value and study the Old Testament, which I love. Especially important to me is the historical accuracy of the Bible, the occurrences described therein, and the Christian concept of salvation that Christ our Lord died on the cross to save us and that good works would never be enough. As a Muslim and then in my practice of Judaism, I wrestled with what it meant to be "good," a constant race against our sins. In Islam, the

22A. "And when he finds it, he joyfully puts it on his shoulders and goes home." Art by John Everett Millais, 1864 (https://creativecommons.org/publicdomain/zero/1.0/).

sin of, say, missing the third prayer in a day, the *Asr*, was equivalent to having intercourse with one's parent! It was so graphic and unforgiving.

I walked over to Pastor Phil's study, handed *Seeking Allah, Finding Jesus* back to him, and said, "This is it. Qureshi answered all the questions I had as a Muslim. There's no turning back." However, it still took me several months before I could take the leap. I started going to church. I remember telling Lee Ann one Wednesday evening when we met for dinner after I had moved out, "I'm standing at the edge of the precipice, and I'm looking down, but I can't take the leap, Lee Ann." She just smiled encouragingly.

Another time, Lee Ann read me the parable of the missing sheep from Luke 15. It took a while for the point of the parable to sink in: that the Lord God would abandon His entire flock to search out the one missing sheep because He loves us that much. And then when the lost sheep is found, "he calls together his friends and his neighbors, saying to them, 'Rejoice with me, for I have found my sheep that was lost.' Just so," Jesus explained, "there will be more joy in heaven over one sinner who repents than over ninety-nine righteous persons who need no repentance" (Luke 15:6-7).

I finally resolved to believe in Jesus and told Pastor Phil and Lee Ann over dinner one night. They embraced me and were so happy. Pastor Phil quoted 2 Corinthians 5:17 (NIV), "Therefore, if anyone is in Christ, the new creation has come: The old has gone, the new is here!" I was baptized the day before my thirty-eighth birthday. Kissing me on my forehead, Lee Ann passed me my birthday gift from her and Pastor Phil: a beautiful Bible with gilded pages. I am still learning. It has been a remarkable journey. This piece of Scripture I hold dear to my heart: "The LORD himself goes before you and will be with you; he will never leave you nor forsake you. Do not be afraid; do not be discouraged" (Deuteronomy 31:8 NIV).

I feel my life's calling is to help others in their respective faith walk, especially that of my immediate family, who are still Muslim. I pray constantly for the Lord's guidance as apostates like me can be killed for leaving Islam. Romans 8:28 (NIV) gives me courage: "And we know that in all things God works for the good of those who love him, who have been called according to his purpose."

From the New Spirituality to New Life in Christ

Marcia Montenegro

It was a chilly Thanksgiving Day, and I was with some neopagans and witches at my chiropractor's house. My chiropractor was a practicing witch and had invited me, her astrologer, for dinner. What she didn't know was that the evening before, after a series of inexplicable events, I had made a huge decision. I was a licensed astrologer and had only ended my term as president of the city's astrological society earlier that year. The evening before, I had decided that I would stop practicing astrology. As I ate, others were chatting, and I had the strange impression that they were all dead. A few other odd things happened, and I left early. What were the events that led to this scenario and to my giving up astrology?

My journey began at age 11, when I had a dream in which I could not find a playmate from childhood. I found out later he had died around that time, and this gave me an interest in the paranormal. This paralleled a growing personal interest in astrology. My sister and I were taken to churches in various overseas locations where we lived, but Bible stories were just nice fairy tales to me.

When we returned to the United States, I became involved in a church. I had questions about the Bible and started doubting its truth and the truth of Christianity itself. In my mind, Jesus's death on the cross had no relevance to my life. In college, I became deeply interested in Eastern religions, and I had further paranormal experiences. After college, I delved into books about communication with the dead and reincarnation, and I came to believe in reincarnation.

In one of my classes, the instructor led us in a guided meditation session. It was this exercise that led me to encounter a spirit guide, a disembodied being that was to be my "spiritual master." I also became involved with Tibetan Buddhism and later Zen Buddhism, learning to practice Eastern meditation. I studied numerology, psychic development, and astrology. I also participated in séances, finally taking a seven-hour exam that allowed me to be licensed as a professional astrologer.

During those years, I read many New Age and "channeled" works (i.e., dictated by disembodied entities). I saw God as a force or energy that we come from and to which we return. I believed that Jesus was an enlightened spiritual master like Buddha and that His teachings in the Bible had hidden meanings. We were all evolving spiritually through reincarnation, headed to a blissful melting into the "One."

Astrology seemed to offer everything I was looking for, and I eventually did it full time. I not only taught astrology but also became president of the local astrological society and chairperson of the board that gave astrology exams for licensure. Therefore, it was a surprise when I had a compulsion to attend a church. I resisted this for several months until I finally gave in, rationalizing that it was unfinished business from a previous life.

I went to a large church and sat in the back, planning to leave early. The service began, and a procession of the ministers and others came down the aisle, led by a young boy carrying a cross. As he passed by me, a strange thing happened. I felt what I call a waterfall of love falling on me and through me. This was very powerful and real and seemed to be from a source I did not believe in—a personal God telling me He loved me.

I stayed for the entire service and returned the following Sunday, telling no one about it. Some people I met in the church asked for my business card, so I thought that maybe I could get some new astrology clients. That gave me one reason to keep attending.

Within a few weeks, I had an impression that this "new" God did not like astrology. I ignored this because it made no sense. Soon, I had the distinct impression that this God wanted me to give up astrology, that it was somehow separating me from Him. This was really crossing the line for me, and I resisted it. But it was so powerful and clear, I actually made the decision to do it without even understanding how I would go through with it.

The story now returns to the time of the Thanksgiving meal, the day after my momentous decision to give up astrology. In the following days, I stumbled along, not sure what life after astrology would be like or how I would cope. I started reading the Bible at Matthew 1:1 and read a little bit each night. I did not understand what I was reading, but the words seemed pure to me. I knew it was different from anything I had read before.

While reading Matthew 8, I was captivated by the account of Jesus rebuking the storm's wild wind and sea. I read this repeatedly, and God opened my eyes. For the first time, I saw who Jesus was and that I needed Him as my Savior. I turned my life over to Him and immediately knew that my life was totally new.

I realized that I had been on a spiritual road leading away from the true God, and I had missed the message of the cross and of the real Jesus. The false beliefs I had cherished were unmasked for the emptiness they were, and the true living God revealed the true Jesus in His Word. It was an astounding revelation!

I became hungry for God's Word and continued to read. I discovered a few months later that a young Christian man in the office where I had worked part-time had been praying for me with a group at his church during the year that I experienced the events leading to my salvation. Prayer glorifies the Lord, and sometimes He burdens us to pray for people so we can see His power and grace at work. I left behind an old life for a new one in Christ and for eternal life with God.

A Japanese Buddhist Meets Jesus

Hajimu Fujii

I was a Buddhist for 35 years. While I was in high school, I decided to follow the teachings of Shinran Shonin (AD 1173–1262), the founder of Jōdo Shinshū Buddhism, one of the most popular schools of Japanese Pure Land Buddhism.

There are two major divisions of Buddhism: Theravada and Mahayana. Theravada followers believe in a single Buddha, the historical Shakyamuni. Mahayana Buddhism teaches that there are many Buddhas who each gave their own scriptures. Pure Land Buddhism is a branch of Mahayana that teaches that there is a realm purified and ruled by the Amida Buddha, also known as Amitābha, the Buddha of Infinite Light. Amida Buddha created the Pure Land and hoped to bring all mankind there. The faithful recite the Nembutsu, *Namu Amida Butsu* (I take refuge in the Amida Buddha). By entrusting their souls to the Amida Buddha, a follower may be purified and enter the Pure Land upon death.

My ancestors were devoted followers and supporters of the Shinshū temple for generations. One day, when I was 35 years old, my friend said something interesting to me. He said that one of the best religions in the world is Christianity. It was noteworthy that he stated this so confidently, seeing as though he was not a Christian. I was irritated that I could not present a reasoned answer to his opinion because I had no knowledge of Christianity. I started reading the Bible for myself so I could find mistakes in the text.

It was difficult for me to find mistakes in the Bible. Several months passed, but one verse remained very significant—the very first verse of the Bible: "In the beginning, God created the heavens and the earth" (Genesis 1:1). It declares that the God of the Bible is Creator of everything. After reading this, I thought that if this God created the whole world, He might be the true God. I believed in many gods up to that time. Most Japanese people believe in the Shinto gods as well as the many Buddhas and bodhisattvas. In Japan, Shintoism and Buddhism coexist; many Japanese have both a Buddhist and a Shinto altar in their homes.

After some reflection, I came to believe that there is only one true God. God is the Creator, and, therefore, I concluded, He must be my creator. The evidence that He exists and that He cares for His creation is demonstrated in many ways. I realized this when considering an individual fingerprint. My fingerprint is unique—there are over seven billion people in this world, but no two people have the same fingerprints. God cares enough to make each person distinct from everyone else.

It was a life-transforming truth when I realized that I am God's unique creation. My endless striving for significance ended because God loves me and I am His workmanship: "For we are His workmanship, created in Christ Jesus for good works, which God prepared beforehand, that we should walk in them" (Ephesians 2:10).

From that time on, my perspective on life was transformed. I left my small, self-centered world, and I entered into God's world as a member of His kingdom. I burned all my religious books besides the Bible.

My life priorities fell into place when I read Jesus's words in Matthew 6:26: "Look at the birds of the air: they neither sow nor reap nor gather into barns, and yet your heavenly Father feeds them. Are you not of more value than they?" The Lord led me to change my life priorities. The most important thing in my life is worshiping and serving God because this is why we were created. Second is family, and the last is my business. This became the new order of priorities in my life, and it has been a special blessing for me that I have been able to keep this order of priorities even up to today.

Not only did my priorities change, but

my relationships were also transformed. In those days, I had been on nonspeaking terms with my father for nearly nine years. Conflict began after I graduated from pharmacy school. I had acquired new skills while serving as an apprentice to a professional pharmacist for two years. I went back to help and improve my father's pharmacy. He rejected my advice and chose not to use my new skills for eight months, so I decided to leave. I came to own my own pharmacy through the help of my classmates from the university. My pharmacy grew and prospered in a short period of time, but my father refused to acknowledge my success.

I had been hating my father for nine years. Jesus taught, "For God so loved the world, that he gave his only Son, that whoever believes in him should not perish but have eternal life" (John 3:16). This verse affirmed my salvation, but it also convicted me that I had committed a sin against God and my father.

Jesus led me to apologize to my father. I went back to my father's house, I got down on my knees, and I apologized to my father for my wrong behavior. I said, "Father, forgive me; I made much trouble for you." He said nothing. I looked up after a moment, and my father was weeping. After a while, he said, "I have given you much trouble..."

He choked up with tears and was unable to speak. He forgave me, and we were reconciled. Reconciliation was impossible for nine years by my efforts, but nothing is impossible for God. When I believed in Jesus, not only were my sins forgiven, but the Lord also changed me so I could forgive and reconcile a broken relationship.

Soon after that, my father and mother drove four hours to visit my pharmacy and house. This was the first and the last time they visited. Several months later, my father was diagnosed with lung cancer. I visited my father in the hospital. I shared John 3:16 with him and led him to Jesus. He accepted Jesus Christ in his heart and passed away two days later.

The Lord continued to prosper my pharmacy business. About six months after I was baptized, I felt my business wouldn't be my life's work. I felt an emptiness about continuing the business. I prayed to God many times, "God, please show me the way I should take." One morning, I made a very impatient prayer: "Please give me an answer today because I am not able to bear the weight upon me." Then I heard a voice: "I will show you the way to take today." In the afternoon without any appointments, three pastors visited me to talk to me about going into the ministry. I felt a shivering sensation thinking of my morning prayer.

I decided to study at a theological school as a special student. There was a rule that the seeker can't formally enter the school until at least one year after baptism, but the seminary accepted me anyway. I studied with ordinary full-time students and earned credits. While I was studying, my wife kept our business and raised our four children. My grandmother lived with us. This continued for eight years. At one point, I suffered from a strained back and got in a completely helpless situation. In that dire situation, I felt God saying, "You can't put on two pairs of shoes at the same time." I had to decide which way to take, either the missionary work or my job as a pharmacist.

The word was given to me: "For it is God who works in you, both to will and to work for his good pleasure" (Philippians 2:13). I found myself still unable to make a final decision, even though I was aware of God's will, until God pushed me again and, two days later, gave me His word: "I can do all things through him who strengthens me" (Philippians 4:13). I understood that God was saying, "It is not you who does it, but it is My plan, and I will do it." My job was to follow Him. It was then that I devoted my life to preach the gospel in full-time ministry.

I eventually moved my family with four children to California, where I attended seminary and planted a church in Fresno, California. As God has transformed my life, it has been a joy to see God transform the lives of my children and the many men and women He has allowed me to teach and disciple. The empty philosophy of Buddhism has been replaced by the truth and transforming power of Jesus Christ.

From Latter-Day Saint to Jesus

Corey Miller

I was raised a sixth-generation Latter-day Saint (LDS) in Salt Lake City, Utah, with ancestors who were directly connected with both Joseph Smith and Brigham Young, the two first and most significant prophets of the Latter-day Saints. Although I felt relatively secure in my religion, I was confused early on with troubling matters in LDS teaching. Like many at the popular level in the LDS Church, I embraced the idea "Try, try your best, and God will make up the rest." Yet I delayed the standard eight-year-old baptism because I also knew that to become worthy of celestial glory in heaven, one had to enter via perfection. Baptism wiped the slate clean, and postbaptismal sins put a clean slate at risk. I figured I'd wait until my death bed when I was about 88 and beat the system by getting baptized without much opportunity for postbaptismal sin. But when I could no longer deal with the stress of possibly dying before being baptized as I ought, I capitulated and was baptized at age nine. I was faithful about going to church and being involved in the community.

In adolescence, I began "living it up" a bit, even while still affirming LDS doctrine. I didn't feel loved by the LDS community, and I found acceptance within the wrong crowd. All the while, I had good intentions that, in time, I'd once again pursue a morally worthy life. At age 16, I was invited to spend the summer with an LDS friend at his father's home in California. His father was not LDS, and he made my stay contingent on our attending a nondenominational Christian camp called Hume Lake. Although I was not living the ideal LDS life at the time, I had no thought of ever leaving my faith. I still understood it to be the one true religion and would become more faithful in the future. I figured that our heavenly father was loving and would forgive my wrongdoing regardless of my temporary adolescent behavior. After all, I surmised that I wasn't really that bad, and I was bound to end up in one of the degrees of glory anyway. Thus I felt no urgency to repent. If it were not for the appeal of spending the entire summer on California beaches, I probably would not have attended the camp at all.

I arrived at Hume Lake without any great expectations. If anything, like many high school guys, I suppose I was looking for cute girls. To my surprise, the camp speaker delivered a message that week on the topic of hell with a robust presentation of the gospel. I'd never heard of the gravity of sin in such a way that made sense of grace. My soul resonated with the message. For the first time in my life, I understood my need for forgiveness. Religion was helpless. Tearfully, I realized I was a sinner and did not deserve forgiveness. Jesus was enough. My fear of leaving what I thought was the truth in the LDS Church was mitigated by the security in Christ. This security was further authenticated when I saw Christ's love displayed in the community of Christians. I was captured by the love of

Christ. Even with my religious upbringing, I had never experienced God's love in that way until I met these people and then met their source, Jesus Christ.

Later that summer, I asked and received approval from my mother to live in California during my junior year of high school. I was baptized and discipled that year. Returning to Utah for my senior year was a challenge. On the one hand, I quickly found fellowship with some young and passionate Christians. We were challenged by the call to evangelism in the New Testament. We spent many nights "street preaching" in Salt Lake City next to the LDS Temple and on the University of Utah campus. On the other hand, I recall feeling confused about whether I had made the right choice. My memories of being LDS began resurfacing with fears that if I were wrong and had left what was indeed the true church, then I was now an apostate, which gave me no comfort in the eternal scheme of things. The tension was such that, while it was hard to deny the life change brought by Christ, I also needed to research and contemplate more.

After extensive research, I became confident that leaving the LDS faith was a good move. But even if LDS doctrine were false, that fact would not in itself make historic Christianity true. Perhaps my newfound Christian faith was just another deception. After all, I had been deceived once before. How was I to know that the Bible was God's Word or that God even exists? How could I know that some other major world religion was not correct? Is any religion correct? Many thoughts like this shook my faith and caused me to dig deep and wide. Consequently, I developed a love for the truth, something that would shape the rest of my life and boost my confidence in Christ.

I went from no interest in academics and a 0.3 GPA on a 4.0 scale to entering academia in order to rigorously pursue truth. In this addictive pursuit of knowing truth, I earned three master's degrees and a doctoral degree. I've been blessed with a wonderful wife and children who have zeal for God and for communicating the truth and love of Christ to people. Having served in pastoral ministry and taught nearly 100 college courses in philosophy, rhetoric, and comparative religions, I'm now president/CEO of Ratio Christi (www.ratiochristi.org), a global campus ministry organization that seeks to equip students and professors with historical, philosophical, and scientific reasons to follow Jesus. For a more in-depth version of mine and others' stories, see my book *Leaving Mormonism: Why Four Scholars Changed Their Minds* (Grand Rapids, MI: Kregel, 2017).

A Seeking Sikh

Sandeep Singh

I was born and raised in the suburbs of Toronto, Canada. I grew up in a conservative Sikh family. I have early memories of conflicts and an emptiness that manifested as a persistent cloud and remained looming over our home emanating the lack of peace we all secretly felt. Growing up in a Sikh home meant I was deeply entrenched in an environment where everything was based on the honor and shame system. It became ingrained early on that tipping the scales of this worldview could result in dire consequences and thus fear seeped into the recesses of my fractured young soul.

The emotional disconnection in my family began to slowly take its toll on me. I was afraid of my father and felt distant from my mother and siblings. I often attended Sikh worship classes in a local Sikh temple and a yearly Sikh youth camp in Michigan. My understanding of obedience was robotic routines of praying words I did not truly understand but that were supposed to yield a sense of holiness and piety. Despite my methodical prayers, I still felt a deep emptiness that seemed to prevail and that I could not shake off.

Sikhism is an Eastern religion that is about 500 years old. It is a union of Sufi Islam and the bhakti movement of Hinduism. Sikhism is monotheistic and does not condone idol worship. The main source of authority is the Sikh holy book, the *Adi Granth*, which was compiled by various saints. Sikhism was created because the founder, Nanak Dev, was disenchanted by various religious practices he observed, notably in Hinduism and Islam. In Sikhism, salvation is more of a product of enlightenment rather than redemption. Enlightenment leads to spiritualism, which inspires man to dedicate his life to the service of humanity, whereas in Christianity, the door to salvation is the redemption from sin through the acceptance of Christ. Therefore, it may be challenging for a Sikh to understand grace as unmerited favor, since it is a performance- and works-based religion. For this reason, it was difficult for me to grasp the concept of grace for many years, even after becoming a believer.

In 1993, change happened quickly in my family environment and in the Canadian economy. I did not want to move out of Canada, the only home I knew, but after losing our home in an affluent suburb, my parents decided it was best for me to move to India. I ended up living in North India for a few years and was exposed to Indian culture. During this time, I began to grow further away from my religious mindset and found myself embracing a newfound cultural identity. It is significant to highlight that religion and culture are so deeply intertwined for those of us from collectivist cultures. However, in my case, there was a constant search for identity that could not be quenched through these avenues, despite my relentless pursuit to make sense of this tiresome internal struggle. Our family issues increased, including financial struggles, familial conflicts, and jealousy from extended family. Amid all the difficulties, there was the saving grace of the Father that seemed to provide glimmers of hope along this journey, although we had yet to discover the Source.

After I moved back to Canada, I struggled to adjust. I didn't feel like I fit in anywhere. My mother met a Sikh woman healed of cancer in Toronto who shared the gospel with her. Surprisingly, my mother accepted Christ quickly. My mindset protested as this conversion called my identity into question. Yet fairly quickly, I began to have dreams about Jesus that confirmed what my mother was trying to tell me about the deity of Jesus. Although it was a sudden revelation for my mother, my journey was different. For such a long time I had suppressed the questions that had plagued me that my soul was heavy with spiritual baggage. Despite my mother's conversion, I was not convinced that I could accept Christ as the sole path of salvation. Internally, I wrestled with anxiety, depression, and suicidal tendencies. I truly felt I had no purpose or hope for my life as an undergraduate student. I had no idea that Christ offered hope, healing, and unconditional love. Those were tenets that seemed to exist only in idealistic literature I read as a way to escape.

After my initial dreams about Jesus, I couldn't deny that He was real, but I did not know how to proceed beyond that initial revelation. I did not have anyone to disciple me or teach me, so I remained in a dry spiritual stage that seemed to last for years. It was easy for me to grasp the holiness of God but not the grace of God. I was afraid of my father, and quite frankly, I was afraid that I would make mistakes in my newfound faith. Learning to grow in the concept of God as a Father was a novel idea. It took time to dismantle my old thinking patterns and embrace the truth about the character of God. I initially moved into legalistic Christianity looking for ways to please Christ, not knowing the power that lies in the freedom of grace.

In 2004, I moved to the United States for graduate school. I did not understand yet how to live a Christian life, and I did not know any believers my age. I began attending a local church occasionally. I wanted to get married at a young age and wanted to marry my boyfriend, who was an unbeliever. Although God sent me warnings, I followed my heart. My short-lived marriage turned into a divorce, which led to a lot of heartbreak and family division.

Finally, I agreed to yield to the Lord, and I cried out, "I will follow you fully!" During the next few years, I lived a very quiet life and began to diligently study Scripture as much as possible. The quiet comfort and solace of the Holy Spirit, along with a handful of intimate prayer partners, became my new world. Inaudible grace became my sustenance to move forward into an unknown world with my newfound faith. I had never known there was a God who cared about intimacy and relationship. These concepts began to heal my heart of the emptiness I grew up with and slowly release the healing power of the love of God.

One insight that has helped me tremendously came through the Song of Solomon. This is ironic because, years earlier, I had decided not to read this book because it pertained to marriage, and I wanted nothing to do with marriage at the time. I also felt a constant void due to the loss of my marriage and alienation from some of my family because of the shame of divorce. I knew my faith mattered, but I did not know that my personal desires mattered to the Lord. One day, as I was driving and listening to worship music, my heart began to stir. I had no idea the worship music was based on the Song of Solomon, even though by this time, I was well versed with the rest of the Bible.

I began to realize that God feels about us the way a husband feels toward his beloved. As I began to understand His unconditional love, I began to heal from my previous religious mindset, a performance mentality, and the pain I felt from my divorce. I felt tangible grace enter my mind, body, and soul, transforming me into a new person full of expectant joy. For the first time in my life, I truly understood that life was beautiful, and my senses became aware of the world of beauty that had been there all along. I began to connect with my family again as my heart healed and I grew in receiving love. I was able to pour out love to new believers who sought me out to ask questions just as I once did as a new believer.

I slowly became bold enough to start to become what God desired for me, a living expression of His fullness. As perfect love continuously washed out fear, hope replaced offense, and wholeness began to blossom. The book I had avoided in the Bible was the one the Lord used to usher me into an unexpected place of intimacy and spiritual maturity. My relationship with God began to build a firm foundation of identity, which triggered a cascade of healing processes necessary for me to truly grasp the extravagant unconditional love of God. Unbeknown to me, God had been directing my steps patiently and affectionately even before I would yield to His relentless pursuit.

Finding Jesus: Leaving the Watchtower and Other False Practices Behind

Cynthia Hampton

I grew up in a nominal Roman Catholic home. I gained an interest in the occult due to my father's and grandfather's deep interest in astrology and the occult. One of their favorite subjects was the prophecies of American clairvoyant Edgar Cayce. I read many books on meditation and visualization, which fueled my interest in witchcraft. I was heavily into occult practices when my mother began to study with the Jehovah's Witnesses.

Due to my interest in prophecy, I was drawn to the apocalyptic teachings of the Watchtower organization, which sounded similar to the teachings of Cayce. Although I really enjoyed astrology and occult practices, the Jehovah's Witnesses view such interests as satanic. Eventually, I threw out much of my occult material and started to seriously study with the Jehovah's Witnesses. I came to believe that the Watchtower was the truth and was baptized in 1972.

There was great excitement at that time because the Jehovah's Witness leaders had predicted that Armageddon was coming in 1975. I remember the speech given by the District Overseer at the International Assembly in Oakland in 1973. He said, "When an alarm clock is ready to ring, there is a click a split second before the alarm actually rings. Well, we are in that time period between the click and the actual ringing of the alarm clock. That's how much time we have left before Armageddon!" All everyone talked about was how little time we had left before Armageddon.

Since there was little time left, many married at a young age. I married a young Jehovah's Witness in 1974 at the age of 18, but we divorced after three years. A year later, I enrolled in community college. At first, I saw no need to study seriously, since Armageddon "was just around the corner." However, it was 1977, and Armageddon had not arrived. I was learning critical thinking skills and believed in asking questions at a time when independent thinking was discouraged. I remember telling an elder's wife that I was enjoying a psychology class. She responded by urging me to quit school because I was studying doctrines of demons. Despite her admonition, I continued with my classes.

By 1979, I quit going to the Jehovah's Witness meetings. In 1980, I disassociated myself from the Watchtower organization. It was then that I decided to go back to practicing New Age philosophies. I thought if the Watchtower did not have the answers for me, surely astrology and meditation would.

In 1982, my neighbor invited me to his church, and I accepted. I discovered that the Christians I met there were warm and caring people who loved Jesus, but I was still scared. Did I really do the right thing by going to this church? Would something bad happen to me because I dared go into what the Watchtower calls "Babylon"? As Jehovah's Witnesses, we were always taught that demons were present in the churches of Babylon.

My questions were answered that day. When the service ended, I looked around and saw a former Jehovah's Witness. Her name was Mary Kling, and she took me under her wing and began to show me the errors of the Watchtower organization. She showed me an old *Watchtower* magazine from April 1, 1979, that taught that Jesus was the mediator for only 144,000! With Mary's guidance, I came to understand that the Watchtower was a false organization and that the truth could only be found in Jesus Christ. Shortly thereafter in May 1982, I gave my life over to Jesus Christ.

It was no coincidence that out of all the

churches in Tucson, Arizona, I happened to visit the one that Mary had been attending. I knew that God had His hand in this the whole time. However, it was not without a price. I told my father about my experience, and he told my mother, who did not take the news well. She told me that I was not welcome in her home ever again! She shunned me for 17 years.

At the end of 1982, I moved to Los Angeles and began a new life. I met Randy Watters, founder of the Free Minds Ministry that helps ex–Jehovah's Witnesses. I got involved in the ministry and learned so much from my brother in Christ.

In 1999, my mother began communicating with me again. In 2000, she and my father came to visit. My two younger children were 10 and 13 when they first met their grandparents. In August 2002, the Watchtower leadership once again instructed their followers to shun the former members, and our communication was severed. It is very sad how the Watchtower separates families.

Upon leaving the Watchtower, many former members ask, "Where else can we go?" This is because members are indoctrinated to believe salvation is dependent upon their good standing with the Watchtower organization. It is important to remember that Jesus never taught that salvation came from associating with an organization. He told His followers to come to Him:

> Jesus said to the twelve, "You do not want to go away also, do you?" Simon Peter answered Him, "Lord, to whom shall we go? You have words of eternal life. We have believed and have come to know that You are the Holy One of God." (John 6:67-69 NASB)

Former members are often haunted by the thought of "What if the Watchtower organization is really the truth?" One way I reassure them is by revealing the Watchtower's own record of false prophecy. Deuteronomy 18:20-22 states,

> "But the prophet who presumes to speak a word in my name that I have not commanded him to speak, or who speaks in the name of other gods, that same prophet shall die." And if you say in your heart, "How may we know the word that the LORD has not spoken?"—when a prophet speaks in the name of the LORD, if the word does not come to pass or come true, that is a word that the LORD has not spoken; the prophet has spoken it presumptuously. You need not be afraid of him.

There is no need to fear a false prophet! The Watchtower is guilty of not only the 1975 false prophecy but many others since their beginning in the late 1800s under Charles Taze Russell.[2]

I've been a Christian now for over 35 years and have never been happier since becoming a Christian and knowing who the true Jesus Christ is. My journey has not been easy, but the joy I have from knowing the true Jesus Christ is amazing.

An Insight to Take from This Chapter

From these stories of coming to Christ, we do well to remember this truth: *It takes patience.*

Relationships take patience. Did you notice how relationships with patient Christians played a crucial role in each of the stories? The pastor and his wife who opened their home and nursed Padmé back to health. A Christian from Marcia's office praying along with a group from his church for her salvation. The three pastors who saw potential in Hajimu. The genuine love Corey discovered among believers in Jesus. The prayer partners who helped along Sandey's faith. The friend from church who showed Cynthia the truth of the gospel and the error of her false beliefs.

Without these Christians' gentle persistence, would Padmé, Marcia, Hajimu, Corey, Sandey, and Cynthia be followers of Jesus today?

We are naive to assume that persuasion happens in a few minutes. Persuasion takes patience. This is all the more so when someone comes from a non-Christian worldview. Often we must do the hard work of first establishing the correct worldview of theism—there is one God who created all things. Hindus, Buddhists, Sikhs, New Agers, and others come from a different worldview and do not immediately understand the doctrines of the Creator, creation, the fall, the sinfulness of mankind, grace, and atonement. Put another way, it is difficult to ask someone to accept John 3:16 until he has come to accept Genesis 1:1.

In Southeast Asia, *The Passion of the Christ* film was shown in several areas. However, it had a very different response there than it did in the West. Steeped in the doctrine of karma, many viewers walked away from the movie concluding that Jesus must have been a very wicked man. They reasoned that He must have committed a heinous crime and attained a large amount of bad karma. For this reason, He was punished with such an awful death. Without the understanding of a holy God and our sinfulness, the atoning work of Christ on the cross does not make sense.

Many Christians have been trained to present the gospel in a few minutes and then call for a decision. However, without taking the time to establish the correct foundation, our presentation can be misunderstood or the need not grasped by individuals from another belief system. Although establishing the correct foundation may take time—perhaps weeks, months, or even years—it will make our evangelism more fruitful and effective in the long run.

"Love is patient."[3] So speak the truth in love. Patiently walk alongside people who are confused and hurting. In so doing, you will not only invite them to our Lord; you will also model what He is like:

> The Lord...is patient toward you, not wishing that any should perish, but that all should reach repentance. (2 Peter 3:9)

Patrick Zukeran (DMin, Southern Evangelical Seminary) is the founder and executive director of Evidence and Answers, a Honolulu-based research and teaching ministry specializing in Christian apologetics. He is also the host of the radio show by the same name. He serves as adjunct faculty for Pacific Rim Christian University. He has authored books including *The Apologetics of Jesus* with coauthor Norman Geisler.

23

How to Treat Our Foreign Neighbors

Taffeta Chime

I recently had a friend tell me she was happy about her new Egyptian neighbors but that she wished they didn't babble away in Arabic when they were on their back porch: "I mean, they've come to America, so don't you think they should use English?" As someone who has worked in an English-language school for several years, of course I support English education for international guests. But I explained to my friend these people were in their *homes* and probably felt more comfortable speaking their first language. After all, they had probably been out at least attempting to speak English all day, and after such mental exhaustion, it feels good to relax and just say what you want to say without having to translate it in your head first. Or maybe her neighbor was talking to a relative or friend back in Egypt who doesn't speak English. I could see from her face that she hadn't considered these things before.

Unfortunately, this attitude toward foreigners is not unusual or new. Animosity toward foreigners has happened practically since the beginning of time! It is natural for people to be cautious of those who are different—especially when the media all too often portrays foreigners in a negative light—but it is not right to hold others as less than or to expect others to conform to your life. In today's tense climate, it is especially important to extend a hand to our foreign neighbors. Leviticus 19:33-34 says, "When a stranger sojourns with you in your land, you shall not do him wrong. You shall treat the stranger who sojourns with you as the native among you, and you shall love him as yourself, for you were strangers in the land of Egypt: I am the LORD your God." This is often the verse quoted when discussing the treatment of foreigners, but many still discredit it because it is from Leviticus, the same book that gives instructions for old covenant laws, like which foods are clean and unclean, how to trim one's beard, and when to offer animal sacrifices. Even so, it is still an applicable instruction: We may not have been strangers in Egypt, but most of us European-blooded Americans were once strangers in the United States. Besides, the sentiment is echoed in the New Testament. For one, Jesus's famous and all-encompassing teaching of the "Golden Rule" very clearly echoes this sentiment: "Love your neighbor as yourself."

Loving foreigners is a practice in empathy, a skill we could all sharpen. Imagine first, as is often the case, a family or an individual who wants to come to the United States in search of more opportunities. Whether fleeing conflict, corruption, or persecution or pursuing education, professional training, medical treatment, and so on, there are many legitimate reasons people desire to live in the United States. And oftentimes, these travelers have to sacrifice a lot to live in this country: They leave families, friends, jobs, cultural comforts, linguistic ease, and so on because they believe the reward is worth giving up these things. By trying to understand both the sacrifices and the dreams of these sojourners, we can more easily see the depths to which we need to pour into them.

Because of cultural differences, it is easy for Americans to leave their empathy behind. We may easily get annoyed or offended because of something foreigners do differently. This can easily morph into an "us versus them" mentality and one-dimensional labels like "that Japanese woman" or "that Mexican worker." But it is vital to remember every human is an intentional creation of our Father God. Every person has history, dreams, and fears; every person has the opportunity to inherit salvation, the gift of the Holy Spirit, and the "peace...which surpasses all understanding" (Philippians 4:7). It was the Pharisees who wanted to hoard God's affection for themselves and not share with outsiders. We should not repeat those mistakes.

So how can we reach out to our foreign neighbors? God in Leviticus and Jesus in Matthew both said to treat them as ourselves. Again, we need to practice empathy. If you were new to the neighborhood, wouldn't you like your neighbors to welcome you? If you didn't know how to use an appliance in your house, wouldn't it help if someone showed you? If you didn't have a car to get to the grocery store, wouldn't it be great if someone would drive you—and better yet, help you navigate through the store? Offer to help often, and empower as you do so; no one likes to be patronized, but most people like to learn how to do something themselves.

Hospitality is also hugely important in most cultures, so invite your foreign friends to experience things. Whether it's just Tuesday lunch, Christmas shopping, or a craft fair, invite people to participate in your life and your culture. And finally, show interest. Ask about their lives, listen to their stories from home, taste their food, learn their language, celebrate their holidays with them, and so on. It is important for foreigners to understand you are not trying to assimilate them; you want to welcome them.

John 13:35 says they will know you are Christians by your love. Not all foreigners are nonbelievers, and in fact, through reaching out to a foreign neighbor, you might learn this is your brother or sister in Christ! But the most important part about reaching out to a foreigner is not to welcome them to the United States but to welcome them to a life in Christ. You love them because Jesus died for them, and it's the right thing to do to serve them.

I love the song "When We All Get to Heaven," and whenever I sing it, I have trouble keeping tears at bay. I can hear the song in the different languages of groups I have worshiped with, in Mandarin, Portuguese, Spanish, and English, of course. I picture the faces of all my dear brothers and sisters whom I may not see again until we are all together in heaven, and I think of my friends in different countries finally meeting each other in the same place. All our differences will beautifully blend into one at the feet of Jesus, and we will do nothing but rejoice. Indeed, what a day of rejoicing that will be!

Taffeta Chime (MA, Middle Tennessee State University) has won multiple awards for her short stories, poems, and essays and has been published in several literary journals. She also has two published young adult novels. Through her 12 years of teaching English as a foreign language, Taffy has built intentional relationships with people from all around the world and continues evangelistic efforts through online Bible/language lessons, homestay for international students and visitors, and volunteer work in the local international community.

Prayer and Fasting

Shodankeh Johnson

Have you by chance heard that Christianity is dying out globally? Don't believe it for a second. We end with this chapter so that you will be encouraged by this snapshot of what God is doing around the world.

I would like to share with you some of what God is doing around the world and to share from God's Word what God is able to do. The stories I will be sharing are not my own. I'm telling *His* story—the testimonies of ordinary men and women whom God has used mightily to bring glory to His name. Jesus said when He is lifted up, He will draw all men and women to Himself (John 12:32). With all our strategies and skills, until God draws them, they are not going to come. So the stories I tell in this chapter are about what God is doing all around the world for His own glory and honor.

If there's anything that Satan is afraid of, it's your fasting-and-prayer link to God. Satan will do anything possible to sabotage this link to God because he knows how much of a game changer prayer and fasting can be. So I encourage you, don't give Satan a chance. Make a daily appointment with God. We make appointments with our doctors, with our lawyers, with our business partners; likewise, it is vital to make a daily appointment with God. When you do that, especially in prayer and fasting, your life will never be the same.

In the first century, in the Macedonian city of Philippi, Paul and Silas were beaten and arrested for casting a demon out of a fortune-telling slave girl, thus depriving her masters of their profit. They were beaten and thrown into the inner prison, where their feet were fastened in the stocks. There, they started to pray and sing unto the Lord. And as they prayed, three things began to happen (Acts 16:16-40).

First, the devil started quaking. As Paul and Silas prayed, suddenly at midnight, there was a mighty earthquake, a disruptive movement on the surface of the earth that caused things to begin to shake. Acts 16:25-26a says, "About midnight Paul and Silas were praying and singing hymns to God, and the prisoners were listening to them, and suddenly there was a great earthquake." When the church begins to make praying and fasting part of their DNA, part of their bloodline, the devil begins to quake. When families begin to pray and fast and make it their daily habit, the devil begins to quake.

Every day, some people will not leave home without coffee or tea. They will drink a cup in the morning, a cup at midday, a cup at night. In the same way, we need to make it a daily discipline to fast and pray. When the church begins to fast and pray—for our families, our children, our nations—the devil begins to quake. There is a volcanic movement that begins to happen. It might be imperceptible to the eyes, but you will feel it.

That's what happened in Sierra Leone in West Africa. Sierra Leone went through a brutal civil war. For ten years, revolutionaries were hacking hands, hacking legs, killing people. It was a senseless war, one of the most brutal wars on this planet. Many groups of fighters converged on Sierra Leone to fight the rebels. For example, there were the Economic Community of West African States Monitoring Group (ECOMOG), which is a conglomerate of about 7,000 West African troops; the Gurkhas from Britain; the Executive Outcomes from South Africa; and the civil militias, which we called the Kamajors. One can imagine the confusion with all these military groups fighting against the rebels. All the while, the rebels were gaining ground, taking villages, and destroying lives. It came to the point where we realized we were not going to win the war with physical weapons. We were going to win it with spiritual weapons.

So we started mobilizing the churches to pray and fast. Men and women, young and old, common and uncommon—they all started fasting and praying for days, weeks, and even months. Although we had used all the conventional weapons, we cried out to God to use His weapons. On our knees, we began praying for His mercy on Sierra Leone. God began to move in the rebel camp, and the devil began to quake. There came a time when the rebel leaders began to talk of peace. I still remember the day the rebels came into town to lay down their arms. The streets were packed full of people who had come to watch. We thought this would never happen, but it did. Some may give all the credit to military might, but we know that whatever physical weapons were used, the children of God were using spiritual weapons. They were asking of God—who is the "Impossibility Specialist"—to step into the battle. And I believe God worked for peace in our nation.

Today, former rebels are following Jesus and planting churches in Sierra Leone. No man can do this, only God. And the foundation God uses is men and women who become faithful in fasting and prayer. As they seek His face, the Impossibility Specialist answers. What man cannot do, God can do. I want to remind you that the God who parted the sea, sent fire from heaven, and shut the mouths of lions still lives today. He's the same God yesterday, today, and forever. The world changes, but He has not changed. And the same promises that Paul stood on, we can stand on today. The same confessions that the early church made, we can make today. And God can do the same things today in the lives of our families, our churches, and our nations. But we must discipline ourselves to fast and pray. In accordance with the Word of God, God will hear us.

Over and over again, I have seen God intervene in situations that seemed impossible. Before I married my wife, I told her that she was about to marry a great troublemaker. I said, "Do you love me? Will you marry me? Even though I am a spiritual troublemaker? I will not keep my mouth shut when it comes to the kingdom of God. Will you marry me?" She said yes. During the civil war in Sierra Leone, I would speak against any evil. There were times that the rebel soldiers would invite me to go to their camp to encourage them. Yet even in their camp, I would speak strongly against the evil I had seen them do.

One day, I was in my small office with two of my disciples. I saw soldiers surround the building. They barged in and began to arrest all three of us. All the while, the other two disciples were crying uncontrollably. I knew the soldiers had been looking for me, so I asked, "Who are you looking for? Are you looking for Pastor Johnson?"

They said, "Yes, we are looking for Pastor Johnson."

I said, "I am Pastor Johnson. These two men just came to visit me." I did not tell them that they were two of my disciples.

So the soldiers let the other two men go, and they ran. They did not even turn back to look at me; they just ran. And that reminded me of what Jesus went through with Peter when officers asked Peter if he knew Jesus, but Peter denied knowing Him (Luke 22:54-62).

The soldiers put me in the truck and brought me back to my house. There, they turned my house upside down; I do not know what they were looking for. They put me back in the truck and told my wife and my neighbors, "You will never see this man again." But I managed to squeeze my head out of the truck and said, "I'm coming back. These are my new best friends. I'm coming back."

They took me to their headquarters and put me in a 40-foot metal container and locked the door. They told me, "We will kill you tonight." The container was extremely hot and had no ventilation, so I took off my shirt. There, I began worshiping and singing praises to God. They did not like me singing, so occasionally they would beat against the container's side, yelling, "Stop singing! Stop singing!" But I answered, "I'm not going to stop singing. I'll continue to sing until I meet my God."

At night, they came to open the container and said, "The colonel wants to see you," and they took me upstairs. When we arrived, the colonel looked at me and smiled. He said, "You are a very brave man. What makes you so bold?"

I asked, "Sir, do you really want to know what makes me so bold?"

He replied, "Yes!"

So I said, "Sir, the Bible says that He who is in me is greater than he who is in the world."

He smiled, shook his head, and said, "Do you know that if you were in the army, you would have been a great man? By your courage, you would have been great in the army."

I responded, "I'm in the army, sir."

His eyes got wide. "Which army?"

"I'm in the army of the Lord, sir."

He looked at me and said, "I'm going to release you tonight. Report here first thing in the morning."

"Yes, sir."

So they released me that night. I went back to my house, and no one was expecting me. When people saw me, they thought I was a ghost. When I convinced them it was me, everyone began advising me, "Pack your bags! Run away! Find a place to go! Don't go back!"

And I said, "I'm going back. They told me to go in the morning."

So first thing in the morning, I got there. And the soldiers at the gate asked me, "So you came back?"

"Yes, because the colonel asked me to come."

I went to the colonel and sat down. "I really admire your boldness," the colonel said. "I want you to do me a favor. Will you please come here every week to talk to my boys? To come and encourage my soldiers?"

I replied, "Yes, sir."

That's how I became a chaplain to the army. It took me going to the container, praying, and worshiping God. As of today, we have trained virtually every chaplain in the army of Sierra Leone, and they are involved in planting churches and making disciples. I want you to know that the enemy's intention when they put me in that container was that I would die. But God turned the situation upside down, working it for His own glory. Because there were men and women praying and fasting, I was spared.

When you devote yourself to praying and fasting, the devil begins to quake.

Second, things began to shake. Because of the earthquake, the foundations of the prison that held Paul and Silas began shaking. Acts 16:25-26 says, "About midnight Paul and Silas were praying and singing hymns to God, and the prisoners were listening to them, and suddenly there was a great earthquake, so that the foundations of the prison were shaken."

When we begin to fast and pray, every faulty foundation of the church begins to shake. Our theologies, philosophies, traditions, and doctrines that have been made by men begin to shake. No wonder the devil doesn't want us to fast and pray! This foundation shaking also explains why a lot of people don't want to fast and pray.

I have seen foundations shake several times. For example, there was a community where we wanted to plant a church. So we went out to look at the place. One of the people knew I was a pastor and identified me. People began to come out and challenge us, saying, "There is no way we are going to allow a church to come into this community." One of the men even began to push me around.

I was just smiling. I told them, "You are too small for God." One of the women became offended and reported me to the police. The police confronted me: "This woman says you said that she was too small for God. Did you say that?"

I replied, "Yes, I said that."

"What do you mean by saying that?"

"Sir," I said, "look at this woman, and look at God. Which one is bigger? Which one is more powerful?"

The officer said, "It's God."

I said, "You've answered it. Is this a crime?"

"No, this is no crime."

So they let me go. At the end of the day, we began praying and fasting for the community. We sent intercessors into the community, who walked through the community without the people knowing. And they renamed the streets: "God, this community will be called a community of salvation. These streets will be called streets of redemption. Your name will be glorified in this community. We bind the strongman in this community. So that Your Word will come in, and Your name will be glorified!"

After weeks of fasting, we found a family of peace. Disciples were made. Baptisms happened. A church was planted. And today, every one of those people who opposed me is part of the church. Their families are a part of the church. And the man who was pushing me around? His son is now a pastor and missionary in Ghana. Who can do that except God?

When we devote ourselves to prayer and fasting, things start to shake. It will be the very foundation, the core, the things you depend on, the things you've believed in all your life that begin to shake. But it is all right. God knows everything. So when God begins to shake things, don't feel offended because God knows what is best.

Third, strongholds began to break. With the doors shut and locked, Paul and Silas were fastened right in the middle of the prison, where jailers put prisoners to die and rot. That was a stronghold. But little did the jailer know that Paul and Silas's God was an Impossibility Specialist. It didn't matter where the jailer put them. As they prayed, "immediately all the doors were opened, and everyone's chains were unfastened" (Acts 16:26). So they had the chance to walk out if they wanted to.

There are so many doors the devil has locked. Some of us are in strongholds, and we don't even realize it. But when we begin to fast and pray, those strongholds begin to topple, and doors begin to open. When God opens a door, no one closes it, and when He closes a door, no one opens it.

Chains of ignorance will fall off when we begin to fast and pray. Chains of tradition will begin to fall off when we begin to fast and pray. Chains of excuses will fall off when we begin to fast and pray. And God's church will begin to move. The impossible will begin to happen.

Amid the chaos of the earthquake, the jailer awoke to see the prison doors open. Assuming all the prisoners had escaped—and being fully aware of the punishment for allowing prisoners to escape—he drew his sword to kill himself. But Paul cried out, "Do not harm yourself, for we are all here" (Acts 16:28). And the very man who had chained them in the inner prison rushed in and fell down before Paul and Silas. The jailer had been one of the strongholds. Now he fell down before them and asked, "What must I do to be saved?" They responded, "Believe in the Lord Jesus, and you will be saved" (Acts 16:31). And that very night, the jailer washed their wounds, after which he and his family were baptized.

We have seen similar things happen in our time. During the civil war, I was openly speaking out against the atrocities, especially those of the Kamajors. The Kamajors were Sierra Leone's civil militiamen, and they numbered over 20,000. Needless to say, they did not like my message. As they looked for me, I went into hiding from place to place. Finally, one day, I was passing by, and one of them recognized me. He said, "That is the man we are looking for." They arrested me, tying my hands in such a way that my fingers could touch the back of my neck. They brought me to their commander. He had his pistol pointed at me, as did his men, who held their AK-47s, waiting for the command to shoot. He told me, "You've been talking about how your God is such a great God. But right now, your God can't do anything for you. Because I am going to kill you."

I bowed my head and said, "God, if this is my time to die, I'm ready to die. But please, God, do me one favor. If I am to die, let me bring one more person to You. Please, let this commander be the one more person who comes to believe. Give me the boldness and courage to talk to him."

I lifted my head and said, "Commander, please give me five minutes to talk to you."

The commander replied, "Go ahead and talk any nonsense. You are already a dead man anyway."

I said, "Commander, I want you to do me a favor. I want you to accept Jesus as your Lord and personal Savior. Right now, if you shoot me, there are angels all around this place waiting to take me into heaven. But if you die, Commander, you don't have a place to go. You will not make it to heaven. So do me a favor. When you accept Jesus right now as your Lord and personal Savior, and then you turn around and shoot me, Jesus will forgive you. And both of us will have a place in heaven. Commander, Jesus loves you. He cares for you. His arms are wide open waiting to receive you."

As I talked, I saw the pistol drop. There was perfect quietness. The commander was at a loss for words. He said to his men, "Untie this man. Let him go. Something is wrong with his head." They untied me and let me go.

But a few weeks later, the commander came looking for me again. He came to the place where I was staying. My wife was outside; I was inside. When he got down from the vehicle, he asked, "Where's your husband?" Trying to hide me, my wife replied that I was not around.

I decided to step out of the house because I was afraid that if I did not, the commander might harm my family. I said, "Commander, what is the problem?"

He said, "I want to talk to you." So we went and stood under a tree. The commander said, "Do you know that the way you spoke to me that day—nobody has ever spoken to me that way? Nobody! And when you spoke to me that day, you told me that if I die, I don't have a place to go. I've been thinking about what you told me. I go to bed and can't sleep. Your voice has been ringing in my ears. That's why I've been looking for you. Can we be friends?"

That's how I became friends with the commander. A few months later, I baptized the commander in the river. Today, he is a follower of Jesus, and two of his men who were holding the AK-47s are part of a church-planting movement.

What man cannot do, God can do. Prayer has the power. It is a game changer. We have seen prayer change communities and transform families.

One day, I was sharing the Word of God with a family, and there was an uncle who did not like me sharing the Word. As I spoke the Word, he came with a bucket filled with water and poured all the water on me. I stood up and smiled. I went back home, changed, and came back. I continued to pray with that family until every one of them got saved. The uncle is still not saved, but we have become friends. When we meet on the streets, I tell him, "I love the way you baptized me that day. I'm looking for the opportunity to also baptize you." Every day, I'm praying for him, that he will become a follower of Jesus Christ.

We have seen difficult homes, families, and communities that have made us say, "There is no way we will ever have the gospel here." But we have seen how the Lord has entered there because men and women were committed to praying and fasting. The same can happen in your home, family, and community. If your church begins to pray and fast and cry out to God for your nation, I believe very strongly that you will see God bring your nation back to Himself. But it's going to start with men and women faithful enough to fast and pray. God will honor His Word.

Father, there is nothing You cannot do. Let Your name be glorified. Let Your name be praised.

Pastor Shodankeh Johnson is the leader of New Harvest Ministries (NHM) in Sierra Leone. Through God's favor, and a commitment to disciple-making movements, NHM has started countless churches and numerous schools in Sierra Leone and has sent long-term workers to the surrounding nations in West Africa. American pastors, discouraged at not experiencing "Acts 2" Christianity, have visited Sierra Leone only to return with reignited passion and renewed vision for what church can be.

Index

Notes

Introduction

1. Christopher Pramuk, "'Something Breaks Through a Little': The Marriage of Zen and Sophia in the Life of Thomas Merton," *Buddhist-Christian Studies* 28 (2008): 67–89, 81.
2. Interfaith scholar John Cobb taught that rather than trying to convert people to our religion, we ought to convert the religions to the point that they no longer contradict one another at core. He writes, "But more important than the conversion of individual Buddhists, Hindus, or Muslims is the conversion of Buddhism, Hinduism, and Islam." See John B. Cobb, *Beyond Dialogue: Toward a Mutual Transformation of Christianity and Buddhism* (Eugene, OR: Wipf and Stock, 1998), 142.

Chapter 1. What in the World God Is Up To (and How You Can Join In)

1. Francis Fukuyama, *The Origins of Political Order: From Prehuman Times to the French Revolution* (New York: Farrar, Straus and Giroux, 2011), 445.
2. A.A. Stockdale, "God Left the Challenge in the Earth," *His* 25 (December 1964): 20.
3. Some of these analogies are taken from John Eldridge, *Epic: The Story God Is Telling* (Nashville: Thomas Nelson, 2004), 35.
4. Edward Shillito, "Jesus of the Scars," *Westminster Gazette*, 1919.
5. These passages are compiled by John Stott in *The Cross of Christ* (Downers Grove, IL: InterVarsity, 1986), 78–79.
6. Samuel Zwemer, *Glory of the Cross* (London: Marshall, Morgan, and Scott, 1928), 6.
7. Richard Powers, *The Overstory* (New York: W.W. Norton, 2018).
8. Arthur Glasser, *Announcing the Kingdom: The Story of God's Mission in the Bible* (Grand Rapids, MI: Baker, 2003), 152.
9. Justo Gonzalez, *For the Healing of the Nations* (Maryknoll, NY: Orbis, 1999), 111–12.

Chapter 2. Tough Questions About Religion

1. John Rumble, *Handbook of Chemistry and Physics*, 93rd ed. (Boca Raton, FL: CRC Books, 2019).
2. In the case of Buddhism, the term is usually thought of as a state of nonexistence, which may not be strictly accurate. For Jainism, nirvana is a state of permanent bliss. Please see the relevant chapters in this book. For more detailed information, here as elsewhere, please see Winfried Corduan, *Neighboring Faiths*, 2nd ed. (Downers Grove, IL: IVP Academic, 2012), 313–57, 358–72.
3. Corduan, 28.
4. For example, E.B. Tylor, *Primitive Culture*, 2nd ed., 2 vols. (London: John Murray, 1889).
5. A leading figure in establishing this path of analysis, called the "culture-historical method," was Fritz Graebner, *Methode der Ethnologie* (Heidelberg, Germany: Carl Winter, 1911).
6. Wilhelm Schmidt, *Der Ursprung der Gottesidee*, 12 vols. (Münster: Aschendorff, 1811–1955); *The Origin and Growth of Religion: Facts and Theories*, trans. H.J. Rose (Proctorville, OH: Whyte-North, 2014); Schmidt, *Primitive Revelation*, trans. Joseph J. Baierl (St. Louis: Herder, 1939).
7. For a detailed account of the debate, see Winfried Corduan, *In the Beginning God: A Fresh Look at the Case for Original Theism* (Nashville: B&H Academic, 2013).
8. Karl Rahner and Herbert Vorgrimmler, "Anonymes Christentum," in *Kleines Theologisches Wörterbuch*, 11th ed. (1936; Freiburg, Germany: Herder, 1971), 23–24; Rahner, *Schriften zur Theologie* (Einsiedeln, Switzerland: Denziger, 1967), 5:183-221.
9. For example, the website *Hinduism Basics*, https://www.hafsite.org/hinduism-101/hinduism-basics. The authors even provide a Sanskrit version of this saying that is supposedly found in the Rig Veda—though it is not, at least not in that form. A more accurate translation of the verse on which this is possibly based focuses on the many gods of later Hinduism, all of which originated with the god Dyaus Pitā, who at one time was considered the

one and only God: "They call him Indra, Mitra, Varu'a, Agni, and he is heavenly nobly-winged Garutmān. To what is One, sages give many a title they call it Agni, Yama, Mātariśvan." Ralph T.H. Griffith, trans., *Rig Veda*, 2nd ed. (Kotagiri, India: Nilgiri, 1896), 1:164, available at *Internet Sacred Text Archive*, accessed March 24, 2020, http://www.sacred-texts.com/hin/rigveda/rv01164.htm. See also Corduan, *In the Beginning God*, 317. The saying is concerned with the explosion of divine names in Hinduism, not with an idea that all religions share the same content with different vocabularies.

10. For why this is actually not a dark and gloomy statement, please see Winfried Corduan, *A Tapestry of Faith: The Common Threads Between Christianity and World Religions* (Eugene, OR: Wipf and Stock, 2002).
11. John Hick, "Religious Pluralism," in *The Philosophical Challenge of Religious Diversity*, ed. Philip L. Quinn and Kevin Meeker (New York: Oxford University Press, 2000), esp. 66–67; Corduan, *Tapestry of Faith*, 138–39. I am devoting such a large amount of space to John Hick, not so much because of his individual contribution, but because he so nicely represents the amazing religious imperialism of some Western academic circles.
12. Where I say "mature," Hick referred to those religions that arose during and after the sixth century BC, a time that he called the "axial age."
13. Please see my detailed discussion of this phenomenon on the website *Christ and Krishna*, win.corduan.net/krishna-christ.html.
14. See the essay by Stuart Redi, "Jesus and Buddha: Same Message, Different Guise? Same Guise, Different Messages?," *Dharma to Grace*, accessed March 24, 2020, http://dharma2grace.net/jesusandbuddha.html.
15. Michio Kaku, "Michio Kaku: Is God a Mathematician?," *YouTube*, January 2, 2013, https://www.youtube.com/watch?time_continue=1&v=jremlZvNDuk.
16. Rudolf Bultmann et al., "Kerygma and Myth," *Religion Online*, https://www.religion-online.org/book-chapter/the-mythological-element-in-the-message-of-the-new-testament-and-the-problem-of-its-re-interpretation-part-i/.
17. No one has studied and written on worldviews more than James Sire. See his *Universe Next Door*, 5th ed. (Downers Grove, IL: InterVarsity, 2009); and *Why Good Arguments Often Fail* (Downers Grove, IL: InterVarsity, 2006).
18. For more on this topic, see "How to Contextualize the Gospel," by I'Ching Thomas in this book (chapter 3).

Chapter 3. How to Contextualize the Gospel

1. While the term *era* typically denotes chronological time, in this case, it would also include mindset or paradigm.
2. Paul G. Hiebert, *Anthropological Reflections on Missiological Issues* (Grand Rapids, MI: Baker, 1994), 54.
3. Hiebert, 57.
4. D.J. Bosch, *Transforming Mission: Paradigm Shifts in Theology of Mission* (New York: Orbis, 1991), 448.
5. Felix Muchimba, *Liberating the African Soul: Comparing African and Western Christian Music and Worship Styles* (Colorado Springs, CO: Authentic, 2007), 14.
6. This era of the Opium Wars and unequal treaties is also sometimes known as China's century of humiliation.
7. Jiang Menglin, quoted in YongTao Chen, "The Sinicization of Christianity: A Chinese Christian's Thoughts," *Chinese Theological Review* 27 (2015): 125.
8. Hiebert, *Anthropological Reflections*, 58.
9. Hiebert, 59.
10. Stephen B. Bevans, *Models of Contextual Theology*, rev. ed. (Maryknoll, NY: Orbis, 2002), 117–18.
11. Hiebert, *Anthropological Reflections*, 63.
12. Hiebert, 63.
13. Winfried Corduan, *Neighboring Faiths: A Christian Introduction to World Religions* (Downers Grove, IL: InterVarsity, 1998), 41.
14. See Jayson Georges, *The 3D Gospel: Ministry in Guilt, Shame, and Fear Cultures* (San Bernardino, CA: Time Press, 2014), for an exploration of the various aspects of the gospel.
15. Karl Reichelt, *Meditation and Piety in the Far East* (Cambridge: James Clarke, 1959), 59.
16. It is a Cultural Chinese belief that every year on the seventh lunar month, the spirits of all departed will be released from hell and allowed to roam among the living. All kinds of rituals are performed to appease these spirits to keep them away.
17. Tan Kang San, "What Is So Theological About Contextual Mission Training?," in *Contextualisation and Mission*

Training: Engaging Asia's Religious World, ed. Jonathan Ingleby, Tan Kang San, and Tan Loun Ling (Eugene, OR: Wipf and Stock, 2013), 8.

18. Jackson Wu, *One Gospel for All Nations: A Practical Approach to Biblical Contextualization* (Pasadena, CA: William Carey Library, 2015), xviii.
19. Corduan, *Neighboring Faiths*, 42.
20. For a helpful answer as to what is contextualization, see the section "What Is Contextualization" in Winfried Corduan's "Tough Questions" chapter in this book (chapter 2).
21. David J. Hesselgrave and Edward Rommen, *Contextualization: Meanings, Methods, and Models* (Grand Rapids, MI: Baker, 1989), 200.
22. Corduan, *Neighboring Faiths*, 42.
23. David Miller, "Here Be Dragons—Some Guidelines for Explorers in Contextual Mission and Theology in Asia," in *Contextualisation and Mission Training*, 33.
24. Corduan, *Neighboring Faiths*, 41.
25. I'Ching Thomas, *Jesus: The Path to Human Flourishing* (Singapore: Graceworks, 2018), 16.
26. James Sire, *Why Good Arguments Fail: Making a More Persuasive Case for Christ* (Downers Grove, IL: InterVarsity, 2006), 140.
27. Tan, "What Is Theological?," 11.
28. Georges, *3D Gospel*.
29. Jayson Georges's website, www.honorshame.com, is a great resource in the discussion of the three cultural orientations.
30. Georges, *3D Gospel*, 13.
31. See Don Richardson, *Peace Child* (Ventura, CA: Regal, 1974).
32. Thomas, *Jesus*, 114.
33. Enoch Wan, "Practical Contextualization: A Case Study of Evangelizing Contemporary Chinese," enochwan.com, accessed October 5, 2017, http://www.enochwan.com/english/articles/pdf/Practical%20Contextualization%20Evangel%20Chinese.pdf.
34. Miller, "Here Be Dragons," 32.
35. Miller, 34.
36. Miller, 28.

Chapter 4. Objections to Cross-Cultural Evangelism

1. John B. Cobb Jr., "Buddhism and Christianity as Complementary," *Eastern Buddhist* 13, no. 2 (1980): 16.
2. Notto R. Thelle, "The 'Humanization' of Buddhism: Aspects of Western Adaptations of Buddhism," *Ching Feng* 10, nos. 1–2 (2010–11): 73.
3. Russell H. Bowers, "Defending God Before Buddhist Emptiness," *Bibliotheca Sacra* 154 (1997): 396.
4. Keith Yandell and Harold Netland, *Buddhism: A Christian Exploration and Appraisal* (Downers Grove, IL: IVP Academic, 2009), 86–87.
5. Bowers, "Defending God Before Buddhist Emptiness," 396.
6. Bowers, 397.
7. Reginald Ray, "From Dialogue to Mutual Transformation: The Third Buddhist-Christian Theological Encounter," *Eastern Buddhist* 20, no. 2 (1987): 115.
8. Frederick Franck, "Upaya: Stratagems of Great Compassion," *Eastern Buddhist* 30, no. 2 (1997): 287–88.
9. Brian Bocking, "Comparative Studies of Buddhism and Christianity," *Japanese Journal of Religious Studies* 10, no. 1 (1983): 94.
10. Paul Grimley Kuntz, "Santayana and Buddhism: The Choice Between the Cross and the Bo Tree," *Buddhist-Christian Studies* 20 (2000): 159.
11. Grace G. Burford, "Asymmetry, Essentialism, and Covert Cultural Imperialism: Should Buddhists and Christians Do Theoretical Work Together?," *Buddhist-Christian Studies* 31 (2011): 150.
12. Daniel J. Adams, "Universal Salvation? A Study in Myanmar Christian Theology," *Asia Journal of Theology* 22, no. 2 (2008): 226.

13. John Makransky, "Thoughts on Why, How, and What Buddhists Can Learn from Christian Theologians," *Buddhist-Christian Studies* 31 (2011): 123.
14. Burford, "Asymmetry," 147.
15. Burford, 154.
16. Paul F. Knitter and Harold A. Netland, "Can Only One Religion Be True? A Dialogue," in *Can Only One Religion Be True? Paul Knitter and Harold Netland in Dialogue*, ed. Robert B. Stewart (Minneapolis: Fortress, 2013), 29–30.
17. Knitter and Netland, 30.
18. Knitter and Netland.
19. Knitter and Netland.
20. Christopher A. Brown, "Can Buddhism Save? Finishing Resonance in Incommensurability," *CrossCurrents* 49, no. 2 (Summer 1999): 167–68.
21. John S. Yokota, "Shin Buddhism and the Christian-Buddhist Dialog: What Is to Be Gained?," *Pure Land* 18–19 (2002): 143.
22. Much of this section, which was originally based on my PhD thesis (Daniel McCoy, "A Comparison of Buddhist Compassion to Christian Love" [PhD diss., North-West University, 2016]), was reworked and printed in a journal article: Daniel McCoy, Winfried Corduan, and Henk Stoker, "Christian and Buddhist Approach to Religious Exclusivity: Do Interfaith Scholars Have It Right?," *HTS Theological Studies* 72, no. 3 (2016): http://dx.doi.org/10.4102/hts.v72i3.3266.
23. *Casablanca*, directed by Michael Curtiz (Burbank, CA: Warner Bros., 1942).
24. As will be made clear below, not all inclusivists believe that all people will be saved. Many believe that there will be a level of sincerity or ethical rightness to be achieved. Hence the statement that "all will be saved (but through my general)" is admittedly too general to describe the beliefs of all inclusivists.
25. This would fall under the category of prescriptive pluralism in the chapter on "Religious Pluralism" (chapter 19).
26. Rita M. Gross, "Religious Identity and Openness in a Pluralistic World," *Buddhist-Christian Studies* 25 (2005): 20.
27. Gross.
28. Amos Yong, "On Doing Theology and Buddhology: A Spectrum of Christian Proposals," *Buddhist-Christian Studies* 31 (2011): 106.
29. John Hick, "Is Christianity the Only True Religion, or One Among Others?," *John Hick: The Official Website*, 2001, accessed March 24, 2020, http://www.johnhick.org.uk/article2.html.
30. Brown, "Can Buddhism Save?," 167–68.
31. Jan Olov Fors, "Mutual Transformation: John Cobb's Theology of Religions and His Dialogue with Buddhism," *Swedish Missiological Themes* 94, no. 1 (2006): 92.
32. Yong, "On Doing Theology and Buddhology," 108.
33. Paul F. Knitter, "A 'Hypostatic Union' of Two Practices but One Person?," *Buddhist-Christian Studies* 32 (2012): 22.
34. John Makransky, "Buddhist Perspectives on Truth in Other Religions: Past and Present," *Theological Studies* 64, no. 2 (2003): 358.
35. Shandao, "Parable of the White Path," in *Popular Buddhism in Japan: Shin Buddhist Religion and Culture*, ed. E. Andreasen (Abingdon, UK: Routledge, 2014), 84–86.
36. "Almost Half of Practicing Millennials Say Evangelism Is Wrong," *Barna*, February 5, 2019, https://www.barna.com/research/millennials-oppose-evangelism/.

Chapter 5. Christianity

1. Conrad Hackett and David McClendon, "Christians Remain World's Largest Religious Group but They Are Declining in Europe," *Pew Research Center*, April 5, 2017, https://www.pewresearch.org/fact-tank/2017/04/05/christians-remain-worlds-largest-religious-group-but-they-are-declining-in-europe/.
2. "Long ago, at many times and in many ways, God spoke to our fathers by the prophets, but in these last days he has spoken to us by his Son, whom he appointed the heir of all things, through whom also he created the world. He is the radiance of the glory of God and the exact imprint of his nature, and he upholds the universe

by the word of his power. After making purification for sins, he sat down at the right hand of the Majesty on high" (Hebrews 1:1-3).

3. John 1:14 recognizes this, saying, "And the Word became flesh and dwelt among us, and we have seen his glory, glory as of the only Son from the Father, full of grace and truth."
4. "And there is salvation in no one else, for there is no other name under heaven given among men by which we must be saved" (Acts 4:12).
5. "For by grace you have been saved through faith. And this is not your own doing; it is the gift of God, not a result of works, so that no one may boast" (Ephesians 2:8-9).
6. "For all have sinned and fall short of the glory of God" (Romans 3:23); "None is righteous, no, not one; no one understands; no one seeks for God. All have turned aside; together they have become worthless; no one does good, not even one" (Romans 3:10-12).
7. "But when the fullness of time had come, God sent forth his Son, born of woman, born under the law, to redeem those who were under the law, so that we might receive adoption as sons. And because you are sons, God has sent the Spirit of his Son into our hearts, crying, 'Abba! Father!' So you are no longer a slave, but a son, and if a son, then an heir through God" (Galatians 4:4-7).
8. "If we confess our sins, he is faithful and just to forgive us our sins and to cleanse us from all unrighteousness" (1 John 1:9).
9. "Go therefore and make disciples of all nations, baptizing them in the name of the Father and of the Son and of the Holy Spirit" (Matthew 28:19).
10. Wayne Grudem, *Systematic Theology: An Introduction to Biblical Doctrine* (Grand Rapids, MI: Zondervan, 1994), 255.
11. "For God so loved the world, that he gave his only Son, that whoever believes in him should not perish but have eternal life" (John 3:16).
12. J.I. Packer, *Knowing God* (Downers Grove, IL: InterVarsity, 1993), 53.
13. "And Jesus increased in wisdom and in stature and in favor with God and man" (Luke 2:52).
14. "For we do not have a high priest who is unable to sympathize with our weaknesses, but one who in every respect has been tempted as we are, yet without sin" (Hebrews 4:15).
15. "But when the fullness of time had come, God sent forth his Son, born of woman, born under the law" (Galatians 4:4).
16. "For by him all things were created, in heaven and on earth, visible and invisible, whether thrones or dominions or rulers or authorities—all things were created through him and for him. And he is before all things, and in him all things hold together" (Colossians 1:16-17); "'But that you may know that the Son of Man has authority on earth to forgive sins'—he then said to the paralytic—'Rise, pick up your bed and go home'" (Matthew 9:6).
17. John Calvin, *Institutes of the Christian Religion*, ed. John T. McNeill (Louisville, KY: Westminster John Knox, 1960), loc. 14204–5, Kindle.
18. "For God so loved the world, that he gave his only Son, that whoever believes in him should not perish but have eternal life" (John 3:16).
19. "Who is to condemn? Christ Jesus is the one who died—more than that, who was raised—who is at the right hand of God, who indeed is interceding for us" (Romans 8:34).
20. "For the grace of God has appeared, bringing salvation for all people, training us to renounce ungodliness and worldly passions, and to live self-controlled, upright, and godly lives in the present age, waiting for our blessed hope, the appearing of the glory of our great God and Savior Jesus Christ, who gave himself for us to redeem us from all lawlessness and to purify for himself a people for his own possession who are zealous for good works" (Titus 2:11-14).
21. There is debate whether Martin Luther actually said it, but a similar sentiment is contained in the Lutheran confession *The Formula of Concord* (1577): "But after man has been justified by faith, then a true living faith worketh by love, Galatians 5:6, so that thus good works always follow justifying faith, and are surely found with it, if it be true and living; for it never is alone, but always has with it love and hope." Henry Eyster Jacobs, Charles P. Krauth, and Charles Frederick Schaeffer, *The Book of Concord, or The Symbolical Books of the Evangelical Lutheran Church* (Philadelphia: General Council Publication Board, 1919), 502.
22. "Jesus answered, 'Truly, truly, I say to you, unless one is born of water and the Spirit, he cannot enter the kingdom

of God. That which is born of the flesh is flesh, and that which is born of the Spirit is spirit. Do not marvel that I said to you, "You must be born again"'" (John 3:5-7); "No one born of God makes a practice of sinning, for God's seed abides in him, and he cannot keep on sinning because he has been born of God" (1 John 3:9).

23. "Then he will say to those on his left, 'Depart from me, you cursed, into the eternal fire prepared for the devil and his angels'...And these will go away into eternal punishment, but the righteous into eternal life" (Matthew 25:41-46).
24. "He will render to each one according to his works: to those who by patience in well-doing seek for glory and honor and immortality, he will give eternal life; but for those who are self-seeking and do not obey the truth, but obey unrighteousness, there will be wrath and fury" (Romans 2:6-8).
25. "For to me to live is Christ, and to die is gain. If I am to live in the flesh, that means fruitful labor for me. Yet which I shall choose I cannot tell. I am hard pressed between the two. My desire is to depart and be with Christ, for that is far better" (Philippians 1:21-23).
26. Harold O.J. Brown writes of the acceptance of "homoousios" (consubstantial) to describe Jesus having the same substance as God the Father, "Only two Arian bishops refused to endorse the *homoousian* creed." See Brown, *Heresies: Heresy and Orthodoxy in the History of the Church* (Peabody, MA: Hendrickson, 2000), 117.
27. Mark A. Noll, *Turning Points: Decisive Moments in the History of Christianity* (Grand Rapids, MI: Baker Academic, 2012), 78.
28. "Overview of Medieval Monasticism," *Dallas Baptist University*, accessed March 24, 2020, https://www3.dbu.edu/mitchell/monasticoverview.htm.
29. Mark Noll speaks of these potential problems in *Turning Points*, 95–96.
30. Innocent III, "Papal Authority: Letter to the Prefect Acerbius and the Nobles of Tuscany, 1198," in *Medieval Sourcebook: Innocent III (r. 1198–1216): Letter on Papal Policies*, available at https://sourcebooks.fordham.edu/source/innIII-policies.asp.
31. "Pastor aeternus," in *A Reformation Reader: Primary Texts with Introductions*, ed. Denis Janz, 2nd ed. (Minneapolis: Fortress, 2008), 14.
32. Anselm, *Cur Deus homo* (n.p.: Ex Fontibus, 2015), 25.
33. Cited in William Placher, *A History of Christian Theology* (Louisville, KY: Westminster John Knox, 2013), 168.
34. "X. Indulgences," *Catechism of the Catholic Church*, accessed March 24, 2020, http://www.vatican.va/archive/ENG0015/__P4G.HTM.
35. Martin Luther, *Christian Liberty* (Philadelphia: Lutheran Publication Society, 1903), 8.
36. David B. Barrett, George T. Kurian, and Todd M. Johnson, *World Christian Encyclopedia* (New York: Oxford University Press, 2001).
37. In Latin, it is "Sacra Scriptura sui ipsius interpres" (WA 7/97.23). Martin Luther, *D. Martin Luthers Werke: Kritische Gesamtausgabe*, 73 vols. (Weimar, Germany: Herman Böhlaus Nachfolger, 1883–2009).
38. Jaroslav Pelikan and Helmut T. Lehmann, eds., *Luther's Works*, American ed., 55 vols. (Philadelphia: Muhlenberg and Fortress; St. Louis: Concordia, 1955–86), 31:341.
39. "How Many Roman Catholics Are There in the World?," *BBC News*, March 14, 2013, https://www.bbc.com/news/world-21443313.
40. "III. The Interpretation of the Heritage of Faith," *Catechism of the Catholic Church*, accessed March 24, 2020, http://www.vatican.va/archive/ENG0015/_PM.HTM.
41. "Interpretation of the Heritage of Faith."
42. "Article 3: The Sacrament of the Eucharist," *Catechism of the Catholic Church*, accessed March 24, 2020, http://www.vatican.va/archive/ccc_css/archive/catechism/p2s2c1a3.htm.
43. "Life and Dignity of the Human Person," *United States Conference of Catholic Bishops*, 2019, accessed March 24, 2020, http://www.usccb.org/beliefs-and-teachings/what-we-believe/catholic-social-teaching/life-and-dignity-of-the-human-person.cfm.
44. The Second Vatican Council helped spell out the church's moral view in its encyclical *Gaudium et spes*.
45. "Article 2: Grace and Justification," *Catechism of the Catholic Church*, accessed March 24, 2020, http://www.vatican.va/archive/ccc_css/archive/catechism/p3s1c3a2.htm.
46. Athanasios N. Papathanasiou, "Some Key Themes and Figures in Greek Theological Thought," in *The Cambridge*

Companion to Orthodox Christian Theology, ed. Mary B. Cunningham and Elizabeth Theokritoff (Cambridge: Cambridge University Press, 2010), 226.

47. Kallistos Ware, *The Orthodox Church* (London: Penguin, 1997), 240.
48. Ware, 258.
49. "The Nature of Sin," *Orthodox Photos*, accessed August 3, 2019, http://www.orthodoxphotos.com/readings/law/sin.shtml.
50. Athanasius, quoted in Ware, *Orthodox Church*, 21.
51. David W. Bebbington, *Evangelicalism in Modern Britain: A History from the 1730s to the 1930s* (London: Unwin Hyman, 1989), 2–5.
52. George M. Marsden, *Understanding Fundamentalism and Evangelicalism* (Grand Rapids, MI: Eerdmans, 2007), 6.

Chapter 6. Islam

1. "Triple Talaq: India Criminalises Muslim 'Instant Divorce,'" *BBC News*, July 30, 2019, https://www.bbc.com/news/world-asia-india-49160818.
2. Jonathan Head, "Quiet End to Turkey's College Headscarf Ban," *BBC News*, December 31, 2010, https://www.bbc.com/news/world-europe-11880622.
3. "Norway Muslims Can Follow Makkah Fasting Hours," *Arab News*, June 8, 2016, https://www.arabnews.com/node/936341/world.
4. Sam Borden, "Observance of Ramadan Poses Challenges to Muslim Athletes," *New York Times*, July 31, 2012, https://www.nytimes.com/2012/08/01/sports/olympics/ramadan-poses-challenges-for-muslims-at-the-olympics.html.
5. "Is It Permissible for Men to Wear Watches Made of Gold?," *Islam Question and Answer*, accessed March 24, 2020, https://islamqa.info/en/answers/148476/is-it-permissible-for-men-to-wear-watches-made-of-gold.
6. Muhammad ibn Adam Darul Iftaa, "Wearing a Watch: Which Hand?," *Islam.ru*, May 6, 2013, http://islam.ru/en/content/story/wearing-watch-which-hand.
7. Although the commentary of Ibn Hajar al-Asqalani is not available in English, the reference can be found in Arabic in a snapshot of the hadith.al-islam website from April 14, 2008, at https://web.archive.org/web/20080414165550/http://hadith.al-islam.com/Display/Display.asp?Doc=0&Rec=23. Another commentary that follows this same interpretation is Sheikh Al-Nawawi in his *Meadows of the Righteous* or, in Arabic, *Riyadh al-Salihin*, *The Book of Miscellany*, chap. 27, "Reverence Towards the Sanctity of Muslims," Hadith 236, accessed March 25, 2020, http://islamicstudies.info/hadith/riyad-us-saliheen/riyad.php?hadith=222&to=239.
8. David Garrison, "Muslims Turning to Christ—a Global Phenomenon," *Premier Christianity*, June 2016, https://www.premierchristianity.com/Past-Issues/2016/June-2016/Muslims-turning-to-Christ-a-global-phenomenon.

Chapter 7. Buddhism

1. "The Birth of the Buddha," translated from the introduction to the Jataka, in "Indian History Sourcebook: Sources on the Buddha's Life and Death," ed. Paul Halstall, *Fordham University*, 1998, accessed March 24, 2020, http://www.fordham.edu/halsall/india/buddha-life.asp.
2. "Birth of the Buddha."
3. "Birth of the Buddha."
4. "Mahapadana Suttanta (DN 14)," translated from the Pali by T.W. Rhys Davids, *Buddhist Library Online*, June 6, 2014, http://buddhistlibraryonline.org/digha-nikaya/digha/dn14-mahapadana-sutta/37-mahapadana-suttanta.
5. "Mahapadana Suttanta (DN 14)."
6. "Sukhamala Sutta: Refinement (AN 3.38)," translated from the Pali by Thanissaro Bhikkhu, *Access to Insight*, 1997, accessed March 24, 2020, http://www.accesstoinsight.org/tipitaka/an/an03/an03.038.than.html.
7. Robert E. Buswell and Donald S. Lopez, *The Princeton Dictionary of Buddhism* (Princeton, NJ: Princeton University Press, 2014), 693.
8. "Maha-Saccaka Sutta: The Longer Discourse to Saccaka (MN 36)," translated from the Pali by Thanissaro Bhikkhu, *Access to Insight*, 2008, accessed March 24, 2020, http://www.accesstoinsight.org/tipitaka/mn/mn.036.than.html.
9. "Dhammacakkappavattana Sutta: Setting the Wheel of Dhamma in Motion (SN 56.11)," translated from the

Pali by Thanissaro Bhikkhu, *Access to Insight*, 1993, accessed March 24, 2020, https://www.accesstoinsight.org/tipitaka/sn/sn56/sn56.011.than.html.

10. "Samannaphala Sutta: The Fruits of the Contemplative Life (DN 2)," translated from the Pali by Thanissaro Bhukkhu, *Access to Insight*, 1997, accessed March 24, 2020, http://www.accesstoinsight.org/tipitaka/dn/dn.02.0.than.html.
11. Buswell and Lopez, *Princeton Dictionary of Buddhism*, 148.
12. "First Events After the Attainment," translated from the introduction to the Jataka, in "Indian History Sourcebook."
13. Paul Williams, Anthony Tribe, and Alexander Wynne, *Buddhist Thought: A Complete Introduction to the Indian Tradition*, 2nd ed. (London: Routledge, 2012), 47.
14. "Dhammacakkappavattana Sutta."
15. "Dhammacakkappavattana Sutta."
16. Andrew Olendzki, "Skinny Gotami and the Mustard Seed (Commentary to Thig 10.1)," *Access to Insight*, 2005, accessed March 24, 2020, http://www.accesstoinsight.org/noncanon/comy/thiga-10-01-ao0.html.
17. Olendzki.
18. Olendzki.
19. "Salayyaka Sutta: (Brahmans) of Sala (MN 41)," translated from the Pali by Thanissaro Bhikkhu, *Access to Insight*, 2011, accessed March 24, 2020, http://www.accesstoinsight.org/tipitaka/mn/mn.041.than.html.
20. "Maha-Sihanada Sutta: The Great Discourse on the Lion's Roar (MN 12)," translated from the Pali by Nanamoli Thera and Bhikkhu Bodhi, *Access to Insight*, 1994, accessed March 24, 2020, http://www.accesstoinsight.org/tipitaka/mn/mn.012.ntbb.html.
21. "Pabbatopama Sutta: The Simile of the Mountains (SN 3.25)," translated from the Pali by Thanissaro Bhikkhu, *Access to Insight*, 1997, accessed March 24, 2020, http://www.accesstoinsight.org/tipitaka/sn/sn03/sn03.025.than.html.
22. "Sunita the Outcaste (Thag 12.2)," translated from the Pali by Thanissaro Bhikkhu, *Access to Insight*, 1994, accessed March 24, 2020, http://www.accesstoinsight.org/tipitaka/kn/thag/thag.12.02.than.html.
23. "Jara Sutta: Old Age (SN 48.41)," translated from the Pali by Thanissaro Bhikkhu, *Access to Insight*, 1998, accessed March 24, 2020, http://www.accesstoinsight.org/tipitaka/sn/sn48/sn48.041.than.html.
24. "Maha-Parinibbana Sutta: Last Days of the Buddha (DN 16)," translated from the Pali by Sister Vajira and Francis Story, *Access to Insight*, 1998, accessed March 24, 2020, http://www.accesstoinsight.org/tipitaka/dn/dn.16.1-6.vaji.html.
25. "Maha-Parinibbana Sutta."
26. "Maha-Parinibbana Sutta."
27. "Maha-Parinibbana Sutta."
28. Williams, Tribe, and Wynne, *Buddhist Thought*, 36.
29. This is a teaching of the meditative, philosophical branch of Hinduism known as Vedanta Hinduism.
30. Buswell and Lopez, *Princeton Dictionary of Buddhism*, 424.
31. For a closer description of various Mahayana schools as well as other important information on Buddhism, see the website *Dharma to Grace*, http://dharma2grace.net/index.html.
32. According to the Buddhist Churches of America, "There were people who asserted that one should strive to say the nembutsu as often as possible, and others who insisted that true entrusting was manifested in saying the nembutsu only once, leaving all else to Amida. Shinran rejected both sides as human contrivance based on attachment to the nembutsu as one's own good act. Since genuine nembutsu arises from true entrusting that is Amida's working in a person, the number of times it is said is irrelevant." "Shinran Shonin," *Buddhist Churches of America*, accessed March 24, 2020, http://www.buddhistchurchesofamerica.org/shinran-shonin/.
33. Cf. the essay by Stuart Redi, "Jesus and Buddha: Different Guise—Same Message?," *Dharma to Grace*, accessed March 24, 2020, http://dharma2grace.net/christandbuddha.html.
34. Lotus Sutra, chap. 2, at *Internet Sacred Text Archive*, accessed March 24, 2020, http://www.sacred-texts.com/bud/lotus/lot02.htm.
35. "The Long Search—Buddhism: Footprint of the Buddha (BBC 1977)," *YouTube*, April 29, 2013, 27:30, https://www.youtube.com/watch?v=C3r202etWLE.

36. Sam Van Schaik, *Tibet: A History* (London: Yale University Press, 2011). From page to page, chapter to chapter, this book chronicles the history of how politics and religion have been entwined in Tibet, and the wars and battles are simply a constant part of the story.
37. This event is documented thoroughly; see, for example, Elliot Sperling, "The Chinese Venture in K'am, 1904–1911, and the Role of Chao Erh-feng," *Tibet Journal* 1, no. 2 (1976): 10–33.
38. Win Corduan, "Basic Buddhist Teaching," *YouTube*, April 12, 2010, https://www.youtube.com/watch?v =O0Q1lrxQlMU.

Chapter 8. Judaism

1. For example, the Roman Catholic Church—citing Romans 11:29 that "the gifts of the calling of God [toward the Jews] are irrevocable"—has declared that it "neither conducts nor supports any specific institutional work directed towards Jews" any longer, though personal evangelism is still encouraged. See "The Gifts and the Calling of God Are Irrevocable," *Commission for Religious Relations with the Jews*, accessed March 24, 2020, http://www.vatican .va/roman_curia/pontifical_councils/chrstuni/relations-jews-docs/rc_pc_chrstuni_doc_20151210_ebraismo -nostra-aetate_en.html#1._A_brief_history_of_the_impact_of_Nostra_aetate_(No.4)_over_the_last_50_years.
2. Chaim Potok, *Wanderings: History of the Jews* (New York: Fawcett Crest, 1978), 263.
3. Flavius Josephus, *The Works of Flavius Josephus, the Learned and Authentic Jewish Historian* (Belfast: Simms and M'intyre, 1841), 991–93.
4. Josephus, 780.
5. Christopher Merrill, *Things of the Hidden God: Journey to the Holy Mountain* (Eugene, OR: Wipf and Stock, 2005), 104.
6. Justin Martyr, "Dialogue with Trypho," chap. 16, *New Advent*, accessed March 24, 2020, http://www.newadvent .org/fathers/01282.htm.
7. "Augustine (354–430)," *Jewish Virtual Library*, accessed March 24, 2020, https://www.jewishvirtuallibrary.org/ augustine.
8. Menachem Posner, "The Baal Shem Tov and the Tavernkeeper," *Chabad.org*, accessed March 24, 2020, https:// www.chabad.org/library/article_cdo/aid/3392231/jewish/The-Baal-Shem-Tov-and-the-Tavernkeeper.htm.
9. Robert M. Seltzer, *Jewish People, Jewish Thought: The Jewish Experience in History* (New York: Macmillan, 1980), 351.
10. Georg Jellinek, *The Declaration of the Rights of Man and of Citizens: A Contribution to Modern Constitutional History* (New York: Henry Holt, 1901).
11. Jellinek.
12. Seltzer, *Jewish People*, 668.
13. Brian Klug, "The State of Zionism: Tracing the Course of Zionism and the Splintered State It Has Created," *Nation*, May 31, 2007, https://www.thenation.com/article/state-zionism/.
14. Klug.
15. "Moses Maimonides' 13 Principles of Jewish Faith," *ORU School of Theology and Missions*, last modified July 9, 2009, http://web.oru.edu/current_students/class_pages/grtheo/mmankins/drbyhmpg_files/GBIB766RabbLit/ Chapter9Maimonides13Princ/index.html.
16. *Jerusalem Talmud Kiddushin* 4:12.
17. *Avot* 4:16, in *Pirke Avot: Torah from Our Sages*, trans. and commentary by Jacob Neusner (Chappaqua, NY: Rossel, 1984). The *Avot* is a popular and highly readable *Mishnah* tractate and an excellent introduction to Judaic values.
18. *Avot* 2:5.
19. *Genesis Rabbah* 92:1. See *A Theological Commentary to the Midrash*, vol. 2, *Genesis Rabbah*, trans. Jacob Neusner (Lanham, MD: University Press of America, 2001).
20. Abraham Joshua Heschel, *The Sabbath* (New York: Farrar, Straus and Giroux, 2005), 74.

Chapter 9. Zoroastrianism

1. Jenny Rose, *Zoroastrianism: An Introduction* (London: I.B. Tauris, 2017), 1.
2. Nietzsche's character in *Thus Spoke Zarathustra* uses the same name as the Zoroastrian founder, but Nietzsche's text is not a record of the historical Zarathustra.

3. Roshan Rivetna, ed., *The Legacy of Zarathustra: An Introduction to the Religion, History and Culture of the Zarathushtis (Zoroastrians)* (Hinsdale, IL: Federation of Zoroastrian Associations of North America, 2002), 12.
4. "3,000 Years of Zoroastrian Culture Is Celebrated by Kluge Center," *Library of Congress*, November 24, 2003, https://www.loc.gov/item/prn-03-196/3000-years-of-zoroastrian-culture-is-celebrated-by-kluge-center/2003-11-24/.
5. Roshan Rivetna, "The Zarathushti World: A 2012 Demographic Picture Compiled," *FEZANA Journal* 27, no. 3 (October 2013): 26.
6. Jenny Rose, *Zoroastrianism: A Guide for the Perplexed* (New York: Continuum International, 2011), 183.
7. Mary Boyce, ed. and trans., *Textual Sources for the Study of Zoroastrianism* (Chicago: University of Chicago Press, 1990), 105.
8. Mary Boyce, *Zoroastrians: Their Religious Beliefs and Practices* (New York: Routledge, 2001), xix.
9. Rivetna, *Legacy of Zarathustra*, 14.
10. Sometimes there are seven when Spenta Mainyu is included.
11. See Rose, *Zoroastrianism: A Guide*, 34.
12. Joseph H. Peterson, "Avesta: Yasna: Sacred Liturgy and Gathas/Hymns of Zarathushtra," *AVESTA—Zoroastrian Archives*, February 13, 2019, http://www.avesta.org/yasna/index.heml#y35.
13. Boyce, *Textual Sources*, 15.
14. Rose, *Zoroastrianism: A Guide*, 34–35.
15. Boyce, *Textual Sources*, 105.
16. Herodotus, *The History of Herodotus*, in *Great Books of the Western World*, trans. George Rawlinson (Chicago: University of Chicago Press, 1991), 31.
17. Rose, *Zoroastrianism: An Introduction*, 20.
18. Rivetna, *Legacy of Zarathustra*, 17.
19. Rivetna, 17.
20. Khosro Kazai, *The Gathas: The Sublime Book of Zarathustra* (Brussels, Belgium: European Centre for Zoroastrian Studies, 2007), 27.
21. Rivetna, *Legacy of Zarathustra*, 15.
22. Rose, *Zoroastrianism: An Introduction*, 20.
23. Rivetna, *Legacy of Zarathustra*, 13.
24. Kazai, *Gathas*, 23.
25. Rose, *Zoroastrianism: An Introduction*, 21.
26. Kazai, *Gathas*, 26.
27. Herodotus, *History of Herodotus*, 92.
28. Rose, *Zoroastrianism: A Guide*, 30.
29. Rivetna, *Legacy of Zarathustra*, 37.
30. Rose, *Zoroastrianism: A Guide*, 105.
31. Rose, 139.
32. Rose, 75.
33. Kazai, *Gathas*, 14.
34. Boyce, *Textual Sources*, 1.
35. Kazai, *Gathas*, 51.
36. Boyce, *Zoroastrians*, 1.
37. Rivetna, *Legacy of Zarathustra*, 25.
38. Sigmund Freud, *Moses and Monotheism* (1939; repr., Mansfield Centre, CT: Martino, 2010), 51.
39. Rose, *Zoroastrianism: An Introduction*, 89.
40. Edwin M. Yamauchi, *Persia and the Bible* (Grand Rapids, MI: Baker, 1991), 466.
41. Kenneth L. Barker, ed., *The NIV Study Bible* (Grand Rapids, MI: Zondervan, 2011), 1862.
42. Rivetna, *Legacy of Zarathustra*, 28.

43. Ali Makki, "Zoroastrian Influences Coming Full Circle," *Chehrenama: Publication of California Zoroastrian Center*, no. 161 (Spring 2012): 11.
44. Makki, 12.

Chapter 10. African Traditional

1. Supyire is part of the Senefo group of languages spoken in northern Mali, western Burkina, and northern Côte d'Ivoire. There are between 350,000 and 500,000 Supyire speakers in Mali. https://www.ethnologue.com/language/spp.
2. The Story of Piifungo is part of an unpublished collection of Supyire stories taped between 1999 and 2002, told by Ali Sanogo, and translated by Robert Carlson. The translation includes occasional interruptions by the original listeners and has been further edited for length but preserves the oral style of Supyire as closely as possible. Professor Carlson writes in his introduction to the collection, "Like most good literature, Supyire stories are meant first of all to be entertaining. But they also have other purposes, one of which is to illustrate the consequences of good and bad behavior." In the previous paragraphs, I have used the romanized spelling "djinn" rather than the derivative "jinn" from the Arabic "al-jinn." Neither of these should be confused with the anglicized "genie," which has entirely different connotations.
3. Langdon Gilkey, *Maker of Heaven and Earth: A Study of the Christian Doctrine of Creation* (Garden City, NY: Doubleday, 1959), 6.
4. John Taylor writes, "Certainly there is not one homogenous system of belief throughout Africa. One tribe gives prominence to an element which is only vaguely conceived in another. In several ways, the traditional culture of the whole Niger basin reveals a sophistication and an individuation that is not known elsewhere. Nevertheless, anyone who has read a number of ethnological works dealing with different parts of Africa must be struck not only by the remarkable number of features that are common but by the emergence of a basic worldview which fundamentally is everywhere the same. To quote an Akan proverb, Man's speech has thirty varieties, but they are slight." John Taylor, *The Primal Vision: Christian Presence amid African Religion* (London: SCM Press, 1963), 27.
5. Gerrie ter Haar, *How God Became African: African Spirituality and Western Secular Thought* (Philadelphia: University of Pennsylvania Press, 2009), 28.
6. John Mbiti, *African Religions & Philosophy* (New York: Praeger, 1969), 29.
7. Mbiti consistently uses "He" for God, and I have carried forward that custom. However, it is pertinent to note that traditional Africans do have varied conceptions of God's "gender." In Supyire folktales, God often has a wife, and in personal interviews with Ali Sanogo, Robert Carlson reported that "Ali said that Kile/God is a man in the dry season and a woman in the rainy season. The reason according to Ali is that in the dry season, the sky does not produce anything, but in the rainy season, it brings fertility." Robert Carlson (head of Linguistics and Translation Studies Department, African International University, Nairobi, Kenya), in discussion with the author, July 2, 2019 (the interview was conducted electronically with the author in Binghamton, New York, and Carlson in Nairobi).
8. See E. Bolaji Idowu's examination of erroneous terminology when discussing ATR. He addresses the following terms: "primitive," "savage," "native," "tribe," "heathenism," "idols," "fetishism," and "animism," dealing with the problems associated with each, and makes a case for the term "diffused monotheism." Idowu, *African Traditional Religion: A Definition* (London: SCM Press, 1973), 136. Kwame Bediako defends, to some degree, Idowu's work, though names some fundamental objections to his overall approach. Bediako, "Understanding African Theology in the 20th Century," *Themelios* 20, no. 1 (October 1994): http://s3.amazonaws.com/tgc-documents/journal-issues/20.1_Bediako.pdf.
9. Mbiti, *African Religions*, 33.
10. "Practically all African peoples associate God with the sky, in one way or another. Some have myths telling of how men came from the sky; or how God separated from men and withdrew Himself into the sky, whence nobody could directly reach him." Mbiti, 33.
11. Evans-Pritchard says, "It would be a mistake to interpret 'of the sky' and 'in the sky' too literally. They may address the moon, but it is God to whom they speak through it." Idowu, *African Traditional Religion*, 154. But this view lacks nuance. The Supyire, according to Robert Carlson, do not "separate Kile/God from kile/Kile, sky/Sky. Note that in their way of thinking, the sky is a *thing* rather than a place. When the people of Satii decided

they would make war on God/sky, they shot up at the sky and some people say blood came down from the sky/God." Robert Carlson, in discussion with the author, June 2019.

12. Taylor, *Primal Vision*, 72.
13. Yusufu Turaki, *Foundations of African Traditional Religion and Worldview* (Nairobi: Word Alive, 2006), 56.
14. Idowu, *African Traditional Religion*, 135.
15. Turaki, *Foundations*, 33.
16. Kwame Bediako, *Christianity in Africa: The Renewal of a Non-Western Religion* (Maryknoll, NY: Orbis, 1995), 95.
17. Arnold Meiring, "As Below, So Above: A Perspective on African Theology," *Theological Studies* 63, no. 2 (2007): 735, https://www.ajol.info/index.php/hts/article/download/41211/8599.
18. Turaki, *Foundations*, 58.
19. Mbiti, *African Religions*, 39.
20. Mbiti, 39.
21. Mbiti, 40.
22. Jacob Olupona, *African Religions: A Very Short Introduction* (Oxford: Oxford University Press, 2014), 8.
23. Mbiti, *African Religions*, 40.
24. Mbiti, 41.
25. Mbiti, 41.
26. Taylor, *Primal Vision*, 67–68.
27. Taylor, 84.
28. Mbiti, *African Religions*, 97.
29. Mbiti, 97.
30. Mbiti, 98.
31. Robert Carlson, in discussion with the author, June 2019.
32. "When I asked," writes Taylor, "a group of church leaders in the Ganda village what a man can do to please God, one of their seniors replied, 'I have never heard a Christian here ask such a question. People do believe in heaven and hell, but most do not care about it. They say, God will forgive me. Their fear is for this life, not the next.'" Taylor, *Primal Vision*, 175.
33. Taylor, 175.
34. Taylor, 176.
35. Robert Carlson, "External Causation in Supyire Culture," *Notes on Anthropology* 3 (1999): 4.
36. Taylor, *Primal Vision*, 180.
37. Taylor, 172–95.
38. Paul G. Hiebert's classic essay "The Flaw of the Excluded Middle" is a brief but invaluable read for those encountering what John Taylor calls "the Primal Vision." Hiebert, "The Flaw of the Excluded Middle," *Missiology: An International Review* 10, no. 1 (January 1, 1982): 35–47.
39. Turaki, *Foundations*, 46.
40. Olupona, *African Religions*, 36–37.
41. Idowu, *African Traditional Religion*, 177.
42. Idowu, 175.
43. Idowu, 175.
44. Robin Horton, *Patterns of Thought in Africa and the West* (Cambridge: Cambridge University Press, 1993), 217.
45. Bediako, *Christianity in Africa*, 100.
46. ter Haar, *How God Became African*, 35.
47. Mbiti, *African Religions*, 83–84.
48. Taylor, *Primal Vision*, 93.
49. Robert Carlson, in discussion with the author, June 2019.
50. Taylor, *Primal Vision*, 100.
51. Taylor, 103.

52. Taylor, 97.
53. P.T.W. Baxter, "Repetition in Certain Boran Ceremonies," *Systems of African Thought: Studies Presented and Discussed at the Third International Seminar in Salisbury, December 1960*, ed. M. Fortes and G. Dieterlen (London: Oxford University Press, 1965), 71–72.
54. Taylor, *Primal Vision*, 102.
55. Taylor, 102.
56. Mbiti, *African Religions*, 124.
57. Mbiti, 126.
58. Olupona, *African Religions*, 30.
59. Taylor, *Primal Vision*, 136–37.
60. Taylor, 135. "The Nyamwezi of Tanzania also associate rain and drought with their king. Indeed, the king's body is seen as extension of the earth itself...If the initial ritual sacrifices do not alter the weather, then the king is beaten to tears. His tears...will invoke the other waters in the sky, which the ancestors ultimately control." Olupona, *African Religions*, 40.
61. Taylor, *Primal Vision*, 140–44.
62. Olupona, *African Religions*, 31–32.
63. Olupona, 31–32.
64. R.E. Bradbury, "Father and Son in Edo Mortuary Ritual," in *African Systems of Thought*, ed. M. Fortes and G. Dieterlen (London: Oxford University Press, 1965), 96–115.
65. Mbiti, *African Religions*, 21–22.
66. Mbiti, 17.
67. Mbiti, 17.
68. A. Scott Moreau, "A Critique of John Mbiti's Understanding of the African Concept of Time," *East Africa Journal of Evangelical Theology* 5, no. 2 (1986).
69. Newell S. Booth Jr., "Time and Change in African Traditional Thought," *Journal of Religion in Africa* 7, no. 2 (1975): 83, https://www.jstor.org/stable/1594752?read-now=1&seq=1#page_scan_tab_contents.
70. Booth, 84.
71. Mbiti, *African Religions*, 19.
72. Booth, "Time and Change," 85.
73. Booth, 85.
74. Bediako, *Christianity in Africa*, 100.
75. ter Haar, *How God Became African*, 2.
76. "According to African thought, our relations within the community determine our relationship with God. And reconciliation starts with humans being reconciled. It is because African theology is much more this-worldly focused and views the affairs of humans as all-important. Instead of a dualistic worldview, African people approach the world holistically, and believe that all creatures in creation are linked. When reconciliation is needed, their solution for it is to reconcile on a horizontal level, and to expect that the vertical dimension will follow from that." Meiring, "As Below, So Above," 737.
77. "Life's essential quest is to secure power and use it. Not to have power or access to it produces great anxiety in the face of spirit caprice and the rigors of life. A life without power is not worth living...Power offers man control of his uncertain world. The search for and acquisition of power supersedes any commitment to ethics or morality (1990: 60)." Turaki, *Foundations*, 35.
78. Mbiti, *African Religions*. "'When an African takes food or drink,' a Nigerian pastor admitted to me recently, 'he feels an almost irresistible temptation to spill a little on the ground before he takes it. For he cannot help remembering.'" Taylor, *Primal Vision*, 159.
79. Carlson, "External Causation," 3.
80. Carlson, 5.
81. Robert Carlson writes, "Living things, in Supyire cosmology, are endowed with a kind of impersonal life-force called *nàmà*. This force can harm other animals or things and is thus potentially the cause of disease and even death. Certain animals and people, such as pythons and albinos, have more *nàmà* than others. You can get sick

even by walking past the place where a python has been coiled up, even if it is no longer there. *Nàmà* is especially dangerous when the animal or person who has it is killed or dies. It may attack the person who killed it. Hunters must protect themselves in various ways against the *nàmà* of their pray…It turns out that you can also be attacked by the *nàmà* of your own actions…The 'consequences' of my action do not arise from myself, but are an external force which I may be able to protect myself from by means of making certain offerings, wearing a certain type of clothing, or enlisting the aid of a fetish." Carlson, 5.

82. Robert Carlson, in discussion with the author, June 2019.
83. Mbiti, *African Religions*, 114.
84. Robert Carlson, in discussion with the author, June 2019.
85. Idowu, *African Traditional Religion*, 175.
86. Taylor, *Primal Vision*, 191.
87. Robert F. Gray, "Parallels in Sonjo and Christian Mythology," in *African Systems of Thought*, 21.
88. Meiring, "As Below, So Above," 738.
89. Arnold Meiring, "African Views on Reconciliation," in "Heart of Darkness: A Deconstruction of Traditional Christian Concepts of Reconciliation by Means of a Religious Studies Perspective on the Christian and African Religions" (PhD thesis, University of Pretoria, 2006), 103.
90. Meiring, 104.
91. Joy Lawn, Pyande Mongi, and Simon Cousens work through the statistics on infant mortality: Lawn, Mongi, and Cousens, "Africa's Newborns—Counting and Making Them Count," in *Opportunities for Africa's Newborns, World Health Organization*, 2006, 11–12, available at https://www.who.int/pmnch/media/publications/aonsection_I.pdf.
92. For statistics and information about female genital mutilation practices in Africa, see "Female Genital Mutilation," *World Health Organization*, accessed March 27, 2020, https://www.who.int/reproductivehealth/topics/fgm/prevalence/en/.
93. Mbiti, *African Religions*, 127.
94. Taylor, *Primal Vision*, 110.
95. Taylor, 111.
96. Taylor, 111.
97. Taylor, 108.
98. World Vision keeps track of the statistics concerning women and water throughout Africa: "Carrying Water Can Be a Pain in the Neck," *World Vision*, accessed March 27, 2020, https://www.worldvision.org/clean-water-news-stories/carrying-water-pain-neck.
99. For an introduction to greetings in Mali, linguist Coleman Donaldson shot a series of videos available at the blog *Bridges from Bamako*: Donaldson, "A Lesson in Sociability," *Bridges from Bamako* (blog), December 21, 2018, https://bridgesfrombamako.com/2018/12/21/a-lesson-in-sociability/.
100. Taylor, *Primal Vision*, 79.
101. Taylor, 79.
102. Taylor, 197.
103. Mbiti, *African Religions*, 3.
104. Taylor, *Primal Vision*, 24.
105. Horton, *Patterns of Thought*, 92–94.
106. Bediako, "Understanding African Theology," 18.
107. Bediako, 18.

Chapter 11. Hinduism

1. Winfried Corduan, *Neighboring Faiths*, 2nd ed. (Downers Grove, IL: InterVarsity, 2012), 269.
2. Corduan, 271.
3. Jeffrey Brodd et al., *Invitation to World Religions*, 2nd ed. (New York: Oxford University Press, 2016), 92.
4. Brodd et al., 100.
5. Brodd et al., 100.

6. Barbara Stoler Miller, *The Bhagavad Gita: Krishna's Counsel in Time of War*, 2nd ed. (New York: Bantam Classic, 2004), 56.
7. Brodd et al., *Invitation*, 108–9.
8. Brodd et al., 109.
9. Brodd et al., 109.
10. Brodd et al., 109.
11. Diane Moca, "Holi Festival Celebrates 10 Years of Welcoming Spring with Flying Colors in Naperville," *Chicago Tribune*, April 6, 2019, https://www.chicagotribune.com/suburbs/naperville-sun/ct-nvs-festival-of-color-naperville-st-0407-story.html.
12. Moca.
13. Brodd et al., *Invitation*, 106.
14. See Bruce Olson, *Bruchko: The Astonishing True Story of a 19-Year-Old American, His Capture by the Motilone Indians and His Adventures in Christianizing the Stone Age Tribe* (Lake Mary, FL: Charisma House, 2006); Tal Brooke, *Avatar of Night* (self-pub., 2015).
15. H.L. Richard, "Evangelical Approaches to Hindus," *Voice of Bhakti*, 2001, accessed March 27, 2020, http://www.bhaktivani.com/volume4/number1/approaches.html.
16. Andy Crouch, "Christ, My Bodhisattva," *Christianity Today*, April 26, 2007, http://www.christianitytoday.com/ct/2007/may/17.34.html.
17. Mitali Perkins, "When God Writes Your Life Story," *Christianity Today*, December 31, 2015, http://www.christianitytoday.com/ct/2016/january-february/jesus-christ-haunted-hindu-testimony.html.
18. Manoj Raithatha, "From Rags to Real Riches," *Christianity Today*, September 23, 2015, http://www.christianitytoday.com/ct/2015/september/money-real-estate-uk-humbled-hustler.html.
19. Brian Nelson, "Perceptions and Experiences of Alienation of Family and Community in Hindu and Jain Evangelism" (DMin diss., Trinity Evangelical Divinity School, 2014), 7.
20. Nelson, 75.
21. Raghav Krishna, "From 'Krishna Bhakti' to 'Christianity' to 'Krista Bhakti,'" *International Journal of Frontier Missiology* 24, no. 4 (Winter 2007): 174.
22. Krishna, 174.

Chapter 12. Jainism

1. Winfried Corduan, *Neighboring Faiths: A Christian Introduction to World Religions*, 2nd ed. (Downers Grove, IL: IVP Academic, 2012), 369.
2. Corduan, 359.
3. The Digambara sect of Jainism maintains that Mahavira never married and never fathered a child. See Manak Chand Jaini, *Life of Mahavira* (Allahabad, India: Indian Press, 1908), v.
4. Hermann Jacobi, trans., "Life of Mahavira, Lecture 5," in *Jaina Sutras, Part II (SBE22)* (1884), *Internet Sacred Text Archive*, accessed March 27, 2020, http://www.sacred-texts.com/jai/sbe22/sbe2285.htm.
5. Jayaram V., "Ajivikas—Their History and Philosophy," *Hindu Website*, accessed March 27, 2020, https://www.hinduwebsite.com/hinduism/concepts/ajivaka.asp.
6. Ameber Pariona, "Countries with the Largest Jain Populations," *WorldAtlas*, April 25, 2017, https://www.worldatlas.com/articles/countries-with-the-largest-jain-populations.html.
7. Pravin K. Shah, "Five Great Vows (Maha-vratas) of Jainism," *Jainism Literature Center*, accessed March 27, 2020, https://sites.fas.harvard.edu/~pluralsm/affiliates/jainism/jainedu/5greatvows.htm.
8. Shah.
9. Nathmal Tatia, "The Jain Worldviews and Ecology," in *Jainism and Ecology: Nonviolence in the Web of Life*, ed. Christopher Chapple (Delhi: Motilal Banarsidass, 2006), 3–4.
10. M. Whitney Kelting, "Jain Traditions: Practicing Tradition Today," in *South Asian Religions: Tradition and Today*, ed. Karen Pechilis and Selva J. Raj (London: Routledge, 2013), 78.
11. Shri Jayatilal S. Sanghvi, "A Treatise on Jainism," *Internet Sacred Text Archive*, accessed March 27, 2020, http://sacred-texts.com/jai/treatise.txt.

12. Peter Heehs, ed., "Jainism," in *Indian Religions: A Historical Reader of Spiritual Expression and Experience* (New York: New York University Press, 2002), 98.
13. Manisha Sethi, *Escaping the World: Women Renouncers Among Jains* (New Delhi: Routledge, 2015), 4.
14. For an in-depth look into why Jain principles and practices have led to Jains' becoming well respected in the area of finance, see Atul K. Shah and Aidan Rankin, *Jainism and Ethical Finance: A Timeless Business Model* (London: Routledge, 2017).
15. "India Jains: Why Are These Youngsters Renouncing the World?," *BBC News*, July 8, 2019, https://www.bbc.com/news/world-asia-india-48879591.
16. "Prayer of Jain Religion," *Jainism Literature Center*, accessed March 27, 2020, https://sites.fas.harvard.edu/~pluralsm/affiliates/jainism/jainedu/prayer.htm.
17. M.T. Saju, "76-Year-Old Scholar Attains Samadhi After Observing 14-Day Santhara," *Times of India*, December 5, 2016, https://timesofindia.indiatimes.com/city/chennai/76-year-old-scholar-attains-samadhi-after-observing-14-day-Santhara/articleshow/55823926.cms.
18. Dhananjay Mahapatra, "Supreme Court Permits Jain Community to Practice Santhara," *Times of India*, August 31, 2015, https://timesofindia.indiatimes.com/india/Supreme-Court-permits-Jain-community-to-practice-Santhara/articleshow/48751751.cms.

Chapter 13. Sikhism

1. "Jagmeet Singh: 'Cut Your Turban Off,' Voter Tells NDP Leader," *BBC News*, October 2, 2019, https://www.bbc.com/news/world-us-canada-49901451.
2. "Sikhs in Canada," *World Sikh*, accessed March 27, 2020, http://www.worldsikh.org/sikhs_in_canada.
3. Ameber Pariona, "Countries with the Largest Sikh Populations," *WorldAtlas*, March 23, 2019, https://www.worldatlas.com/articles/countries-with-the-largest-sikh-populations.html.
4. Manveena Suri and Huizhong Wu, "Sikhs: Religious Minority Target of Hate Crimes," *CNN*, March 7, 2017, https://www.cnn.com/2017/03/06/asia/sikh-hate-crimes-us-muslims/index.html.
5. Tom Rosentiel, "How Many U.S. Sikhs?," *Pew Research Center*, August 6, 2012, https://www.pewresearch.org/2012/08/06/ask-the-expert-how-many-us-sikhs/.
6. *Sikhs in America*, directed by Niall Mckay and Marissa Aroy (New York: Media Factory, 2008), https://www.pbs.org/video/viewfinder-sikhs-in-america/.
7. *Bend It like Beckham*, directed by Gurinder Chadha (Los Angeles: Kintop Pictures, 2002), DVD.
8. "The First Master Guru Nanak (1469–1539)," *Sikhs.org*, accessed March 27, 2020, http://www.sikhs.org/guru1.htm.
9. Nikky-Guninder and Kaur Singh, *Sikhism: World Religions*, 3rd ed. (New York: Chelsea House, 2009), 27.
10. "First Master Guru Nanak (1469–1539)."
11. "The Gurdwara," *BBC*, October 27, 2009, https://www.bbc.co.uk/religion/religions/sikhism/ritesrituals/gurdwara_1.shtml.
12. "Concept of Guru in Sikhism," *Sikh Net*, October 19, 1998, http://fateh.sikhnet.com//sikhnet/discussion.nsf/78f5a2ff8906d1788725657c00732d6c/97F5DAB799D02605872566A2006CA919?OpenDocument.
13. "Concept of Guru in Sikhism."
14. Eleanor Nesbitt and Gopinder Kaur, *Guru Nanak*, Indic Value Series, ed. Julius Lipner (Calgary, Canada: Bayeux Arts, 1999), 46.
15. Ian S. Markham with Christy Lohr, eds., *A World Religions Reader*, 3rd ed. (Chichester, UK: Blackwell, 2009), 238.
16. Winfried Corduan, *Neighboring Faiths* (Downers Grove, IL: InterVarsity, 2012), 377.
17. Kiyotaka Sato, "Divisions Among Sikh Communities in Britain and the Role of Caste System: A Case Study of Four Gurdwaras in Multi-ethnic Leicester," *Journal of Punjab Studies* 19, no. 1 (Spring 2012): 4.
18. Warren Matthews, *World Religions*, 6th ed. (Belmont, CA: Wadsworth Cengage Learning, 2010), 160–61.
19. From September 2001 to January 2002, Kaur and a cameraman traveled across the country, documenting such crimes of prejudice. In 2004, director Sharat Raju turned the footage into a feature-length documentary, *Divided We Fall: Americans in the Aftermath*, produced by New Moon Productions, September 14, 2006. Visit Kaur's blog and watch her TED Talk at https://valariekaur.com.

20. Raja Abdulrahim, "Holding to the Sikh Heritage in the US," *Los Angeles Times*, May 7, 2011, https://www.latimes.com/local/la-xpm-2011-may-07-la-me-beliefs-sikh-20110507-story.html.
21. Jonah Chang, *Shoki Coe: An Ecumenical Life in Context* (Geneva: WCC Publications, 2011), viii.
22. For more on this subject, see Scott A. Moreau, *Contextualizing the Faith: A Holistic Approach* (Grand Rapids, MI: Baker Academic, 2018).
23. William Dyrness, *Insider Jesus: Theological Reflections on New Christian Movements* (Downers Grove, IL: InterVarsity, 2018).
24. See Darren Duerksen, "Ecclesial Identities of Socioreligious 'Insiders': A Case Study of Fellowship Among Hindu and Sikh Communities," in *Understanding Insider Movements: Disciples of Jesus Within Diverse Religious Communities*, ed. Harley Talman and John Jay Travis (Pasadena, CA: William Carey Library, 2015).
25. B. Singh, "I'm a Sikh, and This Is What I Believe," *International Mission Board*, January 26, 2018, https://www.imb.org/2018/01/26/im-a-sikh-and-this-is-what-i-believe/.
26. Singh.
27. W. Owen Cole and Piara Singh Sambhi, *Sikhism and Christianity: A Comparative Study* (New York: St. Martin's, 1993), 50–52.
28. Cole and Sambhi, 52.
29. B. Singh, "I'm a Sikh."
30. For his story, see Phyllis Thompson, *Sadhu Sundar Singh: A Biography of the Remarkable Indian Disciple of Jesus Christ* (Singapore: Armour, 2005).

Chapter 14. The East Asian Complex

1. Eleanor Albert, "Religion in China," *Council on Foreign Relations*, October 11, 2018, https://www.cfr.org/backgrounder/religion-china.
2. Gerald R. McDermott, *The Baker Pocket Guide to World Religions* (Grand Rapids, MI: Baker, 2008), 66.
3. Winfried Corduan, *Pocket Guide to World Religions* (Downers Grove, IL: IVP Academic, 2006), 50.
4. Confucius, *Analects* 15:23, http://classics.mit.edu/Confucius/analects.3.3.html.
5. Julia Ching, *Chinese Religions* (Maryknoll, NY: Orbis, 2002), 66–67.
6. Ching, 65.
7. Ling Feng and Derek Newton, "Some Implications for Moral Education of the Confucian Principle of Harmony: Learning from Sustainability Education Practice in China," *Journal of Moral Education* 41, no. 3 (2012): 345.
8. Ai Guo Han, "Building a Harmonious Society and Achieving Individual Harmony," *Journal of Chinese Political Science* 13, no. 2 (2008):143.
9. Daniel A. Bell, "Reconciling Socialism and Confucianism? Reviving Traditions in China," *Dissident* 57, no. 1 (2010): 91–99.
10. Paul E. Kauffman, *Confucius, Mao and Christ* (Hong Kong: Asian Outreach, 1975), 23.
11. Tsu-kung Chuang, "Communicating the Concept of Sin in the Chinese Context," *Taiwan Mission Quarterly* 6, no. 2 (1996): 49–55.
12. Xinping Zhou, "Original Sin in the East-West Dialogue: A Chinese View," *Studies in World Christianity* 1, no. 1 (2011): 80–86.
13. Chuang, "Communicating the Concept of Sin," 49–55.
14. Kevin J. Wetmore Jr., "The Tao of 'Star Wars,' or, Cultural Appropriation in a Galaxy Far, Far Away," *Studies in Popular Culture* 23, no. 1 (2000): 91–106.
15. For example, see "Taoist Trinity," *China Culture*, December 1, 2014, http://en.chinaculture.org/2014-12/01/content_579145.htm.
16. "Chinese Influence," *Nakasendo Way*, accessed March 27, 2020, https://www.nakasendoway.com/chinese-influence/.
17. Noriko Iwai, "Measuring Religion in Japan: ISM, NHK, and JGSS: Survey Research and the Study of Religion in East Asia," *Pew Research Center*, October 11, 2017, https://www.pewresearch.org/wp-content/uploads/sites/7/2017/11/Religion20171117.pdf.
18. "Funerals in Japan," *Nippon*, July 5, 2015, https://www.nippon.com/en/features/jg00039/.

19. William K. Bunce, *Religions in Japan* (Rutland, VT: Charles E. Tuttle, 1964), 9.
20. John Spacey, "Meet the Gods: 13 Japanese Kami," *Japan Talk*, October 12, 2015, https://www.japan-talk.com/jt/new/kami.
21. "Shrines," *Japan-Guide*, accessed March 27, 2020, https://www.japan-guide.com/e/e2059.html.
22. Angela Lu Fulton, "Shut In and Shut Out: Scores of Young Japanese Have Closed Themselves Off from Society, and Foreign Missionaries May Be in the Best Position to Help Them," *World*, October 25, 2017, https://world.wng.org/2017/10/shut_in_and_shut_out?fbclid=IwAR2tj95NIKoxChUVe5TsGkk63o4TokDTvGLTmhY-dxRgGPhrkP2_n3RmecU.

Chapter 15. Baha'i

1. Robert H. Stockman, *The Baha'i Faith: A Guide for the Perplexed* (London: Bloomsbury Academic, 2013), 1.
2. "A Global Community," *Bahai.org*, accessed March 27, 2020, https://www.bahai.org/national-communities/.Bahai.org is the official website of Baha'is internationally.
3. "Life of the Bab," *Bahai.org*, accessed March 27, 2020, https://www.bahai.org/the-bab/life-the-bab/; *Encyclopedia Britannica*, s.v. "Shi'ite," accessed December 27, 2018.
4. "Life of the Bab."
5. "Life of the Bab."
6. Bab, *Persian Bayan*, vol. 1 (1848), exord., para. 2, 4; Wahid 1, Bab 1, 15; Wahid 2, Bab 2. See the 2017 English translation in the public domain, accessed March 27, 2020, https://archive.org/details/ThePersianBayanVolumeI/.
7. William Miller, whom Baha'is consider an enemy of the faith, attributes this enigmatic aspect to gnostic, Neoplatonic, and Sufi influence on the Bab. See William Miller, *The Baha'i Faith: Its History and Teachings* (Pasadena, CA: William Carey Library, 1984), 48, 52. Miller is cited often in this chapter because his text remains the most comprehensive independent academic account on the subject.
8. Babis are sometimes known as "bayanis" and Babism as "the Religion of Bayan."
9. The Baha'i account of the Bab's execution can be found in "Life of the Bab."
10. Azalis and Baha'is agree that Mirza Yahya held some status of "successor" or "titular head." They disagree, however, about the details of his status. See Bab, *Will and Testament*, trans. Wahid Azal (1849), verses 1–3, available at https://archive.org/details/willtestamentofpoint3/mode/2up; Universal House of Justice (UHJ), "Tablet of the Bab, the Appointment of Azal and His Titles" (memorandum, Haifa, Israel, May 28, 2004).
11. Abdu'l-Baha, *A Traveler's Narrative*, trans. Edward Browne (Wilmette, IL: Baha'i Publishing Trust, 1982), 37.
12. Miller, *Baha'i Faith*, 94–114.
13. Miller, 94–114.
14. D.M. MacEoin, "Azali Babism," in *Encyclopaedia Iranica*, ed. Ehsan Yarshater, gen. ed. (New York: Encyclopedia Iranica Foundation, 1987, last updated August 18, 2011), 3:179–81.
15. "In Baghdad…he lived as the generally-acknowledged head of the community until their removal to Istanbul in 1863. By adopting a policy of seclusion…Sobh-e Azal gradually alienated himself from a large proportion of the exiles, who began to give their allegiance to other claimants, notably Azal's half-brother, Bahā'allāh." See MacEoin, 179–81. See also Miller, *Baha'i Faith*, ix–xvii, 94–114; UHJ, "Tablet of the Bab"; Edward Browne, trans., *The Tarikh I Jadid, or New History of Mirza Ali Muhammad the Bab*, ed. Mirza Huseyn of Hamadan and Edward Browne (Cambridge: Cambridge University Press, 1893), xiv–xxiv.
16. Browne, *Tarikh I Jadid*, xiv–xxiv.
17. Browne, xiv–xxiv.
18. Browne, xiv–xxiv.
19. Miller claims Subh-I-Azal was "for sixteen years…generally considered by the Babis to be the divinely appointed head." *Baha'i Faith*, 94. He argues for a different dating than is conventionally accepted by Baha'is (70–93). A more conservative estimate would allow only 12 years and 10 months, the span between the Bab's death on July 9, 1850, and Baha'u'llah declaration on April 21, 1863.
20. "The Life of Baha'u'llah," *Bahai.org*, accessed March 27, 2020, https://www.bahai.org/bahaullah/life-bahaullah. Baha'is believe the number nine symbolizes perfection as well as the numerical value of *Baha'* (in Arabic, B = 2, A = 1, H = 5, ' = 1) and supposedly indicates the number of years between the Bab and the next manifestation. See UHJ, "The Nine-Pointed Star: History and Symbolism" (memorandum, Haifa, Israel, January 24, 1999).

21. Juan Cole, "The Concept of Manifestations in the Baha'i Writings," *Baha'i Studies* 9 (1982).
22. Cole, 8.
23. Baha'u'llah, *Gleanings from the Writings of Baha'u'llah*, pocket ed. (Wilmette, IL: Baha'i Publishing Trust, 1990), 173–74.
24. Baha'u'llah, *Kitab-i-Iqan* [Book of certitude], trans. Shoghi Effendi (1931; repr., Wilmette, IL: Baha'i Publishing Trust, 1974), 10, 18, 39, 58.
25. Baha'u'llah, 99–100.
26. Baha'u'llah, 66, 103.
27. Baha'u'llah. See also Mushidad Motlagh, *I Shall Come Again*, vol. 1, *Time Prophecies of the Second Coming*, 2nd ed. (Mt. Pleasant, MI: Global Perspective, 2000).
28. A contingent of Babi's persisted at the same time as Baha'is and still exist today. One source estimates no more than 1,000 practicing Azalis might be alive as of 2001. See David Barrett, *The New Believers* (London: Cassell, 2001), 246.
29. Bab, *Persian Bayan*, Wahid 2, Bab 16–17, 61, 69. See Miller, *Baha'i Faith*, 54.
30. Miller, *Baha'i Faith*, 94–114.
31. Miller, 14–15, 53–54; Browne, *Tarikh I Jadid*, 332.
32. "Life of Baha'u'llah."
33. UHJ, "Wives of Baha'u'llah" (letter, Haifa, Israel, October 23, 1993).
34. "The Early Baha'i Community," *Bahai.org*, accessed March 27, 2020, https://www.bahai.org/bahaullah/early-community.
35. "Life of Baha'u'llah."
36. Baha'u'llah, *Summons of the Lord of Hosts* (1868), English trans. (Haifa, Israel: Baha'i World Centre, 2002). The only world leader to respond was Queen Victoria who reportedly said, "If this is of God, it will endure; if not, it can do no harm"; see Shoghi Effendi, *The Promised Day Is Come*, rev. ed. (Wilmette, IL: US Baha'i Publishing Trust, 1980), 65.
37. Baha'u'llah, *Kitab-I-'Ahd* [Book of the covenant], in *Tablets of Baha'u'llah Revealed After the Kitab-i-Aqdas*, pocket-size ed. (Wilmette, IL: US Baha'i Publishing Trust, 1988), 221–22. Baha'is today believe Abdu'l-Baha ordained "twin successors" in Shoghi Effendi and the UHJ; see Baha'u'llah et al., "Covenant," in *Compilation of Compilations*, ed. Baha'u'llah et al. (Mona Vale, Australia: Baha'i Publications Australia, 1991), 1:20–27.
38. "Life of Abdu'l-Baha," *Bahai.org*, accessed March 27, 2020, https://www.bahai.org/abdul-baha/life-abdul-baha.
39. "Life of Abdu'l-Baha."
40. "Life of Abdu'l-Baha."
41. Necati Alkan, "The Young Turks and the Baha'is in Palestine," in *Late Ottoman Palestine: The Period of Young Turk Rule*, ed. Eyal Ginio and Yuval Ben Bassat (London: I.B. Tauris, 2011), 260–78.
42. Alkan, 265.
43. "Life of Abdu'l-Baha."
44. National Spiritual Assembly of the Baha'is of the United States, "The Significance of Abdu'l-Baha's Journey Across America," in *Abdu'l-Baha in America, 1912–2012: Calling America to Its Spiritual Destiny* (Wilmette, IL: National Spiritual Assemblies of the Baha'is of the United States, 2011), https://centenary.bahai.us/abdul-baha-america; Robert Stockman, "Abdu'l-Baha's Visit to North America, 1912: A Preliminary Analysis," in *Lights of Irfan* 13 (Wilmette, IL: Haj Mehdi Armand Colloquium, 2012), 381–99.
45. "The Life and Work of Shoghi Effendi," *Bahai.org*, accessed March 27, 2020, https://www.bahai.org/shoghi-effendi/life-work-shoghi-effendi.
46. "Life and Work."
47. "Life and Work."
48. "Shoghi Effendi's Passing," *Bahai.org*, accessed March 27, 2020, https://www.bahai.org/shoghi-effendi/shoghi-effendis-passing.
49. Shoghi Effendi, *Guardians Seven Year Plan for American Baha'is: 1946–1953* (Wilmette, IL: National Spiritual Assemblies of the Baha'is of the United States and Canada, 1946); Amelia Danesh, Helen Danesh, and John Danesh, "The Life of Shoghi Effendi," in *Studying the Writings of Shoghi Effendi*, ed. M. Bergsmo (Oxford: George Ronald, 1991), 7.

50. Peter Smith, "The Baha'i Faith: Distribution Statistics 1920–1949," *Journal of Religious History* 39, no. 3 (November 26, 2014): 352–69.
51. Baha'u'llah, *Kitab-I-'Ahd*, 222.
52. Abdu'l-Baha, *Will and Testament* (Haifa, Israel: Baha'i International Community, 1922), 1.3–4. Mirza Muhammad Ali went off to start a heretical faction known as Unitarian Baha'is. See *Unitarian Baha'is*, accessed March 27, 2020, https://unitarianbahais.blogspot.com/.
53. Miller, *Baha'i Faith*, 307.
54. Abdu'l-Baha, *Will and Testament*, 5.
55. For example, see Shoghi Effendi, *The Advent of Divine Justice* (1939; repr., Wilmette, IL: Baha'i Publishing Trust, 1990), 1–20.
56. "A Unique Institute," *Bahai.org*, accessed March 27, 2020, https://www.bahai.org/the-universal-house-of-justice/unique-institution.
57. Abdu'l-Baha, *Will and Testament*, 5.
58. UHJ, *Ministry of the Custodians: An Account of the Stewardship and the Hands of the Cause, 1957–1963* (Haifa, Israel: Baha'i World Centre, 1992), 1–2.
59. UHJ, *Ministry of the Custodians*, 25ff.
60. "Shoghi Effendi's Passing."
61. *Baha'i Library Online*, s.v. "Charles Mason Remey," by Robert Stockman, accessed March 27, 2020, https://bahai-library.com/stockman_remey.
62. "Charles Mason Remey."
63. "Charles Mason Remey."
64. Miller, *Baha'i Faith*, 311–19.
65. The following websites reflect the "orthodox Baha'i" view, with guardianship through Remey: www.truebahai.com, http://bahai-guardian.com/ and https://orthodoxbahai.com/.
66. The following information can be found at the Universal House of Justice's official website, https://universalhouseofjustice.bahai.org/. The guardianship is believed to continue through the written legacy of Effendi instead of through Remey or another person.
67. Baha'u'llah, *Epistle to the Son of the Wolf*, trans. Shoghi Effendi, rev. ed. (Wilmette, IL: Baha'i Publishing Trust, 1976), 119.
68. Abdu'l-Baha, *Some Answered Questions*, pocket-size ed. (1984; repr., Wilmette, IL: Baha'i Publishing Trust, 1994), 147.
69. "Essentially a mystical Faith, the Baha'i teachings focus on the soul's relationship with the eternal, unknowable essence of God." See "What Is the Baha'i Faith?," *BahaiTeachings.org*, accessed March 25, 2020, https://bahaiteachings.org/bahai-faith.
70. Stephen Lambden, "The Background and Centrality of Apophatic Theology in Babi and Baha'i Scripture," in *Revisioning the Sacred: New Perspectives on Baha'i Theology, Studies in Babi and Bahai Religions*, ed. Jack McLean (Los Angeles: Kalimat, 1997), 8:37–78, available at http://bahai-library.com/lamden_background_apophatic_theology.
71. Baha'u'llah, *Tablet of Unity* (ca. 1879); "What Is the Baha'i Faith?"
72. "What Is the Baha'i Faith?"
73. UHJ, *One Common Faith* (Haifa, Israel: Baha'i World Centre, 2005).
74. Baha'u'llah appears to use all these distinctions in explaining how Christians fail to recognize Baha'u'llah's status. See Baha'u'llah, *Kitab-i-Iqan*, 78–105, 118.
75. These eras are also known as cycles or dispensations. Abdu'l-Baha, *Some Answered Questions*, 160–70; Baha'u'llah, *Kitab-i-Iqan*, 44–45, 83, 106.
76. Shoghi Effendi, "The Faith of Baha'u'llah: A World Religion" (Palestine, United Nations Special Committee on Palestine, 1947), para. 4, available at https://bahai-library.com/shoghieffendi_faith_bahaullah.
77. Baha'is do not necessarily affirm Scientology, Satanism, or apocalyptic cults like People's Temple (Jim Jones). To my knowledge, however, there is no official list of which religions are sanctioned and which are not.

78. Abdu'l-Baha reportedly said, "To be a Baha'i simply means to love all the world; to love humanity and try to serve it; to work for universal peace and universal brotherhood," quoted in J.E. Esselmont, *Baha'u'llah and the New Era* (Wilmette, IL: Baha'i Publishing Trust, 1980), 71.
79. Abdu'l-Baha, *The Promised Day Is Come* (Wilmette, IL: Baha'i Publishing Trust, 1980), 118.
80. Abdu'l-Baha, *Foundations of World Unity* (1945; repr., Wilmette, IL: Baha'i Publishing Trust, 1979), 9–10.
81. UHJ, *The Promise of World Peace* (Akka, Israel: Baha'i World Centre, 1985), 2.
82. "Heaven and Hell," *Bahai.org*, accessed March 27, 2020, https://www.bahai.org/beliefs/life-spirit/human-soul/heaven-hell.
83. Abdu'l-Baha, *Abdu'l-Baha on Divine Philosophy*, comp. Elizabeth Frasier Chamberlain (Boston: Tudor Press, 1918), 24–28.
84. Abdu'l-Baha, 24–28.
85. Mankind is even believed to be emanations of God from eternity past, an idea reminiscent of Neoplatonism; see Abdu'l-Baha, *Some Answered Questions*, 198–202.
86. Stanwood Cobb, "The Universal State," in *Security for a Failing World* (Washington, DC: Avalon, 1934), 111–22.
87. Baha'u'llah, *Kitab-i-Aqdas* [Most holy book] (Haifa, Israel: Baha'i World Centre, 1992), 88.
88. Baha'u'llah, *Gleanings*, 189–90.
89. Abdu'l-Baha, *Abdu'l-Baha on Divine Philosophy*, 26.
90. UHJ, "Proselytizing, Development, and the Covenant," in *Messages of the Universal House of Justice: 1963–1986: The Third Epoch of the Formative Age* (1982; repr., Wilmette, IL: US Baha'i Publishing Trust, 1996), 513–19.
91. Abdu'l-Baha, Shoghi Effendi, and UHJ, *Political Non-involvement and Obedience to Government*, ed. Peter Kahn (1979; repr., Sydney, Australia: National Spiritual Assembly, 2003).
92. "What Baha'is Do: Response to the Call of Baha'u'llah," *Bahai.org*, accessed March 27, 2020, https://www.bahai.org/action/response-call-bahaullah/.
93. "The Obligatory Prayers," *Bahai.org*, accessed March 27, 2020, https://www.bahai.org/documents/bahaullah/obligatory-prayers.
94. "Obligatory Prayers."
95. Baha'u'llah, *Kitab-i-Aqdas*, 119, 155, 190.
96. Baha'u'llah et al., *Lights of Guidance, Second Part: A Baha'i Reference File*, ed. Helen Hornby (New Delhi: Baha'i Publishing Trust India, 1983; online reprint, 2006, updated February 13, 2018), 344–48; Baha'u'llah et al., *Baha'i Writings on Homosexuality*, ed. Roger Reini and Darren Heibert (Haifa, Israel: Baha'i World Centre, 1996).
97. "Nineteen Day Feast," *Bahai.org*, accessed March 27, 2020, https://www.bahai.org/action/institutional-capacity/nineteen-day-feast.
98. Bahai.org displays only eight standing Baha'i Houses of Worship, or "Mashriqu'l-Adhkar" (Dawning Place of the Mention of God), https://www.bahai.org/action/devotional-life/mashriqul-adhkar-presentation#slide-1, although more have been and are being constructed. See Sonjel Vreeland, "Baha'i Temples: A Brief Introduction," *Baha'i Blog*, July 22, 2018, https://www.bahaiblog.net/2018/07/bahai-temples-a-brief-introduction/.
99. If one home cannot accommodate the size or geographic spread of the group, they may meet in a Baha'i Center instead; see "Nineteen Day Feast."
100. "Nineteen Day Feast."
101. "Walking a Spiritual Path," https://www.bahai.org/action/response-call-bahaullah/walking-spiritual-path.
102. "Walking a Spiritual Path."
103. "Walking a Spiritual Path."
104. "In the estimation of God all men are equal; there is no distinction or preferment for any soul in the dominion of His justice and equity." Abdu'l-Baha, "Talk at Baptist Temple, Broad and Berk Street, Philadelphia, PA," in *The Promulgation of Universal Peace*, 2nd ed. (Wilmette, IL: US Baha'i Publishing Trust, 1982), 81.
105. Shoghi Effendi, "85. Baha'i Funeral Services," in *Directives from the Guardian* (Wilmette, IL: Baha'i Publishing Trust, 1973), 33; UHJ, "Letter Written on Behalf of the Universal House of Justice to an Individual Believer," February 6, 1975, in *Compilation of Compilations*, 1:12–13.
106. "Obligatory Prayers."
107. The Baha'i calendar has 19 months, with 19 days each, totally 361 days, adding 4–5 days of holiday (intercalary

days) to align with the Western or Gregorian calendar. They count years from the Bab's announcement, 1844 AD = 1 BE (Baha'i era). Baha'is also have a month of fasting, New Years, and ten other holidays celebrating key Babi and Baha'i dates. See "About the Baha'i Calendar," http://calendar.bahaiq.com/about/.

108. Abdu'l-Baha, Shoghi Effendi, and UHJ, *Political Non-involvement and Obedience to Government.*

109. Rodney Richards, "Baha'i Administrative Order Explained," *BahaiTeachings.org*, January 4, 2019, https://bahaiteachings.org/bahai-administrative-order-explained.

110. Richards.

111. Richards.

112. Rodney Richards, "What Is Baha'i Consultation?," *BahaiTeaching.org*, July 21, 2018, https://bahaiteachings.org/what-is-bahai-consultation.

113. Besides NSAs, other governing bodies include the 81-member Institution of Counselors, the five Continental Boards, and various Auxiliary Boards. See "Institution of the Counselors," *Bahai.org*, accessed March 27, 2020, https://www.bahai.org/beliefs/essential-relationships/administrative-order/institution-counsellors.

114. Baha'is are, however, discouraged from formal affiliations (membership) with other religions. Shoghi Effendi, "Letter to the Baha'is of Vienna," in *Lights of Guidance*, 159.

115. David Langness, "Independent Investigation of Truth," *BahaiTeachings.org*, September 8, 2003, https://bahaiteachings.org/bahai-principles-independent-investigation-of-truth.

116. Effendi, "Letter to Baha'is of Vienna."

117. Jonah Winters, "Compare: Baha'i Faith, Islam, Christianity, and Judaism" (chart), *Bahá'í Library Online*, August 9, 2009, https://bahai-library.com/comparison_abrahamic_religions. Regarding one-world government, see Charles Lerche, ed., *Emergence, Dimensions of a New World Order* (London: Bahá'í Publishing Trust, 1991).

118. Abdu'l-Baha, *Some Answered Questions*, 146.

119. One source says bluntly that the Baha'i faith is "essentially a mystical Faith" as "Baha'i teachings focus on the soul's relationship with the eternal, unknowable essence of God." See "What Is the Baha'i Faith?" This "mysticism" probably should not be understood in a pantheistic or "Eastern" sense where the mystic seeks the deity within himself, hoping to unite numerically with God. See Farnaz Ma'sumian, "Mysticism and the Baha'i Faith," *Deepen* 6, no. 3 (Spring 1995): 12–17, http://bahai-library.com/masumian_mysticism_bahai.

120. In the doctrine of analogy, the word *good*, for example, means the same thing attributed to God or to man, but it applies differently according man's nature versus God's nature. For a brief explanation, see *Internet Encyclopedia of Philosophy*, s.v. "Religious Language," by Jennifer Hart Weed, accessed July 7, 2019, https://www.iep.utm.edu/rel-lang/.

121. Christianity is normally understood to affirm exclusivism, meaning "one religion has it mostly right and all the other religions go seriously wrong," and to apply this exclusivity to their doctrine of salvation (soteriology). See Philip L. Quinn and Kevin Meeker, eds., *The Philosophical Problem of Religious Diversity* (Oxford: Oxford University Press, 2000), 1, 2, 38–53, 172–92.

122. Granting room for debate on this issue within historic Christianity, Catholics and Eastern Orthodox are known to align with the teaching of Cyprian of Carthage: "Extra ecclesiam nulla salus" (Outside the church there is no salvation; see letter 52 [ca. 258], para. 21). Mainline and evangelical protestants tend to agree, as this point of orthodoxy has a biblical basis. See Norman L. Geisler, *Theology in One Volume* (Grand Rapids, MI: Bethany House, 2011), 1011–51.

123. On natural theology, see William L. Craig and J.P. Moreland, eds., *Blackwell Companion to Natural Theology* (Malden, MA: Wiley-Blackwell, 2012). On *sensus divinitatis*, see John Calvin, *Institutes of the Christian Religion* (1536) 1.3.1. On natural moral laws, or natural law theory, see George Duke and Robert P. George, eds., *Cambridge Companion to Natural Law Jurisprudence* (Cambridge: Cambridge University Press, 2017).

124. Inerrancy doctrine is common, but not universal across Christian churches. It can be argued that Christians have preserved their texts better than Baha'is have preserved theirs. The UHJ is known to substantially redact problematic texts, including Abdu'l-Baha's failed prediction of universal peace by 1957; see J.E. Esselmont, *Baha'u'llah and the New Era* (London: George Allen Unwin, 1923), 278, 288–89; and compare with the same passages in the third edition (Wilmette, IL: Baha'i Publishing Trust, 1970), 248–49.

125. Francis Beckwith, *Baha'i: A Christian Response to Baha'ism: The Religion That Aims Toward One World Government and One Common Faith* (Minneapolis: Bethany House, 1985), 10.

126. For example, Baha'u'llah, *Kitab-i-Iqan*, 25, 33, 43, 61–62, 64, 78–81, 84, 86–87, 89, 105, 118, 120.
127. Baha'u'llah; Motlagh, *I Shall Come Again*; William Sears, *Thief in the Night: The Case of the Missing Millennium* (Oxford: George Ronald, 2002). For a Christian response, see Beckwith, *Baha'i*, 28–37.
128. Baha'u'llah, *Kitab-i-Iqan*, 61.
129. Symbolic interpretations can be justified if the text explicitly calls for it, such as Paul's allegorical interpretation of Hagar and Sarah (Galatians 4:21-31), or if the text offers a key for interpreting the symbols, such as Jesus's explanation of the parable of the sower (Matthew 13:1-23).
130. UHJ, "Resurrection of Christ and the Bible" (memorandum, Haifa, Israel, September 14, 1987), para. 4–5.
131. UHJ.
132. N.T. Wright, *The Resurrection of the Son of God* (Minneapolis: Fortress, 2003); Robert Gundry, *Soma in Biblical Theology with Emphasis on Pauline Anthropology* (1976; repr., Cambridge: Cambridge University Press, 2005); Gary Habermas and Michael Licona, *The Case for the Resurrection of Jesus* (Grand Rapids, MI: Kregel, 2004); Robert R. Bowman and Ed Komoszewski, *Putting Jesus in His Place: The Case for the Deity of Christ* (Grand Rapids, MI: Kregel, 2007), 30.
133. Bowman and Komoszewski, *Putting Jesus in His Place.*
134. Wright, *Resurrection*; Acts 2:14-40; 1 Corinthians 15.

Chapter 16. Church of Jesus Christ of Latter-day Saints

1. In 2018, the Church of Jesus Christ of Latter-day Saints announced that it prefers to be referred to by its full name or by the abbreviated title "The Church of Jesus Christ" or "the Church." (See "Style Guide—the Name of the Church," *Church of Jesus Christ of Latter-day Saints*, accessed March 3, 2020, https://newsroom.churchofjesuschrist.org/style-guide.) Rather than following the church's style guide, this chapter will use long-established, common naming practices observed even by LDS authors but will do so in a way that attempts to show respect. The Church is known familiarly as "the LDS Church," a title I will use, and "the Mormon Church," which I will not use. I will use the term "Mormonism" to refer to the larger cultural movement that arose out of the LDS Church, which is not strictly synonymous with the LDS Church. Members of the Church of Jesus Christ of Latter-day Saints will be referred to as "Latter-day Saints," "Saints," or "Mormons." I will also use "Mormon" and "LDS" as adjectives, such as "Mormon culture" or "LDS worldview." Variation is used mainly to make the chapter more readable.
2. "Statistics and Church Facts: Total Church Membership," *Church of Jesus Christ of Latter-day Saints*, accessed July 15, 2019, https://newsroom.churchofjesuschrist.org/facts-and-statistics.
3. Matthew Bowman, *The Mormon People: The Making of an American Faith* (New York: Random House, 2012), 9–11.
4. Jana Reiss and Christopher Kimball Bigelow, *Mormonism for Dummies* (Hoboken, NJ: Wiley, 2005), 61–63.
5. Matthew J. Grow et al., eds., *Saints: The Story of the Church of Jesus Christ in the Latter Days*, vol. 1, *The Standard of Truth, 1815–1846* (Salt Lake City: Church of Jesus Christ of Latter-day Saints, 2018), loc. 249, Kindle.
6. Church of Jesus Christ of Latter-day Saints, *The Pearl of Great Price: A Selection from the Revelations, Translations, and Narrations of Joseph Smith* (Salt Lake City: Church of Jesus Christ of Latter-day Saints, 2013), 1:20.
7. "The Church of Jesus Christ in Former Times," in *Gospel Principles, Church of Jesus Christ of Latter-day Saints*, accessed July 11, 2019, https://www.churchofjesuschrist.org/study/manual/gospel-principles/chapter-16-the-church-of-jesus-christ-in-former-times.
8. Reiss and Bigelow, *Mormonism for Dummies*, 14.
9. Larry C. Porter, "The Restoration of the Aaronic and Melchizedek Priesthood," *Church of Jesus Christ of Latter-day Saints*, accessed March 25, 2020, https://www.churchofjesuschrist.org/study/ensign/1996/12/the-restoration-of-the-aaronic-and-melchizedek-priesthoods?lang=eng.
10. Grow et al., *Saints*, loc. 359–410.
11. Reiss and Bigelow, *Mormonism for Dummies*, 163–65.
12. Bowman, *Mormon People*, 28–31.
13. Grow et al., *Saints*, loc. 149.
14. Bowman, *Mormon People*, 36–38.
15. Richard Lyman Bushman, *Joseph Smith: Rough Stone Rolling* (New York: Vintage, 2005), 161–63.

16. Bowman, *Mormon People*, 59–61.
17. Reiss and Bigelow, *Mormonism for Dummies*, 188–92.
18. Bowman, *Mormon People*, 61–62.
19. Bushman, *Joseph Smith*, 127–28.
20. Bowman, *Mormon People*, 78–81.
21. Bushman, *Joseph Smith*, 409–10.
22. Bowman, *Mormon People*, 75–78.
23. Reiss and Bigelow, *Mormonism for Dummies*, 196–97.
24. Bowman, *Mormon People*, 88–90.
25. *Encyclopedia Britannica Online*, s.v. "Brigham Young," accessed June 21, 2019, https://www.britannica.com/biography/Brigham-Young.
26. *Wikipedia*, s.v. "Mormon Pioneers," accessed July 13, 2019, https://en.wikipedia.org/wiki/Mormon_pioneers.
27. *Encyclopedia Britannica Online*, s.v. "Brigham Young."
28. Bowman, *Mormon People*, 145–48.
29. Bowman, 148–50.
30. Reiss and Bigelow, *Mormonism for Dummies*, 227.
31. Richard Lyman Bushman, *Mormonism: A Very Short Introduction* (New York: Oxford University Press, 2008), 103–4.
32. Martin S. Tanner, "Schismatic Groups," in *Encyclopedia of Mormonism*, ed. Daniel H. Ludlow (New York: Macmillan, 1992), 1265–67.
33. Max J. Anderson, "Fundamentalists," in *Encyclopedia of Mormonism*, 531–32.
34. "The Fulness of the Gospel: Life Before Birth," *Ensign*, February 2006, 30–31.
35. Joseph Fielding Smith, comp., *Joseph Smith, Teachings of the Prophet Joseph Smith* (Salt Lake City: Deseret Book, 1938), 345.
36. Tad R. Callister, "Our Identity and Our Destiny," *Religious Educator: Perspectives on the Restored Gospel* 14, no. 1 (2013): 1–17.
37. Church of Jesus Christ of Latter-day Saints, *Eternal Marriage Student Manual: Religion 234 and 235* (Salt Lake City: Church of Jesus Christ of Latter-day Saints, 2001), 167.
38. Church of Jesus Christ of Latter-day Saints, *The Doctrine and Covenants* (Salt Lake City: Church of Jesus Christ of Latter-day Saints, 1982), 130:22.
39. "Our Father in Heaven," in *Gospel Principles, Church of Jesus Christ of Latter-day Saints*, accessed July 11, 2019, https://www.churchofjesuschrist.org/study/manual/gospel-principles/chapter-1-our-father-in-heaven.
40. Church of Jesus Christ of Latter-day Saints, *Doctrine and Covenants*, 93:33.
41. Bushman, *Mormonism*, 71–72.
42. Robert L. Millet, "God and Man," in *No Weapon Shall Prosper*, ed. Robert L. Millet (Salt Lake City: Deseret Book, 2011), 356.
43. Reiss and Bigelow, *Mormonism for Dummies*, 45.
44. Reiss and Bigelow, 53.
45. "Plan of Salvation," in *True to the Faith: A Gospel Reference* (Salt Lake City: Church of Jesus Christ of Latter-day Saints, 2004), 115–16.
46. "Jesus Christ, Our Chosen Leader and Savior," in *Gospel Principles, Church of Jesus Christ of Latter-day Saints*, accessed July 11, 2019, https://www.churchofjesuschrist.org/study/manual/gospel-principles/chapter-3-jesus-christ-our-chosen-leader-and-savior.
47. Reiss and Bigelow, *Mormonism for Dummies*, 27–30.
48. For a list of requirements for exaltation, see "Exaltation," in *Gospel Principles, Church of Jesus Christ of Latter-day Saints*, accessed July 15, 2019, https://www.churchofjesuschrist.org/study/manual/gospel-principles/chapter-47-exaltation.
49. Genesis 1:28.
50. Genesis 2:16-17.

51. "The Fulness of the Gospel: The Fall of Adam and Eve," *Ensign*, June 2006, https://www.lds.org/study/ensign/2006/06/the-fulness-of-the-gospel-the-fall-of-adam-and-eve.
52. "Salvation," in *True to the Faith*, 150–53.
53. *The Book of Mormon* (Salt Lake City: Church of Jesus Christ of Latter-day Saints, 2013), 2 Nephi 25:23.
54. Joseph C. Winther, "Because of His Love," *Ensign*, April 2002, 19.
55. Reiss and Bigelow, *Mormonism for Dummies*, 32–33.
56. Church of Jesus Christ of Latter-day Saints, *Doctrine and Covenants*, 138:30.
57. Reiss and Bigelow, *Mormonism for Dummies*, 116–17.
58. Darwin L. Thomas, "Family History, Genealogy," in *Encyclopedia of Mormonism*, 492–94.
59. Paul B. Pixton, "Millennium," in *Encyclopedia of Mormonism*, 906–8.
60. "The Final Judgment," in *Gospel Principles, Church of Jesus Christ of Latter-day Saints*, accessed July 11, 2019, https://www.churchofjesuschrist.org/study/manual/gospel-principles/chapter-46-the-final-judgment.
61. Church of Jesus Christ of Latter-day Saints, *Doctrine and Covenants*, 88:20-32.
62. "Final Judgment." See also Church of Jesus Christ of Latter-day Saints, *Doctrine and Covenants*, 76.
63. Robert L. Millet, "Perdition, Sons of," in *LDS Beliefs: A Doctrinal Reference*, ed. Robert L. Millet et al. (Salt Lake City: Deseret Book, 2011), 488–89.
64. Brent Corcoran, ed., *Multiply and Replenish: Mormon Essays on Sex and Family* (Salt Lake City: Signature, 1994), vii.
65. "The Articles of Faith," in *Pearl of Great Price*, 60.
66. *Book of Mormon*, 1 Nephi 13:26.
67. For an introduction to the Joseph Smith Translation, see Robert J. Matthews, "Joseph Smith Translation of the Bible," in *Encyclopedia of Mormonism*, 763–69; Bushman, *Joseph Smith*, 132, 142.
68. For introductory information about the *Doctrine and Covenants* and its contents, see Roy W. Doxey et al., "Doctrine and Covenants," in *Encyclopedia of Mormonism*, 404–24.
69. Church of Jesus Christ of Latter-day Saints, *Doctrine and Covenants*, 131.
70. Church of Jesus Christ of Latter-day Saints, 76.
71. Church of Jesus Christ of Latter-day Saints, 132.
72. Church of Jesus Christ of Latter-day Saints, 128, 138.
73. Church of Jesus Christ of Latter-day Saints, 84.
74. For an overview of the book of Moses, see Bruce T. Taylor, "Book of Moses," in *Encyclopedia of Mormonism*, 216–17; Bushman, *Joseph Smith*, 132–42.
75. On the origin and contents of the book of Abraham, see H. Donl Peterson, Stephen E. Thompson, and Michael Rhodes, "Book of Abraham," in *Encyclopedia of Mormonism*, 132–38; Bushman, *Joseph Smith*, 285–90.
76. "Introduction," in *Book of Mormon*, vii.
77. "Testimony of the Prophet Joseph Smith," in *Book of Mormon*, ix–xi.
78. Monte S. Nyman and Lisa Bolin Hawkins, "Book of Mormon: Overview," in *Encyclopedia of Mormonism*, 141.
79. *Book of Mormon*, Moroni 10:4.
80. Nyman and Hawkins, "Book of Mormon," 143.
81. Church of Jesus Christ of Latter-day Saints, *Doctrine and Covenants*, 107:57; *Book of Mormon*, 2 Nephi 29:11-13; *Book of Mormon*, 3 Nephi 26:6-8.
82. W.D. Davies and Truman G. Madsen, "Scripture," in *Encyclopedia of Mormonism*, 1278.
83. Jessie L. Embry, *Mormon Wards as Community* (Binghamton, NY: Global Publications, 2001), 135.
84. Spencer J. Palmer, "Comments on Common Ground," in *Mormons and Muslims: Spiritual Foundations and Modern Manifestations*, ed. Spencer J. Palmer, rev. ed. (Provo, UT: Religious Studies Center, 2002), 88.
85. John L. Sorensen, *Mormon Culture: Four Decades of Essays on Mormon Society and Personality* (Salt Lake City: New Sage, 1997), 139–40.
86. Eric A. Eliason, "The Cultural Dynamics of Historical Self-fashioning: Mormon Pioneer Nostalgia, American Culture, and the International Church," *Journal of Mormon History* 28, no. 2 (Fall 2002): 168–69.
87. Mary Ellen Robinson, "Still Circling the Wagons: Violence and the Mormon Self-image," *Sunstone* 40, no. 4 (April 2002): 64–66.

88. Jan Shipps, "Making Saints: In the Early Days and the Latter Days," in *Contemporary Mormonism: Social Science Perspectives*, ed. Marie Cornwall, Tim B. Heaton, and Lawrence A. Young (Urbana, IL: University of Illinois Press, 2001), 73.
89. Shipps, "Making Saints," 74–77.
90. Terryl L. Givens, *People of Paradox* (New York: Oxford University Press, 2007), 26.
91. Sorensen, *Mormon Culture*, 9.
92. "A Portrait of Mormons in the U.S.," *Pew Research Center*, July 24, 2009, https://www.pewforum.org/2009/07/24/a-portrait-of-mormons-in-the-us-religious-beliefs-and-practices/.
93. Jana Reiss, *The Next Mormons: How Millennials Are Changing the LDS Church* (New York: Oxford University Press, 2019), 1–9.
94. Armand L. Mauss, "Mormonism in the New Century," *The Future of Mormonism*, accessed July 10, 2019, www.patheos.com/Resources/Additional-Resources/Mormonism-in-the-New-Century.
95. Church of Jesus Christ of Latter-day Saints, *Doctrine and Covenants*, 1:30.
96. Where there are not enough members to sustain the leadership structure of a ward, smaller "branches" are organized.
97. "How the Church Is Organized," *Church of Jesus Christ of Latter-day Saints*, accessed July 10, 2019, https://www.churchofjesuschrist.org/topics/church-organization/how-the-church-is-organized.
98. Katherine Ball Ross, ed., *The Mission: Inside the Church of Jesus Christ of Latter-day Saints* (New York: Warner, 1995), 139.
99. W.F. Walker Johansen, *What Is Mormonism All About?* (New York: St. Martin's, 2002), 138.
100. Alan K. Parrish, "Keys of the Priesthood," in *Encyclopedia of Mormonism*, 780–81.
101. Bushman, *Mormonism*, 40.
102. Douglas J. Davies, *The Mormon Culture of Salvation* (Burlington, VT: Ashgate, 2000), 68.
103. Embry, *Mormon Wards*, 14.
104. Claudia L. Bushman, *Contemporary Mormonism: Latter-day Saints in Modern America* (Westport, CT: Praeger, 2006), 121.
105. Johansen, *What Is Mormonism All About?*, 95.
106. Johansen, 211.
107. Danielle B. Wagner, "Church Announces Change to Sunday Meeting Schedule, Focuses on Home Gospel Study," *LDS Living*, October 6, 2018, http://www.ldsliving.com/Church-Announces-Change-to-Sunday-Meeting-Schedule-Focuses-on-Home-Gospel-Study/s/89433.
108. Tim B. Heaton, Kristen L. Goodman, and Thomas B. Holman, "In Search of a Peculiar People: Are Mormon Families Really Different?," in *Contemporary Mormonism: Social Science Perspectives*, ed. Marie Cornwall, Tim B. Heaton, and Lawrence A. Young (Urbana, IL: University of Illinois Press, 1994), 88–89.
109. Bushman, *Contemporary Mormonism*, 82.
110. Roger M. Thompson, *The Mormon Church* (New York: Hippocrene, 1993), 197.
111. Thompson, 195.
112. Ross, *Mission*, 34.
113. Davies, *Mormon Culture of Salvation*, 68.
114. "Statistics," *Temples of the Church of Jesus Christ of Latter-day Saints*, accessed July 15, 2019, https://churchofjesuschristtemples.org/statistics/.
115. Davies, *Mormon Culture of Salvation*, 72–79.
116. Bushman, *Mormonism*, 57.
117. Johanson, *What Is Mormonism All About?*, 205.
118. Bushman, *Mormonism*, 57–58.
119. Loren Marks and Brent D. Beal, "Preserving Peculiarity as a People: Mormon Distinctiveness in Lived Values and Internal Structure," in *Revisiting Thomas F. O'Dea's* The Mormons*: Contemporary Perspectives*, ed. Cardell K. Jacobsen, John P. Hoffmann, and Tim B. Heaton (Salt Lake City: University of Utah Press, 2008), 279.
120. William A. Wilson, "Teach Me All That I Must Do: The Practice of Mormon Religion," in *The Marrow of Human Experience: Essays on Folklore*, ed. Jill Terry Judy (Logan, UT: Utah State University Press, 2006), 255.

121. Givens, *People of Paradox*, 238.
122. Jana K. Reiss, "Stripling Warriors: The Cultural Engagements of Contemporary Mormon Kitsch," *Sunstone* 22, no. 2 (June 1999): 44.
123. Calvin L. Rampton, "Toleration of Religious Sentiment," in *God and Country: Politics in Utah*, ed. Jeffery E. Sells (Salt Lake City: Signature, 2005), 87.
124. Davies, *Mormon Culture of Salvation*, 219.
125. "For the Strength of Youth," *Church of Jesus Christ of Latter-day Saints*, accessed July 12, 2019, https://www.churchofjesuschrist.org/study/manual/for-the-strength-of-youth/.
126. Bushman, *Mormonism*, 39.
127. Marks and Beal, "Preserving Peculiarity as a People," 260–64.
128. Johanson, *What Is Mormonism All About?*, 116.
129. "Portrait of Mormons in the U.S."
130. Johanson, *What Is Mormonism All About?*, 100.
131. Armand L. Mauss, "Feelings, Faith, and Folkways: A Personal Essay on Mormon Popular Culture," in *"Proving Contraries": A Collection of Writings in Honor of Eugene England*, ed. Robert A. Rees (Salt Lake City: Signature, 2005), 25–28.
132. Bushman, *Contemporary Mormonism*, 17.
133. "2018 Statistical Report for 2019 April Conference," *Church of Jesus Christ of Latter-day Saints*, April 6, 2019, https://newsroom.churchofjesuschrist.org/article/2018-statistical-report. Along with these proselytizing missionaries, the Church also deploys 38,000 church service missionaries.
134. Thomas S. Monson, "Welcome to Conference," *Liahona*, November 2012, 4.
135. "Preparing for Life as a Missionary," in *Missionary Preparation Teacher Manual* (Salt Lake City: Church of Jesus Christ of Latter-day Saints, 2014), available at https://www.churchofjesuschrist.org/study/manual/missionary-preparation-teacher-manual/lesson-6-preparing-for-life-as-a-missionary.
136. "The Missionary Purpose," in *Missionary Preparation Teacher Manual*, available at https://www.churchofjesuschrist.org/study/manual/missionary-preparation-teacher-manual/lesson-1-the-missionary-purpose.
137. Bushman, *Mormonism*, 46–47.
138. Jana Reiss, "Mormon Growth Continues to Slow, Especially in the US," *Flunking Sainthood* (blog), *Religion News Service*, April 13, 2018, https://religionnews.com/2018/04/13/mormon-growth-continues-to-slow-especially-in-the-u-s/. LDS Church growth has decreased from 5 percent per year in the late 1980s to 1.5 percent per year in 2017.
139. "Religious Switching and Remarriage," in *America's Changing Religious Landscape, Pew Research Center*, accessed March 25, 2020, https://www.pewforum.org/2015/05/12/chapter-2-religious-switching-and-intermarriage/. Of converts to Mormonism, about eight in ten were raised Protestant or Catholic.
140. David Stewart, "LDS Church Growth, Member Activity, and Convert Retention: Review and Analysis," *Cumorah.com*, accessed July 10, 2019, http://www.cumorah.com/index.php?target=church_growth_articles&story_id=8.
141. Jana Reiss, "4 Myths About Ex-Mormons," *Flunking Sainthood* (blog), *Religion News Service*, February 12, 2019, https://religionnews.com/2019/02/12/4-myths-about-ex-mormons/.
142. "A Comprehensive List of Why People Leave the LDS Church" and "What Factors Led or Lead You to Stay Active in the LDS Church Even When You Don't Necessarily Believe in or Enjoy Church?," *Why Mormons Leave*, last modified February 5, 2014, http://www.whymormonsleave.com/.
143. D. Jeff Burton, "The Phenomenon of the Closet Doubter," in *The Wilderness of Faith: Essays on Contemporary Mormon Thought*, ed. John Sillito (Salt Lake City: Signature, 1991), 82.
144. Bushman, *Contemporary Mormonism*, 135.
145. Burton, "Phenomenon of the Closet Doubter," 83.
146. Romans 4:17; Hebrews 11:3.
147. 1 Timothy 1:17; 6:15-16.
148. John 4:24; Luke 24:39.
149. Psalm 90:2; Malachi 3:6.
150. Hosea 11:9; Numbers 23:19.

151. Jude 25; Jeremiah 23:23.
152. God is depicted as having hands in Exodus 7:5, a mouth in Psalm 33:6, and eyes in Psalm 34:15—but compare Psalm 18:2 and Psalm 57:1.
153. Isaiah 43:10; 44:6-8.
154. Ross Anderson, "Understanding the Trinity," *Utah Advance Ministries*, accessed July 15, 2019, http://www.utahadvance.org/writings/articles/understanding-the-trinity/.
155. John 1:1-2.
156. Genesis 1:27.
157. Ephesians 1:5.
158. Isaiah 40:25.
159. Psalm 139:13-15.
160. Genesis 9:6.
161. 1 John 4:1-3.
162. 1 Thessalonians 2:13; 2 Timothy 3:15-16.
163. To understand the transmission of the Bible, see Bruce M. Metzger, *The Text of the New Testament* (London: Oxford University Press, 1964).
164. Luke P. Wilson, "Does Archaeology Support the Book of Mormon? A Survey of the Evidence," *Institute for Religious Research*, December 22, 2011, http://mit.irr.org/book-of-mormon-archaeology-full. Of course, Latter-day Saints would dispute this claim.
165. Ross Anderson, *Understanding the Book of Mormon: A Quick Christian Guide to the Mormon Holy Book* (Grand Rapids, MI: Zondervan, 2009), 76–77.
166. For a critique of the Joseph Smith Translation, see Jerald and Sandra Tanner, *Mormonism—Shadow or Reality?* enlarged ed. (Salt Lake City: Modern Microfilm, 1972), 386–97.
167. Charles M. Larson, *By His Own Hand Upon Papyrus*, rev. ed. (Grand Rapids, MI: Institute for Religious Research, 1992).
168. Hebrews 1:1-2.
169. Deuteronomy 18:21-22.
170. "Failed Prophecies of Joseph Smith," *Institute for Religious Research*, August 16, 2011, http://mit.irr.org/failed-prophecies-of-joseph-smith.
171. Deuteronomy 13:1-3.
172. Bill McKeever and Eric Johnson, *Answering Mormons' Questions: Ready Responses for Inquiring Latter-day Saints* (Grand Rapids, MI: Kregel, 2013), 92–96.
173. Ross Anderson, *Understanding Your Mormon Neighbor: A Quick Christian Guide for Relating to Latter-day Saints* (Grand Rapids, MI: Zondervan, 2011), 69–70.
174. Robert M. Bowman Jr., "The Mormon View of the Church," in *The Bottom-Line Guide to Mormonism, Institute for Religious Research*, August 26, 2013, http://mit.irr.org/mormon-view-of-church.
175. McKeever and Johnson, *Answering Mormons' Questions*, 77–80.
176. Romans 3:23.
177. Colossians 1:21.
178. Ephesians 2:1-3; Romans 3:1-10.
179. Galatians 3:13; 6:14; Ephesians 2:16; Colossians 2:14-15.
180. Romans 11:5-6.
181. Titus 3:3-7.
182. Ephesians 2:8-10.
183. John 14:2-3.
184. Hebrews 9:27; Luke 16:24-26.
185. 2 Thessalonians 1:7-9; Revelation 20:11-15.
186. Jerry Earl Johnston, "Milk Before Meat," *Deseret News*, July 18, 2010, https://www.deseretnews.com/article/705385135/Jerry-Johnston-Milk-before-meat.html.
187. *Book of Mormon*, 3 Nephi 11:2-30.

188. Acts 13:13-43.
189. Acts 14:8-20.
190. Acts 17:16-34.
191. 1 Peter 3:15-16.
192. For a more extended treatment of this question, see Anderson, *Understanding Your Mormon Neighbor*, 115–19.

Chapter 17. Jehovah's Witnesses

1. Throughout this chapter, I will refer to the Jehovah's Witnesses as either JWs or the Witnesses.
2. Robert M. Bowman Jr., *Jehovah's Witnesses* (Grand Rapids, MI: Zondervan, 1995), 9; Fritz Ridenour, *So What's the Difference? A Look at 20 Worldviews, Faiths, and Religions and How They Compare to Christianity* (Ventura, CA: Regal, 2001), 115.
3. Ridenour, *So What's the Difference?*, 115–16.
4. A more detailed discussion about the Witnesses and prophecy will be given later in this chapter under the heading "Prophecy and the Witnesses."
5. Richard Abanes, *Cults, New Religious Movements and Your Family: A Guide to Ten Non-Christian Groups Out to Convert Your Loved Ones* (Wheaton, IL: Crossway, 1998), 231.
6. JWs claim they have the top two magazines in publication worldwide. The monthly *Watchtower* magazine has a distribution of 42 million copies, and their illustrated magazine *Awake!* has a distribution of 41 million. In the US, the top paid-for magazine is *AARP the Magazine*, which has a monthly distribution of 20.4 million copies. For more information, see "*The Watchtower*—No Other Magazine Comes Close," *Jehovah's Witnesses*, accessed June 18, 2019, https://www.jw.org/en/jehovahs-witnesses/activities/publishing/watchtower-awake-magazine/.
7. "Witnesses to Relocate World Headquarters," *Jehovah's Witnesses*, accessed June 18, 2019, https://www.jw.org/en/jehovahs-witnesses/activities/construction/world-headquarters-relocating/.
8. Walter Martin, *The Kingdom of the Cults*, ed. Ravi Zacharias, rev. ed. (Minneapolis: Bethany House, 2003), 53–54. Ross's booklet was called "Some Facts About the Self-styled 'Pastor' Charles T. Russell."
9. Martin, *Kingdom of the Cults*. Russell was challenged to read Greek while on the stand, and he was unable to do so, which led him to admit that he was unfamiliar with the language.
10. Martin, *Kingdom of the Cults*. Russell lied about other things while under oath, including his divorce, alimony payments, and his ability to speak any languages other than English.
11. "Who Is the Faithful and Discreet Slave?," *Jehovah's Witnesses*, accessed July 9, 2019, https://www.jw.org/en/publications/books/jehovahs-will/faithful-discreet-slave.
12. "Who Was the Founder of the Jehovah's Witnesses?," *Jehovah's Witnesses*, accessed June 17, 2019, https://www.jw.org/en/jehovahs-witnesses/faq/founder/.
13. J.F. Rutherford, *Creation* (Brooklyn, NY: Watchtower Bible and Tract Society, 1927), 131. For other examples of the Witnesses' use of Russell's works, see Martin, *Kingdom of the Cults*, 60–63. See also the JW 2010 documentary, "Jehovah's Witnesses—Faith in Action, Part 1: Out of Darkness," *Jehovah's Witnesses*, accessed June 19, 2019, https://www.jw.org/en/publications/videos/faith-in-action-part-1/, which highlights Russell's role in establishing the JW religion and its theology.
14. David Reed, *Jehovah's Witnesses Answered Verse by Verse* (Grand Rapids, MI: Baker, 1992), 59.
15. Ridenour, *So What's the Difference?*, 117.
16. Ridenour, 117.
17. Ron Carlson and Ed Decker, *Fast Facts on False Teachings* (Eugene, OR: Harvest House, 1994), 126.
18. Ridenour, *So What's the Difference?*, 118.
19. Ridenour, 118–19.
20. Ridenour, 120.
21. Ridenour, 120.
22. Abanes, *Cults*, 242–43.
23. "What Is the Governing Body of Jehovah's Witnesses?," *Jehovah's Witnesses*, accessed June 28, 2019, https://www.jw.org/en/jehovahs-witnesses/faq/governing-body/.
24. Refer to the end of this chapter for responses to these four beliefs.
25. *Watchtower*, May 1, 1957, 274, quoted in Rhodes, *Reasoning from the Scriptures with the Jehovah's Witnesses*

(Brooklyn, NY: Watchtower Bible and Tract Society, 1989), 28. Rhodes includes a long list of other examples where JWs are discouraged from thinking independently.

26. Rhodes, 29.
27. Ron Rhodes, *The 10 Most Important Things You Can Say to a Jehovah's Witness* (Eugene, OR: Harvest House, 2001), 23.
28. Rhodes, 23. *Jehovah* does not appear in original Greek manuscripts. Witnesses defend this by saying, "The divine name appears in translations of the Christian Greek Scriptures into Hebrew, in passages where quotations are made directly from the inspired Hebrew Scriptures." See Rhodes, *Reasoning from the Scriptures*, 278.
29. Rhodes, *Reasoning from the Scriptures*, 277. This makes it difficult to review the credentials of the translators. Further, respected biblical linguists have rejected the NWT as a legitimate version of the Bible. See Rhodes, *10 Most Important Things*, 24–25.
30. "Is the *New World Translation* Accurate?," *Jehovah's Witnesses*, accessed June 28, 2019, https://www.jw.org/en/jehovahs-witnesses/faq/new-world-translation-accurate/.
31. *Watchtower*, no. 3 (2016): 16.
32. "The Lie That Made God a Mystery," *Jehovah's Witnesses*, accessed June 20, 2019, https://www.jw.org/en/publications/magazines/wp20131101/lie-made-god-a-mystery-trinity/.
33. Rhodes, *Reasoning from the Scriptures*, 405–6.
34. "Is the Trinity a Bible Teaching?," *Jehovah's Witnesses*, accessed July 11, 2019, https://www.jw.org/en/publications/magazines/wp20120301/Is-the-Trinity-a-Bible-teaching/.
35. "Who Is Jesus Christ?," *Jehovah's Witnesses*, accessed June 20, 2019, https://www.jw.org/en/publications/books/good-news-from-god/who-is-jesus-christ/.
36. "Is Jesus the Archangel Michael?," *Jehovah's Witnesses*, accessed June 20, 2019, https://www.jw.org/en/publications/magazines/wp20100401/Is-Jesus-the-Archangel-Michael/.
37. Rhodes, *Reasoning from the Scriptures*, 150. See also "In What Way Are Jesus and His Father One?," accessed June 20, 2019, https://www.jw.org/en/publications/magazines/wp20090901/way-jesus-and-father-one/.
38. "Did Jesus Die on a Cross?," *Jehovah's Witnesses*, accessed June 26, 2019, https://www.jw.org/en/bible-teachings/questions/did-jesus-die-on-cross/. It is important to note here that some Christians also believe that Jesus died on a stake, not a cross.
39. "The Resurrection of Jesus—Its Meaning for Us," *Watchtower*, November 15, 2014, 4; "After Jesus' Resurrection, Was His Body Flesh or Spirit?," *Jehovah's Witnesses*, accessed July 9, 2019, https://www.jw.org/en/bible-teachings/questions/jesus-body/.
40. "How Can You Be Saved?," *Awake!*, November 8, 1975, https://wol.jw.org/en/wol/d/r1/lp-e/101975807#h=18.
41. "What Is Salvation?," *Jehovah's Witnesses*, accessed June 28, 2019, https://www.jw.org/en/bible-teachings/questions/what-is-salvation/.
42. "Hell: What Is It? Who Are There? Can They Get Out?," *Watchtower* booklet, 1924, http://ia601406.us.archive.org/23/items/WatchtowerLibrary/booklets/1924_hll_E.pdf; "What Really Is Hell?," *Jehovah's Witnesses*, accessed June 28, 2019, https://wol.jw.org/en/wol/d/r1/lp-e/2002521.
43. "What Is the Soul?," *Jehovah's Witnesses*, accessed July 9, 2019, https://www.jw.org/en/bible-teachings/questions/what-is-a-soul/.
44. "Survival or Destruction at the 'Great Tribulation,'" *Jehovah's Witnesses*, accessed July 9, 2019, https://wol.jw.org/en/wol/d/r1/lp-e/1982248.
45. "Why Don't Jehovah's Witnesses Call Their Meeting Place a Church?," *Jehovah's Witnesses*, accessed June 20, 2019, https://www.jw.org/en/jehovahs-witnesses/faq/jehovahs-witnesses-church-kingdom-hall/.
46. "How Are Congregations of Jehovah's Witnesses Organized?," *Jehovah's Witnesses*, accessed June 20, 2019, https://www.jw.org/en/jehovahs-witnesses/faq/congregations-organized/.
47. "What Are Our Meetings Like?," *Jehovah's Witnesses*, accessed June 20, 2019, https://www.jw.org/en/publications/books/jehovahs-will/meetings-of-jehovahs-witnesses/.
48. "What Are Our Meetings Like?" To view a video about Kingdom Halls, see "What Happens at a Kingdom Hall?," *Jehovah's Witnesses*, video, accessed June 20, 2019, https://www.jw.org/en/jehovahs-witnesses/meetings/video-kingdom-hall/.

49. Wilber Lingle, *What the Watchtower Society Doesn't Want You to Know: A Glimpse Behind the Walls of the Kingdom Halls* (Fort Washington, PA: CLC Publications, 2009), 35.
50. "What Is a Pioneer?," *Jehovah's Witnesses*, accessed June 20, 2019, https://www.jw.org/en/publications/books/jehovahs-will/jw-pioneer/.
51. "Why Don't Jehovah's Witnesses Celebrate Certain Holidays?," *Jehovah's Witnesses*, accessed June 26, 2019, https://www.jw.org/en/jehovahs-witnesses/faq/jw-celebrate-holidays/.
52. I do not necessarily disagree with her on this point. Christian churches *should* be focusing on Christ's death and resurrection, but that does not mean that they should always avoid any non-Christian forms of celebration.
53. Interestingly, in 2018, there were 8,579,909 Witnesses worldwide, but 20,329,317 people attended the Memorial service. See "How Many of Jehovah's Witnesses Are There Worldwide?," *Jehovah's Witnesses*, accessed June 17, 2019, https://www.jw.org/en/jehovahs-witnesses/faq/how-many-jw-members/; "2018 Grand Totals," *Jehovah's Witnesses*, accessed June 17, 2019, https://www.jw.org/en/publications/books/2018-service-year-report/2018-grand-totals/. The Memorial is their most widely attended service annually, and they consider it one of their best tools for evangelism.
54. For example, in 2018, out of more than 8.5 million Witnesses, only 19,521 partook in Communion. "2018 Grand Totals," *Jehovah's Witnesses*, accessed June 20, 2019, https://www.jw.org/en/publications/books/2018-service-year-report/2018-grand-totals/.
55. "Why Do Jehovah's Witnesses Observe the Lord's Supper Differently from the Way Other Religions Do?," *Jehovah's Witnesses*, accessed June 20, 2019, https://www.jw.org/en/jehovahs-witnesses/faq/lords-supper/.
56. *You Can Live Forever in Paradise on Earth* (Brooklyn, NY: Watchtower Bible and Tract Society, 1982), 155–65.
57. "Why Don't Jehovah's Witnesses Accept Blood Transfusions?," *Jehovah's Witnesses*, accessed June 26, 2019, https://www.jw.org/en/jehovahs-witnesses/faq/jehovahs-witnesses-why-no-blood-transfusions/.
58. *Keep Yourselves in God's Love* (Brooklyn, NY: Watchtower Bible and Tract Society, 2008), appendix.
59. "Four Things You Should Know About Divorce," *Jehovah's Witnesses*, accessed June 26, 2019, https://www.jw.org/en/publications/magazines/g201002/four-things-about-divorce/.
60. "Marriage Obligations and Divorce," *Jehovah's Witnesses*, accessed July 9, 2019, https://wol.jw.org/en/wol/d/r1/lp-e/1956723.
61. "What About Youth Dance Clubs?," *Jehovah's Witnesses*, accessed June 26, 2019, https://www.jw.org/en/publications/magazines/g20040422/What-About-Youth-Dance-Clubs/.
62. Charles T. Russell, *The Battle of Armageddon*, vol. 4, *Studies in the Scriptures* (Brooklyn, NY: International Bible Students Association, 1925), 621.
63. Charles T. Russell, *The Time Is at Hand*, vol. 2, *Studies in the Scriptures* (Allegheny, PA: Watchtower Bible and Tract Society, 1907), 363.
64. *Watchtower*, January 15, 1892, 22, quoted in Duane Magnani and Arthur Barrett, *The Watchtower Files: Dialogue with a Jehovah's Witness* (Minneapolis: Bethany House, 1985), 78. Although the JW website, JW.org, has a decent archival system for their publications, it does not contain several specific editions, which is why secondary sources can be helpful when researching their prophetic history.
65. *Watchtower*, July 15, 1894, 226, quoted in Magnani and Barrett, *The Watchtower Files: Dialogue with a Jehovah's Witness*, 79.
66. Ridenour, *So What's the Difference?*, 116.
67. J.F. Rutherford, *Millions Now Living Will Never Die* (Brooklyn, NY: Watchtower Bible and Tract Society, 1920), 89–90, 97.
68. *Watchtower*, July 15, 1924, 211, quoted in Abanes, *Cults*, 236.
69. *The 1980 Yearbook of Jehovah's Witnesses* (Brooklyn, NY: Watchtower Bible and Tract Society, 1979), 62, quoted in Abanes, *Cults*, 237.
70. Bowman, *Jehovah's Witnesses*, 12.
71. Ridenour, *So What's the Difference?*, 120.
72. Ridenour, 120.
73. "The Path of the Righteous Does Keep Getting Brighter," *Jehovah's Witnesses*, accessed July 9, 2019, https://wol.jw.org/en/wol/d/r1/lp-e/1981889#h=25.
74. For example, before I finalized this chapter, I had my friend and former Witness, Cynthia Hampton, read it in

order to ensure accuracy. Special thanks for her willingness to do so for this as well as other writings I have done about JWs. You can read her testimony in the chapter "Stories of Coming to Christ" in this book (chapter 22).

75. If you'd like to read more about how to respond to their exclusive use of *Jehovah*, see Ron Rhodes, *Conversations with Jehovah's Witnesses* (Eugene, OR: Harvest House, 2014), 95–104.
76. Rhodes, *Reasoning from the Scriptures*, 148–49 (italics added).
77. For more about how to engage with JWs about the Trinity, see Rhodes, *Conversations*, 169–78.
78. See J. Warner Wallace, "What Was the Shape of Jesus' Cross?," *Cold-Case Christianity*, accessed June 26, 2019, https://coldcasechristianity.com/writings/what-was-the-shape-of-jesus-cross/.
79. Rhodes, *Reasoning from the Scriptures*, 189–94.
80. Rhodes, 293.
81. Glenn Packiam, *Blessed Broken Given: How Your Story Becomes Sacred in the Hands of Jesus* (New York: Multnomah, 2019), 53.

Chapter 18. Unitarian Universalism

1. "UUA Membership Statistics, 1961–2019," *Unitarian Universalist Association*, https://www.uua.org/data/demographics/uua-statistics.
2. Barry A. Kosmin and Seymour P. Lachman, *One Nation Under God* (New York: Harmony Books, 1993), 257–62.
3. "UUA Membership Statistics, 1961–2019."
4. George N. Marshall, *Challenge of a Liberal Faith*, rev. ed. (New Canaan, CT: Keats, 1980), 82.
5. Earl Morse Wilbur, *Our Unitarian Heritage* (Boston: Beacon, 1925), 352.
6. Wilbur, 367–68.
7. Commission on Appraisal of the Unitarian Universalist Association, *Engaging Our Theological Diversity* (Boston: Unitarian Universalist Association, 2005), 24.
8. Commission on Appraisal, 422.
9. "Are You a Unitarian Universalist?," *I Am UU*, accessed March 27, 2020, https://iamuu.net/learn-unitarian-universalism/abcs-of-uu-2/.
10. Paul Kurtz and Vern L. Bullough, "The Unitarian Universalist Association: Humanism or Theism?," *Free Inquiry* 11, no. 2 (Spring 1991): 12–13.
11. "Right to Choose: 1987 General Resolution," *Unitarian Universalist Association*, accessed March 27, 2020, https://www.uua.org/action/statements/right-choose.
12. Gustav Niebuhr, "With a New Spiritualism, Unitarians Welcome People of All Beliefs," *Washington Post*, July 6, 1993, A3.
13. "Unitarian Universalist Worship Services," *Unitarian Universalist Association*, accessed March 27, 2020, https://www.uua.org/beliefs/get-involved/sunday.
14. Harold O.J. Brown, *Heresies: Heresy and Orthodoxy in the History of the Church* (Peabody, MA: Hendrickson, 2000), 120.
15. Phillip Hewett, *The Unitarian Way* (Toronto: Canadian Unitarian Council, 1985), 89.
16. Karl M. Chworowsky and Christopher Gist Raible, "What Is a Unitarian Universalist?," in *Religions in America*, ed. Leo Rosten (New York: Simon & Schuster, 1975), 272.
17. Quoted in Steve Edington, *100 Questions That Non-members Ask About Unitarian Universalism* (Nashua, NH: Transition Publishing, 1994), 1.
18. William F. Schulz, "Our Faith," in *The Unitarian Universalist Pocket Guide*, ed. William F. Schulz, 2nd ed. (Boston: Skinner House, 1993), 4.
19. "The Seven Principles," *Unitarian Universalist Association*, accessed March 27, 2020, https://www.uua.org/beliefs/what-we-believe/principles.
20. Unitarian Universalist Association, *We Are Unitarian Universalists* (Boston: Unitarian Universalist Association, 1992).
21. "Unitarian Universalist Views of God," *Unitarian Universalist Association*, accessed March 27, 2020, https://www.uua.org/beliefs/what-we-believe/higher-power/views.
22. See the Covenant of Unitarian Universalist Pagans website at www.cuups.org.
23. Chworowsky and Raible, "What Is a Unitarian Universalist?," 267.

24. Chworowsky and Raible, 263–64.
25. Tony Larsen with Ellen Schmidt, *A Catechism for Unitarian Universalists Leader Guide* (Boston: Unitarian Universalist Association, 1989), 9.
26. Delos B. McKown, "A Humanist Looks at the Future of Unitarian Universalism," *Religious Humanism* 20, no. 2 (Spring 1986): 59.
27. Barbara Marshman, cited in Daniel G. Higgins Jr. et al., *Unitarian Universalist Views of Jesus* (Boston: Unitarian Universalist Association, 1994).
28. C.S. Lewis, *Mere Christianity* (New York: Macmillan, 1960), 40–41.
29. Quoted in Edington, *100 Questions*, 13.
30. Edington, 1.
31. Edington, 9–10.
32. George N. Marshall, "Unitarian Universalism," in *Encounters with Eternity: Religious Views of Death and Life After-Death*, ed. Christopher Jay Johnson and Marsha G McGee (New York: Philosophical Library, 1986), 302.
33. Quoted in Edington, *100 Questions*, 10.
34. Religious News Service, "'Kindergarten' Writer Says Point Was Missed," *Los Angeles Times*, December 21, 1991, Orange County edition, Special Section, S-7.
35. Charles A. Gaines, "Counting the Ways to 250,000 by 2001," in *Salted with Fire: Unitarian Universalist Strategies for Sharing Faith and Growing Congregations*, ed. Scott W. Alexander (Boston: Skinner House, 1995), 101.
36. Tony A. Larsen, "Evangelizing Our Children," in *Salted with Fire*, 128.
37. Jay Johnson and Marsha G. McGee, eds., *Encounters with Eternity: Religious Views of Death and Life After-Death* (New York: Philosophical Library, 1986), 338, 340.
38. Larsen and Schmidt, *Catechism*, 5.
39. Johnson and McGee, *Encounters with Eternity*, 331, 333, 335.
40. For more on the many philanthropic institutions which find their origin in Christianity, see Alvin J. Schmidt, *How Christianity Changed the World* (Grand Rapids, MI: Zondervan, 2004).

Chapter 19. Religious Pluralism

1. Mark 12:30-31; see also Leviticus 19:18; Deuteronomy 6:4-7; Matthew 22:37; Luke 10:27.
2. Matthew 28:18-20; see also Mark 16:15-19; Luke 24:36-53; Acts 1:6-11.
3. See Paul Copan, *"True for You but Not for Me": Overcoming Objections to Christian Faith*, rev. ed. (Bloomington, MN: Bethany House, 2009), esp. 44–48.
4. *Sahih al-Bukhari* 5:58:266; 8:75:377, accessed March 27, 2020, https://www.sahih-bukhari.com/. For the Qur'an on some Jews and Christians in paradise, see Surah 2:62; 2:111-12; 2:177; 2:253; 2:281; 3:113-14; 6:34; 10:94; 19:51; 22:42; 29:46; 42:15.
5. For example, Dalai Lama, *Answers: Discussions with Western Buddhists*, ed. Jose Ignacio Cabezon (Ithaca, NY: Snow Lion, 2001), 26–31; Gandhi, in *The Ways of Religion: An Introduction to the Major Traditions*, ed. Roger Eastman, 3rd ed. (New York: Oxford University Press, 1999), 65–74.
6. With thanks to Alexis (Lexi) Jordan Salome for recording this interview with Professor Eck and to Karen DeVan for proofreading early drafts of this chapter on pluralism and the chapter in this book on agnosticism/atheism.
7. Chris Stedman, *Faitheist: How an Atheist Found Common Ground with the Religious* (Boston: Beacon, 2012).
8. Genesis 1:26-27; 9:6. For further resources on each topic in this section, see Benjamin B. DeVan, "A Wesleyan Open Inclusivist Approach to Religious Diversity and New Atheism" (PhD diss., Durham University, 2016), 159–85, available at http://etheses.dur.ac.uk/11464/; Benjamin B. DeVan, "How Christians and Muslims Can Embrace Religious Diversity and Each Other: An Evangelical Perspective," *Journal of Religion and Society* 16 (2014): 1–31, http://moses.creighton.edu/JRS/2014/2014-8.pdf.
9. Irenaeus, *Against Heresies* 4:20:7, in *History of Theology: The Patristic Period*, ed. Angelo Di Berardino and Basil Studer (Collegeville, MN: Liturgical Press, 1997), 1:136.
10. Jonathan Sacks, *The Dignity of Difference: How to Avoid the Clash of Civilizations* (New York: Continuum, 2003), 60. For more Jewish-Christian dialogue, see Paul Copan and Craig A. Evans, eds., *Who Was Jesus: A Jewish-Christian Dialogue* (Louisville, KY: Westminster John Knox, 2001).
11. Ibn Arabi, *al-Futuhat al-makkiyya*, ed. O. Yahia (Beirut: Dar Sadir, 1911), 4:4.

12. al-Ghazali, *The Alchemy of Happiness* [*Kimiya-yi sa'adat*], trans. Claud Field (London: J. Murray, 1909), 22–23, available at http://ghazali.org/books/alchemy; al-Ghazali, *Ihya ulum al-din* (Cairo: Dar al-Bayan al-Arabi, 1990), 3:13.
13. Riffat Hassan, "The Qur'anic Perspective on Religious Pluralism," in *Peace-Building By, Between, and Beyond Muslims and Evangelical Christians*, ed. Mohammed Abu-Nimer and David Augsburger (Lanham, MD: Rowman & Littlefield, 2009), 95.
14. United Nations General Assembly, "The Universal Declaration of Human Rights," *United Nations*, December 10, 1948, https://www.un.org/en/documents/udhr.
15. Max Stackhouse, "A Christian Perspective on Human Rights," *Society*, January/February 2004, 25; see also Rodney Stark, *The Victory of Reason* (New York: Random House, 2005), xi.
16. Mary Ann Glendon, *The World Made New: Eleanor Roosevelt and the Universal Declaration of Human Rights* (New York: Random House, 2002); see also Paul Copan, "'Jesus-Shaped' Cultures: How Faithful Christians Have Transformed Societies," *Christian Research Institute* 37, no. 4 (2014), https://www.equip.org/article/jesus-shaped-cultures-faithful-christians-transformed-societies/.
17. "The Universal Declaration of Human Rights," United Nations General Assembly, December 10, 1948, accessed March 27, 2020, https://www.un.org/en/documents/udhr.
18. "Anti-Semitism: Martin Luther—'The Jews & Their Lies' (1543)," *Jewish Virtual Library*, accessed March 27, 2020, https://www.jewishvirtuallibrary.org/martin-luther-quot-the-jews-and-their-lies-quot.
19. Martin Luther, "Concerning Rebaptism, a Letter to Two Pastors," quoted in John S. Oyer, "The Writings of Luther Against the Anabaptists," *Mennonite Quarterly Review* 27, no. 1 (January 1953): 108.
20. On hell fire, see Martin Luther, *Luther's Works: Lectures on the Minor Prophets, II, Jonah, Habakkuk*, ed. Hilton C. Oswald (St. Louis: Concordia, 1973), 19:74–75; Luther, *Luther's Works: Commentaries on 1 Corinthians 7, 1 Corinthians 15, Lectures on 1 Timothy*, ed. Hilton C. Oswald (St. Louis: Concordia, 1973), 28:74–75. For readers interested in competing concepts of hell see, for example, William Crockett, ed., *Four Views on Hell* (Grand Rapids, MI: Zondervan, 1996); Preston Sprinkle, ed., *Four Views on Hell*, 2nd ed. (Grand Rapids, MI: Zondervan, 2016).
21. Balthasar Hubmaier, "Concerning Heretics and Those Who Burn Them," in *The Anabaptist Story: An Introduction to Sixteenth-Century Anabaptism*, ed. William R. Estep, 3rd ed. (Grand Rapids, MI: Eerdmans, 1996), 85.
22. John Leland, "The Rights of Conscience Inalienable," in *The Founding Fathers and the Debate Over Religion in Revolutionary America: A History in Documents*, ed. Matthew L. Harris and Thomas S. Kidd (New York: Oxford University Press, 2012), 146.
23. John Wesley, sermon 102, "Of Former Times," § 20, in *The Bicentennial Edition of the Works of John Wesley* (Nashville: Abingdon Press, 1976), 3:452 (italics added); Donald A.D. Thorsen, *The Wesleyan Quadrilateral: Scripture, Tradition, Reason, and Experience as a Model of Evangelical Theology* (Grand Rapids, MI: Francis Asbury Press of Zondervan, 1990), 40, 256, which references British divine Jeremy Taylor's (1613–1617) "profound effect" on Wesley. Taylor entitled one of his treatises *A Discourse on the Liberty of Prophesying: Shewing the Unreasonableness of Prescribing to Other Men's Faith and the Iniquity of Persecuting Differing Opinions* (London: John Blanchard and Son, 1734).
24. John Wesley, sermon 20, "The Lord Our Righteousness," § II:20, in *Works*, 1:463; see also sermon 39, "Catholic Spirit," § I:6, in *Works*, 2:84–85.
25. Surah 2:256; 6:107; 10:99; 16:82; 18:29; 109:1-6. All Qur'an quotations from M.A.S. Abdel Haleem, *The Qur'an: A New Translation*, Oxford World's Classics (New York: Oxford University Press, 2015).
26. "A Closer Look at How Religious Restrictions Have Risen Around the World: Tenth Annual Report Dives Deeper into the Ways Government Restrictions on Religion and Social Hostilities Involving Religion Have Changed, from 2007–2017," *Pew Research Center*, July 15, 2019, https://www.pewforum.org/2019/07/15/a-closer-look-at-how-religious-restrictions-have-risen-around-the-world/.
27. Peter Beyer, "Constitutional Privilege and Constituting Pluralism: Religious Freedom in National, Global, and Legal Context," *Journal for the Scientific Study of Religion* 42, no. 3 (September 2003): 333–39.
28. See also Paul Copan and Kenneth D. Litwak, *The Gospel in the Marketplace of Ideas: Paul's Mars Hill Experience for Our Pluralistic World* (Downers Grove, IL: IVP Academic, 2014).
29. See, for example, 1 Corinthians 9:1-23; 2 Corinthians 11:7.
30. John Milton, *Aereopagitica*, ed. John Wesley Hales (Oxford: Clarendon Press, 1874), 50–52.

31. William J. Abraham, "Eschatology and Epistemology," in *The Oxford Handbook of Eschatology*, ed. Jerry L. Walls (New York: Oxford University Press, 2008), 587–89.
32. Mehmet Ali Dogan and Heather J. Sharkey, eds., *American Missionaries and the Middle East: Foundational Encounters* (Salt Lake City: University of Utah Press, 2011), xviii.
33. Sudipta Kaviraj, in Bruce Lawrence, "Citizen Ahmad Among the Believers: Salvation Contextualized in Indonesia and Egypt," in *Between Heaven and Hell: Islam, Salvation, and the Fate of Others*, ed. Mohammad Hassan Khalil (New York: Oxford University Press, 2013), 291–92, 307.
34. For analysis, see, for example, Abdullahi Ahmed An-Na'im, *Islam and the Secular State: Negotiating the Future of Shari'a* (Cambridge, MA: Harvard University Press, 2008), 223–63.
35. Compare, for example, Acts 4:19; 5:29.
36. Proverbs 16:25.
37. Owen C. Thomas, "The Atheist Surge: Faith in Science, Secularism, and Atheism," *Theology and Science* 8, no. 2 (May 2010): 204.
38. John Wesley, preface to "Sermons on Several Occasions," §§ 8–10, in *Works*, 1:107; also sermon 39, "Catholic Spirit," § I:4, in *Works*, 2:84: "Every man necessarily believes that every particular opinion which he holds is true (for to believe any opinion is not true, is the same thing as not to hold it), yet can no man be assured that all his own opinions, taken together, are true. In fact, every thinking man is assured they are not, seeing *humanum est errare et nescire*: 'To be ignorant of many things, and to mistake in some, is the necessary condition of humanity.' This, therefore, he understands, applies to himself as well. He knows, generally, that he himself is mistaken; although in what particular opinions he is mistaken, he does not, perhaps he cannot, know."
39. Ralph T.H. Griffith, trans., *Rig Veda*, 2nd ed. (Kotagiri, India: Nilgiri, 1896), 1:89:1, available at *Internet Sacred Text Archive*, accessed August 17, 2019, http://www.sacred-texts.com/hin/rigveda/.
40. Confucius, *Analects* 7:21, Everyman's Library, trans. Arthur Waley (New York: Alfred A. Knopf, 2001), 119.
41. Pontifical Council for Interreligious Dialogue, § 42, quoted in Terrence W. Tilley, "Theologies of Religious Diversity: Toward a Catholic and Catholic Assessment," in *Can Only One Religion Be True? Paul Knitter & Harold Netland in Dialogue*, ed. Robert B. Stewart (Minneapolis: Fortress, 2013), 60.
42. John Wesley, sermon 39, "Catholic Spirit," §§ 4, 5, 2:1, 2, 3, 7, 3:5, in *Works* 2:81–95, quoting 2 Kings 10:15.
43. Graham, quoted in James Michael Beam, "I Can't Play God Anymore," *McCall's*, January 1978, 156; cf. John C. Lennox, *Against the Flow: The Inspiration of Daniel in an Age of Relativism* (Oxford: Lion Hudson, 2015).
44. Amos Yong, "A Heart Strangely Warmed on the Middle Way? The Wesleyan Witness in a Pluralistic World," *Wesleyan Theological Journal* 48, no. 1 (2013): 19.
45. Leymah Gbowee, *Mighty Be Our Powers: How Sisterhood, Prayer, and Sex Changed a Nation at War* (New York: Beast Books, 2011).
46. See George R. Beasley-Murray, *Jesus and the Kingdom of God* (Grand Rapids, MI: Eerdmans, 1986), 308–9, 409: "If he says, 'I have clothed the naked!' it will be said to him, 'This is the gate of the Lord—you who have clothed the naked, enter in the same."
47. Sahih Muslim 32:6232, in, for example, *Divine Word and Prophetic Word in Early Islam*, by William A. Graham, Religion and Society 7 (Berlin: De Gruyter, 2010), 179.
48. Joe Gorman, "John Wesley's Inclusive Theology of Other Religions," *Wesleyan Theological Journal* 48, no. 1 (2013): 47; see also John E. Stanley, "A Theology of Urban Ministry, Supported by the Wesleyan Quadrilateral," *Wesleyan Theological Journal* 38, no. 1 (2003): 138–59.
49. Mills, quoted in Gorman, "John Wesley's Inclusive Theology," 52, citing John 4:10-11.
50. Emperor Julian, quoted in David Ayerst and A.S.T. Fisher, *Records of Christianity*, in the Roman Empire 1 (Oxford: Basil Blackwell, 1971), 179–81.
51. Tilley, "Theologies of Religious Diversity," 73.
52. Phrase from Nancy E. Bedford, "Little Moves Against Destructiveness," in *Practicing Theology: Beliefs and Practices in Christian Life*, ed. Miroslav Volf and Dorothy C. Bass (Grand Rapids, MI: Eerdmans, 2002), 157–81; see also Philippians 1:18.
53. Martin Luther King Jr., "Remaining Awake Through a Great Revolution," in *A Testament of Hope: The Essential Writings and Speeches of Martin Luther King, Jr.*, ed. James M. Washington (San Francisco: HarperSanFrancisco, 1986), 270. See also Ben DeVan, "Martin Luther King, Jr.," in *How to Get a Life: Empowering Wisdom for the*

Heart and Soul, ed. Lawrence Baines and Daniel McBrayer (Atlanta: Humanics / Brumby Holdings, 2003), 28–41.

54. King, "Letter from Birmingham City Jail," in *Testament of Hope*, 292.
55. Martin Luther King Jr., quoted in Coretta Scott King, *The Words of Martin Luther King Jr.* (New York: Newmarket Press, 1987), 51. See also Romans 12:21, "Overcome evil with good."
56. King, *Testament of Hope*, 7, 10, 12, 18, 87, 482, 487.
57. Aenus Silvius Piccolomini [Pope Pius II], *Epistola ad Mahomatem II* [*Epistle to Mohammaded II*], ed. and trans. Albert R. Baca (New York: Peter Lang, 1990), 2; Matthew 5:44; Luke 6:32-36.
58. R. Todd Mangum, "Is There a Reformed Way to Get the Benefits of the Atonement to 'Those Who Have Never Heard?,'" *Journal of the Evangelical Theological Society* 47, no. 1 (2004): 127; compare Jean-Jacques Rousseau, *The Social Contract*, in *Jean-Jacques Rousseau: The Basic Political Writings*, ed. Donald A. Cress and David A. Wootton, 2nd ed. (Indianapolis: Hackett, 2011), 250: "It is impossible to live in peace with those one believes to be damned. To love them would be to hate God who punishes them."
59. 1 Samuel 24–26; 1 Kings 5–6; cf., Exodus 23:4-5; Proverbs 25:21; Isaiah 2:4; Jeremiah 29:7; Jonah 3; Micah 4:3.
60. Martin Luther King Jr., *Stride Toward Freedom: The Montgomery Story* (New York: Harper, 1958), 97.
61. B.R. Ambedkar, who drafted India's constitution, despised Hinduism's oppressive caste system (on Christmas 1927, he ceremoniously burned the caste-promoting *Book of Manu*, while "Untouchables" looked on and cheered). Ambedkar vehemently opposed Gandhi's more sympathetic view of the caste system. A portion of Ambedkar's "Reply to the Mahatma" can be found at *Outlook*, March 10, 2014, https://www.outlookindia.com/magazine/story/a-reply-to-the-mahatma/289692.
62. Wesley, quoted in Martin Forward, "Methodist Theology Among the Religions in the Twenty-First Century," *Epworth Review* 27, no. 1 (2000): 99; compare E. Stanley Jones, *Christ at the Round Table* (New York: Abingdon Press, 1928), 217, suggesting that Jews who bore a "cross of rejection" were nearer, even in their prejudices, to their Jewish brother Jesus than Christians who persecuted Jews.
63. Joel C. Rosenberg, *Inside the Revolution: How the Followers of Jihad, Jefferson, and Jesus Are Battling to Dominate the Middle East and Transform the World* (Carol Stream, IL: Tyndale House, 2009), 367. See also Benjamin B. DeVan, "Joel C. Rosenberg's Jewish-to-Evangelical Perspective on Islam?," *Studies in Interreligious Dialogue* 22, no. 1 (2012): 50–62; Tass Saada, with Dean Merrill, *Once an Arafat Man: The True Story of How a PLO Sniper Found a New Life* (Carol Stream, IL: Tyndale House, 2008).
64. Carl Medearis, *Muslims, Christians, and Jesus: Gaining Understanding and Building Relationships* (Bloomington, MN: Bethany House, 2008), 139–42.
65. Luke 10; see also Luke 9 and 17; John 4 and 8; and virtually any scholarly commentary on these biblical chapters.
66. King, "The American Dream," in *Testament of Hope*, 209.
67. Also called "Alethic parity." See more details on technical vocabulary for §§ 2 and 3 in DeVan, "Wesleyan Open Inclusivist Approach," esp. 49–70.
68. For one example of this tale from antiquity, see John D. Ireland, trans., *The Udana and the Itivuttaka: The Buddha's Sayings* (Kandy, Sri Lanka: Buddhist Publication Society, 2007), 81–84.
69. Eugene F. Gorski, *Theology of Religions: A Sourcebook for Interreligious Study* (Mahwah, NJ: Paulist Press, 2008), 285, deduces, "*All* religions must be seen as partial and incomplete interpretations of a transcendent reality that fully surpasses humankind's ability to name" (italics in original).
70. Compare 1 Kings 8:27; 2 Chronicles 2:6; Acts 17:24.
71. 1 Corinthians 13:9-12.
72. See, for example, John 1:18; 14:9; Colossians 1:15.
73. Joseph Runzo, "Pluralism and Relativism," in *The Oxford Handbook of Religious Diversity*, ed. Chad Meister (New York: Oxford University Press, 2011), 65.
74. See, for example, Protagoras in *Theaetetus* 152a, in *The Collected Dialogues of Plato*, ed. Edith Hamilton and Huntington Cairns (Princeton, NJ: Princeton University Press, 1989), 856; analysis in Copan, *"True for You but Not for Me,"* 20–25, 27; Wilfred Cantwell Smith, *Questions of Religious Truth* (New York: Charles Scribner's Sons, 1967), 89–90: religions become "true" by putting their teachings/narratives into practice.
75. Hans Küng, "Is There One True Religion? An Essay in Establishing Ecumenical Criteria," in *Christianity and Other Religions: Selected Readings*, ed. John Hick and Brian Hebblethwaite, rev. ed. (Oxford: Oneworld, 2001),

122–23, for example, describes the following as the "traditional" view: "Only one single religion is true. Or, all other religions are untrue"; compare Paul Knitter, *No Other Name? A Critical Survey of Christian Attitudes Toward the World Religions*, American Society of Missiology 7 (Maryknoll, NY: Orbis, 1985), 74–113 characterizes this as the "conservative evangelical model."

76. Augustine, *On Christian Doctrine*, trans. D.W. Robertson Jr. (New York: Liberal Arts Press, 1958), 54.
77. Augustine, *De Doctrina Christiana* 2.40.60, as rendered by Paul J. Griffiths, *Decreation: The Last Things of All Creatures* (Waco, TX: Baylor University Press, 2014), 36.
78. C.S. Lewis, *Mere Christianity* (New York: HarperCollins, 2001), 34–35.
79. Compare on this point, Luke Bretherton, *Hospitality as Holiness: Christian Witness amid Moral Diversity* (Aldershot, UK: Ashgate, 2006), 84, 107, cf. 136: "Neither can a single tradition provide…[a] definitive vision of the good life, only Jesus can…[the] work of the Spirit constitutes a rebuttal of any single institution or set of social relations to claim definitive status as the bearer of God's order"; David Marshall, "Towards a Christian Model of Religions: Yuan Zhiming as a Case Study in Fulfillment Theology" (PhD diss., University of Wales, 2012), 94: Christ in the Spirit "brings to fruition central truths within each tradition, which then crowd out harmful propensities."
80. John 14:6.
81. Jones, *Christ at the Round Table*, 11 (italics added).
82. Or demanding that comprehensively correct theology is necessary but not sufficient for salvation, since demons apparently have access to some correct theological beliefs such as "God is one" (James 2:19). See also Paul Copan, "Why Are Christians So Divided? Why So Many Denominations?," in *When God Goes to Starbucks: A Guide to Everyday Apologetics* (Grand Rapids, MI: Baker, 2008), 191–202, 220–21.
83. John Wesley, sermon 130, "On Living Without God," § 15, in *Works*, 4:175. For further thoughts from Wesley, see sermon 4, "Scriptural Christianity," in *Works* 1:159–80; sermon 7, "The Way to the Kingdom," in *Works* 1:218–32; sermon 20, "The Lord Our Righteousness," in *Works* 1:449-65; sermon 38, "A Caution Against Bigotry," in *Works* 2:63–78; sermon 39, "Catholic Spirit," in *Works* 2:81–99.
84. Timothy C. Tennent, *Christianity at the Religious Roundtable: Evangelicalism in Conversation with Hinduism, Buddhism, and Islam* (Grand Rapids, MI: Baker Academic, 2002), 249.
85. Gerald R. McDermott, *Can Evangelicals Learn from World Religions? Jesus, Revelation and Religious Traditions* (Downers Grove, IL: InterVarsity, 2000).
86. Gerald R. McDermott, *God's Rivals: Why Has God Allowed Different Religions? Insights from the Early Church* (Downers Grove, IL: InterVarsity, 2007), 167. McDermott is apparently paraphrasing George A. Lindbeck, *The Nature of Doctrine: Religion and Theology in a Postliberal Age* (Philadelphia: Westminster, 1984).
87. Paul J. Griffiths, *Problems of Religious Diversity*, Exploring the Philosophy of Religion Series (Oxford: Blackwell, 2001), 60.
88. For example, George Grimm, *The Doctrine of the Buddha: The Religion of Reason and Meditation* (New Delhi: Shri Jainendra Press, 1973), 45.
89. John B. Cobb, "Being a Transformationist in a Pluralistic World," *Christian Century*, August 10–17, 1994, 749–50.
90. McDermott, *God's Rivals*, 162–67.
91. Job 1:1.
92. Genesis 14:17-24; Psalm 110:4; Hebrews 5:6-10; 6:19; 7:17.
93. Genesis 20:11.
94. Genesis 16; 21:8-21.
95. Jethro appears in Exodus 3–4; 18.
96. C.S. Lewis, *Reflections on the Psalms* (Orlando: Harcourt, 1986), 86. Acts 7:22 also refers to Moses's Egyptian training.
97. 1 Kings 10:1. Moreover, 1 Kings 4:29-31 declares that God gave Solomon great wisdom, discernment, and breadth of understanding so that his wisdom surpassed all Eastern and Egyptian wisdom: "He was wiser than anyone else…than Ethan the Ezrahite, and Heman, Calcol, and Darda, children of Mahol"; thereby implicitly lauding these non-Israelites' lesser wisdom by esteeming Solomon as even wiser than them.
98. 2 Chronicles 35:21-22.

99. See esp. Jonah 1:1-16; 3:1-4:11.
100. Matthew 2:1-12. The magi's gifts of frankincense and myrrh would have come from trees found only in Arabia. Isaiah 60:6 mentions frankincense and associates it with regions of Arabia to the southeast—Midian and Sheba. This southeasterly region was still considered "East" (Isaiah 60:2)—that is, of the Jordan River—in Jewish thinking. Early church fathers such as Justin Martyr and Tertullian claimed that the magi came from Arabia. See Kenneth Bailey, *Jesus Through Middle Eastern Eyes: Cultural Studies in the Gospels* (Downers Grove, IL: InterVarsity, 2008), 82–83.
101. Matthew 15:21-28; Mark 7:24-30; and Luke 10:25-37 in response to, "What must I do to inherit eternal life?"
102. John 4:22-24.
103. Matthew 8:10-12.
104. Martin Luther King Jr., *The Trumpet of Conscience* (Boston: Beacon, 2010), 29.
105. Benjamin B. DeVan, "As Iron Sharpens Iron, So Does One Religious Tradition Sharpen Another," *Journal of Comparative Theology at Harvard Divinity School* 1, no. 1 (March 2010): 11–21.
106. Francis X. Clooney, *Comparative Theology: Deep Learning Across Religious Borders* (Oxford: Blackwell, 2001), 165.
107. Keith Yandell, "Has Normative Religious Pluralism a Rationale?," in *Can Only One Religion Be True? Paul Knitter & Harold Netland in Dialogue*, ed. Robert B. Stewart (Minneapolis: Fortress, 2013), 171, 179: The supposedly disinterested, apathetic, subjectivist, relativist, or purveyors of religious antipathy can also claim to conceive of all religions as equal or to in principle oppose all religions equally.
108. Gotthold Ephraim Lessing, *Laocoon, Nathan the Wise, Minna von Barnhelm*, ed. William A Steel (New York: St. Martin's, 1967), 167–69.
109. Titus 2:13; 1 Corinthians 13:12; compare Matthew 24:3-14; Revelation 2:25-29.
110. See Genesis 15:6; Romans 4:3; M. Jamie Ferreira, "Faith and the Kierkegaardian Leap," in *The Cambridge Companion to Kierkegaard*, ed. Alastair Hannay and Gordon D. Marino (Cambridge: Cambridge University Press, 1998), 207–34; Blaise Pascal, "The Wager," in *Christianity for Modern Pagans: Pascal's Pensees Edited, Outlined, and Explained*, by Peter Kreeft (San Francisco: Ignatius Press, 1993), 291–316.
111. Compare 1 Corinthians 13:12; Philippians 1:21-23; Hebrews 11; Horatio Gates Spafford, "It Is Well with My Soul" (1873), verse 4, line 1, available at *Hymnary*, accessed August 17, 2019, https://hymnary.org/text/when_peace_like_a_river_attendeth_my_way.
112. On the psychology of atheism, see Paul C. Vitz, "The Psychology of Atheism from Defective Fathers to Autism to Professional Socialization and Personal Convenience," in *The Naturalness of Belief: New Essays on Theism's Rationality*, ed. Paul Copan and Charles Taliaferro (Lanham, MD: Lexington Books, 2018), 175–95. On the place of the will and privileging certain factors over others in (un)belief, see R.W.L. Moberly, *The Bible in a Disenchanted Age: The Enduring Possibility of Christian Faith* (Grand Rapids, MI: Baker Academic, 2018).
113. Luke 12:16-21.
114. Kenneth Barker, ed., *The NIV Study Bible* (Grand Rapids, MI: Zondervan, 2011); Ted Cabal et al., eds., *The Apologetics Study Bible*, 2nd ed. (Nashville: B&H Academic, 2017); Gregory A. Boyd and Edward K. Boyd, *Letters from a Skeptic: A Son Wrestles with His Father's Questions About Christianity* (Wheaton, IL: Victor, 2008); Lane T. Dennis and Wayne Grudem, eds., *The ESV Study Bible* (Wheaton, IL: Crossway, 2008); Timothy Keller, *The Reason for God: Belief in an Age of Skepticism* (New York: Dutton, 2008).
115. Krishna in *The Bhagavad Gita*, Penguin Classics, trans. Juan Mascaro (New York: Penguin, 2003), 23.
116. We see this fulfilled, for example, in Revelation 7:9-10.
117. Revelation 3:9-10.
118. Romans 8:28.
119. Exodus 9:14; 12:12, compare 7:5, 17; 8:10, 22; 9:14; 10:2; 12:12; 14:4, 18; 16:12; Deuteronomy 4:35, 39; 32:39.
120. Joshua 24; Judges 2; 1 Kings 12:25-33; 2 Kings 10:29; 17:16; 2 Chronicles 11:15; 13:8; Psalm 106:19-20; 115; Hosea 13:2.
121. Exodus 20:1-7; 32:4; cf., Exodus 32–34. Deuteronomy 5:1-11; cf. 16:22.
122. Deuteronomy 18:9-12, 20:18.
123. Child sacrifice: Leviticus 18:21; 20:1-5; 1 Kings 11:5; 2 Kings 23:10; Isaiah 57:9; Jeremiah 32:35; cultic prostitution: Deuteronomy 23:17; 1 Kings 15:24; 22:46; 2 Kings 23:7; Hosea 4:14; oppressing the foreigner, orphan, poor, and widow: Job 31:16; Psalm 12:5; 14:6; 82:3; 140:12; Proverbs 14:31; 19:17; 21:1; 22:9, 16, 22; 29:7; Isaiah

3:14-15; 10:2; 61:1; Jeremiah 5:28; 22:16; Ezekiel 16:49; 18:12; 22:12, 22:29; Amos 2:7; 4:1; 5:12; 8:4-6; Zechariah 7:10.

124. Compare Deuteronomy 32:17; 1 Kings 18; 2 Kings 21; Isaiah 37:18-19; 41:21-22; 43:9-10; 44:6-9; 45:6-22; Jeremiah 2:11, 26-28; 3:6-13; 10:1-16; 16:20; Hosea 8:4-7; Amos 5:26; cf. Acts 14:15; 19:26; 1 Corinthians 8:1-13, 10:14-31; Galatians 4:8.
125. 1 Samuel 5:1-7. When set upright, Dagon falls again, breaking into pieces.
126. Daniel 3.
127. Daniel 1–2; 4–6; 10.
128. Luke 11:37-52; compare Matthew 23:1-37. Jesus in Revelation 3:9 rebukes a "synagogue of Satan, who say that they are Jews and are not, but lie" (cf. 2:9).
129. Matthew 7:15-23, compare 21:22-23; 25:31-46; 1 John 4:1. In Matthew 7:22-23 and Luke 13:26-27, some evildoers even claim to work miracles, prophecy, and cast out demons in Jesus' name!
130. For example, Acts 13:6-12; 17:16-29; 19:11-41, even as Paul favorably quotes a Greek philosopher-poet; compare 1 Corinthians 10:14-21; Ephesians 2:2; Revelation 9:20.
131. Acts 14:6-18; compare 1 Thessalonians 1:9.
132. 2 Corinthians 11:14-15.
133. Compare 1 Corinthians 14:29; 1 Thessalonians 5:19-22.
134. Jeremiah 3:23 (KJV).
135. S. Mark Heim, *The Depth of Riches: A Trinitarian Theology of Religious Ends*, Sacra Doctrina (Grand Rapids, MI: Eerdmans, 2001), does cite the Bible but takes much of its inspiration from Dante.
136. John 14:6; 1 Timothy 2:5; Acts 4:12.
137. See one version of this story in Wayne Rice, *More Hot Illustrations for Youth Talks: 100 More Attention-Getting Stories, Parables, and Anecdotes* (Grand Rapids, MI: Zondervan, 1995), 78; compare John 15:15.
138. R.C. Sproul, *Reason to Believe* (Grand Rapids, MI: Zondervan, 1982), 44–45; compare Jesus's famous comments on "rendering unto Caesar" in Matthew 22:15-22; Mark 12:13-17; Luke 20:19-26; 1 Corinthians 1:20-25.
139. For numerous citations corresponding to this definition of Exclusivism, see DeVan, "Wesleyan Open Inclusivist Approach," 52. Just one example is Millard Erickson, "The State of the Question," in *Through No Fault of Their Own? The Fate of Those Who Have Never Heard*, ed. William V. Crockett and James G. Sigountos (Grand Rapids, MI: Baker, 1991), 24: "irrevocably fixed at death."
140. For support for such exceptions for the very young, see, for example, 2 Samuel 12:22-23; Matthew 18:10; 19:13-14; Mark 10:13-16; Luke 18:15-17.
141. See, for example, Jerry L. Walls, *Heaven: The Logic of Eternal Joy* (New York: Oxford University Press, 2002), 63–91.
142. Most famously, Cyprian, "On the Unity of the Church," in *The Ante-Nicene Fathers: Translations of the Writings of the Fathers down to A.D. 325*, vol. 5, *Fathers of the Third Century: Hippolytus, Cyprian, Caius, Novatian, Appendix*, ed. Alexander Roberts and James Donaldson (Buffalo, NY: Christian Literature Company, 1888), 358, 422–23; and satirically Parson Thwackum in Henry Fielding, *The History of Tom Jones, a Foundling*, ed. Douglas Brooks-Davies (London: Dent, 1998), 98: "When I mention [true] religion, I mean the Christian religion; and not only the Christian religion, but the Protestant religion; and not only the Protestant religion, but the Church of England."
143. Charles Hodge, *Systematic Theology* (Grand Rapids, MI: Eerdmans, 1952), 2:646, suggests direct exposure to God's written Word is needed for salvation. For example, Cornelius in Acts 10 hears the gospel from Peter rather than the angel who directed him to Peter.
144. See, for example, Christopher W. Morgan and Robert A. Peterson, *Faith Comes by Hearing: A Response to Inclusivism* (Downers Grove, IL: InterVarsity, 2008), 17–39.
145. For example, Acts 3:19-20; Romans 10:9-10.
146. 2 Corinthians 6:2.
147. C.S. Lewis, *The Great Divorce: A Dream* (New York: HarperCollins, 2001); compare Matthew 16:18; Jerry L. Walls, *Purgatory: The Logic of Total Transformation* (New York: Oxford University Press, 2012); Walls, *Heaven*, 74, 82–85, 89.
148. See, for example, Billy Graham, quoted in Beam, "I Can't Play God Anymore," 158; Billy Graham, quoted

in Nancy and Michael Duffy, "The Political Confessions of Billy Graham," *Time*, August 20, 2007, 44; Billy Graham, "Robert Schuller with the Hour of Power Guest: Billy Graham, Program 1426," *YouTube*, recorded May 31, 1997, accessed September 5, 2019, https://www.youtube.com/watch?v=INPyY0QjgpY.

149. For example, the healing of Rabadash in C.S. Lewis, *The Horse and His Boy* (New York: HarperCollins, 2000), 219; W.H. Lewis, ed., *Letters of C.S. Lewis*, rev. ed. (Orlando: Harcourt, 1988), 428: "Every prayer which is sincerely made even to a false god or to a very imperfectly received true God, is accepted by the true God and that Christ saves many who do not think they know him. In…[Matthew 25,] those who are saved do not seem to know that they have served Christ."
150. See Clark Pinnock, "An Inclusivist View," in *Four Views on Salvation in a Pluralistic World*, ed. Dennis L. Okholm and Timothy R. Phillips (Grand Rapids, MI: Zondervan, 1996), 100.
151. Philippians 2:9-11; compare Romans 14:11. Universalists believe that all will confess Jesus is Lord voluntarily.
152. See Ezekiel 16:53-55; 47:8; Bradley Jersak, *Her Gates Are Never Shut: Hope, Hell, and the New Jerusalem* (Eugene, OR: Wipf and Stock, 2008), esp. 92–97, 165–79.
153. Universalists may here attempt to appeal to 1 Corinthians 15:26, where death is the last enemy to be destroyed.
154. See also Isaiah 66:24; Matthew 3:12; 18:8; Luke 3:17; 12:5; Revelation 17:8; possibly contrast Jeremiah 17:27. One universalist translating "eternal" as involving the next world or age to come is Ilaria Ramelli, *A Larger Hope? Universal Salvation from Christian Beginnings to Julian of Norwich* (Eugene, OR: Cascade, 2019), 215–21.
155. Hitchens, quoted in Ian Katz, "When Christopher Met Peter," *Guardian*, May 31, 2005, http://www.theguardian.com/books/2005/may/31/hayfestival2005.guardianhayfestival; compare Christopher Hitchens, *God Is Not Great: How Religion Poisons Everything* (New York: Twelve, 2007), 247–49.
156. For more on this critique, see Paul Copan, "How Universalism, 'the Opiate of the Theologians,' Went Mainstream: Michael McClymond Decries the Rising Popularity of an Idea Christians Have Rejected for Most of Church History," *Christianity Today*, March 11, 2019, https://www.christianitytoday.com/ct/2019/march-web-only/michael-mcclymond-devils-redemption-universalism.html.
157. Zacharias, quoted in Lee Strobel, *The Case for Faith: A Journalist Investigates the Toughest Objections to Christianity* (Grand Rapids, MI: Zondervan, 2000), 157.
158. Psalm 34:8.
159. See, for example, Copan, "'Jesus-Shaped' Cultures."
160. Dorothy Day, *Selected Writings: By Little and By Little*, ed. Robert Eisberg (London: Darton, Longman & Todd, 2005), 94, 97; compare Mother Teresa, *In My Own Words*, ed. Jose Luis Gonzalez-Balado (London: Hodder & Stoughton, 1980), 94, 97, 30, 36.
161. Compare Revelation 5:1-10.
162. Titus 3:15.
163. 1 John 5:13 (italics added).
164. Patricia St. John, *Patricia St. John Tells Her Own Story*, 2nd ed. (Shoals, IN: Kingsley, 2008), 137.

Chapter 20. New Spirituality

1. Douglas Groothuis, *Walking Through Twilight: A Wife's Illness—a Philosopher's Lament* (Downers Grove, IL: InterVarsity, 2017).
2. Gabrielle Bluestone, "What Does Marianne Williamson Believe?," *New York Times*, June 28, 2019, https://www.nytimes.com/2019/06/28/style/marianne-williamson-debate-president.html.
3. *Encyclopedia Britannica Online*, s.v. "New Age Movement," by Gordon J. Melton, accessed March 27, 2020, https://www.britannica.com/topic/New-Age-movement.
4. For more on the nature and origin of the New Age movement, see Douglas Groothuis, "From Counterculture to New Age," in *Unmasking the New Age* (Downers Grove, IL: InterVarsity, 1986).
5. I reprint such a tract in Douglas Groothuis, *Confronting the New Age* (Downers Grove, IL: InterVarsity, 1988).
6. Francis Schaeffer, *He Is There and He Is Not Silent*, 30th anniversary ed. (Wheaton, IL: Tyndale House, 2001), 8.
7. C.S. Lewis, *The Complete Signature Classics: Miracles* (New York: HarperOne, 2002), 373–74.
8. Joseph Campbell, *The Power of Myth* (New York: Anchor Books, 1991), 58.
9. Campbell, 69.
10. "Purpose," *Whole Earth Almanac*, Fall 1968, 3.

11. Shirley MacLaine, *Dancing in the Light* (Toronto: Bantam Books, 1986), 126.
12. Swami Vivekananda, "Paper on Hinduism," *Ramakrishna Vivekananda*, accessed March 27, 2020, https://www.ramakrishnavivekananda.info/vivekananda/volume_1/addresses_at_the_parliament/v1_c1_paper_on_hinduism.htm.
13. Rhonda Byrne, *The Secret* (New York: Atria Books, 2018).
14. For more on the proper interpretation of biblical texts and others used by New Agers, see James Sire, *Scripture Twisting: Twenty Ways Cults Misinterpret the Bible* (Downers Grove, IL: InterVarsity, 1980).
15. Neale Donald Walsch, audio interview with Daniel McCoy, January 6, 2020.
16. Thomas Ryan, "25 Percent of US Christians Believe in Reincarnation. What's Wrong with This Picture?," *Pew Research Center*, October 21, 2015, https://www.americamagazine.org/faith/2015/10/21/25-percent-us-christians-believe-reincarnation-whats-wrong-picture.
17. See Douglas Groothuis, "Dangerous Meditations," *Christianity Today*, November 4, 2004, https://www.christianitytoday.com/ct/2004/november/10.78.html.
18. See Douglas Van Dorn, *The Five Solas of the Reformation* (Erie, CO: Waters of Creation, 2019), 119–21.
19. Oprah Winfrey, "A New Earth Online Class: Chapter 1 Transcript," *Oprah.com* (n.p.: Harpo Productions, 2008), 12, 14, available at http://images.oprah.com/images/obc_classic/book/2008/anewearth/ane_chapter1_transcript.pdf.
20. Walter Martin, "2003 *Kingdom of the Cults*: Excerpts on Key Doctrinal Issues," *Walter Martin's Religious InfoNet*, accessed March 27, 2020, http://www.waltermartin.com/cults.html#encount.

Chapter 21. Atheism and Agnosticism

1. Frederick Buechner, *Wishful Thinking: A Seeker's ABC: Revised and Expanded* (New York: HarperSanFrancisco, 1993), 1.
2. John Ortberg, *Know Doubt* (Grand Rapids, MI: Zondervan, 2008), 9.
3. Mother Teresa uses the phrase "no faith" at least four times in her book, *Come Be My Light: The Private Writings of the Saint of Calcutta*, ed. Brian Kolodiejchuk (New York: Doubleday, 2007), 169, 187, 193, 238.
4. Billy Graham, "Billy Graham, in His Own Words, About Facing Death and the Lord," excerpt from 1992 interview by Diane Sawyer, *ABC News*, February 22, 2018, https://abcnews.go.com/WNT/video/billy-graham-words-facing-death-lord-53260604.
5. Lorna Mumford, "Living Non-religious Identity in London," in *Atheist Identities—Spaces and Contexts, Boundaries of Religious Freedom*, Regulating Religion in Diverse Societies 2, ed. Lori G. Beaman and Steven Tomlins (New York: Springer, 2015), 153. Nonreligious Londoners often highlighted "emotional events or experiences" rather than rationality, reason, or science as their initial motivation for atheism.
6. For examples of questioning God in the Bible, see Genesis 15:1-6; 17:17-22; 18:20-33; Exodus 3–5; Ruth 1:20-21; 1 Samuel 1:1-18; Job 3; 6–7; 9–10; 12–14; 16–17; 19; 21; 23–24; 26–31; 40; 42; Psalms; Jeremiah 1:6-8; 4:19-26; 8:18-22; 12:1-14; 15:10-2; 18:19-23; 20:7-18; 32:16-25; Lamentations; Habakkuk; Luke 1:26-56.
7. Matthew 27:46; Mark 15:34.
8. Genesis 32:28.
9. Phil Zuckerman, "Atheism: Contemporary Numbers and Patterns," in *The Cambridge Companion to Atheism*, Cambridge Companions to Philosophy, ed. Michael Martin (New York: Cambridge University Press, 2007), 47–65.
10. Ariela Keysar and Juhem Navarro-Rivera, "A World of Atheism: Global Demographics," in *The Oxford Handbook of Atheism*, ed. Stephen Bullivant and Michael Ruse (New York: Oxford University Press, 2013), 556.
11. Ryan T. Cragun, Joseph H. Hammer, and Jesse M. Smith, "North America," in *Oxford Handbook of Atheism*, 603.
12. Todd M. Johnson and Gina A. Zurlo, eds., *World Christian Database* (Leiden: Brill, 2007), http://www.worldchristiandatabase.org/.
13. *Oxford Handbook of Atheism*, 2. See further analysis in Benjamin B. DeVan, "Review Article: *The Oxford Handbook of Atheism*," *Theology and Science* 14, no. 1 (February 2016): esp. 133–35.
14. Stephen Bullivant, "Defining 'Atheism,'" in *Oxford Handbook of Atheism*, 11, 14–15, cf. 612, 624, 660; Paul

Kurtz, *The New Skepticism: Inquiry and Reliable Knowledge* (Buffalo, NY: Prometheus Books, 1992), 194; Alister McGrath, *The Twilight of Atheism: The Rise and Fall of Disbelief in the Modern World* (London: Rider, 2004), 175.

15. For example, Bullivant, "Defining 'Atheism,'" 19; Cragun, Hammer, and Smith, "North America," 608, record some people who identify as "atheists" reporting that they also believe in a personal god!
16. For example, "Nine-in-Ten Americans Believe in a Higher Power, but Only a Slim Majority Believe in God as Described in the Bible," *Pew Research Center*, April 25, 2018, https://www.pewforum.org/2018/04/25/when-americans-say-they-believe-in-god-what-do-they-mean/: "In the U.S., belief in a deity is common even among the religiously unaffiliated—a group composed of those who identify themselves, religiously, as atheist, agnostic or 'nothing in particular,' and sometimes referred to, collectively, as religious 'nones.' Indeed, nearly three-quarters of religious 'nones' (72 percent) believe in a higher power of some kind, even if not in God as described in the Bible."
17. For example, Jack Lee, "Why Evangelicals Need to Stop Saying 'It's a Relationship, Not a Religion,'" *Patheos*, October 15, 2018, https://www.patheos.com/blogs/chorusinthechaos/evangelicals-stop-relationship-not-religion/.
18. Antony Flew, *The Presumption of Atheism: And Other Philosophical Essays on God, Freedom, and Immortality* (New York: Harper & Row, 1976), 14–22. On Flew's conversion, see Antony Flew with Roy Abraham Varghese, *There Is a God: How the World's Most Notorious Atheist Changed His Mind* (New York: HarperCollins, 2007).
19. Ralph W. Hood Jr. and Zhuo Chen, "Conversion and Deconversion," in *Oxford Handbook of Atheism*, 540–41, cf. 612, 660. One example by a philosopher is Anthony Kenny, *What I Believe* (New York: Continuum, 2006), esp. 21–29.
20. Richard Dawkins, *The God Delusion* (New York: Houghton Mifflin, 2006), 53.
21. Ambiguities allow one *New York Times* bestseller to boast high numbers without declaring everyone atheist: Greg Epstein, *Good Without God: What a Billion Nonreligious People Do Believe* (New York: HarperCollins, 2009).
22. Bob Jones, "It's Good to Be King: CNN's Larry King Talks About Objective Journalism, Faith, and Cultural Decline," *World Magazine*, July 28, 2001, https://world.wng.org/2001/07/its_good_to_be_king.
23. "'Godless' Sarah Silverman Says She's 'Fascinated by Religion,'" *HuffPost*, November 23, 2013, video, 3:25–50, https://www.huffingtonpost.com/2013/11/22/godless-sarah-silverman-religion_n_4325262.html.
24. Bertrand Russell, quoted in John R. Searle, *Mind, Language, and Society: Philosophy in the Real World* (New York: Basic Books, 1998), 36–37.
25. Dawkins, *God Delusion*, 354, appealing to Mark Twain without citing an original source.
26. Bruce E. Hunsberger and Bob Altemeyer, *Atheists: A Groundbreaking Study of America's Nonbelievers* (Amherst, NY: Prometheus Books, 2006), 66–68, 119, 126–27.
27. John Bingham, "Richard Dawkins: I Can't Be Sure God Does Not Exist," *Telegraph*, February 24, 2012, https://www.telegraph.co.uk/news/religion/9102740/Richard-Dawkins-I-cant-be-sure-God-does-not-exist.html.
28. Carl Sagan, *Cosmos* (New York: Random House, 1980), 4; Paul Copan, *How Do You Know You're Not Wrong? Responding to Objections That Leave Christians Speechless* (Grand Rapids, MI: Baker, 2005), 47–122.
29. Carl Sagan, *The Demon-Haunted World: Science as a Candle in the Dark* (New York: Ballantine, 1996), 8. Alister E. McGrath and Joanna Collicutt McGrath, *The Dawkins Delusion? Atheist Fundamentalism and the Denial of the Divine* (Downers Grove, IL: InterVarsity, 2007), 31, credit a twentieth-century Christian, the Oxford chemist and Methodist lay preacher Charles A. Coulson, for coining the phrase "the God of the gaps."
30. For further details, see again Copan, *How Do You Know?*, esp. 57–66.
31. Richard Lewontin, "Billions and Billions of Demons," *New York Review of Books*, January 9, 1997, 28–32.
32. Bernard Schweizer, *Hating God: The Untold Story of Misotheism* (New York: Oxford University Press, 2011); "dystheists" in Chad Meister, *Evil: A Guide for the Perplexed* (London: Continuum, 2012), 5.
33. For example, David Berlinski, *The Devil's Delusion: Atheism and Its Scientific Pretensions* (New York: Crown Forum, 2008); Lois Lee, "Western Europe," in *Oxford Handbook of Atheism*, 595; Bradley Monton, *Seeking God in Science: An Atheist Defends Intelligent Design* (Buffalo, NY: Broadview Press, 2009); Bruce Sheiman, *An Atheist Defends Religion: Why Humanity Is Better Off with Religion Than Without It* (New York: Penguin, 2009).
34. Against religion generally, for example, Dawkins, *God Delusion*; Sam Harris, *The End of Faith: Religion, Terror, and the Future of Reason* (New York: W.W. Norton, 2004); Christopher Hitchens, *God Is Not Great: How Religion Poisons Everything* (New York: Twelve, 2007). Three explicitly anti-Christian spin-offs are John W. Loftus, ed., *The Christian Delusion: Why Faith Fails* (Amherst, NY: Prometheus Books, 2010); John W. Loftus, ed.,

Christianity Is Not Great: How Faith Fails (Amherst, NY: Prometheus Books, 2014); John W. Loftus, ed., *The End of Christianity* (Amherst, NY: Prometheus Books, 2011).

35. Graham Oppy, in discussion with the authors, email conversation, April 3, 2019.
36. Graham Oppy, *Naturalism and Religion: A Contemporary Philosophical Investigation*, Investigating Philosophy of Religion Series (New York: Routledge, 2018).
37. J. Clinton McCann, "Psalms," in *The New Interpreter's Bible*, ed. Leander E. Keck (Nashville: Abingdon Press, 1996), 4:729, cf. 716–21, 728–31, 892–93.
38. Matthew 5:22; 2 Corinthians 11:19.
39. Plato, *Apology of Socrates* § 26c, in *Four Texts on Socrates: Plato's Euthyphro, Apology, and Crito and Aristophanes' Clouds*, by Plato and Aristophanes, trans. Thomas G. West and Grace Stary West (Ithaca, NY: Cornell University Press, 1984), 76; Plato, *Laws* § 12.967a, quoted in Jan M. Bremmer, "Atheism in Antiquity," in *Cambridge Companion to Atheism*, 19–25.
40. See again Plato, *Apology of Socrates* §§ 24–27, in *Four Texts on Socrates*, 72–78.
41. Epicurus, *On Nature* § 12, quoted in Bremmer, "Atheism in Antiquity," 19–21.
42. Lucretius, *On the Nature of Things*, from books 1–5, in *The Portable Atheist: Essential Readings for the Nonbeliever*, ed. Christopher Hitchens (Philadelphia: Da Capo Press, 2007), 1–6.
43. Plutarch, *On Superstition* § 10, quoted in Mark M. Edwards, "The First Millennium," in *Oxford Handbook of Atheism*, 154. For a comparison of Plutarch's biographies with the biblical Gospels, see Michael R. Licona, *Why Are There Differences in the Gospels? What We Can Learn from Ancient Biography* (New York: Oxford University Press, 2017).
44. Lucian of Samosata, *Scholia* 75.26–27, quoted in Edwards, "First Millennium," 157.
45. Justin Martyr, *First Apology* 1:6, in *The Apostolic Fathers with Justin Martyr and Irenaeus*, Ante-Nicene Fathers 1, ed. Alexander Roberts, James Donaldson, and A. Cleveland Cose (New York: Charles Scribner's Sons, 1885), 164.
46. Santideva, *The Bodhicaryavatara* 9:118–25, trans. Kate Crosby and Andrew Skilton (New York: Oxford University Press, 1996), 127–28.
47. *Mahapurana* 4:16, in *Sources of Indian Tradition: Introduction to Oriental Civilizations*, ed. William Theodore de Bary (New York: Columbia University Press, 1958), 79.
48. Abu al-'Ala' al-Ma'rri quoted in Reynold Alleyne Nicholson, *Studies in Islamic Poetry* (Cambridge: Cambridge University Press, 2010), 167.
49. Omar Kayyam, *Rubaiyat*, paraphrased from several literal translations in Hitchens, *Portable Atheist*, 8.
50. For example, Bullivant and Ruse have chapters on "Jewish Atheism" and "Hinduism" in *Oxford Handbook of Atheism*; see also Tim Whitmarsh, *Battling the Gods: Atheism in the Ancient World* (New York: Knopf, 2015).
51. Michael J. Buckley, *At the Origins of Modern Atheism* (New Haven, CT: Yale University Press, 1987), 9–10, 199.
52. See Benjamin B. DeVan, "Review of John Suk, *Not Sure: A Pastor's Journey from Faith to Doubt* (Grand Rapids, MI: Eerdmans, 2011)," *Africanus Journal* 5, no. 1 (April 2013): 54–55, https://archive.org/details/africanus5n1apr2013/page/n55.
53. David McLellan, *Karl Marx: His Life and Thought* (New York: Macmillan, 1973), 456–57.
54. Jean-Jacques Rousseau, *Emile, or On Education*, trans. Allan Bloom (New York: Basic Books, 1973), 275–77.
55. Paul-Henri Thiry, Baron d'Holbach, *Good Sense* § 30 (Middlesex, UK: Echo Library, 2007), 26.
56. Baron D'Holbach, *The System of Nature, or Laws of the Moral and Physical World* § 1.18, in *At the Origins*, 421.
57. Naigeon, *Discourses 1–16*, quoted in Alan Charles Kors, "The Age of Enlightenment," in *Oxford Handbook of Atheism*, 202–4, 210.
58. Julien Offray de La Mettrie, *L'Homme Machine*, in *At the Origins*, 418.
59. Edward Gibbon, *The Autobiographies of Edward Gibbon*, ed. John Murray (New York: Fred De Fau, 1907), 223.
60. Hugh Redwald Trevor-Roper, ed., *The Decline and Fall of the Roman Empire: And Other Selections from the Writings of Edward Gibbon*, Great Histories, Historian's Library (New York: Washington Square, 1963), 1:x; compare Baruch Spinoza, *Tractatus Theologico-Politicus*, in *A Secular Age*, by Charles Taylor (Cambridge, MA: Belknap Press of Harvard University Press, 2007), 271.
61. David Hume, *Dialogues Concerning Natural Religion: And Other Writings*, Cambridge Texts in the History

of Philosophy, ed. Dorothy Coleman (Cambridge: Cambridge University Press, 2007), esp. 74–88, 109–12; Thomas H. Huxley, *Science and Christian Tradition: Essays* (New York: D. Appleton, 1894), 249.

62. For example, Dawkins, *God Delusion*, 39, 51–68; Hitchens, *God Is Not Great*, 303; Hitchens, *Portable Atheist*, 155–65; Christopher Hitchens, *Thomas Jefferson: Author of America*, Eminent Lives (New York: HarperCollins, 2005); Christopher Hitchens, *Thomas Paine's Rights of Man*, Books That Change the World (New York: Grove, 2006).
63. Hitchens, *Portable Atheist*, 155–65; versus Walter Isaacson, *Einstein: His Life and Universe* (New York: Simon & Schuster, 2007), 384–93.
64. One representative statement is Ludwig Feuerbach, *The Essence of Christianity*, English and Foreign Philosophical Library 15, trans. Marian Evans, 2nd ed. (London: Trubner, 1881), 270. Freud wrote in a letter to Edward Silverstein on March 7, 1875, in Peter Gay, *Freud: A Life for Our Time* (New York: W.W. Norton, 1988), 28: "Among all philosophers, I worship and admire this man [Feuerbach] the most."
65. Michael J. Buckley, *Denying and Disclosing God: The Ambiguous Progress of Modern Atheism* (New Haven, CT: Yale University Press, 2004), 84–86, for Marx on Feuerbach; Karl Marx, *Contribution to the Critique of Hegel's Philosophy of Right*, in *The Portable Karl Marx*, ed. Eugene Kamenka (New York: Penguin, 1983), 115; Karl Marx and Friedrich Engels, *On Religion* (Mineola, NY: Dover, 2008), 41–42 (italics in original).
66. Huxley, *Science and Christian Tradition*, 239, on agnosticism. On Darwin's bulldog, see Leonard Huxley, *Life and Letters of Thomas Henry Huxley*, Cambridge Library Collection (Cambridge: Cambridge University Press, 2012), 2:62.
67. John William Draper, *History of the Conflict Between Religion and Science* (New York: D. Appleton, 1874); Andrew Dickson White, *A History of the Warfare of Science with Theology in Christendom*, 2 vols. (New York: D. Appleton, 1876).
68. For example, A.J. Ayer, *Language, Truth, and Logic*, 2nd ed. (New York: Dover, 1952); Auguste Comte, *Auguste Comte and Positivism: The Essential Writings*, ed. Gertrud Lenzer (New York: Harper & Row, 1975).
69. Susan Jacoby, *The Great Agnostic: Robert Ingersoll and American Freethought* (New Haven, CT: Yale University Press, 2013).
70. Robert Green Ingersoll, *Lectures of Col. R.G. Ingersoll* (Chicago: Rhodes & McClure, 1898), 551.
71. Charles Darwin, letter to John Fordyce, May 7, 1879, Darwin Correspondence Project, University of Cambridge, accessed June 9, 2019, http://www.darwinproject.ac.uk/letter/DCP-LETT-12041.xml.
72. Sigmund Freud, *New Introductory Lectures on Psycho-analysis*, trans. W.J.H. Sprott (New York: W.W. Norton, 1933), 229; cf. Sigmund Freud, *The Future of an Illusion*, trans. W.D. Robson-Scott (London: Hogarth, 1949).
73. Bertrand Russell, *Why I Am Not a Christian and Other Essays on Religion and Related Subjects* (New York: George Allen & Unwin, 1957), 24.
74. Bertrand Russell, letter to *Humanist*, October 1968, quoted in Charles Pidgen, "Analytic Philosophy," in *Oxford Handbook of Atheism*, 307.
75. John F. Haught, *God and the New Atheism: A Critical Response to Dawkins, Harris, and Hitchens* (Louisville, KY: Westminster John Knox, 2008), contrasts atheist Existentialists with more celebratory New Atheists.
76. Jean-Paul Sartre, *Existentialism and Human Emotions*, trans. Bernard Frechtman and Hazel E. Barnes (New York: Citadel, 1985), 22.
77. Friedrich Nietzsche, *Beyond Good and Evil: Prelude to a Philosophy of the Future*, trans. Walter Kaufmann (New York: Vintage, 1989), 91.
78. Russell, *Why I Am Not Christian*, 107.
79. David Aikman, *The Delusion of Disbelief: Why the New Atheism Is a Threat to Your Life, Liberty, and Pursuit of Happiness* (Nashville: SaltRiver, 2008); Stephane Courtois et al., *The Black Book of Communism: Crimes, Terror, Repression*, trans. Jonathan Murphy and Mark Kramer (Cambridge, MA: Harvard University Press, 1999), available at https://ia800500.us.archive.org/26/items/TheBlackBookofCommunism10/the-black-book-of-communism-jean-louis-margolin-1999-communism.pdf; Aleksandr Solzhenitsyn, *The Gulag Archipelago: 1918–1956: An Experiment in Literary Investigation*, trans. Thomas P. Whitney and Harry Willetts, vols. 1–3 (New York: Harper & Row, 1978), available at https://archive.org/details/AleksandrSolzhenitsynTheGulagArchipelago.
80. Zuckerman, "Atheism," 57.
81. Against Zuckerman, see, for example, David G. Myers, *A Friendly Letter to Skeptics and Atheists: Musings on Why*

God Is Good and Faith Isn't Evil (San Francisco: Jossey-Bass, 2008); Rodney Stark et al., *What Americans Really Believe* (Waco, TX: Baylor University Press, 2008); Bradley R.E. Wright, *Christians Are Hate-Filled Hypocrites... and Other Lies You've Been Told: A Sociologist Shatters Myths from the Secular and Religious Media* (Bloomington, MN: Bethany House, 2010).

82. Thomas J.J. Altizer, *The Gospel of Christian Atheism* (Philadelphia: Westminster, 1966), 111.
83. Jacques Derrida, *Jacques Derrida*, trans. Geoffrey Bennington (Chicago: University of Chicago Press, 1993), 155.
84. See Benjamin B. DeVan, "Landscapes or Sandscapes? New Atheist Grounds for Morality," *Books & Culture*, October 2011, https://www.booksandculture.com/articles/webexclusives/2011/october/morallandscapes.html, and our chapter on pluralism (chapter 19) for critique of cultural and ethical relativism.
85. C.S. Lewis, *Surprised by Joy: The Shape of My Early Life* (Orlando: Harcourt, 1955), 115.
86. Marquis de Sade, *La verite*, in *At the Origins*, 248.
87. David P. Barash, "The DNA of Religious Faith," *Chronicle of Higher Education*, April 20, 2007, 6.
88. For twenty-first-century origins of "New Atheism" and "New Atheists," see Thomas Zenk, "New Atheism," in *Oxford Handbook of Atheism*, 251–54. For a detailed history of the first 12 years of New Atheists and their critics, see Benjamin B. DeVan, "A Wesleyan Open Inclusivist Approach to Religious Diversity and New Atheism" (PhD diss., Durham University, 2016), esp. 4–35, available at http://etheses.dur.ac.uk/11464/.
89. Richard Cimino and Christopher Smith, *Atheist Awakening: Secular Activism and Community in America* (New York: Oxford University Press, 2014), 11, which describes New Atheist books as providing "the cultural content most readily available to be conveyed" by atheist individuals, secular organizations, and networks.
90. Oscar Wilde, *The Picture of Dorian Gray: An Annotated Uncensored Edition*, ed. Nicholas Frankel (Cambridge, MA: Belknap Press of Harvard University Press, 2011).
91. For example, Dawkins, *God Delusion*, 383–87; Hitchens, *God Is Not Great*, 283.
92. Matthew 22:36-40; Mark 12:28-34; Luke 10:25-37.
93. John Gray, *Heresies: Against Progress and Other Illusions* (London: Granta, 2004), 48.
94. Paul Chaffee, "Offering an Overdue Welcome to the Atheist Community," *Interfaith Observer*, April 15, 2013, http://theinterfaithobserver.org/journal-articles/2013/4/15/offering-an-overdue-welcome-to-the-atheist-community.html.
95. Michael Ruse, "A Naturalistic Perspective," in *The Oxford Handbook of Religious Diversity*, ed. Chad Meister (New York: Oxford University Press, 2011), 433–46.
96. John Hedley Brooke and Ronald L. Numbers, eds., *Science and Religion Around the World* (New York: Oxford University Press, 2011).
97. William Lloyd Newell, *The Secular Magi: Marx, Freud, and Nietzsche on Religion* (Lanham, MD: University Press of America, 1995).
98. For example, Paul G. Heibert, Daniel Shaw, and Tite Tiénou, *Understanding Folk Religion: A Christian Response to Popular Beliefs and Practices* (Grand Rapids, MI: Baker, 1999), 35; Lesslie Newbigin, *The Open Secret: An Introduction to the Theology of Mission*, rev. ed. (Grand Rapids, MI: Eerdmans, 1995), 94–120, 160.
99. For example, Peter Boghossian, *A Manual for Creating Atheists* (Durham, NC: Pitchstone, 2013); Dawkins, *God Delusion*, 28; Daniel C. Dennett, *Breaking the Spell: Religion as a Natural Phenomenon* (New York: Viking, 2006), 53.
100. Dawkins, *God Delusion*, 31–50.
101. Our source for Comte and the Soviets is Stephen Bullivant, *The Salvation of Atheists and Catholic Dogmatic Theology*, Oxford Theological Monographs (New York: Oxford University Press, 2012), 31–32.
102. See again Bullivant, 31–32.
103. Bullivant, 33.
104. Gretta Vosper, "Light in the Night Sky: On Becoming a Spiritually Non-Exclusive Congregation," *Interfaith Observer*, April 15, 2013, http://www.theinterfaithobserver.org/journal-articles/2013/4/15/light-in-the-night-sky.html.
105. Katherin Don, "Are Atheists the New Campus Crusaders?," *Religion Dispatches*, February 7, 2013, http://religiondispatches.org/are-atheists-the-new-campus-crusaders/.
106. Chris Stedman, *Faitheist: How an Atheist Found Common Ground with the Religious* (Boston: Beacon, 2012).
107. Epstein, *Good Without God*, xv.

108. Alan Jones, "John Figdor Appointed as Atheist Chaplain at Stanford," *Huffington Post*, December 28, 2012, updated February 26, 2013; http://www.huffingtonpost.com/alan-jones/an-atheist-chaplaincy-a-good-way-to-begin-the-new-year_b_2366663.html.
109. Vanessa Gomez Brake, "The Case for Atheist Chaplains," *Interfaith Observer*, April 15, 2013, http://www.theinterfaithobserver.org/journal-articles/2013/4/15/the-case-for-atheist-chaplains.html.
110. Stephen Prothero, *God Is Not One: The Eight Rival Religions That Run the World—and Why Their Differences Matter* (New York: HarperOne, 2010), 326.
111. See Ninian Smart, *The World's Religions*, 2nd ed. (Cambridge: Cambridge University Press, 1998), 11–29, for ritual, narrative/mythic, doctrinal/philosophical, ethical/legal, experiential, institutional/social, and material aspects.
112. On fiction, for example, see Arthur Bradley and Andrew Tate, *The New Atheist Novel: Fiction, Philosophy and Polemic After 9/11*, New Directions in Religion and Literature Series (London: Continuum, 2010).
113. *Oxford Handbook of Atheism* has chapters on social science, literature, visual art, music, and film.
114. For example, Karl Barth, *Fragments Grave and Gay*, ed. Martin Rumscheidt, trans. Eric Mosbacher (London: Collins, 1971), 31, predicated Christianity as "happy reversal and elimination of all religion," yet twenty-first-century conventions still classify Christianity as a religion.
115. "Humanism and Its Aspirations: Humanist Manifesto III, a Successor to the Humanist Manifesto of 1933" (Washington, DC: American Humanist Association, 2003), § 6, available at http://americanhumanist.org/Humanism/Humanist_Manifesto_III.
116. Denis J.J. Robichaud, "Renaissance and Reformation," in *Oxford Handbook of Atheism*, 179.
117. Grammond, quoted in Robichaud, 192–93, which also quotes "Francois de Rosset" calling Vanini a "mad dog."
118. Steven G. Gey, "Atheism and the Freedom of Religion," in *Cambridge Companion to Atheism*, 260–61, 266.
119. Marie Macey and Alan Carling, *Ethnic, Racial and Religious Inequalities: The Perils of Subjectivity*, Migration, Minorities, and Citizenship (New York: Palgrave Macmillan, 2011), 31.
120. Samuli Schielke, "The Islamic World," in *Oxford Handbook of Atheism*, 647.
121. Shafiq Alam, "'Death to Bloggers': Bangladesh Islamists," *Australian Associated Press*, April 7, 2013, http://www.adelaidenow.com.au/news/breaking-news/death-to-bloggers-bangladesh-islamists/story-e6frea7u-1226613966218.
122. Simon Tomlinson, "Saudi Arabia Declares Atheists Terrorists Under New Laws Targeting Citizens Who 'Call for Secular Thought in Any Form,'" *Daily Mail*, April 1, 2014, http://www.dailymail.co.uk/news/article-2594139/Saudi-Arabia-declares-atheists-terrorists-new-laws.html.
123. Sagan, *Cosmos*, 339.
124. Voltaire attribution in Stephen G. Tallentyre, *The Friends of Voltaire* (London: Smith, Elder, 1906), 198–99.
125. George Orwell, *The Orwell Reader: Fiction, Essays and Reportage*, introduced by Richard H. Rovere (New York: Harcourt, 1984).
126. A.C. Grayling, *The God Argument: The Case* Against *Religion and* for *Humanism* (London: Bloomsbury, 2013), 179–82.
127. As atheist Gina Welch does in Timothy Dalrymple, "Undercover Atheist," *Patheos*, April 2, 2010, http://www.patheos.com/Resources/Additional-Resources/Undercover-Atheist.html.
128. Penn Jillette, "A Gift of the Bible," *YouTube*, July 8, 2010, https://www.youtube.com/watch?v=6md638smQd8.
129. Merold Westphal, *Suspicion and Faith: The Religious Uses of Modern Atheism* (New York: Fordham University Press, 1998), back cover, cf. ix, 3–10, 16.
130. Anthony Campolo, *Partly Right: Christianity Responds to Its Critics* (Dallas: Word, 1985); republished in 2008 as *We Have Met the Enemy, and They Are Partly Right: Learning from the Critics of Christianity*.
131. Grayling, *God Argument*, 139–40.
132. Paul Kurtz and Edwin H. Wilson, "Humanist Manifesto II," *Humanist*, October 1973, http://americanhumanist.org/Humanism/Humanist_Manifesto_II.
133. Chris Stedman, "On Atheists and Theists Together at the Interfaith Table: The Case for Collaboration," *Interfaith Observer*, April 15, 2013, http://theinterfaithobserver.org/journal-articles/2013/4/15/on-atheists-and-theists-together-at-the-interfaith-table.html.
134. Albert Camus, *Resistance, Rebellion, and Death: Essays*, trans. Justin O'Brien (London: Hamilton, 1964), 47–53, in a section entitled "The Unbeliever and Christians."

135. For more on love, see Robertson McQuilkin and Paul Copan, *An Introduction to Biblical Ethics: Walking in the Way of Wisdom* (Downers Grove, IL: IVP Academic, 2014), 27–59.
136. For example, Matthew 5:44; cf. Luke 6:32.
137. "Debate on God," *YouTube*, January 30, 2008, video, 38:54–39:16, http://www.youtube.com/watch?v=vnMYL8sF7bQ, featuring Christopher Hitchens and Shmuley Boteach, moderated by Neil Gillman, Ninety-Second Street Y.
138. Sam Harris, *Waking Up: A Guide to Spirituality Without Religion* (New York: Simon & Schuster, 2014), 46.
139. Robert Ingersoll, *Works* 1:133, quoted in Jacoby, *Great Agnostic*, 145, 217.
140. Stedman, *Faitheist*, 119–22, cf. 128, 168, 178; citing Jesus, 36–39, 45–48, 56, 58, 90–93, 101, 109, 169.
141. Hitchens, *God Is Not Great*, 13, 96.
142. William Shakespeare, *The Tragedy of Hamlet, Prince of Denmark*, act 3, scene 2, available at http://shakespeare.mit.edu/hamlet/hamlet.3.2.html.
143. Hitchens in Jennie Rothenberg Gritz, "Transcending God: Christopher Hitchens on His Beef with Religion, His Faith in Mankind, and His New Bestselling Book, *God Is Not Great*," *Atlantic Unbound*, July 12, 2007, http://www.theatlantic.com/magazine/archive/2007/07/transcending-god/306076/.
144. O'Hair, quoted in Bryan F. Le Beau, *The Atheist: Madalyn Murray O'Hair* (New York: New York University Press, 2003), 250, 356.
145. "Christian's [*sic*] Raise Funds for Ill Atheist Protester," *Tyler Morning Telegraph*, March 20, 2012, http://www.cbs19.tv/story/17199221/christians-raise-funds-for-ill-atheist-protester.
146. Anugrah Kumar, "Atheist Activist Who Became a Christian Returns to Atheism," *Christian Post*, May 5, 2012, https://www.christianpost.com/news/atheist-activist-who-became-christian-returns-to-atheism.html.
147. Al Truesdale with Keri Mitchell, *With Cords of Love: A Wesleyan Response to Religious Pluralism* (Kansas City, MO: Beacon Hill, 2006), 130–32, cf. 119–20, 160–61 for additional anecdotes.
148. Marcas Baram, "Christopher Hitchens Beat Up by Lebanese Thugs During Street Brawl," *Huffington Post / Forbes*, March 31, 2009, http://www.huffingtonpost.com/2009/02/18/christopher-hitchens-beat_n_168035.html.
149. Ayaan Hirsi Ali, *Nomad: From Islam to America: A Personal Journey Through the Clash of Civilizations* (New York: Free Press, 2010), 247; Benjamin B. DeVan, "*Nomad*: A New Memoir by Ayaan Hirsi Ali," *Books & Culture*, July 2010, http://www.booksandculture.com/articles/webexclusives/2010/july/benjaminbdevan.html.
150. Peter Kreeft and Ronald K. Tacelli, *Handbook of Christian Apologetics* (Downers Grove, IL: InterVarsity, 1994), 47–99; William Lane Craig, *Reasonable Faith: Christian Truth and Apologetics* (Wheaton, IL: Crossway, 2008).
151. For example, Paul Copan, *"True for You but Not for Me": Overcoming Objections to Christian Faith*, rev. ed. (Bloomington, MN: Bethany House, 2009), 143–80; Benjamin B. DeVan and Thomas W. Smythe, "The Character of Jesus Defended," *Christian Apologetics Journal* 5, no. 2 (Fall 2006): 109–40.
152. Russell, *Why I Am Not Christian*, 6.
153. For further reading, see Paul Copan, *That's Just Your Interpretation: Responding to Skeptics Who Challenge Your Faith* (Grand Rapids, MI: Baker, 2001), 69–73; Paul Copan, "If God Made the Universe, Who Made God?," *Enrichment Journal*, Spring 2012.
154. For more on naturalism and scientism, see Copan, *How Do You Know?*, 47–84.
155. Michael Patrick Leahy, *Letter to an Atheist* (Nashville: Harpeth River Press, 2007); John Galbraith Simmons, *The Scientific 100: A Ranking of the Most Influential Scientists, Past and Present* (New York: Citadel, 2000).
156. Sana Saaed, "Giants Engaged in Both Science and Religion," *Interfaith Observer*, May 15, 2013, http://theinterfaithobserver.org/journal-articles/2013/5/15/giants-engaged-in-both-science-and-religion.html.
157. Daniel C. Dennett and Alvin Plantinga, *Science and Religion: Are They Compatible?* (New York: Oxford University Press, 2011), 41, 61–63.
158. DeVan, "Wesleyan Open Inclusivist Approach," 196–233.
159. For example, Genesis 50:20; Psalm 23:4; 94:12; 119:71; Proverbs 3:5; 27:6; 28:23; Isaiah 41:10; Hebrews 12:6-11; John 9:1-3; James 1:2-4; Romans 5:3-5; 8:18,28; 2 Corinthians 4:16-18; Philippians 4:12-13.
160. Isaiah 53:4; Hebrews 4:15; and the passion narratives in Matthew 26-27; Mark 14–15; Luke 22–23; John 18–19.
161. See Deuteronomy 31:6; Revelation 21:1-5; and verses in endnote 159 above.
162. For example, Joshua 1:9; Psalm 82:3-4; Isaiah 1:17; 10:1-4; 58:10; Matthew 25; Ephesians 6:10-18; James 2:15-17.

163. Richard Dawkins, *River Out of Eden: A Darwinian View of Life* (New York: Basic Books, 1995), 132–33; Russell, *Why I Am Not Christian*, 107.
164. Thomas C. Oden, *Systematic Theology*, 3 vols. (Peabody, MA: Prince Press, 1998), 3:463.
165. Jerry L. Walls, *Heaven: The Logic of Eternal Joy* (New York: Oxford University Press, 2002), 175–81.
166. Paul Tillich, *Systematic Theology*, 3 vols. (Chicago: University of Chicago Press, 1967), 3:21.
167. For further discussion, see Paul Copan, *"True for You but Not for Me,"* 98–108; Benjamin B. DeVan, "Landscapes or Sandscapes? New Atheist Grounds for Ethics and Morality," *Books & Culture*, October 2011, https://www.booksandculture.com/articles/webexclusives/2011/october/morallandscapes.html.
168. N.T. Wright, *Surprised by Hope: Rethinking Heaven, the Resurrection, and the Mission of the Church* (New York: HarperOne, 2008), 44.
169. Jerome, *Letters* 53, quoted in Oden, *Systematic Theology*, 3:462. So too with heavenly treasures in, for example, Matthew 6:20-21.
170. Andy Crouch, *Culture Making: Rediscovering Our Creative Calling* (Downers Grove, IL: InterVarsity, 2008), 165–67.
171. Crouch, 167–68, referencing Richard Mouw, *When the Kings Come Marching In: Isaiah and the New Jerusalem* (Grand Rapids, MI: Eerdmans, 2002), 20–30 (italics added).
172. Wright, *Surprised by Hope*, 268.
173. Psalm 16:11 conjoins God and God's ways with "pleasures forevermore"; 2 Corinthians 3:18; Philippians 3:12.

Chapter 22. Stories of Coming to Christ

1. Wes Grandberg-Michaelson, "Think Christianity Is Dying? No, Christianity Is Shifting Dramatically," *Washington Post*, May 20, 2015, https://www.washingtonpost.com/news/acts-of-faith/wp/2015/05/20/think-christianity-is-dying-no-christianity-is-shifting-dramatically/ (accessed August 27, 2020).
2. See the section "Prophecy and the Witnesses" in the chapter "Jehovah's Witnesses" in this book (chapter 17).
3. 1 Corinthians 13:4.